Cognitive and Behavioral Interventions

RELATED TITLES OF INTEREST

Handbook of Behavior Therapy with Children and Adults: A Developmental and Longitudinal Perspective
Robert T. Ammerman and Michel Hersen (editors)
ISBN: 0-205-14583-3

Handbook of Prescriptive Treatments for Children and Adolescents
Robert T. Ammerman, Cynthia G. Last, and Michel Hersen (editors)
ISBN: 0-205-14825-5

Behavioral Assessment: A Practical Handbook, Third Edition
Alan S. Bellack and Michel Hersen (editors)
Paper ISBN: 0-205-14277-X   Cloth ISBN: 0-205-14278-8

Cognitive-Behavioral Procedures with Children and Adolescents: A Practical Guide
A.J Finch, Jr., W. Michael Nelson III, and Edith S. Ott
ISBN: 0-205-13435-1

Managed Mental Health Care: A Guide for Practitioners, Employers, and Hospital Administrators
Thomas R. Giles
ISBN: 0-205-14838-7

Social Skills for Mental Health: A Structured Learning Approach
Robert P. Sprafkin, N. Jane Gershaw, and Arnold P. Goldstein
ISBN: 0-205-14841-7

Handbook of Behavior Therapy and Pharmacotherapy for Children: A Comparative Analysis
Vincent B. Van Hasselt and Michel Hersen (editors)
ISBN: 0-205-13949-3

The Practice of Behavior Therapy, Fourth Edition
Joseph Wolpe
Paper ISBN: 0-205-14514-0   Cloth ISBN: 0-205-14515-9

Cognitive and Behavioral Interventions

An Empirical Approach to Mental Health Problems

Linda W. Craighead
UNIVERSITY OF NORTH CAROLINA

W. Edward Craighead
DUKE UNIVERSITY MEDICAL CENTER AND DUKE UNIVERSITY

Alan E. Kazdin
YALE UNIVERSITY

Michael J. Mahoney
UNIVERSITY OF NORTH TEXAS

ALLYN AND BACON

BOSTON   LONDON   TORONTO   SYDNEY   TOKYO   SINGAPORE

For
Ben and Margo Wilcoxon
Glenn and Christine Craighead
Leon N. Kazdin
Daniel and Zita Mahoney

Library of Congress Cataloging-in-Publication Data

Cognitive and behavioral interventions :   an empirical approach to
   mental health problems   /   Linda W. Craighead . . . [et al.].
     p.   cm.
     Includes bibliographical references and index.
     ISBN 0-205-14586-8
     1. Cognitive therapy.   2. Behavior therapy.   3. Cognitive therapy
for children.   4. Behavior therapy for children.   I. Craighead,
Linda W.
     RC489.C63C6227   1993
     616.89′142—dc20   93-31930
                                                                  CIP

Printed in the United States of America
10 9 8 7 6 5 4 3   97 96

CONTENTS

Chapter 21
Applications to Pediatric Psychology   359
L. Peterson, D.D. Sherman, & M. Zink

Part IV
Future Directions

Chapter 22
Future Directions   377

P R E F A C E

As the title indicates, this text, *Cognitive and Behavioral Interventions: An Empirical Approach to Mental Health Problems*, represents a shift in emphasis from its forerunners, the first two editions of *Behavior Modification: Principles, Issues and Applications* by Craighead, Kazdin, and Mahoney (published in 1976 and 1981). At that time, behavior modification and behavior therapy were the terms most commonly associated with interventions derived from the behavioral model. The behavioral approach was identified primarily by its allegiance to scientific methodology and objective assessment, and by applications developed from principles of learning theory. In the present text, our aim is to describe for the reader how behavioral approaches, broadly defined, are being used today. Thus, it is clear that both cognitive and behavioral perspectives must be presented.

The content of interventions that have been evaluated using scientific methodology has broadened considerably over the past decade. In many cases it is difficult, and not very useful, to differentiate between what is and what is not a "behavioral" intervention. Within the ranks of those who identify with the behavioral model are those who label themselves behavior modifiers, behavior therapists, cognitive therapists, cognitive-behavior therapists, multimodal therapists, integrationists, and so on. Obviously, there is considerable variation and often spirited disagreement among these viewpoints concerning specific assumptions about the role of, the relative importance of, or the utility of intervening in the various domains of human functioning.

In this text we discuss both cognitive and behavioral perspectives and present an interactional model that identifies the many variables that constitute human functioning—behavior, biology, cognition, emotion (listed in alphabetical order!)—and outlines how they influence each other and interact with the environment. We then present a variety of specifically behavioral, specifically cognitive, and cognitive-behavioral applications that have been evaluated. New interventions are constantly being developed and evaluated as researchers increase their understanding of other variables and the ways in which those variables interact with behavior and cognition. Each edition of a text such as this will inevitably include more diverse types of interventions as they become empirically validated.

Among those individuals identified with the behavioral model, remarkable consensus remains regarding the necessity of subjecting interventions (however derived) to scientific scrutiny. Methodology becomes increasingly difficult as variables other than overt behavior are included. There will continue to be arguments about what constitutes appropriate method, but the challenge has been to develop new, more sophisticated methodologies for additional aspects of human experience, rather than to conclude that such variables are simply beyond the realm of science.

Part I of this text starts with a brief description of the history of psychology in order to explain the development of behaviorism and the subsequent re-emergence of interest in cognitive phenomena. The push to develop new theories and interventions and the pull toward integration are explored. Chapter 2 provides an overview of the current major clinical models of human behavior, describing both the traditional behavioral and the cognitive-behavioral model. A general integrative model is presented as a framework for thinking about the many variables that affect human functioning. This model should be useful to the reader in conceptualizing how different interventions might be effective in different ways and focusing on the mechanisms through which intervention on one variable may affect other variables.

Chapter 3 first describes the basic behavioral change, principles derived from learning theory, which have formed the cornerstone of the traditional behavioral model. There follows a description of some cognitive change principles that have evolved more recently. These descriptions are just brief introductions; many specific applications and further elucidation of these principles are detailed in chapters on specific disorders in Parts II and III. In many of these areas, many more specific terms are used to refer to various procedures. Due to the difficulty of defining many of these terms out of the context in which they are used, we have not included all of them in the introductory chapters, nor have we provided a separate glossary. Rather, the locations of the definitions of terms are indicated in the subject index.

Parts II and III consist of original contributions by experts in specific problem areas in which cognitive and/or behavioral interventions are already well established—i.e., have demonstrated empirical effectiveness and are widely used. Each author describes the major procedures currently used, summarizes the outcome research, and then focuses on those issues that continue to be problematic and are likely to be the subject of research in that area in the next decade.

In the final chapter, Future Directions, we include some additional areas that were not covered in the chapters on specific disorders. We also discuss areas in which behavioral approaches

appear to be quite promising but in which there is limited empirical support at this time. This chapter includes work on several pressing social problems (e.g., sexual abuse)—areas in which it is extremely difficult to do the type of sophisticated, well-controlled experimental work characteristic of behavioral research. We particularly want to commend those researchers who have tackled these thorny problems, and we hope to inspire some of you who are now considering joining this field to be part of the endeavor to find better solutions for such social problems.

The cognitive and behavioral perspectives presented in this book reflect a way of thinking about human behavior that has led to effective interventions for many clinical problems. We hope they will be equally useful in addressing larger social problems. Nonetheless, our basic premise, the commitment to empirical validation, mandates that we continue to press for rigorous evaluation. Typically, new applications start out on a quasi-experimental basis, but the empirical approach will not be satisfied with "It seems to work well" or even "We tried it in two cities [or with two clients] and got good results."

As is evident in many of the chapters on applications, the process of developing and validating interventions is rarely smooth. Applications that look promising in initial case reports or studies often cannot be replicated or do not fare so well once more rigorous controls are included. Sometimes interventions proven to be effective do not, upon closer inspection, appear to be effective for the reasons initially hypothesized. Efforts to dissect effective packages may fail to identify or clarify the essential ingredients. Although such results are disappointing to researchers, it is useful for the reader to see that even these "negative" findings are essential to the process of scientific inquiry. There are few final answers in these chapters. We hope this book will encourage an appreciation of both the difficulty and the promise of employing scientific methods to ameliorate human problems; we see this cautious optimism as an asset rather than a liability. The abilities to endure uncertainty and to accept change as inevitable are qualities we value as individuals and as researchers.

This text is primarily intended for use by undergraduates in courses on behavioral approaches or applications of social learning theory in departments of psychology, education, human development, nursing, counseling, and law enforcement. With supplementation, it could also be of use in other courses, such as psychopathology or abnormal psychology, learning, adjustment, and counseling. It may also be a useful reference for professionals working in applied settings. References are provided for those who would like to delve more deeply into specific areas, and many of the application chapters list resources that describe in more detail how to carry out the clinical procedures.

Individuals may find this book useful in improving the quality of their own lives through a better understanding of self-management skills and will certainly gain knowledge about skills to help others. Those intending to use these interventions to help people with clinical problems are encouraged to seek additional training and supervision, which provides feedback that is not available in any written format. We see this text as an introduction to the empirical study of mental health problems and an update on the status of outcome research for those who are already familiar with the basic principles.

Many individuals have lent their professional and personal skills to the production of this book,

and it would be impossible to do justice to all of them without adding an entire chapter. We are especially grateful to the late Jerry Frank, who initially encouraged us to take on this project and whose enthusiasm about the value of this approach to a textbook sustained us throughout the process. His untimely death is a loss to us as individuals and to our profession, which has benefited so much from his efforts to bring these viewpoints to the public eye. Mary Grace Luke was invaluable since taking over Jerry Frank's work and assisting us through the final stages. Since Allyn and Bacon purchased the Psychology series, we have been effectively assisted in the completion of this project by Mylan Jaixen and Anne Morrison. We would also like to express our appreciation to Houghton Mifflin, especially Michael DeRocco, for allowing the extensive use of material from *Behavior Modification: Principles, Issues, and Applications* by Craighead, Kazdin, and Mahoney (1976, 1981). We would like to express our appreciation to our secretary, Beverly McNeill, who has worked with us throughout the entire process of writing and editing this book.

Lastly, we thank all of the authors who contributed the chapters in Parts II and III and thereby made possible this textbook, which combines a basic overview of models and principles with specific applications in major areas. The chapters were written by researchers who are currently working in those areas.

Linda Wilcoxon Craighead
W. Edward Craighead
Alan E. Kazdin
Michael J. Mahoney

Linda Wilcoxon Craighead received her Ph.D. in 1976 from Pennsylvania State University. She is an Associate Professor of Psychology at the University of North Carolina-Chapel Hill and Director of the UNC Psychology Clinic. Prior to coming to UNC, she was a postdoctoral Fellow in the Department of Psychiatry at the University of Pennsylvania and on the faculty of Pennsylvania State University. She has published numerous articles on cognitive and behavioral therapies, particularly in the areas of obesity, eating, and affective disorders.

She has been a member of the Board of Directors of the Association for the Advancement of Behavior Therapy and a member of the Board of Directors of the Clinical Division of the American Psychological Association. She has been a member of the editorial board of several scientific journals. In 1988 she was a summer scholar at the Center for Advanced Studies in the Behavioral Sciences. She has received the President's New Researcher Award from the Association for the Advancement of Behavior Therapy and the Student Research Award from the Division of Psychology of Women of the American Psychological Association.

W. Edward Craighead received his Ph.D. from the Department of Psychology at the University of Illinois in Champaign-Urbana in 1970. He joined the Psychology Department faculty at Pennsylvania State University in 1970 and taught there until moving to Duke University Medical Center in 1986. He is currently a Professor in the Department of Psychiatry at Duke University Medical Center and Professor of Psychology at Duke University. He is Chief Psychologist in the Duke University Medical Center Affective Disorders Program and Director of its Cognitive-Behavior Therapy Program. He is also Director of Graduate Studies, Director of Clinical Training, and Director of the Psychology Clinic in the Department of Psychology at Duke University.

Dr. Craighead has been President of the Section of Experimental-Clinical Psychology, on the Board of Directors of the Clinical Division, and a Fellow of the American Psychological Association. He has been a member of the Board of Directors and served as President of the Association for Advancement of Behavior Therapy. He is the author/editor of several books and has published numerous scholarly papers, mostly focusing on cognitive/behavior therapy and depression. He has served as editor of *Behavior Therapy*. He has served on the editorial boards of several scientific journals, including *Cognitive Therapy and Research*, *Journal of Abnormal Psychology*, and *Depression*.

Alan E. Kazdin received his Ph.D. from Northwestern University in 1970. He is Professor of Psychology and Professor in the Child Study Center (Child Psychiatry) at Yale University. He is also Director of the Yale Child Conduct Clinic, an outpatient treatment service for children and their families. Prior to coming to Yale, he was on the faculty of Pennsylvania State University and the University of Pittsburgh School of Medicine.

Currently, his work focuses on assessment, diagnosis, and treatment (particularly concerning antisocial behavior and depression in children) and on psychotherapy outcome. He has been the editor of the *Journal of Consulting and Clinical Psychology, Psychological Assessment,* and *Behavior Therapy,* a Fellow at the Center for Advanced Study in the Behavioral Sciences, and President of the Association for Advancement of Behavior Therapy. He is the author of several books and numerous scientific articles and is among the most widely cited clinical psychologists. He is a Fellow of the American Psychological Association and editor of the Sage Book Series on Developmental Clinical Psychology and Psychiatry.

Michael J. Mahoney received his Ph.D. from Stanford University in 1972. He currently is a Professor of Psychology at North Texas State University; prior to joining the NTSU faculty he was on the faculty at Pennsylvania State University and the University of California at Santa Barbara. The author of several books and numerous scientific articles, Dr. Mahoney helped pioneer the "cognitive revolution" in psychology and is a continuing contributor to the growing interface between the cognitive and clinical sciences. Honored as a Fellow by both the American Psychological Association and the American Association for the Advancement of Science, he was chosen to be a Master Lecturer on Psychotherapy Process in 1981 and a G. Stanley Hall Lecturer in 1988. He has received several professional awards, including a 1984 Fulbright Award, the Faculty Scholar Medal from Pennsylvania State University, and a 1985 Citation Classic from Science Citation Index in recognition of the influence of his 1974 book, *Cognition and Behavior Modification.*

Dr. Mahoney has served on the Editorial Boards of several scientific journals and, since 1978, has worked with the U.S. Olympic Committee in the area of sports psychology. His research interests include basic processes in psychological development and psychotherapy, theoretical and philosophical issues, psychology of science, and health and sports psychology. His 1991 book, *Human Change Processes: The Scientific Bases of Psychotherapy,* integrates the research literatures from several disciplines as they bear on the conceptualization and facilitation of psychological change.

C O N T R I B U T O R S

Russell A. Barkley, Ph.D.
Department of Psychiatry
University of Massachusetts Medical Center
Worcester, Massachusetts

David H. Barlow, Ph.D.
Department of Psychology
State University of New York at Albany
Albany, New York

Jean C. Beckham, Ph.D.
Department of Psychiatry
Duke University Medical Center
Durham, North Carolina

Alan S. Bellack, Ph.D.
Department of Psychiatry
Medical College of Pennsylvania
Philadelphia, Pennsylvania

Michele M. Carter, M.A.
Dept. of Psychology
Vanderbilt University
Nashville, Tennessee

Linda Wilcoxon Craighead, Ph.D.
Department of Psychology
University of North Carolina at Chapel Hill
Chapel Hill, North Carolina

W. Edward Craighead, Ph.D.
Department of Psychiatry
Department of Psychology
Duke University Medical Center
Durham, North Carolina

John F. Curry, Ph.D.
Department of Psychiatry
Duke University Medical Center
Durham, North Carolina

Michael G. Dow, Ph.D.
Department of Community Mental Health
Florida Mental Health Institute
Tampa, Florida

George J. DuPaul, Ph.D.
Department of Psychiatry
University of Massachusetts Medical Center
Worcester, Massachusetts

Charles R. Greenwood, Ph.D.
Juniper Gardens Children's Project
Schiefelbusch Institute for Life Span Studies
University of Kansas
Kansas City, Kansas

David C. Guevremont, Ph.D.
Department of Psychiatry
University of Massachusetts Medical Center
Worcester, Massachusetts

Steven D. Hollon, Ph.D.
Department of Psychology
Vanderbilt University
Nashville, Tennessee

Neil S. Jacobson, Ph.D.
Department of Psychology
University of Washington
Seattle, Washington

Alan E. Kazdin, Ph.D.
Department of Psychology
Yale University
New Haven, Connecticut

Francis J. Keefe, Ph.D.
Department of Psychiatry
Department of Psychology
Duke University Medical Center and Duke
    University
Durham, North Carolina

Betty G. Kirkley, Ph.D.
Department of Nutrition
University of North Carolina at Chapel Hill
Chapel Hill, North Carolina

Mary E. Larimer, Ph.D.
Department of Psychology
University of Washington
Seattle, Washington

Joseph LoPiccolo, Ph.D.
Department of Psychology
University of Missouri
Columbia, Missouri

G. Alan Marlatt, Ph.D.
Department of Psychology
University of Washington
Seattle, Washington

Donna K. McMillan
Department of Psychology
Duke University
Durham, North Carolina

Michael J. Mahoney, Ph.D.
Department of Psychology
University of North Texas
Denton, Texas

Kim T. Mueser, Ph.D.
Department of Psychiatry
Medical College of Pennsylvania
Philadelphia, Pennsylvania

Lizette Peterson, Ph.D.
Department of Psychology
University of Missouri
Columbia, Missouri

Laura Schreibman, Ph.D.
Department of Psychology
University of California at San Diego
La Jolla, California

Daniel D. Sherman, M.A.
Department of Psychology
University of Missouri
Columbia, Missouri

Linda L. Street, Ph.D.
New York State Psychiatric Institute
Columbia-Presbyterian Medical Center
New York, New York

Barbara Terry, Ph.D.
Juniper Gardens Children's Project
Schiefelbusch Institute for Life Span Studies
University of Kansas
Kansas City, Kansas

Jennifer Waltz
Department of Psychology
University of Washington
Seattle, Washington

Dale Walker, Ph.D.
Juniper Gardens Children's Project
Schiefelbusch Institute for Life Span Studies
University of Kansas
Kansas City, Kansas

Karen C. Wells, Ph.D.
Department of Psychiatry
Duke University Medical Center
Durham, North Carolina

Thomas L. Whitman, Ph.D.
Department of Psychology
University of Notre Dame
Notre Dame, Indiana

Michelle Zink
Department of Psychology
University of Missouri
Columbia, Missouri

Cognitive and Behavioral Perspectives:
An Introduction

Psychology is just entering its second century as a recognized science and profession. Nevertheless, it has already exhibited considerable diversification (Hilgard, 1987). To make matters even more complex, there has been recent recognition that early historical accounts of the discipline may have been naive and simplified (Ash & Woodward, 1988; Furomoto, 1989; Scarborough & Furomoto, 1987). Our understanding of theoretical, research, and practical developments in psychology is thus still developing. It is clear, however, that behavioral and cognitive perspectives—and their ongoing integration, both with one another and with other approaches to health services—have played and will continue to play important roles in the development of applied scientific practices in counseling and psychotherapy.

EARLY THEORETICAL
DIFFERENCES

In the first volume of his classic work, *The Principles of Psychology*, William James (1890, p. 224) made the straightforward statement, "The first fact for us, then, as psychologists, is that thinking of some sort goes on." At the turn of the present century, James and Wilhelm Wundt were considered the most influential figures in the field. Wundt's establishment of an experimental laboratory at Leipzig in 1879 was to be cited by later historians as the beginning of scientific psychology. Although these two men exhibited differences in their approaches to human experience, they shared a fascination with the generative or creative aspects of the mind.

Wundt was largely responsible for the early encouragement of "introspection" as a method of studying human experience, for example, and James's writings on the ever-changing "stream of consciousness" remain relevant resources for contemporary researchers. Mary Whiton Calkins, the first woman president of the American Psychological Association, studied with both Wundt and James before her pioneering publications on the psychology of self in 1900.

These developments reflect the fact that a focus on the "inner person"—or the private experience of the individual—was a central theme in the origins of scientific psychology. It was not long, however, before a competing approach would overshadow these efforts and lay claim to a more rigorous expression of the scientific spirit in human studies. Both Wundt and James opposed the tradition of "associationism" that had been popularized by David Hartley in the middle of the eighteenth century. Wundt was fascinated with the structure of the mind and is therefore credited with being a pioneer of the perspective called psychological "structuralism." James and several of his colleagues exhibited more of an interest in the functional and adaptive aspects of human activity and were responsible for the tradition now termed "functionalism." Both of these perspectives emphasized the activity of the individual in his or her learning, adaptation, and experience. By way of contrast, associationism and the closely-allied perspective of "behaviorism" used a more passive portrayal of the organism in the process of learning. This is not to say that the portrayals of early behaviorists and associationists were naive in ignoring the role of physical activity in learning, but only that their conceptualization of basic learning processes—in humans as well as other animals—emphasized (1) *reactivity* rather than *proactivity*, (2) *peripheral* sensation over *central* mechanisms, and (3) *reflexivity* (or automaticity) over *reflectivity* (or mediation).

Table 1.1 shows the major schools of thought in psychology between 1880 and 1950, along with representatives of each. Structuralism and

functionalism were later absorbed into general experimental psychology, which was a wellspring for the later development of cognitive psychology in the second half of the twentieth century. Some associationists, gestalt psychologists, and behaviorists also contributed to that development. What is important to note, however, is that early orthodox behaviorists were outspoken in their discouragement of the study of thoughts, feelings, and private experience. Although John B. Watson (1913, 1924) was not the first person to insist that scientific psychology confine itself to publicly observable behavior, he was one of the most visible and outspoken. In his 1913 manifesto, for example, he argued that "Psychology as the behaviorist views it is a purely objective branch of natural science" (p. 138). It was a move that was meant to liberate psychology from subjectivity and interpretation, and to bring it into closer alignment with the methods and respectability of the physical and biological sciences.

Theories of learning and the experimental analysis of behavior soon became dominant forces in the profession. Led by the works of such individuals as Vladimir M. Bekhterev, Clark L. Hull, Ivan P. Pavlov, B. F. Skinner, and E. L. Thorndike, behaviorism became a central expression of scientific psychology. This fact is reflected in the changing definitions of psychology in the century between 1887 and 1987 (Henley, Johnson, & Jones, 1989). Prior to 1929, introductory texts defined psychology as the science of mind, mental life, or consciousness. Over the next 40 years, however, more than half of the basic texts in the field defined it as the science of behavior. Although this remained the most popular definition through 1987, mind and mental processes had by then shown considerable resurgence as additional and alternative definitions. This has been due in part to the "cognitive revolution" that swept through psychology in the second half of the twentieth century. Before discussing that revolution, however, some of the patterns of development in therapeutic psychology that have both influenced and reflected re-

TABLE 1.1   Schools of thought in psychology, with proponents of each

1880	1890	1900	1910	1920	1930	1940	1950
Structuralism							
Wundt (motor)	Titchener (sensory)						
Functionalism							
	Baldwin	Angell	Carr	McGeoch	Melton		
James							
		Dewey				Underwood	
Associationism							
		Thorndike					Estes
	Ebbinghaus			Woodworth	Guthrie		
		Bekhterev					
Behaviorism							
	Pavlov			Hull	Miller		
		Meyer	Weiss			Spence	
		Watson	Tolman	Skinner	Mowrer		
Psychoanalysis							
		Adler Rank					
Breuer	Janet	Freud		Horney	Sullivan	Fromm	
		Jung Ferenczi					
Existential/Gestalt/Humanist							
		Husserl		Köhler	Heidegger	May	
			Wertheimer	Koffka		Sartre	

SOURCE: © 1989 M. J. Mahoney.

cent changes in theoretical psychology will be briefly described.

SYSTEMS OF PSYCHOLOGICAL PRACTICE

The earliest examples of mental health interventions occurred during ancient times and were largely derived from prevailing mystical and religious views regarding causes and treatments for abnormal behavior. These interventions attempted to rid the individual of evil spirits and demons by exorcism and other means, even including the cutting of holes (*trephine*) in the person's skull to allow the spirits as easier exit.

During the height of the Greek civilization, there were philosophical and practical shifts in the view that behavioral problems were more biological in origin. Abnormal behaviors were studied with the extant scientific methods and were treated by physicians, the most famous of whom was Hippocrates (460–377 B.C.). Even during those times, psychopathological problems continued to be viewed by many as religious problems, and the Greek world had numerous temples at which individuals could be "cured" of their deviant behaviors. Although some emphasis on natural causes and treatments of psychological problems continued during the ascendance and fall of the Roman Empire (e.g., Galen, 130–200 A.D.), such a view never was completely accepted.

With the arrival of the Middle or Dark Ages, the notion that people with mental health problems were suffering primarily from serious religious problems again became the prevailing view. As in ancient times, medieval conceptualizations are based on the assumption that individuals were inhabited by evil spirits as retribution for their wickedness and sins. Exorcism was required to treat abnormal behaviors. Often, harsh and inhumane procedures, such as flogging and starvation, were used to make the body uninhabitable for the evil spirits. A variety of other religious activities (religious ceremonies) and pseudoreligious treatments (e.g., enforced copying of parts of the Bible) evolved in an effort to help people with their problems. One of the major treatments during this period required the afflicted person to travel to religious shrines where healing supposedly occurred. Gradually communities with shrines (e.g., Gheel near Antwerp in Belgium) became centers where people stayed and lived. Similarly, many monasteries became treatment and housing centers for people with psychological disorders. From this situation evolved the concept of an asylum as a long-term residential facility that served to isolate such individuals from the strain and stress of everyday life. However, the conditions were quite deplorable in most cases, and deprived these people of the usual freedoms and choices of life.

Around the beginning of the nineteenth century the influence of various doctors and humane leaders, such as Pinel in France, Tuke in England, and Rush in the United States, led to the development of more humane treatment approaches, which were based largely on practical problem-solving approaches. Some of the best treatment programs, such as the one at Worcester State Hospital in Massachusetts, have been referred to as "moral treatment" (Bockoven, 1963), and resulted in fairly normal living styles and very successful (up to 70% discharge rates) treatment programs.

Because of the success and relatively humane treatment of mental patients in the hospital setting of the nineteenth century, the latter half of that century witnessed the building of larger state hospitals. These soon became overcrowded and understaffed, however, and this precluded the continuation of "moral treatment." Bigger hospitals required larger staffs, who were not adequately trained, perhaps due to a general lack of an adequate model for intervention and the continued absence of a knowledge base for treating such problems. About this time (late 1900s), within the context of large mental hospitals, the medical model of psychiatric disorders began to prevail.

This *medical model* maintained that the residents in the large hospitals had an illness (although the nature of the disorders was largely unknown and methods of treatment were of limited effectiveness), and that a physician should do the treating. The staff, rather than providing a therapeutic community, were seen as a custodial staff to provide for the patient's physical needs. Treatment in the United States continued under the direction of the medical model for several decades.

The first major shift toward emphasizing the role of psychological factors in the origins and treatment of behavioral problems was Freud's psychoanalytic model. Freud had his major initial impact on treatments in the 1920s and 1930s; forms of psychoanalytic or psychodynamic theory still play a major role in the mental health field.

As noted, psychology emerged as a discipline in the last quarter of the nineteenth century, and behaviorism emerged in the 1930s and 1940s. Psychologists' major role in the mental health arena until World War II was as assessors of intelligence and personality. After that time psychologists played a larger role in the conceptualization and treatment of psychological disorders. As they became involved in the treatment of practical problems, behaviorally oriented psychologists brought their scientific methodology and recently derived principles of learning with them. As these principles were applied to behavioral problems, the field of behavior therapy or behavior modification rapidly emerged. This behavioral viewpoint has gradually intertwined with cognitive approaches to the study of humans and the treatment of human problems. This integration has developed into the broadly based treatments described and reviewed in this book as cognitive-behavioral interventions.

To understand better these behavioral and cognitive-behavioral systems of intervention, they should be considered in the broader context of psychological therapies. Although there may now be over 400 different approaches to psychotherapy (Mahoney, 1991a), this diversity can be simplified if conceptually similar approaches are clustered together. Ideas can be expressed very differently and yet share core assumptions and assertions about human nature and psychological change. The diversity reflected in over 400 psychotherapies, for example, can be reduced to fewer than six families of theories that endorse different "root metaphors" about how best to study human experience (Pepper, 1942). At the beginning of the present century there were three dominant perspectives shaping professional services in psychology: psychoanalysis, behaviorism, and some of the seeds of modern cognitive therapies. Eclecticism, the idea that the best parts of rival theories should be selected and integrated, was not popular in the first half of the century. This situation changed dramatically after 1950.

In the recent proliferation of psychotherapies there has been considerable elaboration and integration. Fifteen surveys of U.S. clinical psychologists over almost four decades reflect the changing popularity of different perspectives (Figure 1.1). The early dominance and more recent decline of psychoanalysis is noteworthy, as is the relative growth of eclecticism. Both cognitive and behavioral perspectives have established themselves to a lesser degree and their integration has become increasingly popular over the last quarter of a century (Craighead, 1982, 1990; Kazdin, 1978; Mahoney & Arnkoff, 1978).

The unfinished integration and convergence of theoretical views has been a major factor in late twentieth-century psychology. Although it is an oversimplification, there is some truth in the characterization of twentieth-century psychology as a multifaceted, dynamic tension among three powerful forces in human experience: doing, thinking, and feeling. The essence of the theoretical struggles that have characterized psychology in our century can be cast as a conceptual triangle (Figure 1.2). The relative power or primacy of each of the three forces has been a major criterion for distinguishing theoretical views. Clustering around their preferred "prime mover" (first cause), adherents of different theories gravitated toward corresponding concepts. Those who thought behavior was the primary source of power called themselves "behaviorists" and argued that action and its consequences determine human thinking and feeling. Those who endorsed the power of thinking and imagination argued that cognition is the prime mover: "As you think, so shall you act and feel." They became known as "cognitivists." The emotive theorists argued that feeling is primary and most powerful. Their therapies—often labeled experiential—have focused on the experience and expression of affect as the most promising path to health and well-being.

G. Terence Wilson, past president of the Association for the Advancement of Behavior Therapy (AABT), described a similar three-way contrast of emphases in the evolution of clinical behavior therapy over the last three decades. The 1960s, he noted, were the decade of behavior: therapies based on learning theory and reinforcement contingencies were considered the essence of behavior therapy. The decade of the 70s was marked by the cognitive revolution in clinical psychology and the integration of cognitive and behavioral theories and therapies. With the 1980s came yet another evolution: a shift in focus to emotional processes in learning and adaptation. With the opening of the final decade of the century there has been a marked increase in eclectic and intergrative models that acknowledge the complex interdependence of these three realms. The human being has been put back together, so to speak, and there is considerably more breadth in therapeutic concepts and techniques.

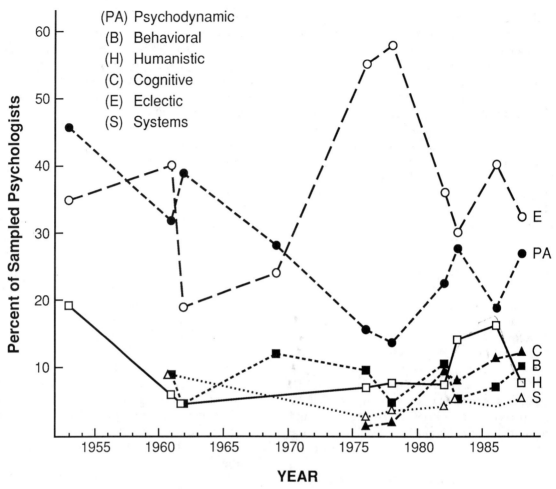

FIGURE 1.1

Surveys of clinical psychologists' perspectives
SOURCE: ©1989 M. J. Mahoney.

CONTRASTS IN COGNITIVE AND BEHAVIORAL PERSPECTIVES

It would be misleading to suggest, however, that all important theoretical differences have been reconciled in the sweep of eclecticism and psychotherapy integration. The late B. F. Skinner, for example, remained uncompromising in his rejection of the cognitive sciences and their potential contributions to psychology. Three

years before his death in 1990 he labeled cognitive psychology, psychotherapy, and humanistic psychology as "major obstacles" to the development of psychology as a science (Skinner, 1987). When it was argued that scientific psychology is much broader than the study of behavior and its consequences (Mahoney, 1989), intensely emotional defenses of Skinner and his views were provoked (Lonigan, 1990; Mahoney, 1990, 1991a, 1991b).

Only days before he died, Skinner focused his

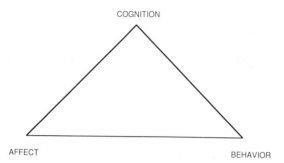

COGNITION

AFFECT

BEHAVIOR

FIGURE 1.2

Conceptual triangle
SOURCE: ©1989 M. J. Mahoney.

TABLE 1.2   Original (1977) survey participants

Gene G. Abel	Arnold A. Lazarus
W. Stewart Agras	Richard S. Lazarus
Nathan H. Azrin	Harold Leitenberg
Donald M. Baer	Robert P. Liberman
Albert Bandura	Michael J. Mahoney
David H. Barlow	G. Alan Marlatt
Aaron T. Beck	Donald H. Meichenbaum
Daryl J. Bem	K. Daniel O'Leary
Sidney Bijou	Gordon L. Paul
J. Paul Brady	E. Jerry Phares
Joseph R. Cautela	David C. Rimm
Gerald C. Davison	Julian P. Rotter
Albert Ellis	Irwin G. Sarason
Charles B. Ferster	Martin E. P. Seligman
Jerome D. Frank	Jerome L. Singer
Cyril M. Franks	George Spivack
Donna Gelfand	Bonnie Strickland
Marvin R. Goldfried	Carl E. Thoresen
Frederick H. Kanfer	Leonard P. Ullmann
Alan E. Kazdin	G. Terence Wilson
Leonard Krasner	Joseph Wolpe

SOURCE: ©1989 M. J. Mahoney.

waning energies in a public attack on cognitive science, which he called "the creationism of psychology," because of its search inside rather than outside the organism for the causes of human behavior. "Cognitive science," said Skinner, "is an effort to reinstate that inner initiating-originating-creative self or mind which, in a scientific analysis, simply does not exist." (Bales, 1990, p. 6). According to his daughter, Skinner spent his last evening alive working to complete the written version of his attack on cognitive scientists (Fowler, 1990).

What is at stake here that has motivated such strong claims and such dramatic "dying breath" expressions? Is this yet another swing of the conceptual pendulum between the extremes of environmentalism and self-determinism (Buss, 1978)? How representative was Skinner of present-day behaviorists? Some partial answers to such questions were offered in a longitudinal study of leading experts in cognitive and behavioral perspectives (Mahoney & Gabriel, 1990).

In 1977 a sample of 42 influential behaviorists and cognitivists (Table 1.2) completed a questionnaire about psychological issues and the causes of human change. Eight years later they again responded to the 12 items that had most dramatically distinguished between behaviorists and cognitivists in the earlier survey. The results of this pair of studies were very interesting (Tables 1.3, and 1.4). In the 1985 testing, the experts sorted themselves into three (not two) groups: behavioral, cognitive-behavioral, and cognitive. The 12 items that had distinguished the earlier cognitive and behavioral groupings were also very successful in distinguishing the three-way clusters (Table1.4); significant group differences were observed on 75% of the items. (Although large numbers of statistical tests may inflate the probability of a "spuriously significant" result, procedures like the Bonferroni correction compensate for the number of tests employed and guard against such inflation.)

Not surprisingly, the behaviorists sampled were more accepting of a conditioning model of learning, granted relatively more power to the environment than to the organism, and were less tolerant or accepting of the cognitive sciences.

TABLE 1.3   Questionnaire items and descriptive statistics (©1989 M. J. Mahoney)

Item	Year	Behavioral (n = 8)		Cognitive-Behavioral (n = 17)		Cognitive n = 12	
		M	SD	M	SD	M	SD
1. At present, there is considerable evidence to suggest that private events (e.g., patterns of thought) may be very influential factors in human adjustment.	1977	7.29	0.5	8.65	1.5	9.50	0.9
	1985	6.38	2.9	7.06	1.9	8.83	1.3
2. Thoughts and mental images are probably conditioned mediating responses that act as stimuli for subsequent behavior.	1977	8.00	1.7	4.88	2.5	4.00	3.1
	1985	7.00	1.7	4.31	2.6	4.09	3.95
3. Unconscious processes probably play a minor role (if any) in human behavior.	1977	4.86	3.2	4.35	3.1	2.33	2.2
	1985	4.13	4.5	4.77	3.0	1.46	1.0
4. The term "self-control" is an enigma in that all control begins with the environment.	1977	7.86	1.8	3.06	2.3	1.08	1.6
	1985	5.57	3.4	2.13	2.2	1.17	0.7
5. When the behaviorist begins to infer private events from observable performances, he or she has abandoned behaviorism.	1977	3.57	3.2	2.82	2.6	3.00	3.0
	1985	4.63	4.7	3.35	3.5	2.75	2.7
6. I feel satisfied with the adequacy of my current understanding of human behavior.	1977	1.29	1.3	2.18	2.7	0.92	1.6
	1985	2.13	2.9	2.47	2.3	2.08	1.7
7. Private events (thoughts, images, etc.) offer little promise in enhancing our understanding and control of human behavior.	1977	4.29	2.1	1.24	1.3	0.17	0.6
	1985	4.75	4.3	1.12	0.8	0.82	1.4
8. Conditioning models offer the most adequate contemporary perspective on human learning.	1977	7.63	2.6	4.47	3.1	1.67	2.6
	1985	5.75	3.4	3.24	2.9	1.25	1.3
9. Cognitive psychology may have much to offer the behavior therapist.	1977	4.71	2.4	7.47	2.6	10.00	0.0
	1985	4.63	4.2	6.77	1.9	9.25	0.8
10. The recent interest in "cognition" among behavior modifiers is an unfortunate and counterproductive development.	1977	5.71	2.8	1.47	1.5	0.17	0.6
	1985	5.25	4.0	2.29	2.0	0.46	0.8
11. The basic process in clinical behavior change is conditioning.	1977	5.88	3.6	3.35	2.4	1.33	1.6
	1985	5.00	3.1	3.24	2.8	1.83	1.7
12. Unless they can be operationalized, "feelings" are of little use in a scientific analysis of human behavior.	1977	6.57	3.3	4.69	2.8	3.58	3.1
	1985	6.57	3.9	5.12	3.8	3.50	3.2

TABLE 1.4   Summary of item ANOVAs (©1989 M. J. Mahoney)

Item	Year	F Value (df)	p Value	Post Hoc Comparisons
1	1977	7.73(2, 33)	<.002	CB>B; $t = 3.34$** C>B; $t = 6.93$**
	1985	4.53(2, 34)	<.02	C>B; $t = 2.38$* C>CB; $t = 3.07$**
2	1977	5.50(2, 33)	<.01	B>CB; $t = 3.51$** B>C; $t = 3.60$**
	1985	3.25(2, 32)	<.05	B>CB; $t = 2.67$** B>C; $t = 2.19$*
3	1977	2.43(2, 33)	NS	
	1985	5.48(2, 33)	<.01	CB>C; $t = 4.64$**
4	1977	25.91(2, 33)	<.0001	B>C; $t = 8.38$** B>CB; $t = 5.50$** CB>C; $t = 2.75$*
	1985	10.31(2, 32)	<.0004	B>CB; $t = 2.59$* B>C; $t = 3.58$**
5	1977	0.17(2, 33)	NS	
	1985	0.79(2, 34)	NS	
6	1977	1.31(2, 33)	NS	
	1985	0.13(2, 34)	NS	
7	1977	23.41(2, 33)	<.0001	B>C; $t = 5.18$** B>CB; $t = 3.65$* CB>C; $t = 3.09$*
	1985	10.62(2, 33)	<.0003	B>CB; $t = 2.67$* B>C; $t = 2.76$*
8	1977	10.72(2, 34)	<.0002	B>C; $t = 5.09$** B>CB; $t = 2.68$* CB>C; $t = 2.65$*
	1985	8.02(2, 34)	<.001	B>C; $t = 3.80$** CB>C; $t = 2.65$**
9	1977	15.17(2, 33)	<.0001	C>B; $t = 5.92$** C>CB; $t = 4.09$**
	1985	11.65(2, 34)	<.0001	C>B; $t = 3.49$** C>CB; $t = 5.05$**
10	1977	27.26(2, 33)	<.0001	B>C; $t = 5.16$** B>CB; $t = 3.79$* CB>C; $t = 3.33$**
	1985	10.46(2, 30)	<.0004	B>CB; $t = 2.11$* B>C; $t = 3.66$* CB>C; $t = 3.12$**
11	1977	7.92(2, 34)	<.002	B>C; $t = 3.38$* CB>C; $t = 2.68$*
	1985	3.51(2, 33)	<.05	B>C; $t = 2.48$*
12	1977	2.21(2, 32)	NS	
	1985	2.17(2, 33)	NS	

* $p <.05$ = Bonferroni $p <.017$.   ** $p <.01$ = Bonferroni $p <.003$.
Note: B = behaviorists, CB = cognitive-behaviorists, C = cognitivists.

Cognitivists, on the other hand, were more critical of conditioning models, more inclined to grant power to the organism, and more optimistic about the promise of cognitive studies. Cognitive-behavioral respondents scored midrange on most of these issues. Interestingly, cognitive respondents were substantially less skeptical of unconscious processes.

This research also illustrates a point emphasized by early (and many modern) behaviorists—namely, that statistical measures of central tendency (means, medians, and models) may obscure or misrepresent the importance of variability and individual differences. On closer examination, for example, it was found that there were wide-ranging differences in the responses of behavioral, cognitive and cognitive-behavioral respondents. Moreover, when the same kinds of statistical tests were performed on variances (individual differences within groups), it was found that there were significant differences in the variability within the three groups at the second (but not the first) testing. Overall, behaviorists demonstrated more variability in their 1985 responses than did either cognitive or cognitive-behavioral respondents. Thus, although behaviorists had shown no substantial change in their *average* responses to items, they demonstrated relatively more diversity in their views at the second testing. These findings can be interpreted in a number of ways, of course, and it is logically impossible to known which (if any) is the "right" or most reasonable interpretation.

Yet another ambiguous but interesting set of data was based on the responses of the first 21 presidents of the Association for Advancement of Behavior Therapy. The presidents estimated their own "cognitiveness" (see Figure 1.3). But how representative is the ideology of a president in terms of his or her constituency and what inferences can be drawn from such data? Is the critical question whether cognitive or behavioral perspectives are more or less popular rather than whether the dialogue across these conceptual contrasts is likely to be productive? In increasing numbers, modern psychological researchers and practitioners are less focused on which theoretical system is "good" or "bad" and more interested in what the study of diverse systems may

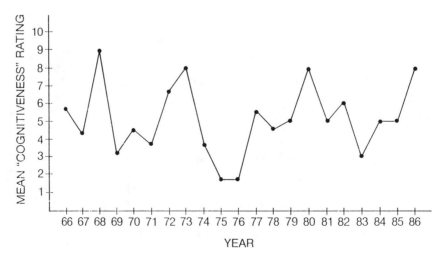

FIGURE 1.3

Estimates of their own "cognitiveness" by 21 past presidents of the Association for the Advancement of Behavior Therapy (©1989 M. J. Mahoney)

contribute to our understanding and facilitation of human development. This point is, in fact, illustrated by examining the changes within cognitive and behavioral theories over the last few decades. Let us therefore shift to a sketch of some of the general directions and new paths being forged by theorists, researches, and therapists who endorse cognitive and behavioral metatheories.

THE MULTIPLICITY OF MODERN BEHAVIORISMS

To begin with, it should be acknowledged that behaviorism has been characterized by a plurality of views for some time now, and that broad generalizations about its essence have become increasingly inaccurate in representing the range of views and practices that are now labeled "behavioral" and "behavioristic." Indeed, it has been these differentiations that have drawn some of the heaviest criticism from those who describe themselves as "orthodox" or "radical" behaviorists. This is hardly surprising, of course, given that the proponents of differentiation have been eager to refine and "reconstruct" behaviorism, and "orthodoxy" entails an unwavering fidelity to the "right opinion" of first authorities. The spectrum of changes that have been underway in behaviorism and the range of reactions to those changes are now popular topics of both research and commentary (Hayes, 1987; Killeen, 1984; Zuriff, 1985). Consider, for example, the important shift away from John B. Watson's radical behaviorism and toward the modern expressions of "interbehaviorism" and "emergent behaviorism." These newer versions of behaviorism acknowledge their reliance on inference, concede the conceptual power of mediational concepts, and endorse the wisdom of dialogue across the shifting ideological sands of cognitive and behavioral perspectives (Kleinginna & Kieinginna, 1988; Martin &

Levey, 1985; Piattelli-Palmarini, 1989; Rachlin, 1989). Among other things, these writers and others have moved toward a common ground that simultaneously acknowledges the biological embodiment of the organism, social and symbolic contributions to human experience and expression, and the fundamental role of exploratory behavior in affording opportunities for learning. It is therefore not surprising that some of the most significant developments in "postmodern" experimental psychology have themselves emerged from novel explorations and creative methodologies.

To illustrate, consider some of the recent studies of "animal cognition" (Dore & Dumas, 1987), especially comparative studies of conceptual behavior in life forms ranging from pigeons to people. Until recently, the stimuli used to signal and study rats, pigeons, and virtually all other experimental subjects were simple geometric shapes and colors. However, Herrnstein and Loveland (1964) were pioneers in the discovery of "natural concepts" in animals—i.e., that many animals can distinguish among complex stimuli that occur in the natural environment. They were the first to demonstrate, for example, that pigeons can readily discriminate between pictures with and without humans in them. Later work has shown that our feathered friends can also discriminate and categorize pictures of trees, leaves, water, other pigeons, the letter "A" and the number "2" (regardless of font), and aerial photographs with and without human-made objects in them (Bhatt, Wasserman, Reynolds, & Knauss, 1988; Roberts & Mazmanian, 1988; Wasserman, Kiedinger, & Bhatt, 1988). As Roberts and Mazmanian (1988, p. 259) put it, studies of natural concept learning in animals "have demonstrated that monkeys and pigeons can conceptualize at a more abstract level than has been revealed in previous animal studies, but the basis for this ability remains unclear."

What *is* increasingly clear, however, is the fact that experimental psychology is alive and well, and that it is still making important contributions to our understanding of basic learning processes.

Even if the lesson is only a deeper appreciation for the abstraction and complexity exhibited by many living organisms, it is an important invitation to move beyond our earlier conceptual constraints. In coming up with novel methods and questions in the study of animal behavior processes, provocative new findings have emphasized that our prior assumptions unnecessarily limited our research and theories.

EVOLUTIONS BEYOND THE COGNITIVE REVOLUTION

Just as there are many contemporary variants of behaviorism, there are also different forms of cognitivism. At last count, for example, there were over 20 distinguishable forms of cognitive psychotherapy, and there have been at least two (and some say three) major theoretical developments subsequent to the first cognitive revolution in psychology.

Information Processing

The first cognitive revolution is now said to have taken place in the decade between 1955 and 1965. That was the "information processing" revolution, and it remains the best known splash of the cognitive sciences. Information processing models were essentially based on the developing technology of computers, and the first wave of cognitive theories in psychology borrowed extensively from computer metaphors. Thus, for example, stimuli were said to enter a "sensory register" and then to be processed through short-term or long-term memory banks. For many years, the terms "information processing" and "cognitive psychology" were used as virtual synonyms. With more recent developments in cognitive studies, however, the limitations of these models became increasingly apparent. Because of their emphasis on computation and computer

metaphors for knowledge representation, for example, information processing approaches have been found to be very limited in their conceptual scope.

Connectionism

The second cognitive revolution, which is still underway, has been called "connectionism," but it should not be confused with E. L. Thorndike's learning theory of the same name. The basic features of modern connectionism are: (1) a shift away from computers and toward biological studies of the nervous system as the primary source of metaphors for model building; (2) a rejection of exclusively linear (serial) models of information processing, with a shift toward the greater power and flexibility of modern supercomputers and their "massively distributed parallel processing;" and (3) the acknowledgment of "subsymbolic" processes that cannot be expressed in explicit symbolic form. Although connectionist models have demonstrated greater power than their information processing predecessors, they remain excessively tied to computational logic, and many modern observers believe that their promise may be compromised by this continuing subservience to (rather than of) the computer.

Hermeneutics

Hermeneutics has recently received recognition as a field of study relevant to both cognitive science and psychology (Madison, 1988; Messer, Sass & Woolfolk, 1988; Palmer, 1969). Technically, the term "hermeneutics" refers to the complex process of interpretation. It originated in theology, where interpretations of religious writings became prominent during and after the Enlightenment. (The term itself refers to the Greek god, Hermes, whose responsibilities included interpreting the messages of gods to humans). Hermeneutics is often described as a multidisciplinary approach that acknowledges that "meaning" resides neither in the reader nor in the text, but, rather, in the dynamic engagement of both, with each encounter necessarily unique. An important debate in hermeneutics is that between the objectivists and what might be termed the constructivists. Playing with both temporal and spatial elements in the act of exchange (e.g., dialogue) and aimed toward solving the mystery of (personal) meaning in human experience, modern hermeneutics scholars contend that significance does not reside in the meaning of the text per se, but rather in the fact that the meaning draws out of us what had been previously sealed. The concept of the "reader in the text" is now well respected, and the narratives and interpretations that permeate our lives have seldom been so salient. Among other things, modern work in hermeneutics has contributed to the decline of naive objectivism and to a deeper appreciation for the limitations of human inquiry.

Constructivism

Although the perspective now called "constructivism" has been around for some time, its greatest impact on cognitive and clinical studies has been very recent and is ongoing. Briefly stated, constructivism is characterized by three fundamental features: (1) the assertion that knowing is proactive and participatory; (2) the acknowledgment of tacit (unconscious) processes in all learning and knowing; and (3) the acknowledgment that learning and knowing are comprised of complex, developmental, and dynamic self-organizing processes. The assertion that knowing is proactive and participatory is consistent with the metaphor of the "active organism," a metaphor that was elaborated by Sir Charles Sherrington in experimental physiology just after the turn of the century. It places greater emphasis on the "motor" (efferent) aspects of learning activities than has been traditionally conceded by "sensory" (afferent) metatheories of

knowing. This assertion is a theme shared by constructivists and behaviorists (both traditional and "emergent").

The third assertion of constructivism is also a theme of potential concordance, especially given the recent attention to complexity evidenced by some behaviorists (e.g., Kleinginna & Kleinginna, 1988; Rachlin, 1989). The second feature of constructivism, however—the acknowledgment of "deep structures" and tacit (unconscious) processes in the organization of living systems—may be an obstacle to reconciliation. This is particularly evident in criticisms of constructivism that mistake this assertion as a conceptual embrace of psychoanalysis. The term "unconscious" is an emotionally loaded one for those whose professional identity and socialization has included a disparagement of and distancing from anything resembling psychodynamic thinking.

There are at least two significant issues embedded here: (1) whether psychodynamic approaches have made important contributions to our understanding, and (2) whether the "unconscious processes" acknowledged by constructivists are similar to those proposed by Freud. Briefly stated, modern psychodynamic theories—which are themselves exhibiting substantial differentiations from Freud's first assumptions (Roazen, 1976)—are raising important questions in theory, research, and practice, particularly in the domain of self-psychology and the therapeutic relationship (Mahoney, 1991). At the same time, however, the core (or "deep structure") self-organizing processes discussed by constructivists are very different from Freud's portrayal of the unconscious, and it is a regrettable error to presume that this domain is an unbridgeable gap between behavioral and cognitive formulations. Until psychologists make peace with the issues of limited awareness and the long-standing animosity between psychodynamic and cognitive-behavioral approaches, however, they are unlikely to find merit in the bridge-building process.

Summary

Cognitive and behavioral perspectives have made important contributions to theoretical psychology and modern conceptualizations of psychological services. At the present time, there are signs of increasing integration both between these perspectives and, more generally, with other approaches to human experience. The remaining chapters of this book elaborate on these contributions and offer illustrations of the practical relevance of cognitive and behavioral perspectives.

CHAPTER 2

Models of Clinical Change

Utilization of any psychotherapy procedures to alter personality or produce behavioral or cognitive change assumes some model or conceptualization of human nature. The model includes assumptions about motivational forces; the processes that contribute to and shape attitudes, thoughts, and behaviors; the degree to which external events influence an individual's life; and the degree to which the influence of such events can be modified. In addition, the model dictates the way behavior is viewed, the causes to which behavior is ascribed, and the procedures considered appropriate to produce clinical change.

Many models have been posed to explain "normal" and clinical behavior (Hall & Lindzey, 1970; Mahoney, 1991). It is beyond the scope of this chapter to review in detail the entire range of approaches. However, to understand better the developments described in Chapter 1 and put cognitive-behavioral interventions in an appropriate conceptual perspective, this chapter will describe in considerable detail the models that have had a major impact on the conceptualization

of clinical disorders and psychological treatment procedures. The models will include the medical, psychodynamic, and behavioral models, and an integrative conceptual model, within which current cognitive-behavioral interventions can best be understood.

THE MEDICAL MODEL

The medical model of abnormal behavior is patterned after views adhered to in medicine. The medical model assumes that deviant behavior is the result of a disease. As with any disease, there is a specific group of symptoms (deviant behaviors) that go together, and each group of symptoms is the result of a specific disease that has a specific etiology or course of development. Such a cluster or group of behaviors is referred to as a syndrome. To explain the implications of such a position and the current form of the medical model, which is a source of controversy, the

15

forms of disease in medicine must be discussed briefly. In medicine, at least three types of disease can be distinguished (Buss, 1966). First are infectious diseases, which are attributed to some pathogen such as bacteria or virus, as in the common cold. Second are systemic diseases, resulting from a failure or malfunction of a physiological-system organ. A particular organ may fail to function and cause a severe medical problem such as, appendicitis. Third are traumatic diseases, which result from some external event, such as a physical blow or ingestion of a toxic substance; an example would be lead poisoning.

This conceptualization of the three types of disease has been extended to the study of deviant behavior. The infectious-disease model advanced considerably with the discovery of the etiology of general paresis. Research by Krafft-Ebing in 1897 and Noguchi and Moore in 1913 supported the idea that neural degeneration resulted from the syphilitic spirochete. Since some of the behaviors associated with general paresis resembled forms of mental illness (i.e., psychoses), it was thought that other infections might account for other deviant behavior. Generally, infectious diseases are not presently considered to be responsible for most deviant behavior, although various infectious diseases do have behavioral concomitants. Rather, the systemic-disease model is used in research on deviant behavior. For example, some investigators are examining whether various forms of abnormal behavior, such as schizophrenia, represent a breakdown of bodily functions, as in a failure to metabolize certain substances, a lack of specific enzymes, or a malfunction of neurochemical processes. The traumatic-disease model has also been extended to abnormal behavior. Some deviant behaviors clearly result from externally induced trauma, including birth difficulties and severe head injury.

During the past 40 years enormous advances have been made in understanding the biological factors involved in psychiatric or psychological problems. For example, the classification system of problems has been greatly improved. Broad categories of major disorders can be fairly reliably diagnosed, which means the syndromes have been more clearly and adequately defined with inclusion and exclusion criteria for each disorder more specifically stated. This is contained in the *Diagnostic and Statistical Manual* published by the American Psychiatric Association (APA, 1987). As with any classification system, it regularly undergoes revision as new data are forthcoming. The revised third edition (DSM-III-R) is currently in use, and field trials are now being conducted as part of the development of DSM-IV. As will be seen in later sections of this book, cognitive-behavioral interventions can be organized around the disorders identified within this diagnostic manual. As will be noted later, the use of the diagnostic categories and labels derived from the medical model is an ongoing controversial issue within cognitive-behavior therapy.

Less progress has been made in identifying the specific biological underlying causes of behavioral problems. Nevertheless, the available data do strongly suggest that neurochemical dysfunctions may be a partial cause or at least a maintaining factor in several serious disorders, including schizophrenia, manic depressive disorder, and some forms of depression. Furthermore, increasingly effective medications have been developed to alleviate or at least ameliorate some of these difficulties. At the current time these may most accurately be viewed as broad-spectrum medications whose exact method of reducing problems is not known. This observation does not detract from the substantial and ongoing progress made by biological psychiatrists and psychologists in understanding the brain and its dysfunctions. Indeed, as will be noted later, there is reason to be excited about some of the philosophical and scientific assumptions and compatible treatment procedures developed from both biological (medical model) and cognitive-behavioral perspectives.

Within the realm of medicine and physiology, each of the three major approaches of the medical model is useful and not a major source of contention. Investigating the physiological causes (infection, systemic defect, exogenous trauma) of correlates of abnormal behavior has led to important discoveries. However, for many behaviors considered deviant, there is no known organic cause, and in order to account for many of these behaviors, aspects of the medical model have been extrapolated and altered. Specifically, the model has been extended beyond the search for biological causes of deviant behavior. The current controversy focuses on the questionable utility of such a model in explaining deviant behavior that has not been shown to have a clear physiological basis. The medical model suggests that there must be some underlying disease to which symptoms can be attributed. Thus, a model that posits that physical symptoms are due to underlying physical disorders has been extended to psychology where "psychological symptoms" are seen as resulting from "psychological disorders." In these cases, the supposed causal agent underlying "abnormal" or deviant behaviors is a set of "diseased" personality attributes. This extrapolation of the medical model, which utilizes the model but not its content, has been labeled the intrapsychic model or the quasi-medical model (Bandura, 1969).

INTRAPSYCHIC OR QUASI-MEDICAL MODELS

The quasi-medical model of abnormal behavior focuses on personality and intrapsychic processes and is based on assumptions that have been useful in physical medicine. First, it assumes that "symptoms" (deviant behaviors) result from some underlying "disease" process. The "psychological diseases," while not considered to be real entities, except as a result of reification, are seen as functioning analogously to the systemic or traumatic disorders in the medical model. Second, to arrive at the root of the

problem, treatment must focus on the underlying psychic state. To understand the extrapolation of the medical model to the realm of behavior disorders requires explanation of the intrapsychic or quasi-medical model in general, and of psychoanalytic theory in particular.

The intrapsychic model focuses on psychological forces that are assumed to exist within the individual. A number of personality theorists have posited an assortment of such psychic forces, including drives, needs, impulses, motives, personality traits, and other attributes. These forces are assumed to propel behavior. The many versions of the intrapsychic view differ on the precise forces and motives to which behavior is ascribed.

Psychoanalytic Theory

Sigmund Freud (1856–1939) provided an elaborate theory to explain the supposed motivational underpinnings of behavior, and emphasized those causes to which abnormal behaviors might be traced. Regarding many psychological disorders, Freud accepted the structure of the medical model itself, but not its content. These psychological disorders were viewed as analogous to physical disorders; thus, failure of the personality to function appropriately would be analogous to systemic disease, and psychological trauma (for example, sexual abuse) would correspond to traumatic disease.

Freud traced behaviors to psychological impulses, drives, forces, and unconscious processes occurring within the individual. According to psychoanalytic theory, all behavior can be traced to some underlying psychological process. The processes described by Freud are referred to as psychodynamic processes, and the theory frequently is referred to as a psychodynamic theory.[1] Freud's psychodynamic view of person-

---

[1] Dynamics is a branch of mechanics in which phenomena are explained by referring to energy forces and their relation to motion, growth, and change in physical matter.

ality describes behavior in terms of psychological energies, or motivating forces, drives, and impulses, and their expression at various stages early in the individual's development.

Freud proposed three structures of personality; the id, the ego, and the superego. The *id* is the reservoir of all instincts and is the source of psychic energy (libido) for all psychological processes and behavior. The *ego* mediates between the demands of reality and the id's need to fulfill instinctual wishes. Finally, the *superego* represents the internalization of social and parental standards and ideals of behavior. These personality structures are in continuous conflict, which usually occurs at an unconscious level. Each structure contributes to determining whether and how an impulse will be expressed. As the child develops, the expression of psychic energy goes through different phases, each with its own focus for instinctual gratification.

Freud delineated four stages of psychosexual development through which everyone supposedly passes. At each stage, the focus or source of pleasure or instinctual gratification is associated with different areas and functions of the body (oral, anal, latency, and genital). As the child develops, the expression of psychic energy invariably leads to conflicts both with reality and within the structures of the personality. Anxiety reactions, defense mechanisms, and alternate modes of behaving result from instincts that do not obtain direct and immediate expression. Impulses, such as attraction toward the opposite-sexed parent, may not be resolved and may result in a breakdown of normal personality development. Normal behavior develops from the appropriate expression of impulses, wishes, and desires. Deviant behavior, according to the psychoanalytic view, is due to an internal, unconscious conflict resulting from the disruption of normal development and expression of drives and needs and their gratification. Psychological drives can fail to find expression in socially appropriate ways. Drives and unresolved conflicts may find symbolic expression in aberrant behaviors, which are considered symptoms of the real underlying problem. According to Freud's theory, normal, everyday behaviors, as well as abnormal behaviors, can be traced to particular personality processes and the expression of psychic impulses. For example, cigarette smoking is not merely an unwanted or bothersome habit but also a reflection of an individual's need for oral gratification; it might result from insufficient or overindulgent stimulation early in life.

The intrapsychic model, and primarily the psychoanalytic approach, has had a tremendous impact on clincial psychology and psychiatry and, indeed, has dominated the field of mental health. This is evident in a variety of ways, such as the language associated with the development, occurrence, and amelioration of deviant behavior. Terms like etiology, treatment, mental hospital, patient, clinic, psychopathology, and mental illness reflect the carryover from the medical model. As was seen in Figure 1.1, the relative significance of psychodynamic approaches has attenuated somewhat with emerging data supporting the effectiveness of shorter-term, directive therapies, many of which are described later in this book.

Other Intrapsychic Approaches

Psychoanalytic theory has been referred to as an intrapsychic position because it posits that psychological forces within the organism account for behavior. There are a number of other intrapsychic views of personality and behavior. These views also explain behavior by looking into underlying psychological processes. In contrast to the psychoanalytic model, many of these models were designed to account for all of human behavior, normal and abnormal; much less emphasis has been given to the development and alleviation of abnormal behavior.

In some theories, traits are posited as the psychological features that account for behavior. Behaviors are attributed to different amounts of a given trait, such as kindness, or to different traits across individuals. In trait theories, an individual's behavior is explained by the dispositions or traits he or she possesses (Allport, 1961). In other intrapsychic positions, the self-concept, or notion of the self, is believed to be an important basis for behavior (Rogers, 1959). The assumption is that one's behavior is dictated by one's perception of oneself in relation to others and of various experiences of the world. In yet another intrapsychic position, a taxonomy of needs is posited to account for behavior (Maslow, 1966). The needs are internal psychological processes that give rise to overt behavior. Behavior can be traced to a diverse series of needs. Knowledge of specific needs and the ways in which they are expressed is necessary in order to understand behavior. Perhaps the most fruitful intrapsychic model for clinical intervention has been the interpersonal model (Klerman, Weissman, Rounsaville, & Chevron 1984). Although its general clinical utility remains to be demonstrated, Interpersonal Psychotherapy, focusing on the psychodynamic-based constructs of guilt, has been demonstrated to be an effective treatment for major depression (Elkin et al., 1989) and bulimia (Fairburn, 1988). It may well be that as such short-term treatments utilizing psychodynamic constructs are developed for other specific disorders, such as Horowitz's treatment (1986) for trauma survivors, these models will become more useful and valued. This is likely to encourage and facilitate the developing theoretical integration noted in Chapter 1. Other examples of clinical integration of personality factors with behavioral treatments will be highlighted in the final chapter of this book. Although various forms of intrapsychic theories could be elaborated, additional knowledge of their unique features is not required in order to discuss the implication of this approach.

Implications of Intrapsychic Models

Adoption of the medical model and intrapsychic models has significant implications not only for

conceptualizing personality but also for psychological assessment, the labeling of behavioral problems (diagnosis), and for altering behavior (treatment).

The intrapsychic model has strongly influenced psychological assessment and diagnosis of behavioral disorders. Within this framework, assessment focuses on underlying processes that explain behavior, and thus a client's overt behavior is not of direct interest. For example, an individual may seek therapy to overcome anxiety that arises in social situations. The focus is not on specific situations that appear to precipitate anxiety. Assessment focuses on the client's psychodynamics or personality attributes to which the anxiety is assumed to be traceable. Through psychodynamic assessment, the psychologist attempts to provide global descriptions of personality; to reconstruct the individual's psychological development; and to determine how the person reacted in the past to important psychological impulses such as sex and aggression, what defense mechanisms have developed, and what basic characteristic traits or psychological defects account for behavior. Assessment searches for the underlying psychological processes that are considered to be the sources of behavior problems.

Projective tests are an example of the diagnostic tools of traditional personality assessment. These tests attempt to assess personality indirectly through reactions in ink blots, stories created in response to ambiguous stimuli, free associations, or other unstructured tasks. Projective tests provide the client with ambiguous stimuli onto which he or she must impose meaning and structure. The responses are considered as signs that reveal personality structure, psychodynamics, and unconscious motivation. Conclusions are reached by interpreting the meaning of the behavioral signs and inferring underlying processes. Interpretation of projective tests requires clinical judgement to extract meaning from responses. There has been serious criticism of the reliability and validity of these interpretations in predicting behavior. Individuals often disagree on the interpretation of test responses and about the psychological processes to which the responses are attributed. In fact, a number of authors have questioned the utility of projective tests (Lanyon & Goodstein, 1971; Mischel, 1968, 1979; Peterson, 1968; Sechrest, 1963).

Many other psychological tests and inventories have been designed to assess aspects of the client's personality, character traits, and psychological needs, deficits, or defects; these include tests of anxiety, depression, paranoid tendencies, extroversion, impulsiveness, brain damage, and intelligence. Psychological assessment with various inventories attempts to provide a profile of traits and to identify problem areas in personality or psychological development. In clinical use, the purpose of such tests is to help the clinician understand behavior and describe or diagnose disorders. Behaviorally oriented clinicians and researchers have gradually increased their employment of these traditional assessment techniques. However, special attention must be given to the psychometric properties of these assessment scales, and consequently most projective tests are still not used by behavioral researchers. Subsequent chapters will note and evaluate many of the relevant assessment instruments employed in the study of disorders discussed. Radical behaviorists still insist on the study of observable behaviors, and remain the harshest critics of other types of assessment devices, a criticism that is frequently warranted, since many assessment instruments have failed to demonstrate adequate basic psychometric qualities.

The medical and intrapsychic models assume that problematic behaviors are symptomatic of some underlying disorder. In medicine, of course, internal conditions, such as infection or organ dysfunction that are responsible for such symptoms as fever or discomfort are treated. However, treatment of symptoms alone is insufficient if the underlying condition is not altered as well. In medicine, symptomatic treatment is employed and a disease is allowed to run its course only in cases where there is no acceptable cure for the underlying disorder, as with the common cold or a terminal illness. In these cases, symptoms may be ameliorated with decongestants or painkillers. However, in cases where a cure for the underlying physiological problem is known (for example, rabies, gallstones, ruptured appendix), symptomatic treatment alone is obviously inappropriate.

From a psychodynamic perspective, when treatment focuses on the actual problematic behavior, the individual will not be cured. The notion of *symptom substitution* has been suggested as a possible consequence of symptomatic treatment. This concept suggests that if a maladaptive behavior is altered without treatment of the underlying disorder, other symptoms might be substituted for the problematic behavior. Symptom substitution is expected from a *psychodynamic position* because impulses, drives, and psychological forces not resolved through normal channels of behavior seek release through the formation of symptoms such as anxieties, obsessions, tics, and so on. Alteration of the symptom, through which release of a psychological impulse was sought, will not alter the underlying impulse. So the impulse may seek re-expression in another form or another symptom. Cure can result only from the removal or reduction of the impulse, drive, or conflict that led to the maladaptive behavior.

There has been considerable dispute about symptom substitution. Disagreement has centered around these points: whether symptom substitution occurs, whether it can be assessed empirically, whether substitute symptoms can be predicted in advance, and whether the occurrence necessarily supports a psychodynamic position (Bandura, 1969; Kazdin, 1982; Kazdin & Wilson, 1978; Ullmann & Krasner, 1975). At present there is little evidence indicating deleterious effects following treatment of specific behavior problems, and behavioral and cognitive-behavioral therapies have been so widely instituted that if this were a serious clinical problem, it would be readily apparent. Indeed, as discussed later, beneficial side effects frequently are associated with the alteration of specific behaviors, which have been viewed by the psychodynamic perspective as symptoms.

Critiques of the Intrapsychic Model

Among the contributions of the Freudian and intrapsychic models have been: (1) early focus on a scientific approach to the study of psychological processes; (2) focus on psychological causes of disorders; and, (3) the use of psychological (vs. somatic) procedures in the treatment of psychiatric problems.

The quasi-medical or intrapsychic model, however, has been challenged on several grounds. Some authors have noted that pessimism results from diagnosis and traditional formulations of deviant behavior (Stuart, 1970). For example, Goldfried (1990) and his colleagues, in studying the therapy process, found that behavior therapists typically encourage clients to test reality by communicating the message that, "Things are not as *bad* as you think," and psychodynamic therapists communicated, "Things are not as *good* as you think." The problems that clients express are reformulated in terms of personality or characterological defects, deficits, inabilities, or deeply rooted causes. The labels imply a permanent, complex psychological state that is not readily alterable. Behavioral problems are attributed to defects in personality or psychological development. The defects are considered to be deeply rooted, making treatment an extremely elaborate endeavor. Of course, behavior change may never be a simple matter, but attributing behavior to reified and complex inferred states makes behavior change even less straightforward than might otherwise be the case. Indeed, psychodynamic formulations of behavior probably have discouraged the direct alteration of behavior because of its inability to alter supposedly underlying causes in the individual.

The most frequent and significant criticisms of the intrapsychic model have been leveled against Freud's psychodynamic position. Several authors have noted: (1) the difficulty in scientifically establishing several of its propositions; (2) the inconsistencies within the theory itself and in the therapeutic procedures derived from the theory; and (3) the lack of empirical support in many areas (for example, some features of child development) in which relevant research has been conducted (Bandura, 1969; London, 1964; Mischel, 1976; Ullmann & Krasner, 1975). More lamentable, perhaps, is the relative sparsity of qualitative research on the viability of psychodynamic formulations. Some of its strongest supporters have noted their disappointment in this continuing scarcity of rigorous experimental evaluation (Luborsky & Spense, 1978). As noted, however, psychodynamically oriented short-term approaches designed to treat specific problems, although still limited in scope and focus, may eventually prove more effective than traditional, long-term, psychoanalytic therapies.

As this is a textbook on cognitive-behavioral interventions, it would be easy (and tempting) to render a lopsided evaluation, portraying psychodynamic approaches as misguided and unpromising and discussing behavioral approaches with glowing optimism; such a polarity would be both inaccurate and misleading. Although some of the conjectures of Freud and his followers have not survived rigorous experimental scrutiny, their enduring influence and stimulating hypotheses have been major contributions to the field. Whatever else it may be, the enterprise of helping human beings is not a horse race between distinct ideologies. As noted in Chapter 1, there are increasing signs of collaborative exchange and mutual respect between behavioral and psychodynamic theorists; this may well be a promising sign of productive future integration (Mahoney, 1991; Wolfe & Goldfried, 1988). A relatively new organization, the Society for Exploration of Psychotherapy Integration, has been developed to explore possible avenues of integration of conceptual models and practical procedures from the various approaches to psychological intervention.

THE BEHAVIORAL MODEL

The behavioral approach departs from the medical model and the intrapsychic views of behavior in a number of ways. As noted, some unique features of the behavioral approach are methodological in terms of emphasis on assessment of behavior, objectification of concepts, evaluation of treatment interventions, and minimization of inferred variables. The behavioral approach tries to avoid unverifiable, unobservable inner states. However, it would be inaccurate to state that internal states are avoided altogether. Within the behavioral approach, various viewpoints differ on the extent to which inferred variables and inner states should be utilized. For example, among radical behaviorists, inferred variables are usually totally rejected. The focus is entirely on overt or publicly observable behavior. On the other hand, some behavior modifiers posit inferred or mediating variables to account for some overt behaviors. It is important to distinguish between inferred variables posited by some behaviorists and those used in intrapsychic notions. Inferred variables posited by behaviorists are amenable to objective assessment or have empirical ramifications. Anxiety, posited by some behavioral theorists (Wolpe, 1958), can be assessed objectively, through physiological means or a rating of observed behaviors on an avoidance test. Some behaviorists (especially as they have become more cognitive) stress covert events, such as thoughts, self-verbalizations, and imagery, which mediate overt behavior. Yet internal or private events are also amenable to assessment, at least through self-report by the individual experiencing them. In fact, Swan and McDonald (1978) reported that behavior therapists used client's self-report in an interview in 89% of their cases, self-monitoring by the client in 51% of their cases, and written self-report in 27% of their cases. Moreover, overt procedures that alter private events can be observed publicly.

Despite differences among behaviorists, it is generally correct to state that the focus is on behavior rather than on underlying states. The inferred variables posited by behavior modifiers generally are more accessible than are psychodynamic states, both to the client who comes for treatment and to the therapist who undertakes a program of behavior change. For example, a client may wish to eliminate obsessive thoughts or undesirable urges. Although these are not overt behaviors, the behavioral focus would be on the occurrence of these thoughts or urges. Indeed, the client can observe the frequency of these thoughts, to provide data for the therapist. The private event focused on here is accessible, at least to the client. Moreover, behavioral treatment will focus on the thoughts and urges themselves, rather than on supposed sources of these covert events. In contrast, a psychodynamic view of the obsessional thoughts would hold that they reflect underlying dynamic processes; the thoughts would be considered signs of something else and would not be treated as the problem itself.

The behavioral approach is concerned with the development, maintenance, and alteration of behavior. Abnormal behavior is not regarded as distinct from normal behavior in terms of how it develops or is maintained. Abnormal behavior does not represent a dysfunction or a disease process that has overtaken normal personality development. Rather, certain learning experiences or a failure to receive or profit from various learning experiences accounts for behavior. Behavior develops according to the same principles, whether it is labeled normal or abnormal.

Behavior modification assumes that behavior, whether labeled abnormal or normal, depends to a great extent on environmental factors. The processes through which adaptive behaviors usually develop can also explain the development of maladaptive or deviant behaviors. Moreover, therapeutic interventions involve training clients to engage in certain behaviors and not to engage in others: to learn new modes of behaving. A goal of behavior modification is to provide learning experiences that promote adaptive and prosocial behavior.

To demonstrate how behavior is learned and how new behaviors can be taught, the next chapter will outline three types of learning (classical conditioning, operant conditioning, and observational learning) that have played a major role in conceptualizing behavior and generating treatment techniques. Although behavior modifiers have historically drawn heavily from the learning area of psychology, current views are much broader, and it would be incorrect to assume that behavior modification is merely the application of principles of learning. However, for historical reasons and because of the widescale effective applications, the next chapter will describe and discuss basic learning principles in detail.

Implications of the Behavioral View

The behavioral approach to assessment of behaviors departs from traditional diagnostic assessment (Barlow, 1981; Mischel, 1968), although they have some problems in common, such as psychometric characteristics (e.g., reliability). The behavioral approach focuses directly on the behaviors that are to be altered, rather than on the underlying personality. Although a problem may be described in vague or general terms (e.g., hyperactivity), the behavior modifier seeks to observe the behavior that requires change and the events that prompted the diagnosis, the frequency of these behaviors, and the antecedent and consequent events associated with any outbursts. In short, assessment focuses on the behavior of the client as well as on environmental factors. Assessment of the behavior to be changed (referred to as the target behavior) is essential to ascertain the extent of change required or the extent of the problem. Behaviors are not considered to reflect underlying psychological problems but are of direct interest in their own right. Sometimes the factors that precede and follow behavior are assessed. These factors may be useful in altering the target behavior. Events that precede behavior may include the presence of a particular person, instructions, and other cues in the environment that affect the response. The relevant variables for each disor-

der will be discussed in the chapters on those specific disorders.

Behavior modifiers emphasize external environmental events that can be used to alter behavior. This is not to say that events within the individual do not influence behavior. Indeed, internal events and covert behaviors, such as thoughts, feelings, and perceptions, can directly influence behavior. Behavior modifiers, however, differ on the extent to which internal events are to be regarded as determinants of behavior.

It is important to distinguish the internal events that are sometimes central to behavior modification from the seemingly similar processes that are the focus of psychodynamic theorists. Psychodynamic theorists make inferences about underlying states that represent complex abstractions far removed from behavior. It is difficult (frequently impossible) to verify that such an internal state is or could be related to overt behavior. Few predictions can be made that could be subjected to scientific scrutiny. In contrast, behavior modifiers attempt to relate covert or underlying events closely to observable phenomena. In addition, predictions are made about the relationship between covert events and overt behavior. For example, some behavior modifiers (broadly defined) believe that things people say to themselves privately ("I can't do that" or "I am incompetent") affect performance. The influence of self-statements can be examined empirically by altering what people say to themselves and evaluating whether this affects overt behavior (Beck, 1976; Craighead & Craighead, 1980; Meichenbaum, 1977). The next section of this chapter will discuss the role of such "cognitive" events.

Behaviorists consider it unlikely that altering a problematic behavior will result in its replacement by another problem behavior, as in symptom substitution. Behaviorists do not consider problematic behavior a reflection of supposed psychic impulses that seek expression. In fact, behaviorists predict that once a particular problem behavior is altered for an individual, other aspects of his or her life may improve as well. The beneficial effects of treating one behavior may generalize to other behaviors. If a stutterer is trained to speak more fluently, it can be expected that additional positive changes will result. The person may become more confident and extroverted and less shy. Resolution of one problem may begin a series of favorable changes in a person's life. The notion of symptom substitution has little empirical support. Several studies with diverse behavioral techniques confirm the generalization of beneficial effects to behaviors not originally included in treatment (Kazdin, 1982; Mahoney, Kazdin, & Lesswing, 1974). Of course, it is possible that a person who has altered one behavior will still have additional problems, and other problems may seem more salient once the initial problem behavior has changed. However, this is far removed from the notion of symptom substitution. Even if new problematic behaviors develop, they are not necessarily re-expressions of psychic conflicts. Treatment, whether medical or psychological in nature, is no guarantee against the development of further problems. For example, repairing a broken limb does not guarantee the absence of future injuries of a similar nature. Problematic behaviors may appear as a result of psychological treatment. It is possible, for example, that once deviant behavior is reduced, the person may have no appropriate response in his or her repertoire to take its place. This deficit may be evident in continued inappropriate social behaviors. If this occurs, it is frequently the result of poor assessment in which all the problem areas were not evaluated, and thus the treatment program employed was inappropriate and too limited. This deficit can be corrected by a treatment program that develops appropriate behaviors while eliminating inappropriate ones.

AN INTEGRATIVE MODEL FOR INTERVENTIONS

As outlined in an earlier edition of this book (Craighead, Kazdin, & Mahoney, 1981), behavior therapy employs two basic assumptions in its clinical application: behavior therapy utilizes findings from both experimental psychology and clinical practice to develop testable clinical procedures; and clinical interventions implemented under the rubric of behavior therapy should be among those with demonstrated efficacy. Since experimental psychology was focused on learning theory in the late 1940s through the 1960s, when behavior therapy began in earnest and gradually received widespread utilization, clinical applications derived from experimental psychology at that time were based on learning theory.

As we have seen, however, the broader field of experimental psychology has undergone dramatic paradigmatic shifts over the past 20 years. Cognitive and even emotional variables have become (or returned) to being the focus of study in experimental psychology (Izard, Kagan, & Zajonc, 1984; Mahoney, 1991). These findings were occurring simultaneously with major developments in biological psychiatry and psychophysiological and physiological psychology. Such developments have increased our understanding of the role of biological variables in causing various problems of living for humans and the importance of biological or somatic treatments for some disorders. As will be seen in the discussions of specific disorders, the combination of biological and cognitive-behavioral treatments is an important new direction in treatment-effectiveness research.

The available evidence regarding the role of biological, cognitive, and even emotional variables in causing, maintaining, and changing behaviors has necessitated modifications in the basic behavioral model. Of course, there is no one "final" or "true" model of change; there are only attempts to develop models, based on the available evidence, to explain and predict change. The following model is based on the developments of the past two decades as behavior therapy has evolved into cognitive-behavior therapy; 69% of the members of the Association for Advancement of Behavior Therapy label themselves cognitive-behavioral (Craighead, 1990).

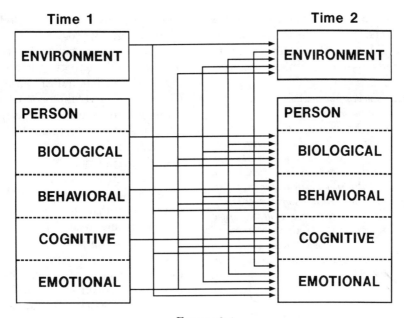

FIGURE 2.1

The cognitive-behavioral model. SOURCE: Craighead, Meyers, & Craighead, 1985.

Although the title "cognitive-behavioral model" is still being used, greater importance has gradually been ascribed to biological and emotional variables, and perhaps a new title or label for this integrative model will soon be forthcoming.

At a basic level, the cognitive-behavioral model in Figure 2.1 assumes a *reciprocal determinism* (Bandura, 1977, 1986) between the environment and the individual. A person lives in an environmental context so that the environmental variables (e.g., school, work) and the person (individual) variables reciprocally influence one another. It further assumes that for each individual, the person variables are reciprocally interdependent, i.e., every person variable affects each of the other person variables as they interact with the environment. For example, depressed persons may focus on the thought, "I am tired all the time; I'm just too tired to do anything," which may then serve to increase their actual fatigue (a biological characteristic of depression) and decrease their social interaction (a

behavior), which changes the impact the environment has on their thinking (they then interact less with others), which increases their depressive thoughts about no one liking them. Thus, the variables continuously and reciprocally interact in normal behavior patterns, in abnormal patterns, and in the process of therapeutic change.

In Figure 2.1, each event occurs within an environmental setting, which may be home, family, school, social event, and so on. The environmental variables of most importance probably vary across disorders, e.g., social situations for social phobics, intimate interactions for people suffering from sexual dysfunction, and home interactions for family and/or marital discord. The person variables of importance depend upon the individual and the disorder. Craighead (1990) recently provided the following examples of the applicability of this model for depression. To understand this specific application of the model, begin by assuming Time 2 is the current time; then the characteristics of depression can be assessed and described within the broad categories of Environment and Person. The Environmental variables to consider are job, social, family, financial, and religious (morals, ethics) variables.

The Person factors in depression include biological (e.g., sleep, appetite, sex drive, energy), behavior (e.g., social isolation, crying), cognitions (e.g., distortions, concentration, memory), and emotions (e.g., depression, anger, and anxiety). Factors at Time 1 (some preceding point in time), then, may be studied and identified as causative of the Time 2 factors. Furthermore, with treatment studies, changes in depressive characteristics (symptoms) at Time 2 may be viewed as resulting from changes in the various factors during treatment (Time 1). Of course, this is an ongoing interaction and dynamic process model with Times 1 and 2 representing any discrete points in time at which an assessment might be made (Craighead, 1990, pp. 16–17).

Implications of the Integrative Model

Based on the material presented thus far, it is easy to see that each of the major models of change has focused on one of the components of this interactive model. For example, the medical model has focused on the biological component and assumed that changes in the other domains are brought on by the primary interventions and resultant changes in the biological domain. Behavior therapists have focused on environmental and behavioral change, cognitive therapists on cognitive change, and intrapsychic models on emotional change. At times, proponents of each model have argued for the exclusive and superior nature of the variables they consider primary and prepotent; thus behaviorists, for example, might have argued that observable behavior was what needed to change and environmental manipulations represented *the* method of change. (Behaviorists, of course, have not had a corner on this exclusivity position.)

As noted earlier, there has been a gradual move toward an integrative approach to clinical research and practice, represented by this inte-

grative and interactional model. The major tenet of the integrative cognitive-behavioral model is that all domains of human functioning and their interactions are important in assessing, describing, and treating human problems in living. Clearly the focus of this book and the psychological interventions described here is on the environmental, behavioral, and cognitive variables, which are important in the assessment and treatment of dysfunction. However, the comprehensive, interactive model also underscores the importance of biological and emotional variables; this implies that they need to be considered, evaluated, and treated either directly or indirectly when they are a part of the problem. As will be seen, much more is known about biological factors and more progress has been made in discovering effective biological treatments than has been the case with emotion, although progress is being made in that area. This interface of cognitive-behavioral and biological treatments will be discussed in the chapters on depression, eating disorders, sexual dysfunction, and future directions. The increasing compatibility between treatments derived from the various domains, which can be understood within the integrative model, is one of the most exciting developments in the mental health field. An important conclusion from the acceptance of such a model is that not only cognitive-behavioral treatments but other psychological and certainly biological or somatic treatments may also be effective. Furthermore, it may be important simultaneously to assess and give treatments in several domains. Throughout this book, chapters will describe various treatments that have been derived from components of this model and illustrate the way the model explains how these treatments relieve suffering due to clinical problems and/or improve human functioning.

The emphasis of cognitive-behavior therapy has clearly been on environmental, behavioral, and cognitive variables. Some procedures (e.g. relaxation training and biofeedback) in the biological domain have also been part of behavior therapy, but most of the somatic treatments for psychological dysfunction have fallen into the medical arena. Most therapies that focus on emotion have either been psychodynamic or are very recent in origin and therefore have limited data regarding their effectiveness. This book describes psychological interventions that have focused largely on behavioral and cognitive change, although they may best be explained within an interactive model. Thus, the next chapter will focus attention on the principles of learning employed to produce behavioral change and the principles involved in cognitive change. These principles will frequently be employed in the clinical procedures described later in this book.

SUMMARY

This chapter provides an outline of different models of behavior. The medical model can be broken down into three types: infectious, systemic, and traumatic. The quasi-medical model or intrapsychic model is based on the systemic and traumatic medical models, but only the structure of the medical model and not its content is utilized. Just as physical symptoms are considered to have underlying physical causes, the intrapsychic model assumes that deviant behavior has underlying psychological causes. The most popular intrapsychic model has been the psychoanalytic model proposed by Freud. In both assessment and treatment, the emphasis has been on the underlying psychological causes rather than on the deviant behavior.

The behavioral model assumes that all behaviors (normal as well as abnormal) develop according to the same principles. In both assessment and treatment the emphasis is on the problem behavior and the internal and external events associated with it. The importance of learning has been stressed in the behavioral model. More recently, this model for human change has been broadened to include cognitive, biological, and emotional variables in addition to the environmental and behavioral variables, which were emphasized in the earlier behavioral model. An example of such an interactive model was presented.

CHAPTER 3

Principles of Behavior and Cognitive Change

As the field of behavior therapy and behavior modification emerged after World War II, clinical procedures were based on the findings from experimental psychology, which during that time was focused on theories of learning. Behaviorists generally accepted the view that normal and abnormal behaviors were learned according to the same principles of learning. Three types of learning were considered important in explaining and altering behavior: classical or respondent conditioning, operant conditioning, and observational learning.

Psychologists working within the behavioral framework accepted the idea that the clinical enterprise draws from basic psychological findings in the development of innovative interventions and that clinicians should evaluate empirically the effectiveness of the procedures they develop. Thus, it was natural that as basic psychological research shifted from a learning to a cognitive emphasis, behaviorally oriented clinicians began to develop procedures with a cognitive flavor (Mahoney, 1974; Meichenbaum, 1977).

This increased focus on cognitive change coincided with the developing fields of rational-emotive therapy (Ellis, 1962) and cognitive therapy (Beck, 1976), which developed somewhat separately and in more purely clinical arenas. The empirical emphasis and evaluation of cognitive therapy (Rush, Beck, Kovacs, & Hollon, 1977) set well with behaviorally oriented clinicians, so the two major approaches were fairly compatible and, as previously noted, have gradually become integrated. Because of the increased emphasis on cognitive procedures, in addition to the principles of learning, we will describe some of the basic principles of cognitive change so that the later descriptions of cognitive therapy procedures can be more easily understood.

CLASSICAL CONDITIONING

Classical conditioning, extensively investigated by Ivan Pavlov (1849–1936), is concerned with stimuli that automatically evoke reflex responses. Some stimuli in the environment, such as noise, light, shock, and taste of food (referred to as unconditioned stimuli), elicit reflex responses (referred to as respondents). Respondents frequently are considered involuntary or autonomic responses that are not under control of the individual; this has recently become a much-debated point. Examples of respondents include pupil constriction in response to bright light, flexing a muscle in response to pain, or a startle reaction in response to loud noise. The relationship between the unconditioned stimulus and the response is automatic or unlearned. A neutral stimulus, referred to as a conditioned stimulus, may be associated with the unconditioned stimulus that elicits the response. If a conditioned stimulus is paired (presented simultaneously) with an unconditioned stimulus, the conditioned stimulus alone eventually elicits the response. Classical conditioning refers to the process whereby new stimuli gain the power to elicit respondent behavior. In classical conditioning, events or stimuli that precede behavior are seen as controlling reflex responses.

An example of classical conditioning has been provided by Watson and Rayner (1920), who demonstrated that fears could be learned. An eleven-month-old boy named Albert served as the subject. Albert freely played with a white rat without any adverse reaction. Prior to the actual conditioning, the investigators noted that a loud noise (unconditioned stimulus) produced a startle and fear reaction in Albert. To condition the startle reaction in response to the rat, the presence of the rat (neutral or conditioned stimulus) was immediately followed by the noise. When Albert reached out and touched the rat, the noise sounded and Albert was startled. Within a relatively short time, the presence of the rat alone elicited a startle reaction. The conditioned stimulus elicited the fear response (conditioned response). Interestingly, the fear generalized so that objects Albert had not feared previously, including a rabbit, a dog, a Santa Claus mask, a sealskin coat, cotton, and wool,

also produced the fear reaction. This demonstrated that fears can be acquired through classical conditioning. (Of course, whether fears evident in everyday experience are in fact acquired through classical conditioning is difficult to say, because one rarely observes an individual at the time that fear develops.)

OPERANT CONDITIONING

Much of human behavior is not involuntary or elicited by stimuli in the sense of reflexive reactions. Rather, behavior is emitted and is controlled primarily by the consequences that follow. Behaviors amenable to control by a change in the consequencs that follow them are referred to as operants, because they are responses that operate on or have some influence on the environment and generate consequences (Skinner, 1953). Operants are strengthened or weakened as a function of the events that follow them. Most behaviors performed in everyday life are operants. They are not reflex responses elicited by stimuli. Operant behaviors include talking, reading, walking, working, smiling, or any response freely emitted.

The principles of operant conditioning describe the relationship between behavior and various environmental events (antecedents and consequences) that influence behavior. Although both antecedents and consequences can alter behavior, most applications of operant-conditioning principles emphasize the consequences that follow behavior. Behavior change occurs when certain consequences are contingent on performance. A consequence is contingent when it is delivered only after the target behavior is performed.

In everyday life, many consequences are contingent on behavior. For example, wages are contingent on working and good grades are contingent on studying for exams. A contingency refers to the relationship between behavior and the events that follow the behavior. The notion of contingency is important because behavior-modification techniques often alter behavior by altering the contingencies that control or fail to control a particular behavior.

It may be helpful to clarify some common misconceptions by presenting an overview of the principles of operant conditioning. In order to avoid confusion of terms, it is essential to distinguish between the label for an event or stimulus and the label for the principle that describes what occurs when an event or stimulus is used in a contingent manner. For example, the confusion surrounding the principle of negative reinforcement has largely resulted from the failure to distinguish between a negative reinforcer—that is, a stimulus or event—and negative reinforcement. Events or stimuli traditionally have been classified as positive reinforcers and negative reinforcers (aversive stimuli). Each class of stimuli or events may have different effects on the frequency of a behavior; the effect is determined by whether a stimulus or event is applied or removed following the occurrence of a behavior.

As can be seen in Figure 3.1, positive reinforcement, an increase in the frequency of a behavior, occurs when a positive reinforcer is contingently applied or presented. Negative reinforcement, also an increase in the frequency of a behavior, occurs when a negative reinforcer is contingently removed. Thus, the principle of reinforcement always refers to an increase in the frequency of a response when it is followed by a contingent stimulus or event. Likewise, the principle of punishment always refers to a decrease in the frequency of a response when it is followed by a contingent stimulus or event. Again, as shown in Figure 3.1, there are two types of punishment.[1] Several labels have been suggested for the two types of punishment; the following ones

[1] These distinctions regarding punishment and questions regarding whether punishment by removal is in fact punishment have been much argued. Because of the practical advantages and because much of the research has been based on the distinctions presented in Figure 3.1, the material is presented in this fashion.

seem most clearly related to the procedures. Punishment by removal, a decrease in the frequency of a response, occurs when a positive reinforcer is contingently removed. Punishment by application, also a decrease in the frequency of a response, occurs when a negative reinforcer is contingently applied.

Positive Reinforcement

Reinforcement refers to the presentation of a positive reinforcer or the removal of a negative reinforcer after a response, to increase the frequency of that response. The event that follows the behavior must be contingent upon the behavior. Again, there are two types of reinforcement: positive reinforcement and negative reinforcement.

Positive reinforcement refers to an increase in the frequency of a response that is followed by a positive reinforcer. It is important to distinguish the term positive reinforcer from reward. A *positive reinforcer* is defined by its effect on behavior. If an event follows behavior and the frequency of behavior increases, the event is a positive reinforcer. Any event that fails to increase the behavior it follows is not a positive reinforcer. An increase in the frequency of the preceding behavior is the defining characteristic of a positive reinforcer. In contrast, rewards are defined as something given or received in return for service, merit, or achievement. Although typically rewards are subjectively highly valued, they do not necessarily increase the frequency of the behavior they follow. Many events that a person evaluates favorably may serve as reinforcers, yet this cannot be known on the basis of verbal statements alone. Moreover, there may be many reinforcers available for an individual, ones which he or she is unaware of or does not consider as rewards. For example, in some situations, verbal reprimands inadvertently serve as positive reinforcers because they provide attention for a response. Behaviors followed by reprimands may increase (Madsen, Becker, Thomas, Koser, & Plager, 1970). Even though reprimands

	Applied	Removed
Positive Reinforcer	Positive Reinforcement	Punishment By Removal
Negative Reinforcer	Punishment By Application	Negative Reinforcement

FIGURE 3.1

Operant conditioning

may sometimes serve as positive reinforcers, most people would not refer to them as rewards. Thus, a reward is not synonymous with a positive reinforcer. Whether an event is a positive reinforcer is empirically determined. Only if the frequency of a particular behavior increases when the event immediately follows the behavior is the event a positive reinforcer.

There are many examples of positive reinforcement in everyday life, although it is rare that anyone systematically measures whether a favorable event that followed behavior increased the frequency of that behavior. A student who studies for an examination and receives an A is probably reinforced, and studying is likely to increase in the future because it was reinforced by an excellent grade. Winning money at a slot machine usually increases the frequency of putting money into the machine and pulling the lever. Money is a powerful reinforcer that increases performance of a variety of behaviors.

Positive reinforcers include any event that increases the frequency of the behavior it follows.

There are two categories of positive reinforcers: primary or unconditioned and secondary or conditioned reinforcers. Stimuli that do not require a person to learn their reinforcing value are *primary reinforcers*. For example, food and water serve as primary reinforcers to hungry and thirsty people. Primary reinforcers may not be reinforcing all of the time; food will not usually reinforce someone who has just finished a large meal. However, when food does serve as a reinforcer, its value is automatic, or unlearned, and does not depend on previous association with any other reinforcers.

Some events that control behavior, such as praise, grades, money, and completion of a goal, become reinforcers through learning. *Secondary reinforcers* are not automatically reinforcing. Events that once were neutral in value acquire reinforcing properties as a result of being paired with events that are already reinforcing (either primary or other conditioned reinforcers). If a neutral stimulus is repeatedly presented prior to or along with a reinforcing stimulus, the neutral stimulus becomes a reinforcer. For example, praise may not initially be reinforcing for some people; it may be a neutral stimulus for them, rather than a positive reinforcer. If praise is to be established as a reinforcer, it must be paired with an event that is reinforcing, such as food or money. After several pairings of the delivery of food with praise, the praise alone serves as a reinforcer and can be used to increase the frequency of other responses.

Some conditioned reinforcers are paired with several other reinforcers and are referred to as *generalized conditioned reinforcers*. Generalized conditioned reinforcers are extremely effective in altering behaviors because they are paired with a variety of events rather than just one. Money is a good example of a generalized conditioned reinforcer. It is a *conditioned* or *secondary* reinforcer because its reinforcing value is acquired through learning. It is a *generalized* reinforcer because a variety of reinforcing events contribute to its value. Additional examples of generalized conditioned reinforcers include attention, approval, and affection from others (Skinner, 1953). These are generalized reinforcers because their occurrence is often associated with a variety of other reinforcing events. For example, attention from someone may be followed by physical contact, praise, smiles, affection, or delivery of tangible rewards such as food.

In behavior-modification programs, generalized reinforcers in the form of tokens are used frequently (Kazdin, 1977). The tokens may be poker chips, coins, tickets, stars, points, or check marks. Tokens serve as generalized reinforcers because they can be exchanged for other things or events that are reinforcing. For example, in a psychiatric institution, long-term residents may receive tokens for attending group activities, socializing with others, grooming, and bathing. The tokens may be exchanged for snacks or for privileges such as watching television and attending social events. The strength of tokens derives from the reinforcers that back up their value. Generalized conditioned reinforcers, such as money or tokens, are more powerful than any single reinforcer because they can purchase a variety of back-up reinforcers.

Antecedent as well as consequent events affect the occurrence of behaviors. Antecedent stimuli serve as cues signaling that the reinforcer will follow a behavior. Such a stimulus, which marks or indicates the time and place that a response will be reinforced, is called a *discriminative stimulus* or an S^D. Such stimuli affect our lives every day. One needs only to visualize the grocery market to see how buying behavior is affected by the stimuli that precede it; for example, think of the cookie shelf or the check-out counter. Both contain stimuli that are likely to increase buying responses.

Negative Reinforcement

Negative reinforcement refers to an increase in the frequency of a response following removal of a negative reinforcer (aversive event or stimulus) immediately after the response occurs. An event is a *negative reinforcer* only if its removal after a response increases performance of that response. Events that appear to be annoying, undesirable, or unpleasant are not necessarily negative reinforcers. A negative reinforcer is defined solely by its effect on behavior.

It is important to note that reinforcement, whether positive or negative, always *increases* a behavior. Negative reinforcement requires an ongoing aversive event that can be removed or terminated after a specific response occurs. A familiar example of negative reinforcement is putting on a coat while standing outside on a cold day. Putting on a coat (the behavior) usually terminates an aversive condition, namely being cold (negative reinforcer). The probability of wearing a coat in cold weather is increased. Similarly, taking medicine to relieve a headache may be negatively reinforced by the termination of pain. Of course, whether negative reinforcement occurs in the foregoing examples depends on whether or not the behavior that terminates the undesirable condition increases.

An interesting example of negative reinforcement was reported in a study with a socially withdrawn psychiatric patient (Fitcher, Wallace, Liberman, & Davis, 1976). The purpose of treatment was to increase the patient's voice volume and duration of speech because he spoke inaudibly and only for brief intervals. Nagging was the aversive event and consisted of staff constantly reminding the patient to speak louder or for longer periods during conversations with them. If the patient did not comply within three seconds, he was nagged again. From the patient's perspective, the appropriate behavior (louder and longer speech) terminated nagging and avoided further nagging. Thus, termination of the aversive event was the basis for changing behavior. The results showed that each of the behaviors that the staff nagged a client to perform increased with the termination contingency.

Negative reinforcement requires some aversive event, such as shock, noise, or isolation, which is presented to the individual before he or she responds. The event is removed or reduced immediately after a response. As with positive reinforcers, there are two types of negative reinforcers: primary and secondary. Intense stimuli, such as shock or loud noise, which impinge on the sensory receptors of an organism serve as *primary negative reinforcers.* The aversive response to them is unlearned. Secondary negative reinforcers, or *conditioned aversive events,* become aversive by being paired with events that already are aversive. For example, a disapproving facial expression or the word "no" can serve as aversive events after being paired with events that are already aversive (Lovaas, Schaeffer, & Simmons, 1965).

One type of negative reinforcement occurs when an individual escapes from an aversive situation. Both classical and operant conditioning may be involved. An aversive stimulus or event may elicit an escape response (classical conditioning) that serves to terminate the aversive stimulus or event (operant conditioning). Escape behaviors gradually occur earlier and earlier as the individual approaches the aversive stimuli, and eventually the individual avoids the aversive situation. This avoidance response is maintained and the individual stays out of the aversive situation. *Escape and avoidance responses* may be learned by a combination of a number of the factors summarized. In everyday life, various secondary negative reinforcers may gain the power to elicit escape responses and therefore lead to avoidance responses. These factors interact in simple ways at some times and in complex ways at others.

As with positive reinforcement, antecedent or discriminative stimuli may affect behavior. Such stimuli signal the individual that negative reinforcement will follow a response; that is, if the response occurs, a negative reinforcer will be terminated or removed. Thus, a camper who hears a bear growl may make an avoidance response, or a new mail carrier who sees your Beware of Dog sign may not deliver your mail. Several other examples from everyday experience show that avoidance behavior is under the control of antecedent stimuli, such as air raid sirens, screeching car tires, threats, and traffic signals.

Punishment

Punishment refers to the presentation of an aversive stimulus or event or the removal of a positive event after a response; such procedures decrease the probability of the response it follows. This definition diverges from the everyday use of the term, in which punishment refers merely to a penalty imposed for performing a particular act. For an event to meet the technical definition of punishment, the frequency of the response it followed must decrease (Azrin & Holtz, 1966). Because of the negative connotations frequently associated with punishment, it is important to dispel some stereotypic notions that do not apply to the technical definition of punishment. Punishment does not necessarily entail pain or physical coercion. Punishment is neither a means of retribution nor a retaliation for misbehaving.

Sometimes in everyday life, punishment is employed independently of its effects on subsequent behavior. For example, children are "taught a lesson" for misbehaving if they are required to make a sacrifice of some kind. Similarly, criminals may receive penalties that do not necessarily decrease the frequency of their criminal acts. In the technical sense, punishment is defined solely by its effect on behavior. Punishment is operative only if the frequency of a response is reduced.

There are two types of punishment. First, an aversive stimulus can be applied after a response; this is *punishment by application*. Familiar examples include being reprimanded or spanked after engaging in some behavior, or being burned by touching a hot stove. Whether these examples from everyday life qualify as punishment depends on whether they decrease the frequency of the preceding response. Second, a positive reinforcer can be removed after a response; this is *punishment by removal*. Examples include losing privileges after staying out late, being fined for misbehaving, and having one's driver's license revoked.

A variety of conditions may influence the effectiveness of punishment. The separation of these conditions in nonlaboratory applications of punishment is often quite difficult. Generally, each of the following enhances the suppressive effects of punishment:

1. Immediate application or removal of the contingent stimulus after the undesired response

2. Punishment of every occurrence of the response

3. Introduction of the contingent punishing stimulus at maximal intensity, rather than with gradual increases in severity

4. Removal of motivation for the undesired response

5. Training of an alternative, acceptable response, especially when the motivation for the undesired response cannot be eliminated

6. Reinforcement of responses that are incompatible with the punished response

7. For humans, providing a description of the punishment contingency

Aside from the question of its effectiveness, a number of side effects from punishment have caused its use in applied settings to be questioned. Some of these side effects are: (1) increased emotional responding, (2) avoidance of the punishing agent, and (3) imitation of the use of punishment. (In many instances, positive side effects have also been reported.) It is frequently argued that, whenever possible, positive reinforcement of a behavior incompatible with the one to be decreased should be employed. Another alternative to punishment is the use of extinction. However, some situations require the use of punishment. For example, since head-banging must be decreased quickly, punishment is frequently employed. Even in such cases, positive reinforcement programs for alternative behaviors should be used concurrently with punishment procedures.

To summarize, behaviors are affected by contingent consequences. Reinforcement refers to procedures that increase the frequency of a response, whereas punishment refers to procedures that decrease a response. There are two kinds of reinforcement: positive and negative. There are two kinds of punishment: punishment by application and punishment by removal. Note the distinction between negative reinforcement and punishment. Behaviors may also increase or decrease as a function of their antecedents; such processes are referred to as stimulus control.

Operant Extinction

Operant extinction refers to a reduction in response frequency following the cessation of reinforcement. A previously reinforced behavior will decrease when it ceases to produce positive reinforcers or to terminate negative reinforcers.[2] Technically speaking, extinction is the process of disconnecting the prior relationship between a response and its consequences. It is common, however, for people to use the term in reference to its effects. When this occurs, the term extinction may be inappropriately used as a synonym for reduction. For example, parents might say that they "extinguished" their child's swearing behavior. This usage is misleading for two reasons. First, it overlooks the fact that other procedures, such as punishment, also reduce behavior but would hardly be called extinction. Bear in mind that in punishment, a response is followed by the presentation or removal of a stimulus. In extinction, no such event occurs—the response is *not* followed by any contingent environmental event.

Extinction should also be kept distinct from *recovery*. Recovery refers to the increase in behavior that may occur with cessation of punishment. A previously punished response may increase when it ceases to produce negative stimuli or to cause the removal of positive stimuli. For example, in the absence of any other changes, the suspension of fines for speeding may increase the frequency of speeding. Recovery undoubtedly occurs in applied settings, but usually there is an attempt to minimize its effect. On the other hand, extinction is a widely used principle upon which several clinical procedures are based.

In everyday life, the most common use of extinction is ignoring a behavior that may have been reinforced previously with attention. A parent may ignore a whining child. A physician may ignore the complaints of a hypochondriac. A teacher may ignore children who talk without raising their hands. A therapist or counselor may ignore self-defeating statements made by the client. In each of these examples, the prior rein-

forcer (attention, approval, or sympathy) for the response is no longer presented. The following are additional examples of extinction: putting money into vending machines (the behavior) will cease if gum, food, or drink (the reinforcer) are not forthcoming; turning on a radio will cease if the radio no longer functions; and attempting to start a car will stop if the car will not start. In these examples, the consequences that maintain the behavior are no longer forthcoming. The absence of reinforcing consequences reduces the behavior.

In clinical applications, the stimuli or events that previously reinforced the behavior must be identified so that their occurrence can be controlled. Once the reinforcer is withheld, a temporary increase in behavior may occur. This increase, referred to as an *extinction burst*, usually subsides quickly and the behavior decreases. Such an extinction burst, a temporarily increased response rate, does not always occur when extinction is employed. For example, Wright, Brown, and Andrews (1978) treated a nine-month-old girl who constantly engaged in ruminative vomiting (regurgitating food after eating). The girl weighed only eight pounds, although normal weight for her age would be about twenty pounds. The girl received little nourishment from her meals because of her excessive vomiting. Constant attention was provided to the girl for her vomiting. An extinction contingency was initiated in which the staff was instructed to leave the child's presence and not attend to her when she began to vomit. At the beginning of the extinction, there was an increase in episodes of vomiting. Fortunately, the burst lasted only two days and was followed by a decrease in vomiting and an increase in weight. The gains achieved in treatment were evident over a year later when follow-up information was obtained.

Shaping

New behavior cannot always be developed by reinforcing a response. In many cases, the de-

---

[2] The situation described here is one in which a response has previously terminated an ongoing negative reinforcer. In extinction, the negative reinforcer would be ongoing, but the previously learned response would no longer terminate it. This should not be confused with the situation wherein the organism, by totally avoiding the negative reinforcer, precludes the opportunity for extinction to occur.

sired response may never occur. The behavior may be so complex that its component elements are not in the repertoire of the individual. For example, developing appropriate eating behavior requires, among other things, selecting and using appropriate utensils, which may not be in the repertoire of very young children. *Shaping* refers to reinforcing small steps or approximations toward a terminal response rather than reinforcing the terminal response itself. Responses that resemble the final response or that include components of that response are reinforced. Through reinforcement of these *successive approximations* of the terminal response, the final response is gradually achieved. Responses that are increasingly similar to the final response (goal) are reinforced and they increase; responses dissimilar to the final response are not reinforced and they extinguish.

One of the most familiar examples of shaping is training animals to perform various tricks. If the animal trainer waited until the tricks were performed to administer a reinforcer, the reinforcer might never be delivered. However, by shaping the response, the trainer can achieve the terminal goal. Initially, food may be delivered for running toward the trainer. As that response becomes stable, the trainer may reinforce running up to the trainer when he or she is holding the hoop. Other steps closer to the final goal would be reinforced in sequence, such as walking through the hoop on the ground, jumping through the hoop when it is slightly off the ground, and jumping through the hoop when it is high off the ground. Eventually, the terminal response will be performed with a high frequency, whereas the unnecessary responses or steps developed along the way will have extinguished.

Shaping requires the reinforcing of behaviors that resemble the terminal response or approximate the goal. As the initial approximation is performed consistently, the criterion for reinforcement is altered slightly so that the next response resembles the final goal more closely than did the previous response. This procedure is continued until the terminal response is developed.

Prompts

Antecedent events, such as cues, instructions, gestures, directions, examples, and models can facilitate development of a behavior. Events that help initiate a response are referred to as *prompts*. Prompts precede a response. When the prompt results in the response, the response can be reinforced. When a prompt initiates behaviors that are reinforced, the prompt becomes a discriminative stimulus (S^D) for reinforcement. For example, if a parent tells a child to return from school early and the child is reinforced for doing so, the instruction or prompt becomes an S^D. Instructions signal that reinforcement is likely when certain behaviors are performed. Eventually, instructions alone are likely to be followed by the behavior. As a general rule, when a prompt consistently precedes reinforcement of a response, the prompt becomes an S^D and can effectively control behavior.

Developing behavior can be facilitated in different ways by using various kinds of prompts, such as physically guiding the behavior, instructing the person to do something, gesturing to the person, and observing another person (a model) performing a behavior (e.g., watching someone play a game). Prompts play a major role in shaping. Developing a terminal response using reinforcement alone may be tedious and time-consuming. If the person is prompted to begin the response, more rapid approximations to the final response can be made.

Although prompts may be required early in training, they can be withdrawn gradually, or faded, as training progresses. If a prompt is abruptly removed early in training, the response may no longer occur. But if the response is performed consistently with the prompt, the prompt can be progressively reduced and finally omitted. Gradually removing a prompt is referred to as *fading*. To achieve behavior without continued dependence on prompts, the fading of prompts and reinforcement of responses in the absence of cues or signals is required. For example, prompts may be used to train children to feed themselves. Initially, a trainer may guide the child's arm to help the child place a spoon into the food and bring the food to the mouth. At the beginning of training, prompts may be essential to initiate performance of the appropriate behavior. The completion of the behavior, accompanied by prompts, is reinforced. Gradually, guidance by the trainer is reduced. Perhaps the trainer will exert less physical strength in initiating movement of the spoon to the food. Eventually, the trainer may fade all touching of the child and merely point or say to the child, "Eat." Ultimately, the trainer may eliminate prompts and merely reinforce the child for completing the eating sequence. Thus, although prompts may figure heavily in the development of the behavior, at the end of training they may be omitted. It is not always essential to remove all prompts or cues, because much of ordinary behavior is controlled by such cues. For example, it is important to train individuals to respond to the presence of certain prompts, such as instructions, that exert control over a variety of behaviors in everyday life.

Distinguishing between Classical and Operant Conditioning

The distinction between classical and operant conditioning is obscure in many situations (Kimble, 1961). Earlier thought had been that classical conditioning was restricted to involuntary behaviors and operant conditioning was restricted to voluntary behaviors. However, a great deal of research has shown that such supposedly involuntary responses as heart rate, blood pressure, galvanic skin responses, intestinal contractions, and vasomotor reflex can be altered through operant conditioning (Kimmel, 1967, 1974).

In everyday experience, the difficulty in distinguishing respondent and operant behaviors is

evident. A response may be elicited (classical conditioning); it may also be controlled by the consequences that follow it (operant conditioning). For example, a child may cry in response to a painful fall. This crying is a respondent or a reflexive response to pain. Once the crying begins, it may be sustained by its consequences, such as cuddling and effusive sympathy, and become an operant. It is sometimes difficult to separate operant from respondent crying.

This distinction between classical and operant conditioning also seems vague because operant behavior can be controlled by preceding stimuli. Operant behaviors are performed in certain situations with various cues present. When the consequences that follow behavior consistently occur in the presence of a particular set of cues, such as a certain person or place, the cues alone increase the probability that the behavior will be emitted. The stimuli that precede the response set the occasion for the response, or increase the likelihood that the response will occur. For example, the sound of music on the radio may serve as a stimulus for singing or dancing. This is not an example of classical conditioning because the preceding stimulus (music) does not force (elicit) the response (singing) to occur. In operant conditioning, the stimulus does not elicit or produce a response; it only increases the probability that the response will occur. The following major difference between classical and operant conditioning should be kept in mind. In classical conditioning, the primary result is a change in the power of a stimulus to elicit a reflex response. In operant conditioning, the primary result is a change in an emitted response.

OBSERVATIONAL LEARNING

Observational or vicarious learning, also called modeling (Bandura & Walters, 1963), includes both types of responses, respondents and operants. In observational learning, an individual observes a model's behavior but need not engage in overt responses or receive direct consequences. By observing a model, the observer may learn a response without actually performing it. Modeling can develop new responses and can alter the frequency of previously learned responses as well (Bandura, 1969; Rosenthal & Bandura, 1978).

To understand the effects of modeling, it is useful to distinguish *learning* from *performance*. The requirement for learning through modeling is the observation of a model. The modeled response is assumed to be acquired by the observer through a cognitive, or covert, coding of the observed events (Bandura, 1971). However, whether a learned response is performed may depend on response consequences or incentives associated with that response. The role of response consequences in dictating performance has been demonstrated by Bandura (1965). Children observed a film where an adult modeled aggressive responses (hitting and kicking a large doll). For some children, the model's aggression was rewarded; for others, aggression was punished; and for others, no consequences followed the model's behavior. When children had the opportunity to perform the aggressive responses, those who had observed the model being punished displayed less aggression than those who observed the aggression being rewarded or ignored. To determine whether all children had learned the responses, an attractive incentive was subsequently given to children for performing aggressive responses. There were no differences in aggressive responses among the three groups. Apparently all groups learned the aggressive responses, but consequences to the model and observer determined whether they would be performed.

The effect of modeling on performance depends on other variables in addition to the consequences that follow the model's performance (Flanders, 1968; Rachman, 1972; Rosenthal & Bandura, 1978). Observers imitate models who are similar to themselves more than models who are less similar. Certain model characteristics also facilitate imitation. For example, greater imitation usually results from models who are high in prestige, status, or expertise. Imitation is also greater after observation of several models than after observation of a single model.

A classic example of modeling for purposes of treatment was reported by Jones (1924). A young boy, Peter was afraid of a rabbit and several other objects (rat, fur coat, feather, cotton, wool). Peter was placed with three other children in a play situation in which a rabbit was present. The other children, who were unafraid of rabbits, freely interacted with the animal. Peter touched the rabbit immediately after observing others touching it. The example suggests the importance of modeling. However, other procedures were employed with Peter, such as associating the rabbit with the presence of food, so the precise contribution of modeling in reducing his fear is unclear.

The behavioral approach considers the majority of behaviors to be learned or alterable through the learning procedures outlined here. Treatment is designed to alter behaviors that have been learned or to develop new behaviors rather than to alter psychological processes that traditionally have been assumed to underlie behavior.

PRINCIPLES OF COGNITIVE CHANGE

Recently, cognitive psychology has made significant contributions to the development of clinical change efforts. The cognitive position emphasizes the role of mediation in learning, the cognitive and symbolic processes that influence behavior, biology, emotion, and the environment. The effects of these processes are evaluated according to the demands of scientific investigation. The cognitive processes that have been studied include perception and interpretation of environmental events, belief systems, verbal and imaginal coding systems, thinking, planning, problem solving, and others. These processes are crucial to understanding the interrelationship between the individual and environmental events. Understanding either cognitive processes of the individual or environmental events alone without understanding their interaction provides an insufficient account of many behaviors. The importance of the reciprocal interactions between environmental consequences and behavior change was emphasized in the previous section. This section focuses on principles of cognitive change.

Principles of cognitive change are not as easily organized as principles of learning. However, this section will summarize those that have received widespread clinical applications and underlie many of the procedures described in later chapters. They will be presented under the headings of problem solving, attributions, and cognitive therapy.

Problem Solving

Frequently, individuals in therapy learn how to resolve a particularly difficult situation. It is not uncommon, however, that a person is subsequently unable to use that knowledge to deal with additional problems. Recently, attempts have been made to teach individuals more general problem-solving skills so that they not only can manage the reported problem situation but also can apply the learned problem-solving skills to other situations (D'Zurilla & Goldfried, 1971).

Problem solving has been defined as "a behavioral process, whether overt or cognitive in nature, which (a) makes available a variety of potentially effective response alternatives for dealing with the problematic situation, and (b) increases the probability of selecting the most effective response among these various alternatives" (D'Zurilla & Goldfried, 1971, p. 108). The goal in developing problem-solving skills is to train an individual in how to resolve new problems as they arise, rather than merely to solve a single problem. It is assumed that through training the client will develop a strategy to manage or cope

with virtually all problems encountered. This does not mean that a client will effectively solve all problems, but only that he or she will have the skills to develop, select, and attempt solutions.

D'Zurilla and Goldfried (1971) divided problem solving into five stages or components. To resolve a problem, an individual must:

1. Develop a general orientation or set to recognize the problem
2. Define the specifics of the problem and determine what needs to be accomplished
3. Generate alternative courses of action that might be used to resolve the problem and achieve the desired goals
4. Decide among the alternatives by evaluating their consequences and relative gains and losses
5. Verify the results of the decision process and determine whether the alternative selected is achieving the desired outcome

Problems may arise in everyday life if any of these steps is omitted. A person may not recognize that there is a problem and may even deny its presence; may not recognize specific features of the problem that, if noted, might be more manageable; may not generate viable solutions to the problem; or may pursue unsuccessful courses of action without recognizing their futility. For example, a student may have deficits in social skills in relation to the opposite sex. Rather than conceptualizing this as a problem (i.e., a failure to initiate interactions) for which solutions could be generated, the individual may think of it as a personal trait (i.e., undue shyness) or attribute it to other people being snobbish. Even if the individual recognizes the problem, he or she might not know which specific encounters are problematic or how to formulate alternative courses of action to remedy the problem.

Training in problem-solving skills would be most appropriate for individuals who show response deficits or inhibitions that transcend a single situation. Training is accomplished by progressively shaping problem-solving skills in the client. Simulated and actual problems can be introduced in therapy, and the requisite component skills outlined above can be gradually developed. Initially, minor problems are used and the therapist models the skills. As the client masters the skills, more difficult problems are tackled. The final goal is for the individual to approach all problematic situations with the problem-solving strategy. First, the client practices adopting a problem-solving set and controlling impulsive reactions that short-circuit the problem-solving sequence. After the general problem is formulated, specific aspects of the problem are defined. By identifying specific features of the overall problem—that is, external events that account for the problem and internal reactions that contribute to its status as a problem—the client finds solutions more readily available. An explicit definition of the problem also helps to clarify goals. Once the goals are clear, alternatives for specific action may be posed. Then the individual, in conjunction with the therapist, weighs the consequences associated with each alternative. The long- and short-term advantages and disadvantages of each alternative are evaluated. Next, one alternative is selected in light of its probable consequences. Once a specific plan is decided on, the client develops concrete procedures for implementing the plan. When the plan is finally implemented, the client must evaluate whether the intended effect is achieved and whether he or she is satisfied within the constraints of the available alternatives.

Other variations of problem solving place more emphasis on the interpersonal processes involved in problem solving. In Spivak and Shure's work (1974), one important part of being able to generate effective solutions for interpersonal situations is the ability to identify accurately the problem from the other person's point of view. Therefore, specific skills in other-person perspective-taking are taught.

These therapeutic strategies emphasize improving the client's cognitive abilities to handle problems. Thus, the principles of problem solving may be viewed as basic principles of cognitive change.

Attribution

Another focus of fundamental research that is relevant for human cognitive change is the area of attribution. *Attribution* refers to explanations of and perceptions about the cause of particular events. The causal agents to which events are attributed account for many behaviors. The role of attribution in clinical change is particularly interesting because it points out the importance of cognitions or thoughts regarding observed events. The importance of cognitions is readily apparent when a specific environmental event receives differing interpretations from different people. For example, a simple sound, such as the ticking of a clock, may be interpreted by one person as a harmless clock and by another person as a time bomb. Such attributions placed upon events may dictate different behaviors.

A classic experiment in the area of attribution was performed by Schachter and Singer (1962). These authors demonstrated that an individual's report of his or her emotional state depends on physiological arousal plus cues in the environment to which this arousal might be attributed. In the experiment, some subjects received an injection of epinephrine (adrenalin), which results in physiological arousal, and others received placebo injections of salt water. One-third of the subjects in each group received correct information regarding the effects of epinephrine (for example, that heart rate increases), one-third received incorrect information (about irrelevant effects, such as itchy feet), and one-third received no information. After the injection, subjects were exposed to someone who was behaving in either a euphoric or an angry manner. The latter individuals were confederates working for the experimenter. The euphoric confederate appeared elated and played games (such as throwing crumpled paper into the wastebasket), sang, and so on. The angry confederate made nasty remarks and appeared generally upset. The main issue was the reaction of subjects exposed to the euphoric or angry confederates. The results indicated that those who received the injection of epinephrine and had no other explanation for their arousal described their feelings in terms of the cues available to them, that is, in terms of the actions of the confederate. Thus, the attributions made about their own feelings were dictated not only by a physiological state but by interpretations of the environment.

Another classic study (Davison & Valins, 1969) explored the role of attribution in maintaining behavior change after drugs were withdrawn. Individuals whose behavior is altered with the use of drugs may show behavior change only while the drugs are administered. Once the drugs are withdrawn, the gains may no longer be maintained. Quite possibly, individuals attribute changes in their own behavior to the drugs rather than to themselves. Such attributions may account for whether behavior is maintained once the drugs are withdrawn. One important question in understanding behavior change is the effect of having individuals attribute behavior change to themselves rather than to extraneous factors.

Davison and Valins gave subjects a series of shocks and then administered a placebo drug. Next, subjects were given a series of milder shocks and led to believe that they were now able to tolerate more pain. The implication, of course, was that the drug helped the individuals tolerate greater pain. After this, some subjects were told that the drug actually was a placebo. Those who were led to believe in the power of the drug were told that the real effects of the drug were wearing off. During the final series of shocks, the two groups differed in their pain tolerance. The subjects who attributed their increased tolerance to the drug did not tolerate as much pain as did those who attributed their increased tolerance to themselves. In short, the putative increased tolerance of some subjects could not be attributed to the drug, for they were told that it was only a placebo. These individuals, in fact, were able to tolerate more pain subsequently because of the self-attribution.

In clinical practice, attribution may play a major role in clinical change. As a part of therapy, individuals may learn to alter the attributions that they impose upon themselves, others, and events in their environment. Individuals may learn to attribute to themselves greater control over their own behavior and view themselves as agents who can affect the world rather than as passive objects victimized by environmental factors. This is, in fact, one of the focal issues in Bandura's self-efficacy theory (1977). *Self-efficacy* is one's perceived capacity to meet some challenge or perform a particular response. According to Bandura,

> expectations of personal efficacy determine whether coping behavior will be initiated, how much effort will be expended, and how long it will be sustained in the face of obstacles and aversive experiences. (p. 191)

Self-efficacy is a mediational variable that may be useful in refining our ability to predict and understand the processes by which humans change.

Another clinical application of attributions is the reformulated learned-helplessness model of depression (Abramson, Seligman, & Teasdale, 1978). Although the theory is not seen as applicable to all depressions, the depressive attributional style it describes does seem to characterize many depressives. The theory maintains that depressed individuals attribute the causes of negative events in their lives to themselves (internal), believe that they always have and always will cause negative things to happen to them (stable), and that they cause negative things to happen in all aspects of their lives (global). In contrast, the same depressed individuals maintain that positive events are due to external (e.g., luck), unstable, and specific events. Even if this attributional style is only descriptive of depression rather than causative, modifying this style of explaining events so an individual may take more credit for positive events and blame him- or herself less for negative events may be an important aspect of successful cognitive-behavior therapy for depression, as Hollon and his colleagues have shown (Evans et al., 1992). Thus, a number of studies regarding attributions suggest that teaching clients about attributional patterns and how to change this aspect of cognitive style are important principles of therapeutic cognitive change.

Cognitive Therapy

The first two sets of principles of cognitive change were drawn from areas (problem solving and attribution) of basic cognitive psychology. As already noted, another major contributor to cognitive-behavior therapy is cognitive therapy (Beck, 1976; Beck, Rush, Shaw, & Emery, 1979), which developed more within the clinical arena. Nevertheless, its principles of cognitive change have received considerable empirical validation and have become central principles that underlie much of cognitive-behavior therapy. These principles of cognitive therapy will be briefly summarized.

The most basic tenet of cognitive therapy is that individuals develop and maintain beliefs about themselves as they mature. Individuals view themselves, the world, and the future in light of these beliefs. These beliefs organize themselves around important themes in a person's life and are reflected in the self-talk in which individuals engage. For example, a depressive[3] man may maintain a basic belief that he is worthless. This may be reflected in statements he makes to himself about his competence as a

father, spouse, friend, employee, and so on. These self-statements may be categorized around such themes as "perfectionism" or "need for approval from others." The ultimate goal of cognitive therapy is to change the beliefs that the individual holds about himself. A part of the therapy process will be to get the individual to see how he talks to himself (self-statements) around these themes and how he, in that process, attributes responsibility to positive and negative events. The primary goal, however, remains the changing of the client's basic beliefs rather than just changing the self-statements associated with those beliefs. One way to change the connections between self-statements and beliefs is the identification and modification of dysfunctional and distorted assumptions the client is making about himself or herself. Table 3.1, from Beck et al. (1979), identifies the kinds of distorted assumptions that characterize depressive thinking and what cognitive therapy attempts to do to correct those maladaptive assumptions.

The process of change in cognitive therapy initially involves the use of behavioral strategies to increase activities, especially those that give the client a sense of mastery and pleasure. The cognitive procedures include (1) identification of dysfunctional and distorted cognitions and realization that they produce negative feelings and maladaptive behaviors; (2) self-monitoring of negative thoughts, or self-talk; (3) identification of the relationships of thoughts to underlying beliefs and to feelings; (4) identification of alternative (functional and nondistorted) thinking patterns; (5) hypothesis testing regarding the validity of the person's basic assumptions about self, world, and future. In addition, specific methods of changing negative cognitions (adapted from Bedrosian & Beck, 1980) include (1) *distancing* (teaching the client to re-evaluate ingrained beliefs and judgments by making them more explicit and testing their validity); (2) *decentering* (getting clients to see that they are not the focus of all events); (3) *reattribution* (getting clients to change their attributional style—much like the attribution retraining noted ear-

---

[3] The examples given in this section are based largely on the cognition of depressed individuals. Although cognitive therapy was developed to treat major depression and much of the research evaluating the cognitive therapy model has been done with depressed subject, the model has been applied to other disorders in recent years. Later chapters will illustrate this increased and broader application.

TABLE 3.1   Cognitive errors derived from assumptions

Cognitive Error	Assumption	Intervention
1. Overgeneralizing	If it's true in one case, it applies to any case which is even slightly similar.	Exposure of faulty logic. Establish criteria of which cases are "similar" and to what degree.
2. Selective abstraction	The only events that matter are failures, deprivation, etc. Should measure self by errors, weaknesses, etc.	Use "log" to identify successes patients forgot.
3. Excessive responsibility (Assuming personal causality)	I am responsible for all bad things, failures, etc.	Disattribution technique.
4. Assuming temporal causality (Predicting without sufficient evidence)	If it has been true in the past, then its always going to be true.	Expose faulty logic. Specify factors which could influence outcome other than past events.
5. Self-references	I am the center of everyone's attention— especially my bad performances. I am the cause of misfortunes.	Establish criteria to determine when patient is the focus of attention and also the probable facts that cause bad experiences.
6. "Catastrophizing"	Always think of the worst. It's most likely to happen to you.	Calculate real probabilities. Focus on evidence that the worst did not happen.
7. Dichotomous thinking	Everything either is one extreme or another (black or white; good or bad).	Demonstrate that events may be evaluated on a continuum.

SOURCE: Beck et al. (1979, p. 261). Reprinted by permission.

lier); (4) *decatastrophizing* (getting clients to broaden the information and time frame used in making evaluative decisions—most "catastrophes" can be viewed as tolerable and time-limited).

Cognitive therapy is a collaborative endeavor of the therapist and client (patient) as a team. For example, Bedrosian and Beck (1980) noted that, "In order to achieve a consensual definition of the cognitive distortions that require modification, the therapist and patient must work as co-investigators of the patient's thought processes" (p. 141). Clients are taught to identify explicitly the thoughts, assumptions, and beliefs that they hold about themselves, the world, and the future, and then to collect data to test (hypothesis testing) the validity and usefulness of those cognitions. In so doing, the cognitive therapist is teaching the client to be a "personal scientist" (Kelly, 1955)—i.e., using the scientific method to test behavioral skills and cognitions. Beck and his colleagues, in adopting Kelly's idea of teaching the client (patient) to be a personal scientist, employed a process that appealed to many clinicians trained in an empirical perspective. By teaching clients that the basic principles of scientific evaluation include data collection and hypothesis testing for both behavioral skills and cognitions, cognitive therapy utilizes the empirical model that behavior therapists have always advocated. Thereby, the integration of the two therapeutic approaches has been further facilitated.

As can be determined from this description of the principles of cognitive therapy, such treatment teaches individuals to identify and change basic beliefs they hold about themselves. Currently, these principles, along with those derived from problem-solving and attribution, constitute the most important principles of the cognitive-change component of cognitive-behavior therapy. Undoubtedly, the understanding and development of principles of cognitive change will continue, just as recent cognitive and post-cognitive developments in basic psychology have continued to emerge (see Chapter 1).

SUMMARY

Although behavior modification has borrowed extensively from a number of other areas of psychology, it has relied most heavily on the psychology of learning, including classical conditioning, operant conditioning, and observational learning (modeling). In addition to brief discussions of classical conditioning and observational learning, the present chapter has described in more detail the principles of operant conditioning, which have served as the cornerstone for so many behavioral interventions.

Contingent consequences affect behavior. Two reinforcement procedures increase the frequency of a response: application of a positive reinforcer (positive reinforcement) and removal of a negative reinforcer (negative reinforcement). Two punishment procedures decrease the frequency of a response: application of a negative reinforcer (punishment by application) and removal of a positive reinforcer (punishment by removal). Extinction is a reduction in response frequency following the cessation of reinforcement.

Shaping refers to reinforcing small steps or approximations toward a terminal response. Prompts are events that precede a response and help to initiate it; prompts may gradually be faded. Antecedent stimuli or events may also affect behavior, and when this occurs, a response is under stimulus control.

This chapter has also outlined several areas relevant to human change that reflect research in the cognitive tradition. Principles of cognitive change derived from problem solving, attribution, and cognitive therapy were described. The applications of these principles will be described in later chapters. To explain and account for behavior change, both cognitive and environmental influences should be considered. However, even these two influences should not be considered as exhausting the factors that control behavior, since other obvious factors, such as emotion and biological influences are also important. Nonetheless, at this point, scientific findings from the areas of learning and cognition have proven particularly valuable in the development of effective procedures to change behavior.

The next focus will be the basic methods of scientific inquiry that have been employed in both the development and evaluation of cognitive and behavioral interventions.

CHAPTER 4

Evaluation in Behavioral Research

The hallmark of behavior modification is a firm commitment to research and experimental investigation of alternative treatments. A scientific approach to treatment evaluation entails several components. Critical steps include assessment and data collection, research design, and data evaluation (Kazdin, 1992). These steps have as their goal the demonstration of the effects of treatment in ways that can be replicated by others. Stated generally, scientific research seeks to understand orderly relations among various phenomena. The phenomena consist of independent variables (conditions of interest that usually are altered) and dependent variables (the measures that reflect the effect of the altered conditions).

Establishing relationships between independent and dependent variables is not as straightforward a task as it might seem. Special care must be taken to assess performance, evaluate whether change has occurred, and arrange conditions so that conclusions can be drawn about what caused the changes. This chapter discusses some of the methods used to investigate behavioral treatment interventions.

ASSESSMENT AND DATA COLLECTION

An initial step in the evelation process is the measurement of the construct or domain of interest. Assessment requires specifying the domain of interest and the precise measures or operations that define that domain. Typically, research in behavior modification relies on assessment in three broad domains: affect (feeling), cognition (thought), and behavior (action). The utility and relevance of these different domains vary among clinical problems of interest to the investigator. For example, in the treatment of depression, it is useful to include measures in each of these domains because depression is evident in how people feel (e.g., sad, worthless), think (e.g., helpless to change their situation, hopeless about the future), and act (e.g., engage in activities, interact with others). Thus, the construct "depression" is operationalized with different types of measures.

Assessment in behavior modification is a critical topic because it is fundamental to evaluation (Ciminero, Calhoun, & Adams, 1986; Mash & Terdal, 1988). The topic is broad because measures must satisfy a variety of different needs. First, measures are required to assess a wide range of *clinical problems* (e.g., disorders of children and adults) and *areas of functioning* (e.g., classroom performance, marital communication, social skills). Second, *different types of measures* are used, including those based on various questionnaires and inventories, psychophysiological responses, direct observations of behavior, and others. Third, several different *sources of information* are used as well, such as ratings or reports by the clients themselves and reports by significant others (e.g., parents, spouses). Finally, information about performance in *different settings* may also be obtained (e.g., child functioning at home, at school, and in the community).

Assessment of clinical dysfunction relies on a variety of different measurement strategies and methods. The reason has to do primarily with findings that different methods and domains yield different information. For example, parent and teacher reports of how children behave at home and at school are not highly related (Achenbach, McConaughy, & Howell, 1987). Child behavior is likely to vary in different situations; in addition, perspectives of parents and teachers are likely to be quite different. In general, behavioral assessment includes diverse measures to capture multiple characteristics of performance.

A unique feature of assessment and evaluation within behavior modification has been the measurement of overt behavior. Studies often include or rely heavily on measures of how the individual actually performs in everyday life. For example, in the treatment of clients with extreme anxiety, it is useful to know how anxious people report themselves to be on a self-report measure of anxiety. In addition, direct observation of behavior provides critical information that might show that the clients can in fact enter situations they previously avoided and show little or no overt sign of anxiety. One measure does

not replace the other. However direct observation adds important information about actual performance and hence complements other methods of measurement.

The purposes of measurement are to operationalize the construct of interest and to translate the construct into quantitative terms. In behavior modification studies, several measures are used to operationalize the construct or area of focus. It is useful to highlight this process by considering direct observation of overt behavior.

Classes of Behavioral Data

Direct observations of overt behavior require a special format so that the data are quantifiable. Usually, one of four classes of behavioral data are used: magnitude data, temporal data, frequency data, and categorical data. *Magnitude data* include any measures that involve the strength or intensity of a response. For example, if one were to record the pressure exerted on a lever, one would obtain a magnitude datum. Weight and height are also magnitude data. *Temporal data*, as the name suggests, involve measurement of time. The elapsed time between two events is an example of a temporal datum. Such measures include response latency and response duration. *Frequency data* involve discrete responses whose occurrences can be counted and used to make objective comparisons. Thus, such responses as the number of times a child hits herself on the head or bites her little brother, or the number of bar presses a laboratory animal makes, may be classified as frequency data. Note that frequency data often are temporally bound. For example, one may wish to report the number of occurrences of particular behavior during some specified time period or the rate of responding. For this purpose, the data would still quality as frequency data. Response rate would be classified as a frequency measure even though it involves frequency divided by time. *Categorical data* involve measurements differentiating one response from another. In the simplest instance, such categorization may involve recording the presence or absence of a particular response. Likewise, recording whether response A or B occurred constitutes the accumulation of categorical data. Thus, for example, a right instead of a left turn in a maze would be a categorical datum. The presence of a bar press in situation A and its absence in situation B is another categorical datum.

The four data classes are not employed in a mutually exclusive manner. One may record whether a right or left turn occurred in a maze (categorical data), the number of right and left turns that were made (frequency data), and the running speed associated with each (temporal data). The foregoing data classification system is not intended as an ideal schema, but rather as a means of familiarizing the reader with the wide range of data types employed in the field of behavior modification.

Methods of Behavioral Observation

An investigator must decide if he or she will collect data for the entire time period in which a target behavior may occur or collect data only for some portion of the time. This decision leads to the use of one of the two methods of data collection: continuous or sampling. In the *continuous* method, data are collected continuously over a period of time. In the *sampling* method (also known as *time sampling*), data are collected only for a portion of the total time. For example, one might want to know how many cars cross a particular intersection in one year's time. If the continuous method of data collection were used, the number of cars crossing the intersection would be recorded 24 hours a day for an entire year. Such an undertaking would, of course, be expensive, but it would provide complete data. A less expensive approach would be the sampling method. In the sampling method, one would choose a number of representative days or weeks, and the number of cars crossing the inter-

section would be recorded only during those times. From the data obtained, one could generalize to the entire year by multiplying appropriately. Note that in the sampling method one gathers data only for some fraction of the total time during which the variable of interest is potentially recordable. Thus, one measures a sample of the total time in question.

Each of these methods of data collection has had extensive application in behavior modification. The continuous method is most often utilized when the time period in question is relatively short. The sampling method, on the other hand, is used in situations where the behavior of interest is evaluated over a relatively long time period. For example, one might wish to measure the amount of tantrum behavior emitted by a child in a month. The sampling method would be more useful, because the behavior of interest is to be measured over a long time period. It would be very expensive, if not impossible, to station an observer in the child's home 24 hours per day.

There are several varieties of the sampling method. One can employ either *fixed* or *randomized* time samples. For example, one might sample the behavior in a classroom every day from noon until one o'clock. This would be a fixed time sample. A randomized time sample would entail sampling during randomly selected one-hour periods throughout the school day. The relative advantages of the latter method should be obvious. Unless one is interested in the behaviors that occur during some fixed time, the randomized method usually provides a more representative sample of the behavior in question. In the above example, it may well be that classroom behaviors between eight and nine o'clock are quite different from those between noon and one o'clock.

Both continuous and sampling methods have their relative advantages and disadvantages. The continuous method is more accurate, as it entails full coverage of the behavior in question. The sampling method can be very misleading of one's choice of time samples is unrepresentative. For example, if one were to monitor the traffic at an intersection only on weekdays and from that generalize to the entire year, such a projection would probably be grossly inaccurate. Likewise, if one were to sample a student's studying behaviors only on weekends, an inaccurate representation might result. The advantage of the sampling method is that it is much less expensive than the continuous method and is also helpful in the measurement of nondiscrete behaviors. In general, the continuous method of data collection is to be preferred when it is practical. However, when correctly applied, the sampling method is also a reliable means of data collection.

Data Collection Formats

Within both the continuous and sampling methods a data collection format must be chosen. Two of the most frequently used data collection formats are *actual counts* of the behavior and an *all-or-none-classification*. Actual counts involve the recording of discrete units or instances of behavior. The occurrences of the behavior or units of behavior are simply tallied. Actual counts of performance have been used to measure such responses as the number of social responses (instances of saying hello), self-stimulatory behavior (rocking), seizures, calories consumed, cigarettes smoked, and so on. Occasionally, counts are made of persons rather than specific responses. For example, behavioral interventions have been evaluated on the number of persons who litter, come to work on time, complete homework, and commit crimes.

In all-or-none classifications of behaviors, observations are completed during a period of time. At the end of the period, performance is scored as occurring or not occurring. The time period is scored in an all-or-none fashion. Usually, performance is observed for several time periods (or intervals), each of which is relatively brief (for example, fifteen seconds). If behavior occurs at all during the interval, the entire interval is scored as an occurrence. This method, some-

times called *interval recording*, has been used to monitor many behaviors, such as whether persons are smiling, talking, working, or hitting others. Interval recording is well suited for ongoing responses that cannot easily be counted as single units. For example, a person may interact with others for fifteen minutes on one occasion and two minutes on another. The different durations make these interactions difficult to score as simply two instances of the response. However, several brief time intervals could be scored in terms of the presence or absence of social behavior.

Assessment and data collection play a critical role in behavioral research. As evident from this brief overview, several assessment options and decisions are possible for a given area of interest or clinical problem. The critical feature of assessment is not necessarily the specific method. Rather, it is essential that the method is one that can be described to other researchers and conducted in ways that yield reliable data.

RESEARCH DESIGN

In behavior modification, assessment and data collection are essential because they permit one to determine whether performance has changed over the course of treatment. With assessment, the investigator can identify whether persons have improved, become worse, or remained at their original level of functioning. Although assessment is necessary to the evaluation process, by itself it is insufficient. The reason is that we not only wish to achieve change but to understand the reasons for that change. For example, clients treated for anxiety may improve on several measures over the course of treatment, but change in performance can occur for a variety of reasons other than the treatment we provide. Reductions in stressful events in everyday life, comfort from a friend, greater emotional distance from the event, and a variety of other events and maturational processes might also lead to reductions in anxiety.

Although data can indicate whether behavior has changed, they do not explain *why* it has changed. Clients may improve in their performance on the dependent measures after receiving treatment or while treatment is in effect, but this does not necessarily mean that the treatment *caused* the change. To determine the cause of behavior change requires more than merely gathering data. The investigator must arrange a situation so that a causal relation can be demonstrated between certain conditions, such as treatment, and behavior change. The manner in which the situation is arranged to evaluate the effect of treatment intervention or some independent variable is referred to as the *research design*. The purpose of the research design is to structure or to arrange the situation so that the cause of behavior change can be unambiguously demonstrated.

The importance and the essential features of research design can be seen by how it aids in drawing inferences about interventions and their effects. Consider the ambiguity that often arises or could arise from ordinary experience. We might recommend an intervention to a friend who has a cold. The intervention could be to consume a special soup (chicken) and to watch special television shows (soap operas). Knowing the importance of assessment, we administer a few measures of how our friend is feeling when the cold has begun but before treatment begins. Treatment is then provided, with daily prescriptions of our special soup and a regimen of watching soap operas. After 10 days, we readminister our measures and note that our friend is greatly improved. For the moment, let us grant that the measures reflect actual change and the person is well. The change may even be dramatic. Does the change support the effects of our treatment (soup and soaps)?

We know in this example that causal inferences about treatment cannot be made. The reason is that colds tend to improve on their own within several days. The change we attribute to

our special treatment might well reflect the natural course of the body's response to the cold. Our soup and soap hypothesis may well be worth testing. However, to evaluate the impact of this intervention, the situation must be arranged to separate the effects of our treatment from other competing explanations of why the change might occur. Research design is directed at planning an experiment in such a way as to identify the reason for the change. This is accomplished by arranging how treatment is delivered, to whom it is delivered, and when it is delivered (Kazdin, 1992).

In behavior modification, a variety of research designs is used to determine whether a given intervention is responsible for behavior change. Two major classes of designs are used: *control group* and *single-case* designs. In control group designs, the performance of two or more groups is evaluated. Each of the groups is exposed to different interventions or control conditions. The effects are evaluated by comparing the average performance of the two groups. In single-case designs, the performance of an individual or group of individuals is compared across different conditions over time. Behavior of the individual or group is assessed under two or more conditions. The two design categories do not represent uncompromising extremes. Indeed, they are often combined in various ways. The present discussion will focus on major versions of control group and single-case designs. We will not imply that one design is inherently better and should always be used. An experimental design is a research tool and the experimenter should utilize the one that addresses the experimental question of interest as well as the circumstances of the intervention.

GROUP EXPERIMENTAL DESIGNS

The most commonly used research designs in clinical research, and in psychological research more generally, are based on group comparisons.

The designs are referred to as control group designs because of the use of groups that are exposed to or receive different conditions. The basic design requires at least two groups, one of which receives the intervention (the experimental group), and the other that does not (the control group). To determine if the intervention is effective, performance of the experimental and control groups is compared. If the intervention is effective, one would expect that performance of individuals in the experimental group, on average, would be better than the performance of persons in the control group.

To be sure that any difference between the two groups is due to the intervention, the groups must be similar to begin with. The best procedure to control for systematic differences between groups before the program is implemented is to assign clients randomly to one of the two groups. This may be accomplished by using numbers drawn from a random-numbers table, selecting numbers from a hat, and so on. If subjects are not randomly assigned to groups, the likelihood is greater that the groups may be different in their performance before the program is implemented and may differentially change over time for some reason other than the effect of the program.

Basic Control Group Designs

There are a variety of control group designs and variations that are distinguished by the specific types of control and comparison groups and whether groups are assessed at pretreatment or at both pretreatment and posttreatment (Cook & Campbell, 1979; Kazdin, 1992). The control group experimental design includes at least two groups whose subjects have been randomly assigned. One group receives treatment; the other does not. Both groups are usually assessed before and after treatment on the dependent measure. The differences between groups at the end of treatment can then be evaluated to determine the effect of treatment.

If only a single group is used, any changes in its performance over time cannot be definitively attributed to treatment. For example, a group of depressed clients may complete psychological measures of depression, undergo treatment for several weeks, and then complete the measures again. Posttreament performance may reveal that depression has substantially decreased. Was treatment responsible for the change? The question cannot be answered in the situation described here. With the same amount of elapsed time between initial and final assessment, an untreated group might experience a similar reduction in depression. Having the group retake the test might have resulted in improved performance whether or not treatment was provided. A reduction in depression may occur for other reasons as well. Some individuals may be less depressed because they are no longer preoccupied with events that were once viewed with despair. Furthermore, events other than therapy, such as new social acquaintances, changes in employment, or world or local events, may influence performance. There are a number of other interpretations of such changes over time (Kazdin, 1992). The point remains that without a no-treatment control group, a single group measured before and after treatment is equivalent to an uncontrolled case study. The use of an equivalent control group excludes a variety of alternative interpretations of the results. To show the effects of treatment for depression, clients can be assigned randomly to the treatment or no-treatment control group. When the treatment subjects complete therapy, both groups are reassessed on the dependent measures. If there are differences in the reassessment data, it is likely that treatment accounted for the change.

The control group design requires at least two groups, as already noted. However, in most research additional groups are included to permit the investigator to make further comparisons that will elaborate the basis for group differences. As an example, Longo, Clum, and Yaeger (1988) evaluated a multifaceted behavioral treatment for adults with recurrent genital herpes. Herpes is a sexually transmitted viral disease with no known cure. Psychological treatment was considered to be appropriate because episodes of the disease are associated with and apparently fostered by stress and the experience of emotional distress. Individuals with recurrent herpes were assigned randomly to one of three groups. The behavioral intervention consisted of group meetings that provided training in stress management, relaxation, imagery, and planned exercises in these areas outside of the group treatment sessions. A second group was included in the design as an "attention placebo" control condition. Individuals also attended group treatment sessions; instead of specific training experiences, persons in this group discussed interpersonal conflicts. This intervention was not considered by the investigators to be a procedure likely to produce change, but the investigators wished to control for the possible impact that would result merely from attending treatment sessions. A final group consisted of a waiting-list control condition. This group did not receive the treatment until the investigation was completed. The purpose of this group was to evaluate changes that might occur over time without any intervention.

The results indicated that episodes of herpes were fewer, less severe, and of a shorter duration for members of the group who received the treatment program, relative to each of the other groups. A similar pattern favoring the intervention group was evident for measures of depression, stress, and emotional distress. These results suggest that treatment produced greater change than the passage of time and attending sessions that resembled treatment.

Evaluation of the Control Group Design

The basic control group design can determine a causal relationship between treatment and behavior change. The basic design can be expanded by adding groups to answer different questions. The major purpose of adding groups is to control for various events that may account for behavior change and to exclude rival interpretations of the results (Kazdin, 1992). In the case of intervention research, a variety of different groups can be

used to identify which components of treatment are the crucial ingredients in altering behavior and what variations of treatment can be made to enhance treatment outcome.

Factorial Designs

In many instances, merely elaborating the basic control group design will not answer all the questions of interest. Factorial designs are control group designs in which two or more variables are examined simultaneously, permitting evaluation of separate and combined effects of each variable. For example, the investigator may wish to evaluate combined and separate effects of two independent variables, such as the duration of psychotherapy (5 sessions versus 20 sessions) and material discussed in the session (emotionally significant material versus mundane topics). This would require four groups (see Figure 4.1). At the end of treatment, it will be possible to determine the effect of length of treatment duration alone by comparing groups 1 and 2 with

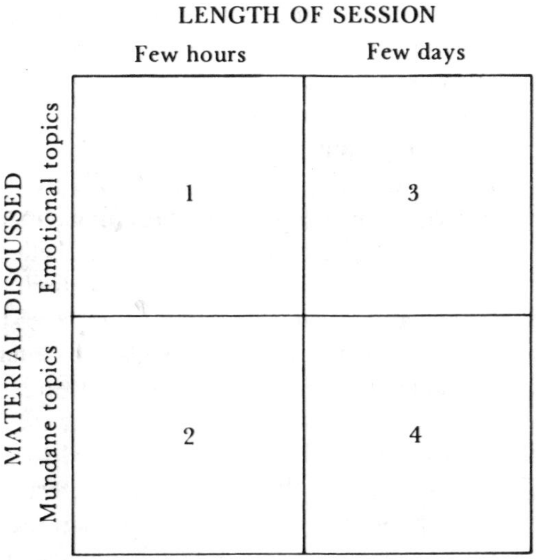

LENGTH OF SESSION

FIGURE 4.1

Factorial design with four groups, examining the effect on treatment outcome of the topic discussed in therapy and the length of the session

groups 3 and 4. It will also be possible to examine the effect of the material discussed during the session by comparing groups 1 and 3 with groups 2 and 4. Finally, it will be possible to examine whether the effect of treatment duration depended on the kind of material discussed (that is, the combined or interactive effects). It may be that discussing emotionally significant material is helpful only when the session is extended and individuals can resolve some of the problems and anxieties that are aroused. Thus, discussion of emotionally significant material might be helpful in group 3 but not in group 1. The groups must be compared to determine this.

Evaluation of Factorial Designs

The strength of a factorial design is that it can assess the effects of separate variables in a single experiment. This advantage is one of economy because different variables can be studied with fewer subjects and observations in a factorial design than in separate experiments for the single-variable study of each of the variables, one at a time. In addition, the factorial design provides unique information about the combined effects of the independent variables. The importance of interactions cannot be overestimated in conducting research. Essentially, interactions indicate qualifications about treatment and its effects. A given treatment may not be simply effective or ineffective but may depend on a host of qualifiers such as who administers treatment, type of client problem, conditions of administration, length of treatment, and so on. These qualifiers refer to variables with which treatment is likely to interact. Finding that the effect of an independent variable does or does not interact with the levels of another variable is more than the evaluation of the generality of the experimental intervention. The implications may have important theoretical or practical value. In general, factorial designs can address more complex and sophisticated questions than do single-variable experiments.

SINGLE-CASE EXPERIMENTAL DESIGNS

Single-case experimental designs represent another approach to structuring the situation to draw inferences about treatment. The designs have been referred to by different terms, such as *intrasubject-replication designs* and *N = 1 research*.[1] The unique feature of these designs is the capacity to conduct experimental investigations with the single case (i.e., one subject).

The underlying rationale of single-case experimental designs is similar to that of group experimentation. All experiments compare the effects of different conditions (independent variables) on performance. With group designs, the comparison is made between groups of subjects who are treated differently. In single-case research, inferences are usually made about the effects of the intervention by comparing different conditions presented to the same subject over time.

Fundamental to single-case designs is the collection of data continuously over time. This means that the client's performance is observed on several occasions, usually before the intervention is applied and continuously over the period while the intervention is in effect. Typically, observations are conducted on a daily basis or at least on multiple occasions each week. Continuous assessment allows the investigator to examine the pattern and stability of performance before treatment is initiated. The pretreatment

---

[1] Although several alternative terms have been proposed to describe the designs, each is partially misleading. For example, single-case and $N = 1$ designs imply that only one subject is included in an investigation. This is not accurate and hides the fact that large numbers of subjects and entire communities and cities have been included in some "single-case" designs (Kazdin, 1989). The term "intrasubject" is useful because it implies that the methodology focuses on performance of the same person over time; the term is also partially misleading because some of the designs depend on looking at the effects of interventions across subjects. The term "single-case designs" has been adopted here to draw attention to the unique feature of the designs, i.e., the capacity to experiment with individual subjects, and because it enjoys the widest use.

information over an extended period provides a picture of what performance is like without the intervention and provides baseline data. Baseline information is used to characterize performance in the present and to predict the probable level of performance in the future. The impact of the intervention is evaluated in light of changes in this pattern of continuous assessment and baseline performance. Alternative designs accomplish this in different ways.

Reversal or ABAB Design

In a number of programs, the effects of different procedures are evaluated by comparing the performance of an individual or several individuals under different experimental conditions. Specifically, data are collected on the frequency (or some other measure) of a certain behavior, such as tantrums, in a single individual or group. Observations are usually made for several days prior to any treatment intervention. The rate of behavior prior to treatment or intervention is referred to as the *baseline* or *operant rate*. The period during which the baseline rate of behavior is assessed is referred to as the *baseline* or *A phase*. After a pattern of behavior emerges and performance is relatively stable, a particular program is implemented to alter behavior. The phase during which a program or treatment intervention is being implemented is referred to as the *treatment* or *B phase*. Data are gathered throughout baseline and treatment phases to determine whether behavior changes. If behavior changes after the program is implemented, this does not necessarily mean that the program was responsible for the change. Additional phases are required to determine what caused the change. After the program has been in effect for some time and a consistent pattern is evident, the program may be withdrawn temporarily. This third phase is referred to as a *reversal phase* and is usually a reintroduction of the conditions that were in effect during the initial baseline phase. If behavior reverts to baseline levels when the program is withdrawn, this strongly suggests that the program was responsible for change. To increase the plausibility of this conclusion, the treatment program is reinstated in the final phase of the experiment. If behavior again changes when the intervention is implemented, this is a clear demonstration that the intervention was responsible for the change. Of course, in an applied setting where one is attempting to modify an undesirable behavior, it is always essential to undertake this final phase.

The design is referred to as a reversal design because the phases are alternated or reversed; after baseline the program is first implemented, then withdrawn or altered in some fashion, and then implemented again. Behavior usually reverses as the phases are altered. The design is also referred to as an ABAB design because baseline (A) and treatment (B) phases are alternated to demonstrate that treatment was responsible for the observed change.

The reversal design is nicely illustrated in a study designed to reduce the aggressive behavior of elementary school children (Murphy, Hutchison, & Bailey, 1983). The children included 344 first and second graders who played outside prior to the beginning of school. The purpose of the study was to develop and evaluate an intervention to reduce the relatively high rates of aggressive behavior (e.g., striking, slapping, tripping, kicking, pushing, or punching others) on the playground. During baseline, students were observed for 12 days to assess the number of aggressive behaviors during the 20-minute period before school began. After baseline, the intervention began and included several components. The major component was to provide organized game activity including rope jumping and foot races supervised by playground aides. Aides led these organized activities to structure play for the children. Aides were also instructed to praise appropriate play behavior (reinforcement) and to use a mild punishment procedure (placing disruptive children on a bench for 2 minutes for particularly unruly behavior). The intervention was discontinued after 7 days in a reversal phase to see if the program was responsible for behavior change. Finally, the intervention phase was reinstated again. The results, presented in Figure 4.2, provide the data for the class treated as a whole. The number of aggressive incidents during each intervention phase decreased relative to baseline and reversal phases, respectively. By showing changes in behavior when the experimental condition is presented, withdrawn, and re-presented, it is unlikely that other influences accounted for the results.

Evaluation of the Reversal Design

The reversal design has been used extensively in behavior modification. Although the design can determine a causal relationship between behavior and an experimental intervention, there are some limitations in its use. First, behaviors sometimes do not reverse when the program is temporarily withdrawn. Behavior may remain at the level achieved during treatment. If the behavior does not reverse or approach baseline

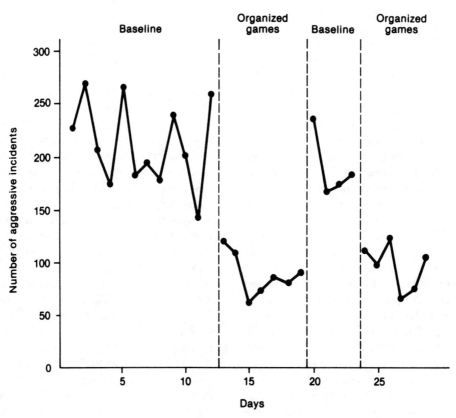

FIGURE 4.2

Number of incidents of aggressive behavior recorded on the playground before school started. Baseline—no intervention. Intervention—organized activities, praise, and time-out. Reversal—return to baseline conditions. Intervention—return to the activities, praise, and time-out procedures

SOURCE: Murphy, Hutchison, & Bailey, 1983. ©*Journal of Applied Behavioral Analysis.*

when treatment is withdrawn or altered, this suggests that the program may not be responsible for the change. Behavior change may be a function of some event occurring concurrently with the program.

Behavior may not reverse during withdrawal of treatment, for another reason. Often, changes in behavior alter the environment in a way that supports and maintains the behavior change. For example, a child might be trained to interact socially with peers by receiving praise from a teacher or parent. When praise is withdrawn, this behavior may not reverse because the favorable consequences associated with peer interaction now maintain the behavior. Although teacher or parent praise may have been responsible for the initial behavior change, the behavior may now be maintained by consequences provided by peers. Because of failure of the behavior to reverse, a reversal design would not show what caused the behavior change.

A second problem with the reversal design is that it is often undesirable or even unethical to show reversal in a behavior. For example, a program might be effective in altering extremely aggressive behavior in a child. However, few people would be willing to withdraw the program temporarily and risk an increase in aggressive behavior. There may be no clear justification for making the individual "worse" and possibly endangering others by encouraging an increase in aggressive behavior.

Reversal designs have been used extensively in situations where a temporary reversal in behavior is not harmful to the individual. The reversal phase need not be long. Sometimes the program need only be altered or withdrawn for a few days. Once the behavior reverts toward baseline, treatment can be reinstated immediately. It should be emphasized that the purpose of the reversal design is to obtain causal knowledge about behavior change. This knowledge is essential for scientific validation of treatment. In many instances, temporary worsening of behavior must be avoided. Fortunately, other designs can be used to avoid the aforementioned limitations.

Multiple-Baseline Designs

In multiple-baseline designs, a causal relationship between treatment and behavior is demonstrated by showing that behavior changes when treatment is introduced at several different points in time. This is accomplished without a reversal procedure. Although there are several variations, three versions of this design are commonly used.

One variation is the multiple-baseline design across individuals. In this version, baseline data are gathered for a particular behavior across two or more individuals. After data are gathered separately for each individual, treatment is applied to the behavior of one individual. Baseline observations are continued for the others. After the behavior of each individual shows a stable pattern, treatment is applied to another individual. The intervention is introduced to all individuals at different points in time, until everyone has been included in the program.

As an example, a cognitively based, problem-solving, skills training procedure was evaluated with mothers who neglected their children (Dawson, de Armas, McGrath, & Kelly, 1986). Neglect refers to a chronic pattern in which parents fail to meet the needs of their children in relation to physical safety, health, nutrition, and emotional development. For legal purposes, neglect is often considered along with physical abuse, in the sense that both reflect extreme, harmful, and maladaptive child-rearing practices. Neglectful parents may have deficits in judgment and behavior because they fail to anticipate the needs of their children and the consequences of their neglect. In this study, problem-solving skills training was applied to three mothers (ages 20–27) who had been adjudicated for their neglect and referred for treatment. Several vignettes related to the care of children were constructed, based on past reports and the mothers' descriptions of situations in which they failed to meet their children's needs. Each situation was read aloud to the parent, who was asked to engage in the problem-solving approach—to define the problem, consider possible solutions, describe the consequences and obstacles of each solution, and choose the best solution. A sample vignette is as follows.

> *You and your mother have an argument on the phone. She tells you that you can just forget about bringing your children over tonight for her to babysit while you go out with your boyfriend (husband). It's 5:00 P.M. You don't have any money to hire a babysitter. The story ends with you and your boyfriend (husband) going out for the evening. (Dawson et al., 1986, p. 213)*

During baseline, problem situations were presented to see how each mother managed the care of her children—i.e., whether she identified a plan to solve the problem, selected various means or steps toward the goal, and identified obstacles that would interfere with completing appropriate behaviors. Problem-solving skills were then taught individually to each mother by using modeling, shaping, and feedback. The effects of training were evaluated in a multiple-baseline design across individuals (3 parents). As shown in Figure 4.3, each mother's solutions to the problems (vignettes) included more of the problem-solving skills components than did baseline performance. Ratings were also completed by social workers associated with each case, to assess the extent to which the parent improved in her child-rearing practices, as reflected in solutions to child-related problems in the home; performance of responsibilities; providing food, clothing, and child care; and similar activities. Effectiveness ratings increased after treatment for each of the mothers. At follow-up 15 months later, only one parent was available for reassessment on the vignettes. This parent continued to show high levels of problem-solving skills. The other two parents, who had moved, had full custody of their children returned by the child welfare department, with no further reports of neglect.

Other variations of the multiple-baseline design rely on the same logic: staggered presentation of the intervention across different baselines in an effort to show that behavior change is achieved whenever the intervention is introduced. In the *multiple-baseline design across behaviors*, baseline data are gathered across two or more behaviors in a given individual or group. After the behaviors have stabilized, treatment may be introduced for the first behavior, and baseline data continue to be gathered for the other behaviors. The first behavior should change while the other behaviors should not. If this is the case, the experimental intervention is introduced for the second behavior. Treatment for other behaviors is introduced at different points in time. The treatment effect is demonstrated if each behavior changes only when the treatment intervention is introduced and not before then.

In a *multiple-baseline design across situations*, baseline data are gathered across a given behavior for one individual or a group of individuals across two or more situations. After baseline data are obtained across all situations, treatment is introduced to alter behavior in the first situation. The program is introduced at different points in time for the remaining situations. For example, the recess privilege might be used to change academic behavior across two different class periods, namely morning and afternoon class sessions. Baseline data would be gathered on academic performance during the morning and afternoon each day. Then the students would be informed that 10 extra minutes of recess could be earned by a predetermined amount of improvement in academic performance during the morning. The privilege would initially be withheld from the afternoon session. Eventually it would be extended to the afternoon session. Behavior should change when and only when the recess privilege is introduced for each session.

Evaluation of Multiple-Baseline Designs

Multiple-baseline designs demonstrate the effect of an intervention without using a reversal phase. With such designs there is no need to return to baseline conditions and temporarily lose the gains made during the program. A causal rela-

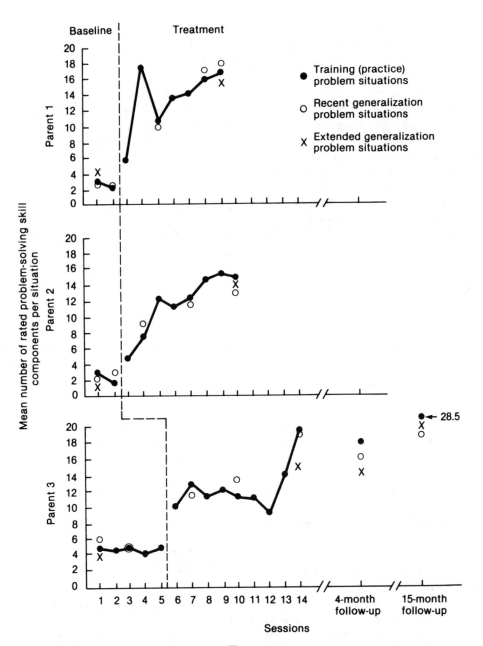

FIGURE 4.3

Mean (average) number of problem-solving skill elements included in responses to problem situations for each parent

SOURCE: Dawson, de Armas, McGrath, & Kelly, 1986. Reprinted by permission.

tionship is demonstrated if behavior changes when and only when treatment is introduced.

Under some circumstances, the design may not demonstrate a causal relation between treatment and behavior (Kazdin, 1982). This occurs when the introduction of the treatment has widespread effects, so that implementing the intervention for one of the baselines (e.g., individuals, behaviors, or situations) has a broad effect that spreads to other baselines. In such instances, the specificity of the effect of the intervention is not clear and it is difficult to rule out influences other than the intervention in accounting for change. Although broad effects of an intervention occasionally are evident, the problem has not hindered effective use of the designs. In general, multiple-baseline designs are quite useful, particularly in situations where a reversal phase could present problems or where behavior change is desired across different behaviors, different individuals, or different situations.

Changing-Criterion Design

Another single-case design to demonstrate the effect of treatment is the changing-criterion design. No reversal is required nor are data gathered across several (i.e. multiple) baselines. The design begins with a baseline phase when data are gathered for a single behavior. After the baseline rate is established, treatment is introduced, which may consist of rewarding a particular behavior. Early in the program the criterion for receiving the reward might be relatively easy to meet. As behavior changes, the criterion for earning the reward is changed. As further progress is shown, the criterion is continually changed. If behavior changes as the criterion for the reward is altered, one may conclude that the program is responsible for the change.

For example, a changing-criterion design was used to evaluate a program designed to reduce cigarette smoking in a 65-year-old male named Joe, who lived far (200 miles) away from the clinic (Belles & Bradlyn, 1987). Through arrangements made by phone, a program was devised to alter the number of cigarettes smoked daily. Baseline began with self-monitoring the number of cigarettes smoked. These counts were corroborated by Joe's wife, who observed his smoking unobtrusively. After baseline, the program began in which Joe rewarded himself for a reduced number of cigarettes smoked. Specifically, for each day he met or fell below the criterion number of cigarettes smoked, he provided $3.00 to a fund for items he wished to buy. On days he exceeded the criterion, he agreed to send a personal check for $25.00 to a charity he disliked. To verify this procedure, the check was to be mailed to the investigator, who then forwarded the contribution to the charity.

The program was evaluated in a changing-criterion design so that in many separate phases, the criterion for the number of cigarettes per day was set progressively lower. As shown in Figure 4.4, the criterion (horizontal line) was closely approximated in each phase (B through U). When Joe reached the criterion of 5 cigarettes per day, he indicated he wished to remain at that level. This level was maintained and the program was terminated. Follow-up conducted up to 18 months later indicated that smoking remained at this level, obviously well below and safer than the rate of 80–100 cigarettes each day before the intervention began. The pattern of the results suggests that changes in the criterion were associated with reductions in cigarette smoking.

Evaluation of the Changing-Criterion Design

The changing-criterion design provides a fairly clear demonstration of a causal relationship if a behavior change correlates closely with changes in criterion as the latter is altered throughout treatment. The design is suited to situations in which performance can be changed gradually and the final goal is reached in a series of steps. The performance criterion can be repeatedly altered, and attainment of the goal must be gradual. Certainly, there would be a problem in the design if the performance criterion required a

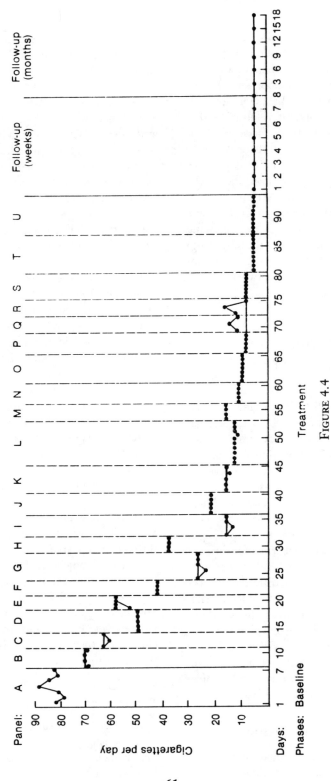

FIGURE 4.4

Number of cigarettes smoked per day from baseline (A phase) through each intervention phase (B–U phases) in which the criterion was altered. The criterion within each phase of the self-reward/self-punishment program is indicated by a horizontal line

SOURCE: Belles & Bradlyn, 1987. Reprinted by permission of Pergamon Press, Inc.

moderate change, such as reduction in the number of cigarettes smoked or alcoholic beverages consumed, but the behavior change was dramatic, such as the elimination of smoking or drinking. In cases where the behavior does not closely follow the criterion, it is possible that something other than treatment accounted for the behavior change. Even when the criterion is followed by a change in behavior, it is possible that some concurrent event is responsible for the change. If behavior changes in the desired direction during the program for reasons other than the program, it may appear to be following changes in the criterion. Thus, the changing-criterion design may not give the clearest demonstration of a causal relationship between the behavior and the program.

METHODS OF
DATA EVALUATION

Assessment and data collection provide information about whether behavior or performance has changed. Alternative research designs provide the methods of arranging the administration of treatment so that inferences about the impact of treatment can be drawn. The investigation yields data about performance of the clients. These data reflect the measures obtained for subjects in the different groups, as in control group designs or continuous performance over time for the subject(s) in single-case designs.

The data can be examined in different ways to draw conclusions about treatment. The alternative ways to evaluate the meaningfulness of observational data or experimental evidence are referred to as the *methods of data evaluation*. Three methods are often used in behavior-modification research: statistical, nonstatistical, and clinical evaluation of therapeutic change (Kazdin, 1992).

Statistical Evaluation

In most research, statistical evaluation examines whether groups receiving different conditions can be distinguished statistically on the dependent measure(s). Statistical evaluation consists of applying a test to assess whether the difference obtained on the dependent measure is likely to have occurred by chance. Typically, a level of confidence (such as .05 or .01) is selected as the criterion for determining whether the results are statistically significant. The difference between groups on the dependent measure is evaluated with a statistical test that yields a probability value. A statistically significant difference indicates that the probability level is equal to or below the level of confidence selected—for example, .05. That is, the probability is .05 or some other value lower than that (for example, .03). This means that if the experiment were completed 100 times, a difference of the magnitude found in the experiment would occur only five times on a purely chance basis. If the probability obtained in the study is lower than .05, most researchers would admit that group differences probably were not the result of chance but reflected a real relationship between the independent and dependent variables.

To state that a relationship in an experiment is statistically significant does not mean that there is necessarily a genuine relationship between the variables studied. Even a statistically significant difference could be the result of a chance event. Chance can never be completely ruled out. That is, there may be no relationship between the variables in reality but a statistically significant difference appears in the experiment because of sampling of subjects and other factors. However, by tradition, researchers have agreed that when the probability yielded by a statistical test is as low as .05 or .01, that is a sufficiently conservative level of confidence to permit one to conclude that there probably is a relationship between the independent and dependent variables.

Problems and Considerations

Essentially, statistical evaluation provides a criterion to separate probably veridical from possibly chance effects. Although subjectivity and bias can enter into the process of statistical evaluation, for example, in terms of the tests that are applied and the criteria for statistical significance, the goal of statistics is to provide a *relatively* bias-free and consistent method of interpreting results. The prevalent use of statistics does not imply that agreement on their value is universal. Diverse facets of statistical evaluation have been challenged, including the arbitrary cirterion that a particular confidence level such as $p < .05$ represents; the all-or-none decision making based on that criterion; the absence of information regarding the strength or practical value of the relationship, whether or not statistical significance is attained; the likelihood that the null hypothesis, upon which tests are based, is never really true; and others (Chow, 1988; Rosnow & Rosenthal, 1989). Nevertheless, hypothesis testing and statistical evaluation to detect relations among variables dominate current research. The dominance is not the result of unfortunate circumstances with no clear rationale. Methods of statistical evaluation provide consistent criteria for determining whether an effect is to be considered as veridical. This advantage is critically important.

Consider the fundamental value of a consistent criterion. Consider, for example, the development of a new therapy technique in clinical work. It is likely that a proponent of the new therapy will allege that therapeutic effects are produced and that the effects are superior to those produced by other treatments. In more experimentally based terms, the new treatment is proposed to produce greater personality or behavior change than no treatment and than other treatment conditions. Claims that a treatment is effective (e.g., in facilitating dieting or reducing cigarette smoking), as advocated in trade books and magazine articles, are rarely based on experimental methods and statistical criteria, testimonials by proponents of the technique or those who have participated in the program serve as the basis for evaluation. It would be valuable in these cases to apply experimental methods and to evaluate the results statistically. Statistics provide a tool to help separate veridical effects from those that might have occurred by

chance. Endorsement of statistical evaluation does not mean that statistics provide "the answer," "real truth," and so on. Statistical evaluation is subject to all sorts of abuses, ambiguities, and misinterpretation. Yet an advantage is that these ambiguities can often be made explicit, studied, and understood. The explicitness of statistical procedures helps us raise questions and understand the limits of the conclusions. Statistical evaluation is strongly emphasized in psychology; indeed, statistical significance often is regarded as the definitive test of whether the variables under investigation are important or worth pursuing. Yet there are additional criteria to consider, ones frequently used in behavior-modification research.

Nonstatistical Evaluation

In areas of clinical research where single-case designs are used, data are usually evaluated without relying upon statistics. Nonstatistical evaluation usually refers to examining the data and determining by visual inspection whether the intervention had an effect. Visual inspection is commonly used in single-case research where continuous data are available for one or several subjects. With single-case designs, the investigator has the advantage of seeing the data for a single subject for consecutive periods without the intervention, followed by similar data with the intervention in effect. If the intervention abruptly changes the pattern of data, an inference about the effect of the intervention is clearer than simply looking at pre- and postintervention differences across two observations. Assessment of the individual's performance on several occasions makes examination of the data through visual inspection less arbitrary than the method might appear at first glance.

Evaluation of data nonstatistically has the same goal as statistical analysis: to identify if the effects are consistent, reliable, and unlikely to have resulted from chance fluctuations between conditions. Although visual inspection is based on subjective judgment, this does not mean that decisions are by fiat or vary with each person making the judgment. In many uses of single-case designs, where visual inspection is invoked, the applied or clinical goals are to achieve marked intervention effects. In cases where intervention effects are very strong, one need not carefully scrutinize or enumerate the criteria that underlie the judgment that the effects are veridical. In applied research, several situations arise in which intervention effects are likely to be so dramatic that visual inspection is easily invoked. For example, whenever the behavior of interest is not present in the client's repertoire during the baseline phase (e.g., social interaction, exercise, reading) and increases during the intervention phase, a judgment about the effects of the intervention is easily made. Similarly, when the behavior of interest occurs frequently during the baseline phase (e.g., reports of hallucinations, aggressive acts, cigarette smoking) and stops completely during the intervention phase, the magnitude of change usually permits clear judgments based on visual inspection.

Visual inspection depends on many characteristics of the data, but especially those that pertain to the magnitude of the changes across phases and the rate of these changes. The two most salient characteristics related to magnitude are changes in *mean* and *trend* in the data. *Changes in means* across phases are shifts in the average rate of performance. Consistent changes in means across phases can serve as a basis for deciding whether the data pattern meets the requirements of the design. A hypothetical example showing changes in means across the intervention phase is illustrated in an ABAB design in Figure 4.5. As evident in the figure, performance on the average (horizontal dashed line in each phase) changed in response to the different baseline and intervention phases. Visual inspection of this pattern suggests that the intervention led to consistent changes.

Changes in trend are of obvious importance in applying visual inspection. Trend, or slope, refers to the tendency for the data to show systematic increases or decreases over time. The alteration of phases within the design may show that

the direction of behavior changes as the intervention is applied or withdrawn. Figure 4.6 illustrates a hypothetical example in which trends have changed over the course of the phase in an ABAB design. The initial baseline trend is reversed by the intervention, reinstated when the intervention is withdrawn, and again reversed in the final phase. A change in trend would be an important criterion even if there were no trend in baseline. A change from no trend (horizontal line) during baseline to a trend (increase or decrease in behavior) during the intervention phase would also constitute a change in trend.

Other features of the data also enhance visual inspection. For example, if the shift in data points from one phase to the next is abrupt at the point that the phase changes or if the effects of a new phase seem to be rapid, this further suggests that reliable change is associated with the intervention. In general, changes in several characteristics of the data frequently occur as phases are changed. Visual inspection is conducted by judging the extent to which changes in the different characteristics are evident across phases and whether the changes are consistent with the requirements of the particular design.

It is important to note that invoking the criteria for visual inspection requires judgments about the pattern of data in the entire design and not merely changes across one or two phases. Unambiguous effects require that the criteria mentioned above be met throughout the design. To the extent that the criteria are not consistently met, conclusions about the reliabilty of intervention effects become tentative. For example, changes in an ABAB design may show nonoverlapping data points for the first AB phases but no clear differences across the second AB phases. The absence of a consistent pattern of data that meets the criteria mentioned above limits the conclusions that can be drawn.

Problems and Considerations

Visual inspection has been quite useful in identifying reliable intervention effects in both experimental and clinical research. When intervention

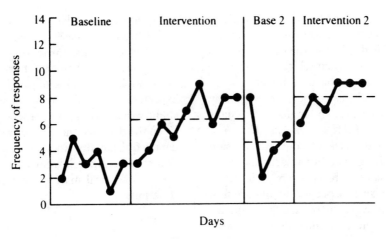

FIGURE 4.5

Hypothetical example of performance in an ABAB design, with means in
each phase represented by dashed lines

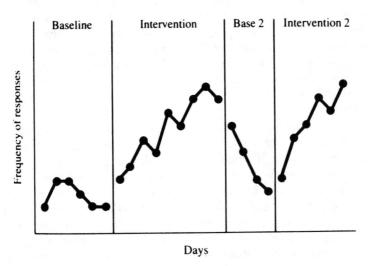

FIGURE 4.6

Hypothetical example of performance in an ABAB design, with changes
in trend across phases. Baseline shows a relatively stable or possibly
decreasing trend. When the intervention is introduced, an accelerating
trend is evident. This trend is reversed when the intervention is
withdrawn (Base 2) and is reinstated when the intervention is
reintroduced.

effects are potent, the need for statistical analysis is obviated. Intervention effects can be extremely clear from graphic displays of the data, in which persons can judge for themselves whether the previously noted criteria have been met.

The use of visual inspection as the primary basis for evaluating data in single-case designs has raised major concerns. Perhaps the major issue pertains to the lack of concrete decision rules for determining whether a particular demonstration shows or fails to show a reliable effect. The process of visual inspection would seem to permit, if not actively encourage, subjectivity and inconsistency in the evaluation of intervention effects. Studies of how individuals invoke the criteria for visual inspection have shown that judges, even experts in the field, often disagree about particular data patterns and whether the effects were reliable (DeProspero & Cohen, 1979).

Another criticism levied against visual inspection is that it regards as significant only those very marked effects. Many interventions might be consistent in the effects they produce but are statistically relatively weak. Such effects might not be detected by visual inspection and would be overlooked. Overlooking weak but reliable effects can have unfortunate consequences. First, weak but reliable effects may have theoretical significance in relation to understanding personality, dysfunction, or treatment. Second, the possibility exists that interventions when first developed may have weak effects. It would be unfortunate if these interventions were prematurely discarded before they could be developed further, as they might eventually achieve potent effects. If the stringent criteria of visual inspection discourage the pursuit of interventions that do not have potent effects, these criteria may be a detriment to developing a technology of behavior change. On the other hand, stringent criteria may encourage investigators to develop interventions to the point that they do produce marked changes before making claims about demonstrated efficacy.

A final problem with visual inspection is that

it requires a particular pattern of data in baseline and subsequent phases so that the results can be interpreted. Visual inspection criteria are more readily invoked when data show little or no trend or trend in directions opposite from the trend expected in the following phase and indicate slight variability. However, trends and variability in the data may not always meet the idealized data requirements. In such cases visual inspection may be difficult to invoke. Other methods, such as statistical analyses, may be of use in these situations.

Clinical Significance of Therapeutic Change

One problem with statistical evaluation, especially in clinical research, is that is detracts from the question of the applied importance of therapeutic change. By searching for statistically significant effects, it is easy to lose sight of the fact that one goal is to produce clinically important behavior changes. In contrast, visual inspection draws attention to the importance of achieving marked changes. However, marked changes evident graphically by sharp changes in slopes and means do not necessarily signal that improvements are meaningful or important in the experience of the client.

Behavior modification research has attempted to assess the extent to which changes in behavior are important for the client. Evaluation of the clinical or applied importance of the change is usually used as a supplement to statistical or nonstatistical methods of determining whether group differences in changes are reliable. Once reliable changes are evident, further efforts are made to quantify whether treatment moves the client appreciably closer to adequate functioning, that is, whether the change is important.

For some behaviors, one may be able to tell readily without special methods whether this is the case. For example, treatment that eliminates self-destructive behavior such as the headbanging of an autistic child would be regarded as producing a clinically significant change. All self-destructive acts would be regarded as maladaptive and their elimination as an important change. However, reducing self-destructive behavior from, say, 500 to 200 instances per day might not be regarded as clinically important. Without a further reduction or complete elimination, the client might still self-inflict serious damage. The change might meet criteria for statistical significance or a reliable difference by criteria for visual inspection, but its clinical value could be challenged. Virtual or complete elimination would be needed to effect a clinically important change. Of course, in many cases, the presence or absence of a behavior is not necessarily the criterion for deciding whether an important change was achieved. Other criteria are necessary.

Several different criteria for evaluating the clinical significance of treatment effects have been elaborated (Kazdin, 1992). In the most commonly used methods, comparisons are made between clients who have received treatment and others who are functioning well or have no problems in everyday life. These latter persons provide normative data, i.e., information on the measures of interest and the level of functioning of these measures among persons who are not referred or who do not seek treatment.

The issue for clinical significance is to evaluate the extent to which the clients who have received treatment compare with others who are functioning well in everyday life. Prior to treatment, the client sample presumably would depart considerably from their well-functioning peers in the area identified for treatment (e.g., anxiety, social withdrawal, aggression). One measure of the extent to which treatment produced clinically important changes would be the demonstration that at the end of treatment the clients were indistinguishable from or within the range of a normative, well-functioning sample on the measures of interest. Evaluating the extent to which individuals perform at or within the normative range is the most commonly used method of evaluating clinical significance (Kazdin, 1992).

Other methods to evaluate the clinical significance of intervention include examining whether individuals have made marked changes of a certain magnitude and whether the persons are significantly different from a dysfunctional sample after treatment, as well as within the normal range (Jacobson & Revenstorf, 1988). The point of these alternative methods is similar: to see if the level of changes somehow places persons into a more normal realm of functioning.

Problems and Considerations

The use of normative data represents an important step toward quantifying the extent to which behavior change produced with treatment has really made an important change. However, identifying a normative group, the commonly used method, raises critical questions. For example, in intervention research, to whom should mentally retarded individuals, chronic psychiatric patients, or prisoners be compared in evaluating treatment or training programs? Developing normative levels of performance might be an unrealistic ideal in treatment, if that level consists of individuals functioning normally in the community. Also, what variables would define a normative population? It is unclear how to match subjects included in the normative group along the diverse variables. The normative group might well be defined differently.

Even if a normative group can be identified, exactly what range of their behaviors would be defined as within the normative level? Among individuals whose behaviors are not identified as problematic there will be a range of acceptable behaviors. It is relatively simple to identify deviant behavior that departs markedly from the behavior of "normal" peers, but as behavior becomes slightly less deviant, it is difficult to identify the point at which behavior is within the normative range. Is the normative range within some measure of variability of the average (mean) behavior of the normal peers, say plus or minus one standard deviation? A subjective judgment is required to assess the point at which the individual has entered into the normal range of performance.

Another issue has to do with the criterion for normative functioning. For many behaviors and measures of interest, bringing individuals into the normative range is a questionable goal. Consider for example the reading skills of elementary school children. A clinically significant change might well be to move children with reading dysfunction so that they fall within the normal range. However, perhaps the normal range itself should not be viewed as an unquestioned goal. The reading of most children might potentially be accelerated from current normative levels. Thus, normative data itself needs to be considered. More extreme would be bringing youths who abuse drugs and alcohol to the level of their peers. For some groups, the peer group itself might be engaging in a level of deviant behavior that is potentially maladaptive.

Finally, it is quite possible that performance falls within the normative range or departs markedly from a deviant group but does not reflect how the individual is functioning in everyday life. Paper-and-pencil measures, questionnaires, interviews, and other frequently used measures may not reflect adaptive functioning for a given individual. Even for measures with high levels of established validity, performance of a given individual does not mean that he or she is happy, doing well, or adjusting in different spheres of life.

INTERPRETATION
OF THE DATA

Inferences from the Investigation

Once the data have been evaluated, they are interpreted in terms of their implications for the topic under study. When the experiment has been derived from a formal hypothesis, the data are evaluated in light of that hypothesis. When experimentation has been of purely exploratory nature, the data are interpreted in terms of their meaning for behavioral research. Note, however, that data interpretation is sometimes less objective when hypothesis testing is involved. This may be because a researcher with a vested interest or a pet hypothesis is often biased toward viewing the data as being favorable to that interest. In a sense, he or she may be reluctant to state that the hypothesis was not supported. This is especially apparent when the data do not present a clear-cut or consistent pattern among several measures. To avoid personal biases in such instances, the researcher should either adopt stringent criteria or solicit an independent colleague to assist in interpretation.

One might conceptualize the purposes of data interpretation as being twofold: (1) to evaluate the implications of the data for the particular situation from which they were drawn; and (2) to evaluate their implications for similar future situations. The first purpose pertains to relations within the experiment; the second pertains to the generality of such relationships.

The interpretation of data is a somewhat nebulous area. Except for the organizational outlines and decision procedures of statistical methods, no standard formula for data interpretation exists. This lack of an agreed-upon standard often results in differing interpretations of the same data. Surprising as it may seem, it is not unusual to find researchers citing the same experiment in support of contradictory hypotheses. For example, many of the early studies on the effectiveness of psychotherapy were interpreted in opposite manners by researchers.

Perhaps the most important point to be stressed in data interpretation is the option of abstention. When the data are insufficient or ambiguous, the researcher should refrain from drawing conclusions. This emphasizes the importance of conservatism in the evaluation of evidence. The researcher should always be inclined to doubt the implications of data. Interpretations must be considered only in a tentative and cautious manner.

Replication

Interpretations of the results of a single investigation are always tentative. Advances in a given area of behavioral research, and of course scientific research more generally, derive from the accumulation of studies. This does not detract in any way from the importance of assessment, design, and analysis for any single investigation. However, interpretation of data extends to a body of research in general rather than any single study. The reliability or repeatability of a finding across studies greatly enhances evaluation of any particular investigation. Critical to the scientific enterprise and interpretation of data is the concept of *replication*.

Replication refers to repetition of the results of an experiment. Studies are designed to duplicate the conditions of a previous experiment in various ways. Occasionally, investigators try to adhere to the original procedures and experimental conditions as closely as possible. On other occasions, investigators alter some of the conditions to see if the results can be repeated under slightly different circumstances. For example, the study may be repeated with subjects who are older or younger than those in the original experiment; with subjects of different diagnoses; with the treatment varied slightly; with less experienced therapists; and so on.

The importance of replication in scientific research cannot be overemphasized. If the results of the original study are successfully replicated, the confidence we can place in the findings is greatly increased. At the same time, replications are tests of the generality of the original finding. Such tests evaluate whether changes in conditions support the relation between the independent and dependent variables. From the standpoint of the accretion of knowledge and the interpretation of findings, replication plays a special role. Studies that replicate prior findings increase one's confidence that the relationship originally found is reliable and not likely to be due to a particular artifact. Replications that vary the original conditions suggest that the original

relationship holds across a wider range of conditions. Essentially, the greater the divergence of the replication from the conditions of the original experiment, the greater the generality of the relationship that was demonstrated.

SUMMARY

Assessment and data collection are prerequisites to scientific research. In behavior modification, assessment usually entails multiple measures that involve different formats, domains of functioning, and sources of information. The unique feature of assessment has been the evaluation of overt behavior or samples of performance that are considered to reflect the construct of interest or clinical problem directly. Direct observation of overt behavior can be accomplished in a variety of ways. Four classes of data are magnitude, temporal, frequency, and categorical data. Continuous data collection and sampling procedures are two methods of data collection. The format of data collection may vary; two frequently employed formats are actual counts and all-or-none classification. Data collected in behavior-modification programs tell the investigator whether behavior is changing. Because the goal of treatment is to alter behavior, careful assessment of change is essential. However, evidence of behavior change does not explain *why* behavior changes.

To assess the reasons for behavior change, research design is necessary. Research design consists of the plan or manner of arranging the experimental conditions to permit drawing inferences about the impact of those conditions. Two general categories of experimental design are useful to distinguish. In control group designs, comparisons are made between alternative groups. Typically, groups receive alternative intervention and control conditions and are assessed after treatment is completed. The impact of treatment is evaluated by comparing differences between groups. The basic control group design and factorial designs were highlighted. In single-case designs, the impact of treatment is evaluated by observing performance over time. Continuous assessment and changing experimental conditions help to establish that the intervention, rather than extraneous influences, was responsible for behavior change. Alternative designs that were highlighted include reversal (ABAB), multiple-baseline, and changing-criterion designs. Although control group and single-case designs can be distinguished, they are often combined in behavioral research.

Data evaluation usually encompasses statistical, nonstatistical, or clinical evaluation. With statistical evaluation, tests are used that yield probability levels, to judge whether the findings are statistically significant. Nonstatistical evaluation or visual inspection of the data has been used in single-case research. Single-case designs help draw inferences from visual inspection because continuous data are available for the subject(s). Another method of evaluation is to assess the clinical importance of experimental findings. Even the fact that the effects of an intervention may be statistically significant really does not address whether the changes in the subjects are important for their everyday functioning. Typically, clinically significant change is examined by seeing if performance of the clients after treatment falls within the range of a normative comparison sample or departs markedly from the level of functioning that characterizes a sample who evince the problem for which treatment was applied.

Data analysis, by whatever method, leads to interpretations about the investigation and its effects. Interpretations serve to evaluate the implications of the data. Conclusions are reached about the basis for the data, given the particular experiment and the possible generality or lack of generality of the findings to persons, situations, and behaviors not included in the experiment. Interpretation of any individual study is always risky. The field advances by the accumulation of several studies that support the effectiveness of a given intervention. Replication, or repetitions of the results of a previously conducted study, greatly enhances the inferences that are drawn about a given intervention. Replication research is exceedingly important because it is the most reliable test of whether a finding is veridical.

RESOURCES

Barlow, D. H, Hersen, M. (1984). *Single-case experimental designs: Strategies for studying behavior change* (2nd. ed.). New York: Plenum.

Ciminero, A. R., Calhoun, K. S., & Adams, H. E. (Eds.). (1986). *Handbook of behavioral assessment* (2nd ed.). New York: Wiley.

Cook, T. D., & Campbell, D. T. (Eds.). (1979). *Quasi-experimentation: Design and analysis issues for field settings.* Chicago: Rand McNally.

Kazdin, A. E. (1992). *Research design in clinical psychology.* Needham Heights, MA: Allyn & Bacon.

Kazdin, A. E. (Ed.). (1992). *Methodological issues and strategies in clinical research.* Washington, DC: American Psychological Association.

CHAPTER 5

Anxiety Disorders

Linda L. Street

David H. Barlow

For most people, anxiety and fear are a part of everyday life. Whether experienced as anxiety concerning failure, which motivates one to study more efficiently for an examination, or as concern with social evaluation, which restricts one from entering a room full of strangers, anxiety and fear are clearly universal phenomena. What remains less clear, however, is where the differentiation lies between "normal" and "pathological" anxiety or fear. In some instances, this distinction can be made easily. For example, if an individual lives in a tropical rainforest that is inhabited by many poisonous snakes, exhibiting fear and avoidance of tall grass and old tree stumps is likely to increase his or her chance of survival; this illustrates the adaptive function of fear. On the other hand, if one who lives in a New York City high-rise apartment will not venture outside for fear of encountering snakes on the street, this fear is clearly excessive.

In many other instances, the distinction between functional and/or normal anxiety and pathological anxiety is far less obvious and is dependent on a variety of factors. For example, a large proportion of the population has a fear of public speaking. Whether or not an individual will receive a diagnosis of social phobia is likely to depend not only on the level of fear he or she experiences in this situation but also on his or her job description. Obviously, this type of phobia would cause more extreme impairment for a politician than for a construction worker. Compulsive behaviors, such as rechecking that one's doors are locked or one's checkbook is correctly balanced are also frequently observed in the normal population. However, the prevalence rate of obsessive-compulsive disorder (OCD) has been estimated to be between only 1.8% and 2.5% (Marks, 1987) of the population. In only a small proportion of cases do these behaviors cause the marked distress and/or interference in functioning required to receive a psychiatric diagnosis. Thus, one may view anxiety-related pathology as spanning a continuum, ranging from "normal" anxiety, in which "the emotional response is proportional to the perceived risk or danger" (Tuma

& Maser, 1985, p. xxii), to "pathological" anxiety in which irrational thinking, excessive worry, and avoidance of anxiety-provoking situations lead to a restricted lifestyle and poor quality of life.

In today's society, where tranquilizers are among the most widely prescribed of all medications and "stress management" has become a household phrase, it is often overlooked that up to a point the presence of anxiety can enhance our ability to perform a variety of activities, from test-taking to becoming sexually aroused (Barlow, Sakheim, & Beck, 1983). Evolutionary theorists such as Darwin (1872) pointed out that anxiety served an adaptive function for our ancestors by preparing them to flee or defend themselves from predators in a dangerous environment. However, in the technologically advanced twentieth century, men and women face relatively few physical threats. According to Beck (1985), we are like animals in a zoo, caged by the social and environmental restraints of our time that prevent us from utilizing our genetically prepared action tendencies ("fight or flight"). As a result, we are prone to experience maladaptive levels of anxiety that can interfere with our ability to function successfully.

FEAR AND ANXIETY

One key question that arises from the previous discussion concerns the issue of why some individuals go on to develop maladaptive levels of anxiety and others do not. In order to address this question adequately, another issue must first be clarified: the distinction between fear and anxiety. Some researchers argue that these constructs are indeed separate phenomena (Izard & Blumberg, 1985), yet others contend that they are on a continuum (Ehlers & Margraf, 1989; Lang, 1985). Although the terms *anxiety* and *fear* have thus far been used interchangeably in the present discussion and are, in fact, overlapping constructs, they do differ in several important ways.

In our view, fear is an innate, primitive alarm response that is often accompanied by the behavioral manifestations of "fight or flight" (Barlow, 1988). A "true" alarm is the term used to describe this response when it occurs during a dangerous or life-threatening situation, and a "false" alarm is characterized by marked fear in the absence of a life-threatening stimulus (i.e., it occurs unexpectedly). We refer to this false alarm as a *panic attack*.

Fear or panic are frequently experienced by individuals who do not go on to develop an anxiety disorder. Norton, Harrison, Hauch, and Rhodes (1985), for example, found that of 186 normal adults questioned, over one-third reported having experienced at least one panic attack in the past year. Obviously, alarms, in and of themselves, are not problematic. Rather, it is the development of "anxious apprehension" over the future occurrence of an alarm (in various situations) that marks the majority of the anxiety disorders.

As suggested elsewhere (Barlow, 1988), anxiety is a loose construct consisting of both cognitive and affective (emotional) components. The term "anxious apprehension" refers to this future-oriented mood state characterized by high negative affect combined with a sense that internal and external events are occurring in an unpredictable, uncontrollable manner. This sense of uncontrollability is accompanied by: (1) a rapid shift in the focus of attention away from external activities to internal self-evaluative content, (2) increases in arousal, (3) narrowing of attention, and (4) hypervigilance regarding the source of the apprehension. At mild or moderate levels, anxiety is adaptive, as it helps us to become ready for a challenge, such as a test. Without anxiety, our performance would probably not be as good, but when this cycle escalates to a significant degree, concentration and performance are disrupted, and an individual may begin to experience significant impairment in daily life. At this point, the anxiety has become a clinical problem and, depending on the focus of the anxious apprehension, is likely to meet the criteria for one or more of the anxiety disorders.

In summary, most of us occasionally experience the alarm of fear, which is the activation of our basic action tendency to escape ("I've got to get out of here") when in a dangerous situation and occasionally when there is nothing to fear (unexpected panic). In addition, most of us experience anxiety when we feel that something bad is about to happen that we will not be able to deal with (control). We may constantly worry and be alert for signs of such an upcoming negative event, so that when it occurs we will be ready to act. This state of alertness is characterized by increased arousal, narrowing of attention, and hypervigilance. For example, many of us worry about taking tests, but view them as negative events that are going to happen, for which we need to prepare, rather than as a present danger that would activate our escape response. How the combination of fear (panic) and anxiety contribute to the various anxiety disorders is discussed below.

THE ANXIETY DISORDERS

Specific Features

The most recent revision of the Diagnostic and Statistical Manual (DSM-III-R) (American Psychiatric Association [APA], 1987) specifies the existence of eight distinct anxiety disorder categories, as well as a residual category for anxiety or phobic disorders that do not meet the criteria for a previously specified diagnosis. For example, a DSM-III-R diagnosis of *social phobia* is a "persistent fear of a circumscribed object or situation in which the person is exposed to possible scrutiny by others and fears that he or she may act in a way that will be humiliating or embarrassing" (p. 243). The essential features of *panic disorder* (PD) are "recurrent panic attacks, i.e., discrete periods of intense fear or discomfort, with at least four characteristic physical or cognitive symptoms" (p. 235), such as heart palpitations, dizziness, and a fear of dying or going crazy. Panic disorder may also be accompanied

by *agoraphobia* (PDA), defined as "fear of being in places or situations from which escape might be difficult or in which help might not be available, which leads to either travel restrictions or need for a companion when away from home" (p. 236). *Generalized anxiety disorder* (GAD) is characterized by unrealistic or excessive worry about two or more life circumstances, such as health, family, or future. *Obsessive-compulsive disorder* (OCD) specifies the existence of recurrent obsessions or compulsions that cause distress, are time-consuming, or interfere with a person's functioning. *Posttraumatic stress disorder* (PTSD) is characterized by the development of a particular symptom picture following an unusually traumatic event.

Common Features

Although each of the anxiety disorder categories in DSM-III-R emphasizes a particular key feature, recent evidence has accumulated to suggest that these categories also share several common characteristics. For example, Barlow et al. (1985) assessed the prevalence of panic in 108 individuals with social and simple phobia, GAD, OCD, and agoraphobia with panic. They found at least 83% of patients in each diagnostic category had previously experienced at least one panic attack. Worry also appears to occur frequently across the anxiety disorders, either in the form of anticipatory anxiety about a specific event (e.g., a panic attack, a job interview) or in the form of more global concerns, including one's health, family, and future.

Both panic and anxious apprehension are obviously central features of all anxiety disorders, with the exception of GAD, in which panic is not the central focus. However, what does appear to differ among the diagnostic categories is the focus of this anxious apprehension (i.e., what one is worried about), the perception of cues associated with panic, and whether panic is expected or not (Barlow, 1988). For example, if a person develops a simple phobia of driving, it is likely that he or she previously experienced either a true alarm (e.g., a car accident) or false alarm (unexpected panic while driving) and subsequently became anxious over the possibility of re-experiencing this intense fear while in a driving situation. Obviously, the cues for panic in simple phobia are much more circumscribed than those in other anxiety disorders, such as panic disorder. With regard to OCD, on the other hand, an individual might panic to the cue of an intrusive thought about killing one of her children and might then become apprehensively anxious about the occurrence of the next uncontrolled intrusive thought.

Avoidance

Another dimension that manifests itself in varying degrees across the anxiety disorders is avoidance, which can be cognitive and/or behavioral in nature. Individuals with OCD, for example, frequently engage in a variety of bizarre, cognitive rituals in an attempt to avoid the disruptive thoughts, images, and self-doubts that characterize the obsessive component of this disorder. One woman, who was treated at the Phobia and Anxiety Disorders Clinic at the State University of New York at Albany, spent several hours each day imagining that her kitchen utensils and other household objects were covered with a purifying blue light. When questioned about the purpose of this ritual, she reported that it was an attempt to neutralize or avoid her recurrent obsession that these objects were contaminated by semen from the tap water used for washing. Behavioral avoidance, on the other hand, usually occurs in its most severe form as a complication of PD. In some instances, persons become essentially housebound because of fear that if they leave home they will experience a panic attack. In recent years, there have been many advances made in the treatment of this disorder, and even severe cases often show substantial improvement. In view of the vast amount of new research on the assessment and treatment of this disorder, the remainder of this chapter

will focus primarily on issues related to the assessment and treatment of PD and panic disorder with agoraphobia (PDA). Treatments for OCD and PTSD are discussed in the last chapter of the book (Future Directions).

ASSESSMENT

To conduct a comprehensive evaluation of a particular anxiety problem, several primary goals must be accomplished. The first goal involves determining whether or not an individual's symptomatology meets the criteria for any of the previously specified anxiety disorder categories listed in DSM-III-R. Second, it is necessary to go beyond diagnostic classification, to assess the specific characteristics and maintaining variables associated with each unique anxiety case.

Prior to making a diagnosis, it is essential to rule out several physical disorders that can mimic panic. These disorders include hypoglycemia, hyperthroidism, insulin-secreting tumors, mitral valve prolapse, and audiovestibular disturbances (Jacob & Rapport, 1984). To do this, a thorough evaluation of these symptoms by a physician is often recommended. In some instances, a physical disorder may coexist with panic disorder, and in that case, both conditions should be treated (Barlow, 1988).

Once these preliminary considerations have been attended to, the initial step in conducting a thorough evaluation typically involves assessment of three response systems: physiological, cognitive, and behavioral (Lang, 1968). Physiological evaluation commonly consists of monitoring changes in various indicators of autonomic nervous system arousal, including heart rate, galvanic skin response, and respiration rate. Cognitive or subjective features that require assessment include subjective distress, anxiety focused on panic, and the content of panic-related catastrophic cognitions. Third, the individual's level of behavioral avoidance should be assessed, as well as the degree of impairment that he or she is experiencing with regard to performing specific tasks (e.g., activities at work, household chores).

Finally, the therapist should obtain information about the functional relationship between internal and external cues for panic, the occurrence of panic, and the pattern of cognitive and behavioral avoidance that has developed. Conducting such a functional analysis allows the therapist to tailor a standard treatment package to the individual needs of the client and to alter the antecedents and/or consequences of panic that may be contributing to the maintenance of the disorder. For example, in many instances, patients who perceive that their panic attacks are cued by external phobic stimuli (e.g., stores, work) are able to maintain a high level of agoraphobic avoidance because they have persuaded their family members that they cannot work, shop, or perform other activities that would require them to leave the home. Typically, the first step taken toward obtaining the information is to conduct a clinical interview. Next, depending on the specific questions that are asked, a variety of self-report, self-monitoring, behavioral, and/or physiological measures (described below) are usually conducted.

Clinical Interview

During the initial interaction between client and therapist, a great deal of useful information can be learned about the nature of the presenting problem(s), and whether or not the reported symptomatology meets the criteria for a particular anxiety disorder. In addition, the therapist can assess information about the individual's cognitive, somatic, and behavioral patterns of responding during periods of anxiety.

To make a DSM-III-R diagnosis of PD, the therapist must find evidence that the patient experienced one or more panic attacks that were unexpected and not triggered by situations in which he or she was the focus of others' attention. At least one of these attacks must have

involved four or more characteristic symptoms of panic that developed suddenly and increased in intensity within 10 minutes of the beginning of the first symptom. Finally, at least four attacks must have occurred within a 4-week period, or one or more attacks must have been followed by a period of at least a month of persistent anxiety over having another attack, according to the DSM-III-R (APA, 1987).

The diagnosis of PDA is made when an individual meets the criteria for panic disorder and has a "fear of being in places or situations from which escape might be difficult (or embarrassing) or from which help might not be available in the event of a panic attack" (APA, 1987, p. 238). Frequently, these situations involve travel outside the home, driving, and shopping in malls and grocery stores. As a result of this fear, the person's mobility is restricted or he or she endures such situations with dread.

Once the determination of a DSM-III-R diagnosis has been made, information about the frequency, intensity, and duration of the somatic and cognitive accompaniments of panic and anxiety can be obtained. Specifically, patients can be questioned about the frequency and intensity of the thoughts and physical sensations they experience before and during episodes of panic, as well as how fearful or worried they are about the recurrence of another panic attack. Most often, catastrophic cognitions center around themes of dying, going crazy, or losing control.

Many persons with PDA are likely to report that there are one or more "safety" cues in their lives (Barlow, 1988). A "safe person," for example, is frequently someone who is aware of the disorder and whom the patient believes is capable of helping him or her in the event of a panic attack. These cues can also take the form of a place (e.g., the home), object (e.g. medication, food, or drink), or even a child or pet that in some way allows the patient to feel either more in control or better able to cope with a panic attack, should one occur. A clinician must assess for the presence of these cues in order to develop an effective strategy for eventually reducing the patient's attachment to them.

Finally, the therapist should learn not only about the patient's presenting problem but also about his or her history, other existing problems, current living situation, and daily level of functioning. For example, the discussion of treatments that intervene in the psychosocial context will demonstrate that issues pertaining to an individual's marital relationship may be intrinsically related to the development and/or maintenance of his or her disorder. Similarly, additional diagnoses of depression or dependent personality, often present in individuals who exhibit strong patterns of avoidance, must be carefully considered when planning an efficacious treatment.

At the Center for Stress and Anxiety Disorders in Albany, New York, a structured interview was developed for the purpose of diagnosing the major anxiety disorder categories in DSM-III-R and for ascertaining other clinically relevant information that can be used to plan an effective treatment. This instrument, called the Anxiety Disorders Interview Schedule - Revised (ADIS-R) (Di Nardo & Barlow, 1988) has been shown to be a reliable measure for diagnosing both PD and PDA (Barlow, 1988) and, in addition, allows the interviewer to obtain information about the history and course of the disorder, patients' currently utilized coping strategies, and their level of agoraphobic avoidance.

Questionnaires

Questionnaire measures are inexpensive, can be completed by the patient either at home or at the therapist's office, and require minimal instruction. They also provide a useful measure of therapeutic change when administered on a pretreatment and posttreatment basis, as they have the advantage of asking the same questions in an identical manner, over repeated trials. The following questionnaires have adequate psychometric properties and are among the most useful developed to date.

The Fear Questionnaire (Marks & Mathews, 1979) was developed to assess changes in phobic severity over time. It provides a global measure of phobic disturbance, a measure of avoidance with regard to the patient's primary phobia, and a score that reflects total avoidance level across 15 common phobias. It also provides three useful subscales (agoraphobia, blood-injury phobia, social phobia) and a measure of anxiety-depression that assesses degree of general affective disturbance.

The Body Sensations Questionnaire and Agoraphobia Cognitions Questionnaire (Chambless, Caputo, Bright, & Gallagher, 1984) were designed to assess fear of the physical sensations (e.g., heart palpitations, dizziness) and frequency of the catastrophic thoughts (e.g., passing out, going crazy) that are commonly experienced during panic attacks. These measures provide an efficient means of identifying each patient's most feared sensations and cognitions so they can be effectively targeted in therapy, via cognitive techniques and/or interoceptive exposure.

The Mobility Inventory for Agoraphobia (Chambless, Caputo, Jasin, Gracely, & Williams, 1985) ascertains information about the tendency for an individual to avoid (alone and accompanied) a variety of situations (e.g., elevators, restaurants) that are commonly feared by agoraphobics. This scale can be used not only for providing an overall index of avoidance but also for targeting those situations that need to be practiced with *in vivo* exposure during treatment.

The Anxiety Sensitivity Index (Reiss, Peterson, Gursky, & McNally, 1986) measures the belief that anxiety symptoms have harmful consequences beyond their immediate discomfort, such as additional anxiety, illness, embarrassment, and loss of control. For example, an individual who scores high on this measure is likely to fear that nervousness may lead to mental illness.

The Fear and Avoidance Hierarchy (FAH) was developed at the Phobia and Anxiety Disorders Clinic to assess the degree of fear and avoidance associated with a variety of different activities and situations that patients encounter in their daily lives. Each FAH is individually prepared by patient and therapist to contain 10 rank-ordered items ranging from those that cause minimal fear and are rarely avoided to those that cause extreme fear and are always avoided. For example, a FAH for a client who is fearful of driving and shopping in grocery stores would include activities such as "driving one block from home" and "purchasing one item at a local convenience store" at the bottom of the hierarchy; "driving three exits on the highway" and "buying a full cart of groceries at a large supercenter" would be located at the top. If constructed to reflect the client's overall therapeutic goals, this instrument can be used throughout treatment to aid in the development of weekly exposure practices and to provide the client with feedback about his or her therapeutic progress.

Self-Monitoring Measures

In recent years, self-monitoring techniques have increasingly been utilized in clinical research and practice. Researchers in particular have attempted to obtain reliable and valid information about the frequency and intensity of panic attacks and the general levels of anxiety, depression, and other subjective emotional states that are experienced by patients as they progress through treatment. These measures are extremely useful because they eliminate many of the problems associated with retrospective recall that are inherent in most questionnaire and interview assessments. For example, when patients are asked to describe the intensity of a panic attack experienced 2 weeks earlier, their report of that event may be colored by their emotional state at the time of the evaluation.

At our clinic, therapists currently use three types of self-monitoring forms. The first type,

the Panic Attack Record, is an extremely practical, non-obtrusive, pocket-sized pad that patients are instructed to carry with them at all times. They are asked to complete one sheet on the pad during or immediately following each panic attack they experience, and to record the intensity and duration of the attack, the number of symptoms they experienced, the presence of cues for panic, and other descriptive information. A sample is presented in Figure 5.1.

The second type of self-monitoring form (presented in Figure 5.2), the Weekly Record of Anxiety and Depression, is completed by patients in the evening, before bedtime. They are asked to reflect about their day and rate the average and maximum levels of anxiety, the average levels of depression and pleasant feelings, and the average fear of panic they experienced throughout the course of the day.

A third useful self-monitoring device, the Daily Activity Monitoring Form, is used to assess behavioral avoidance. It requires patients to record the duration of, and the (maximum and minimum) level of anxiety experienced during each activity they perform (e.g., driving, shopping, staying home alone) on a daily basis.

Although self-monitoring measures are useful in resolving many of the disadvantages associated with retrospective recall, they have several problems of their own. The first and perhaps most notable is patient compliance. If distributed without instruction and close supervision, these forms are likely to be forgotten or ignored. Thus, it is essential to emphasize conscientious recordkeeping, to provide clear instructions, and to give feedback to patients about their accuracy. For the Panic Attack Record to accurately reflect changes in frequency of panic over the course of treatment, the therapist should also provide patients with a clear definition of panic. At our clinic, they are told to complete one record sheet each time they experience a sudden rush of intense fear or anxiety, or a feeling of impending doom that is accompanied by a number of physical sensations.

PANIC ATTACK RECORD

Name: _____

Date: _____   Time: _____   Duration: _____ (mins.)

With: Spouse _____   Friend _____   Stranger _____   Alone _____

Stressful situation: Yes/No   Expected: Yes/No

Maximum anxiety (*Circle*)

0 _____ 1 _____ 2 _____ 3 _____ 4 _____ 5 _____ 6 _____ 7 _____ 8

    None   Moderate   Extreme

Sensations (*Check*)

Pounding heart	_____	Sweating	_____	Hot/cold flash	_____
Tight/painful chest	_____	Choking	_____	Fear of dying	_____
Breathless	_____	Nausea	_____	Fear of going crazy	_____
Dizzy	_____	Unreality	_____	Fear of losing control	_____
Trembling	_____	Numb/tingle	_____		

FIGURE 5.1

Panic Attack Record. Developed at the Phobia and Anxiety Disorders Clinic, State University of New York at Albany.

Behavioral Measures

Because of the subjective nature of self-report information, many researchers suggest that an objective measure of behavioral avoidance should be obtained through direct observation of the patient in his or her environment. At our clinic, a therapist typically visits the patient's home and requests that he or she perform three feared activities (of low, medium, and high intensity). One example of such an activity might be, "to walk three blocks from home, unaccompanied." Immediately after completion of the task, patients are asked to rate the average and maximum levels of fear they experienced and whether or not they panicked.

Although this is a more objective measure of behavioral avoidance than are self-report instruments, it is also subject to demand characteristics and is a costly use of therapist time. One useful strategy might be to train paraprofessionals as therapists, with the instruction that patients should try to perform as many of the feared activities as they possibly can, but not to push themselves far beyond their normal level of functioning.

Name _____   Week ending _____

WEEKLY RECORD OF ANXIETY AND DEPRESSION

Have you had any panic attacks this week?   _____ Yes _____ No

Each evening before you go to bed please rate your <u>average</u> level of anxiety (taking all things into consideration) throughout the day, the <u>maximum</u> level of anxiety which you experienced that day, your <u>average</u> level of depression throughout the day, and your average feeling of pleasantness throughout the day. Use the scale below. Next, please list the dosages and amounts of any medication you took. Finally, please rate, using the scale below, how worried or frightened you were, on average, about the possibility of having a panic attack throughout the day.

Level of Anxiety/Depression/Pleasant Feeling

0 _____ 1 _____ 2 _____ 3 _____ 4 _____ 5 _____ 6 _____ 7 _____ 8

| None | Slight | Moderate | A lot | As much as you can imagine |

Date	Average Anxiety	Maximum Anxiety	Average Depression	Average Pleasantness	Medication (Type, dose, number (mg))	Fear of Panic Attack

FIGURE 5.2

Weekly Record of Anxiety and Depression. Developed at the Phobia and Anxiety Disorders Clinic, State University of New York at Albany.

Physiological Assessment

By definition, physiological arousal is a primary component of panic disorder and also plays a large role in the other anxiety disorders. Thus, it has frequently been argued that measurement of this response system is necessary to conduct a thorough evaluation of a particular anxiety problem (Barlow & Wolfe, 1981). Although some evidence has suggested that panic patients are more physiologically aroused than normal control subjects while at rest (Gorman et al., 1988; Lader & Mathews, 1968) and that pretreatment heartrate may be predictive of treatment outcome (Vermilyea, Boice, & Barlow, 1984), standard physiological measures have not been reliable when used as an index of therapeutic change (Holden & Barlow, 1986; Michelson & Mavissakalian, 1985).

Interoceptive Assessment Procedures

A final technique for assessing PD involves directly measuring fear of internal bodily sensations that are similar to those experienced during natural panic. A series of physical exercises have been developed to elicit these sensations, including voluntary hyperventilation, spinning in a swivel chair, holding one's breath, running in place, and shaking one's head from side to side. From these exercises, subjective ratings of anxiety and symptom intensity and measures of escape and avoidance can be obtained. An example of the utility of this assessment strategy was demonstrated by Zarate, Craske, Rapee, and Barlow (1988) when they identified an individual with simple phobia of driving, who was fearful of the sensations produced by performing step-ups on a small stool. Interestingly, they were able to achieve a reduction in the patient's fear of driving solely through repeated exposure to the step-up task. Clearly, this technique has important implications in the areas of both assessment and treatment of anxiety disorders that involve fear of interoceptive stimuli.

TREATMENT OF PANIC DISORDER/AGORAPHOBIA

Unfortunately for many, the first major advance in the treatment of agoraphobia did not occur until the late 1960s (Agras, Leitenberg, & Barlow, 1968; Stern & Marks, 1973). Not until this period of time did psychologists and psychiatrists first began to arrange in a systematic way for their patients to approach and remain in the situations they feared, rather than to avoid them. This type of treatment, known as *in vivo* exposure, has since been shown to be the treatment of choice for reducing behavioral avoidance (Barlow & Wolfe, 1981), and it is probably one of the most effective psychological therapies developed to date.

Following this initial discovery, researchers interested in agoraphobia began to focus on identifying those variables that enhance the efficacy of exposure-based principles in clinical practice. For example, studies were conducted to determine the optimum number and duration of exposure practices that should be conducted, the necessity of therapist assistance during exposure, and the benefit of including the patient's spouse or significant other in treatment. More recently, there has been a shift in attention toward the development of strategies that target panic more directly. For example, cognitive restructuring, relaxation training, exposure to interoceptive cues, and breathing retraining have been applied directly to reducing patients' fears of internal bodily sensations, which is at the heart of panic disorder.

Variations of Exposure Treatment

In Vivo Exposure

During *in vivo* exposure, patients are instructed to expose themselves repeatedly to situations or activities (1) which they fear and/or avoid because of the fear of experiencing a panic attack, or (2) in which escape would be difficult or help unavailable in the event of panic or incapacitation. Exposure practices can be conducted in a variety of different ways, ranging from prolonged, massed practices to short, graduated, self-paced exposures.

Imaginal Exposure

Because of the early success of *imaginal exposure* (i.e., systematic desensitization and imaginal flooding) in the treatment of specific phobias, several studies were initially conducted to compare its effectiveness with that of *in vivo* exposure in reducing the behavioral avoidance associated with agoraphobia. With the exception of one study that found no differences between these procedures (Mathews et al., 1976), *in vivo* exposure has repeatedly been demonstrated to be superior to imaginal exposure in treating this disorder (Emmelkamp & Wessels, 1975; Stern & Marks, 1973; Watson, Mullett, & Pillay, 1973).

Graduated Exposure

Although early research found a superiority of more intensive forms of exposure (McFayden & Presly, 1977; Sterns & Marks, 1973), in recent years, graduated, self-directed therapy has become increasingly popular in clinics around the world. In *graduated exposure*, patients initially expose themselves only to situations that evoke minimal anxiety, and then gradually progress toward those that are more difficult. Barlow (1988) has outlined several factors that are likely to have contributed to this recent shift in popularity. First, two studies conducted by Rachman and colleagues (de Silva & Rachman, 1984; Rachman, Craske, Tallman, & Solyom, 1986) found evidence that agoraphobics who were allowed to escape a phobic situation (at a previously determined level of fear) during therapist-assisted exposure fared as well on a variety of phobic measures as subjects who were required to remain in a feared situation until their anxiety level peaked and subsequently decreased by 50%. Second, individuals treated with graduated exposure appeared to drop out of therapy less frequently (Jannoun, Munby, Catalan, & Gelder, 1980; Mathews, Teasdale, Munby, Johnston, & Shaw, 1977) and to exhibit greater continued improvement over follow-up

than those who were treated with more intensive exposure (Emmelkamp & Wessels, 1975). Third, some have suggested that because most prolonged exposure is therapist-assisted, this type of treatment may produce unwanted dependency on the therapist (Mathews et al., 1977). Fourth, the abrupt nature of the changes resulting from such intensive treatment may have detrimental effects on the marital relationship (Himadi, Cerny, Barlow, Cohen, & O'Brien, 1986). Milton and Hafner (1979), for example, reported that marital dissatisfaction increased in 60% of couples they treated with intensive graded exposure during the 6-month period following therapy. Intensive exposures have also been found to involve high relapse rates (Jansson & Ost, 1982; Milton & Hafner, 1979). Finally, some researchers have suggested (Barlow, 1988; Michelson, Mavissakalian, Marchione, Dancu, & Greenwald, 1986) that because graduated, self-directed exposure involves a conscious effort from clients to confront the situations they fear, this procedure may lead to increased feelings of control and/or self-efficacy with regard to clients' ability to cope with panic.

Additional Components

In addition to identifying the specific parameters of exposure therapy that increase its effectiveness in clinical practice, several researchers have attempted to enhance treatment outcome of agoraphobia by adding components, such as relaxation, cognitive therapy, and marital communications training, to standard exposure-based therapy. Despite the fact that maladaptive cognitions are frequently present in individuals who suffer from agoraphobia, studies that have evaluated the effectiveness of cognitive restructuring (e.g., Emmelkamp & Mersch, 1982; Meichenbaum, 1975), either alone or in combination with *in vivo* exposure, have demonstrated: (1) that *in vivo* exposure is superior to cognitive restructuring (Emmelkamp, Kuipers, & Eggeraat, 1978), and (2) that cognitive restructuring does not appear to enhance the effectiveness of the former treatment (Emmelkamp & Mersch, 1982).

Treatments Involving the Interpersonal System

PDA can be an extremely pervasive disorder, impairing both social and occupational functioning. Although research has shown that in many ways, the marriages of agoraphobics are similar to those of nonagoraphobics (Buglass, Clark, Henderson, Kreitman, & Presley, 1977; Marks, 1987), in at least some cases, symptoms of the disorder probably affect the marital relationship and vice versa. For example, when the spouse of an agoraphobic becomes responsible for the majority of financial as well as domestic responsibilities, he or she may not only feel resentful and overwhelmed, but may also be unintentionally contributing to the maintenance of the agoraphobic problem.

Several researchers have investigated the effects of including the spouse or other significant partner in therapy (Arnow, Taylor, Agras, & Telch, 1985; Jannoun et al., 1980; Mathews et al., 1977). At our clinic, a treatment outcome study was conducted in which 28 women who met the DSM-III (APA, 1980) criteria for agoraphobia with panic attacks were treated in a graduated, self-initiated, exposure-based program that also included cognitive restructuring (Barlow, O'Brien, & Last, 1984). Half of these women were treated in small groups, accompanied by their husbands, and the other half were provided with an identical treatment without their husbands. In the spouse group, husbands were asked to serve as coaches to assist their wives in coping with their anxiety, and in planning and carrying out exposure practices. In addition, couples were made aware of the possibility that the husband-wife relationship can serve as a maintaining factor in the disorder.

The overall results of this study showed that at posttest, a greater number of women in the spouse group showed clinical improvement when compared to the non-spouse group. For marriages that were rated as well-adjusted at pretreatment, increases in marital satisfaction, based on client's and spouse's scores on the Locke-Wallace Marital Adjustment Test (Locke & Wallace, 1959), occurred during treatment, regardless of whether or not the spouse was included. Agoraphobics from poorly adjusted marriages, however, obtained greater increases in marital satisfaction and were more improved on the clinician's rating of phobic severity when their spouses participated in treatment than when they did not (Barlow, O'Brien, Last, & Holden, 1983). Results of a follow-up study indicated that the 27 agoraphobics who were treated with their spouses continued to show an improving course for 24 months after treatment. The 14 patients treated without their husbands did not continue to improve at 1-year follow-up, although at 2 years, they resumed an improving trend (Cerny, Barlow, Craske, & Himadi, 1987).

The obvious question that arises about these findings concerns the specific components in the couples treatment of agoraphobia that are responsible for its effectiveness. Research is needed not only to identify these essential ingredients but also to develop strategies for maximizing their potential benefits. Arnow et al. (1985) investigated the effects of adding marital communications training to a standard exposure-based group treatment. They treated 25 agoraphobic women and their partners in a standard protocol for 4 weeks and then divided them into two groups that were matched according to degree of patient improvement. One group was taught marital communication skills and the other group received relaxation training. Their results showed that patients in the marital communication group exhibited greater improvement on behavioral and self-report measures at posttest and follow-up.

At our clinic, we are also examining the effectiveness of adding marital communications and problem-solving training to the standard, exposure-based couples treatment described earlier. This treatment package is also being compared to another multicomponent package that contains the basic ingredients of the standard protocol and a variety of psychological techniques (described below) specifically designed for treating panic attacks (e.g., interoceptive exposure, breathing retraining, visualization exercises). Finally, a comparison is being made between each of these treatments and a combined package containing both communications training and panic management components.

Effectiveness of Exposure-Based Treatment

The development of *in vivo* exposure has had a large impact on the treatment of agoraphobia. Although this procedure has been implemented somewhat differently across research settings, it is a relatively consistent finding that between 60% and 70% of individuals with PDA who complete an exposure-based treatment show some degree of clinical improvement (Jansson & Ost, 1982), and that in many cases, these gains are maintained over follow-up (Jansson & Ost, 1982; Munby & Johnston, 1980).

Somewhat less impressive, however, is the fact that the median dropout rate is approximately 12% (Jansson and Ost, 1982), and when exposure is conducted on a highly intensive basis, the dropout rate increases to between 25% and 40% (Zitrin, Klein, & Woerner, 1980). Combined with the 30% to 40% of treatment completers who do not show substantial improvement, the total proportion of people who fail to benefit from this treatment is considerable. In addition, although *in vivo* exposure appears to be somewhat effective in reducing the frequency of panic, a considerable number of patients continue to panic at posttreatment and follow-up (Arnow et al., 1985; Michelson, Mavissakalian, & Marchione, 1985). Recent attempts at enhancing effectiveness of this treatment have included the incorporation of techniques that intervene in

the patient's interpersonal system (e.g., marital problem-solving and communication skills training) as well as those that are geared toward treating panic directly.

Panic Control Therapy (PCT)

Traditionally, agoraphobia was viewed as a fear of leaving the home or of going to public places. Only since the early 1980s has panic been recognized as a central feature of this disorder, with avoidance as a secondary complication. The limited success achieved by *in vivo* exposure in treating panic, combined with the reconceptualization of agoraphobia as a variant of panic disorder, has prompted researchers to develop treatment strategies that target the panic phenomenon more directly, although these techniques have most frequently been tested in patients who exhibit no more than mild agoraphobic avoidance. Along these lines, we developed a new treatment consisting of cognitive restructuring, interoceptive exposure (exposure to somatic cues associated with panic attacks), and breathing retraining. The treatment is referred to as *panic control treatment* (PCT).

The results of a large-scale treatment outcome study conducted at the Phobia and Anxiety Disorders Clinic at SUNY-Albany were recently reported (Barlow, Craske, Cerny, & Klosko, 1989). In this study, PCT was compared to a condition in which relaxation training was taught to patients, who used this strategy whenever they felt anxious or panicky. The third condition combined PCT and relaxation, and the fourth condition was a wait-list control. The results indicated that all three active treatment conditions were effective in reducing the frequency of panic attacks and in producing overall improvement across a composite measure of overall functioning. Specifically, 87%, 85%, 60%, and 35% of patients in the PCT, combined, relaxation, and wait-list conditions, respectively, were free of panic attacks at posttest. However, significantly more dropouts occurred from the relaxation condition (33%) than from the combined (17%), PCT (6%), or wait-list (6%) conditions. One phenomenon that may partially account for this finding is that of "relaxation-induced" panic. It has been found that a proportion of PD patients experience feelings of anxiety and/or panic while attempting to engage in relaxation exercises. For example, Adler, Craske, & Barlow (1987) recently demonstrated that patients who listened to a relaxation tape felt more out of control and rated the symptoms they experienced as more similar to natural panic than did patients who listened to a neutral tape or a tape with instructions to tense their muscles. In addition, a frequently made clinical observation is that merely asking these patients to focus their attention on their internal bodily sensations (as is required during relaxation exercises) can be anxiogenic.

Recently, we have completed a 2-year follow-up of patients treated in this study. Our findings indicated that patients treated with PCT alone maintained their gains, with 80% continuing to be free of panic attacks 2 years after treatment. They were significantly more improved than patients from relaxation or wait-list conditions, and somewhat surprisingly, significantly more improved than patients who received the combined treatment of relaxation plus PCT. Patients in the latter condition may have felt overwhelmed with the task of attempting to master too many anxiety-reduction techniques at the same time.

The results of the aforementioned studies indicate that PCT is effective in ameliorating symptoms of panic in individuals who suffer from panic disorder without agoraphobia. Only recently have researchers attempted to dismantle these strategies and to isolate the components that target specific features of panic. Currently, studies are underway in our clinic to ascertain the relative contribution of various components of treatment such as cognitive therapy or breathing retraining. A major treatment component emphasized in our clinic is exposure to the somatic sensations associated with panic (interoceptive exposure).

Interoceptive Exposure Procedures

Early in the 1960s, Russian physiologists discovered a principle that has since been recognized as important in our understanding of PD. They demonstrated that fear or anxiety could be conditioned to internal physiological sensations. By providing electric shock simultaneously with stimulation of the colon in dogs, they were able to produce conditioned fear in these animals during natural defecation (Razran, 1961). This principle has since been utilized by researchers such as Barlow and Cerny (1988), who hypothesized that individuals who develop PD have learned an association between internal cues and false alarms in much the same way that true or false alarms become associated with external cues in simple phobia.

Evidence showing that frequency of panic can be reduced during *in vivo* exposure therapy suggests that during this procedure, exposure occurs not only to characteristics of the external environment but also to the feared internal sensations of arousal that characterize the disorder. However, although *in vivo* exposure remains a plausible means of producing these physiological sensations in individuals who have developed fears of specific external situations, it does not seem to be effective for those who have not. Finally, there remain a substantial number of agoraphobics who continue to experience panic attacks throughout *in vivo* exposure therapy (Arnow et al., 1985; Michelson et al., 1985).

A variety of strategies (e.g., CO_2 inhalation, infusion of sodium lactate and isoproterenol, yohimbine injection, hyperventilation) have been developed by researchers to produce physiological sensations that mimic natural panic in the laboratory, although in only a few cases have these procedures been used for treatment purposes. Several early studies (Bonn, Harrison, & Rees, 1973; Haslam, 1974; Orwin, 1973) demonstrated that repeated exposure to sodium lactate, CO_2, and exercise, respectively, resulted in a reduction in symptoms of anxiety, although measures of panic were not obtained. More recently, two controlled studies were conducted in which repeated trials of CO_2 inhalation were found to reduce frequency of panic from pre- to posttreatment (Griez & van den Hout, 1986) and to reduce subjective anxiety during CO_2 inhalation (van den Hout, van der Molen, Griez, Lousberg & Nansen, 1987).

In recognition of the relationship between interoceptive fears and panic disorder, a variety of physical exercises have been developed at our clinic to enable patients to reproduce and expose themselves to the specific physiological sensations they fear. For example, we begin therapy with an assessment of interoceptive fear in the manner previously described. Subsequently, we develop homework assignments that require the patient repeatedly to induce and cope with those particular sensations that were identified as anxiety-provoking. The following example of a woman who was treated with PCT illustrates this procedure:

> M.R. experienced her first panic attack approximately 5 years before seeking treatment. It occurred on a hot sunny day in late July when she had walked into her backyard to chlorinate her new swimming pool. Upon opening the lid on the canister that contained the chlorine, she became sickened by the odor and felt unable to breathe. She proceeded to hyperventilate uncontrollably for approximately 10 minutes before getting the attention of her husband, who was working in the yard. She requested that he call an ambulence as she felt she would smother and die. Although M.R. did not develop a specific pattern of behavioral avoidance, she become intensely afraid of being "hot." She adjusted the temperature in her home to remain at 60° in both summer and winter, wore only sleeveless blouses, and was afraid of bathing or showering in hot water. Through interoceptive assessment, it also became apparent that she was extremely fearful of sensations, such as dizziness and breathlessness, that are experienced during hyperventilation. In treatment, M.R. was initially educated about the physiology of anxiety, and then taught to challenge her catastrophic thoughts about smothering and losing control with more realistic evidence. Next, she was assigned a series of interoceptive exposure practices that included riding in a hot car without air conditioning, practicing hyperventilation while sitting in a tub of warm water, wearing a turtleneck sweater in July, and standing near an open container of chlorine on a hot, sunny day. Part of each therapy session was also conducted in a small room containing a portable electric heater that was turned on one-half hour before M.R. arrived at the clinic. After 11 sessions of PCT, her fear of heat and of hyperventilatory sensations had greatly subsided.

CONCLUSIONS AND FUTURE DIRECTIONS

Since DSM-III was published more than 10 years ago (APA, 1980), tremendous strides have been made in understanding the nature and treatment of pathological anxiety. PCT and other similar treatments have been found effective in ameliorating the symptoms of panic disorder. However, because the majority of outcome studies evaluating these treatments have been multicomponent in nature, the efficacy of each particular strategy remains undetermined. Thus, one focus of current and future research is to identify the essential therapeutic components that target specific features of panic. For example, research may discover, through self-report and interoceptive assessments, that breathing retraining is an effective treatment only for those patients who exhibit fear of the symptoms of hyperventilation. Furthermore, it remains to be seen whether interoceptive exposure is, in fact, the most essential component in reducing the fear of internal sensations, and what specific contributions are made by each of the other treatment strategies in enhancing the ability to cope with panic (e.g., increasing sense of control, increasing self-efficacy, providing cognitive distraction, altering the processing of information about panic, reducing overall level of arousal).

With regard to reducing the behavioral avoidance associated with PDA, in vivo exposure has been found to be an effective treatment. However, further research is needed to assess the effects of adding therapeutic components to in vivo exposure designed specifically to treat panic.

In addition to investigating variables that affect treatment outcome, a large focus of research within the anxiety disorders has been on the identification of etiological factors. Some theorists argue that panic is primarily a biological phenomenon (Klein, 1980; Klein, 1993; Sheehan, 1982), and others attempt to identify psychological contributory factors. Biological researchers generally assume that spontaneous panic (i.e., a sudden burst of intense fear that arises without an obvious precipitant) represents a physiologically unique state. That is, panic attacks are qualitatively, rather than quantitatively different from generalized anxiety. Second, they claim that panic is associated with a specific, genetically transmitted biological vulnerability.

Other researchers have emphasized the importance of separation anxiety (Weissman, Leckman, Merikangas, Gammon, & Prusoff, 1984) and stress (Last, Barlow, & O'Brien, 1984) as predisposing factors that make persons vulnerable to experiencing panic attacks. Cognitive theorists such as Beck and Emery (1985) suggest that cognitive schema that develop in childhood may play an important role in increasing the probability that panic will develop in adulthood. In recent years, a trend of integration appears to be developing, in that researchers have begun to incorporate aspects of both biological and psychological models into their conceptualizations of panic. Barlow (1988), for example, argues that people who develop full-blown panic disorders are susceptible to developing anxious apprehension due to a combination of factors, including high baseline levels of arousal, poor coping skills, a lack of social support, and perceptions of uncontrollability and unpredictability regarding the experience of a false alarm. He suggests that the reduction of anxious apprehension and the prevention of escapist action tendencies associated with false or learned alarms are both necessary ingredients in any successful panic treatment.

One biologically based therapy for anxiety and panic that has not been discussed is medication. Several classes of drugs have been studied with regard to their effectiveness in treating PD: antidepressant medications (including tricyclic and monoamine oxidase inhibitors), benzodiazepines, and beta blockers; see Barlow (1988) for a review. Many studies have also been conducted to compare the effectiveness of drug and psychological treatments. At our clinic, a large clinical outcome study evaluated the relative efficacy of PCT compared to therapeutic doses of Xanax (alprazolam). These treatments were also compared to placebo and a wait-list control. The results indicated that on most measures, PCT was significantly more effective than wait-list or placebo, whereas Xanax was not significantly different from PCT or placebo/wait-list. The percentages of patients who were panic-free at posttest were 78%, 50%, 36%, and 33% for PCT, Xanax, placebo, and wait-list, respectively (Klosko, Barlow, Tassinari, & Cerny (1990).

More recently, David Clark and colleagues (Clark, Salkovskis, Hackmann, Middleton, Anastasiades, & Gelder, 1992) compared cognitive therapy to applied relaxation, imipramine, or a wait-list in 64 panic disorder patients. Cognitive therapy, as developed independently by Clark and his colleagues, is procedurally very close to PCT. All three treatments also contained some homework assignments in which patients practiced exposing themselves to feared situations. Patient and therapist ratings were taken before treatment and after 3, 6, and 15 months. All three treatments proved to be effective. However, cognitive therapy was significantly more effective than either applied relaxation or imipramine in reducing panic, anxiety, and avoidance behavior not only at the end of treatment but also at follow-up.

These results, in combination with those of other treatment outcome studies mentioned in this chapter, suggest that PD and PDA are responsive to a variety of diverse treatment strategies, although exposure (*in vivo* and interoceptive) appears to play a central role. Despite the fact that effective treatments exist for these disorders, it is clearly necessary to attempt to isolate their effective therapeutic ingredients, develop improved treatments, and learn more about the etiological and maintaining factors that contribute to these disorders.

TREATMENT RESOURCES

Barlow, D.H., & Craske, M.G. (1988). *Mastery of Your Anxiety and Panic*. Albany, NY: Graywind. This is a manual containing all details of panic control treatment, intended to be handed to the client with panic disorder, who could then work through this program, preferably under clinical supervision.

Craske, M.G., & Barlow, D.H., (1990). *Therapist's Guide for the Mastery of Your Anxiety and Panic*. Albany, NY: Graywind. A therapist's guide for administration of the panic control treatment developed at the Center for Stress and Anxiety Disorders at the State University of New York at Albany.

Craske, M.G., & Barlow, D.H. (in press). Panic disorder and agoraphobia. In D.H. Barlow (Ed.), *Clinical handbook of psychological disorders*. NY: Guilford. This manual describes how to incorporate the spouse into a comprehensive *in vivo* exposure treatment for agoraphobic avoidance.

CHAPTER 6

Depression in Adults

Steven D. Hollon

Michele M. Carter

Over the last two decades, few disorders have been as extensively and successfully studied as depression. As recently as the mid-1970s, it was not possible to identify even a single study indicating that psychotherapy, typically dynamic-eclectic, was effective in the treatment of depression (Hollon & Beck, 1978; Weissman, 1979). Although the antidepressant medications had been shown to be clinically effective in over a hundred controlled trials (Klein & Davis, 1969; Morris & Beck, 1974), in no study had traditional dynamic-eclectic approaches done better than inert pill-placebos in terms of acute symptom reduction.

This situation has changed during the ensuing years. A variety of psychosocial interventions, several drawn from the behavioral and cognitive-behavioral domains, appear to be at least as effective as the antidepressant medications in the treatment of clinical depression (Hollon & Beck, 1986). Further, there are some indications that these interventions, all predicated on a skills-training model, may be even more suc-

cessful than the pharmacological approaches at preventing the return of symptoms after treatment cessation (Hollon, Shelton, & Loosen, 1991).

Clearly, the behavioral and cognitive-behavioral interventions have added to the clinician's repertoire for dealing with depression. They represent no panacea; they do not work for everybody and there is currently no compelling evidence that they work in precisely the manner presumed by theory. However, those same caveats apply to every other available intervention, including the pharmacologic, somatic, and other psychosocial approaches. Although, as we will discuss, we still do not consider the evidence for the efficacy of the behavioral and cognitive-behavioral interventions to be conclusive, there can be little doubt that the development of these approaches represents a major advance. It is a clear example of the value of integrating theory-driven basic research with clinical experimentation (Hollon & Garber, 1988, 1990), long a hallmark of the behavioral perspective.

In this chapter, we describe the various behavioral and cognitive-behavioral approaches. In particular, we emphasize Beck and colleague's cognitive therapy for depression (Beck, 1964, 1967, 1970, 1976; Beck, Rush, Shaw, & Emery, 1979), since it is the most extensively tested approach and the one that we know best, but we also describe more purely behavioral and self-control interventions as well. Throughout, we try to attend to both the basic clinical strategies of which they are comprised and the empirical evidence evaluating their efficacy.

NATURE OF DEPRESSION

Depression is one of the oldest recognized disorders and one of the most prevalent. It has been estimated that at least 1 person in 10 will experience a major affective disorder at some point in his or her lifetime (American Psychiatric Association [APA], 1987). Depression can range in severity from mild mood disruptions to wholly debilitating psychotic episodes. It is closely linked to suicide and, if inadequately treated, can increase the risk for mortality associated with other physical conditions (Avery & Winokur, 1976; Wells, et al., 1989). It tends to be self-limiting, which means that most afflicted individuals eventually recover from any given episode, even in the absence of treatment. It also tends to be recurrent, as the majority of individuals who become depressed at least once experience multiple episodes during their lifetimes (Zis & Goodwin, 1979). Although there is considerable variability across individuals, the typical episode is likely to last about 6 to 9 months in outpatients and about 9 to 12 months in inpatients (Beck, 1967). Approximately one-quarter to one-third of all depressed individuals will exhibit a chronic course with little or no symptomatic relief. Some episodes appear to be triggered by external events, such as the loss of a loved one or a major career disappointment. Other episodes appear to arise in the absence of any clear external precipitant.

As a syndrome, depression is marked by distress in five areas: (1) distressed affect, usually experienced as sadness; (2) cognition, including negative beliefs about the self and pessimism regarding the future; (3) behavior, with marked passivity and a reduction in the number of activities undertaken; (4) motivation, including a pervasive loss of interest and suicidal ideation; and (5) vegetative disturbances, such as loss of appetite, insomnia, and loss of interest in sex. The syndrome of mania typically involves change in each of these same five areas in the opposite direction to that found in depression. It has long been known that depression and mania tend to occur in the same individuals, suggesting that they might be opposite manifestations of the same underlying disorder (Kraepelin, 1913).

There is an important distinction between bipolar and unipolar affective disorders. The former involves individuals who exhibit one or more manic (or hypomanic) episodes, either alone or in combination with depressive episodes, and the latter involves individuals who exhibit depression only. Evidence for the genetic transmission of the bipolar affective disorders is quite strong, but considerably more equivocal with respect to the unipolar affective disorders (Bertelson, Harvald, & Hauge, 1977; Perris, 1966; Winokur, 1979). Studies that have restricted their attention to severely depressed hospitalized samples of patients with multiple recurrent episodes have been the most likely to find evidence of genetic transmission in unipolars. Considerable heterogeneity is also evident among the unipolars with respect to manifest symptomatology, course, prognosis, and treatment response (Craighead, 1980). Females predominate among the unipolars, being anywhere from two to three times more prevalent than males. Females and males are about evenly represented among the bipolars (Weissman & Klerman, 1977). Approximately 8 out of every 10 diagnosed depressed individuals are unipolar. Given the evident heterogeneity among the numerically more common unipolars, some researchers, ourselves included, prefer the term "nonbipolars" to describe these individuals, since this category is likely to be composed of several etiologically distinct subpopulations.

Only about 1 depressed patient in 10 will ever exhibit an affective episode of psychotic proportions, using the current convention of requiring either hallucinations, delusions, or stupor for such a designation (APA, 1987). To date, the bulk of the psychosocial treatment literature has focused on nonpsychotic, nonbipolar depressed outpatients. Whether these interventions have anything to offer with respect to bipolar, psychotic, or even inpatient populations remains to be determined.

ASSESSMENT OF DEPRESSION

It is first important to recognize that the term *depression* tends to be used to describe three distinct levels of organization within the field of psychopathology (Beck, 1967; Lehmann, 1959). At the simplest level, that of a single symptom, the term refers to an unpleasant affective state, usually synonymous with sadness. At a more complex level, it refers to a clinical syndrome, a collection of signs and symptoms that co-vary with greater than chance frequency. At this level we talk about depression as involving affective, cognitive, behavioral, motivational, and vegetative signs and symptoms. Finally, at the most complex level, that of a nosological disorder, the term implies not just a common manifest symptomatology, but also some consistency in course, prognosis, treatment response, and, presumably, etiology. Transient states of sadness probably occur in most people at some time or other. Depression as a syndrome is less common, but still one of the more ubiquitous forms of psychopathological distress. Depression as a discrete nosological entity is less common still, but remains one of the most prevalent of the major psychopathological disorders. The syndrome of depression, found in conjunction with some other diagnosable disorder, is often considered to be secondary to that other disorder, particularly if its onset came later (Robins & Guze, 1972).

Self and Clinician Rating Scales

Instruments for assessing depression exist at all three levels. At the level of a discrete affective symptom, the various adjective checklists (Lubin, 1967; Zuckerman & Lubin, 1965) and the visual analogue scales (Aiken, 1969) are typically the instruments of choice. These instruments provide a simple, psychometrically sound basis for measuring fluctuations in mood over short periods of time.

At the level of the syndrome, a variety of self-report and clinician-rated instruments all appear to do an adequate job. Among the many self-report instruments, scales such as the Beck Depression Inventory (BDI) (Beck, et al., 1961), the Zung Self-Rated Depression Inventory (Zung, 1965), and Scale 2 (Depression) from the Minnesota Multiphasic Personality Inventory (Hathaway & McKinley, 1951) are all popular choices. Among the clinician-rated measures, the Hamilton Rating Scale for Depression (HRSD) (Hamilton, 1960) and the Raskin Depression Scale (RDS) (Raskin, Schulterbrandt, Reatig, & McKeon, 1970) are among the most widely used syndromal rating instruments. Many other alternatives exist; see Rehm (1981) for a review. Each provides a continuous total score indexing the degree to which the various signs and symptoms that comprise the syndrome of depression are present. As such, they represent the most popular measures of change in controlled treatment outcome trials in this area.

Diagnostic Interviews

What these measures do not do is to differentiate between a diagnosable nosologic disorder and an affective syndrome secondary to some other disorder, and they do not provide chronicity data necessary for a clinical diagnosis. For diagnostic purposes, most investigators use one of the various semi-structured diagnostic clinical interviews. Chief among them in current usage are the Present State Examination (Wing, Cooper, & Sartorius, 1974), chiefly used in Europe; the Schedule for Affective Disorders and the Schizophrenias (SADS) (Endicott & Spitzer, 1978); and the Structured Clinical Interview for DSM-III-R (SCID) (Spitzer & Williams, 1985). By asking questions regarding various symptoms and their severity and chronicity, and combining this information with clinical observations, an interviewer using these instruments can make a determination of whether the syndrome of depression is present and, if so, whether it represents a nosological entity in its own right or the secondary manifestation of some other disorder.

TREATMENT OF DEPRESSION

We now turn to a discussion of the leading behavioral and cognitive-behavioral interventions for the treatment of depression in adults. We focus on three approaches, cognitive therapy for depression (Beck, et al., 1979); the more purely behavioral approaches, including the recent development of a psychoeducational approach (Lewinsohn & Clarke, 1985); and self-control therapy (Rehm, 1977). Since cognitive therapy has received the greatest attention in the controlled treatment evaluation literature, we focus the bulk of our attention on that approach.

Cognitive Therapy

Rationale

Beck's approach is predicated on a cognitive theory in which depression is viewed, at least in part, as a consequence of pervasive negative beliefs and maladaptive information processing (Beck, 1963, 1967, 1976). Depressed individuals are seen as exhibiting a negative cognitive triad; they regard themselves as inadequate, their environments as nonreinforcing, and their futures as devoid of hope (Beck, 1967). Their information processing is seen as being dominated by depressotypic schemata that lead them to interpret ambiguous information in the most negative way

possible and that differentially bias recall against positive information. A variety of information processing distortions, including a tendency to overlook positive information (selective abstraction), a tendency to arrive at negative inferences in the absence of any real evidence (arbitrary inference), and a tendency to overemphasize the negativity of the implications of any given event (magnification), are seen as maintaining this negative set in the face of evidence to the contrary. The propensity to think in such a fashion is presumed to be latent until triggered by some negative life event (Beck, 1984). Once triggered, this propensity then leads to the negative affect and behavioral passivity noted in the larger syndrome.

Cognitive therapy is an integrated set of cognitive and behavioral interventions designed to identify, evaluate, and change erroneously negative beliefs and modify maladaptive information processing styles (Beck, 1964, 1970, 1976; Beck et al., 1979). In this approach, clients are trained to treat their beliefs as hypotheses to be evaluated, frequently by relying on behavioral experiments that they design, in conjunction with their therapists, to test those notions. Although the approach makes use of many of the same behavioral activation strategies developed in the more purely behavioral approaches, it tends to do so in the context of testing the accuracy of beliefs. In this sense, it is truly integrative with respect to its inclusion of both cognitive and behavioral procedures. The two are not so much done sequentially over time as they are joined in the empirical hypothesis testing process (Kendall & Hollon, 1979).

Clinically, the practice of cognitive therapy typically involves seven roughly overlapping stages. In the first, the therapist attempts to provide a cognitive rationale for the problems the client has encountered. Examples are solicited and examined to see if they fit within a cognitive theory of emotion, in which the nature and intensity of the affect experienced is seen as a function of the interpretation made of the particular event (Schachter & Singer, 1962). The nature of

TABLE 6.1   Weekly self-monitoring record from a depressed male

Time (hrs)	Sunday 1/15	Monday 1/16	Tuesday 1/17	Wednesday 1/18	Thursday 1/12	Friday 1/13	Saturday 1/14
9–10	Sleep	Did dishes(40), breakfast	Drove to class, eat(50)	Meeting with sales agent(50)	Therapy session (25P)*	Up, out to dentist, nauseous(25)	Up early(60), to work, working with J. (M)*
10–11	Sleep	Went to bookstore(45P)	Sculpture class(55M)	Meetings(55)	Mail out brochures, eat(50M,M)	Dentist, toast at diner	Apply hardwall, finish wall(65P)
11–12	Read paper(25)	Filled gas, read paper(45)	Sculpture class(55M)	Meeting(55)	Make business calls (M,P)	Home, read magazine(25)	Off to store(60P)
12–1	Read magazine(30)	Looked at mail, real estate ads(45), system(55P)	Looked at boots stores(40), guilty	Fill car, buy paper(55)	Read mail(60), phone calls(45)	Call models, truck relay out(25)	Work on alarm system(55P)
1–2	Read magazine, eat(30)	Went to work(40)	Went to work(50)	Make calls(45), yard(35)	Work at lumber(40P,M)	Replace relay, mail, talk to J.(45)	Come home, read
2–3	Watch tube(30)	Cut end rows(45P)	Talked with boss(50)	Go to work(45)	Lumber yard & hardware store(25)	Work on sculpture,(50P)	Eat lunch(30), wash dishes
3–4	Watch tube(30)	Painted end rows(50P,M)	Head for home(45)	Install fixtures(30)	Repair tires(25)	Off to work(50)	Clean home(30)
4–5	Watch tube(30), eat	Install grill plates (60P,M)	Leave for night class(45)	Home to eat(35)	Replace tiles & clean up(25)	Patching wall & clean up(50)	Clean home(25), wash clothes, relax
5–6	Watch tube(30)	Install grill plates & mike	Sculpture class(50P)	Go to movie(45)	Clean up, head for home(25)	Work on wall, to store(50P)	Relax, make drinks, dinner(25)
6–7	Watch tube(30), read	Come home(50)	Sculpture(50)	Movie(45P)	Eat, watch tube(25)	Home to eat(25), read magazine	Eat, talk, drink wine(35)
7–8	Took bath(30-45)	Eat dinner(45), talk to J.	Head home, talk to J.(50)	Movie(35), fight with J.	Watch tube, called therapist(25)	Talk to J.(25), out for ice cream	Relax, talk(35)
8–12	Read magazine bed.10:30(35)	Watch tube(45), made molds	Work on sculpture(50)	Coffee out(45), then home	Watch tube, talk to J.(20)	Back home(35), tooth still hurts	Relax, talk(35)

* M = Mastery Behavior
P = Pleasure
(0–100) = Current mood: 0 is the worst you've ever felt, 100 is the best you've ever felt.
SOURCE: Hollon & Beck, 1979. Reprinted with permission from Academic Press.

self-fulfilling prophecies is also described, in which expectations are seen as influencing actions, regardless of what is desired (Darley & Fazio, 1980), and recent life experiences are examined for the operation of such a process.

Self-Monitoring

The client is typically trained next in the use of systematic self-monitoring techniques, as in many purely behavioral approaches. Table 6.1

presents a representative self-monitoring sheet. This particular client was a middle-aged physical sculptor who had lost his teaching position at a small liberal arts college when that institution had to close its art department in the face of financial retrenchment. The client presented for treatment, saying that he had a reality-based depression that he could not imagine remitting until he found suitable employment in another college setting.

In self-monitoring, the client was encouraged to record his mood on an hourly basis, using a 0–100 point scale, in which 0 represented the worst he had ever felt and 100 the best he had ever felt. He was also instructed to record a brief description of what he had done over the preceding hour and to record a P for each pleasant event and an M for each mastery experience.

After several days of self-monitoring, it became evident that he was in the best spirits when he was at his current job, working as a handyman at a condominium complex. His mood was clearly the worst on the weekends and evenings, when he tended to lounge around the house ruminating about the negativity of his current employment situation. These observations alone led him to reconstrue his distress as being the consequence of his negativity about his current job, rather than any direct consequence of the job itself.

Behavioral Activation

These self-ratings also provide the basis for the next step in therapy, which is typically to use a variety of behavioral activation strategies to increase the client's level of activity and overcome behavioral passivity. Examples include activity scheduling, breaking large tasks into manageable units ("chunking"), and structuring complex tasks so that the easiest steps are undertaken first ("graded tasks"). With the client just described, one of the first tasks selected was to schedule activities for those nonworking hours when he tended to be least active and most dysphoric.

Upon inquiry, he indicated that if he were not so depressed, he might have wanted to take his family to an art exhibit that was then showing in town. This larger task was broken up into several smaller steps, the first of which could be accomplished during the therapy session (calling to see if the exhibit was still showing), and a record was made of his initial expectations regarding the venture (i.e., he didn't think that he could do it and, if he could, he didn't think he would enjoy it). The client was encouraged to carry out the necessary steps despite his negative expectations, simply as a means of testing their accuracy.

At a subsequent session, the client indicated that he had indeed been able to take the family to the exhibit and that they had all enjoyed the outing, despite his negative expectations. His affective ratings for that Sunday afternoon were considerably higher than they had been for the prior Sunday (depicted in Table 6.1), and he was beginning to entertain the possibility that his distress was more a product of his way of responding to the loss of his academic position than the loss itself. He next turned his attention to using the behavioral and cognitive strategies to ready his portfolio for submission to prospective employers, something he had not been able to accomplish during the preceding several months, but which he succeeded in doing over the next week. What he found was that when he broke any large task into its constituent parts and focused on completing just one step at a time (purely behavioral strategies), then reminded himself that the best way to deal with a negative expectation was to suspend judgment as to its accuracy and just see what he could accomplish (a cognitive strategy), he was far more likely to accomplish what he set out to do than if he did not. In the process, his initial perception of himself as someone with minimal competency began to give way to a perception of himself as someone who could be fairly effective when he chose the correct strategies and did not allow his self-doubts to disrupt his efforts.

Identifying Beliefs

Clients frequently need assistance in identifying beliefs related to negative affects and behavioral passivity. Although some negative beliefs are readily accessible, others are not. Many reactions have become so routine that they appear to occur almost automatically and outside of awareness. In such instances, it is often helpful to role-play the situation in question, or to encourage the client to seek out the situation in question with an eye to monitoring carefully his or her own reactions to it. It is then helpful to start with whatever initial beliefs can be accessed and to explore their implications by asking just what they mean to the client. This process is continued until a full accounting can be given for any affect experienced in the situation, an accounting that would lead anyone to experience the same affect in that situation if he or she believed the same things that the client believed. Even when specific automatic thoughts that "make sense" out of the affects experienced are readily accessible, it can be useful to proceed through this strategy (referred to as the "downward arrow"), since the same surface beliefs may mask a wholly different set of underlying meanings.

Evaluating Beliefs

The next major step is to evaluate the accuracy of the beliefs thus identified. Clients are typically trained to ask one or more of the following three questions about any given belief: (1) What is the *evidence* for or against that belief?, (2) Is there any *alternative* explanation for that event?, and (3) What are the real *implications* if that initial belief is true? In some instances, simply inquiring about the evidence supporting a given belief undermines its apparent validity. Frequently, it is useful to collect additional evidence by running a behavioral experiment, as was described earlier for the client who took his family to the art exhibit.

Table 6.2 presents a Dysfunctional Thoughts Record (DTR) completed by that same client after several weeks of therapy. In the first example in the table, the client, who by this time was more active with his family on the weekends and had succeeded in compiling his portfolio and circulating it to several prospective employers, had decided to put his neglected financial affairs in order. He had gone down into his basement early one morning with the intent of organizing his tax records (he had neglected to file his most recent return), when he was overcome by the magnitude of the task (see Situation column). He found himself ruminating about his own incompetence (see Automatic Thoughts column), and found his mood becoming increasingly negative (see Emotion(s) column). After several minutes, he went back upstairs and began to work the situation through on the DTR.

As can be seen in the Rational Response column, he first applied the evidence question to his belief that "I can never get my work done," reminding himself of his recent experiences, including the completion of his portfolio. He next applied the question about alternatives, to remind himself that his "failure" that morning was more a result of choosing the wrong strategy (i.e., trying to do everything at once, rather than breaking it up into small, manageable steps) than of any character flaw (e.g., "I'm no good"). In this fashion, he was able to reduce his negative affect and return to the task, taking only a small portion at a time; he was able to complete the project over the course of the next several days. At the bottom of Table 6.2 is an example of a misapplication of the approach, substituting the repetition of a little-believed aphorism for a more fully developed effort at empirically based hypothesis testing.

Another example of this process includes a client in a recent controlled trial who, after having had a full hysterectomy in her earlier twenties, became convinced that no one she fell in love with would ever want to have a long-term relationship with her because she could not bear children. As a consequence, she had fallen into a pattern of withdrawing from anyone who started

TABLE 6.2   Evaluating automatic negative thoughts: client's daily record of dysfunctional thoughts

Date	Situation	Emotion(s)	Automatic Thought(s)	Rational Response	Outcome
	Describe: 1. Actual event leading to pleasant emotion, or	1. Specify sad, anxious, etc.	1. Write automatic thought(s) that preceded emotion(s)	1. Write rational response to automatic thought(s)	1. Rerate belief in automatic thought(s), 0–100%
	2. Stream of thoughts, daydream, or recollection, leading to unpleasant emotion.	2. Rate degree of emotion, 1–100%	2. Rate belief in automatic thought(s), 0–100%	2. Rate belief in rational response, 0–100%	2. Specify and rate subsequent emotions, 0–100%
2/5	Not getting filing and lots of other stuff done.	Anxious-Sad-Angry. 85%	A failure again, I can never get my work done, I'm no good. 85%	I have gotten filing and other work done in the past, but usually in smaller bites, not all at once. 80%	1. 45% 2. Anxious-Sad. 50%
2/7	Sitting & idly looking thru some old books. 6:30 A.M.	Depressed. 75%	Feeling guilty because I'm not doing work. I'm going to slip	After 12 hrs. of high-energy work yesterday (phone work,	1. 10% 2. Joyful, Exuberant. 95%

to show any real interest in her, so as to forestall the eventual pain of having them terminate the relationship when they learned of her "disability." Following discussions with her therapist, she decided to conduct a "poll" of male co-workers. To protect her privacy, she presented the scenario as the plot of a recent daytime soap opera. What she found was that the majority of the males she talked to indicated that they would not let the inability to have children interfere with the development of a relationship with someone in whom they were becoming interested. A minority did indicate that they would terminate the relationship, but they were matched by a comparably sized minority who indicated that they would prefer not having children and would consider infertility in a potential spouse to be a source of relief.

Underlying Assumptions

The bulk of treatment involves working through instances in which specific beliefs are identified and examined with respect to their accuracy, with the client's behaviors frequently used to test the validity of those beliefs. In many instances, general patterns begin to emerge that constitute underlying themes of the client. These more

TABLE 6.2   Continued

Date	Situation	Emotion(s)	Automatic Thought(s)	Rational Response	Outcome
			back into funk if I'm not careful. 70%	building, filing, letter, driving), I think its OK to relax from 5:30 P.M. to 6:30 A.M. the following day. 95%	

(Example of misapplication: Applies "Rational Response" in rote fashion without examining belief. Note the lack of rated belief in the "Rational Response" and the lack of subsequent effect on belief and emotion in "Outcome.")

Date	Situation	Emotion(s)	Automatic Thought(s)	Rational Response	Outcome
2/9	I can't handle it any more, too much in the past to undo, lack of setting priorities, misuse of time, plus the present seems untenable	Depressed. 80%	No options— either direct job in my specialty or nothing at all	The present does not predict the future. 20%	1. 95% 2. Depressed. 95%

EXPLANATION: When you experience an unpleasant emotion, note the situation that seemed to stimulate the emotion. (If the emotion occurred while you were thinking, daydreaming, etc., please note this.) Then note the automatic thought associated with the emotion. Record the degree to which you believe this thought: 0% = not at all; 100% = completely. In rating degree of emotion: 1% = a trace; 100% = the most intense possible.
SOURCE: Hollon and Beck, 1979. Reprinted with permission from Academic Press.

general beliefs, referred to as underlying assumptions, typically constitute basic world views that are rarely recognized as idiosyncratic. Examples include such beliefs as, "It is necessary to be loved and approved of at all times," or "It is important to be successful in one's chosen career." As Ellis (1962) has suggested, such outcomes would be nice, but they are hardly necessary for life to be rewarding and meaningful. In the later stage of therapy, the client and therapist typically start to look for general patterns that have emerged across a variety of specific situations. This is frequently a point at which historical reconstruction is employed in an effort to determine how the client may have come to adopt his or her particular underlying assumptions.

Termination and Relapse Prevention

The final stage of treatment involves preparation for termination and relapse prevention. In fact, this preparation typically begins in the initial session and is used throughout treatment as a justification for the extensive between-session homework. It is suggested that cognitive therapy is a skills-training approach, the goal of which is to teach the client to become his or her own therapist. This stance doubtless slows the progress of therapy during its early stages, but may contribute to its apparent preventive capacity.

Finally, in the last several sessions considerable time is spent having the client imagine himself or herself encountering particularly stressful life situations after therapy is over and practicing what to do about them, an adaptation of stress inoculation training (Meichenbaum, 1977).

Empirical Evaluations of Cognitive Therapy

Cognitive therapy has been evaluated in a number of controlled trials (for reviews, see Hollon, 1981; Hollon & Beck, 1986; Hollen et al., 1991; Jarrett & Rush, 1985). It has typically outperformed minimal treatment or attention placebo controls in studies involving analogue or college student populations (McNamara & Horan, 1986; Shaw, 1977; Taylor & Marshall, 1977). It has also performed well in comparison with tricyclic antidepressant pharmacotherapy, the current standard of effective treatment, in studies involving clinical outpatient samples. In the first such trial, Rush, Beck, Kovacs, and Hollon (1977) found cognitive therapy superior to imipramine pharmacotherapy over a 12-week treatment course. However, in that trial, medication withdrawal was begun 2 weeks before the end of treatment (to ensure that all patients would be drug-free at the posttreatment evaluation), a strategy that may have led to an underestimation of pharmacotherapy's efficacy. In a subsequent study, Blackburn and colleagues (Blackburn, Bishop, Glen, Whalley, & Christie, 1981) found that cognitive therapy was superior to pharmacotherapy in a general medical setting and comparable in an psychiatric outpatient setting. However, the rate of response to pharmacotherapy in the former setting was so low (14%) as to raise questions about the adequacy of the operationalization of that approach. In a subsequent trial, Murphy and colleagues (Murphy, Simons, Wetzel, & Lustman, 1984) similarly found comparable outcomes for cognitive therapy alone versus nortriptyline pharmacotherapy. In that trial, blood plasma levels were used to ensure that medication levels were indeed adequate. Hollon and colleagues (Hollon, DeRubeis, Evans, Wiemer, Garvey, Grove, & Tuason, 1992) similarly found comparable outcomes for cognitive therapy and imipramine pharmacotherapy across a 12-week active treatment period in a study in which both plasma medication levels and the quality and fidelity of adherence to cognitive therapy were monitored. In each of these trials, patients were fully clinically representative and selected on the basis of careful diagnostics, outcome was measured from multiple perspectives, and therapists were generally experienced in the delivery of their respective modalities.

Although each of these trials appears to speak to the efficacy of cognitive therapy, in the most ambitious trial to date, the NIMH Treatment of Depression Collaborative Research Project (Elkin, Parloff, Hadley, & Autrey, 1985; Elkin et al., 1989), cognitive therapy failed to exceed a minimal treatment pill-placebo control and, although not significantly different, did less well than imipramine pharmacotherapy in terms of producing acute response in more severely depressed outpatients. Although this trial, the first to include a minimal treatment control in a fully clinically representative design, appears to be less than fully supportive of the comparative efficacy of cognitive therapy, it should also be noted that the supervision provided for the recently trained cognitive therapists during the study proper was markedly less frequent (about once per month) than that provided in other recent trials. Whether that reduced the competency with which cognitive therapy was executed remains to be determined, and indeed can be, since ratings were made of actual therapist behaviors on both the Cognitive Therapy Scale (CTS) (Young & Beck, 1981), a measure of therapy competence, and the Collaborative Study Psychotherapy Rating Scale (CSPRS) (Hollon, Evans, Elkin, & Lowery, 1984), a measure of the fidelity of adherence. A full appreciation of the results of the NIMH trial must await the report of these latter measures.

Several of these studies have followed the treated samples for extended periods after treatment termination. Kovacs, Rush, Beck, and Hollon (1981) found some, albeit nonsignificant, indications of greater maintenance of treatment gains in patients who had been treated with cognitive therapy in the earlier trial by Rush and colleagues (Rush et al., 1977). It is important to remember that the pharmacologically treated patients in that trial had medications withdrawn before the end of the active treatment period and evidenced an increase in symptomatology over the final 2-week period. In effect, it may be that that early withdrawal procedure had the effect of confounding response and relapse, overestimating the difference between cognitive therapy and pharmacotherapy with respect to acute treatment, and underestimating the difference with respect to relapse prevention.

In a 24-month follow-up of the trial by Blackburn and colleagues (1981), Blackburn, Eunson, and Bishop (1986) found evidence that prior cognitive therapy reduced the rate of subsequent relapse relative to prior pharmacotherapy. Simons, Murphy, Levine, and Wetzel (1986) observed a similar phenomenon over a 12-month follow-up of the Murphy et al. (1984) sample, as did Evans et al. (1992) in a 24-month follow-up of the Hollen et al. sample (1992). In the latter trial, patients who received prior cognitive therapy during active treatment, whether alone or in conjunction with medications, evidenced relapse rates as low as patients maintained on medication over the first 12 months of that 24-month follow-up period.

These findings, although far from unequivocal (the samples in each study were relatively small and the results in each instance marginal), are potentially quite important. Clinical practice with respect to pharmacotherapy is increasingly coming to regard brief treatment (e.g., of 3 to 4 months duration) as adequate to reduce symptoms but not to block their return, and is shifting to the provision of up to 10 to 12 months of pharmacotherapy on a routine basis. Although the studies just cited compared prior cognitive therapy to pharmacotherapy of inadequate length, they do document a preventive effect for the psychosocial approach. Advocates of psychosocial interventions have long argued that their interventions should prevent future occurrences of disorder, but only recently has such an effect begun to be demonstrated.

Behavior Therapy

Rationale

The behavioral approach is based largely on a social learning theory analysis proposing that depressive episodes are related to a decrease in pleasant and an increase in unpleasant interactions between the person and his or her environment (Ferster, 1965, 1973; Lewinsohn, 1974; Lewinsohn & Atwood, 1969; Lewinsohn, Biglan, & Zeiss, 1976; Lewinsohn, Youngren, & Grosscup, 1979). The central tenet is that a low rate of response-contingent positive reinforcement is a causal antecedent to the occurrence of depression. Environmental interactions that yield positive outcomes are invariably strengthened through reinforcement. In the case of depression, it is suggested that the individual's behavior does not lead to positive reinforcement at a level sufficient to maintain that behavior. Similarly, the deficit of positive reinforcement is seen as leading directly to the negative affective states that are the hallmark of the disorder. Depression may also result from a high rate of punishment. Punishment (defined as interactions yielding aversive consequences) may lead to depression by interfering with potentially rewarding activities (Lewinsohn, Antonuccio, Steinmetz, & Teri, 1984).

In general, there are two major sets of explanations to account for why a person might experience either of the above conditions. First, the person's environment may have too few available positive reinforcers or too many punishers, or the impact of positive events may be reduced and/or the impact of negative events may be heightened for some individuals; (Lewinsohn,

Lobitz & Wilson, 1973). Second, the person may lack the skills necessary to obtain positive reinforcement from the environment and/or cope effectively with aversive events. The goal of treatment within this framework is either to (1) increase the quantity and quality of positive reinforcement and decrease the quantity and quality of punishment via contingency management, or (2) increase the person's ability to engage in effective behaviors via skills training. In this latter regard, explicit social skills training models have been developed, based on the notion that interpersonal deficits and conflict are responsible for the initiation and maintenance of depressive behavior; a deficit in social skills is seen as keeping the individual from eliciting the necessary positive reinforcement from the environment (Becker, Heimberg, & Bellack, 1987). In such instances, teaching the social skills necessary to increase the quality of interpersonal behavior, thereby increasing response-contingent positive reinforcement by eliminating maladaptive and stressful interactions, is seen as one means of increasing nondepressed behavior and decreasing depressed mood.

Procedures

The actual procedures employed can be quite diverse, depending on the aspect of behavioral deficit targeted. Efforts to manipulate contingencies are typically carried out in a straightforward fashion, with particular attention paid to having the client (or significant others in the client's life) arrange for an increase in positive events or a decrease in negative events (Lewinsohn, 1974; Lewinsohn & Atwood, 1969; Lewinsohn et al., 1976). Social skills training typically involves a combination of didactic and model-guided presentations, with a heavy reliance on structured role-playing experiences with corrective feedback (Becker et al., 1987).

Psychoeducational Group Treatment

These intervention procedures have hardly been static. In recent years, both have been melded together, with cognitive strategies often incorporated in the mix. One particularly exciting innovation has been Lewinsohn and colleagues' efforts to develop a psychoeducational group approach designed to teach coping skills to individuals who might be at risk but are not necessarily currently depressed (Lewinsohn et al., 1984). This highly structured psychoeducational approach, called the Coping with Depression (CWD) course, is usually taught in a group format and consists of 12 two-hour sessions conducted over 8 weeks. The first two sessions are used to provide the rationale of the social learning view of depression and give instruction in self-change skills, Homework assignments begin in the first session and include recording pleasant events, mood monitoring, and reading a handbook entitled *Control Your Depression* (Lewinsohn, Munoz, Youngren, & Zeiss, 1986). Several self-change skills are taught, including monitoring specific behaviors to be changed, setting realistic goals, and developing a plan to make changes in behavior. Participants are taught to identify antecedent situations for distress, develop ways to control those situations, and identify the consequences of those efforts. Subsequent sessions are utilized to teach specific skills in each of the following four areas: relaxation training, increasing pleasant activities, control of negative thinking, and social skills. The final sessions are used to integrate the skills learned, so as to maintain therapeutic gains and prevent relapse. During these sessions, the participant develops a written emergency plan that details what steps are to be taken to counteract depressive feelings, should they occur in the future (Clarke & Lewinsohn, 1989).

Empirical Evaluations of Behavior Therapy

There have been several efforts to evaluate the various behavioral intervention packages. Zeiss, Lewinsohn, and Munoz (1979) compared behavioral treatment targeted at increasing pleasant events to three other conditions: interpersonal skills training, cognitive training, and a nonspecific control, all in an analogue sample. All three interventions outperformed the control but did not differ from one another, suggesting that their effects were largely nonspecific. McLean and Hakstian (1979) compared behavior therapy (including contingency management, social skills training, and some cognitive training) to relaxation training, dynamic-eclectic psychotherapy, or tricyclic pharmacotherapy in a fully clinical sample and found the behavioral intervention to be generally superior. Bellack and colleagues (Bellack, Hersen, & Himmelhoch, 1981, 1983) compared social skills training (either combined with pill-placebo or active medication) to medication alone or traditional psychotherapy in a clinical sample and found some minimal evidence suggestive of greater gains in the skills training group, albeit only when combined with placebo. In an evaluation of the CWD course, Brown and Lewinsohn found no differences relative to either individual treatment or a minimal phone contact procedure, although all three active conditions evidenced substantially greater improvement at posttreatment relative to a waitlist control, with improvement maintained at a subsequent follow-up (Brown & Lewinsohn, 1984). In a later investigation, similar results were obtained in a comparison between CWD and individual behavior therapy, indicating little difference between the psychoeducational course and individual treatment (Teri & Lewinsohn, 1985).

In general, the results have tended to support of the more purely behavioral interventions but have been somewhat sparse and inconclusive. The psychoeducational course, in particular, has been the least powerfully evaluated to date, since such prospective prophylactic trails are particularly difficult to execute. Overall, as for cognitive therapy, it would appear that the behavioral interventions are also quite promising but still not conclusively proven to be effective treatments for depression.

Self-Control Therapy

Rationale

This model posits that depressive episodes are the result of deficits in self-control (Rehm, 1977). Self-control is defined as the capacity to alter the probability of a response in the absence of (or despite contrary) external contingencies (Kanfer, 1971). Poor self-control skills are believed to make people susceptible to depression and to make it difficult for them to overcome depressive symptomatology once it is initiated. Unless they encounter an exceptionally rewarding environment, individuals with severe self-control deficits are expected to be chronically depressed and characterized by a strong dependence on others.

Specific deficits at different stages of self-control (self-monitoring, self-evaluation, and self-reinforcement) are seen as the basis for the development of depressive symptomatology. With respect to the self-monitoring phase, depressed persons are seen as either selectively attending to negative events to the exclusion of positive events or selectively attending to the immediate versus the delayed consequences of their behavior (Rehm, 1977). With respect to the self-evaluation phase, depressed persons are characterized as making inaccurate attributions of causality, similar to those described in the reformulated learned-helplessness phenomenon (Abramson, Seligman, & Teasdale, 1978), or as setting excessively stringent criteria for self-evaluation. The greatest emphasis of this theory is placed on the self-reinforcement phase. In this phase, depression is characterized by low rates of self-administered reward relative to rates of self-administered punishment. The lowered rates of self-reward are thought to be associated with the vegetative symptomatology (psychomotor retardation, lack of initiative) commonly associated with depression. Excessive self-punishment serves to suppress potentially effective behavior. Once depressed individuals begin to set stringent self-evaluation criteria and to selectively abstract negative events, they tend to wax and wane between response strategies because the alternative is self-punished early in the response chain (Rehm, 1977).

Procedures

Therapy, often conducted in a group format, consists of didactic presentations of self-control concepts and behavioral assignments in three phases, corresponding to the three aspects of self-control. In the first phase (self-monitoring), homework consists of monitoring positive activities with immediate and delayed reinforcement value (Rehm, 1977). During this phase four points are emphasized: (1) that mood is related to activity, (2) that depressed persons often do not attend to positive activities, (3) that depressed persons tend to focus on the immediate rather than the delayed effects of their behavior, and (4) that gaining control over positive activities and increasing them can overcome depression.

In the second phase (self-evaluation), clients are taught to utilize self-monitoring data to specify realistic and obtainable goals in behavioral terms. It is also in this phase that they are taught to make accurate attributions for their successes and failures.

In the third phase (self-reinforcement), clients are helped to set up self-administered reinforcement programs. During this phase it is stressed that behavior is controlled by rewards and punishments, that it is possible to control one's own behavior through contingent rewards and punishments, and that depressives tend to self-punish too much and self-reward too little. In this phase subjects construct individual self-reinforcement programs aimed at maintaining and increasing the level of positive activities in which they engage (Rehm, 1977).

Empirical Evaluations of Self-Control Therapy

Self-control therapy has been evaluated in five controlled trials. Hilford (1975) compared a self-control program to both nondirective therapy and a no-contact condition in an inpatient psychiatric population. Results indicated that the self-control program was superior to the other treatments on measures of self-reported depression, verbal behavior, and ward behavior ratings. In a study involving depressed female community volunteers, Fuchs and Rehm (1977) compared self-control therapy to a nonspecific therapy condition and a wait-list control and found the self-control program superior to each. Rehm, Fuchs, Roth, Kornblith, and Romano (1979) compared self-control therapy to assertion skills training in yet another sample of depressed female community volunteers. In that study, subjects provided with assertiveness training evidenced greater gains on social skills variables, whereas subjects treated with self-control therapy evidenced greater gains on self-control measures, behavioral measures of depression, and self-report measures of depression. Rehm and colleagues (Rehm et al., 1981) compared each of the three components of their self-control program to each other and each to the full program and to a wait-list control in an effort to evaluate the contribution of the individual components. Results indicated that all treatment conditions were superior to the wait-list control on measures of self-report and clinician-rated measures of depression. There were, however, no consistent differences in outcome for the separate components. Finally, Roth, Bielski, Jones, Parker, and Osborn (1982) provided the first evaluation of the self-control approach in a fully clinical population, comparing the intervention alone to the combination of self-control training and antidepressant medication. Although both conditions evidenced a marked decrease in depressive symptomatology, combined treatment resulted in more rapid improvement on self-report measures of depression. Treatment gains were maintained by both groups at a 3-month follow-up.

The evidence to date suggests that self-control therapy produces some beneficial therapeutic effects, although the sparse number of controlled investigations precludes any convincing statements concerning its efficacy. Before such statements can be made, further studies comparing self-control therapy to other methods of treatment (e.g., cognitive therapy, pharmacotherapy) are in order. The preliminary results, however, suggest that this approach, like the more clearly behavioral interventions, possesses sufficient promise as to make such studies worthwhile.

ISSUES FOR FUTURE RESEARCH

There are several key issues that deserve further consideration. First, although the controlled comparisons are often quite encouraging, it is still not clear that the various behavioral and cognitive-behavioral interventions actually work as well as their proponents would like to claim, at least in the sense of exceeding the benign effects of simply entering into a therapeutic relationship. The tricyclic antidepressants clearly do, and the behavioral and cognitive-behavioral interventions have typically not differed from those interventions in controlled trials, but the bulk of those trials have not contained the kinds of controls necessary to sustain a claim of specific treatment efficacy. In the absence of group differences, tie scores might as readily reflect comparable inefficacy as comparable efficacy. It remains possible that either pharmacologically nonresponsive depressives have been consistently oversampled or that pharmacotherapy has repeatedly been inadequately executed (Meterissian & Bradwejn, 1989). Although we do not think that either is likely, each remains a possibility that the existing scientific literature has not adequately ruled out.

In short, we now believe that the tendency to eschew minimal treatment controls in pharmacotherapy-psychotherapy comparisons (a practice previously endorsed and followed by the senior author) represents a systematic error in design logic (Hollon, Shelton, & Loosen, 1991). In the late 1970s, when many of the first generation of post-Rush trials were planned, this seemed to be

a reasonable strategy. In retrospect, it appea[r] have retarded the acquisition of information ιⱨαι would have allowed us to make more definitive statements than we can now make. We would predict that such studies will support the clinical efficacy of these interventions, the NIMH Treatment of Depression Collaborative Research Project notwithstanding, but those trials remain to be done.

Second, and closely related, we also think that recent efforts to determine whether any benefit is derived from combining behavioral or cognitive-behavioral interventions with pharmacotherapy, our own included, have similarly been flawed. In particular, we think most prior efforts have simply used samples that were too small to answer the question of interest. As described by Kazdin and Bass (1989), most controlled outcome trials have not used large enough samples to detect the kind of small-to-moderate additive effects likely to be associated with combined treatments.

Third, the accumulating evidence for some kind of prophylactic effect for cognitive therapy is, if anything, stronger than the evidence supporting its specific efficacy in the treatment of the acute episode (Hollon, Shelton, & Loosen, 1991). In general, this is because the magnitude of the difference between prior cognitive therapy and prior pharmacotherapy is typically quite large. At the same time, only a single study has unambiguously demonstrated this effect (Evans et al., 1992). Although differences in posttreatment relapse rates in the other trials have usually been quite large, they have typically been only marginally significant due to the small sample sizes involved.

Fourth, with respect to prevention, we regard the work by Lewinsohn and colleagues with psychoeducational approaches directed toward "at risk" populations to be particularly exciting (Hollon, DeRubeis, & Seligman, 1992). There can be no question that being able to forestall the emergence of a disorder is preferable to treating it once it has emerged. Although such efforts will prove particularly difficult to evaluate, we think they are of such potential importance that special attention should be devoted to their pursuit.

Fifth, to the extent that the behavioral and cognitive-behavioral interventions prove to be clinically effective, it becomes relevant to ask whether different groups of patients respond differentially to those approaches than to the tricyclic antidepressants or other psychosocial approaches. Although we certainly want to encourage such efforts, we feel compelled to point out that such research is, if anything, even more difficult to conduct than simple outcome research. It is not sufficient to examine covariation between pretreatment individual differences and subsequent response in a series of patients treated with a single type of intervention in order to determine who responds best to that approach. Such information, which we have labelled prognostic, is indeed predictive, but only in the sense that it allows the selection of the kinds of patients who will make the treatment look good (Hollon, in press). If the goal is to select the best treatment for a given patient, then it is necessary to look for differential response to different treatments among patients similar in pretreatment characteristics; i.e., the typical outcome study. A fully prescriptive design, one that would best generate information for matching patients to treatments, would allow individual differences to vary but randomize patients sharing similar characteristics to different treatment. In effect, efforts to determine the best treatment for a given patient require all of the logical controls needed in typical treatment outcome research and larger samples than are typically used, carefully selected and assessed so as to contain variation on the potential predictors of interest.

Finally, we need more research on precisely how the behavioral and cognitive-behavioral interventions produce change, to the extent that they do produce change, both with respect to the treatment of the acute episode and the prevention of future episodes. Such research should focus on precisely which aspects of the larger treatment packages are causally active (components) and precisely what processes in the clients they act through (mechanisms). Such process research is notoriously difficult to conduct but ultimately quite valuable. We suspect that such efforts will require a continual movement between underlying theory and empirical observation, at times demanding refinements in those theories and at others requiring modifications in our clinical practice. In a disorder like depression, where causal heterogeneity is likely the rule, such an effort will probably also require a change in the very way we pose our questions of interest (Hollon, DeRubeis, & Evans, 1987).

CONCLUSIONS

There is no doubt that the behavioral and cognitive-behavioral interventions hold great promise, both for the treatment of depression and perhaps its prevention as well. Nonetheless, these approaches have still not been established in a manner that the canons of scientific inquiry require. Prior trials have generally been encouraging but remain inconclusive. The approaches are well-defined and have become quite popular clinically. We hope that the next decade will see an extension and improvement upon the empirical bases required to justify interest in these approaches.

TREATMENT RESOURCE

Beck, A. T., Rush, A. J., Shae, B. F., & Emery, G. (1979). *Cognitive therapy of depression: A treatment manual.* New York: Guilford.

Schizophrenia

Alan S. Bellack
Kim T. Mueser

It would be impossible to present a comprehensive review of the nature and treatment of schizophrenia in this brief chapter. One could easily fill several volumes on each of these topics. Consequently, our goal here will be to highlight key issues in current conceptualizations of the disorder and its assessment and provide a description of the most widely used behavioral treatment strategies. In addition, we will include a cursory historical overview and conclude with some suggestions about future directions in research and treatment.

SYMPTOMS OF SCHIZOPHRENIA

Schizophrenia is the most severe of all psychiatric disorders. It is marked by significant disruptions in thought processes, behavior, and affect, each of which can become incapacitating. The primary symptoms of the disorder are generally grouped into two categories: (1) positive symptoms, which are exaggerations of normal functions, and (2) negative symptoms, which reflect diminutions or deficits of normal functions (Andreasen & Olsen, 1982). A listing of positive and negative symptoms is presented in Table 7.1 Although positive symptoms are more florid and disconcerting, negative symptoms are often more pernicious. They tend to be associated with poorer social functioning, poorer response to treatment, and a worse course of illness (Carpenter, Heinrichs, & Wagman, 1988). In addition to the positive and negative symptoms of schizophrenia, most patients with the illness experience significant depression. As many as 50% of persons with schizophrenia attempt suicide and 10% complete it (Roy 1986; Roy, Schreiber, Mazonson, & Picker, 1986).

Schizophrenia typically begins in late adolescence or early adulthood. It affects approximately 1% of the world population without regard for race, culture, or socioeconomic status, although women experience a milder course of the illness (Goldstein, 1988). About 25% of afflicted individuals will have a good recovery from the initial episode and return to premorbid levels

TABLE 7.1   Diagnostic variables in the two classes of schizophrenia

Diagnostic variable	Finding in negative schizophrenia	Finding in positive schizophrenia
Premorbid functioning	Poor	Good
Characteristic onset	Insidious	Often acute
Symptoms	Alogia Affective flattening Avolition Anhedonia Attentional impairment	Delusions Hallucinations Positive formal thought disorder Bizarre behavior
Sensorium	Impaired	Intact
Response to treatment	Poor	Good
Pathophysiology	Structural	Neurochemical
Etiology	Neuronal loss and atrophy	Hyperdopaminergic transmission in limbic system

SOURCE: Andreasen, N. C. (1988). *Schizophrenia*. Kalamazoo, MI: Upjohn Company. Reprinted by permission.

of functioning. Another 25% will never recover and suffer a declining course. The remaining 50% will have an intermediate course, marked by periodic relapses and an inability to function effectively for more than brief periods (Harris, 1984). This latter group contains the patients most likely to be seen by behavior therapists. The best predictor of the course of illness is premorbid social competence: better premorbid adjustment is associated with a better outcome (Mueser, Bellack, Morrison, & Wixted, 1990).

EARLY BEHAVIORAL TREATMENT: THE TOKEN ECONOMY

The treatment of schizophrenia has played a key role in the history of behavior therapy. Beginning in the 1950s, Ogden R. Lindsley and B. F. Skinner, Israel Goldiamond, Teodoro Ayllon, and other behavioral pioneers conducted an innovative series of case studies demonstrating that conditioning procedures could have a significant impact on psychotic behavior (Kazdin, 1978). These studies were among the first illustrations that therapeutic techniques based on laboratory principles could play a role in the treatment of significant human problems. The studies also illustrated the possibility that even such bizarre behaviors as catatonic rigidity, self-abuse, and autistic gestures could be produced and maintained by environmental factors. Expanding on these initial findings, Ayllon and Azrin (1968) applied operant principles to organizing the entire living environment of chronic patients living in Anna State Hospital in Illinois. Their program, the token economy, proved to be much more effective and humanistic than the pattern of neglect and abuse that characterized institutional care in the 1960s and 1970s. The classic study by

Paul and Lentz (1977) later provided empirical evidence of the efficacy of token programs. They demonstrated that a comprehensive token environment could rehabilitate profoundly impaired patients and facilitate post release adjustment. Token systems remain the most effective approach for structuring inpatient environments and stand as a monument to the power of behavioral techniques. Unfortunately, these programs are not as widely used for adult patients as their therapeutic power might suggest (Glynn, 1990). They are comparatively costly, require considerable staff effort, and sometimes limit the constitutional rights of patients by withholding guaranteed resources (e.g., by making access to religious sevices, bedding, etc., contingent on desired behavior). They are also not well-suited to the short-term hospitalizations and outpatient care characteristic of the current mental health system (see below).

Social impairment is one of the cardinal symptoms of schizophenia (Bellack, 1989; Morrison & Bellack, 1987). Even when primary psychotic symptoms are in remission, a majority of schizophrenics are left with residual social disability. Through the 1960s, it was assumed that this pattern of impairment could not be remediated. However, beginning in the early 1970s, Hersen, Eisler, Miller, and others demonstrated that: (1) poor social functioning could be operationalized as a series of discrete behaviors, (2) these behaviors could be conceptualized as learnable skills, and (3) that even severely impaired patients could be taught these skills with a behavioral technique called social skills training. It has since been demonstrated that social skills training can produce durable changes in behavior and have a significant impact on overall functioning and the risk of relapse (Morrison & Wixted, 1989).

More recently, the principles and techniques of social skills training have been applied to the families of schizophrenia patients. Behavioral family therapy has proven to be highly effective in reducing relapse rates and improving the emotional climate within the family (Mueser, 1989).

Social skills training and behavioral family therapy are the most effective psychosocial procedures available for the outpatient treatment of schizophrenia. They are widely regarded as essential components of a comprehensive treatment program (Bellack, 1989). We will discuss social skills training and behavioral family therapy at greater length in subsequent sections of this chapter.

ASSESSMENT

Schizophrenia is characterized by multiple handicaps, and there are many different perspectives from which to evaluate treatment outcome (Strauss & Carpenter, 1977). Thus, the patient must be assessed across a variety of domains, including symptomatology, role functioning, exacerbations and relapses, medication dose and side effects, impact on the family, quality of life, and other factors. Assessment of these diverse domains is a sufficiently complex topic to warrant its own chapter. The following section is intended to provide a brief overview of the predominant approaches to assessment.

Diagnosis

Prior to the 1970s, schizophrenia was an ill-defined and vastly overused label, serving as a "wastebasket" category for difficult, psychotic patients. As a result, the label had little reliability, validity, or utility. This situation improved dramatically with the publication of the Research Diagnostic Criteria (RDC) (Spitzer, Endicott, & Robins, 1978) and the DSM-III (American Psychiatric Association [APA], 1980). Key symptoms are now defined objectively, and there are operational criteria for making the diagnosis. Although specific criteria are bound to change as our knowledge about the disorder increases, recent studies employing current criteria have documented that there are substantial differences in treatment needs, course of illness, outcome, and psychopathology between schizophrenia and other psychotic disorders such as bipolar disorder and schizoaffective disorder (Levitt & Tsuang, 1988). The reliability of diagnosis has been substantially increased by the use of standardized, structured interviews, such as the Schedule for Affective Disorders and Schizophrenia (SADS) (Endicott & Spitzer, 1978) and the Structured Clinical Interview for DSM-III (SCID) (Spitzer & Williams, 1985). Interrater agreement for schizophrenic diagnoses derived from these instruments by trained interviewers is upwards of $r = .80$ (Spitzer, Forman, & Nee, 1979), which is comparable to agreement figures for behavioral coding systems. Such structured interviews are mandatory for research, and desirable for clinical purposes as well.

Behavioral Observation

Direct observation is the hallmark of behavioral assessment. Perhaps the most elaborate and sophisticated of all observation systems was developed specifically for work with psychiatric inpatients, including those with schizophrenia: the Time-Sample Behavioral Checklist (TSBC) (Paul & Licht, 1988). The TSBC was designed to provide a comprehensive picture of behavior on an inpatient ward or other controlled environment. It contains 69 codes, covering almost every aspect of a patient's behavior, including location on the unit, body position, whether patient is awake or asleep, facial expression, social orientation, appropriate concurrent activities, and crazy behavior. Each code is rated in successive 2-second observation periods. A skilled observer can code an entire ward of patients in 20–30 seconds (Paul & Licht, 1988). The resultant mass of data can be stored and analyzed on-line. The TSBC has excellent reliability and has proven to have considerable validity for evaluating the outcome of treatment programs, including prediction of postdischarge functioning.

Despite these positive features, the TSBC is not widely used. As is the case with many other extensive observational systems, the TSBC appears to have two fatal flaws: high cost and low relevance. It would be highly useful for a behavioral study in which specific behaviors were the primary subject of interest, but that is not the case in most clinical outcome studies. As indicated above, schizophrenia is marked by multiple handicaps requiring multifaceted treatment, and outcome must be evaluated across a variety of domains. Such research is difficult and expensive to conduct. Staff time, the assessment burden on patients, and costs must be carefully controlled. Observational systems like the TSBC are expensive and time-consuming to employ, and account for only a small proportion of unique variance in overall outcome. They provide high-fidelity information that is not otherwise available, but domains of outcome such as relapse and role functioning in the community, which have more clinical and social relevance, can be assessed more cheaply and conveniently (e.g., by interviewer ratings). Moreover, detailed behavioral codes have limited acceptability by the broader scientific and clinical community. It is unlikely that direct observation will ever have widespread acceptance unless and until it is shown to be cost-efficient *and* clinically useful.

One area in which observational strategies are frequently employed is in studies evaluating social skills training and family interactions. Although they have a number of limitations, role-play tests and structured conversations remain the standard for assessing interpersonal behavior (Bellack, 1979, 1983). These strategies reliably differentiate targeted populations and are related to other measures of social functioning (Bellack, Morrison, Wixted & Mueser, 1990; Bellack, Morrison, Mueser, & Wade, 1989; Mueser, Bellack, Morrison, & Wixted, 1990).

Structured conversations have proven to be particularly useful for assessment of family interaction patterns. The characteristic strategy requires the patient and a significant other to participate in two 10-minute discussions in which they attempt to resolve family conflicts (Goldstein & Doane, 1982). The interaction is videotaped for subsequent rating on a behavioral coding system. This technique has proven useful for prediction of relapse and identification of behavioral correlates of Expressed Emotion (Miklowitz, Goldstein, Falloon, & Doane, 1984) and for evaluation of the effects of behavioral family therapy (Doane, Falloon, Goldstein, & Mintz, 1985). However, the use of these procedures as generic outcome measures may be limited, due to the high cost of rating the interactions.

Self-Report Inventories

Self-report is a controversial source of information for the assessment of schizophrenia patients. Although patients are generally the only source of information about their inner world (e.g., delusional beliefs), they are notoriously unreliable reporters. In addition to the characteristic limitations of self-report, such as inaccurate recollection and response bias (Bellack & Hersen, 1977), schizophrenics have a number of cognitive impairments that further restrict their ability to provide accurate information. They often are disorganized and have some thought disorder, even between acute episodes (Harrow & Quinlan, 1985), and they generally have marked impairments in information processing and attention span (Neuchterlein & Dawson, 1984) that may interfere with responses on self-report inventories.

Despite the limitations of self-report inventories for schizophrenic patients, there has been a recent growth in interest in the clinical validity of these instruments. Several studies have suggested that self-report measures of mood in schizophrenia may be more predictive than interview-based measures of outcomes such as relapse (Hogarty et al., 1979), thought disturbance (Blanchard, Mueser, & Bellack, 1992), and suicide (Cohen, Test, & Brown, 1990). Although this research awaits replication, it raises the interesting possibility that the self-reports of schizophrenia patients may be more clinically valid than was previously thought.

Interviewer Rating Scales

Although self-report inventories are suspect, self-report plays a critical role as a source of data for clinician judgements. The primary difference is that the skilled interviewer can evaluate and interpret patient behavior and ask leading questions. Interviewer rating scales are the most important instruments in research on schizophrenia. They are used for assessing symptomatology (e.g., Brief Psychiatric Rating Scale [BPRS] by Overall & Gorham, 1962 and Scale for the Assessment of Negative Symptoms [SANS] by Andreasen & Olsen, 1982); ability to fulfill social roles (e.g., Social Adjustment Scale-II [SAS] by Schooler, Hogarty, & Weissman, 1978); overall adjustment (e.g., Global Adjustment Scale [GAS]); and medication side effects (e.g., Abnormal Involuntary Movement Scale [AIMS]—see Guy, 1976). Carefully constructed interview scales have been shown to be highly reliable and have good criterion and predictive validity (Morrison, 1988). They characteristically serve as the primary measures in comprehensive assessment batteries.

Significant-Other Reports

Significant others are often the only source of information about the patient's functioning outside of the hospital. Family members can report on the patient's role functioning in the community, social competence, compliance with medication, symptomatology, medication side effects, illicit drug use, and other factors. Recently, families have also been enlisted to report on subtle behavioral changes that forewarn of impending relapse (Herz & Melville, 1980). Family reports can be assessed by paper and pencil inventories, such as the Katz Adjustment Scales (Katz & Lyerly, 1963), or by interview.

Another focus of assessment is the family (or significant other) itself. Attitudes about the patient and styles of interaction within the family can play a critical role in relapse. One particular measure of family attitudes, Expressed Emotion

(EE), has proven to be among the most potent predictors of outcome (Hooley, 1985; Halford, 1991). Patients living with relatives rated as high in EE are 3 to 4 times more likely to relapse than patients living with low EE relatives (see discussion of family therapy, below). EE is assessed by the Camberwell Family Interview (CFI) (Vaughn & Leff, 1976), a semistructured interview designed to facilitate the expression (and assessment) of feelings and attitudes about the patient. The interview is coded on three dimensions: number of critical comments, hostility, and emotional overinvolvement. High EE is characterized by high hostility and critical comments *or* high overinvolvement. As the CFI requires more than 1½ hours to administer and several more hours to score, several alternative procedures have been developed, including the Short CFI (Mueser, Bellack, & Wade, 1993), the Five Minute Speech Sample (Magana et al., 1986), and the Patient Rejection Scale (Kreisman, Simmens, & Jay, 1979). Preliminary research with these instruments (especially the speech sample) has yielded promising results, but their utility in predicting relapse remains to be demonstrated.

INFLUENCE OF CONCEPTUAL MODELS ON TREATMENT

Historical Perspective

When Ayllon and Azrin were developing their token program, state psychiatric hospitals provided nearly 50% of all psychiatric care in the country (Sharfstein, 1984). As reflected in movies such as *Snakepit* and *One Flew over the Cuckoo's Nest*, these institutions were almost all overcrowded and understaffed, and placed greater emphasis on control and management of patients than on treatment. The result was often mistreatment or maltreatment and the so-called "institutionalization syndrome" of withdrawal, apathy, and infantile behavior (Wing & Brown,

1970; Paul & Lentz, 1977). Fortunately, this situation has changed substantially in the last 25 years, following the discovery of antipsychotic medications (Kane, 1989). These medications significantly improve symptoms in as much as 90% of patients, and lower the risk of symptom relapses from over 70% to under 30%. The widespread use of antipsychotic medications resulted in a dramatic shift from primary reliance on long-term hospitalization in state facilities to short stays and community-based treatment. The number of state hospital beds decreased from a high of 559,000 in 1955 to 138,000 in the late 1970s, and is lower today (Sharfstein, 1984). The average length of stay dropped from 6 months to 3 weeks during that period, and by the late 1970s, state hospitals provided only 9% of all mental health care in the country (Sharfstein, 1984).

Unfortunately, these dramatic changes reflect differences in how and where treatment is provided, not in the prevalence or effects of chronic mental illness. The reduction in state hospital beds has been paralleled by a dramatic increase in short-term psychiatric beds in general hospitals, Veteran's Administration Hospitals, community mental health centers, and private psychiatric hospitals (Goldman, Adams, & Taube, 1983). Since 1955, there has been a tremendous increase in readmissions to hospitals. Almost 70% of all admissions now involve patients with a previous history of hospitalization (Sharfstein, 1984). In the 1950s, patients entering a psychiatric hospital could expect a multi-year stay. Today they enter through a "revolving door," and can expect to have multiple admissions of several days to several weeks. The 2 million or so schizophrenics in this country accumulate as many as 500,000 hospital admissions per year (Goldman, 1984). The numbers would be even higher if current commitment laws were more lenient. The cornerstone of current treatments for the chronic mentally ill was the Community Mental Health Centers Act of 1963, the goal of which was to develop local centers to provide treatment in the community, rather than in large, geographically isolated institutions. It was expected that living in the community would allow patients to be reintegrated into family and peer groups and to find employment, as well as allow them to enjoy the many privileges and benefits our society has to offer. These expectations were fulfilled for some patients, but the majority have traded the distressing conditions in state hospitals for marginal lives in the community (Klerman, 1977; Lehman, 1983).

Chronic Problems Associated with Schizophrenia

The majority of schizophrenia patients (and other chronic patients as well) living in the community are chronically unemployed and have little hope of finding work. They are dependent on the social service system for money, food, and shelter. They often suffer from poor nutrition and health and have shortened life expectancies. Only a small proportion of chronic patients are capable of living independently; most require some form of supervised living arrangements (Goldstrom & Manderscheid, 1981). A great many live in run-down apartments or rooming houses in decaying areas of cities, or have no residence whatsoever. As many as one-half of the homeless people in our country are chronically mentally ill (Cordes, 1984) and upwards of 10% have schizophrenia (Susser, Struening, & Conover, 1989). Many other mentally ill individuals find shelter in prisons, having been arrested for their odd or annoying behavior rather than being brought to psychiatric facilities by police (Belcher, 1988).

Most chronic patients have a poor quality of life, even aside from housing. They are easy prey for street criminals, and thus are frequent victims of violent crime. A majority are unable to perform basic tasks necessary for daily living in the community; fewer than 60% are able to perform household chores or prepare meals independently; fewer than 50% can manage their own money or take medication as prescribed.

They also are unable to take advantage of social and recreational opportunities available in the community because they lack the money, skills, and motivation to participate in such activities. Recreation for most patients is limited to watching television or listening to the radio. Many are socially isolated and spend endless hours sleeping, walking the streets, or sitting idly in community mental health center day rooms. An increasing number of chronic patients abuse illicit drugs, which often worsen their primary illness as well as having the usual deleterious consequences of substance abuse (Mueser et al., 1990). To a great extent, the current plight of schizophrenia patients in our society is a tragedy and a national embarrassment.

Chronic Illness Model of Treatment

The interested reader is referred to Bellack (1989) for a broader discussion of why a well-intentioned plan for dealing with the chronic mentally ill has failed so miserably. One factor that is particularly germane to the role of behavior therapy is the unrealistic model of illness that has characterized both behavioral and nonbehavioral approaches. The mental health community (including behavior therapists) has generally subscribed to an infectious disease model of illness, in which treatment is viewed as a short-term process for dealing with a circumscribed, temporary disturbance. This model is inappropriate for schizophrenia, which generally is multiply handicapping, lifelong disorder. As indicated above, only a small proportion of patients will have a substantial recovery with a return to premorbid levels of functioning (Strauss & Carpenter, 1981). The majority will have residual handicaps even when the primary symptoms are well-controlled. Most patients will have periodic exacerbations of psychotic symptoms and require short-term rehospitalization. Relapse is a natural part of the illness for most patients and cannot be viewed as a sign of treatment failure.

To some extent, the mental health system has been frustrated by the fact that schizophrenics do not get better and go away. The "up and out" philosophy of treatment resulting from such expectations is not only ineffective for schizophrenics, but may actually increase stress and precipitate relapse (Schooler & Spohn, 1982). Schizophrenia is best conceptualized by a chronic illness model, similar to that employed for individuals suffering from renal disease, juvenile diabetes, and Down's syndrome. These disorders require long-term, multidimensional treatment, the goals of which are management of symptoms, teaching living and coping skills, and enhancing quality of life, not curing the illness.

The chronic illness model provides a dramatically different perspective on the needs of the schizophrenia patient. It is not reasonable to think of treatment in the traditional sense of the patient coming to the clinic for brief visits and receiving a single intervention for a limited period of time. Treatment *per se* is only one component of a system of services, each of which serves an essential role in the overall care of the patient (Bellack, 1989; Test, 1984). The variety of services required is illustrated in Table 7.2. Behavioral techniques such as social skills training and behavioral family therapy are prominent components of the treatment module. Moreover, behavioral strategies can also make significant contributions to other aspects of the overall program, including medication compliance (Bellack, 1986; Wallace, Boone, Donahue, & Foy, 1985), and rehabilitation (Anthony & Nemec, 1984). Behavioral interventions for schizophrenia patients may not produce the demonstrable changes associated with treatment of anxiety disorders or depression, but are no less valuable.

Stress-Vulnerability Model of Etiology

The precise etiology of schizophrenia is not known, but the most widely accepted working hypothesis is Zubin and Spring's (1977) stress-

TABLE 7.2   A comprehensive program of care

Treatment
Medication
Family therapy
Social skills training
Medical care
Crisis intervention

Rehabilitation
Housekeeping
Nutrition and hygiene
Job training
Transportation

Social Services
Income support
Housing
Social support
Recreation

Continuity of care
Active coordination of above services

SOURCE: Bellack, A. S. (1989). *A Clinical Guide* for *the Treatment of Schizophrenia* (New York: Plenum).

vulnerability model. According to their formulation, schizophrenic symptoms emerge as a result of the combined influence of psychobiological vulnerability and environmental stress. "Vulnerability" is a construct that entails a sensitivity or predisposition to decompensate under stress and experience a range of psychotic symptoms. It is determined primarily by genetic and developmental factors, and varies along a continuum from low to high. Individuals with low vulnerability are unlikely to develop the illness unless faced with the most extreme circumstances but those with high vulnerability are susceptible to decompensation even under moderate stress. Stressors are environmental events that have a negative impact on the individual, including life events (Rabkin, 1980), negative ambient family emotion (Koenigsberg & Handley, 1986), or an unstructured, impoverished environment (Wing & Brown, 1970; Wong et al., 1987). Internal "events," such as physical illness and the effects of psychostimulants or hallucinogens can also serve as significant stressors.

The effects of stress on vulnerability are moderated by the individual's coping skills. Coping skills are a diverse set of abilities that enable an individual to resolve problems, reduce arousal, and achieve instrumental or socio-emotional goals that maximize adaptation and include social skills, problem-solving skills, skills needed for daily living (e.g., ability to use public transportation and manage money), and basic self-care skills (e.g., ability to maintain personal hygiene and grooming). Coping skills can reduce the consequences of negative events by enabling the person to circumvent potential stressors entirely and by decreasing the severity of the impact. Behavioral techniques can often play a useful role in enhancing the coping skills of schizophrenia patients. The biological limitations imposed by the disorder (e.g., restricted attention and information processing capacity, lack of interest and energy) may limit the effectiveness of some behavioral procedures that are useful with less impaired populations, such as problem-solving training and self-control techniques (Bellack, Morrison, & Mueser, 1989). There are numerous demonstrations in the literature of the utility of individualized behavioral interventions (Curran, Monti, & Corriveau, 1982).

BEHAVIORAL INTERVENTIONS
IN THE TREATMENT
OF SCHIZOPHRENIA

The stress-vulnerability model of schizophrenia has important implications for developing interventions to improve the outcome of the illness, including symptomatology, social adjustment, quality of life, the ability to care for oneself, and frequency of relapses and rehospitalizations. Ac-

cording to the model, effective treatments for schizophrenia must modify at least one of the three hypothetical constructs presumed to influence outcome: (1) biological vulnerability, (2) environmental stress, or (3) coping skills that mediate the noxious effects of stress. Behavioral interventions can play a key role in improving outcome via each of these three constructs. Vulnerability is assumed to be determined mainly by genetic and biological factors, although it can be lowered by antipsychotic medications and increased by alcohol or drug abuse. Behavioral interventions may influence vulnerabilty by fostering compliance with antipsychotic medications, teaching patients information regarding the effects of medication, and training social skills for discussing medication issues with one's physician. Additionally, the deleterious effects of substance abuse can be minimized by application of any number of behavioral techniques developed for the treatment of addictive disorders.

Socioenvironmental stressors impinging on the patient can be lessened directly by a variety of different behavioral interventions. Stress emanating from hostile, critical, or intrusive family interactions can be reduced by teaching family members strategies for communicating less stressfully and solving everyday problems associated with the multiple handicaps of schizophrenia (e.g., behavioral family therapy). Furthermore, stress in non-family environments, such as day treatment programs, board-and-care homes, and foster homes can be minimized by providing rehabilitation programming that remediates deficits and teaches skills for independent living over an extended period of time, and does not attempt to produce rapid change (Linn, Klett, & Caffey, 1980). Stress can result from environmental overstimulation, but chronic understimulation, a lack of structure, and an absence of social contacts can also produce stress, leading to an increase in symptoms (Rosen, Sussman, Mueser, Lyons, & Davis, 1981; Wong et al., 1987). Interventions can minimize the stress due to understimulation by adequately structuring social rehabilitation programs and by teaching skills to enable patients to structure their own time meaningfully, such as with leisure and recreation skills.

The enhancement of coping skills is the third strategy commonly used to improve the outcome of schizophrenia. Generally, two different approaches have been applied to bolster patients' ability to cope more effectively with stress: (1) *teaching social skills* to enable patients to obtain instrumental and social needs, as well as to reduce interpersonal conflict; and (2) the application of *behavioral self-management techniques* to reduce the negative effects of stress on the patients. Since chronic symptoms such as persistent auditory hallucinations, delusions of reference, and paranoid delusions are often experienced as stressful and can lead to anxiety and depression, behavioral self-management methods can be fruitful when focused on these secondary symptoms of the illness (Tarrier et al., 1993).

Despite the array of behavioral interventions that can be utilized to improve the outcome of schizophrenia, relatively few treatment techniques have been systematically replicated, and the impact of many methods on widely accepted domains of the illness (e.g., relapse rate, social adjustment) remains to be demonstrated. Paul and Lentz's (1977) study on the effects of the token economy on chronic patients remains a classic to this day. However, their remarkably strong findings supporting the efficacy of the token economy, including improvements superior to standard treatment and an equally intensive milieu treatment in adaptive behavior, need for medication, discharge into the community, and community survival, have never been replicated in another setting, although this method continues to be the treatment of choice for many severely ill schizophrenics (Glynn & Mueser, 1992). Similarly, a broad range of different cognitive-behavioral strategies has been applied successfully in the treatment of schizophrenic symptoms, including systematic desensitization (Slade, 1972), aversive conditioning (Turner, Hersen, & Bellack, 1977), covert sensitization (Moser, 1974), contingency management

(Liberman, Wallace, Teigen, & Davis, 1974), overcorrection (Sumner, Mueser, Hsu, & Morales, 1974), thought stopping (Fisher & Winkler, 1975), self-monitoring (Adams, Malatesta, Brantley, & Turkat, 1981), self-instructional training (Bentall, Higson, & Lowe, 1987), and cognitive restructuring of irrational beliefs (Perris, 1989). These successes notwithstanding, little research has documented the relative efficacy or feasibility of these behavioral methods for the population of schizophrenic patients. Most studies have been reports of successfully treated single cases, and the relevance of illness characteristics (e.g., premorbid social functioning, symptomatology) to determining clinical response remains unknown. At the present, only two approaches to the behavior modification of schizophrenia have been supported by research that is both controlled (i.e., random assignment of patients to treatment groups) and replicated: social skills training and behavioral family therapy. These findings represent significant advances in the field; as recently as 10 years ago, neither of these interventions had been supported by even a single controlled study. For this reason, we will focus here on describing recent developments in these treatments for schizophrenia.

Social Skills Training

Social skills training (SST) refers to a set of behavioral procedures derived from learning theory that are combined in a treatment "package" designed to improve social functioning. SST has its historical roots in conditioned reflex therapy (Salter, 1949) and assertion training (Wolpe, 1958), and evolved to incorporate the principles of observational learning or social learning theory (Bandura, 1969). Social skills are the specific verbal, non-verbal (e.g., facial expression, eye contact), and paralinguistic (e.g., voice loudness, tone, and fluency) behaviors used in interpersonal situations to attain instrumental and affiliative needs. Over the past decade, impairments in social perception skills (e.g., the ability to recognize relevant social parameters, such as facial expression) (Morrison & Bellack, 1987; Morrison, Bellack, & Mueser, 1988) and information processing skills (e.g., the ability to generate possible responses and anticipate their probable consequences) (Wallace et al., 1980) have been recognized as prevalent among persons with schizophrenia and are frequently targeted for modification, in addition to the overt behaviors described above.

Description of SST Procedures

The clinical procedures involved in SST, whether conducted in group or individual format, generally adhere to the following basic steps:

1. The patient's behavioral assets, deficits, and excesses in social situations are systematically assessed, through such methods as role-plays, naturalistic observation, and interviews.

2. Specific social behaviors are targeted for modification and a rationale for learning these behaviors is provided to the patient.

3. The therapist models the skill in a role-play.

4. Specific instructions are given to the patient to rehearse the skill.

5. The patient practices the skill in a role-play.

6. Positive feedback is given to the patient for specific components of the skill performed well, and corrective feedback is given to improve performance.

7. Repeated rehearsal and feedback take place.

8. A homework assignment is given to practice the skill in the natural environment, to facilitate generalization of the skill.

Additional training in social perception skills can be integrated into the training by asking patients to identify specific emotions exhibited during role plays. Information processing or problem-solving skills can be taught by asking patients to compare and evaluate different possible response options in a social situation. The nuances of SST are described further in several books (Kelly, 1982; Liberman, DeRisi, & Mueser, 1989).

Specific Skills Taught in SST

Numerous studies have been conducted to examine the efficacy of SST with schizophrenic and other chronically mentally ill persons (Donahoe & Driesenga, 1988). Many of these studies suffer methodological flaws that limit the conclusions that can be drawn, including failure to specify diagnostic criteria such as those from DSM-III, (APA, 1980) or to use structured interviews to establish diagnoses (e.g., the Structured Interview for DSM-III) (Spitzer & Williams, 1985), absence of control groups, failure to use broadly accepted outcome criteria (e.g., relapse rate, social adjustment, symptomatology) (Strauss & Carpenter, 1977), and lack of attention to the possible confounds of psychotropic medications. Despite these limitations, early research on SST yielded a consistent pattern of results suggesting that this approach may be efficacious. First, it has been established that schizophrenic patients can be taught a range of socially adaptive skills, including nonverbal behaviors such as smiles and eye contact (Edelstein & Eisler, 1976; Kolko, Dorsett, & Milan, 1981); paralinguistic skills such as voice loudness and tone (Eisler, Hersen, & Miller, 1973; Finch & Wallace, 1977); conversational skills (Holmes, Hansen, & St. Lawrence, 1984; Urey, Laughlin, & Kelly, 1979); assertive responses (Eisler, Blanchard, Fitts, & Williams, 1978; Hersen, Bellack, & Turner, 1978); independent living skills (Brown & Munford, 1983); job interviewing skills (Furman, Geller, Simon, & Kelly, 1979; Kelly, Laughlin, Claiborne, & Patterson, 1979); and job maintenance skills (Mueser, Foy, & Carter, 1986). Topic areas commonly addressed in SST programs are summarized in Table 7.3. Second, at least moderate generalization of acquired skills to similar situations can be expected from training, with more complex skills showing less general-

TABLE 7.3   Social skill topic areas

Interpersonal skills

Conversation skills

Dating and friendship

Assertiveness

Problem solving

Self-care and maintenance skills

Vocational rehabilitation

Home finding and maintenance

Medication management

Leisure and recreation

Self-care and personal hygiene

Use of public transportation

Food preparation

Money management

Use of community agencies

ization and severely ill patients acquiring fewer skills more slowly (Bellack, Hersen, & Turner, 1976; Frederickson, Jenkins, Foy, & Eisler, 1976).

Controlled Evaluations of SST

Early studies on the effects of SST on schizophrenic patients did not address the broad issue of the impact of this treatment on specific domains of the illness and its long-term outcome. However, the results indicating that social behaviors can be broken down into specific component skills that can be effectively taught to patients through behavioral rehearsal were sufficiently encouraging to lead to several controlled studies of SST with schizophrenic patients. The research designs employed in these controlled studies have methodological limitations, but they provide the first strong evidence that this approach can play an important role in the social rehabilitation of schizophrenic patients (Benton & Schroeder, 1990; Halford & Hayes, 1991). The studies are briefly reviewed below.

Bellack, Turner, Hersen, and Luber (1984) examined the effects of SST conducted in groups as treatment for schizophrenic patients participating in an outpatient day treatment program. Patients were randomly assigned to either SST plus day treatment or day treatment alone. The skills-training program was conducted over a 3-month period, with follow-up assessments conducted after 6 months and 1 year. At the 6-month follow-up, patients who had received SST, compared to those who did not, continued to show significant improvements in social adjustment and symptoms over and above functioning at the end of the 3-month treatment period. One-year relapse rates, however, did not differ between the two groups, suggesting that the duration of treatment may have been too brief to create sustained improvements in overall functioning.

Liberman, Mueser, and Wallace (1986) evaluated the efficacy of SST for schizophrenics in a study design that compared this approach with an equally intensive holistic health treatment. Patients were randomly assigned to treatment groups, which were conducted in a state hospital over a 9-week period with patients who were awaiting discharge into the community. Each treatment included multiple sessions conducted daily, trips into the community, and weekly family therapy sessions. The holistic health treatment focused on helping patients understand schizophrenia as a valuable personal experience, and on teaching meditation, yoga, and physical exercise (e.g., jogging). Results based on assessments conducted after 2 years provided stronger support for the SST intervention on several measures of symptoms and social adjustment. Cumulative relapse rates at 2-year posttreatment slightly favored the SST over holistic health treatment, although the differences were not statistically significant (50% versus 78%, respectively). However, two features of the study design limited the conclusions that could be reached. First, the absence of a no-treatment (or minimal treatment) control group obscured the evaluation of whether both groups or neither group improved patient's functioning. The demonstration of improvements in social functioning and symptoms during a treatment following a hospitalization is not sufficient to conclude that treatment has been effective, since such improvements typically occur in the absence of psychosocial intervention (Mueser, Bellack, Morrison, & Wade, 1990). Second, SST and holistic health treatments were confounded with family treatment, because the relatives of patients receiving SST also received behavioral family therapy, which has independently been found to improve outcome (Falloon, Boyd, & McGill, 1984), and the other relatives received holistic health-oriented treatment, the efficacy of which has not been previously determined. Despite these limitations, these results provide additional support for the clinical utility of SST.

The third controlled study of SST in schizophrenia compared SST with three other treatments: no psychosocial treatment, psychoeducational family treatment, and SST plus psychoeducational treatment (Hogarty et al., 1986; Hogarty et al., 1991; Hogarty, Anderson, & Reiss, 1987). All patients were recovering from a recent symptom exacerbation, received antipsychotic medications, were residing with high Expressed Emotion (EE) family members, and were hence assumed to be at high risk for relapse. SST was provided on an individual basis weekly for one year and biweekly for a second year. One-year relapse rates supported the efficacy of SST (20%) and SST plus psychoeducation (0%) over no treatment (41%); the psychoeducational treatment had a relapse rate of 19% after 1 year. Two-year relapse rates were less supportive of SST (42%), but suggested some improvements over no psychosocial treatment (67%); the 2-year relapse rates for the combined treatment were 25% and for the psychoeducational treatment were 32%. Although this study represents a significant advance in outcome research on SST, it also has its limitations. Since all patients were living with high EE relatives, and family EE has been found to be a strong predictor of relapse (Koenigsberg &

Handley, 1986), one might expect that patients whose families did not receive any family counseling, such as those in the SST and no-treatment groups, would continue to be at high risk for relapse, regardless of individual-based interventions. A second problem with this study concerns the frequency of sessions in the SST group. Although treatment lasted longer than in the Bellack et al. (1984) and Liberman et al. (1986) studies, the frequency of sessions in the Hogarty study was lower (weekly for first year, biweekly for second year). No data were presented to indicate that patients' social skills actually improved in the SST group, raising the question of whether the intervention succeeded in its most basic goal. A final limitation of this study is that follow-up data on domains of functioning other than relapse were obtained only for those patients who did not relapse over the course of the study, resulting in unacceptably low sizes for the follow-up analyses (Bellack & Mueser, 1991). The outcome of schizophrenia is multidimensional, and a single outcome criterion such as relapse rate is unlikely to be an accurate reflection of other domains of the illness (e.g., social adjustment, quality of life).

In sum, controlled research on the efficacy of SST has provided strong encouragement that this treatment approach may be clinically useful with schizophrenic patients. None of the three studies provides unambiguous support for SST, and each had methodological limitations. The general pattern of results is favorable, however, especially when considering the evidence that psychodynamic treatments may have deleterious effects on schizophrenics (Mueser & Berenbaum, 1990), and client-centered therapy has not been found to have beneficial effects in this population (Rogers, Gendlin, Kiesler, & Truax, 1967). Future research is necessary to compare SST conducted over an extended period of time to no psychosocial treatment. Controlled research is also needed to examine the importance of frequency and length of treatment sessions on treatment outcome. Finally, the role of social skills as mediators of environmental stress, as hypothesized in the stress-vulnerability model of schizophrenia, needs to be evaluated by determining whether improvements in patient social skills during SST are correlated with or predictive of a favorable outcome.

Cognitive Rehabilitation

Recent years have witnessed a growth in interest in cognitive approaches to the treatment of schizophrenia. A variety of different models of cognitive therapy or rehabilitation have been proposed, and the theoretical rationales for these interventions have stimulated a lively debate that is likely to continue for several years (Bellack, 1992; Braff, 1992; Brenner, Hodel, Roder, & Corrigan, 1992; Hogarty & Flesher, 1992; Liberman & Green, 1992; Spaulding, 1992; Spring & Ravdin, 1992). Perris (1989) has developed a model of cognitive therapy for schizophrenia that is based on Beck's (1976) approach to depression, focused mainly on teaching patients to identify and dispute their irrational cognitions. Liberman and colleagues (e.g., Wallace, Liberman, McKain, Blackwell, & Eckman, 1992) have developed an approach in which cognitive remediation occurs in the context of training problem-solving skills embedded within a social skills training program. Brenner et al. (1992) employ a different model, in which the initial focus of treatment is on the remediation of basic cognitive deficits, such as cognitive differentiation and social perception, followed by training on motor and cognitive-motor areas, such as verbal communication and interpersonal problem solving. All of these approaches share the common assumption that cognitive deficits in schizophrenia are modifiable through training, although data to support this assumption are notably absent at present. An alternative possibility, although less sanguine, is that most cognitive deficits in schizophrenia are not reversible and that efforts at social rehabilitation need to focus on teaching patients how to manage these deficits in social situations, rather than to overcome them (Bellack, 1992).

Behavioral Family Therapy

Early theories of the etiology of schizophrenia postulated that it was a result of disturbed family relationships. Sullivan (1927) attempted to treat schizophrenia by recreating the family in an inpatient setting, in order to provide corrective emotional experiences. Fromm-Reichman (1948) believed that the illness was due to a pattern of overbearing, emotionally insecure behavior on the part of the mother, and coined the term "schizophrenogenic mother." The "double-bind" theory of schizophrenia theorized that children who are habitually exposed to contradictory messages from parents eventually develop the illness (Bateson, Jackson, Haley, & Weakland, 1956). Other theories suggested that the illness was the result of immature parents forcing their children to remain childlike to bolster their own self-esteem (Bowen, 1961), or due to the transmission of "irrationality" (Lidz, Fleck, & Cornelison, 1965) or "communication deviance" (Wynne & Singer, 1963) from parents to offspring.

As evidence accumulated that schizophrenia has a predominantly biological basis and that the transmission of the illness is determined by genetic rather than social factors, early theories of the family's role in etiology became obsolete. Furthermore, the discovery of antipsychotic medications fundamentally changed the nature of the illness, enabling most patients to be treated in the community. More than 60% of the schizophrenic patients in the community are living with families (Goldman, 1982; Minkoff, 1978), resulting in a burden on family members who are poorly equipped to cope with the stressful behavior of a chronically ill person at home (Dearth, Labenski, Mott, & Pellegrini, 1986). Impairments in patient social functioning, such as poor self-care skills, social withdrawal, and lack of motivation, are particularly irksome to family members and are more likely to promote criticism than delusions or hallucinations (Leff & Vaughn, 1985). These criticisms, or high Expressed Emotion, have been found to increase patients' risk of symptomatic relapses following an acute hospitalization (Koenigsberg & Handley, 1986).

Behavioral family therapy (BFT) was developed both to reduce the burden on family members of caring for the illness and to minimize the negative impact of family Expressed Emotion on the course of the patient's illness (Falloon, Boyd, & McGill, 1984; Falloon et al., 1988; Mueser, 1989). Ultimately, the goal of BFT is to enable the family to manage independently, without ongoing family therapy, most of the daily stresses involved in living with a chronic illness, although in some cases maintenance treatment may be necessary.

Similar to social skills training, BFT is a structured intervention that resembles more a classroom than a traditional therapy setting. Sessions are based on preplanned agendas and involve the active participation of all family members, including the patient. Homework is given to foster generalization of skills to the natural environment. Sessions can be conducted with individual families or in multiple-family groups at either the home or the clinic, and usually occur on a declining contact basis for at least a year. BFT can be divided into five separate stages, although there is considerable recycling of each stage throughout the treatment: (1) assessment of all family members, (2) education about schizophrenia, (3) communication skills training, (4) problem-solving training, and (5) special problems.

Assessment/Education

The behavioral analysis of the family system is an ongoing process that is interwoven throughout therapy. The therapist conducts an assessment by identifying the assets and deficits of each family member, the family as a unit, and the role that specific problem behaviors play in the functioning of the family. Assessment information is obtained through individual interviews, observation of family members interacting with one another, and the performance of the family on structured problem-solving tasks. During the educational sessions, common mis-

conceptions about the cause of schizophrenia are refuted, such as the schizophrenic having a "split personality" or that families cause the illness. Families are informed about the symptoms of schizophrenia, its diagnosis, prevalence, course, the biological theories, and the influence of drug abuse. The nature of antipsychotic drugs is explained, including their beneficial effects on acute symptoms and prevention of relapses, as well as side effects and coping strategies. Families learn about the stress-vulnerability model of schizophrenia, and are taught to recognize prodromal signs of symptom relapses. Information is presented to family members by using flipcharts, posters, or blackboards, and is summarized in handouts entitled "What is Schizophrenia?," "Medication for Schizophrenia," and "The Role of the Family."

Communication Skills Training

Communication skills training focuses on lowering family tensions by improving empathic listening, teaching effective skills for expressing positive feelings to others, making requests of others, and expressing negative feelings. These skills are taught by using the procedures of social skills training, which employ modeling, behavioral rehearsal, feedback, social reinforcement, and homework for generalization. Additional communication skills are taught on an as-needed basis, including compromising with others and requesting time out from a stressful interaction. Families containing a schizophrenic member with severe cognitive impairments often benefit from learning how to ask the patient questions to determine whether he or she is tracking the conversation.

Problem Solving

Training in problem-solving skills builds on the communication skills previously taught, and aims at teaching a sequence of steps for resolving a problem or attaining a goal, to minimize negative emotional undercurrents and maximize the identification and implementation of effective solutions. The steps of problem solving are: (1) identify the problem or goal to all members' satisfaction; (2) brainstorm a list of possible solutions; (3) evaluate the advantages and disadvantages of each solution; (4) select the best solution(s); (5) plan how to implement the best solution by considering necessary resources, roles, time-frames, etc.; and (6) review implementation of the solution at a later date. Family members are taught how to lead the family discussion, record the various solutions, and write and monitor the steps of the implementation plan. As part of their homework assignments from the beginning of therapy, families are instructed to have weekly family meetings. These family meetings are then used to problem-solve on individual and family goals, to resolve conflict between family members and to pinpoint and modify stressors within and outside of the family.

The last stage of BFT is oriented to resolving problems that remain. This may involve teaching a range of behavioral techniques, depending on the specific needs of the family, including the token economy for extreme social withdrawal, contingency contracting to increase socially desirable behavior, social skills training for interpersonal deficits, or relaxation training or exposure for anxiety. Usually the entire family is involved in planning and implementing these special interventions.

Outcome Evaluation

The clinical efficacy of BFT has been strongly supported by a controlled study comparing this intervention with individual treatment and case management (Falloon, 1985; Falloon et al., 1985; Falloon, McGill, Boyd, & Pederson, 1987). All patients were living with high Expressed Emotion relatives and were treated with antipsychotic medication by psychiatrists who were blind to their treatment assignment. BFT was provided in the family's home weekly for 3 months, biweekly for 6 months, and monthly thereafter for a 2-year period. At the 2-year

point, only 17% of the patients receiving BFT had relapsed, compared to 83% of the individually treated patients. These differences were also reflected by the lower rate of rehospitalization and greater gains in social and vocational functioning in the BFT patients. Finally, the family treatment was successful in reducing the burden of the illness on the relatives and in decreasing critical and intrusive statements made by family members to the patient during problem-solving discussions.

These results indicate that BFT may be a powerful treatment for schizophrenia, and several replication studies are currently under way, including the National Institute of Mental Health Collaborative Study on the Treatment of Schizophrenia and the Brentwood VA Hospital Study (Randolph et al., 1990). Recently, a variation on BFT has been described and validated in a controlled clinical trial (Barrowclough & Tarrier, 1987, 1990; Tarrier et al., 1989). This study also provided support for behavioral methods of working with families of schizophrenic patients. Two-year relapse rates of patients living with high Expressed Emotion relatives were significantly lower in patients receiving the behavioral family treatment (33%) than in those receiving routine treatment (59%).

The two controlled studies conducted on BFT both demonstrated significant treatment effects compared to less or no psychosocial intervention. Although these differences represent important clinical advances, the precise role of behavioral methods in improving outcome beyond gains that would occur from education alone remains to be determined. Two nonbehavioral family interventions have been reported to reduce relapse rates of schizophrenics in controlled studies similar to the ones performed on BFT, suggesting that education alone may be an important factor in the treatment of families (Hogarty, Anderson, & Reiss, 1987; Leff, Kuipers, Berkowitz, & Sturgeon, 1985). Table 7.4 summarizes the results of controlled outcome studies conducted on families containing a schizophrenic member. Future research should di-

TABLE 7.4   Summary of controlled outcome studies of family therapy

Study	Theoretical Orientation	Goals of Treatment	Number of Patients	Cumulative 2-year Relapse Rates (%)	
				Standard Treatment	Family Therapy
Falloon et al., 1985	Educational-Behavioral	To teach the interpersonal skills necessary for families to solve their own problems	36	83	17
Tarrier et al., 1989	Educational-Behavioral	To reduce relapse rates and improve patient social functioning through stress management and goal setting	53	59	33
Leff et al., 1985	Educational-Eclectic	To lower expressed emotion in relatives and reduce amount of patient-relative contact	24	78	14
Hogarty et al., 1986	Educational-Systems	To work with the family until patient has achieved successful re-entry into social and vocational mainstream	57	67	32

rectly compare BFT with purely educational treatments for families, to evaluate the importance of behavioral methods for enabling families to manage a schizophrenic relative more effectively.

A final area in need of research concerns the issue of the durability of behavioral and other family therapy approaches. To date, only the Tarrier et al. (1989) study examined clinical differences between treatment groups after the treatment had been terminated, whereas the other three studies did not. The behavioral methods postulate that relapses can be prevented by teaching family members the skills necessary to successfully ward off the negative effects of stress. Others have argued that relapses can only be temporarily postponed and that treatment must be indefinite (Hogarty et al., 1986). This question can only be resolved by controlled outcome studies of family interventions for schizophrenia that collect follow-up data at least 1 year posttreatment.

CONCLUSIONS AND FUTURE DIRECTIONS

Our knowledge about schizophrenia has increased dramatically since the period when behaviorists first reported success in working with schizophrenics. The genetic transmission of at least some forms of the illness is now well-established (Schulz & Pato, 1989). There is considerable evidence for the existence of both neurochemical and structural brain impairments, which may eventually prove to be the cause(s) of the disorder(s) (Keith & Mathews, 1988). We have pointedly used the terms "illness" and "disorder" to describe schizophrenia. Social learning models and functional analyses of psychotic symptoms are no longer viable. Similarly, simple conditioning techniques for controlling psychotic symptoms cannot be considered appropriate except in the most unusual cases. As previously indicated, treatment demands a comprehensive mix of pharmacological and psychosocial interventions, administered over an extended period of time. Pharmacotherapy is demonstrably effective for symptom control (Kessler & Waletzky, 1981), and behavioral strategies can play a vital role in rehabilitation and stress management.

The last 25 years have seen a major change in where patients live and the nature of their most pressing needs. In contrast to the period between 1950 and 1975, most patients now reside in the community. Token programs were uniquely suited for transformation of pernicious state hospital milieus, but such programs are not easily translated to the unstructured community settings in which most patients now live. Consequently, the current focus of behavioral programs is delaying and/or preventing relapse, by teaching patients and their families coping skills to deal with the interpersonal stresses of daily life. In the future, more attention should be paid to increasing medication compliance, enhancing quality of life, and facilitating stabilization and readjustment to the community after acute hospitalizations.

The future for behavioral interventions for schizophrenia is exceedingly bright. New pharmacological interventions, such as clozapine, promise to make patients more receptive to behavioral rehabilitation strategies (Kane, Honigfeld, Singer, & Meltzer, 1988). At the same time, increasing knowledge about the information processing deficits that underlie functional impairments will make it possible to devise more effective interventions (Bellack, Morrison, & Mueser, 1989). Behavior therapists have neglected schizophrenia in favor of treating milder disorders. Given the tremendous need for services for the chronic mentally ill and the demonstrated potency of behavioral interventions, that has been a serious mistake. Behavioral clinicians and scientists need to rediscover the disorder and help rectify one of society's most serious public health problems and a major human tragedy.

TREATMENT RESOURCES

Bellack, A. S. (Ed.). (1989). *A clinical guide for the treatment of schizophrenia*. New York: Plenum.

Dearth, N., Labenski, B. J., Mott, M. E., & Pellegrini, L. M. (1986). *Families helping families: Living with schizophrenia*. New York: Norton.

Falloon, I. R. H., Boyd, J. L., & McGill, C. W. (1984). *Family care of schizophrenia: A problem-solving approach to the treatment of mental illness*. New York: Guilford.

Falloon, I. R. H., Mueser, K. T., Gingerich, S., Rappaport, S., McGill, C., & Hole, V. (1988). *Workbook for behavioural family therapy*. Buckingham, UK: Buckingham Mental Health Service.

Kelly, J. A. (1982). *Social skills training: A practical guide for interventions*. New York: Springer.

Liberman, R. P., DeRisi, W. J., & Mueser, K. T. (1989). *Social skills training for psychiatric patients*. New York: Pergamon.

Paul, G. L., & Lentz, R. J. (1977). *Psychosocial treatment of chronic mental patients: Milieu versus social-learning programs*. Cambridge, MA: Harvard University Press.

Perris, C. (1989). *Cognitive therapy with schizophrenic patients*. New York: Guilford.

CHAPTER 8

Social Inadequacy and Social Skill

Michael G. Dow

As behavioral treatment models became more prevalent in the 1960s and early 1970s, a number of influential papers questioned the relevance and importance of various target behaviors within the emerging field of behavior therapy (Cooper, Furst, & Bridger, 1969). Studies on snake phobia drew the heaviest criticism. These concerns led Borkovec, Stone, O'Brien, and Kaloupek (1974) to propose several criteria that might be used to judge the clinical relevance of various target problems. These criteria included: (1) a clinically relevant target behavior should occur at some reasonable frequency among the psychiatric population; (2) the target behavior should be a source of discomfort or interference in daily life; (3) the target behavior should not be influenced by demand or suggestion effects; (4) physiological arousal should occur in anticipation of, and in response to, the feared situation; and (5) there should not be marked habituation of physiological arousal upon exposure to the feared situation. Borkovec et al. (1974) recommended that social anxiety be considered an appropriate target behavior for clinical research and treatment. From that time to the present, the related constructs of social anxiety, speech anxiety, reticence, minimal dating, communication apprehension, assertiveness, social skill, social phobia, and social inadequacy have received extensive empirical and theoretical attention.

Curran (1977) presented the first major review of the subject, in which he argued that this megaconstruct might best be viewed as involving three etiological processes: conditioned anxiety, skills deficits, and faulty cognitive-evaluative self-appraisals. In large measure, the field still emphasizes these three major areas.

In a later review, Curran and Wessberg (1981) proposed an alternate model that is largely compatible with the first model, although more descriptive in nature and less theoretical. The later model assumes that an individual has either an adequate or inadequate social skills repertoire, and either does or does not have additional interference operating that may reduce social performance. Social skills repertoire really refers to whether the requisite skills could ever be utilized, as in a nonthreatening environment. In other words, does the individual currently have the response capabilities to exert socially skilled behavior? Interference mechanisms would include negative self-statements, attributional errors, selective attention to negative events, inappropriate emotional arousal, lack of interest in other people, among other possibilities. These factors might decrease social performance in some individuals below the expected level, based on skill alone. Thus, this descriptive model suggests that individuals might best be viewed as representing one of the 2-by-2 quadrants that show the possible combinations of skill level and interference mechanisms. Social inadequacy might occur in three of the four quadrants, namely: interference mechanisms occur although adequate skills are present; skills are inadequate, no additional interference occurs; or inadequate skills are present and interference occurs.

A similar model was proposed by Trower, Yardley, Bryant, and Shaw (1978), who made a distinction between social skills deficits and interference mechanisms that limit the expression of competent social behavior. Their term "primary social failure" refers to the loss or failure to acquire competence, and "secondary failure" refers to the disruption or inhibition of performance.

Further complicating the theory of social inadequacy is the fact that there is wide agreement that social effectiveness is situation-specific and response-mode specific. By situation-specific, we mean that a certain individual may have difficulty with some types of social situations but not others. For example, some individuals who are able to make effective public speeches may have difficulty asking a co-worker out on a date. By response-mode specificity, we mean that the experience of social difficulty may emphasize cognitive-subjective factors such as negative self-evaluations, behavioral factors such as unskilled verbal and nonverbal behavior, and/or physical factors including overarousal, sweating, rapid breathing, increased heart rate, and physical unattractiveness. Individuals who experience social interpersonal difficulties may have problems in one or more of these three areas.

It should be apparent from these complexities that while the term "social skill" is probably the most frequently used term to describe this area of research and writing, many authors are somewhat uncomfortable emphasizing only social skills, given the breadth and complexity of this area. To be sure, the advantage of the term "social skill" is that is acknowledges the role that this approach has in enhancing social performance among nonclinical normal individuals (Goldsmith & McFall, 1975). However, it has the disadvantage, because of the word "skill," of implying that only behavioral mechanisms are involved in social competence. The term "social inadequacy", used by Curran and Wessberg (1981) and by Arkowitz (1981), has the advantage of being theoretically neutral and also suggests a broad construct. Hence, both of these descriptive terms (social inadequacy, social skill) are used to name this chapter.

ROLE OF SOCIAL INADEQUACY IN CLINICAL DISORDERS

Zigler and Phillips (1961) are often credited with the notion that level of social competence is an important factor in the development of psychopathology and is predictive of treatment effectiveness. Research conducted by Zigler and Phillips (1961) found that psychiatric patients who were relatively low in social competence averaged a longer period of institutionalization and were more likely to be rehospitalized than patients who were relatively high in social competence. Later research by Lentz, Paul, and Calhoun (1971) confirmed that level of social functioning is related to discharge from the hospital and to rehospitalization.

Although the work of Zigler and Phillips was instrumental in emphasizing the relevance of social competence for psychopathology, the variables they used as summary indices of this construct were far removed from the active dynamics of interpersonal behavior. Later formulations of social competence were more consistent with the cognitive-behavioral model and emphasized the execution of complex motor skills (Argyle & Kendon, 1967; Lentz, et al., 1971).

Socially inadequate behavior appears to be fairly prevalent within the psychiatric population. Curran, Miller, Zwick, Monti, and Stout (1980) found that 7.4% of a large group of psychiatric inpatients were judged by a professional staff to be socially inadequate; Bryant, Trower, Yardley, Urbieta, and Letemendia (1976) found that 16.3% of a large outpatient sample were judged to be socially inadequate. Moreover, the prevalence of inadequate social behavior appears fairly uniform among the major psychological disorders (Bryant et al., 1976; Curran et al., 1980; Youngren & Lewinsohn, 1980). The prevalence rates may be somewhat similar, but there have been clear areas of emphasis in each of the major clinical areas that have been investigated.

Depression

Diagnostic criteria for depression usually include social withdrawal, diminished interest or pleasure from daily activities, and reduced level of activity (motor retardation). It should be clear from these criteria that depression often involves a reduction in the quality and frequency of social interaction. Overt social behavior has been implicated as an important causal factor in two etiological models of depression. Lewinsohn (1974) argued that depression results from reduced rates of positive reinforcement. The amount of reinforcement available to the individual is presumed to be related to the number of reinforcing events in the person's immediate environment, the reinforcing potential of these events for the individual, and the individual's level of social skill. Social skill was defined by Libet and Lewinsohn (1973) as the ability to emit behavior that is rein-

forced by others and to refrain from emitting behavior that is punished by others. Studies relevant to this model have generally shown that depressed individuals engage in fewer pleasant activities and are perceived as somewhat less socially skilled than nondepressed normal individuals. The level of pleasant activities, many of which are social in nature, has also been shown to correlate with mood ratings. Specific overt behaviors that may distinguish depressed and normal individuals have not been clearly established (Dow & Craighead, 1987; Jacobson, 1981).

Coyne (1976b) argued that a specific interpersonal style, characterized by complaining and inappropriate self-disclosure, plays a causal role in the development and maintenance of depression. Depressed individuals may be reinforced when others listen to them and their problems; however, eventually the listener typically becomes annoyed, tired, or frustrated and distances him- or herself from the depressed individual. Although research has shown that naive observers react in a relatively negative way to depressed persons in an introductory social conversation (Dow & Craighead, 1987; Lewinsohn, Mischel, Chaplin, & Barton, 1980) and during a phone conversation (Coyne, 1976a), the specific behaviors responsible for these negative evaluations remain unclear. One of the difficulties in evaluating Coyne's model is that most studies in this area have examined the overt behavior of depressed persons in the context of introductory conversations with strangers. Difficulties in interpersonal behavior with friends, spouses, or confidants may be theoretically much more relevant to this model (Doerfler & Chaplin, 1985).

An important study of family interaction by Biglan et al. (1985) found that when depressed mothers displayed dysphoric affect, fathers and children were less likely to display irritated and sarcastic behavior, but caring behavior was also reduced. This study provides some support for Coyne's interactional model of depression (cf. Coyne, Kahn, & Gotlib, 1987).

The cognitive aspects of social inadequacy are particularly relevant among depressed persons.

The chapter by Hollon in this volume has already outlined a number of cognitive self-evaluative tendencies that appear to be involved in the etiology of depression. Given the perceived importance of social behavior and social relationships in our culture, it seems clear that many of the negative thoughts, depressive attributions, and cognitive distortions present in depression involve social situations. Research using a social conversational task with a stranger has shown that depressed individuals evaluate themselves and their social performance more negatively than do normal control subjects (Dow & Craighead, 1987; Lewinsohn et al., 1980). Depressed people are also ready to describe their social relationships as lacking sufficient support. Research by Brown and Harris (1978), Costello (1982), and Billings and Moos (1984) has found that a lack of supportive relationships is associated with depression. However, the extent to which these differences reflect perceptions of lack of support (cognitive differences) or actual relationship differences is still somewhat unclear.

Other research has indicated that marital discord, per se, is associated with the development of depression (Coyne et al., 1987). Thus, it may not be surprising that many aspects of marital therapy are similar to social competence enhancement in such areas as communication skills training, expression of feelings, assertiveness training, social problem-solving, modifying negative thoughts during interpersonal communication, reducing social withdrawal, increasing social activities, and cognitive restructuring. It seems clear that a promising, relatively new line of research involves focusing on interpersonal difficulties in the intimate relationships of depressed individuals (see Chapter 11, on couples therapy).

Anxiety

The current classification system of the American Psychiatric Association, the *Diagnostic and Statistical Manual of Mental Disorders* (3rd. ed., rev.) (DSM-III-R), (American Psychiatric Association, 1987), includes the category of social phobia under the anxiety disorders. The definition of this disorder emphasizes a persistent fear of one or more situations in which the person is exposed to possible scrutiny by others and fears that he or she may do something humiliating or embarrassing. As such, this disorder emphasizes the cognitive self-evaluative aspects of social inadequacy.

Other anxiety disorders listed in DSM-III-R, such as panic disorder with agoraphobia, agoraphobia without history of panic disorder, and generalized anxiety disorder, also have some overlap with the issues discussed in this chapter, since many of these anxiety disorders center around social situations. Thus, it should not be surprising that the term "social anxiety" has been used as a comprehensive term in a number of research studies in this area.

As already described in this volume, the cognitive-behavioral approach to anxiety assumes that negative past experiences may condition an anxiety reaction to otherwise neutral stimuli, such as social situations. Future avoidance of those situations may maintain or worsen the fear reaction. In addition, cognitive self-statements may magnify the anxiety and fear reaction. The types of specific symptoms that are often associated with social anxiety would include behavioral reactions such as trembling, fidgets, pacing, poor eye contact, avoidance of social situations, and limited hand gestures; cognitive symptoms such as negative self-statements, selective attention and recall of negative experiences, and negative self-evaluations; and physical symptoms such as sweating, increased heart rate, and blushing.

One difficulty in this area is that several of the behavioral codes that have been characterized as skills deficits seem to be explained equally well by the construct of anxiety. Low talk time, more pauses, few hand gestures, and low eye contact have been described as evidence of social skill deficits as well as evidence of social anxiety.

Mowrer (1947) suggested that the relationship between a conditioned stimulus (CS) such as a social situation and a conditioned response such as anxiety is maintained when the individual avoids the CS, so that extinction of the conditioned response is not allowed to occur. Treatments such as systematic desensitization, flooding, and implosion, all involve exposure to the conditioned stimulus. However, social skills training also involves increasing the degree of exposure to the CS because it involves graduated practice of social interaction. Thus, the distinction between anxiety behaviors and skills deficits becomes somewhat blurred, as all treatments involve exposure to social situations. Social skills training is currently utilized more often than the traditional anxiety reduction techniques such as systematic desensitization and relaxation. This may be because social skills training provides the common element of exposure and the added element of response acquisition. Also, social situations tend to be so broad that focused hierarchies or focused images, which are needed in systematic desensitization, are not always possible. However, there may still be a subset of clients who would respond best clinically to relaxation or systematic desensitization procedures.

Schizophrenia

Research on basic social skills training and social-interpersonal difficulties between schizophrenic individuals and their families is described in the chapter on schizophrenia in this volume, so will not be emphasized here.

SOCIAL INADEQUACY AND SOCIAL SKILL WITHIN A NORMAL POPULATION

Much of the writing and research in the area of social skill has concerned social difficulties in a normal population. Unlike research on depression, where some authors have questioned the use of college students to conduct "analogue" research, this is one area where research on nor-

mal populations is considered appropriate. In fact, Goldsmith and McFall (1975, p. 51) originally characterized "social skills training" as "a general therapy approach aimed at increasing performance competence in critical life situations. In contrast to the therapies aimed primarily at the elimination of maladaptive behaviors, skills training emphasizes the positive educational aspects of treatment." The three major areas that have been covered are dating, assertiveness, and social skill.

Dating

Several research studies have shown that dating is viewed by a significant proportion of the population as difficult and anxiety-producing. For example, a British survey of Oxford University students by Bryant and Trower (1974) found that 36% of the sample indicated that approaching others was moderately difficult or worse, and 35% stated that going to dances or discotheques was moderately difficult or worse. This compares with the 1% of the sample who indicated that going into shops, walking down the street, using public transportation, or being with friends was at least moderately difficult. In a study reported by Glass, Gottman, and Shmurak (1976), dating was rated as difficult by 54% of males and 42% of females. Likewise, Martinson and Zerface (1970) found that difficulty in dating was the single most frequent problem mentioned by undergraduates who were seen in a college counseling center.

Cognitive and Behavioral Factors

Several research studies conducted in the 1970s attempted to characterize differences between high- and low-dating students—both males and females. Arkowitz, Lichtenstein, McGovern, and Hines (1975) concluded that a sample of dating-shy men had adequate social skills when interacting with a female in a behavioral assessment task but appeared to have considerable anxiety about their performance. Other research by Clark and Arkowitz (1975) found no behavioral difference between high and low socially anxious males on a simulated dating task. Cognitive differences were identified by O'Banion and Arkowitz (1977) to suggest that socially anxious females were more negatively affected by negative feedback and criticism that was provided, compared with less socially anxious females. Steffen and Redden (1977) found that high and low socially competent men differed in their reaction to negative feedback from a female, but did not differ in their reaction to positive feedback. As a result of these studies, there seems to be general agreement that cognitive factors may be particularly relevant for individuals who experience problems with dating. This seems understandable from the point of view that the dating process inevitably involves personal rejection. Being able to accept rejection without feeling bad about oneself and not being anxious when being evaluated by members of the opposite sex are crucial components in the dating process. This is not to say that behavioral skills are irrelevant, however. The response-specificity principle mentioned earlier still applies. In clinical practice, one has to consider the combination of cognitive, behavioral, and physical capacities with which an individual presents. All relevant deficits should be addressed in treatment.

Physical Attractiveness

One difficulty with interpreting research in the area of dating anxiety and dating skills is that relatively few studies have comprehensively considered the role of physical attractiveness. Studies that have compared high- and low-frequency daters on measures of physical attractiveness have found that high-frequency daters (both males and females) are rated as more attractive (Glasgow & Arkowitz, 1975; Greenwald, 1977). In the study by Greenwald (1977), ratings made by confederates, raters, and peers indicated that differences in physical attractiveness between high- and low-frequency female daters could account for many of the differences that distinguished these groups. Although Greenwald concluded that many of the differences might reflect poor grooming that could be targeted for change in social skill training programs, she did not assess specific aspects of physical attractiveness. In the study by Dow (1985), socially inadequate subjects each interacted in a social conversation with three different, randomly selected college students. After the interaction, these peer raters completed an open-ended question that asked them what suggestions, if any, might improve the physical attractiveness of the person with whom they interacted. For 31% of the sample, at least two of the peers independently volunteered the same suggestion for change in the socially inadequate person. The suggestions made most often in this regard were: hair style change, 24%; losing weight, 5%; improving posture, 5%; shaving off facial hair, 5%; dressing differently, 5%; and getting contact lenses or different glasses, 2%. Many of these changes could be targeted for change in a comprehensive social competency program.

Initially Getting Dates

Another concern in this area of research is the lack of attention to what may be two relatively independent processes: the process of initially getting a date and the skills enhancements that presumably help someone to appear more skilled once he or she is on a date. Important research by Muehlenhard and colleagues has focused on the specific issue of how to convey interest in dating as a way of increasing one's chances of being asked out. This research has indicated that men would like it if a woman asked them on a date or hinted that she would like to go out with them (Muehlenhard & McFall, 1981). This research also indicated that simply waiting and hoping that the man would ask her out was not effective for a woman. Not all women are comfortable asking men for dates, but it seems likely that this will become more and more common as sex roles continue to change. Women who are interested in hinting might engage in a variety of behaviors demonstrated by Muehlenhard, Koralewski, Andrews, and Burdick (1986) to be effective in conveying interest in dating. These behaviors included: making compliments, being helpful, talking more, indicating interest in rescheduling a date if asked out for a time when she is busy, not talking as if she is busy much of the time, asking questions, initiating conversation during a pause, mentioning a social activity that she would like, making it clear she has noticed him in the past, providing eye contact, smiling, touching while laughing, showing attentiveness, and using speech inflections. Many of these behaviors can be taught in social skills training programs.

Assertiveness

A significant proportion of the research and theoretical writing in the broad area of social inadequacy and social skill has emphasized assertiveness. Assertive behavior has been defined in a number of ways, but most current definitions acknowledge that assertiveness provides a way to respond to problematic situations by making requests for behavior change and refusing inappropriate requests (Schroeder & Black, 1985). These aspects of assertiveness are often described as negative assertion, since they involve dealing with negative situations. A second major aspect of assertiveness is often referred to as positive assertion and involves expressing positive feelings. In general, an assertive person stands up for his or her rights and responsibilities, expresses his or her opinion, and expects to be treated fairly by others. Assertiveness can be contrasted with passivity and aggressiveness. A passive person generally does not express opinions, does not refuse unreasonable requests, and typically lets others have their way much of the time. An aggressive person may overreact to problematic situations, become angry, and attempt to hurt or abuse others in retaliation. Aggressive individuals want things to be done their way and are not interested in taking turns or negotiating fairly.

Although most approaches acknowledge that assertive behavior is often desirable, it is generally acknowledged that there are times when passive behavior or aggressive behavior are more desirable. For example, if approached by a mugger with a gun, it might be best to turn over one's money passively, as opposed to using this time to practice one's assertiveness skills. Likewise, most people would agree that there are situations in which it is acceptable to escalate into aggressive behavior to protect one's rights, especially if assertive behavior is tried first and is not effective.

Most research studies in the area of assertiveness have adopted a skills-deficit model and have dealt with asking for behavior change or denying unreasonable requests. By practicing the behavioral skill of assertive responses, one might also be reducing the anticipatory anxiety and negative self-statements associated with making an assertive response. Research and clinical assessment should include a hierarchical task analysis in which distinctions are made concerning at least three general levels that a social skills deficit might involve: (1) the inability to emit the behavior effectively in a protected environment; (2) the inability to emit the behavior effectively in the context of the targeted social situation, although the behavior could be emitted in a protected environment; and (3) the ability to emit the relevant behavior effectively in the targeted social situation, but with failure to do so (Bruch, 1981; Schwartz & Gottman, 1976). In the study by Bruch (1981), nonassertive subjects did not differ significantly from high-assertive subjects in their ability to construct a written assertive response or to deliver the assertive response in a safe, hypothetical situation. Based on these results, Bruch argued that cognitive factors, including negative self-statements and the lack of positive self-statements, may be an important but underemphasized aspect of assertiveness training. This is consistent with the research by Eisler, Frederiksen, and Peterson (1978), which showed that high-assertive subjects expected more favorable consequences from others in social situations, compared with low-assertive subjects.

Behavioral Components of Social Skill

Much of the basic research in the general area of social competence has attempted to identify behavioral components of social skill. As mentioned earlier, many of the initial studies using high and low daters were not able to show significant behavioral differences. However, in a broader review that includes individuals who describe themselves as socially anxious and avoidant, based on questionnaire responses, some preliminary conclusions about the behavioral components of social skill can be made. Dow (1985) reviewed the results of 18 studies in this area, and concluded that there is moderate evidence for the social skill relevance of nine conversational behaviors: more eye contact; more smiles; more personal attention (e.g., talking about the other person and asking questions); fewer overt or verbal indicators of anxiety such as trembling, stammers, or fidgets; more talking time; more hand gestures; fewer pauses or long latencies; more compliments; and more positive statements about third persons or things.

Obviously, not everyone who has social difficulties is low in overt behavioral skill, and not everyone who is overtly unskilled has deficits in each of these specific behaviors. However, the list does provide an overview of the types of behaviors that are often targeted for change in social skills training programs.

ASSESSMENT

Clinical Interview

Some reviews in the area of social skill have neglected to emphasize the importance of a comprehensive, behaviorally oriented clinical interview in the assessment process. Arkowitz (1981) provided an excellent review of social skills assessment procedures, in which he noted that clinicians of all orientations, including behavioral clinicians, use the clinical interview as a

major source of clinically related information. Arkowitz presented an excellent interview guide that outlined the following major areas in assessing social inadequacy:

1. Physical description of the patient
2. Behavioral observation of the patient
3. Patient's description of presenting problems and treatment goals
4. Operational definitions of problems and goals
5. Major problems other than social inadequacy
6. Effects of the social dysfunction on the person's life functioning
7. Assessment of social functioning in specific areas (i.e., same sex versus opposite sex interactions; casual versus intimate relationships; public speaking)
8. Estimates of social skill, social anxiety, and self-evaluations in each area covered above
9. Cognitions relating to social functioning
10. Sexual knowledge, experiences, and fears
11. Current living situation, with particular reference to potential social encounters
12. Description of typical day, with particular reference to social contacts
13. Current employment and educational situation
14. Current family situation
15. Interests and pleasurable leisure activities
16. Obstacles to effective social funtioning
17. History (i.e., social difficulties, education, work, family, health)

Behavioral Assessment

Social Interaction Tasks

Research studies in this area often include an analogue assessment social interaction task in which subjects interact in a brief conversation (usually 5 minutes) with a research assistant or confederate in a typical getting-acquainted, first-time conversation (Arkowitz et al., 1975; Dow, Biglan, & Glaser, 1985). Studies have differed in the extent to which these confederates are trained. In some cases, confederates have been taught to be minimally responsive—only talking for a few minutes or only talking in response to comments from the subject. It is often difficult to arrange such an assessment situation in outpatient mental health clinics—the setting most likely to attract clients requiring focused treatment for social inadequacy. Informal observation of how the client interacts with the therapist, clinic secretaries, or other clients in a group setting may provide a less desirable but more easily collected source of information.

Role-Play Situation Tasks

A number of other studies have used orally presented conversational prompts or tape-recorded prompts to elicit conversational segments from clients. Typically a situation is described: You are leaving your statistics class and the girl sitting next to you says, "I didn't understand a thing the professor said." The subject is instructed to respond out loud to the conversational prompt as if he or she were actually in the situation. The responses are tape-recorded and coded for later analysis. Variations on this basic methodology have been used by Arkowitz et al. (1975), Dow et al. (1985), and Rehm and Marston (1968), among others. A taped situations test dealing exclusively with assertive situations for women was developed by MacDonald (1978). The primary advantages of this approach include the opportunity to assess responses to a number of specific social situations by using a standardized format. The potential drawback of this approach is that since the task assesses a series of unrelated responses or conversational segments, results may not generalize well to a typical conversation (Bellack, Hersen, & Lamparski, 1979; Bellack, Hersen, & Turner, 1978, 1979).

Peer Ratings

Ratings or evaluations by peers in the socially inadequate individual's natural environment are a somewhat underused source of data—in both clinical research and clinical treatment. In the study by Arkowitz et al. (1975), which investigated differences in high- and low-frequency daters, subjects were asked to provide the names of two male and two female peers who would complete a rating form to estimate dating frequency, comfort, initiative, skill, and frequency of different types of interactions with females, as well as global social skill in heterosexual situations. Subjects were not allowed to see these ratings. An adaptation of this form was also used in the study by Dow et al. (1985).

Self-Report Assessment

Questionnaires

Virtually every research study in the area of social skill has used one or more self-report questionnaires that assess various aspects of social functioning. The use of these measures is also quite common in clinical practice among behaviorally oriented practitioners who work with socially inadequate individuals. Some of the more commonly used questionnaires would include the Social Avoidance and Distress Scale (Watson & Friend, 1969), the Fear of Negative Evaluations Scale (Watson & Friend, 1969), the Rathus Assertiveness Scale (Rathus, 1973), the College Self-Expression (Assertiveness) Scale (Galassi, DeLo, Galassi, & Bastien, 1974), the Conflict Resolution Inventory (McFall & Lillesand, 1971), and the Social Performance Survey Schedule (Lowe & Cautela, 1978). A recent scale by Beidel, Turner, Stanley, and Dancu (1989), entitled the Social Phobia and Anxiety Inventory, was designed to assess the DSM-III-R social phobia disorder.

Self-Monitoring

One of the easier ways to assess the client's social behavior in his or her natural environment is for the client to record on a daily basis the frequency of various social behaviors. Clients might be given forms that ask them to record the number of male and female individuals that they spoke with each day, the number of dates that they had each week, or instances of their assertively requesting behavior change from others. A caution in the use of these measures is that they can easily be distorted intentionally or unintentionally because of reactivity effects, demand effects, and the difficulties inherent in recalling past events accurately (Nelson, 1977). However, their use does provide the opportunity to gather data directly relevant to the client's targeted social behavior within a natural environment.

Treating Social Inadequacy and Enhancing Social Skill

Social Skills Training

At this point in time, there seems to be agreement on the relevant components of social skills training. It is unclear whether all of these components are necessary for each individual, or more specifically, it is unclear when certain components can be eliminated. Most programs are presented in a somewhat packaged format and may even be presented in a group format. In the organizational format and terms presented by Twentyman and Zimering (1979) in their research review, the major components of social skills training are as follows: (1) behavioral rehearsal of desired responses, both overt and covert; (2) modeling; (3) coaching, which involves instructing clients in appropriate behaviors; (4) feedback and reinforcement, through which successive approximations to the desired behavior are shaped; (5) homework assignments, typically to engage in certain social behaviors; (6) projected positive consequences, in which the client is taught to imagine positive reactions to

assertive responses or other social behaviors; and (7) cognitive modifications, such as self-statement retraining. At least some evidence has been found for the relevance of each of these components.

The next phase of research in this area should help concretize the process by which treatment can be tailored to the specific needs of specific socially inadequate individuals. It is unclear which aspects of social inadequacy, as assessed by which measures, are best treated by the various components. A basic distinction in this area, as described by Curran and Wessberg (1981), would be to determine whether skills deficits and/or cognitive interference mechanisms were present and to tailor treatment to the nature of the disorder that was present.

Assertiveness Training

Assertiveness skills training typically involves seven steps: (1) a didactic presentation that involves definitions of assertiveness, passiveness, and aggressiveness, as well as a discussion of basic guidelines of assertive behavior; (2) identification of specific instances of behavior change desired in the client's life, with further discussion of these instances, to help the client identify the specific changes in behavior that can be requested; (3) role-playing of the assertive request; (4) feedback about verbal and nonverbal aspects of the performance; (5) additional practice and appropriate modeling of assertive behavior by the therapist or another person; (6) real-life practice of assertive behavior (homework); and (7) discussion and feedback to determine the effectiveness and appropriateness of follow-up interventions. Support and encouragement are given throughout. In some instances, videotaping client role-plays to provide direct interpersonal feedback may be desirable.

Basic Guidelines

An example of basic guidelines that the author uses when teaching a client how to ask for specific behavior change is illustrated below.

Make sure your request is reasonable. Even if an unreasonable request were to be made skillfully—using appropriate verbal and non-verbal behavior—the request should not be viewed as assertive. It is an aggressive act to ask for something that is not appropriate, given the level of intimacy and duration of a relationship.

Speak in a clear, calm tone of voice. An angry, sarcastic tone may elicit anger and defensiveness from another person. A clear, calm tone invites serious discussion of a problem and may provide a greater opportunity to achieve changes in the other person's behavior.

Talk about how the problem makes you feel. If you emphasize your own feelings, the other individual may not feel that he or she is being criticized. For example, I might invite an argument if I said, "It is hot today," but it would be much less likely for someone to argue with me if I were to say, "I feel hot." People approach interpersonal relationships with very different ideas about how people should behave toward one another. Rather than become involved in an argument about how people should act, it is better for me to keep the conversation focused on how the other person's behavior affects me and how I would like him or her to act toward me.

Ask for specific behavior change. People are often very general when asking other people to change their behavior. W say things like, "I want you to treat me with more respect." What does that mean? For one person it may mean that, "I would like you to say hello to me when you come home from work." For another person it may be, "I don't want you to raise your voice to me and call me names." The failure to specify exactly what the other person is doing that we find unacceptable is the surest way to guarantee that the assertive process will be unsuccessful.

Don't make assumptions or mind-read. Often we assume reasons for other people's negative behavior toward us, and these assumptions may keep us from acting assertively. For example, we might say, "He's obviously mad at me and is irritating me on purpose." Sometimes we go so far as to say, "I shouldn't have to ask him for this, because he knows how I like to be treated." By making assumptions or mind-reading, we make it more difficult to communicate important feelings to others.

Don't ask why the other person acts as he or she does, or ask other questions about motives. One of the most common tendencies in conflict situations is to blame others or to ask another person, "Why do you treat me so badly?" This emphasis on why and motives often interferes with the primary goal of asking for specific behavior change.

Try to say something positive about the other person. The people who irritate us the most are often close friends and loved ones. Sometimes it is precisely because we love someone that their behavior is irritating to us. At times, it is best to support our assertive statements by putting them in the context of our positive feelings about the other person. For example, "I really like going to the movies with you, but I feel irritated and upset when we're late. I'd appreciate it if you would be ready on time."

The sample assertive statement just given shows the basic format of assertively asking for behavior change and integrates each of the guidelines mentioned in this section. The abbreviated format is: I feel _____ when you _____ ; I'd appreciate it if you would _____ .

Case Study

The approach advocated in this chapter is that the therapist should conduct a comprehensive assessment of all social difficulties, taking into consideration behavioral, cognitive, and physical factors (grooming, attractiveness, somatic symptoms, etc.), as well as a thorough assessment of other clinical disorders such as depression and anxiety that may affect the effort to provide social competence enhancement. Then a treatment plan is developed and implemented gradually, and the therapist continues to assess the effectiveness of the approach and make modifications in the plan, based on any new information that becomes available during the course of treatment. The following case study outlines this approach.

Presenting Problem and Identifying Information

Jim was a 19-year-old college sophomore who came to the outpatient clinic and reported vague feelings of loneliness and depression. He had never been involved in counseling or mental health treatment and had no family history of mental problems. He was majoring in philosophy and enjoyed reading and watching movies. He had a few close friends, both male and female, that he knew from high school, but he had not developed any close friends at college. Jim had briefly dated one girl in high school, but they had not become close. Jim had an older brother who was 23, married, and worked as a postal inspector. Jim's parents lived and worked in a city about 50 miles from the college community. Jim typically drove to visit them every other Saturday and would stay overnight. Jim was raised as a Methodist and felt that religion was important to him, although he was not involved in any church activities.

Assessment

The initial interview emphasized three major goals. First, the therapist sought to ask a wide variety of questions about psychiatric and behavioral problems, in order to rule out various disorders such as drug/alcohol abuse, agoraphobia, major depression, and psychotic symptoms. Second, the interviewer attempted to focus on social and interactional difficulties, in order to learn the antecedents, behaviors, and consequences that were involved in the feelings of loneliness and other social difficulties. Third, the interviewer attempted to develop good rapport with the client and to help the client feel comfortable. At the

end of the session, the client was given the Social Avoidance and Distress Scale (SADS), the Rathus Assertiveness Scale, and the Beck Depression Inventory (BDI) to complete in the waiting room and give to the receptionist. In addition, the client was asked to keep self-monitoring records of the number of male and female individuals that he spoke with each day for the next week.

At the second session, the assessment data were discussed briefly. The self-report inventories indicated a high level of social avoidance and distress (SADS = 22), a mild to moderate level of depression (BDI = 17), and a fairly normal level of assertiveness (Rathus = 11) (see Table 8.1). The self-monitoring records indicated that the client spoke with an average of 10 males per day and 2 females. When this information was presented to the client, it helped focus the discussion on heterosocial anxiety. The client acknowledged feeling most anxious in the presence of females—particularly attractive females. The client was asked to describe the types of thoughts that came into his mind whenever he would be likely to interact with a female, and it was discovered that he frequently engaged in negative thoughts such as, "I shouldn't look at her, she's too pretty for me," "She probably thinks I look funny," and "It's not fair that I can't have someone like her as a girlfriend."

Since the therapist was involved in conducting research studies on social competence, he had student assistants available who regularly engaged in social interaction task conversations with research subjects. After explaining the purpose of these assessments and assuring the client that the student assistant would not know that he was a therapy patient, the therapist arranged for the client to be involved in a taped social interaction task with a female assistant. Results of this assessment confirmed that the client had some difficulty interacting with a female, although the low level of his self-evaluation was more striking. The confederate rated the subject as physically attractive, which confirmed the therapist's impression that the client was average to above average in physical attractiveness.

TABLE 8.1   Treatment results

Measure	Pretest	Posttest
Self-Report Tests		
Social Avoidance and Distress Scale	22	13
Beck Depression Inventory	17	9
Rathus Assertiveness Scale	11	10
Self-Monitoring (One Week)		
Daily average # of women spoken to	2	6
Daily average # of men spoken to	10	11
Number of dates in last month	0	3
Social Interaction Task Ratings (7-Point Scales)		
Self-rating, attractiveness	1	3
Self-rating, social skill	1	3
Confederate rating, attractiveness	5	5
Confederate rating, social skill	3	4

Treatment

At the beginning of the third session, the therapist provided the client with a problem formulation and treatment plan. The therapist informed the client that he seemed to be experiencing a form of social anxiety that appeared most problematic when in the presence of females. A significant part of this anxiety involved overly strict and negative self-evaluations. The client was told that his basic level of social skill and physical attractiveness seemed to be in the normal range, but some additional experience in social interaction seemed warranted, along with a focus on improving negative self-evaluations. Through discussing these issues, a tentative treatment contract was developed whereby the client agreed to be seen for a total of 20 sessions that would focus on heterosexual social anxiety. The door was left open to renegotiate the contract as needed or to discuss other problems.

Some of the specific therapeutic activities conducted are shown in Table 8.2. Results of treatment on pre and post measures are shown in Table 8.1. Basically, the subject showed some improvements on his self-report scales and self-monitoring, as well as on the self-ratings and confederate ratings from the social interaction task. The posttest conversation was held with a different female assistant who was blind to the subject's situation.

EVOLVING TRENDS AND AREAS OF FUTURE EMPHASIS

Unlike many of the other problem areas discussed in this volume, there appears to be a recent decline in research interest concerning social skill and social inadequacy, although it is still a major area of clinical focus for a wide variety of problems. Corrigan (1990) plotted the total number of published articles and empirical reports in this area, per year from 1972 to 1987, and found a steady increase from 1972 to 1980, a peak from

TABLE 8.2   Therapeutic activities

Activity	Week Number
Client self-monitors actual social conversations.	1–20
Client completes relevant self-report assessments.	1
Behavioral assessment (social interaction task) is conducted.	2
Behavioral formulation and initial treatment plan are presented.	3
Relaxation skills are taught.	3–5
Problematic social situations that occurred in the past week are discussed, focusing on thoughts, images, and behavior.	3–20
Using interpretation, feeling reflection, and direct questioning, therapist helps client to identify specific negative thoughts that interfere with social interactions.	3–20
Cognitive therapy techniques are used to help client rationally reject those thoughts and replace negative thoughts with positive or neutral thoughts.	4–20
Client reads handouts on increasing relevant conversational skills: asking questions, giving compliments, improving nonverbal behavior. Client role-playing social conversations that utilize these skills.	7–15
Client is encouraged to engage in more frequent social situations while self-monitoring relevant target behaviors.	7–20
Therapist and client examine environmental barriers to social situations, such as the conflicting demands of going home every other weekend versus trying to develop a college social life.	8–9
Therapist and client problem-solve ways to meet more people, particularly women and develop a plan to join relevant clubs or organizations. Therapist gives homework assignment of casually asking five male friends how they met their girlfriends.	9–10
Using female graduate student, therapist assigns practice social conversations, to take place in student union.	12, 15
Therapist discusses client's grooming patterns, provides constructive feedback on dress and grooming habits.	13
Therapist encourages client to pursue more active relationships with acquaintances and to role-play asking out any women he may want to date. Therapist provides support and encouragement. Client reviews any dates he had and therapist provides suggestions and feedback, and challenges negative thoughts.	13–20
Therapist and client discuss termination issues, renegotiate treatment plan if needed.	19
Therapist conducts posttest assessments and discusses results.	20

1980 to 1984, and a steady decline from 1984 to 1987. Other authors have noted that the field appears to be growing somewhat weary of this problem and its complexities (Curran, 1979b; Dow & Craighead, 1984; McEwan, 1983), despite the demonstrated success of social skills training (Twentyman & Zimering, 1979).

The paradox of this area is that conceptual models and assessment practices have not met traditional standards of rigor for the experimental analysis of behavior, but treatment seems effective anyway. Moreover, it has been noted frequently that naive observers appear to be more effective at discriminating high and low competent groups on global ratings of social skill, as compared with trained observers using better operationalized and psychometrically superior indices of the frequency or duration of various behaviors (Conger, Wallander, Mariotto, & Ward, 1980). Additionally, it can easily take over 1,000 hours of total personnel time to record social interactions, develop a reliable behavioral coding system, train coders, and have two independent coders reliably rate all videotapes or tape recordings for one study. In short, behavioral researchers in the area of social skill appear to be on an extinction schedule. There has been little contingency between the results of basic assessment research and the effectiveness of social skills training. In fact, to the dismay of the rigorous experimental researcher, the general behaviors, such as eye contact and smiles, that were selected a priori in the early studies without research support appear to be as relevant to social skill as any other behaviors. Curran's (1979b) lament seems most appropriate: "Everyone seems to know what good and poor social skills are but no one can define them adequately" (p. 321).

The Definitional Problem

The reduction of research interest in this area stems from several sources that involve both methodological and conceptual issues. The con-

ceptual criticisms seem to focus around what Curran (1979b) referred to as the definitional problem. There have been few attempts to characterize the construct of social skill, and previous theories have largely not been responsible for the treatment and assessment methodologies that are most commonly employed. A continuing trend in this area over the next several years will be a re-examination and re-evaluation of models of social skill and competence.

The most widely accepted definition of social skill was offered by Libet and Lewinsohn (1973), who argued that social skill is the complex ability to elicit positive reinforcement and to minimize punishment received from others. Curran (1979b) criticized this definition, not for what it says but for its lack of specificity. For example, do behaviors have to be primarily social in nature to be social skills, or can any behavior qualify? Do social skills have to be overt behaviors, or should private events involved in the process of social perception be included in this definition? To what extent can one differentiate the effects of anxiety, such as behavioral avoidance and behavioral interference, from skill deficits per se? These questions, collectively, constitute a major part of the definitional problem in the area of overt social skill. Behaviorists seem relatively satisfied with the broad outline of Libet and Lewinson's definition; the problem occurs when one attempts to fill in between the lines. Future research and writing will have to wrestle with these questions.

Reinforcement in Context: A Social-Ethological Perspective

A further requirement for the field is to regain the link between social skills development and social relationship development.

The process of reinforcement and punishment is inextricably tied to the historical and current environmental contingencies that promote survival of the individual and survival of the species. Social approval is often an important reinforcer because one's survival is dependent on the cooperation of others and because reproduction of the species is dependent on the establishment and maintenance of social/sexual bonding. If social skills are behaviors that elicit reinforcement from others, then social skills, like all behaviors that directly elicit reinforcement, must be tied to the survival of the individual organism and/or the survival of the species. It appears that social interaction plays an instrumental role in developing social and cultural bonds between individuals. Social skills are simply behaviors that facilitate the development of these bonds.

Social behaviors should be considered socially skillful if they facilitate the development of social bonds and therefore increase an individual's likelihood of obtaining social reinforcement, even if those social behaviors are not directly rewarded in the conversational setting. Conversely, an individual who tells racist jokes and elicits nervous laughter from others may be reinforced by the nervous laughter. However, the net result may be that others avoid this individual and reduce their requests to engage in pleasurable or mutually supportive activity. Thus, social-affiliative bonding (and ultimately, social reinforcement) is reduced, so telling racist jokes would not be viewed as socially skillful.

Unfortunately, the ultimate goal of this broad research area cannot be achieved unless we put greater emphasis on outcome variables such as increases in social behavior in the natural environment, friendships developed, and close relationships initiated and maintained. We hope that future research will refocus on this aspect of social relationship enhancement.

The Need for Idiographic Research

Most major reviews in this area have pointed to the fact that socially inadequate individuals may not all be the same and may represent different etiological mechanisms (such as behavioral skills deficits, conditioned anxiety, cognitive interference, or physical unattractiveness). However, few studies have tried to match subject charac-

teristics to treatment. Moreover, few studies have developed assessment techniques to describe the profile of social difficulties with which a client presents. These issues must receive emphasis in order for the field to advance. Unfortunately, these types of analyses are difficult.

Dow (1985) used a complicated analysis of variance model and generalizability analysis (Cronbach, Gleser, Nanda, & Rajaratnam, 1972), to provide a way of characterizing a group of socially inadequate subjects as follows: 59.5% had no reliably indicated overt social skill problems, 11.9% had general difficulties across a set of 9 behaviors nominated as relevant to social inadequacy, and 28.6% had specific differential difficulties in overt social behavior. This approach has not yet been linked with treatment outcome research, but it provides an example of a way to conduct individually based or "idiographic" outcome research.

BEHAVIORAL CONSISTENCY AND BEHAVIORISM

The terms social skill and social inadequacy both seem to imply a certain consistency in human behavior. One might not bother to target a potentially problematic conversational behavior if the difficulty occurred infrequently or in only one narrow type of setting. This raises the question of how social skills training can be consistent with the theoretical perspectives of behaviorism and cognitive-behaviorism, both of which minimize the role of general personality traits (Curran, 1979a; McFall, 1982). In the view taken here, the primary distinction between trait theory and behavioral models is not in the degree of consistency in human behavior, although behaviorists do generally argue for less consistency in human behavior than do trait theorists. The primary distinction is that trait theory construes consistency in behavior as evidence of hypothetical entities that cause behavior (Wiggins, 1973, p. 366), and behaviorists argue that behavioral consistency, to the extent it occurs, is due to the same cognitive-behavioral factors that determine all behavior.

At least three specific mechanisms may be involved. First, some degree of behavioral consistency would be predicted by cognitive-behavioral models if for no other reason than that a person's physical appearance and voice qualities are relatively consistent across time. Consistency in these stimulus conditions may elicit relatively consistent behavior from others, which further serves to elicit relatively consistent behavior from an individual. Other stimuli that remain relatively constant in a person's life and may promote a certain consistency in behavior would include: home, members of the family, job, friends, and other aspects of the social and physical environment.

A second factor that may promote consistency in behavior is that a person's history of reinforcement changes only gradually over time. Individuals who have been reinforced for certain behavior will not immediately stop emitting that behavior simply because the schedule of reinforcement changes or because reinforcement is terminated. Extinction and the modification of behavior in accordance with different schedules of reinforcement both take place over time. Thus, there may be some consistency in behavior due to the history of reinforcement and the ambiguity over what behaviors are reinforced in different settings.

A third factor that may promote consistency in behavior involves the direct reinforcement of consistent behavior as a response class and the punishment of inconsistent behavior. As agents of social control, we appear to reinforce consistency and punish inconsistency selectively in our friends and associates all the time:

It's good to see that you're back to your old self again.

Who are you trying to fool anyway? You don't know how to dance.

I thought you didn't like pistachio ice cream.

I made your favorite dinner today, honey.

I hate it when you're so hard to predict.

It seems easier to deal with someone who is consistent. In other words, we can best elicit reinforcement and avoid punishment when the schedule of reinforcement is consistent. Thus, it is in our best interest to reinforce consistency and punish inconsistency in others.

All three of these arguments were designed to show that some consistency in behavior is not antithetical to a cognitive-behavioral perspective. In fact, there are good reasons to predict a certain degree of consistency, based on learning theory. The essential difference between trait and operant models concerns different conceptualizations of what causes behavior—consistent or otherwise. It is on a secondary level of importance that some behaviorists and trait theorists have argued about the degree of consistency in human behavior.

Within a cognitive-behavioral perspective, social skill may be viewed as a label for a variety of social behaviors that often elicit reinforcement and minimize punishment from others. Such a label could be characterized as an intervening variable, in the language of MacCorquodale and Meehl (1948). Intervening variables merely serve to describe empirical relationships in a summary or abstract way, and hypothetical constructs refer to presumed entities or processes that are not observable.

Recent discussions of these issues have pointed to a serious problem: the degree of behavioral consistency and situational specificity of social skills has not been adequately investigated. Additional empirical research is needed, as it is the only way to determine the degree of consistency in human behavior.

CONCLUSIONS

There is clear evidence that social-interpersonal problems are relevant to most types of psychopathology and are an important problem in their own right among normal individuals. Much research has been conducted in this area and effective treatments have been developed. However, many researchers have realized in the last 10 years that this area presents a number of complicated conceptual and methodological problems that are difficult to resolve, and there has been a recent decrease in research in this area. Future research will require theoretical and methodological advances in order to move the field beyond its current level of knowledge and understanding.

Treatment Resources

Alberti, R. E., & Emmons, M. L. (1986). *Your perfect right: A guide to assertiveness training*. San Luis Obispo, CA: Impact.

Becker, R. E., Heimberg, R. G., & Bellack, A. S. (1987). *Social skills training for depression*. New York: Pergamon.

Glaser, S. R. (1980). *Toward communication competency: Developing interpersonal skills*. New York: Holt, Rinehart and Winston.

Kelly, J. A. (1982). *Social-skills training: A practical guide for interventions*. New York: Springer.

Lange, A. J., & Jakubowski, P. (1976). *Responsible assertive behavior: Cognitive/behavioral procedures for trainers*. Champaign, IL: Research Press.

Liberman, R. P., DeRisi, W. J., & Mueser, K. T. (1989). *Social skills training for psychiatric patients*. New York: Pergamon.

Wilkinson, J., & Canter, S. (1982). *Social skills training manual: Assessment, programme design, and management of training*. New York: Wiley.

CHAPTER 9

Obesity and Eating Disorders

Linda Wilcoxon Craighead

Betty G. Kirkley

Obesity and the eating disorders, anorexia nervosa and bulimia nervosa, are discussed here together because of their common foci on weight, weight-related cognitions, and eating and exercise behaviors. Although bulimia nervosa and anorexia nervosa are established psychiatic disorders, obesity is not, and there is no evidence that overweight people in general display greater psychopathology than the general population or can be characterized by any particular personality traits. However, about half of the obese who seek treatment report binge eating, and for about half of these it is of sufficient severity to warrant a diagnosis of bulimia. Despite many differences, the goals of behavioral treatment for obesity and the eating disorders are similar: to normalize eating and exercise behaviors and to alter maladaptive weight-related cognitions. This chapter will first describe various problems related to eating behavior and indicate how they may be related. Then specific treatment approaches for each type of problem will be discussed and the research

evaluating those treatment approaches will be reviewed.

TYPES OF EATING PROBLEMS

Obesity is a medical condition characterized by excess body fat. In practice, however, it is typically defined as overweight, excess body weight relative to a particular standard, i.e. the Metropolitan Insurance Company's height-weight tables (1983). Generally, 20% to 40% above desirable weight is considered moderately overweight, 40% to 100% is moderate to severe, and over 100% is morbidly overweight. Measures of body fat (e.g., skinfold or underwater weighing) are available but are usually not necessary to determine health risk or evaluate treatment response. Clinical outcomes are usually discussed in terms of pounds lost or decreases in percent overweight. Body Mass Index (BMI), which is weight/height^2, correlates better with body-fat measures and is sometimes reported in research studies.

About 15% of men and 20% of women are at a weight (i.e., more than 20% above desirable weight) that increases their risk for cardiovascular disease and a number of other medical disorders. Losing weight has clearly been demonstrated to result in improved glucose tolerance, decreased blood pressure, and decreased cholesterol and triglycerides. The negative health consequences of obesity generally increase with degree of obesity but vary with individual characteristics. For example, fat deposits above the waist, more often found in men, are more of a health risk than fat deposits around the hips, which are more characteristic of women. Although the health risks due to mild overweight are typically minimal, if a person is mildly overweight *and* has diabetes, high blood pressure, or high cholesterol, a weight loss of even 10 pounds may significantly reduce the need for medication and reduce risk for additional health problems. Thus, from a behavioral medicine perspective, obesity would be treated to improve health, and treatment would focus on those with the most health risk, primarily men and the severely overweight.

In actuality, most people who seek to lose weight are women who do so primarily, if not entirely, for cosmetic/social reasons. By adolescence, a clear sex difference in weight focus and eating has emerged. For girls, higher weights are associated with lower self-esteem, and by age 18, as many as 80% of females report they "feel" fat or wish to lose weight. Young males are more likely to want to gain weight. It appears that cultural pressures lead young women to try to maintain low weights that require considerable "restraint"—that is, conscious efforts to ignore internal hunger cues and restrict intake. Paradoxically, such restraint increases the likelihood of binge eating and subsequently becoming upset or depressed over dieting failures. Thus, it is women who are most vulnerable to negative appraisals of overweight, most likely to initiate weight loss efforts, and as a result, most likely to develop eating disorders.

Bulimia nervosa is characterized by loss of control over eating. It takes the form of recurrent binge eating (large amounts in short periods of time) accompanied by compensatory behavior such as self-induced vomiting, purgative or diuretic abuse, strenuous exercise, and/or strict dieting. Through these extreme measures, most individuals with the disorder are able to maintain a normal body weight, so the extreme concern over body shape and weight, rather than actual overweight, is the salient aspect of the disorder.

Bulimia nervosa is found primarily in young women. Although no adequate epidemiological study of the disorder has been conducted, surveys of young women attending colleges and in medical clinics have generally found that from 1 to 2% report symptoms that are consistent with the diagnosis, and a much larger percentage report less severe binge eating (Cooper & Fairburn, 1983; Pyle et al., 1983). It is impossible to determine from the data what proportion of these may have only a transitory problem. The prevalence among males appears to be substantially lower (Halmi, Falk, & Schwartz, 1981).

The negative physical consequences of bulimia nervosa are primarily those of the purging method(s) used. Frequent vomiting, diuretics, and purgative use can cause electrolyte disturbance, which can lead to cardiac arrhythmias and cardiac arrest in otherwise healthy people (Mitchell, Pyle, Eckert, Hatukami, & Lentz, 1983). Individuals who induce emesis frequently experience erosion of the dental enamel and chronic sore throat; those who use purgatives often experience constipation and diarrhea.

In most cases the psychological symptoms of the disorder are more severe than the physiological results. Since most bulimics find their eating pattern and loss of control very distressing, it is not surprising that numerous investigators have documented low self-esteem and high rates of depression among individuals seeking treatment (Fairburn, Kirk, O'Connor, & Cooper, 1987; Kirkley, Schneider, Agras, & Bachman, 1985).

The primary characteristic of anorexia nervosa is the refusal to maintain a minimal normal weight (i.e., less than 85% of expected weight for age/height). In addition there is intense fear of weight gain, distorted body image, a very restricted eating pattern (often accompanied by excessive exercise), and amenorrhea. Frequently, depression is also present. About half can be described as bulimic anorectics since they do binge and purge. However, what anorexics consider a binge is often small compared to what bulimics label a binge. Anorexia usually starts in adolescence. If left untreated, the person may die from starvation or related medical problems. Anorexics typically minimize the severity of their illness and must be compelled by others to receive treatment. Approximately half of anorexics have a single episode and recover but for many, anorexia becomes a chronic life-threatening condition in which the individual continues to have social and psychiatric problems and struggles to maintain a healthy weight. Individuals often report a history with multiple problems associated with eating, i.e., various periods of obesity, anorexia, and bulimia. The incidence of anorexia is low; studies report a range of .1% to 1% of females between the ages of 12 and 25.

ASSESSMENT OF EATING BEHAVIOR AND COGNITION

Daily self-monitoring records are the primary method used to assess eating patterns. These records can be simple or very comprehensive, providing information about caloric levels, nutrient intake, exercise, number of binges and purges, types of food chosen, when and where food is eaten, and emotional states. Such information is used both to plan interventions and to assess the effects of treatment.

Structured interviews based on DSM-III-R criteria are typically used to confirm a diagnosis of anorexia or bulimia. Several self-report measures are also available to assess the behaviors and cognitions associated with these problems. Among the most widely used are the Bulit (Smith & Thelan, 1984), the Binge Eating Scale (Gormally, Black, Darton, & Rardin, 1982), the Eating Attitudes Test (Garner, Olmstead, & Polivy, 1983), and the Eating Inventory (Stunkard and Merrick, 1985).

BEHAVIORAL TREATMENT FOR OBESITY

The behavioral approach to weight loss was based on work done in the 1970s in which operant principles, in the form of stimulus control techniques, were applied to eating behavior. The assumptions were that overweight people "overeat," i.e. have an obese eating style. Changes in these eating behaviors were expected to allow people to lose weight at a slow, steady rate and maintain that loss. However, it is now unclear whether there is an "obese" eating style or that the overweight typically "overeat."

Regardless of prior eating style, to achieve weight loss, behavioral programs must establish a negative energy balance (fewer calories ingested than energy expended), not just a controlled current eating style. Weight reflects both past and current eating behaviors. Adaptive dieting strategies are taught, to restrict intake to a modest degree; maladaptive strategies (severe restriction) are strongly discouraged, as they tend to trigger unplanned eating. Behavioral strategies do appear to be effective in setting up a negative energy balance, but it seems to be difficult to maintain that level of restraint without ongoing group support. Few participants continue to lose weight once behavioral programs are over.

On the other hand, to achieve weight maintenance (prevent weight gain) only a zero energy balance needs to be maintained. This does not appear to be quite as difficult. Many participants maintain well for at least the first year after a program. It is not clear if this is due primarily to continued mild restraint. Some data suggest the previously overweight may have to maintain a slightly subnormal intake indefinitely to maintain any weight loss. However, increased activity levels could maintain a zero energy balance even if calorie intake returned to pretreatment or "normalized" levels.

At the present time, increased activity appears to play the larger role in maintenance; strategies to restrict food intake and motivation to adhere to those strategies appear to play a larger role in initial weight loss.

Behavioral programs for obesity are typically conducted in small groups that meet weekly with a trained leader for a specified period, usually from 12 to 24 weeks. Treatment is presented within a psycho-educational model and focuses on changing daily habits. The participant learns a general strategy for making changes in his or her behavior (the self-control model), as well as specific techniques proven useful in changing weight-related behaviors. Research has not specified the particular contribution of any technique. The only technique that seems to be indispensable is self-monitoring and that, by itself, is not sufficient for more than a few weeks. Clients are encouraged to try all the techniques and then to identify and focus on those that are most helpful to them. At the current time, there is little research to identify subtypes of obesity or specific client characteristics that predict response to treatment. However, researchers hope to develop measures to screen out individuals unlikely to respond to behavioral treatment and to match patients most likely to benefit from specific treatment components.

Adherence (determining whether individuals actually use the techniques they learn) is a major issue in behavioral treatment. Self-reports of use of techniques must usually be relied on and may be inaccurate. Self-reports typically indicate high use of techniques during treatment but little continued use after treatment. Also, reports of

habit change appear to correlate only modestly with weight loss in treatment. Stalonas, Johnson, and Christ (1978) suggested that behavioral programs may be effective primarily because the techniques continuously prompt attention to weight loss. If that is the case, many techniques could work.

Brownell's (1989) *Learn to Eat* program will be used to illustrate a state-of-the-art, comprehensive, cognitive-behavioral treatment. Readers are referred to this manual and others listed at the end of the chapter for greater details on implementation. This program consists of the components described below.

Lifestyle Techniques

Personal Behavioral Analysis

These techniques set up self-monitoring of weight, food intake, and so forth, in order to do detailed behavioral analyses that identify problematic patterns.

Altering Eating Style

These techniques are used to slow the rate of eating so less will be consumed during a normal mealtime. Regular, planned meals and snacks are emphasized, since most people overeat if they wait until they are very hungry.

Stimulus Control

These techniques minimize exposure to food cues, make it harder to eat impulsively, and introduce new cues for healthy, controlled eating. The goal is to refocus the client on internal hunger cues rather than environmental cues for eating.

Altering Behavioral Chains

These techniques focus on ways to disrupt behavior sequences that lead to eating. Typical problem behavior chains involve eating when tired, lonely, bored, depressed, or anxious. The goal is to identify high-risk situations and teach the client to avoid, escape, or distract with other activities. It is easier to interrupt the chain early, before an urge to eat occurs. Introducing a 10-minute delay once an urge occurs is also used, since many urges subside if not acted on.

Exercise

Jeffrey and Wing (1979) found self-reported exercise was unrelated to weight loss during treatment. Adding an exercise component to traditional behavioral programs produces only slightly better weight loss during treatment. However, programs including exercise have demonstrated better maintenance (Craighead & Blum, 1989; Dahlkoetter, Callahan, & Linton, 1979; Stalonas, Johnson, & Christ, 1978). In addition, a number of correlational analyses have shown that maintenance of weight loss was associated with continuing exercise (Hoiberg, Berard, Watten, & Caine, 1984; Marston & Criss, 1984). Exercise has the additional benefits of improved muscle tone and health, reduction in negative moods, and improved self-esteem.

The major problem with exercise is adherence. Reviews of exercise adherence (Martin & Dubbert, 1982) indicate that fewer than half of people beginning an exercise program will be exercising after 3 to 6 months. Of obese subjects, only about one-third continue to exercise at recommended levels after one year (Katahn, Pleas, Thackrey, & Wallston, 1982). Supervised exercise groups have been used to support and reinforce exercise; participation in this type of exercise group is typically quite high. It may be that supervised exercise is important initially to establish exercise as a habit, but that individualized programs compatible with a person's lifestyle are more likely to be maintained in the long run.

Attitude Techniques

The role cognitions may play in overeating has not been clearly specified. O'Connor and

Dowrick (1987) reported significant differences between normal weight, overweight, and previously overweight groups on a measure of eating-relevant self-statements. Also, adaptive cognitions have been shown to correlate with success in treatment (Sjoberg & Person, 1979; Straw et al., 1984). However, treatment programs including strong cognitive elements have not proved to be superior to more traditional programs (Collins, Wilson, & Rothblum, 1986; Mahoney, Rogers, Straw, & Mahoney, 1977).

The role of emotions is more clearly established than the role of cognitions specifically. Lingswiler, Crowther, and Stephens (1987) found that overweight subjects report greater fluctuations over the day in anxiety, hostility, and depression than do nonoverweight subjects. In a review of the literature, Ganley (1989) concluded that obese subjects may be more likely than normal-weight subjects to eat to reduce negative affect, but individual differences on a number of variables must be taken into account. No simple model explained emotional eating in the obese. Cognitive techniques are frequently used to cope with negative affect and may turn out to be useful for those who eat in response to negative affect.

Relapse prevention strategies were first developed and validated in the treatment of alcohol abuse and have now been modified to apply to overeating. Marlatt and Gordon's (1985) relapse model has received some empirical support in studies of dietary lapses among obese diabetics (Kirkley & Fisher, 1988; Grilo, Shiffman, & Wing, 1989). It was notable that most lapses occurred in a limited range of predictable high-risk situations and that situations involving negative affect were most likely to lead to overeating. A combination of both cognitive and behavioral coping responses was reported to be most effective in handling urges to eat.

Relationship Techniques

It has been difficult to document a specific effect of relationship techniques on weight loss, although they are widely used. Since many clients have difficulty being assertive around food issues or asking for help in avoiding or coping with high-risk situations, behavioral rehearsal is typically used to teach new ways to respond to these social situations. Brownell, Heckerman, and Westlake (1979) found a strong, positive effect on both subjects' and spouses' weights when spouses were included in treatment, but others have not replicated these results. In a program that did not include spouses, Black and Threlfall (1988) found that overweight subjects with normal-weight partners lost more weight than those with overweight partners. Thus overweight spouses may particularly need to be included in treatment in order to enlist their support more effectively.

Nutrition

Behavioral programs initially paid little attention to nutrition and avoided specific diet plans, as the focus was on changing eating style and habits. The most effective current programs include flexible, exchange-type diets and daily calorie goals of approximately 1500 for men and 1200 for women. Jeffrey and Wing (1979) found that self-reported calorie intake was the single best predictor of weight loss in behavioral treatment.

In addition to greater awareness of calories, increased attention has been paid to nutrient values. Rats given access to a varied diet high in fat and sugar gain weight quickly, although they remain at normal weight when given unlimited access to plain rat chow (Sclafani & Springer, 1976). High fat was more problematic than high sugar. Drewnowski and Greenwood (1983) report that in taste tests obese persons typically prefer higher fat content than normal-weight persons but not higher sweetness. Thus, reduction in fat intake has become a major focus. Many individuals find it easier to alter content than to restrict amounts, so this focus may help moderate some of the negative effects of prolonged restraint.

Outcome of Behavioral Treatment of Obesity

Brownell and Wadden (1986) surveyed controlled trials of behavior therapy for obesity and found that: (1) average weight loss and weight maintenance had gradually improved over two decades of research, and (2) the primary factor explaining the improvement was longer treatment. Similarly, Bennett (1986) analyzed results from 105 behavioral studies and found weight loss was positively associated with treatment duration, hours of contact, and therapist experience. Treatment length rather than content may be the critical factor. Perri, Nezu, Patti, and McCann (1989) found that extending treatment from 20 to 40 weeks (by introducing the same procedures but more gradually) resulted in larger losses both at 40 weeks and at follow-up.

Average weight-loss data are useful but do not accurately reflect the failure of dropouts or the variability in outcome for those who complete treatment. Although average losses are much lower, Kirschenbaum (1988) reported that the 44% categorized as "responders" in his program lost an average of 46 pounds over 3 months. Depending on exact criteria used, 30% to 50% of individuals in behavioral programs would be considered "nonresponders" (do not lose at the expected rate of $\frac{1}{2}$ pound per week). Thus, behavioral treatment appears to be the treatment of choice, but new approaches for nonresponders are clearly needed.

Follow-ups of more than one year are a fairly recent addition to the literature. Brownell and Jeffrey (1987) reported that follow-ups beyond 2 years showed a consistent trend toward weight regain. It is difficult to interpret long-term results since many individuals repeatedly gain and lose weight, and others seek additional treatment. The fact that weight regain reaches an asymptote near or slightly below the individual's baseline weight has led some researchers (Kramer, Jeffrey, Forster, & Snell, 1989) to conclude that biological processes exert pressure toward a "set" weight that gradually overrides effects of efforts to change habits. As there are no long-term control groups, it is not clear if people who never received treatment would have continued to gain or stayed about the same weight. Clearly a small percentage of behaviorally treated patients keep weight off over the long run, but that is more the exception than the rule. Jordan, Canavan & Steer (1987) reported that subjects who maintained their losses 6 to 10 years later were characterized by use of carefully planned snacks, more regular exercise, and use of alternative activities to displace eating.

Current thinking views obesity as a chronic condition that requires long-term, perhaps lifetime, maintenance treatment. The work of Perri and colleagues (Perri et al., 1988) illustrates the best of current approaches. Their program involved 20 weeks of weekly treatment followed by a year-long maintenance program of 26 bi-weekly, therapist-led, problem-solving sessions, plus a social influence program involving peer support and financial incentives, an aerobic exercise program, or both. Groups receiving any type of posttreatment program maintained an average of 83% of their losses at the end of the year (23 pounds), significantly more than those receiving no maintenance program (7 pounds). The group receiving all components demonstrated essentially perfect maintenance (30 pounds).

Bjorvell and Rosner (1985) described a program for the severely overweight, involving 6 weeks of "day treatment" that included a 600-calorie diet, exercise, behavior therapy, and training in cooking, followed by a 4-year maintenance program in which weekly booster sessions and weigh-ins were provided. In addition, participants could return for 2-week stays in the day treatment program, as needed to avoid relapse. Average losses of 28 pounds were reported at the end of the 4-year program. Thus, long-term, flexible programs that provide continued support, monitoring, and access to additional help as needed appear to be necessary for successful long-term management for many, particularly the more severely obese.

Enhancing Standard Treatment

Behavior therapy has frequently been combined with more aggressive weight-loss approaches in the hope that behavioral strategies would serve to maintain losses no matter how the weight was initially lost. Current efforts have been disappointing, suggesting that maintenance of weight loss is far more complex than originally anticipated.

In a review of controlled trials that combined behavior therapy with anorexiants, Craighead and Agras (1991) concluded that although appetite suppressants increase initial weight loss, weight regain occurs once medication is withdrawn. In the long run, combinations were never more effective than behavior therapy alone. Similar results were reported in the first study of a new antidepressant, fluoxetine, combined with behavior therapy (Marcus et al., 1990). However, it is possible that long-term treatment with medications may be useful for some individuals not able to manage internal appetitive cues with behavioral strategies alone.

Similar patterns have been reported in controlled trials of behavior therapy, very low-calorie diet, and their combination (Wadden & Stunkard, 1986; Wadden, Stunkard, & Liebschutz, 1989); at 3-year follow-up there were no differences. It may be that aggressive weight-loss approaches are inherently incompatible with a behavioral approach, but further work may find effective ways to utilize behavioral methods to achieve maintenance after large, rapid weight losses produced by other methods.

The presence of binge eating has been noted as a predictor of poorer response to standard behavioral treatment programs (Keefe, Wyshogrod, Weinberger, & Agras, 1984). In an effort to be more effective with obese bingers, Marcus, Wing, and Hopkins (1988) modified their standard program to emphasize meal regularity, intake of complex carbohydrates, and activity as an alternative to overeating, but it was no more effective than their standard program. Obese binge eaters were more likely to drop out of treatment than nonbinge eaters, but those who remained in treatment lost as much weight as nonbinge eaters. Binge eaters showed more weight regain at 6-month follow-up, but by one year there were again no differences. At all points, binge eaters reported greater depression and distress, and more maladaptive diet behavior than nonbinge eaters. Future work will probably involve additional modifications, drawing more from techniques developed for bulimia nervosa.

Prevention/Early Intervention

The difficulty of sustaining weight loss and the fact that behavioral techniques appear to be more effective for normalizing habits than for losing weight have led some researchers to focus on treating overweight children and on preventing obesity. Most overweight children do not "grow out of it" and do become obese adults; their health and self-esteem are often adversely affected. However, it is not healthy to restrict children's calories too severely while they are still growing. If the rate of weight gain can be slowed, a goal compatible with behavioral treatment, the child's increases in height allow the child to become gradually less overweight.

Child programs include the same major components as adult programs but typically include parental involvement. Epstein and his colleagues (1985) have provided the most systematic study of variables affecting family-based treatment for pre-adolescent obesity.

Two-thirds of obese adults were not obese as children but became obese as adults, usually by adding 1 to 2 pounds per year between the ages of 20 and 50 (Garn & Clark, 1976). Forster, Jeffrey, Schmid, and Kramer (1988) demonstrated the feasibility of a low-cost program for normal-weight adults interested in preventing weight gain. The program included newsletters, return postcards, financial incentives (returning participants' own money), and an optional 4-week educational course. Participants averaged a 2-pound loss over the year in the program while the control group stayed essentially the same in weight. Likewise, one large-scale community educational campaign, designed to reduce cardiac risk factors, demonstrated no weight gain in the intervention town, but the control town showed a gain of one pound over a year-long period. Thus, efforts to establish low-cost, easily available programs for the not-yet-overweight and the mildly overweight, focusing more on increasing fitness than on restraint, may be an effective public health approach to obesity. Teaching adolescents and adults appropriate, healthy ways to prevent creeping weight gain, and to avoid maladaptive dieting strategies that promote an unhealthy pattern of weight loss and gain may prevent obesity and eating disorders.

Worksite Programs

Harnessing the power of the social environment appears to be the major factor to consider in developing large-scale efforts for weight loss/obesity prevention. Brownell (1986) has shown that clinic programs are not as effective when offered conveniently at low cost at the worksite. Attrition is high, often 50%, and weight losses are smaller. These problems appear to be similar to those reported for various self-help and commercial groups (e.g., Weight Watchers), although little empirical evaluation of such programs has been done. Large-scale programs appear to attract more people who are less motivated than do clinic programs. A different approach pioneered by Brownell is to set up highly publicized group weight-loss competitions at worksites, such as comparing employees at two local banks or setting up two teams at a factory. Cost and attrition are usually very low and losses are similar to those of clinic programs. Apparently the competitions provide high motivation and group support, which appear to be more important than educational or behavioral stategies, at least for these samples.

Cognitive-Behavioral Treatments for Bulimia Nervosa

Cognitive Model of Treatment

The cognitive perspective on bulimia nervosa conceptualizes the bulimic's tendency to evaluate herself largely in terms of her shape and/or weight as the central feature in the disorder (Fairburn, 1988a). This tremendous over-concern with body size is thought to lead to the formation of rigid food and calorie rules. Paradoxically, dietary restraint and rigid food rules have been shown to contribute to the development of binge eating (Polivy & Herman, 1985). When it becomes clear that dietary restraint alone is not adequate to maintain a satisfactory weight within the context of binge eating, then self-induced vomiting, purgatives, extreme exercise, or other strict weight-control measures seem to be perfect solutions. Unfortunately, such approaches exacerbate the dietary restraint and over-concern with weight that contributed to the initial binge eating. A vicious cycle is established, in which binge eating and purging become increasingly out of control. Cognitive-behavioral treatment attempts to interrupt this cycle in both the cognitive and behavioral dimensions. Fairburn's (1984) program is an example of such a treatment conducted on an outpatient basis.

Description of Cognitive-Behavioral Procedures

The first phase of Fairburn's treatment program typically lasts about 8 weeks and focuses on reestablishing self-control over eating. Sessions are usually scheduled twice weekly, although severe cases may require three or four appointments per week. During this phase the rationale for treatment is provided, and the danger of self-induced vomiting and purgative abuse is explained. The patient is asked to weigh weekly and to self-

monitor her food intake; these practices are continued throughout treatment. The patient is then instructed to restrict eating to three or four conventional mealtimes and one or two planned snacks. Since many bulimics have adopted a pattern of frequent meal-skipping, the regular meal pattern often results in a significant reduction in hunger. In order to limit eating outside of mealtimes, strategies that limit the availability of food and provide for incompatible activities are utilized. At each session the patient defines behavioral goals that are followed up at the next session. During this phase the frequency of binge eating and vomiting typically reduces substantially. Significantly, vomiting is not directly addressed, as the cognitive view of bulimia nervosa suggests that vomiting will usually cease when overeating stops. Once a regular eating pattern is established and binge eating becomes intermittent, the emphasis shifts to examining the factors that maintain the eating problem. Fairburn advocates that patients who fail to make sufficient progress during Stage 1 should be transferred to another form of treatment (e.g., inpatient), as they are unlikely to make progress with continued cognitive-behavioral treatment.

Stage 2 of treatment usually consists of eight weekly appointments and is more cognitively oriented. During this phase the patient identifies the circumstances in which loss of control typically occurs and is aided in developing more adaptive coping strategies and problem solving (Goldfried & Goldfried, 1975). Thoughts and beliefs that are interfering with behavior change are identified, and the patient is trained to replace them with more adaptive thoughts by using cognitive procedures similar to those employed by Beck (1976). The maladaptive thoughts usually center around an irrational over-concern with body size. Finally, the patient is encouraged to introduce "forbidden" foods into her diet gradually and to confront avoided situations.

Stage 3 typically consists of three sessions at 2-week intervals. The patient is encouraged to continue to relax food rules and dieting and to maintain a regular eating pattern. In addition, she is encouraged to develop and adopt strategies for dealing with future lapses.

Cognitive-behavioral bulimia treatment, as applied in practice, often differs significantly from the protocol laid out by Fairburn. For example, it has frequently been adapted to a group format, treatment sessions are often held weekly throughout, and many therapists continue treatment for significantly more than the 20 weeks suggested by Fairburn. Unfortunately, no research has compared the effectiveness of group versus individual treatment or massed versus spread-out sessions, although trends suggest that group treatment may be somewhat less effective than individual sessions.

Evaluation of Cognitive Model of Treatment

A number of controlled research studies have consistently shown cognitive-behavioral treatment to be a reasonably effective approach that results in significant reductions in binge eating, vomiting, depression, and weight-related misconceptions (Wilson, 1987; Garner, Fairburn, & Davis, 1987). A review by Craighead & Agras (1991) indicates that cognitive-behavioral treatment results in significant reductions of binge eating and vomiting (mean reduction of binges ranges from 63% to 96%) at the end of treatment, with 20% to 80% of subjects abstaining from vomiting. Bulimics placed on waiting lists have in every study failed to improve (Lacey, 1983; Huon & Brown, 1985; Lee & Rush, 1986; Freeman, Barry, Dunkeld-Turnbull, & Henderson, 1988). Furthermore, Kirkley et al. (1985) found cognitive-behavioral treatment to be significantly more effective at posttreatment and to have fewer dropouts than a nondirective treatment plus self-monitoring.

The maintenance of therapeutic effects with cognitive-behavioral treatment is promising but somewhat inconsistent across studies. Whereas some studies have shown deterioration in patient symptoms at follow-up (Kirkley et al., 1985), most have reported good maintenance or enhanced progress (Fairburn, Kirk, O'Conner, & Cooper, 1986; Wilson, Rossiter, Kleinfield, & Lindholm, 1986). Indeed, the longest follow-up period to date (3 years) suggests that most patients can maintain or improve their results over time (Fairburn, 1988b).

Anxiety-Reduction Model of Treatment

Rosen and Leitenberg's exposure and response-prevention (ERP) treatment (Rosen & Leitenberg, 1984) is based on an anxiety-reduction model of bulimia nervosa and is derived from current behavioral treatments for obsessive-compulsive disorders (Foa & Steketee, 1979). The anxiety-reduction model, like the cognitive model, posits that bulimics have an extreme fear of weight gain that leads to extreme anxiety following binge eating. According to this model, vomiting reduces this anxiety and eventually comes to serve an escape function similar to obsessive-compulsive rituals. Once the escape response is established, the bulimic has little reason to resist her urges to eat, and binge eating usually becomes more frequent and severe. Thus, according to this model, the anxiety-escape response of vomiting becomes the driving force that must be controlled in bulimia nervosa.

Exposure and Response-Prevention Procedures

Exposure and response-prevention treatment (ERP) has two basic components: 1) exposure to the feared stimulus (e.g., eating forbidden foods), and 2) prevention of the escape response (i.e. vomiting). It is usually not conducted with patients who primarily use laxatives.

In order to conduct ERP treatment, the therapist must determine what foods are avoided when the bulimic cannot vomit and the types and quantities of food that typically lead to vomiting.

This is done through self-monitoring and test meals. The bulimic is asked to record all food and liquid intake, the amount of anxiety associated with each eating episode, and whether she considered it a binge. Based on the self-monitoring results, three test meals are tailored to the individual. The first is usually a large dinner and occurs in the clinic, although the bulimic is left alone. The other test meals usually consist of a high-carbohydrate food (e.g., spaghetti) and a sweet snack (e.g., ice cream or candy bar). The patient is instructed to eat as much as she can without vomiting afterwards, and during the meal the patient periodically relates her thoughts into a tape recorder. She is instructed to not vomit for at least $2\frac{1}{2}$ hours after the test meal. The test meals provide an indication of the severity of food avoidance.

At the beginning of treatment (e.g., first 6 weeks), sessions are typically massed (e.g., scheduled three times per week) in order to speed up the learning process, and session frequency is reduced as improvement occurs. During treatment sessions the patient is encouraged to eat an amount of a forbidden food that would normally cause her to vomit, while the therapist focuses the bulimic's attention on her thoughts and feelings, which are usually about weight gain. Through this process the therapist can challenge the patient's cognitions and provide relevant information. The therapist stays with the patient until the urge to vomit passes; this is often up to 2 hours in the beginning but shortens with time. Once the bulimic has shown improvement in session, she is encouraged to change her eating habits at home, and progress is followed via patient self-monitoring. This usually focuses on moving toward a regular meal pattern and including previously forbidden foods.

Evaluation of Exposure plus Response-Prevention Treatment

The efficacy of exposure plus response-prevention (ERP) treatment in bulimia has been investigated with both single-subject designs and controlled studies, although small subject numbers have been typical. This is probably due to the relative difficulty of adapting this treatment strategy to a group format. In general, however, these investigations have suggested that ERP also is a reasonably effective treatment for the majority of subjects. For example, Leitenberg, Gross, Peterson, and Rosen (1984) reported that four of five women receiving ERP substantially reduced binge eating and vomiting, and two of them completely stopped. Only one subject showed no improvement. Similarly, Rossiter and Wilson (1985) found that two of three patients receiving ERP stopped binge eating and vomiting and one failed to improve. These results were generally confirmed in an open clinical trial of ERP, conducted in a private practice (Giles, Young, & Young, 1985). Of 34 women entered into ERP treatment, 79% were improved (50% to 79% reduction in vomiting) and 62% were significantly improved (80% to 100% reduction). Excluding dropouts (18%), 89% improved and 75% improved significantly, including 11 patients who stopped vomiting completely. These results were maintained at follow-up.

Controlled Evaluations: Combining and Comparing Treatments

The apparent success of two treatment approaches for bulimia nervosa inevitably led to investigations designed to determine if a combination treatment would be superior to the single treatments alone. Leitenberg, Rosen, Gross, Nudelman, and Vara (1988) compared four groups: ERP conducted in a single setting (i.e. the clinic); ERP conducted in multiple settings (i.e. clinic, home, and restaurant); a no-exposure group that was said to be similar to cognitive-behavior therapy; and a waiting list group. In this investigation the treatment was conducted in groups of three. Again, the waiting list failed to improve and all three treatments did improve. Both the multiple and single-setting ERP treatments were found to be effective, resulting respectively in 67% and 73% reductions in vomiting at posttreatment and 85% and 72% reductions at follow-up. These differences were not significantly different, suggesting that the expected advantage for multiple settings did not materialize. Subjects in the no-exposure condition reduced vomiting at posttreatment and follow-up by 40% and 39% respectively. Leitenberg et al. (1988) concluded that "these results are tentative indications that the ERP procedure may add to the effects of a cognitive therapy intervention but probably only in regard to actual vomiting and eating behavior."

Agras and his colleagues (Agras, Schneider, Arnow, Raeburn, & Telch, 1989) attempted to determine if the addition of ERP would enhance the effects of cognitive-behavioral treatment. They compared four groups: wait-list control; self-monitoring plus nondirective treatment; cognitive-behavioral treatment; and cognitive-behavioral and ERP. Treatment was conducted in 14 one-hour sessions held over 4 months. Although all three treatments showed significant reductions in vomiting from pre- to posttreatment, only the cognitive-behavioral group produced significantly greater reductions in purging than the wait-list control. Of the cognitive-behavioral group, 56.3% had ceased purging at the end of treatment; abstinence rates for the ERP and self-monitoring groups were 23.5% and 31.2%, respectively. At 6-month follow-up, 59% of the cognitive-behavioral group were abstinent from purging, compared with 20% and 18% for the ERP and self-monitoring groups. Thus, in this investigation the addition of ERP appeared to reduce the efficacy of cognitive-behavioral treatment.

Unfortunately, neither of these investigations permits firm conclusions regarding what form or combination of cognitive and behavioral treatments is most effective for bulimia. Both suffer from the problems that typically plague comparisons of different treatment modalities. The no-exposure or cognitive-behavioral treatment in Leitenberg's study simply excluded the actual therapist-led exposure sessions from Leitenberg's overall treatment package. Although the treatment then included many of the features that are found in Fairburn's cognitive-behavioral treatment, the condition was designed as a control for ERP, not as the most effective form of cognitive-behavioral treatment. Similarly, the Agras (1989) investigation did not utilize ERP as it is usually conducted by the Leitenberg group. Exposure sessions were introduced in the seventh session, were less than one hour in length, and were held on no more than eight occasions. Furthermore, it appears that the subjects were encouraged to consume less food than is typically the case in ERP.

Given these methodological differences, it is no surprise that Leitenberg et al. (1988) found somewhat greater benefit to be derived from ERP, and Agras (1989) found that ERP did not enhance cognitive-behavioral treatment. It is perhaps more surprising that the differences each found between the treatments were not larger. The results do suggest that for a treatment modality to be effective it must be conducted well, and the inclusion of an additional treatment component without increasing treatment time may reduce overall treatment efficacy.

Although cognitive-behavioral treatment and ERP appear to be quite different at first glance, they actually share a number of features: self-monitoring of food intake and purging, exposure to avoided and anxiety-producing foods, and instructions to maintain a regular meal pattern. Exposure plus response prevention treatment tends to emphasize the exposure process, and cognitive behavioral treatment emphasizes the maintenance of a regular meal pattern. Given this significant overlap, it is likely that much of the success in these two treatment approaches is due to these common features. This conclusion is supported by the Kirkley et al. finding (1985) that a nondirective group treatment that included self-monitoring but no specific behavioral recommendations for eating and exposure yielded significant reductions in bulimic symptoms but was inferior to cognitive-behavioral therapy. Also, Freeman et al. (1988) found that cognitive restructuring did not enhance the efficacy of a purely behavioral treatment that included monitoring, exposure, and eating instruction, which suggests that these key behavioral features may be essential to cognitive-behavioral treatment's efficacy. If these results are verified in further investigations, they will challenge the basic assumptions of the cognitive model of bulimia.

PHARMACOLOGIC TREATMENT FOR BULIMIA NERVOSA

Antidepressant drugs are the third form of bulimia treatment that has received extensive research investigation. This treatment approach was originally based on the hypothesis that bulimia was a variant of major affective disorder. Several subsequent studies, however, have failed to find a relationship between pretreatment depression levels and treatment outcome with antidepressants (Agras, Dorian, Kirkley, Arnow, & Bachman, 1987; Mitchell & Groat, 1984). These results suggest that some alternative mechanism, such as a direct serotonergic effect on appetite, may be the key method of action.

A number of placebo-controlled trials of tricyclic antidepressants and monoamine oxidase inhibitors have been conducted. The vast majority of these studies have found the antidepressants to be superior to placebos, with reductions ranging from 64% to 91% in binge eating and abstinence rates ranging from 30% to 68% (Craighead & Agras, 1991). No studies of the long-term efficacy of antidepressants in bulimia have appeared, but short-term studies indicate that relapse typically occurs when medication is withdrawn (Pope, Hudson, & Yurgelun-Todd, 1983).

A recent investigation (Mitchell et al., 1990) has shed some light on the relative merits of antidepressants and cognitive-behavioral treat-

ment for bulimia. Mitchell and his colleagues compared 12-week trials of four conditions: (1) imipramine hydrochloride, (2) placebo, (3) imipramine hydrochloride plus cognitive-behavioral therapy, and (4) placebo plus cognitive-behavioral group therapy. At the end of treatment, all three active treatments yielded results superior to the placebo, and the condition including cognitive-behavioral therapy resulted in greater improvement than imipramine alone. The addition of the antidepressant to the cognitive-behavioral therapy did not significantly improve eating-behavior results (i.e., binge eating and purging) but did enhance treatment effects on depression and anxiety. Interestingly, the conditions with antidepressants had significantly higher dropout rates (36 versus 10) than those with placebo. These results led the investigators to conclude that cognitive-behavioral treatment alone is effective, is acceptable to more patients, and is more effective than antidepressants alone in controlling bulimic symptoms.

In the short run, antidepressants appear to enhance cognitive-behavioral treatment by alleviating depression. However, the long-run effectiveness of combined treatment is unclear. Evidence from Rossiter, Agras, Losch, & Telch (1988) suggests that these modalities work through different mechanisms. Cognitive-behavioral treatment appears to work by increasing calorie intake (decreased dietary restraint), thereby reducing the urge to binge. Antidepressants appear to work by reducing the urge to binge (presumably a serotonergic effect) as subjects continue a subnormal calorie intake. Since the bulimic's maladaptive dietary practices are not altered, this may explain why relapse is common after antidepressants are withdrawn. Additional studies are needed to determine if subjects receiving combined treatment do learn to alter their dietary practices and thus avoid relapse, or whether medication may undermine the long-run effectiveness of cognitive-behavioral treatment, as was found in the treatment of obesity.

Behavioral Treatment for Anorexia Nervosa

Treatment for anorexia nervosa must often be done in an inpatient setting because of the patient's extreme aversion to weight gain.

A number of single-subject (e.g., ABAB) experimental designs have been used to establish the specific effectiveness of various behavioral techniques in promoting weight gain (see review in Agras, 1987). Due to the relative rarity of the disorder, it is difficult to set up controlled trials or to evaluate the long-term effect of any specific behavioral intervention. Thus, research has focused primarily on the short-term goal of initial weight restoration.

Agras and Kraemer (1983) reviewed the available case studies of anorexia and concluded that behavior therapy enhanced the *rate* of weight gain compared to medically oriented therapy (including psychotherapy), resulting in shorter hospital stays; there were no differences in total weight gain. This may be related to the fact that in most cases patients were not allowed to leave the hospital until they reached an acceptable weight. That contingency is itself an application of negative reinforcement, as most patients find the hospital environment aversive. One large-scale clinical trial (Eckert, Goldberg, Casper, & Halmi, 1979) comparing behavioral treatment to milieu therapy did not find overall differences in weight gain at the end of a 35-day period. However, those patients who had not received previous outpatient therapy (presumably less chronic cases) did appear to respond better to behavior therapy.

Behavioral treatment consists primarily of explicit, contingent positive reinforcement for weight gain. The patient's access to privileges (visits, passes, TV, reading material) and physical activity is determined by meeting daily weight goals. For example, the patient is weighed each morning and is restricted to the dayroom if the goal, typically $\frac{1}{4}$ *or* $\frac{1}{2}$ pound above the previous high weight, is not met. In addition, negative reinforcement may be added. For example, after 2 days of no gain, the patient may be restricted to her room and after 3 days be restricted to bed or possibly even tube-fed. Patients are not forced to eat, but all meals are supervised; staff do not comment on amounts eaten. Patients must sit at the table for specified periods. Typically, patients must remain under observation for an hour afterward to prevent opportunities for purging. Patients are allowed to select items from the hospital menu, but a dietitian supplements their selections if necessary to insure that at least 4,000 calories per day are presented to the patient. Serving large meals has been found to increase calorie intake even though the patient never eats all that is served. Specific informational feedback to the patient (daily weight, calorie intake, and/or self-monitoring of mouthfuls eaten) enhances the effectiveness of the contingencies, presumably by allowing the patient to adjust the amount eaten in order to meet the weight-gain goals.

Once normal body weight has been restored, outpatient therapy is typically instigated to prevent relapse and to address other aspects of the disorder such as distorted body image, rigid food rules, distorted beliefs about food, and interpersonal problems. A specific weight criterion that would necessitate readmission to the hospital is set (a negative reinforcement contingency), with patients being weighed weekly.

Cognitive-behavioral treatment for anorexia based on the treatments developed for bulimia has been described (Garner, Garfinkel, & Berris, 1982); however, no empirical evaluations are currently available. The approach is similar to treatment of bulimia and is focused on identifying and challenging the distorted cognitions associated with body image and food intake.

Conclusions

Cognitive and behavioral interventions for eating disorders have been extensively evaluated and are now well-established in the treatment of those disorders. The fact that fairly objective outcome variables were easily available encouraged early researchers, especially in obesity. However, more sophisticated assessments of the actual behaviors associated with eating, rather than indirect assessments of outcome (such as weight), will be needed if we are to make progress in understanding the mechanisms through which the interventions work and to use that understanding to improve treatment effectiveness.

Behavioral intervention is clearly the treatment of choice for mild to moderate obesity. Long-term maintenance and effective alternatives for nonresponders and the more severely obese remain the most pressing issues. Current behavioral interventions are actually best suited for prevention and early intervention, because they appear to be more effective for establishing normalized eating and exercise patterns than they are for establishing the subnormal calorie intake needed to lose substantial weight. A specific additive effect for cognitive interventions has not been demonstrated at this point.

In contrast, when treating bulimia, both cognitive-behavioral and behavioral interventions (exposure and response-prevention) have demonstrated effectiveness, and many professionals consider them the initial treatments of choice. These interventions re-establish a more normal calorie intake. Medical treatment (antidepressants) appears to reduce appetite so that binge eating/purging is reduced but dietary restriction continues. Preliminary evidence suggests that these differing mechanisms could explain the poor maintenance after medical treatment. In all treatments, purging is typically greatly reduced, but researchers hope to increase the percentage totally abstinent. In addition, a large number of bulimics have substance abuse problems or are diagnosed as having borderline personality disorder. Such clients are typically excluded from research studies, but clinical reports indicate they are particularly difficult to treat and do not respond well to behavioral approaches.

Explicit behavioral contingencies are now an integral part of most inpatient treatment programs for anorexia. Empirical research in this area has been limited because of the low incidence of the disorder and the comprehensive programs typically required. Behavioral techniques have been shown to increase calorie intake, but there is little data regarding the effects of cognitive interventions with anorexics.

For all eating problems, behavioral and cognitive interventions demonstrate superior effectiveness relative to other alternatives, but unfortunately this is frequently due to the ineffectiveness of other treatments. Further, many people with eating disorders are not helped sufficiently by behavioral and cognitive interventions, nor do they find the benefits to be well-maintained. Thus, much work remains to be done, and we believe it will require considerable interdisciplinary collaboration because of the significant role of biological variables, which are now poorly understood.

TREATMENT RESOURCES

Agras, S. (1987). *Eating disorders: Management of obesity, bulimia, and anorexia*. New York: Pergamon.

Archer, G. (1989). *Big kids: A parent's guide to weight control for children*. Oakland, CA: New Harbinger.

Brownell, K. D. (1989). *Learn to eat*. Dallas, TX: Brownell & Hager Publishing Co. (Participant and Leader Manuals available).

Fairburn, C. G., & Wilson, G. T. (Eds.). (1993). *Binge eating: Nature, assessment and treatment*. New York: Guilford.

Edgette, J. S., & Prout, M. F. (1989). Cognitive and behavioural treatment of anorexia nervosa. In A. Freeman, K. Simon, L. B. Beutler, & H. Arkowitz (Eds.), *Comprehensive handbook of cognitive therapy*. New York: Plenum.

Kirschenbaum, D. S., Johnson, W. G., & Stalonas, P. M. (1987). *Treating childhood and adolescent obesity*. New York: Pergamon.

Wadden, T. A., & Van Itallie, T. B. (1992). *Treatment of the seriously obese patient*. New York: Guilford.

CHAPTER 10

Addictive Behaviors

Mary E. Larimer

G. Alan Marlatt

Substance abuse, including smoking, drug abuse, and alcohol abuse, is the focus of much concern in our society. The consequences both for individuals who engage in these behaviors and for society are many and serious. They include, but are not limited to, increased health care costs, lowered productivity of the addicted individual, higher crime rates, and premature death.

The *Diagnostic and Statistical Manual of Mental Disorders* (3rd ed., Rev.) (DSM-III-R) (American Psychiatric Association [APA], 1987) defines two classes of problems with psychoactive substances: abuse and dependence. For the diagnosis of psychoactive substance dependence to be made, the individual must have at least three symptoms from a list including consuming more of the substance than he or she wants to (i.e., loss of control); persistent desire or unsuccessful efforts to cut down or control the substance use; spending large amounts of time engaged in substance-related activities; frequent intoxication or withdrawal that interferes with respon-

sibilities; giving up other important obligations because of substance abuse; continued substance use despite knowledge of a persistent or recurrent problem caused or exacerbated by the substance; tolerance; withdrawal (although there may not be withdrawal associated with all substances); and use of substance to relieve withdrawal symptoms. In addition, the symptoms must have persisted for at least one month or have occurred repeatedly over a longer period of time.

The diagnostic criteria for psychoactive substance abuse require that the individual either continues to use the substance despite knowledge of problems related to that use or that there be recurrent use in situations in which use is physically hazardous. Again, the symptoms must have a duration of at least one month, and in addition, the diagnosis of psychoactive substance dependence must not apply.

The DSM-III-R reports prevalence rates for psychoactive substance use disorders, based on a community study conducted in the United

States from 1981–1989 using DSM-III criteria (similar to DSM-III-R). Approximately 13% of the adult population reportedly have met criteria for alcohol abuse or dependence at some time in their lives. An estimated 4% have met criteria for cannabis abuse or dependence, .7% have had opioid abuse or dependence, and 1.1% have had sedative, hypnotic, or anxiolytic dependence or abuse. Although no estimates of prevalence rates for nicotine abuse or dependence are reported in DSM-III-R, the Surgeon General's report (U.S. Surgeon General, 1988) estimated that 51.4 million people nationwide were addicted to nicotine. Prevalence of cocaine abuse or dependence is difficult to estimate, but according to the National Institute on Drug Abuse (NIDA) household survey on drug use, (NIDA, 1985) 4,710,000 individuals used cocaine on an average of once per month. Although the percentage of more frequent users in the general population was less than .5%, 1.4% of the population between ages 12 and 17 (an estimated 330,000 individuals) and 1.8% of individuals between 18 and 25 (610,000 people) used cocaine at least once per week.

The relatively high rates of substance abuse in our society, combined with the serious health and social consequences, make development of appropriate treatment for these individuals extremely important. Unfortunately, few traditional treatment programs have been successful in producing lasting change. Relapse to alcohol, cigarettes, heroin, and other substances is estimated to occur in 50% to 90% of cases, usually within the first 3 months following treatment (Brownell, Marlatt, Lichtenstein, & Wilson, 1986; Marlatt and Gordon, 1985).

Most traditional therapies are based on a medical or disease model and assume that substance abuse has a biological or genetic etiology (Jellinik, 1960). This model typically focuses on the phenomena of "loss of control" consumption (i.e., the individual is unable to limit the amount of consumption), tolerance (experiencing fewer effects at the same dosage of substance over time), craving, and withdrawal. All are thought to be largely biological or physiological processes triggered by the activity of the substance in the body and are therefore presumed to be beyond the volitional control of the individual. This disease process is thought to be progressive, and the only way to halt the progression is through complete abstinence. Ironically, this abstinence is achieved, not through some medical treatment, but by the user's essentially voluntary commitment to refrain from using substances.

CONCEPTUAL BASES FOR COGNITIVE-BEHAVIORAL APPROACHES

The development of behavioral and cognitive-behavioral strategies for the treatment of addictive behaviors stems from research challenging many of the basic assumptions of the disease model of addiction. First, there is convincing evidence that tolerance to alcohol and other drugs can be both operantly and classically conditioned. Siegal (1983) reviews evidence from both animal and human studies indicating that most tolerance is not mediated by tissue adaptation or other biological mechanisms. Rather, observed tolerance (defined as functional tolerance) only develops when the drug is administered in a situation that has been previously associated with drug use. Regardless of the amount of previous experience with the drug, animals do not show tolerance to the behavioral effects of a drug if it is administered in a novel setting. In addition, animals who are repeatedly given alcohol prior to a maze task, when compared with animals given the same amount of alcohol after running the maze, were able to perform better at a subsequent trial when both groups received alcohol before the trial. This indicates that practice while impaired is essential to the development of behavioral tolerance. Cross-tolerance to other drugs can also be acquired in this way. Not only can tolerance be conditioned, but it will extinguish when the drug cues are paired repeat-edly with a placebo rather than the drug. When a placebo is administered in a setting that has pre-viously served as a cue for drug administration, the animal responds physiologically in a direc-tion opposite to the physiological effects of the drug (i.e., animal temperature will decrease if the drug would normally cause it to increase). This conditioned compensatory response may help explain functional tolerance.

Cognitive factors have also been shown to play a role in influencing substance abuse. Re-search using a balanced-placebo design (Marlatt & Rohsenow, 1980) that crosses actual content of a beverage (alcohol versus placebo) with subject's expectation of beverage content (i.e., told alcohol or told placebo) indicates that alcoholics who believed they had consumed alcohol experienced more craving and consumed more alcohol than did those who believed they had received a pla-cebo, regardless of actual beverage content (Marlatt, Demming, & Reid, 1973). It seems that the belief that they had consumed alcohol was enough to trigger the loss-of-control phenome-non in alcoholics, but the actual consumption of alcohol had no such effect. The role of beliefs and expectations about alcohol and other substances extends well beyond the experience of craving or loss of control, and will be discussed in more detail later in the chapter.

Operant conditioning principles also play a role in substance abuse. Both animal and human studies indicate that alcohol, nicotine, and other drugs may be powerful primary reinforcers, so much so that animals sometimes forego food, water, and sex in favor of drug use (Johanson & Schuster, 1982). Alcohol, nicotine, heroin, and other psychoactive substances are positively re-inforcing, due to their initial pleasant effects, which are experienced by the user as a "high" or a type of euphoria. Psychologically, the individ-ual's expectancies about the effects of the sub-stance can influence his or her perception of the reinforcing effects of a substance, and this in turn can influence his or her level of consumption. Studies of expectancy effects for alcohol use indi-cate that subjects with more positive expectan-cies for the effects of alcohol tend to drink more (Marlatt & Rohsenow, 1980; Rohsenow, 1983). Because the positive effects of substance use are closer in time to the actual ingestion of the sub-stance than are the more delayed aversive effects, their salience for affecting the behavior is in-creased (Solomon, 1977). Therefore, individuals are likely to continue to use the substance even after the aversive effects become larger than the positive effects.

Psychoactive substance use can also be nega-tively reinforced. The negative reinforcement value of substances is again both physiological and psychological. Alcohol, nicotine, and other drugs do have some physiologically relaxing and analgesic effects. Therefore, they can be nega-tively reinforcing through their use to escape stress and pain, a factor that becomes more im-portant with the advent of dysphoric withdrawal symptoms. The use of the substance is thereby negatively reinforced because it relieves these aversive symptoms. Psychologically, substance use can be seen as a maladaptive attempt to es-cape from an unpleasant situation, or to cope with interpersonal conflict and negative affect. In their study of relapse situations of alcoholics, heroin addicts, and smokers, Marlatt and Gor-don (1980, 1985) found that nearly half of the relapse episodes reported by alcoholics, heroin addicts, and smokers took place in situations in-volving negative affect.

Finally, there is evidence that addicts have skills deficits that interact with the reinforcing properties of substances. Shiffman (1982, 1984) has shown that individuals who fail to cope ap-propriately with stressful situations are more likely to relapse to cigarettes than are individuals who have and utilize a coping repertoire. Simi-larly, studies with alcoholics have shown that when the individual is unable to express negative feelings appropriately, he or she is more likely to drink (Marlatt, Kosturn, & Lang, 1975), and that alcoholics have deficits in a variety of social skills, including assertive behavior (Levine & Zigler, 1973). Similar links have been found between social skills deficits and opioid abuse (Monti, Abrams, Binkoff, & Zwick, 1986). Given these deficits, individuals are more likely to use substances in an attempt to cope with stressful situations, including interpersonal situations where assertiveness or other socially appropriate responses are called for (Alexander & Hadaway, 1982); this use of substances as coping responses is likely to be negatively reinforced.

Based on research findings that support the role of classical conditioning, operant conditioning, and cognitive factors in the etiology and maintenance of substance abuse, a variety of techniques have been developed to treat these problems. Although these techniques vary on a number of dimensions, all share the common assumption that substance abuse is a learned behavior (addictive behavior), and that through the use of behavioral principles, what has been learned can be unlearned. The recovery process is also viewed as a learning process: learning to cope with life without drugs.

ASSESSMENT

Issues Concerning Self-Report

Detailed assessment of the behavior in question is the key to successfully implementing a cognitive-behavioral treatment program for addictive behaviors (Donovan & Marlatt, 1988). Assessment of addictive behaviors for the purposes of implementing and evaluating a cognitive-behavioral program faces several methodological hurdles. First, much of the information must be collected via self-report methods. There is a great deal of controversy within the field of addictive behaviors concerning the reliability and validity of these data. Much has been written about the reliability and validity of alcoholics' self-reports. The concept of denial, defined as the addicted person's inability or refusal to recognize his or her own problem, has been used to assert that addicted persons cannot give

valid reports of their own behavior. Unfortunately, often the individual is the only one who has access to that information; significant others, if they exist at all, are unable to observe the individual consistently. Physiological measures such as urinalysis can be used to detect some chemicals, but for the most part they cannot give the specific and detailed information necessary for treatment planning and evaluation. Some self-report measures are clearly necessary.

A recent review of the literature on self-report (Babor, Stephens, & Marlatt, 1987) provides some encouragement to the clinician and researcher faced with this dilemma. The authors found that although addicted individuals' self-reports were not always valid and reliable, they were not necessarily always invalid or unreliable either. For instance, even when the patient's report differed from that of a significant other, it was about as likely that the patient reported more substance abuse as that he or she reported less. Additionally, although reports of the patient and spouse were only moderately correlated for very specific information, more global measures achieved better consensus, indicating that the patient does seem to be capable of accurately reporting his or her behavior.

Babor et al. (1987) also make several suggestions for improving the validity and reliability of self-report data. In particular, reliability can be improved by either avoiding retrospective accounts as much as possible, or providing anchors to help the individual place the substance use in context. Interviews and daily diaries appear to be more reliable than certain retrospective questionnaires. Validity of data can be improved by collecting information from significant others in addition to the patient, by including physiological measures, and by assessing other objective information such as hospitalizations, job performance, or time spent in jail. It may be that these other forms of data collection serve primarily as "bogus pipeline" procedures; that is, they encourage the patient to report accurately because he or she knows the answers will be checked.

Multiple Assessment Modalities

In summary, it appears that self-report measures can give valid and reliable, as well as extremely useful, information under certain circumstances. It is important to consider the method of assessment both when evaluating the effectiveness of a program in general and when implementing it with a specific patient. Ideally, an assessment of the problem should consider all factors relevant to successfully designing and implementing a treatment program for the behavior in question (Donovan, 1988). To achieve this goal, a variety of measures will be needed. These include:

1. *Measures of consequences of the addictive behavior.* The Michigan Alcoholism Screening Test (MAST) (Selzer, 1971) and the Rutgers Alcohol Problem Inventory (RAPI) (White & Labouvie, 1989) are examples of this type of measure used with alcohol abusers, and both have been found to be reliable. The Addiction Severity Index (McLellan, Luborsky, & O'Brien, 1980) can be used for a variety of drugs. Each of these measures gives the clinician information on the consequences the individual is experiencing from his or her substance abuse, which can serve as a measure of the severity of the problem.

2. *Self-report measures of consumption.* Retrospective measures of consumption are necessary to provide the clinician with information on the pattern and amount of consumption prior to treatment, and to serve as a starting point for the analysis of the antecedents and consequents of the addictive behavior. The Time Line Follow-Back interview (TLFB) (Sobell et al., 1980) provides anchors for the individual, to assist in retrospective recall of substance use habits for one year following treatment; reported reliability of alcohol consumption data using this technique has been quite high (Vuchinich, Tucker, & Harllee, 1988).

If possible, a daily diary of consumption should be kept for a minimum baseline period of 2 weeks and throughout the treatment and follow-up periods.

3. *Collateral reports of consumption.* Significant others, if the client's permission is obtained, should be asked to provide information on their observations of the client's behavior.

4. *Objective measurements of problem involvement.* Hospital records, jail records, employment or school records, and so forth can be used.

5. *Behavioral observation.* Whenever possible, direct observation of the behavior in question is best. This can be used, for instance, to assess the individual's social and assertiveness skills through role-play.

6. *Physiological measures.* Many drugs, including marijuana, nicotine, heroin, and cocaine, can be detected through simple, relatively nonintrusive physiological tests (i.e., saliva or urinalysis). These are important measures to collect, both because they serve as validity checks and because they can be used to facilitate maintenance.

Issues Concerning Outcome Assessment

Although establishing baseline levels of consumption and problem involvement is important, a second assessment issue involves evaluating treatment outcome. Traditional treatment approaches emphasize total abstinence as the only acceptable goal of treatment. Therefore, treatment outcomes have typically been dichotomous: abstinent or relapsed. With the advent of behavioral treatments, it has become increasingly important to evaluate a number of dimensions of outcome (Sobell & Sobell, 1982). In particular, at least for alcohol, the goal of moderate consumption may be acceptable for some clients. In order to evaluate successful moderation, it is important to assess not only the amount and pattern of consumption, but also whether there is improvement in other life areas such as occupational and interpersonal functioning, health, and psychological wellbeing. Assessment of these variables should include multiple data sources, as described above, and in addition, an attempt should be made to define improvement operationally, or to use continuous measures rather than categorical ones.

Although assessment is a vital and necessary part of all behavioral and cognitive-behavioral programs, the actual treatment components vary widely. The following review of behavioral and cognitive-behavioral therapies for addictive behaviors is by no means comprehensive; rather, it is intended as an introduction to the field and an overview of some of the more common therapies.

THERAPY TECHNIQUES

Aversion Therapy

Aversion therapy was one of the first behavioral therapies to emerge in the treatment of addictive behaviors. It is based on the classical conditioning principle of conditioned aversion; in short, if substance cues are repeatedly paired with noxious stimuli, the substance itself will take on aversive properties. In general, aversive therapies pair either actual consumption of the substance or cues associated with consumption (i.e., pictures of the substance, drug paraphernalia, cigarette packages) with negative or aversive stimuli.

Chemical aversion, commonly used to treat alcohol abuse, involves ingestion of a chemical that induces nausea and vomiting when alcohol is consumed. Common chemicals include disulfiram (Antabuse) and emetine. *Rapid smoking* is an aversive technique that involves forcing the individual to chain-smoke cigarettes until he or she becomes ill. *Electrical aversion* involves the administration of mild to moderate electric shock in the presence of cues for consumption or actual consumption. *Covert sensitization* is similar to aversion therapy, in that it attempts to produce a conditioned aversion to the substance. However, covert sensitization does not rely on chemical or electrical stimuli to produce this aversion but relies on negative imagery.

Data on the effectiveness of aversion therapy has been equivocal. Wiens and Menustik (1983) report an abstinence rate of 63% at one year posttreatment for male alcoholics treated with chemical aversion. However, a recent review of the literature (Riley, Sobell, Leo, Sobell, & Klajner, 1987) noted that chemical aversion is most successful with individuals who are married, employed, and from higher socio-economic backgrounds. A comparison of data on chemical aversion therapy administered at private hospitals versus public hospitals (with clients of lower socio-economic status) indicates that much of the promising data is more a function of patient characteristics than of successful therapy (Neuberger, Matarazzo, Schmitz, & Pratt, 1980; Neuberger et al., 1982). Similarly, a review of the literature on both chemical and electrical aversive conditioning with drug abusers (Stitzer, Bigelow, & McCaul, 1985) concluded there was no evidence that this type of therapy was effective. Electrical aversion therapy has been largely discontinued, due to ethical concerns and lack of evidence for its effectiveness. Covert sensitization has achieved some success for promoting abstinence among alcoholics (Elkins, 1980). However, much more research on this technique is necessary.

The literature on aversive conditioning with smoking has been more promising. Erickson, Tiffany, Martin, and Baker (1983) found the addition of rapid-smoking procedures to a behavioral counseling package produced significantly higher abstinence rates, and these results were maintained through 1-year follow-up. Other studies (Hall, Sachs, & Hall, 1979; Lichtenstein, Harris, Birchler, Wahl, & Schmahl, 1973) have similarly found positive effects for rapid-smoking techniques. Although negative findings for rapid smoking also exist (Raw & Russell, 1980), most studies indicate that rapid smoking as an aversive technique can be effective for promoting abstinence from nicotine.

Although the data on aversion therapies have been equivocal, the technique is worth mentioning because it is based on classical conditioning principles. Unfortunately, it seems likely that the years of positive conditioning that occur prior to the aversion therapy outweigh the time-limited artificial pairings made during treatment.

Contingency Management

Based on operant learning principles, contingency-management procedures seek to restructure the addicted individual's enviroment in such a way that positive behaviors are reinforced, and nondesirable behaviors (i.e., excessive consumption) are met with neutral or negative consequences. Contingency-management principles have been used to encourage the individual to enter and remain in treatment, to continue use of disulfiram (Antabuse), and to remain abstinent from substances. Typical examples of contingency-management techniques involve payment of a "motivational fee" that is refunded if the individual is compliant with treatment, social reinforcement of desired behaviors through enlisting the spouse or friends of the individual, and other techniques.

Hunt and Azrin (1973) designed a community-based contingency-management program for hospitalized male alcoholics, which included vocational, marital, and social reinforcement. In particular, subjects in the contingency-management group ($N = 8$) were assisted in obtaining satisfactory employment, with counselors providing everything from suggestions to encouragement to transportation. Marital functioning was the focus of couples counseling, with spouses instructed to provide a variety of positive consequences only when the alcoholic was sober and to withdraw all affection and attention when the individual was drinking. A social club was set up for the use of the clients, so that they had a place to interact and receive positive social reinforcement, which again was withdrawn when the individual was not sober. In addition, counselors assisted with the development of an enriched home environment, through encouraging the clients to obtain televi-

sion sets and radios, install telephones in their homes, and subscribe to newspapers and magazines. In many cases, the program would assist with the initial financial arrangements; the individuals were expected to make subsequent payments on their own, which served as an additional incentive to continue working rather than drinking.

The control group was matched on a number of variables, but received only the standard hospital treatment. The results of the study were quite positive. The community contingency-management group had fewer drinking days, more working days, more social interactions, fewer days institutionalized, higher monthly income, and greater marital satisfaction ($p < .005$ for all results). These gains were maintained throughout the 6-month follow-up.

The success of this community-based intervention is impressive. However, the study involved a relatively small number of patients ($N = 8$) and the intensive treatment involved is very costly and difficult to implement. Still, the results point to the success of operant techniques for the treatment of substance abuse.

Skills Training

Behavioral skills-training techniques are based on the assumption that substance abusers are deficient in certain skills, and that these deficiencies promote or maintain excessive consumption. Based on this rationale, a variety of skills-training procedures have been developed. These include training in drinking skills and blood alcohol level (BAL) discrimination, training in interpersonal skills, and vocational skills training. Not all studies are supportive of the assumption that substance abusers have skills deficits. Regardless, the data on skills training have been generally favorable.

Drinking skills training and BAL discrimination are typically incorporated as part of multimodal therapy programs; in their review of the literature from 1978–1983, Riley et al. (1983)

found no data on the use of these techniques alone. However, as part of other programs, this type of skills training includes drink-refusal skills, analysis of the antecedents of drinking, and planning strategies for moderating alcohol consumption.

The data on interpersonal skills training are somewhat more comprehensive. First, there is evidence that some individuals may abuse substances as a way of coping with stressful interpersonal situations (Higgins and Marlatt, 1975). Second, although few methodologically sound studies have investigated the relative effectiveness of interpersonal skills training, those that have been done obtained generally positive results. Chaney, O'Leary, and Marlatt (1978) compared a skills-training group, a discussion group, and a no-treatment control group, and found that at 1-year posttreatment, subjects from the skills-training group were drinking on fewer occasions, consumed less alcohol, and had shorter drinking episodes than did subjects in the other two groups. In a recent review of the literature on behavioral treatment for alcohol addiction, Ingram and Salzberg (1988) concluded that the data generally supported the utility of skills training. Stitzer et al. (in press) reviewed the literature on the use of skills training with drug abusers and reached a similar positive conclusion.

Evaluation of Comprehensive Cognitive-Behavioral Programs

Cognitive-behavioral treatment programs are generally broad-band treatment packages that incorporate some or all of the techniques previously discussed. In addition, these programs include an emphasis on cognitive factors in substance abuse, including the power of outcome expectancies. Sanchez-Craig, Annis, Bornet, and MacDonald (1984) implemented a cognitive-behavioral program with 70 early-stage problem drinkers, who were randomly assigned to an abstinence or controlled drinking goal. Results indicated significant reductions in drinking for

subjects in either group, demonstrating that cognitive-behavioral strategies are as applicable to abstinence goals as to controlled-substance-use goals. Oei and Jackson (1982) compared combined social skills training (SST) and cognitive restructuring (CR) to either technique alone and to a traditional supportive-therapy control group. They found the combined program and CR-only to be more effective than SST-only in producing reductions in drinking at 6- and 12-month follow-ups; all three behavioral groups were superior to the traditional therapy group.

Relapse Prevention

Cognitive-behavioral relapse prevention (RP) (Marlatt & Gordon, 1980, 1985; Marlatt & George, 1990) is a program designed to be applied to a number of addictive behaviors, either as an adjunct to behavioral or traditional treatment, or alone. The program combines skills training, cognitive therapy, and lifestyle change, and is primarily designed to help the individual anticipate and cope with relapse situations.

RP teaches individuals to observe the antecedents and consequents of substance abuse, and to identify personal high-risk situations (i.e., those situations in which they are most likely to use substances). Once high-risk situations have been identified, the individual is trained to identify the discriminative stimuli associated with an approaching high-risk situation. These discriminative stimuli serve as cues that coping is ncessary. The individual can be taught skills for coping with these high-risk situations without using the substance. The coping skills include both behavioral coping (i.e., assertive behavior, alternative activity, leaving the situation) and cognitive coping (i.e., thinking about commitment to abstinence).

In addition to skills training, RP attempts to combat the negative cognitions and emotions associated with lapses (episodes of substance use following some period of abstinence); cognitive restructuring is used to challenge the individual's global, stable, internal attributions for lapses; and lapse episodes are framed as opportunities for learning new coping responses.

Data from balanced placebo research are used to challenge individual expectancies relating to substance abuse. RP promotes increased self-efficacy (the belief that the individual has the ability to handle a given situation) through increasing the individual's perception of control in high-risk situations.

Finally, the RP program encourages the development of a balanced lifestyle. Meditation, relaxation, and aerobic exercise are encouraged, and are framed as "positive addictions" (Glasser, 1976) to replace the negative addiction of substance abuse. Other lifestyle changes encouraged in the RP program include developing more supportive social networks, leaving substance-abusing environments, and potentially developing more spiritual lifestyles.

NEW DIRECTIONS

Cue Exposure

Cue exposure is a relatively recent addition to the field of addiction treatment. Based on classical and operant conditioning principles, cue exposure involves presenting the addict with cues for consumption, such as the sight or smell of the drug, but preventing consumption from taking place. Coupled with skills-training procedures, this technique theoretically involves extinction of the emotional and physiological reactions of craving for consumption, which have been conditioned to the drug cues, and trains the individual to use these same cues as discriminative stimuli for the initiation of a coping response (Monti, Abrams, Kadden, & Cooney, 1989). Although this procedure has not been tested enough to be considered valid, results from case studies with alcoholics (Blakely & Baker, 1980; Hodgson & Rankin, 1983) and controlled treatment-outcome studies with heroin addicts

(McLellan, Childress, Ehrman, & O'Brien, 1986) have been encouraging.

Brief Interventions

Brief interventions for substance abuse and dependence are relatively new. As outlined by Sanchez-Craig and Wilkinson (1989), the techniques have arisen out of the behavioral tradition, in response to the lack of support for more intensive treatments, as well as to economic concerns and the pressure for early identification and treatment of substance abusers.

Brief interventions may consist of simple advice given by a medical professional to an identified substance abuser, or they may involve a more structured presentation of a rationale for reduction of substance use and some guidelines for achieving such a reduction. In either case, brief interventions share the assumption that people can be responsible for changing their behavior, and some will do so if given good reasons that make sense to them.

Although still in their infancy, brief interventions represent a significant new direction in the addiction field, particularly as they apply to less severely addicted individuals. These early-stage substance abusers often reject formal treatment, due to its insistence on lifelong abstinence as the only goal and due to the disruption to work and social functioning necessitated by inpatient treatment (Sanchez-Craig & Wilkinson, 1987). For these individuals, brief interventions presented in an outpatient format are often more acceptable and are therefore more likely to be utilized.

Treatment Matching

Treatment matching, or assigning clients to a specific type of treatment based on pretreatment characteristics, has recently begun to be investigated in the field of addictive behaviors. This approach stems from the idea that there needs to be a fit between client and therapy in order to maximize the potential for a successful outcome.

Matching characteristics might include certain types of psychopathology, such as depression. Sociopathy and the severity of the addiction are other potential matching variables, as is the attitude of the individual toward treatment. In fact, any number of variables might be used to match individuals to treatment, and much research needs to be done to attempt to determine reliable matching variables.

Kadden, Cooney, Getter, and Litt (1989) present data from one such study, which assessed subjects' levels of sociopathy, psychopathology, and neurological impairment, then compared outcomes for more- and less-severely impaired individuals when treated with coping-skills training or interactional therapy. Individuals with higher levels of psychopathology and sociopathy had better outcomes when treated with coping-skills training; interactional therapy was more effective for low-sociopathy subjects; and individuals with a higher degree of neurological impairment fared better in interactional therapy than in skills training. These findings support the utility of assessing psychopathology, sociopathy, and neurological impairment during the planning phase of therapy.

Prevention

Cognitive-behavioral treatments for addictive behaviors have gained increasing respect and popularity in the last two decades. Although carefully controlled treatment-outcome studies are still necessary, in general the results of outcome studies have been favorable. Even so, relapse rates following treatment remain high. Relapse prevention (RP) provides some encouragement, but it seems likely that even the best treatment programs will be unable to help some portion of addicted individuals.

Prevention may be the key to reducing the percentage of substance abusers in our society. Secondary prevention refers to halting the progression toward substance abuse in individuals who are at risk for alcohol problems, due either to their current behavior or to other risk factors (i.e., family history of substance abuse, etc.).

The application of cognitive-behavioral strategies to prevention of substance abuse is fairly recent (Marlatt, 1988). It stems from data supporting the use of cognitive-behavioral strategies for treatment of addictive behaviors, as well as data implicating social modeling (Collins & Marlatt, 1981), reinforcement, and cognitive factors in the development of substance abuse problems. Additional supportive data include findings that younger, early-stage problem drinkers are more amenable to treatment with cognitive-behavioral therapy than are older, more chronic alcoholics (Sanchez-Craig et al., 1984), and that smokers with less chronic smoking histories are less likely to relapse than are older, heavier smokers (Shiffman, 1989). In general, data support the contention that secondary prevention using cognitive-behavioral strategies has a good chance for success.

Few empirical studies have been done in this area to date. Gilchrist, Schinke, Bobo, and Snow (1986) compared a cognitive-behavioral skills-training program with placebo (standard health class) and no-intervention control groups for prevention of smoking with 714 school children (mean age = 11.4 years). At a 15-month follow-up, skills-training subjects were reporting significantly less weekly smoking than subjects in the other two groups. Botvin, Baker, Renick, Filazzola, and Botvin (1984) conducted a cognitive-behavioral skills-training program targeted at reducing smoking, drinking, and marijuana use among seventh grade students ($N = 1,311$). They found that a skills-training program implemented by older peer leaders (10th and 11th grade students) was very effective in reducing substance use, but that the same program implemented by regular classroom teachers had no effect when compared to an assessment-only control condition. These findings may be explained by a difference in the training and monitoring of the different group leaders.

Two studies have looked at the effects of cognitive-behavioral secondary prevention efforts with heavy-drinking college students. The first study (Kivlahan, Marlatt, Fromme, Coppel, & Williams, 1990) compared an eight-session skills-training program (the Alcohol Skills Training Program, ASTP) to a standard alcohol information school program (AIS) and an assessment-only control group. The second study (Baer, Kivlahan, Fomme, & Marlatt, 1991) looked at three different methods of presenting the ASTP. Group format (six sessions) was compared to a correspondence format and a one-session professional advice format. Basic information in all formats included BAL discrimination, moderate-drinking skills, limit setting, alcohol outcome expectancies, and lifestyle balance. Preliminary results indicate that subjects in all groups reduced their alcohol consumption, and these reductions were maintained through 1-year follow-up; 2-year follow-up data are in the process of being collected, to assess stability of change.

Although there is clearly a need for more controlled research in the area of substance abuse prevention, the data so far are encouraging. Cognitive-behavioral methods are the first to yield data indicating actual behavior change, rather than merely the changes in attitudes and knowledge achieved by standard prevention programs. Given the enormous problems associated with substance abuse, and the difficulty in treating substance abuse problems, prevention efforts offer our best hope of minimizing substance abuse in this society.

CONCLUSIONS

The development of behavioral and cognitive-behavioral strategies for the treatment of addictive behaviors has challenged many of the basic assumptions of the traditional, disease model of addiction. These strategies share the common assumption that substance abuse is a learned behavior and can be unlearned. Thus, the recovery process is viewed as a process in which a person learns to cope with life without drugs. Many of the earliest efforts utilized aversive conditioning therapies; however, only in the case of rapid-smoking procedures have aversive procedures received strong support as a useful component of treatment. The majority of empirical work on behavioral approaches has focused on problems of alcohol abuse, although conceptually and clinically the model is appropriate for many other types of addictive behaviors.

The most established behavioral procedures focus on contingency management, training appropriate drinking skills, and training skills needed to develop alternatives to drinking (social skills, vocational skills, etc.). It has been demonstrated that these strategies can be applied either to abstinence goals or to controlled-use goals. Cognitive-behavioral relapse prevention programs that include skills training, cognitive therapy, and lifestyle change are designed to help the individual anticipate and cope with relapse situations. A procedure called cue exposure is perhaps the most interesting new addition to the skills-training approach. By exposing the addict to consumption cues while preventing consumption, the technique is designed to extinguish conditioned emotional and physiological responses to those cues, which are experienced as urges/cravings, and to replace those responses with positive coping responses.

Recent efforts have targeted early intervention, particularly since younger or less severely addicted individuals appear to be particularly amenable to cognitive-behavioral approaches. In addition, cognitive-behavioral prevention studies with school children have shown great promise by demonstrating actual behavioral change (lower rates of smoking or reductions in drinking behavior) rather than merely changes in attitudes and knowledge such as those resulting from traditional educational approaches. Thus, cognitive-behavioral approaches are having a significant impact at all levels: treatment for the more severely addicted, moderation training for the problem drinker, and prevention.

TREATMENT RESOURCES

Baer, J. S., Kivlahan, D. R., Marlatt, G. A., Fromme, K., Larimer, M. E., Dimeff, L. A., Williams, E., & Tapert, S. F. (1992). *Alcohol skills training manual*. Unpublished manuscript.

Miller, W. R., & Rollnick, S. (1991). *Motivational interviewing: Preparing people to change addictive behavior*. New York: Guilford.

Wanigarane, S., Wallace, W., Pullin, J., Francis, K., & Farmer, R. (1990). *Relapse prevention for addictive behaviours: A manual for therapists*. Oxford, UK: Blackwell Scientific Publications.

CHAPTER 11

Behavioral Couples Therapy

Jennifer Waltz

Neil S. Jacobson

Intimate relationships are a central aspect of many people's lives. Understanding why some couples are happy and others are not and how to help unhappy couples improve their relationships is a daunting process. Many couples look for therapy after years of developing behavior patterns that produce extremely dissatisfying relationships. The sections of this chapter explicate: (1) a behavioral conceptualization of relationship distress, (2) methods used to assess couple distress, (3) important techniques used in behavioral couples therapy, (4) research on the effectiveness of behavioral couples therapy, and (5) some future directions in the field.

BEHAVIORAL FORMULATIONS OF RELATIONSHIP DISTRESS

Behavioral formulations of relationship distress have evolved continuously since behavioral researchers and clinicians first began speculating about the causes of relationship problems and unhappiness. This evolution has resulted in a richer understanding of a complex phenomenon, a phenomenon that has tested the limits of behavioral theory. Because relationship distress is multifaceted, a behavioral conceptualization must be multifaceted as well.

Each partner in a relationship can be thought of as a salient part of the other partner's environment (Jacobson & Margolin, 1979). Each partner's behavior has a consequence for the other partner, whether that consequence be rewarding or punishing. Since behavior in a relationship occurs in an ongoing, continuous stream of acts, each person is simultaneously being affected by and affecting the partner. In happy couples, the type of influence each person has over the other is generally positive, resulting in a situation in which each person increases positive behaviors in the other through the reinforcing behaviors emitted. In unhappy couples, an aversive control situation develops and the main way that partners affect each other's behavior is through negative reinforcement and/or punishment. (Jacobson & Margolin, 1979). Consistent with behavioral theory, such aversive control situations result in negative affective states (Skinner, 1974).

Couples seek treatment for a variety of behavioral and affective concomitants of relationship distress. They may identify frequent arguments, lack of closeness, sexual problems, feelings of dissatisfaction with their partner, or problems with communication as the basis for seeking treatment. They may be experiencing symptoms such as depression or anxiety and are ostensibly seeking treatment for these symptoms, with relationship problems as an underlying issue. The couple may have experienced some recent escalation in their problems, such as the occurrence of physical violence. The duration and intensity of dissatisfaction in one or both partners and the level of commitment to the relationship are important factors in understanding the nature of their problems.

Communication Behaviors

Some characteristics have been found to differentiate between distressed and nondistressed couples. Overall, distressed couples behave more negatively, both verbally and nonverbally, when interacting with each other in a variety of laboratory tasks (Schaap, 1984). Schaap's review of 26 studies lists many examples of negative behaviors distressed couples have been found to use more than do nondistressed couples, such as put-downs, criticisms, disapproval, and disagreeing statements (Hahlweg et al., 1979; Revenstorf, Vogel, Wegener, Hahlweg, & Schindler, 1980), and positive behaviors they show less of, such as responsiveness to their partner in the form of paraphrasing, agreeing, or acknowledging (Wegener, Revenstorf, Hahlweg, & Schindler, 1979); supportive behaviors (Sprenkle, 1975); and "reconciling acts" such as using humor (Raush, Barry, Hertel, & Swain, 1974). Non-

verbally, members of distressed couples smile less (Gottman, 1979), keep more distance between themselves and their partners and have more closed body posture (Beier & Sternberg, 1977). Distressed couples show more negative behaviors during problem solving (Billings, 1979).

Attributions

Partners in distressed and nondistressed couples differ not only in terms of how they behave while communicating with each other, but also in how they describe the relationship and their partner. For example, distressed partners describe their partners as being more negative than do members of nondistressed couples (Gottman, 1979). Compared to nondistressed couples, distressed partners asked to explain their partner's behavior tend to give reasons that are likely to maintain their dissatisfaction with the relationship (Fincham, Beach, & Baucom, 1987; Fincham & Bradbury, 1987; Holtzworth-Munroe & Jacobson, 1985). That is, when asked why a partner did something they did not like, the reasons given tend to emphasize that it was due to the partner (e.g., his or her personality traits) rather than something about the situation, and that the partner did it intentionally and is likely to do it again in the future. In contrast, nondistressed partners tend to give more benign reasons for a partner's negative behaviors and suggest that the partner's behavior was not intended to harm them, is not likely to happen again, and had more to do with external circumstances than to something about the partner. For example, when asked why his partner did not smile at him when she got home from work, a distressed husband might say, "Because she's an irritable person and she's always trying to get me down," and a nondistressed husband would be more likely to say, "Because she had a bad day."

Similarly, when asked to explain a partner's behaviors that are pleasing, distressed couples tend to discredit their partners by giving distress-maintaining reasons (e.g., due to external circumstances, was not intentional, is not likely to happen in the future). Nondistressed partners are more likely to attribute the behavior to relationship-enhancing causes (e.g., something about the partner, done intentionally, likely to happen again).

Interaction Patterns

Distressed and nondistressed couples also differ in their typical interaction patterns. Members of distressed relationships are more likely to respond to a negative statement from their partner with another negative statement. Nondistressed couples are less rigid; a negative statement is less likely to be responded to with another negative (Gottman, 1979). Nondistressed couples tend to respond to a partner's anger with neutral or positive statements, but people in unhappy relationships tend to reciprocate with negativity, which results in continuation and escalation of negative interactions.

Not surprisingly, these negative interactions have a significant impact on how members of distressed couples feel about their relationships. Distressed partners seem to be more reactive to negative events than happy partners. Such events have a larger detrimental effect on overall satisfaction with the relationship than such events have for nondistressed couples (Jacobson, Follette, & McDonald, 1982). Happy couples seem more able to disregard such events, at least in terms of their feelings about the relationship as a whole, than do distressed couples.

Ways of Handling Conflict

Recent research has provided a more fine-grained analysis of the types of negative communication related to relationship satisfaction and how these might function over time. Certain types of communication behaviors that are characteristically associated with couple distress in the present have, somewhat paradoxically, been found to be related to improvements in couple satisfaction over time (Gottman & Krokoff, 1989). More specifically, research on married couples found that couples who displayed a pattern including "positive verbal behavior and compliance" on the part of the wife tended to be happier in the present, but to display decreases in marital satisfaction over time. Engaging in the conflict and expression of anger (as opposed to withdrawing) were associated with low levels of marital satisfaction in the present but increased marital satisfaction over time. Finally, "defensiveness, stubbornness, and withdrawal from interaction" were related to low satisfaction both in the present and over time. These results suggest that rather than always being destructive for a relationship, some amount of conflict and the ability to express anger without withdrawal occurring seem to be, in the long run, important aspects of satisfactory relationships.

ASSESSMENT

A variety of methods are available to assess various aspects of couples' behavior. The means of assessment employed depend largely on the purpose of the assessor and the time and resources available to do the assessment. One may be interested in characterizing a couple in an overall way, for example: "How satisfied is each partner with the relationship." One may want to characterize the couple in terms of how they interact with each other or how they discuss and attempt to solve problems. When a couple enters therapy, a more thorough understanding of the couple's specific problems and some knowledge of the history of the relationship are necessary.

Self-Report

To characterize a couple's overall satisfaction with their relationship, researchers often use paper and pencil measures such as the Dyadic Adjustment Scale (Spanier, 1976) or the Marital Adjustment Scale (Locke & Wallace, 1959). These scales yield scores that reflect a person's level of satisfaction with his or her relationship. Normative data are available on these instruments, making interpretation of scores relatively straightforward. These measures are useful in that they yield an objective score that can be used in empirical research, for example to mark change pre- and post-therapy. They can also be useful markers for therapists in identifying a global level of satisfaction of each partner.

Paper and pencil measures are also used to assess specific relationship issues. For example, checklists ask respondents to indicate which of various areas (e.g. money, communication, in-laws, etc.) they feel are problematic in their relationship. Other measures, such as the Areas of Change questionnaire, provide lists of partner behaviors and ask respondents to indicate which ones they would like their partner to engage in more often or less often (Weiss, Hops, & Patterson, 1973). There are also paper and pencil measures that assess physically (Strauss, 1979) and emotionally abusive behaviors (Tolman, 1987).

Direct Observation

Behavioral observation methods are widely used in behavioral research to study couples' interaction patterns and communication behaviors. The most commonly used task is one in which couples are asked to discuss and attempt to resolve a problem in their relationship. Problems may be standardized or specific to the relationship. These interactions are typically video- or audiotaped and then coded for different types of behaviors. Coding systems such as the Marital Interaction Coding System (MICS) typically categorize behaviors into such categories as "complain," "criticize," "smile/laugh," "interrupt," "(offer a) positive solution," and so

forth (Hops, Wills, Patterson, & Weiss, 1971). These codes are then aggregated into larger categories such as positive versus negative behaviors.

Direct assessment of couples' communication is useful for several reasons. First, this method does not rely on the couples' own subjective reports but offers an objective look at their behavior. In addition, couples' interaction patterns are predictive of how satisfied they are likely to be with their relationship in the future. For example, "whining" behavior by the wife accompanied by "withdrawal" on the part of the husband predicted long-term diminished marital satisfaction (Gottman & Krokoff 1989).

Clinically, a sample of a couple's behavior while interacting with each other can be of use to a therapist in attempting to form a conceptualization of the couple's problems. Often a more complete picture of the behaviors preventing successful problem solving emerges from such an assessment. For example, the partners may not focus on one particular problem at a time but move from topic to topic without any resolution. Alternately, a couple may be unsuccessful in problem solving because they focus on blaming each other rather than generating solutions. Another couple may simply withdraw and avoid engaging in any conflict. Knowledge of these recurrent patterns may improve the therapist's ability to develop an effective intervention plan for the couple.

Interviews

In a clinical setting, assessment is also accomplished via a therapist's interviews with the couple reporting for therapy. Typically, a therapist will conduct 2 or 3 assessment sessions at the outset of therapy to determine whether couples therapy seems appropriate and what the important issues and problems are for a given couple. In the first meeting with a couple, the therapist explains that the first few sessions will be for assessment only, not treatment, so the couple does not have unfulfilled expectations that things will change in the first weeks of therapy. The therapist then asks each partner to explain why they are seeking help and what they think the important issues are. This discussion is kept brief so the couple does not get bogged down in focusing solely on problems. Next, the therapist engages the couple in a discussion of their relationship history, focusing primarily on how they met, what first attracted them to one another, and why they got married (if they did), as well as general information about how their relationship has gone since. This discussion provides the therapist with important information about the couple's history and frequently has the additional benefit of helping the couple generate or revive some positive feelings about one another.

The second session is often conducted with each partner being seen individually. During this session the therapist explores in greater depth each person's view of what the problems in the relationship are. The therapist discusses each partner's level of commitment and his or her conceptualization of the problems, and attempts to develop rapport with each partner.

In the third session, the therapist presents the couple with a conceptualization of the relationship problems. The therapist presents a model of the relationship, stressing the reciprocal nature of problems: the ways in which both partners contribute to each problem in a way that makes it less likely that either partner will change.

THERAPY TECHNIQUES

Behavioral couples therapy (BCT) is associated with techniques derived from behavioral theory that are applied to the problems causing conflict or unhappiness in a relationship. They may be employed in a more or less structured way. These techniques are used within the context of a warm and collaborative therapeutic re-

lationship. The therapist is open about discussing the purposes for various activities and the format therapy will take. The therapist is responsive to client needs by adapting techniques to the individual couple while structuring the sessions and maintaining direction.

Collaborative Set

The first and probably most important goal of BCT is to induce a "collaborative set" within the couple. Members of distressed relationships often focus on what their partner does that they do not like, rather than on what they themselves can do to improve the relationship. They are reluctant to change their own behavior until they see their partner making changes first, which often results in a stalemate. The collaborative set embodies the notion that each member of the couple must focus on changing his or her own behavior, rather than waiting for his or her partner to change. The therapist discusses this concept directly with the couple and asks them each to agree to adopt this new theory of relationship change. The therapist refers to this idea throughout therapy.

Behavior Exchange

Many studies have demonstrated that partners in distressed relationships tend to engage in fewer behaviors that are pleasing to their partners than do happy couples (Gottman, 1979; Jacobson, Follette & McDonald; 1982; Levenson & Gottman, 1983; Margolin, 1981; Vincent, Weiss & Birchler, 1975). Although couples usually come into therapy expecting to focus immediately on problems, this lack of positive feelings about the relationship makes work on problems difficult. The goal of the first module of behavioral couples therapy, behavior exchange (BE), is therefore to try to increase positive feelings and thereby enhance the reinforcing value of each partner for the other by having each partner engage in behaviors pleasing to the other. Often couples experience increases in satisfaction in a short period of time during behavior exchange.

To set BE in motion, the therapist asks each partner to make a list of behaviors that they think would be pleasing to the other. They are then asked to engage in a few of these behaviors during the week and to observe the reaction of their partner. They are also asked to express appreciation for their partners' attempts. An additional assignment may be given for each partner to make a list of things the other could do that would please him- or herself, and lists are exchanged. Partners are asked to focus only on behaviors they will feel comfortable with and will not resent doing. The therapist may need to emphasize that each partner is choosing to do things they want to do, rather than doing it out of a sense of obligation to the therapist.

Communication Skills Training

Typically the behavioral therapist will choose to work on communication skills as the second module of treatment. It is often important to improve a couple's basic communication skills before attempting to resolve problems in the relationship, so the couple will be able to talk effectively with each other about other problems. This module involves a series of exercises of increasing complexity, designed to shape the couple's verbal and nonverbal communication behaviors to be more effective. The therapist models each skill as it is covered, has each partner practice it, gives feedback, and then gives a homework assignment that includes practicing the skill at home.

First, the therapist makes a distinction for the couple between the roles of "speaker" and "listener," and describes skills involved in each role. Emphasis is placed on the importance of good listening skills, including attending both verbally and nonverbally, not interrupting, and using paraphrasing. Skills of the speaker role include being clear and direct in stating feelings, being concise, not blaming, not mind-

reading, etc. The couple is first instructed to have each partner take a turn discussing something innocuous, such as a hobby or how their day went, while the other partner listens and paraphrases. Topics assigned for discussion become increasingly emotional and relationship-focused, such as talking about something that happened during the day and how it made the partner feel, about something pleasant that one partner did during the week and how that made the other partner feel, and so on.

Problem-Solving Training

Problem-solving training, frequently the third module of treatment, involves teaching the couple a structured format for discussing conflict areas in their relationship. The therapist instructs the couple to begin by working on relatively minor problems. The therapist participates in the couple's early attempts by modeling, coaching, and reinforcing approximations of the desired behavior. The format of problem solving includes two parts: problem definition and problem solution. In the problem-definition phase, one partner raises a problem by describing what's bothering him or her without blaming, ascribing negative intent, or raising numerous examples, and also acknowledges his or her role in the problem. The other partner paraphrases and expresses his or her willingness to work on the problem. The couple works together to develop a concrete definition of the problem, which they then write down. The problem-solution phase begins with brainstorming possible solutions, which are also written down. Couples are encouraged to be as creative as possible and not to evaluate the solutions as they are generated. After a list of solutions has been created, the pros and cons of each solution are discussed and a decision is made as to whether the solution should be kept or dismissed. Then a change agreement is written up to include all solutions that have been retained. The change agreement also specifies how solutions will be carried out and a date when the efficacy of the agreement will be re-evaluated.

The following is a brief sample of how a problem-solving discussion might proceed:

PROBLEM DEFINITION

W: I really appreciate it when you come and pick me up from work when it's raining, but when you're late it makes me feel frustrated and like you don't really care.

H: You like it that I come and pick you up when the weather's bad but when I'm late you feel frustrated and like I don't care about you very much?

W: Yes. I know I contribute to this by sometimes not being ready when I said I would be.

H: You think the fact that you're sometimes not waiting when I get there contributes to the problem. Is that right?

W: Yes.

H: I can really see how this is a problem, and I'm willing to work with you on it.

PROBLEM SOLUTION—BRAINSTORMING

W: I could call you 10 minutes before I'm ready to go, so I'd be ready when you get there.

H: I could call and let you know if I'm going to be late.

W: I could take the bus home when the weather's bad.

H: You could wait in your office and keep working, so if I'm late it won't be so frustrating. Then when I get there I could come in and let you know I'm there.

The couple then discusses the pros and cons of each solution and comes up with the following change agreement.

Cindy will wait for James in her office when he's coming to get her. James will call to let Cindy know if he's going to be late. Agreement will be reviewed in one month.

Many distressed couples experience specific sexual dysfunctions or generally decreased pleasure in their sexual relationship. Alleviation of other problems in the relationship and increases in overall satisfaction with the relationship sometimes result in increased pleasure in sexual activity as well. The therapy may also directly address issues of affection and sexual enrichment through use of techniques such as sensate focus, application of communication and problem-solving skills to discussions of sex and affection, or guided fantasy. For couples experiencing specific sexual dysfunctions, behavioral couples therapists use a range of behavioral techniques commonly used in sex therapy (see Chapter 12, on sexual dysfunction).

Frequently couples arrive at a therapy session after having had an argument or still feeling too angry from a not-so-recent argument to work productively on whatever the therapist had planned for the session. The therapist may then choose to forego the original agenda and do troubleshooting with the couple about the argument. The purposes of troubleshooting are to defuse the argument and to help the couple better understand the process of the argument so they can identify ways to avoid similar arguments in the future. The therapist first asks each spouse to explain his or her position to the therapist while the other spouse listens but does not comment. Each person thereby hears the other's position and may gain a better understanding of what is actually bothering the partner, without reengaging in the argument. The therapist then may go through the original argument step by step with the couple, asking each partner what he or she could have said or done differently at each point, as well as coaching and giving suggestions.

Identifying Negative Interaction Patterns

This step-by-step analysis of an argument can sometimes lead to the identification of a negative interaction pattern that recurs in the relationship. An interaction pattern describes a typical process that the couple repeats across fights or arguments, regardless of the particular content area. For example, a pattern might involve the following steps: (1) wife brings up a complaint or concern, (2) husband ignores her, (3) wife repeats her complaint, (4) husband responds angrily, (5) wife withdraws and drops her complaint. Once a therapist begins to recognize such a pattern, he or she may help the couple identify it by describing the pattern to them and asking them to monitor their daily interactions and arguments to identify the pattern on their own. The goal of such an exercise is for couples to be able to recognize the pattern when it arises during the week. Sometimes the act of recognition itself is sufficient to break or alter a pattern. When this is not the case, the therapist will also work with the couple to generate alternative ways of behaving that meet both partners' needs but break the pattern.

An example of an argument following the above pattern is as follows: Theresa mentions that Peter hasn't taken out the garbage; Peter grunts and continues to watch TV; Theresa waits and fumes for about 15 minutes, then mentions it again; Peter yells at her, "All you ever do is nag!"; Theresa leaves the room crying. A BCT therapist working with Theresa and Peter hears this description and recognizes this as a pattern; he describes the pattern to the couple, using examples of other fights they've had in the past that follow the same pattern. The therapist would also work with Peter and Theresa to develop alternate responses such as: rather than bringing up her complaints while Peter is watching TV, Theresa could do so at some agreed-upon time, or Peter could respond to Theresa's initial statement of concern about some household task by telling her when he plans to complete the task. This discussion may help Peter and Theresa to be more able to identify what they each need in this situation and enable them to reach a compromise, rather than each of them repeating the usual behavior pat-

tern and consequently keeping the pattern in motion.

EVALUATION OF THERAPY OUTCOME

Behavioral couples therapy has been the focus of much empirical research. A recent review reports on 17 controlled outcome studies on the efficacy of behavioral couples therapy (Hahlweg & Markman, 1988). Research has focused on the effectiveness of the therapy, the importance of various components of the treatments, use of co-therapists versus an individual therapist, group versus conjoint BCT, the format of the therapy, and characteristics of couples that predict how well they will do in BCT.

In addition to looking at factors that affect how and why BCT works, researchers have studied various types of changes that the therapy may produce. In other words, different dependent measures are used in evaluating behavioral couples therapy. These measures include various types of changes in communication behaviors, as assessed by observational techniques; changes in self-reports of satisfaction; and changes in reports of specific problems in the relationship. In addition, changes in individual psychopathology of partners following behavioral couples therapy have also become the focus of empirical research.

Recent reviews of controlled clinical trials that compare BCT to wait-list controls have concluded that BCT does produce changes relative to wait-list control groups (Baucom & Hoffman, 1986; Hahlweg & Markman, 1988). Couples receiving BCT have been found to be more satisfied with their relationships relative to the wait-list group and to identify fewer problem areas in their relationships after treatment. A recent meta-analysis, which combines the results from multiple studies, concluded that the chances of getting better while on a wait-list are about 30%, whereas the chance of the relationship improving by the end of a behavioral treatment is 70% (Hahlweg & Markman, 1988). In terms of changes in communication, BCT seems to reduce the number of negative communications couples make, but the findings are mixed with respect to increasing positive statements. In fact, most studies have not demonstrated that couples receiving BCT actually show an increase in the number of positive statements they make (Baucom & Hoffman, 1986).

Baucom also reports on three studies that compared BCT to a nonspecific control therapy. Use of a nonspecific therapy condition controls for the effects of receiving all of the inactive components of BCT, such as the time spent together with a therapist, the attention from the therapist, and so forth. Couples are not taught skills in these treatments, but simply spend time talking about their problems with a therapist. Couples receiving BCT showed more improvement in communication (Jacobson, 1978), but the findings have been mixed in terms of the relative effectiveness of BCT in improving relationship satisfaction. Two studies found BCT to be more effective (Azrin et al., 1980; Jacobson, 1978); another study found no differences at posttest but better results for the BCT group at follow-up (Crowe, 1978).

The findings regarding the relative importance of the different components of BCT (e.g., communication training, behavior exchange, problem-solving training, behavioral contracting) do not lend themselves to definitive conclusions. For example, two studies examined the roles of behavior exchange, communication/problem-solving training, and behavioral contracting (Baucom, 1982; Jacobson, 1984). These studies did not find significant differences in reported relationship satisfaction across treatments, suggesting that the various components of BCT are not differentially important to the outcome of the treatment. There was some indication, however, that couples who received only behavior exchange were less satisfied with

their relationships 6 months after therapy was completed, suggesting that the skills acquired in communication/problem-solving training may help couples maintain their gains in satisfaction.

In most studies that examine the effectiveness of BCT, the therapy is done in a highly structured format, with a set order of modules and set number of sessions. In contrast, practitioners using BCT in nonresearch settings probably do not follow such a structured format. One study compared BCT done in the structured, research-setting format to BCT administered in a more flexible way (Jacobson et al., 1989). In this flexible BCT condition, therapists tailored the therapy to individual couples: they had as many or few sessions as they chose and administered BCT interventions in any order they chose, omitting those they did not think were appropriate. No differences were found between these treatments at posttest, but at 6-month follow-up, the couples from the structured condition were more likely to have deteriorated, suggesting that couples who receive an individualized form of BCT are more likely to maintain their treatment gains over time.

Predictors of Outcome

A few characteristics of couples have been found to be predictors of how much a couple will benefit from behavioral couples therapy. For example, younger couples seem to achieve better outcomes in BCT than do older couples (Baucom, 1984; Hahlweg, Schindler, Revenstorf, & Brengelmann, 1984). Not surprisingly, couples who seem to lack affection for each other at pretreatment are less likely to benefit from BCT, regardless of their problem-solving ability (Hahlweg et al., 1984). Finally, some interesting results based on communication patterns as predictors of therapy outcome have also been found. For example, Hahlweg et al. (1984) found that negative communication behaviors at pretreatment were positively correlated with satisfaction at posttreatment. It may be that the capacity to continue discussing an issue, although it may be aversive, results in high levels of negative behaviors in the communication assessment situation, but ultimately also produces a more satisfying relationship.

Use of Co-Therapists

Working with two people simultaneously in a psychotherapy format is quite different from working with an individual. A common problem that arises in such a therapy modality is that the therapist may be seen by one or both of the spouses as more sympathetic to one of them, or the therapist may in fact become more aligned with one spouse. For this and other reasons, it has been suggested that BCT can be more effectively done with two co-therapists rather than with a single therapist. The empirical evidence does not support this notion, however. A study comparing BCT with one therapist versus BCT with co-therapists found no differences on a number of dependent variables at either posttreatment or follow-up (Mehlman, Baucom, & Anderson, 1983) Because the use of co-therapists requires greater resources than a single therapist, unless special circumstances warrant otherwise, the evidence points to use of a single therapist as the more efficient choice.

There is mixed evidence for the differential effectiveness of BCT done conjointly, that is, with one couple present, versus BCT done in a group format, with more than one couple present. There is some evidence that conjoint BCT is more effective than group BCT, at least in altering certain areas. Hahlweg et al. (1984) compared conjoint BCT to conjoint-group BCT and found that couples in both treatment conditions improved in terms of their satisfaction and their communication. However, conjoint BCT couples reported more change in relationship problems and overall happiness with the relationship than group couples did. In contrast, a recent study (Wilson, Bornstein, & Wilson,

1988) comparing group to conjoint BCT found both treatments to be equally effective, relative to a wait-list control, except in terms of the number of positive statements couples made in a posttest communication assessment. Group therapy couples emitted more positive statements to their partners during this task than did conjoint therapy couples. No differences were found at 6-month follow-up.

Maintenance of Effects

Relapse is the recurrence of symptoms or problematic behaviors at some point after an individual or couple has successfully changed in therapy. Since the point of behavioral couples therapy is to help couples make lasting changes in their relationships, it is important for researchers to assess how couples are doing, not just at the end of therapy, but over a span of time as well. Most studies do not include follow-up assessments with couples for more than 6 months. One study that followed couples over a 2-year period found that about one-third of couples who showed improvement at the end of treatment had returned to their baseline level of distress two years later (Jacobson, Schmaling, & Holtzworth-Munroe, 1987). A recent review cites five studies that included follow-up assessments at 9 to 12 months and concluded from a meta-analysis of these studies that BCT actually does produce long-lasting change for couples who remain married (Hahlweg & Markman, 1988). Methodological problems in studies that follow couples over time may be producing the discrepant findings. Many couples drop out over the course of treatment and follow-up, including couples who split up. Often these data are simply excluded from analyses, resulting in an artificially inflated representation of treatment effects that does not take into account couples who have divorced or simply dropped out.

Research in couples therapy has produced some methodological advances that have influenced research in other areas of behavioral research as well. The development of clinical significance statistics has been largely the contribution of couples therapy researchers. Although most studies find statistically significant changes in several dependent variables, this does not tell us how much couples are actually changing, only that the changes are reliable and therefore not likely to have been due to chance alone. Recently, investigators have begun to consider not only the reliability of the change that occurs, but also the extent to which couples who enter therapy distressed actually come out of therapy nondistressed (Jacobson, Follette, & Revenstorf, 1984). Since most couples probably enter therapy with the desired goal of achieving a level of satisfaction with their relationship that is not just slightly higher than what they have but is at a level that most people would consider "satisfied," the clinical significance statistic is a meaningful measure of change. Using this statistic, results of several studies show that about half of couples who receive BCT in a research setting improve to an extent that they can be considered nondistressed (Jacobson, Follette, Revenstorf, Baucom et al., 1984).

FUTURE DIRECTIONS

This section will discuss some important areas of exploration in behavioral couples therapy and research. These include: therapeutic techniques aimed at preventing relapse, prevention of relationship distress, the impact of BCT on individual functioning, and new therapeutic interventions, including cognitive interventions and more holistic therapeutic techniques derived from behavioral therapy.

As discussed above, the issue of relapse and maintenance of treatment gains over time is a salient one in behavioral couples therapy research. Some new innovations in the format of therapy are now directly addressing this issue (Whisman, 1989). Traditionally, most therapies

are conducted in a discrete block of time, and the importance of a well-defined termination of treatment has been stressed. Behavioral therapies typically follow this pattern, with relatively short-term therapy being applied and viewed as complete when symptoms have remitted and the client or couple is viewed as recovered. The notion of introducing booster or maintainence sessions into the therapy was formulated to address the problem of recurring distress directly. Many couples face stressful life changes that adversely affect their relationship at some point following therapy. Maintenance sessions help couples cope with these changes and reinforce continued use of skills already acquired in therapy. Maintenance sessions can be implemented in various ways, including appointments scheduled at regular intervals after therapy is over or regularly scheduled phone call check-ins, with appointments scheduled as needed. The efficacy of maintenance treatments is currently being investigated in a clinical trial (Whisman, 1989).

Some work is now specifically addressing the issue of prevention of marital distress by focusing on couples preparing for marriage (Markman, 1979; Markman, Floyd, Stanley, & Lewis, 1986). The purpose of prevention is to provide treatment for couples before they become distressed, in order to reduce the likelihood that they will become distressed. Probably the best-researched program, the Premarital Relationship Enhancement Program (PREP), includes the following treatment components: communication and conflict-resolution skills training, cognitive restructuring, and sensual/ sexual enrichment. This program is administered in a group format with couples planning to be married.

The effectiveness of the PREP program has been evaluated in a clinical trial with remarkable results (Markman, Floyd, Stanley, & Storaasli, 1988). Couples who received the PREP intervention showed higher relationship satisfaction, higher sexual satisfaction, and fewer relationship problems than couples in the control group, both immediately following treatment and at follow-up. There is also some evidence that participation in the PREP program reduced divorce rate (Markman, 1989).

Family-systems-oriented therapists have for some time addressed their therapy to dysfunctional family patterns that they see as maintaining individual psychopathology. Behaviorally oriented therapists are now also taking an interest in the relationship between marital or relationship distress and individual functioning. It may be that distressed relationships cause or maintain problems in some members of such relationships. Although the primary goal of most couples therapy programs is to effect relationship change, researchers are beginning to investigate the impact of couples therapy on the functioning of the individuals in the relationship. The goal of such programs is to alleviate the relationship distress that may be maintaining individual psychopathology.

Two studies have examined the effect of behavioral couples therapy on depression in the female partner among married couples (Beach & O'Leary, 1986; Jacobson, Dobson, Fruzzetti, Schmaeling, & Salusky, 1991). Both studies have found support for the idea that doing BCT with distressed marital partners alleviates depression in the wife. A recent review also concluded that there is evidence to support the use of couples therapy in the treatment of agoraphobia and alcoholism (Jacobson, Holtzworth-Munroe, & Schmaling, 1989). One study found that the addition of communication training to a standard exposure therapy program for agoraphobics enhanced the progress of the therapy (Arnow, Taylor, Agras, & Telch, 1985). Although the results are somewhat equivocal in the area of treatment of alcoholism (O'Farrell, Cutter, & Floyd, 1985), McCrady et al. (1986) found that alcoholics provided with social-learning-based couples therapy improved more quickly and maintained their improvements longer than a control group who received couples therapy that focused on alcohol-related problems. In addition, Dadds, Schwartz, and Sanders (1987) found that BCT done as an adjunct to parent training with maritally distressed parents of a conduct-disordered child improves the effectiveness of the parent training. These studies suggest that alleviating relationship distress can have broader effects than simply improving the relationship.

Interventions derived from cognitive theory are now being applied in the couples therapy setting (Baucom & Epstein, 1989; Epstein, 1982). According to this model, dysfunctional ways of thinking about one's partner or relationship tend to maintain relationship distress. The type of thoughts these interventions address are primarily the reasons distressed partners give to explain their partner's behavior. As described above, distressed couples tend to give negative reasons for their partners' behaviors. Cognitive interventions are designed not necessarily to get couples to change these beliefs but to improve their ability to entertain more than one possible option. In other words, rather than rigidly sticking to the negative reason that comes to mind first, cognitive interventions promote being able to generate a range of things that may have influenced one's partner and to recognize that any of these may have been active. The intended goal is to defuse the negative emotions associated with the original, negative reason the person gave by coming up with alternative reasons.

One study that compared standard BCT to BCT with the addition of cognitive interventions did not find that the addition of the cognitive techniques improved outcomes (Baucom & Lester, 1986). Although the empirical evidence does not suggest that cognitive interventions improve the quality of BCT, many clinicians find them appealing and such techniques seem to be one wave of the future.

CONCLUSIONS

This chapter has attempted to highlight some important issues in the study and practice of behavioral couples therapy, including a behavioral conceptualization of relationship distress, an overview of how behavioral couples therapy addresses relationship problems, and a review of some of the research on couples therapy. The contribution of behavioral researchers and practitioners to the understanding of relationship distress and its treatment has obviously been significant. The application of behavioral theory in the couples therapy setting has created a structure to help understand the sometimes overwhelming plethora of behavior the couples therapist is faced with organizing and changing. The continued exploration of behavioral the-

ory, as applied to relationship distress, should produce even more effective therapeutic interventions in the future.

TREATMENT RESOURCES

Jacobson, N. S., & Christianson, A. (In press). *Integrative behavioral couples therapy*. New York: Martin.

Jacobson, N. S., & Margolin, G. (1979). *Marital therapy: Strategies based on social learning and behavior exchange principles*. New York: Brunner/Mazel.

CHAPTER 12

Sexual Dysfunction

Joseph LoPiccolo

This chapter will review the history and current status of behavioral treatment focused on problems of sexual functioning in heterosexual couples. This type of treatment, once a secondary component of marital therapy, individual psychotherapy, and sex education, has come to be a more or less independent type of behaviorally oriented treatment, popularly referred to as "sex therapy."

Behavioral sex therapy is a type of therapy in which the therapist actively and directly educates the patient about sexual physiology and sexual techniques, restructures maladaptive behavior patterns and cognitions regarding sexuality, and uses anxiety-reduction and skill-training techniques to improve the patient's functioning. The history of the application of behavioral techniques to sexual dysfunction is a long one that much predates the rise of formal behavior therapy. In the late eighteenth century, a British physician, Sir John Hunter (cited in Comfort, 1965), described a treatment program for erectile failure that is similar to the

program described by Wolpe (1958) and by Masters and Johnson (1970). At the turn of the century, hypnotherapists such as Schrenk-Notzing (1895/1956) used direct sex education and instruction in sexual techniques to treat sexual dysfunction successfully.

In the early behavioral view of sexual dysfunction, anxiety was considered to be the major causal factor. That is, anxiety was posited to be incompatible with, or reciprocally inhibitory to, sexual arousal. The basic treatment strategy was progressive relaxation and systematic desensitization.

Although the behavioral movement gained considerable force within American psychology and, to a lesser degree, psychiatry, it had no real impact on how the average educated layman thought about sexual dysfunction. The primary cultural view of sexual dysfunction remained a psychoanalytic one, until the landmark publication of Masters and Johnson's works (1966, 1970). Masters and Johnson proposed a relatively atheoretical scheme for treatment of sexual dysfunction. In their discussion of the causes of sexual dysfunctions, they stressed a type of informal social learning theory approach. That is, they suggested that exposure to certain critical events in childhood, adolescence, and adulthood resulted in sexual dysfunction. Masters and Johnson stressed the role of religious, cultural, and familial negative messages about sex and the anxiety induced by traumatic first sexual experiences; they introduced the notion of sexual dysfunction as a self-maintaining vicious cycle mediated by anxiety (Masters & Johnson, 1970). That is, Masters and Johnson basically proposed that while a variety of early life experiences might result in the first occasion of sexual dysfunction, the anxiety attendant upon sexual failure and the development of an anxious, self-evaluative, spectator role serve to maintain the occurrence of sexual dysfunction.

Following the publication of Masters and Johnson's *Human Sexual Inadequacy* in 1970, a number of other accounts of behavioral or quasi-behavioral approaches to treatment of sexual dysfunction have appeared (Hartman & Fithian, 1972; Kaplan, 1974; Lobitz & LoPiccolo, 1972; LoPiccolo & Lobitz, 1972). These accounts all differ greatly in the degree to which behavioral terminology is used and in the theoretical framework that is presented. However, if differences in language are ignored, all of these reports seem to describe fairly similar treatment procedures (LoPiccolo, 1977b). Although there are unique elements in various programs, the *reduction of performance anxiety* (often through implicit counterconditioning and cognitive-behavioral strategies), *sex education, skill training in communication and sexual technique*, and *attitude change procedures* remain elements common to both behavior therapy and sex therapy approaches to sexual dysfunction.

In the late 1970s, within the field of behavior therapy, there was a renewal of interest in cognition as well as overt behavior. In the field of sex therapy, this cognitive-behavioral emphasis led to a focus on the patient's *thinking* about sex.

Therapy came to include modification of the patient's cognitions regarding sexual issues. Unrealistic expectations, negative self-images, distorted views of the opposite sex's needs and requirements, and tendencies to catastrophic thinking became a major focus of therapy (Lazarus, 1978). Interestingly enough, much of this cognitive-behavioral approach to sex therapy had been anticipated in somewhat different theoretical terms by the work of Albert Ellis 20 years earlier (Ellis, 1958, 1962). While Ellis's theoretical label for this procedure is "rational-emotive therapy," the procedures described by Ellis for sexual dysfunctions are extremely similar to procedures advocated as "new" procedures by the cognitive-behavior therapists in recent years.

CLASSIFICATION OF SEXUAL DYSFUNCTION

As Szasz (1960) has repeatedly pointed out, accepting any person into therapy validates the idea that a problem exists. Consequently, although social values can remain implicit in the descriptive factors thought to contribute to adequate sexual functioning, the classification of sexual dysfunctions forces explicit statements about what sexual behaviors are valued.

The impact of the historical period and the individual investigator's beliefs has been dramatic in the sexual diagnosis area. Clitoral stimulation was considered immature by Freud (1905/1962) but normal and desirable by Masters and Johnson (1970). Premature ejaculation was considered biologically "superior" in the 1940s (Kinsey, Pomeroy, & Martin, 1948) and a dysfunction in the 1970s (Kaplan, 1977; Masters & Johnson, 1970).

The *Diagnostic and Statistical Manual of Mental Disorders* (3rd ed., rev.) (DSM-III-R) classifies sexual dysfunctions according to the phases of the sexual response cycle, as first described by

Masters and Johnson (1966) and modified by Kaplan (1974, 1977). In this classification (American Psychiatric Association [APA], 1987), sexual dysfunctions are defined as "psychosomatic disorders which make it impossible for the individual to have and/or enjoy coitus." Dysfunctions can affect any of the first three phases of the sexual response cycle: the *desire phase*, the *arousal phase*, and the *orgasm phase*.

The desire phase consists of feeling an urge to have sex, having sexual fantasies or daydreams, and feeling sexually attracted to others. There are two dysfunctions associated with the desire phase: *hypoactive sexual desire* and *sexual aversion*. The former is a lack of interest in sex, and, as a result, a low level of sexual activity. When a person with hypoactive sexual desire does have sex, however, he or she often functions normally and may even enjoy the experience, or at least not find it unpleasant. In contrast, patients with sexual aversion find sex to be actively unpleasant. Instead of experiencing arousal and pleasure, these patients often feel revulsion, disgust, anxiety, and fear.

The sexual arousal phase is marked by general physical arousal; increases in heart rate, muscle tension, blood pressure, and respiration; and specific changes in the pelvic region. Blood pooling in the pelvis (pelvic vasocongestion) leads to erection of the penis in men, and to swelling of the clitoris and labia and the production of vaginal lubrication in women. Dysfunctions during this phase, in the DSM-III-R system are *male erectile disorder* (previously called impotence) and *female arousal disorder* (previously referred to as frigidity). Earlier versions of the DSM did not differentiate between physical arousal and the subjective experience of emotional arousal, but sex therapists pointed out that a more specific classification system was needed (Schover, Friedman, Weiler, Heiman, & LoPiccolo, 1982). For example, as one patient put it, "Oh, I get very aroused and excited, the problem is just that my damn penis won't get hard!" Conversely, there are patients (more typically women) who report the occurrence of all the physiological components of arousal but who do not experience any accompanying excitement, pleasure, or arousal. In recognition of this distinction, the DSM-III-R defines sexual arousal disorders as involving either a failure of lubrication or genital swelling in woman, the absence of penile erection in men, or the lack of a subjective sense of sexual excitement and pleasure in either men or women.

The orgasm phase of the sexual response cycle consists of reflexive muscular contractions in the pelvic region. The most common male sexual dysfunction in this phase is *premature ejaculation*, which is defined as "ejaculation with minimal sexual stimulation before, upon, or shortly after penetration and before the person wishes it." (APA, 1987, p. 295). Much rarer is the male inability to reach orgasm despite adequate stimulation, called *inhibited male orgasm* in DSM-III-R, but usually referred to by sex therapists as inhibited ejaculation, ejaculatory incompetence, or retarded ejaculation.

Female orgasm phase disorder is called *inhibited female orgasm* in DSM-III-R. There is some ambiguity in DSM-III-R about whether lack of orgasm during intercourse is a sexual dysfunction, provided the woman can reach orgasm with her partner during direct stimulation of the clitoris, with caressing by her partner's hand or mouth. However, almost all contemporary sex therapists and researchers feel that the evidence is clear that women who have such clitoral orgasms are entirely normal and healthy (LoPiccolo & Stock, 1987).

There are two other dysfunctions listed in the DSM-III-R that do not fit neatly into a specific phase of the arousal cycle. *Vaginismus*, spastic contractions of the muscles around the outer third of the vagina, prevents entry of the penis. *Dyspareunia* (from Latin words meaning "painful mating") refers to pain in the genitals during sexual activity. Although dyspareunia does occasionally occur in men, it is much more common in women.

As the DSM-III-R categories of sexual dysfunction are rather broad, two additional di-

TABLE 12.1   Multiaxial problem-oriented system for sexual dysfunction

Desire Phase

Low sexual desire

Aversion to sex

Arousal Phase

Decreased subjective arousal

Difficulty achieving erections

Difficulty maintaining erections

Difficulty achieving and maintaining erections

Decreased subjective arousal and difficulty achieving erections

Decreased subjective arousal and difficulty maintaining erections

Decreased subjective arousal and difficulty achieving and maintaining erections

Decreased physiological arousal, female

Decreased physiological arousal, male

Orgasm Phase

Premature ejaculation, before entry

Premature ejaculation, less than 1 minute

Premature ejaculation, 1–3 min.,

Premature ejaculation, 4–7 min.,

Inhibited ejaculation

Anhedonic orgasmic

Orgasm with flaccid penis

Anhedonic orgasm with flaccid penis

Rapid ejaculation with flaccid penis

Anhedonic orgasm with rapid ejaculation

Inorgasmic

Inorgasmic except for masturbation

Inorgasmic except for partner manipulation

Inorgasmic except for masturbation

Infrequent coital orgasms

Inorgasmic except for vibrator or mechanical stimulation

Coital Pain

Vaginismus

Dyspareunia

Pain on ejaculation

Pain after ejaculation

Other pain exacerbated by sexual activity

Frequency Dissatisfaction

Desired frequency much lower than current activity level

Desired frequency much higher than current activity level

Qualifying Information

Prefers gender other than that of partner

Transvestism

Fetishism

Voyeurism

Exhibitionism (male)

Sexual pleasure from inflicting pain

Sexual pleasure from experiencing pain

Sexual pleasure from humiliating partner

Sexual pleasure from being humiliated

History of severe psychopathology

Current severe psychopathology

Severe marital distress

History of substance abuse

Current active substance abuse

History of physically abusing spouse

Currently physically abusing spouse

Active extramarital affair

Medical condition possibly affecting sex

Medication possibly affecting sex

No dysfunction

No diagnosis

mensions are often used to define a patient's specific problem. The dysfunction may be described as either lifelong or not lifelong, and as either global or situational. Thus, a woman with lifelong, global orgasmic dysfunction has never experienced an orgasm during any form of sexual activity. A man with not lifelong, situational erectile failure previously had erections during sex with his wife, but now only has erections during his solitary masturbation or with another partner.

Although the DSM-III (third edition of DSM) was a multiaxial system, the psychosexual dysfunction diagnoses were a small set of rather broad categories, which combined often dissimilar problems under the same label. A more specific, problem-oriented diagnostic system for sexual dysfunctions (Schover et al., 1982) formed the basis for many of the changes made from DSM-III to DSM-III-R.

The system contains six axes and is shown in Table 12.1. Diagnostic categories within the first five axes are mutually exclusive and exhaustive. Thus, only one diagnostic category may be used per axis. The last axis is reserved for qualifying information, descriptors that include information on unusual sexual preferences that may affect the individual's compatibility with partners. Other descriptors, such as severe marital problems, traumatic sexual experiences, substance abuse, or interfering medical problems that may affect prognosis of sex therapy, are also listed in this sixth axis. This axis ensures that clinically relevant information is not ignored because it does not fit into a specific category.

The first five axes that make up the system are as follows.

1. *Desire.* This axis includes low desire and aversion to sex.

2. *Arousal.* This category has more specificity than the DSM-III. Signs of physiological arousal are listed separately from the subjective emotional experience of arousal.

3. *Orgasm.* Again, this category is more specific than other classification systems and, for exam-

ple, includes several behavioral problems with male orgasm not specified in other systems, such as anhedonic orgasm (no pleasure during orgasm), orgasm with flaccid penis, and rapid ejaculation with a flaccid penis. Female orgasmic dysfunctions are classified according to the particular sexual activities during which the female client can experience orgasm.

4. *Coital Pain.* This axis includes genital pain during sexual activity, but also back pain, arthritis, and other factors that may interfere with sexual activity. Vaginismus is also included, as attempts at intercourse may be extremely painful for the woman with vaginismic muscle spasms.

5. *Dissatisfaction with Frequency.* This axis describes discrepancies in partner's satisfaction with the frequency of sexual activity. These discrepancies often arise if one partner has a dysfunction, or there is disagreement as to preferred types of activities or time of day to have sex.

ASSESSMENT OF SEXUAL DYSFUNCTION

Some sex therapy programs historically have included direct observation of the couple's sexual behavior (Serber, 1974; Hartman & Fithian, 1972) or direct sexual stimulation of the clients by the therapist (Hartman & Fithian, 1972). Although such procedures may seem to offer the advantage of direct recording of actual sexual behavior, the reactive nature of the situation, the potential for abusive exploitation of clients, and the negative reactions of most clients (and therapists!) have virtually eliminated such procedures in present-day therapy.

Sex History Interview

One common assessment strategy is the sex history interview (Masters & Johnson, 1970; Kaplan, 1974; Hartman & Fithian, 1972). The format of such an interview is usually that of an extended face-to-face, semi-structured interview, often lasting several hours.

The utility of such extensive history-taking has not been empirically demonstrated and is open to question in terms of the most efficient use of therapeutic time. Certainly many of the questions asked in the more extensive interviews has minimal clinical utility, in that treatment procedures remain the same regardless of the varying nature of the patient's answer. It should also be noted that causal explanations of etiology based on occurrence of supposedly pathogenic life history events must be viewed with caution. Such explanations are likely to be oversimplified at best, as research indicates that such events are of high base-rate occurrence in our society, and appear frequently in life histories taken from sexually functional adults (Heiman, Gladue, Roberts, & LoPiccolo, 1986).

Self-Report Questionnaires

Two very useful questionnaire inventories are the Sexual Arousal Inventory (Hoon, Hoon, & Wincze, 1976) and the Sexual Interaction Inventory (LoPiccolo & Steger, 1974). The Sexual Arousal Inventory is specific to females. The Sexual Interaction Inventory attempts to describe a couple's sexual relationship in terms of frequency and enjoyment of specific sexual activities. Both instruments are statistically sophisticated and provide guidelines for treatment, in that they identify arousal deficits and problem behaviors for therapeutic focus.

Physiological Assessment

Despite the fact that the majority of sexually dysfunctional patients are organically intact, it is becoming clear that there are a large number of biological processes that can be implicated in sexual dysfunction (LoPiccolo, 1992). The assessment of mixed biogenic and psychogenic etiology of sexual dysfunction is especially crucial in male erectile failure and female dys-

pareunia (painful intercourse). Organic factors do not, at the present stage of our knowledge, seem as clearly implicated in premature ejaculation or female orgasmic dysfunction.

A complete evaluation of the patient's biological status requires consideration of a number of parameters not included in routine physical examinations. Obviously, complete and thorough pelvic examinations by a consultant urologist or gynecologist are indicated. Current medications should be carefully assessed, as many commonly prescribed agents dramatically interfere with sexual functioning (LoPiccolo & Daiss, 1988). Beyond this, tests for thyroid function, endocrine status (especially testosterone), and glucose tolerance are needed, especially in low sex drive and erectile failure cases. An examination for neurological disease and blood flow to the pelvis is also especially important in erectile failure cases. In assessing physiological etiology of erectile failure, recording of nocturnal erection during REM (rapid eye movement or dreaming) sleep has been found to be a useful measure (Schiavi & Fisher, 1982).

To summarize, behavioral assessment of sexual dysfunction includes problem-focused, multi-method evaluation of functioning via interviewing, paper and pencil questionnaires, and physiological assessment. The goal of the assessment is to understand the factors that originally established and currently maintain the sexual dysfunction. Although treatment of sexual dysfunction is basically a cognitive-behavioral enterprise, the role of intrapsychic defenses cannot be ignored in many cases. In occasional erectile failure cases, for example, the client may be struggling with the issue of an unacceptable and therefore consciously denied homosexual orientation. Similarly, the importance of considering the role of the sexual dysfunction in the couple's broader emotional relationship cannot be overemphasized. For some couples, the dysfunction plays a functional role in the maintenance of their emotional relationship and lifestyle. A dysfunction may be a means of avoiding intimacy, of expressing hostility, of maintaining control in the relationship, or of retaliating for other grievances in the relationship.

TREATMENT TECHNIQUES

Low Sexual Desire

Low sexual desire is a disorder that is seen with increasing frequency in clinical practice. Desire disorders now constitute the largest group of complaints voiced by patients seeking therapy (LoPiccolo & Friedman, 1988). Furthermore, although low-desire disorders were more frequently seen in women in years past, the current cases are male and female in equal numbers (LoPiccolo & Friedman, 1988). In much of the current literature, there is no empirical basis given for the diagnosis of low sexual desire. Rather, the diagnosis seems to be based on the clinician's unspecified global judgment. Some studies have used an arbitrary behavioral index, such as frequency of intercourse. All such definitions have a number of problems. Normative studies on frequency of sex indicate that age, number of years married, socioeconomic status, religiosity, marital happiness, and a host of other factors all influence the frequency of marital coitus in couples. Even allowing for the confounding effects of such variables, it is difficult to equate low sexual desire with a low frequency of marital coitus. Some cases of low sexual desire involve relatively high frequencies of coital activity, because the low-desire spouse has been given an ultimatum by the other spouse that unless they have sex more frequently, a divorce or an affair will result. In other cases involving a low frequency of sexual activity with the spouse, the low-desire client may engage in daily masturbation. Diagnostic criteria therefore need to include frequency of occurrence of sexual fantasies, masturbation, noncoital sexual activity, coitus with the partner, and any nonpartner-related sexual activity.

The occurrence of spontaneous sexual drive and interest, as reflected in the initiation of sexual activity, must be differentiated from receptivity to partner's initiation.

There is little published outcome research on the treatment of low sexual desire. Two studies (Friedman, 1983; Schover & LoPiccolo, 1982), using a complex cognitive-behavioral treatment program (LoPiccolo & Friedman, 1988), found generally good treatment results. These studies indicate the need for a treatment focused specifically on low desire, as standard sex therapy often fails to raise sexual desire (Kaplan, 1979).

Affectual Awareness

The first component of the LoPiccolo and Friedman (1988) treatment program is called affectual awareness. In this phase of therapy, the focus is on getting the client in touch with any negative attitudes, beliefs, and cognitions regarding sex. For example, clients will report that although they were raised by their parents or their religion to have negative attitudes toward sex, they have overcome these attitudes. Close examination, however, reveals that although this change has occurred at an intellectual level, it is not a true "gut-level" feeling change. Making the person aware of these lingering negative residues of earlier indoctrination constitutes the affectual awareness stage of therapy.

Insight-Oriented Therapy

The second phase of sex therapy for low sexual desire involves insight-oriented therapy. In this phase of therapy, clients are helped to gain an understanding of why they have the negative emotions that were identified in the affectual awareness phase. Steps 1 and 2 are in some sense only preparatory for the more active interventions of Steps 3 and 4.

Cognitive Therapy

The third phase of treatment involves cognitive therapy. The cognitive phase of therapy is designed to alter irrational thoughts that inhibit sexual desire. Patients are helped to identify self-statements that interfere with sexual desire. They are taught that unrealistic or irrational beliefs may be the main cause of their emotional reactions, and that they can change these unrealistic self-statements.

Individualized coping statements are generated, with the help of the therapist, to help the patient cope with, rather than avoid, emotional reactions to particular sexual situations. Typical coping statements might include, "When I was younger I learned to feel guilty about engaging in sex and I don't want to, nor do I have to, feel that way anymore," or, for a low-drive woman raised in an alcoholic-father family, "My husband is not like my father. I deliberately picked a man I can trust, who is dependable and who is not an alcoholic."

Behavioral Intervention

The fourth element of this treatment program consists of behavioral interventions. Behavioral assignments are used throughout the therapy process and include basic sex therapy *in vivo* desensitization procedures (Masters & Johnson, 1970), as well as other sexual and nonsexual behavioral procedures. First, behavioral assignments are used early in therapy to help evoke feelings in patients during the experiential/sensory awareness exercises. Second, behavioral interventions are used to help patients change nonsexual behaviors that may be helping to cause or maintain the sexual difficulty. Assertion training, communication training, and skill training in negotiation are examples of such behavioral interventions. Third, behavioral assignments are used for skill training to build good sexual techniques that make sex more rewarding.

A particularly useful behavioral intervention for low sexual desire is drive induction or "priming the pump." This can be done with the help of a desire checklist or a desire diary, in which the patient records all sexual stimuli,

thoughts, and emotions. Another such intervention is the assignment of fantasy breaks during the day, in which the patient is asked to spend several minutes consciously having a sexual fantasy. Patients are also assigned to go to films with sexual content, read books with sexual content, rent erotic videos, look at erotic magazines, read collections of sexual fantasies, and so forth. Similarly, the patients are also assigned to engage in casual, low-intensity physical affection. In most low-drive cases, there is very little kissing, hugging, and petting. This affection deficit develops because of the low drive, as the low-drive partner learns not to be affectionate for fear that the spouse will misinterpret casual affection as sexual initiation (LoPiccolo & Friedman, 1988).

Premature Ejaculation

There are no objective criteria for what constitutes premature ejaculation. In terms of actual duration of intercourse, the Kinsey report found that "for perhaps three-quarters of all males, orgasm is reached within two minutes" of initiating intercourse (Kinsey, Pomeroy, & Martin, 1948, p. 580), but Hunt's 1974 study found that the average duration of intercourse had increased dramatically, to 10 to 14 minutes, in the intervening 26 years.

It is perhaps easier to describe what is not premature ejaculation: Both husband and wife agree that the quality of their sexual encounters is not negatively influenced by efforts to delay ejaculation.

The standard treatment for premature ejaculation involves the "pause procedure," developed by Semans (1956) and modified into the "pause and squeeze" procedure by Masters and Johnson (1970). In the Semans's procedure, the penis is stimulated until ejaculation is imminent. At this point, stimulation is stopped. The male pauses until the sensation of high arousal subsides, then begins stimulation of the penis again. This procedure is repeated over and over again, until the male has experienced a massive amount of stimulation, but without the occurrence of ejaculation. The number of pauses required to sustain stimulation and delay ejaculation rapidly decreases over successive occasions with this procedure, and the male soon gains the capacity for penile stimulation of great duration.

Masters and Johnson (1970) have modified this procedure by having the wife stimulate the husband's penis and then squeeze firmly where the shaft of the penis joins the glans (head of the penis) when a pause in stimulation is needed. This squeeze technique is said to eliminate immediately the urge to ejaculate, and may also cause a partial loss of erection. Although there has not been a controlled experimental study of the relative effectiveness of the pause procedure versus the squeeze procedure, at a clinical level both procedures seem to be quite effective.

The underlying mechanism in the Semans and Masters and Johnson procedures may be Guthrie's (1952) "crowding the threshold" process for extinguishing stimulus-response connections, in this case, the connection between minimal stimulation and ejaculation. According to Guthrie, such extinction is produced by gradually exposing the subject to progressively more intense and more prolonged stimulation, but always keeping the intensity and duration of the stimulus just below the threshold for elicitation of the response.

Inhibited Ejaculation

Inhibited ejaculation has received very little attention in the therapeutic literature. As initially reported by Masters and Johnson (1970), this remains a relatively rare dysfunction, and the cause of the problem often remains unclear. Clinical case studies suggest a variety of psychological factors as causes, but there is virtually no supporting empirical research (Dow, 1981; Schull & Sprenkle, 1980).

Inhibited ejaculation can result from a number of physiological conditions, such as multiple sclerosis (Kedia, 1983). Similarly, several medications, including antihypertensives, sedatives, antianxiety, antidepressive, and antipsychotic agents, may have the side effect of preventing ejaculation (Ban & Freyhan, 1980). One aspect of the "postconcussion syndrome" may be inability to ejaculate, apparently caused by damage to the hypothalamus, which regulates production of sex hormones (Kosteljanetz et al., 1981).

Relatively little has appeared in the literature regarding treatment of inhibited ejaculation. The standard treatment strategies, involving elimination of performance anxiety and ensuring adequate stimulation, remain the state-of-the-art treatment approaches. In this approach, the couple is instructed to caress the penis manually (and, if acceptable to the couple, orally) until erection is attained, but to cease stimulation whenever arousal is increasing or approaching the point of impending orgasm. This paradoxical instruction reduces goal-focused anxiety about performance and allows the male to enjoy the sexual pleasure provided by this caressing. Elements from the treatment program for inorgasmic women, including the use of electric vibrators, behavioral maneuvers called "orgasm triggers" (such as holding one's breath), and having the patient role-play an exaggerated orgasm, do seem to have some success with this disorder (LoPiccolo, 1977a).

For cases caused by neurological diseases or medication side effects, more physiologic interventions are indicated. There is some success reported with the use of drugs that activate the sympathetic nervous system, such as ephedrine sulfate (Murphy & Lipshultz, 1988). At a behavioral level, increased stimulation of scrotal, perineal, and anal areas tends to trigger orgasm. Most effective is the use of an anal insertion probe, which can be either vibratory or providing a mild electric current, and indeed this type of anal stimulation is the only effective treatment for severely neurologically impaired patients (Murphy & Lipshultz, 1988).

Erectile Failure

The major focus of recent work on erectile failure has been on *differential diagnosis*. In 1970, Masters and Johnson stated that 95% of all erectile failure was purely psychogenic in origin and did not involve any physiological problems. More recent studies have indicated that neurologic diseases, hormonal abnormalities, or failure of blood flow to the penis are involved in a considerable percentage of cases of erectile failure (Tanagho, Lue, & McClure, 1988).

Although a complete evaluation of such organic factors is necessary before undertaking behavioral treatment of erectile failure, the presence of some degree of organic impairment does not always argue against behavioral treatment. There are many cases in which a man has a mild organic impairment, which then makes his erection more vulnerable to being disrupted by psychological, behavioral, and sexual technique factors. Many such cases with some partial organic impairment can be treated successfully by behavioral therapy. If psychological and behavioral difficulties are eliminated, the patient's mildly impaired physiologic capacity may be sufficient to produce full erection.

The behavioral treatment program for erectile failure consists of two basic components: (1) ensuring that the patient is receiving a high level of physical and psychological sexual stimulation from his wife, and (2) eliminating anxiety and performance demands that interfere with erection despite adequate stimulation.

Some cases of erectile failure are at least partially the result of the wife's poor sexual technique and her strong demands on the male to have erections. In such cases of insufficient stimulation and the wife's excessive demands for performance, the demands on the husband and the wife's frustration can both be reduced by instructing the couple to assure orgasm for the wife by means of manual, oral, or electric vibrator stimulation of her genitals, none of which require the male to have an erect penis.

Explicit films and books can be used to train the wife in effective stimulation techniques.

An equally powerful source of anxiety, independent of the wife's reaction, stems from the male's own attitude towards sex, once erectile failure has begun to occur. A male with erectile failure tends to enter his sexual encounters as an anxious observer rather than as an aroused participant. That is, he watches closely for signs of erection and is upset by any lag in gaining erection or any signs of partial loss of erection. Since this anxiety about erection obviously prevents arousal from occurring, one therapeutic approach is prescribing a course of homework activities for the couple, to preclude performance anxiety and ensure adequate stimulation for the male. For example, the first set of activities might require the couple only to massage each other's nude bodies, not including any stimulation of the male's genitals. The male is paradoxically instructed that, "The purpose of this exercise is for you to learn to enjoy sensual pleasures, without focusing on sexual goals. Therefore, you should try to not get an erection. Erection would mean you are being sexual rather than sensual." Obviously, a nude massage *is* a sexually stimulating experience. The paradoxical demand to not get an erection in this setting effectively frees the man from anxiety about getting an erection.

Over successive occasions, the couple's repertoire of sexual activities is rebuilt. The next assignment might be for the wife to stimulate the male's penis, but to stop such stimulation immediately should an erection occur. Only when the penis is flaccid should stimulation be resumed. Next, penile insertion into the vagina is allowed, but only with the female physically pushing the male's flaccid penis into her vagina while she sits astride his supine body. Again, the couple is told, "This procedure works best with a flaccid penis. If you can't avoid an erection, it's all right, although not as good, to go ahead and insert anyway. But please try not to have an erection." Once the male has been unable to avoid an erection during vaginal containment, slow pelvic thrusting, vigorous intercourse, and finally, coital ejaculation can be allowed.

Although this procedure works well with most cases, it has not been found successful in cases where the male has a homosexual orientation (Masters & Johnson, 1970, p. 273). In such cases, lack of psychological stimulation (rather than the male's anxiety and the wife's poor technique) may be a factor. If a male is more aroused by men than by women, removing his performance anxiety may still leave him unaroused in response to his wife's lovemaking, regardless of how nondemanding and skilled she may be. For such cases, addition of a classical conditioning procedure to increase heterosexual arousal seems to increase effectiveness of the basic treatment strategy (LoPiccolo, Stewart, & Watkins, 1972). In this procedure, the male masturbates with his currently arousing homosexual fantasies and explicit stimuli, such as pictures of nude males. Just prior to orgasm, the male is instructed to switch his focus to fantasies of heterosexual activities with his spouse. This procedure ensures that the pleasure of orgasm occurs in a heterosexual context. On subsequent occasions, this switch can be made earlier in masturbation, until fantasies and activities involving the wife become effective sexual stimuli in their own right. This stimulus-switching procedure can also be used by the couple in their series of prescribed sexual activities.

Arousal and Orgasm Dysfunctions in Women

The most effective treatment to date for lifelong, global lack of orgasm in women is a program of directed masturbation developed by LoPiccolo and his students (LoPiccolo & Lobitz, 1972; LoPiccolo, 1977a; Heiman, LoPiccolo, & LoPiccolo, 1976, Heiman & Lo-

Piccolo, 1988; LoPiccolo & Stock, 1986, 1987). The basic components of this treatment program for lack of orgasm include education, self-exploration and body awareness, and directed masturbation. The use of directed masturbation has been questioned by some, and is not a component of all treatment programs for global, lifelong lack of orgasm. Masters and Johnson (1970), for example, instead stressed couple-focused sensate exercises and addressing historical issues that result in a sex-negative orientation. However, a number of studies (Kohlenberg, 1974; Riley & Riley, 1978) have shown that a program of directed masturbation training is a more effective treatment method for the woman who has never had an orgasm.

The directed masturbation program developed by LoPiccolo forms the basis for a popular self-help book and film, titled *Becoming Orgasmic* (Heiman & LoPiccolo, 1988). Morokoff and LoPiccolo (1986) compared the effectiveness of this self-treatment book and film with regular sex therapy. Regular therapy involved weekly hour-long meetings with a therapist for 15 consecutive weeks. Self-help involved only three sessions with the therapist, spaced 5 weeks apart, with the woman using the book and film on her own between sessions with the therapist. Results indicated that the self-help program was fully as effective as regular therapy in helping the women obtain orgasm and in producing gains in overall marital and sexual satisfaction.

The directed masturbation/behavior therapy program described in *Becoming Orgasmic* (Heiman & LoPiccolo, 1988) involves nine steps:

In Step 1, the woman learns to identify the various parts of her genitals and is encouraged to do some attitudinal work on acceptance of female sexuality and to examine her own sexual history in terms of pathogenic influences.

In Step 2, the woman explores her body and genitals by touching.

In Step 3, the woman locates erogenous zones, including the clitoris, as the focus for sexual pleasure.

In Step 4, the woman is directly instructed in techniques of masturbation.

In Step 5, an attempt is made to make this procedure more erotic and sexual. The woman is encouraged to develop sexual fantasies, to read popular anthologies of women's sexual fantasies (for example, Friday, 1973), and to use this material as an aid to facilitate her arousal.

In Step 6, if the woman has not yet reached orgasm, the use of the electric vibrator is introduced. Those women who do have their first orgasm with the vibrator usually go on to have orgasms in other forms of sexual stimulation, but the vibrator is a useful means of obtaining the first orgasm.

In Step 7, the woman demonstrates for the male partner the technique she has learned that produces arousal and orgasm for her. The male partner first demonstrates his masturbation techniques for the woman, to help disinhibit the woman and to ensure that this is a truly co-equal and reciprocal learning process.

In Step 8, the woman instructs her male partner in his caressing and touching of her genitals, to produce orgasm through his direct stimulation.

In Step 9, the couple resumes penile-vaginal intercourse with the woman and/or the man continuing direct manual stimulation of the clitoris to facilitate orgasm during penetration.

Situational Lack of Orgasm

In dealing with situational lack of orgasm, one must raise the issue of just what is an appropriate focus for treatment. Sex therapists do not consider lack of orgasm during coitus to be an indication for treatment, provided that the

woman can have orgasm in some way with her partner, and that she enjoys intercourse. However, for couples who would like to experience coital orgasm, not out of a feeling that it is pathologic not to do so, but simply as an experience they would like to have, there are some techniques that can be tried.

Some couples complain that the woman can only have orgasm in one narrowly restricted way, and this pattern constricts their enjoyment of sex. For example, the woman may only be able to have an orgasm during oral stimulation by her husband, or during masturbation by lying face down with her ankles crossed and pressing her thighs together while rhythmically rocking. In such cases, one treatment strategy (LoPiccolo & Stock, 1986) attempts to capitalize on the arousal produced by the activity that will produce orgasm, to enhance arousal during coitus. That is, if the woman is able to become highly aroused and have an orgasm during oral sex, she can be advised that the couple should engage in oral sex until she is just on the verge of orgasm. At that point, the couple can shift activities and engage in intercourse. If she should lose her arousal during intercourse, she can shift back to oral sex until high arousal is reestablished, and then switch back to coitus.

Another approach to a restricted range of female orgasm has been described by Zeiss, Rosen, and Zeiss (1977). In this stimulus generalization approach, a more sequential series of changes is made in effective stimulation. Consider, for example, a woman who can masturbate herself to orgasm and wants to have orgasm during intercourse. As a first step, the woman might be instructed to masturbate as she always has, but simply with a finger passively inserted in the vagina, right from the beginning of the masturbation sequence. This procedure will enable her to learn to experience orgasm with something contained in the vagina. Once this has been accomplished, she can be instructed to masturbate while thrusting the finger in the vagina. Once success is achieved in this procedure, a change can be made to having the male partner manipulate her clitoris, again with nothing in the vagina. Once he is able to produce orgasm for her in this way, this can be repeated, but first with her finger, and then his finger, inserted in the vagina. If these steps are successful, the progression can be made to having his penis passively contained in the vagina while she masturbates to orgasm. The next step would involve passive penile containment while he stimulates her to orgasm manually. As the final step, thrusting of the penis in the vagina with direct manual stimulation may now succeed in producing orgasm. Thus, by breaking down the differences between masturbation and coitus into a series of very small and discrete changes, there is much greater success in broadening the woman's range of orgasmic responsivity (Zeiss, Rosen, & Zeiss, 1977).

Vaginismus

Vaginismus refers to involuntary spastic contraction of the vaginal musculature, such that intercourse cannot be accomplished or can only take place with great difficulty and pain. If physical examination reveals no organic basis, vaginismus is usually an anxiety response. The woman may fear penetration because of prior painful attempts at coitus due to lack of lubrication, rape, or extreme fear and guilt during the first attempt at coitus. LoPiccolo and Stock (1987) note that women who have a history of incestuous molestation in childhood or adolescence are especially likely to present with vaginismus as part of their sexual dysfunction. Often these women present with an aversion to sex, inability to become aroused, and inability to have orgasm, and also have vaginismus.

The effective treatment program for vaginismus is a combination of relaxation training and progressive dilation of the vagina (Fuchs, Hoch, & Paldi, 1978; Sarrel & Sarrel, 1979; Pridal and LoPiccolo, 1993). The female patient can be given relaxation instructions or urged to buy one of the many commercially available books, audiotapes, or videotapes that demonstrate deep

muscle relaxation techniques. Dilation can be done by a gynecologist in the office, or by the therapist sending the woman home with a set of progressively larger dilators, which are typically plastic cylinders. Available research does not indicate that one procedure is more effective than the other. The important element is that the dilation be *under the woman's control*, and done at her own pace so that she does not experience pain or fear during dilation. When the woman can easily insert a dilator that is larger than the penis, the patient couple begins gradual insertion of the penis. In this procedure, the couple is instructed that the man is to lie on his back and not to move or thrust. The woman is to kneel above him, grasp his penis, and very gradually and slowly insert just the tip into the vagina. If all goes well, on successive occasions, she can progressively insert more and more of the penis, until full containment is accomplished. She can then begin some pelvic thrusting, and finally the husband can be allowed to initiate pelvic movements.

CONCLUSIONS AND FUTURE DIRECTIONS

This review has focused on the clinical techniques currently in use by behaviorally oriented sex therapists. Unfortunately, much of this knowledge is based on clinical experience rather than on empirical research. Many articles published as experimental reports are, in reality, demonstration projects that do not involve random assignment to experimental conditions, manipulation of independent variables, and assessment with objective, quantified dependent variables (LoPiccolo, 1980).

In many studies, patients are identified only as having sexual dysfunction or orgasm problems. In such studies, differences between heterogeneous patients probably have much greater impact on treatment outcome than do any differences in treatment techniques. Much more fine-grained, multiaxial diagnosis, as proposed by Schover et al. (1982) is necessary before one can expect variations in treatment to show differential outcomes.

Sex therapy treatment interventions consist of broad-spectrum, multifaceted combinations of a variety of procedures (LoPiccolo, 1980). There have been few studies attempting to identify which components of the total sex therapy package are active ingredients and which are "inert fillers."

Failure to specify clearly the criterion for therapeutic change is a recurring problem. A clinical, global judgment of outcome is often all that is reported, especially in the medical and psychiatric journals. This issue surfaced in a popular-press publication (Zilbergeld & Evans, 1980) in regard to the outcome results reported by Masters and Johnson. Nonspecific and placebo effects in sex therapy need to be further elucidated, although studies of psychotherapy placebo effects present difficult practical and ethical problems (LoPiccolo, 1980; O'Leary & Borkovec, 1978). Further studies of the role of biological and physiological factors in sexual problems are badly needed, as are more long-term studies of the lasting effects of sex therapy. Although our research base is not as strong as we would wish, most of the behavioral techniques described in this article do produce results in the majority of cases, and, as such, have been validated in a meaningful way.

TREATMENT RESOURCES

Recommended for Patients

Heiman, J., & LoPiccolo, J. (1988). *Becoming orgasmic: A personal and sexual growth program for women* (rev. exp. ed.). Englewood Cliffs, NJ: Prentice-Hall. (For women).

Kaplan, H. S. (1989). *PE: How to overcome premature ejaculation*. New York: Brunner/Mazel.

LoPiccolo, L., & Heiman, J. R. (1974). *Becoming orgasmic*. New York: Focus International. (Videotape).

LoPiccolo, J. *Treating erectile problems*. (1980). New York: Focus International. (Videotape).

LoPiccolo, J. *Treating vaginismus*. (1984) New York: Focus International. (Videotape).

Zilbergeld, B. (1978). *Male sexuality*. New York: Bantam. (For men).

Recommended for Professionals

Bancroft, J. (1989). *Human sexuality and its problems*. New York: Churchill-Livingston.

Leiblum, S., & Rosen, R. (1988). *Sexual desire disorders*. New York: Guilford.

Leiblum, S., & Rosen, R. (1989). *Principles and practice of sex therapy: Update for the 1990s*. New York: Guilford.

LoPiccolo, J., & LoPiccolo, L. (1978). *Handbook of sex therapy*. New York: Plenum.

Schover, L. R., & Jensen, S. B. (1988). *Sexuality and chronic illness*. New York: Guilford.

CHAPTER 13

Behavioral Medicine

Francis J. Keefe

Jean C. Beckham

Behavioral medicine is a field that is attracting a great deal of attention from behavioral clinicians and researchers. The field of behavioral medicine is broad and appeals not only to behavioral scientists but also to biomedical scientists. The breadth of behavioral medicine is evident in the following definition arrived at by the Yale Conference on Behavioral Medicine:

> Behavioral medicine is the field concerned with the development of behavioral science knowledge and techniques relevant to the understanding of physical health and illness and the application of this knowledge and these techniques to prevention, diagnosis, treatment and rehabilitation . . . (Schwartz & Weiss, 1978, p. 7).

Although behavioral medicine is a broad, interdisciplinary field, many of the intervention strategies used are cognitive or behavioral in nature. Techniques such as relaxation training, biofeedback training, cognitive restructuring, and self-instructional training are mainstays in most behavioral medicine treatment programs. Such cognitive-behavioral interventions have been found to be effective in the treatment of a wide variety of medical conditions, including diabetes, coronary heart disease, hypertension, asthma, and cancer (Blumenthal & McKee, 1987).

Cognitive-behavioral interventions offer an important alternative to traditional medical and surgical treatments. Patients referred for cognitive-behavioral intervention often have limited medical or surgical treatment options. Medications have major side effects that limit their use in many patients. For example, in patients having chronic diseases, the long-term use of pain medications poses special problems because these medications may interact with other medications and/or affect the central nervous system, renal blood flow, or gastric mucosa (Keefe et al., 1987a). Although surgical treatments can benefit some patients, these treatments are often either contraindicated or reserved as a last resort.

The purpose of this chapter is to provide an introduction to cognitive-behavioral interventions used in behavioral medicine. A thorough review of the applications of cognitive-behavioral techniques in behavioral medicine is beyond the scope of this chapter. The interested reader is referred to several recent books that provide such comprehensive overviews (Blumenthal & McKee, 1987; Melamed & Siegel, 1980; Wickramasekera, 1988). This chapter will illustrate some of the basic components of cognitive-behavioral interventions in behavioral medicine by focusing on two common clinical applications: pain management and stress management. For each application we will review the conceptual foundations underlying cognitive-behavioral intervention, describe specific assessment and treatment methods, and highlight future directions for clinical and research efforts.

BEHAVIORAL APPROACHES TO PAIN MANAGEMENT

In the past two decades, there has been increasing interest in behavioral and psychological approaches to pain management. Training in pain management methods is now available in many inpatient and outpatient facilities devoted to the treatment of chronic pain. Although pain management training has been applied to the management of acute pain (Jay, Elliott, Katz, & Siegel, 1987), it is more commonly utilized with persistent pain conditions such as low back pain or arthritis pain.

Most therapists involved in pain management rely on treatment protocols consisting of a combination of cognitive and behavioral interventions. Well-controlled treatment outcome studies have documented the efficacy of such multimodal treatment protocols in the management of chronic low back pain (Turner & Clancy, 1988), arthritis pain (Bradley et al., 1987; Keefe et al., 1990a; 1990b), and migraine and muscle contraction headaches (Blanchard et al., 1982).

CONCEPTUAL BASES FOR TREATING PAIN

Ideally, the treatment of any pain condition consists of identifying the underlying somatic cause of the pain and correcting it (Urban, 1982). Although this ideal is approached for some acute pain conditions, it is rarely met for chronic or persistent pain conditions. Indeed, many of the individuals presenting for pain management have long histories of failure to respond to biomedical interventions designed to alleviate the somatic basis of their pain. There is growing recognition among pain specialists of the limitations of somatic models in understanding chronic pain phenomenon (Bonica, 1977; Fordyce, 1976; Melzack, 1988).

Cognitive-behavioral approaches to pain management are based on the notion that pain is a complex phenomenon that can be best understood and treated in a multimodal fashion (Karoly, 1985; Keefe & Gil, 1986; Turk, Meichenbaum, & Genest, 1983). Although the behavioral-science concepts underpinning cognitive and behavioral pain management efforts are varied (Keefe & Gil, 1986), they can be grouped into three broad categories: behavioral, cognitive, and psychophysiological. Since many patients have multiple interacting problems, it is often necessary to integrate concepts from several of these categories to provide an adequate conceptual understanding of the patient's pain.

Behavioral Concepts

Fordyce (1976) described how behavioral processes such as conditioning and modeling can affect the acquisition and maintenance of pain behaviors. Fordyce uses the term "pain behavior" to refer to those overt actions that communicate to others the fact that pain is being experienced. These behaviors can be varied and may include resting in bed, taking medications, seeking health care, or exhibiting facial expressions of pain, guarded movement, or verbal complaints of pain.

Because pain behaviors are overt, they are particularly subject to operant conditioning influences. Positive social reinforcement can be one of the major factors maintaining maladaptive pain behaviors (Fordyce, 1976). Well-meaning family members or friends, for example, may respond to the display of pain behavior with increased attention or offers of assistance. These reinforcing consequences may, in some cases, maintain displays of pain behavior long after the normal healing time for injury.

Classical or respondent conditioning can also exert control over pain behavior. Nociceptive input from damaged nerves may serve as an unconditioned stimulus eliciting unconditioned behavioral responses to pain. Environmental stimuli that are routinely associated with increased pain can produce classically conditioned pain behavior patterns (Fordyce, 1976). The burn patient undergoing painful wound debridement, for example, may learn to associate the sight of the treatment room or the physical therapist with increased pain (Keefe & Gil, 1986). These previously neutral stimuli may, over the course of repeated treatment sessions, come to evoke behavioral responses such as excessive guarding or withdrawal of the limb or body area to be treated.

A recent study by Rickard (1988) found that children of chronic low-back-pain patients exhibited a higher frequency of maladaptive health-related behaviors likely to be learned through observation than did children of diabetic patients or of healthy parents. A classic study of cultural influences on pain perception was carried out by Sternbach and Tursky (1965). These investigators found that there were significant differences in responses to painful electric shock among housewives having Yankee, Irish, Jewish, or Italian cultural backgrounds. The Yankees had a matter-of-fact orientation to pain, and the Italians expressed a desire for pain relief. The Jewish subjects expressed a concern for the implication of pain, and the Irish tended to inhibit expressions of suffering. Taken together, these studies suggest that pain behaviors are not only influenced by operant and respondent conditioning, but can also be affected by modeling and cultural conditioning.

Cognitive Concepts

A large body of experimental literature demonstrates that cognitive factors such as beliefs, expectations, and attentional focus can influence the perception and reaction to pain stimuli in normal subjects (Chapman, 1978; McCaul & Malott, 1984). Clinical studies of acute and chronic pain patients also suggest that cognitive factors strongly influence pain perception and behavior (Tan, 1982).

In the chronic pain area, three sets of cognitive variables have received a great deal of research attention (Keefe & Williams, 1989). The first is pain-related cognitive distortions or errors (Lefebvre, 1981). Research has demonstrated that chronic pain patients have a tendency to distort their evaluations of their own behavior and performance in an overly negative fashion. Sanders (1983), for example, found that chronic low-back-pain patients systematically underestimated the amount of time they spent standing and walking compared to normal controls. Research by Lefebvre (1981) indicated that chronic low-back-pain patients who were prone to overgeneralization, catastrophizing, and many of the other cognitive errors described by Beck (1973) were more likely to report symptoms of depression. Smith, Follick, and Ahern (1986) found that low-back-pain patients who scored high on a questionnaire measuring a variety of pain-related cognitive distortions not only had higher levels of depression but also had significantly higher levels of physical and psychological disability.

Beliefs about pain are a second cognitive variable that appear to affect the pain experience. A recent study by Williams and Thorn

(1989) suggests that certain pain beliefs may have an adverse affect on pain treatment. Chronic pain patients who believed that their pain would endure had much poorer compliance with behavioral and physical therapy interventions. Patients who viewed their pain as an unexplained mystery also showed poorer compliance with physical therapy. Some chronic pain patients have beliefs about their pain (e.g., "I'm sure this pain is a sign that I have cancer") that fail to match the medical explanations for their pain. Such beliefs may be supported by close relatives and friends, and these beliefs may lead to "doctor shopping," fruitless searches for miracle cures, and poor compliance with cognitive or behavioral interventions.

The use and perceived effectiveness of cognitive pain-coping strategies are cognitive variables that can also have an important effect on the pain experience (Keefe et al., 1987a). Research on pain-coping strategies in osteoarthritis patients having persistent knee pain, for example, has shown that patients who rate the effectiveness of their coping strategies as high and who avoid irrational catastrophizing cognitions cope much more effectively with their pain (Keefe et al., 1987a, 1987b). High scores on a questionnaire factor measuring these cognitive variables were found to be a stronger predictor of pain, physical disability, and psychological disability than medical variables such as evidence of osteoarthritis, obesity, or age.

Given the growing recognition of the importance of cognitive factors in chronic pain, it is not surprising that behavior therapists have expanded their repertoire of pain management techniques beyond the confines of operant-behavioral intervention to include a broader variety of cognitive-behavioral interventions (Keefe & Gil, 1986).

Psychophysiological Concepts

Cognitive-behavioral therapists believe that stress and muscle spasm can play an important role in the pain experience (Keefe & Gil, 1986). Stress is hypothesized to be a causative factor in many pain conditions. Stress may produce pain by heightening autonomic responses leading to pain (e.g., as in migraine headache patients) or by increasing muscle activity (e.g., as in temperomandibular joint pain patients) (Bonica, 1977). A painful injury such as whiplash often produces muscle spasms that in turn can cause increased pain. Muscle spasms produce pain by producing vasoconstriction and releasing pain-producing substances (Bonica, 1977). When spasms are persistent, they can lead to changes in posture, muscular asymmetries, and abnormal patterns of movement (Dolce & Raczynski, 1985), all of which can cause or exacerbate pain.

Psychophysiological concepts such as the stress-pain hypothesis and the pain-spasm-pain cycle have had a major impact on pain management efforts. These concepts are widely accepted and serve as the basis for such common pain control methods as progressive relaxation training, biofeedback, and meditation.

Assessment of Pain

Given the complex and interacting factors that may contribute to the pain experience, it is not surprising that cognitive-behavioral therapists rely on a comprehensive battery of assessment procedures. The typical battery includes a structured interview, a pain diary, questionnaires, and direct observations of pain behavior.

Structured Interviews

Structured behavioral interviews are probably the most widely used behavioral assessment technique in the pain management area (Keefe, Brown, Scott, & Ziesat, 1982). A variety of structured interview formats for evaluating pain patients have been described (Fordyce, 1976; Keefe, 1988). Topics covered in the interview typically include a discussion of factors that increase or decrease pain, a review of daily activity patterns, a discussion of the effects of tension on pain, and an attempt to identify environmental contingencies for pain and "well" behaviors.

Interviewing the patient allows the therapist to pinpoint behavioral problems that may serve as key targets for behavioral intervention. Because of personality features (Bradley, Prokop, Margolis, & Gentry, 1978) or anxiety (Long & Webb, 1980), patients may fail to mention or be reluctant to discuss important pain-related behavioral problems at the time of their initial medical evaluation. A structured interview that covers a broad range of topics, however, can often pinpoint important behavioral problems that may be amenable to behavioral intervention. These problems include an overly sedentary lifestyle, overdependence on medication or family members, or poor understanding of the cause and future trajectory of pain.

Pain occurs in a social context, and interviews with spouse or family members are considered essential in identifying social factors that may contribute to the etiology or maintenance of pain behavior (Fordyce, 1976). An overly solicitous spouse may enforce inactivity, take over tasks, and limit the patient's social activities, thus reinforcing high levels of pain behavior and physical disability. Family members or friends also may pass on to the patient their own inaccurate beliefs about pain and its treatment.

Pain Diaries

Ongoing recording of pain and related behaviors is a key feature of cognitive-behavioral treatment programs for pain. Many programs require patients to complete 2 to 4 weeks of daily diary sheets prior to starting treatment; therapists use these records to pinpoint problems and establish a pretreatment baseline (Keefe, Gil, & Rose, 1986).

Pain diary records typically focus on one or more of four major areas: pain level, medication intake, activity level, and a cognitive appraisal of the environment, such as ratings of perceived tension or stress. Examining the relationships among these areas can be quite revealing.

One common pattern, called *pain cycling* (Gil, Ross, & Keefe, 1988), is characterized by the patient continuing with an activity such as sitting or walking until pain becomes intolerable, and only then resting or taking pain medication. Patients who show such a pattern learn to associate activity with increased pain, and as a result may avoid activities and develop an overly sedentary lifestyle. These patients often can benefit from learning to pace their activities through a structured behavioral program.

Ratings of tension and pain are often highly correlated. A patient may report a substantial increase in pain when working under the time pressure of an important deadline or after having an argument with his or her spouse. Patients showing such a pattern may benefit from training in tension-reducing methods such as progressive relaxation or biofeedback.

One of the major applications of pain diaries is in evaluating treatment outcome. Blanchard and his colleagues (Blanchard & Andrasik, 1985) have developed and refined a pain diary for use in behavioral treatment studies of headache patients. This diary requires patients to rate headache intensity and record medication intake four times a day (at mealtimes and bedtime). Scores derived from the diary include: (1) a headache index, reflecting average daily headache intensity; (2) headache-free days, indicating the number of pain-free days; (3) a peak headache rating, indicating the single highest weekly rating; and (4) a medication index, providing a quantitative measure of medication intake. This pain diary format has been used in biofeedback treatment outcome studies with headache patients and has been shown to be sensitive to treatment effects (Blanchard et al., 1982). Blanchard, Andrasik, Neff, Jurish, and O'Keefe (1981) also found support for the social validity of the diary, in that ratings of improvement by significant others correlated significantly with patient diary records of improvement.

Direct Observations of Pain Behavior

Although direct observation has long been considered the most fundamental and objective form of behavioral assessment (Nelson & Hayes, 1979), only recently have observation methods been applied to the assessment of pain behavior in chronic pain patients (Keefe, Crisson, & Trainor, 1987). Patients having lower or upper back pain, musculoskeletal pain syndromes, or arthritis exhibit observable pain behaviors (e.g. guarding, facial grimacing) as they participate in simple daily activities such as walking, stair climbing, or rising from sitting. Although physicians often informally observe such behaviors during physical examinations, they do not usually systematically record or quantify these behaviors.

Over the past 9 years, Keefe and colleagues have carried out a series of studies to develop and refine a systematic approach to recording and quantifying motor pain behaviors. Initial studies (Keefe & Block, 1982) took a 10-minute videotaped behavior sample from chronic low-back-pain patients as they performed a standard sequence of sitting, standing, walking, and reclining. The videotapes were subsequently scored by trained observers who recorded the occurrence of five motor behaviors: guarding, bracing, rubbing of the painful area, sighing, and facial grimacing. Data analysis revealed that independent observers were highly reliable in coding these behaviors. The motor behaviors also appeared to be valid measures of pain behavior, in that they correlated with patient self-reports of pain, discriminated pain patients from pain-free controls, and decreased significantly following pain treatment. These findings have been subsequently replicated in studies of rheumatoid arthritis patients (Anderson et al., 1987).

Pain behavior observation methods are mainly used in clinical research settings. Direct observations of pain behavior have been carried out during physical examinations and daily clinical rounds, and over the course of hospitalization on a specialized, behaviorally oriented, inpatient pain management unit (Keefe, Crisson & Trainor, 1987). Because of the time and costs involved in direct observation, this method has not become widely used in clinical settings. Advances in observation methodologies, such as the use of hand-held data recorders and portable microcomputers or the development of simpler coding schemes, hold the promise of increasing the clinical utility of pain behavior observation systems. At present, observation appears to offer clinical researchers an objective, reliable, and valid method of studying social and environmental variables controlling pain behavior and of evaluating treatment outcome (Keefe, 1989).

COGNITIVE-BEHAVIORAL PAIN MANAGEMENT PROGRAMS

The cognitive-behavioral approach to pain management invariably relies on a variety of intervention techniques. Although specific techniques vary somewhat from one pain problem to the next, several basic elements can be delineated. These include a treatment rationale, methods for changing activity patterns, methods for changing cognitions, and methods for altering psychophysiological responses.

Treatment Rationale

Many individuals referred for behavioral pain management initially view their pain as a relatively simple problem that can be cured with appropriate medical or surgical treatment (Long & Webb, 1980). Patients often deny the influence of psychological variables and fail to recognize the value of their own coping efforts in managing pain. Acknowledging these beliefs and discussing an alternative conceptualization of pain is a key component of any cognitive-behavioral pain treatment program (Fordyce, 1976; Turk et al., 1983).

A simplified version of the gate control model of pain (Melzack & Wall, 1965) is a widely used rationale for cognitive-behavioral treatment. The gate control model of pain views pain as a complex phenomenon that can be affected by thoughts, feelings, memories, and behavior. The model postulates that such cognitive and behavioral influences can modify the physical transmission of pain signals from the site of pain through pain pathways to the brain. According to gate control theory, there is a gating mechanism located in the spinal cord that can be either closed or open. If the gate is open, pain signals are free to pass through to the brain and the patient experiences pain. If the gate is closed, pain signals are interrupted and little or no pain is experienced. Cognitive factors believed to open this gating mechanism include depression, anxiety, and preoccupation with somatic symptoms (Turk et al., 1983). Cognitive-behavioral treatment techniques may provide a means of closing the gating mechanism, as they alter cognitive, emotional, and behavioral responses to pain.

Many patients find the gate control model helps them better appreciate the role of cognitive and behavioral factors in pain. Providing this rationale early in treatment increases patients' willingness to become involved in behavioral assessment efforts. It may also increase compliance with behavioral treatment interventions.

Changing Activity Patterns

Daily activity patterns are a major target behavior for behavioral treatment interventions (Fordyce, 1976). The level and range of activity can have an important influence on pain. Many patients having chronic pain live sedentary and very restricted lifestyles. These patients become deconditioned and frequently depressed because of their lack of involvement in pleasant or distracting activities. Behavioral programs are often used to activate such patients.

Activity-rest cycling is a particularly effective way to increase activity in chronic pain patients and break the tendency toward pain cycling (Gil, Ross, & Keefe, 1988). Activity diary records kept by the patient can be used to establish a baseline level of activity that the patient is able to tolerate. The patient is then asked to break down the daily schedule into cycles of activity and rest. An extremely deactivated patient might be placed on an hourly activity-rest cycle consisting of 15 minutes up and out of bed, followed by 45 minutes reclining in bed. The patient is encouraged to adhere to this schedule each hour if possible and, at a minimum, for 11 to 12 hours of the waking day. Activity level is increased each day, and time spent resting is decreased. Most behaviorally oriented inpatient programs use activation programs similar to the activity-rest cycle (e.g., the activity quota system developed by Fordyce, 1976). Although controlled studies of activation are lacking, inpatient programs using such techniques have been able to achieve increases in uptime (time up and out of the reclining position) of 50% to 100% in patients having long histories of chronic pain (Keefe, Gil, & Rose, 1986).

Changing Cognitions

To change maladaptive pain-related cognitions, cognitive-behavioral therapists use techniques such as cognitive restructuring, self-instructional training, distraction and imagery. Turk, Meichenbaum, and Genest (1983) have described in detail how techniques such as cognitive restructuring and self-instructional training can be used to help patients identify and change maladaptive thoughts and beliefs related to pain. Their approach to cognitive restructuring involves: (1) helping patients recognize the relationship between thoughts, feelings, behavior, and pain; and (2) teaching them to identify irrational, maladaptive thoughts and replace these cognitions with alternative, rational, coping thoughts. Catastrophizing and other self-defeating cognitions that commonly occur in patients having pain include "I am worthless" and "I'll never be able to cope with pain, so why bother?" Alternative, rational thoughts that can help individuals cope with pain more effectively are identified through therapy sessions, and patients are encouraged to practice countering irrational thoughts with more positive coping thoughts.

Self-instructional training (Turk et al., 1983) is particularly appropriate for the management of time-limited episodes of severe pain such as the pain associated with an invasive medical procedure. Self-instructional training teaches patients how to divide painful situations into three phases and use self-reflection and positive self-statements to maintain coping efforts throughout these phases. The three phases are: (1) preparing for intense stimulation before it becomes too strong, (2) confronting and handling intense stimulation, and (3) coping with thoughts and feelings that arise at critical moments. Patients are often given a list of self-statements to use during each of these phases and asked to identify the self-statements that are most relevant to their coping style. Through behavioral rehearsal they are then taught how to use these statements during episodes of increased pain.

Systematic training in distraction techniques is a key component of pain management training (McCaul & Malott, 1984). Patients may be taught how to use a focal point to focus on their physical surroundings or how to focus on a video game (Corah, Gale, & Illig, 1979) or auditory stimuli such as music (Lavine, Buchsbaum, & Poncy, 1976). Counting backward slowly is another commonly employed distraction technique.

Training in imagery techniques is typically presented as an adjunct to relaxation training (Turner & Clancy, 1988). Patients are asked to identify pleasant images such as walking on a beach or reclining under a shady tree on a warm day, and to rehearse using these images to divert their attention from pain. Some patients find training in imagery for reinterpreting pain sensations to be quite helpful (Rybstein-Blinchik, 1979). Reinterpretation strategies involve imagining the pain as a different sensation, e.g., as a dull or warm sensation.

The efficacy of cognitive interventions for managing chronic pain has been reviewed by several authors (Turk et al., 1983; McCaul & Malott, 1984). Although there are relatively few controlled studies of cognitive restructuring in chronic pain, a number of studies have found self-instructional training effective in managing acute pain or pain secondary to invasive medical procedures (Turk et al., 1983). Although much of the research on distraction and imagery methods has been carried out with normal human volunteers, clinical studies of these techniques have proliferated in the past 10 years. Studies of distraction and imagery reveal that these techniques are more effective than control conditions and that they work best for the control of pain stimuli of low intensity (McCaul & Malott, 1984). Interestingly, reinterpretation strategies have been found to be more effective than distraction for severe clinical pain. Reinterpretation strategies may be effective because they help patients learn to reframe cognitively a perceptual experience that is difficult to ignore when using distraction.

Changing Psychophysiological Responses

Relaxation training is probably the single most frequently employed cognitive-behavioral intervention for pain. Although a variety of forms of relaxation training are employed, progressive relaxation is the most common. Most therapists use a variant of Jacobson's original approach, similar to that described by Bernstein & Borkovec (1973).

Biofeedback is a second approach used to modify psychophysiological responses in chronic pain patients. Biofeedback is the major form of behavioral treatment for pain syndromes such as muscle contraction or migraine headaches and is often part of a treatment package for chronic pain syndromes such as low back pain or arthritis pain (Keefe & Hoelscher, 1987).

Biofeedback consists of providing an individual with information about a physiological response in order to enable the person to gain control over that response. A typical biofeedback training session begins with placement of noninvasive sensors on the patient's body to record a target physiological response. For a muscle contraction headache patient, electrodes might be attached to the skin to record the activity of muscles in the forehead or neck. The sensors are connected to an amplifier that in turn drives a feedback display that provides information to the patient regarding moment-to-moment changes in the physiological response. Feedback typically consists of a visual display (e.g., a needle on a meter) and an audio signal (e.g., a tone that varies in pitch as the target response changes). Biofeedback training is usually carried out in a series of 6 to 10 hour-long sessions. Initial sessions are focused on helping patients gain control over the target response under relatively easy conditions (e.g., reclining in a quiet room), and later sessions are focused on helping patients gain control over the target response while they are engaging in activities (e.g., walking or stair climbing) that tend to increase their pain.

There is a large body of research literature on biofeedback applications to chronic pain syndromes. A recent review of this literature (Keefe & Hoelscher, 1987), reached two major conclusions. First, controlled studies have demonstrated the efficacy of biofeedback for muscularly based low back pain and dysmenorrhea. Second, promising results have been obtained in uncontrolled studies using biofeedback in the treatment of central pain and rheumatoid arthritis. Biofeedback has been utilized as a treatment component in many multidisciplinary treatment programs for patients having intractable pain syndromes. However, the lack of component analyses does not allow evaluation of the specific contribution that biofeedback makes to treatment outcome.

FUTURE DIRECTIONS IN PAIN MANAGEMENT

Several recent papers have identified important new directions for cognitive-behavioral pain management (Keefe & Gil, 1986; Keefe & Williams, 1989). This section will highlight several of these areas.

One of the most important areas for future clinical and research efforts is the use of cognitive-behavioral treatment as an early intervention for pain. Cognitive-behavioral interventions have mainly been used in treating patients who have suffered from constant daily pain for years. From a learning perspective, one could argue strongly for intervening earlier in the development of chronic pain behavior patterns. Cognitive and behavioral responses to pain are less likely to be entrenched when patients have shorter histories of pain.

Recent studies suggest that early behavioral intervention may reduce pain and disability in patients who are at risk for chronic pain. Fordyce, Brockway, Bergman, and Spengler (1986), for example, carried out a controlled comparison of behavioral and medical treatments in the management of low back pain. Patients in this study worked for a large aircraft manufacturer and had back pain that was of recent origin (within 7 days of onset). Patients were randomly assigned to receive either a traditional medical treatment for back pain or a special behavioral treatment program. Those receiving medical treatment were given analgesics, back exercises, and bedrest and were instructed to "let pain be their guide" in using these treatments. Patients receiving behavioral treatment received the same treatments, but in each case the treatment was delivered according to a pre-set schedule, rather than on the basis of pain. Thus, analgesics were taken at fixed time intervals, and patients were told to increase their exercises and time out of bed according to specific guidelines. Although there were no significant differences in outcome at 6 weeks, at the 9- and 12-month follow-up evaluations the behavioral group had significantly lower levels of health care utilization and reported fewer impairments and less body area affected by pain.

A second important area for future investigation is extending cognitive-behavioral pain management methods to underserved populations such as young children and older adults. The treatment of pain in children has only recently received systematic attention from clinicians and researchers (Ross & Ross, 1988). For years children were thought to experience less severe pain than adults. As a result, children often received inadequate pharmacologic treatments for pain.

Behavioral methods may offer a practical treatment alternative for managing both acute and chronic pain problems in children. Jay and Elliott (1983), for example, demonstrated the efficacy of a cognitive-behavioral treatment package for pediatric cancer patients undergoing painful bone marrow aspirations. Training techniques used in their intervention included a film of another child successfully coping with the procedure, a small trophy as a reinforcer, breathing exercises, emotive imagery such as imagining a superhero coping with the same pain, and behavioral rehearsal. Jay et al. (1987), in a major, controlled outcome study, demonstrated that this combination of cognitive and behavioral interventions significantly reduced behavioral, self-report, and physiological indices of distress in pediatric cancer patients.

Recent studies of children having chronic migraine headaches also support the utility of cognitive-behavioral interventions. Richter et al. (1986) reported that relaxation training and cognitive restructuring were both superior to attention-placebo control in the treatment of pediatric migraine. Kabela and Andrasik (1988) reported that biofeedback techniques are also quite effective in the management of migraine headaches in children.

Although pain is a common problem in older adults, there are few controlled studies of cognitive-behavioral interventions with older populations. Keefe and colleagues have recently evaluated a cognitive-behavioral pain management intervention for older adults (mean age=64 years) who have persistent osteoarthritic knee pain. Preliminary findings indicate that patients receiving cognitive-behavioral intervention had significantly lower levels of pain and psychological disability posttreatment than patients receiving an education intervention or standard medical care (Keefe et al., 1990a). At the time of a 6-month follow-up evaluation (Keefe et al., 1990b), patients receiving the pain-coping skills intervention had significantly lower levels of psychological and physical disability than patients receiving the arthritis education. The pain-coping skills intervention also showed marginally lower levels of psychological disability ($p < .052$) and physical disability ($p < .13$) than patients in the standard care group. Interestingly, patients who rated the effectiveness of their coping skills as high at the end of initial treatment had lower levels of pain, physical disability, and pain behavior at the 6-month follow-up.

One of the most important directions for future research in pain management is toward the study of the large population of individuals in the general population who appear to cope well with persistent pain (Keefe & Williams, 1989). Most of what we know about cognitive and behavioral approaches to pain has been learned from studying chronic pain patients who present to pain clinics and pain management programs because they are coping poorly. An intensive study of individuals in the general population who are coping successfully may help identify effective coping strategies and the social and environmental factors that support such coping. Epidemiologic studies such as those being carried out by Von Korff, Dworkin, LeResche, and Kruger (1988) can provide a better understanding of cognitive and behavioral pain-coping strategies in the general population. Information gathered through such studies could be used to develop new methods of pain assessment and treatment that might be helpful for many chronic pain sufferers.

ROLE OF STRESS MANAGEMENT IN MEDICAL TREATMENT

Stress management training (SMT) can be broadly defined as anything done professionally to prevent or ameliorate debilitating stress and coping inadequacies (Lazarus & Folkman, 1984). SMT is not considered to be a simple set of procedures but an individualized process in which assessment and treatment are designed to help the client discover origins of maladaptive coping and its maintaining factors, and acquire more effective coping responses. Although SMT varies widely, it usually includes (1) assessment; (2) a rationale and information regarding stress, the disorder, and the skills to be learned; and (3) coping-skills training involving physiological arousal reduction (e.g., progressive muscle relaxation) and/or cognitive interventions (e.g., problem solving). Ideally, SMT intervention is designed to address the physiological systems and specific deficits associated with a particular disorder.

Over the past decade, SMT has been increasingly utilized to supplement medical treatment. Sometimes SMT is only one component in a multimodal treatment program. For example, the treatment of hypertension can include weight reduction, sodium restriction, smoking cessation, and medication compliance, along with SMT. For other disorders such as irritable

bowel syndrome, in which medical management of the disorder has been unsatisfactory, SMT may be one of few treatments available to patients (Almy, 1977).

SMT has been shown to be significantly beneficial in the treatment of many stress-related disorders. Controlled outcome studies have supported the use of SMT in inflammatory bowel disease (DeGossely, Konicky, & Lenfant (1975); irritable bowel syndrome (Cohen and Reed, 1968; Giles, 1978; Hedberg, 1973; Susan, 1978); peptic ulcer disease (Chappell, Stefan, Rogerson, & Pike, 1936); modification of Type A behavior pattern to prevent coronary heart disease (Powell & Thoresen, 1987); hypertension (Crowther, 1983; Drazen, Nevid, Pace, & O'Brien 1982; Patel 1977); Raynaud's disease (Freedman, Ianni, & Wenig, 1983; Freedman, Lynn, Ianni, & Hale, 1981); genital herpes (Longo, Clum, & Yaeger, 1988); and diabetes (Surwit & Feinglos, 1983).

Physicians estimate that emotional stress plays an important role in more than half of all medical problems (Atkinson, Atkinson, Smith, & Hilgard, 1987). There is increasing evidence linking changes in emotion to biochemical changes. Recent studies, for example, have documented the mediating role played by immune competency in the stress-infection relationship (Jemmott & Locke, 1984; Glaser et al., 1986; Glaser, Rice, Speicher, Stout, & Kiecolt-Glaser, 1987; Kennedy, Kiecolt-Glaser, & Glaser, 1988; Kiecolt-Glaser & Glaser, 1987; Kiecolt-Glaser & Glaser, 1989).

Much of the evidence in the area of stress and physiological disorders is correlational because it is difficult to develop adequate research methodologies to measure the interaction between stress and physiological changes. Although direct links between stress and physical disease have not yet been identified, there is compelling evidence that: (1) stress is related to the etiology and symptom occurrence of several physical disorders, and (2) stress management interventions can be helpful in reducing the symptomatology of these disorders.

Definitions of Stress

In considering stress-related disorders and stress management training, it is first necessary to establish definitions of stress and stress-related disorders. In two traditional models of stress, generally termed the trait approach and the life event approach, stress has been conceptualized as either a stimulus (person-generated) or a response (environment-generated). In the trait approach, stable underlying personality constructs or developmental conditions predisposing individuals towards illness were thought to explain a link between stress and disease. In the life event approach, the association between major life events (e.g., divorce, retirement) and illness was investigated to explain a connection between environmental stressors and illness.

The most recent theoretical formulation considers stress to be "neither in the environment nor in the person but a product of their interplay" (Lazarus & Folkman, 1984, p. 354). According to this conceptual model, an individual's cognitive appraisal system is an important variable in the physiological adaptive process. Included in cognitive appraisal is the way in which a person perceives and appraises daily life events, forms beliefs about those events, and then reacts on the basis of those beliefs. Cognitive appraisal is believed to form a crucial link between life events and illness. According to this viewpoint, stress occurs when an individual appraises events as overtaxing coping resources and endangering well-being.

Stress-Related Disorders

Stress and Etiology

Medical disorders are defined as stress-related when stress is involved in the etiology or exacerbation of symptoms. Stress has been demonstrated to be involved in the etiology of disease in a number of controlled laboratory investigations. Laboratory rats subjected to un-controllable random shock, for example, have been shown to be more likely to exhibit elevated blood glucose levels after streptozotocin-induced diabetes, (Huang, Plaut, Taylor, & Wareheim, 1981). Uncontrollable shock also has been shown to lead to increased stomach ulceration in rats (Weiss, 1972).

Stress may interact with other etiological factors to trigger or hasten the onset of disease. An individual may have a biological predisposition to develop a particular problem, and stress, in conjunction with other factors, may elicit the development of that disorder. Falkner, Onesti, and Angelakos (1981), for example, documented differential effects of 14 days of salt loading on normotensive adolescents with positive or negative family histories of hypertension. Normotensive subjects with a positive family history of hypertension showed significantly higher stress-induced systolic and diastolic pressures after salt loading than prior to salt loading. However, salt loading did not affect blood pressure response to stress in individuals with no family history of hypertension.

Stress and Symptom Variability

Once a disorder is present or established, stress can adversely effect the disorder in several ways. First, stress may affect physiologic regulatory functions. In peptic ulcer disease patients, stress has been associated with increases in gastric acid secretion (Peters & Richardson, 1983). Stress has also been associated with increased severity and duration of herpes simplex virus for patients with recurrent genital herpes (VanderPlate & Aral, 1987).

A second way that stress may negatively affect an established disorder is that when patients are under stress, they may be less effective in self-management of their condition. For example, a diabetic patient may overeat or undereat, resulting in deregulation of blood glucose. Occurrence of symptoms, regardless of the cause, may increase anxiety and distress in the patient and, along with the symptoms themselves, may disrupt functional ability, making adherence or effective self-intervention more difficult or impossible.

ASSESSMENT OF STRESS RESPONSES

The purpose of assessment in SMT is to identify physiological, behavioral, and cognitive aspects of maladaptive coping and to understand how these behavioral and cognitive coping responses are maintained. Assessment methods typically employed in SMT include self-monitoring, psychophysiological assessment, and questionnaire measurements of life events and daily hassles.

Self-Monitoring

Participants in stress-management programs are often asked to self-monitor their activities. This might take the form of a behavioral diary in which they record antecedents (such as a scheduled meeting with a boss), their behavior (losing temper with boss), and the consequences of their behavior (losing special assignment and feeling guilty) for stressful situations. Cognitive and physiological responses are sometimes included as part of the self-recording. For example, the patient might be asked to record thoughts before an anticipated stressful situation, such as, "I know I'm going to fail that test," and physiological reactions during the stressful events, such as sweaty palms or shortness of breath.

Self-monitoring serves multiple purposes (Keefe, Kopel, & Gordon, 1978). It establishes the patient as an active participant in treatment from the outset of intervention and encourages the patient to begin learning important skills for management of symptoms. In addition, documenting specific antecedents, behaviors, and consequences can identify important target areas for intervention.

Psychophysiological Assessment

In a psychophysiological assessment, physiological responses are recorded under controlled laboratory conditions. The patient is typically placed in a subject room that is controlled for noise level, lighting and temperature. Monitoring devices are attached to record physiological responses such as respiration, heart rate, digital temperature, blood pressure, and electromyographic (muscle) activity. These responses are recorded when the patient is resting and during the performance of stressful tasks such as public speaking, mental arithmetic, or a cold pressor task in which the hand is immersed in ice water.

Several response patterns may be identified in psychophysiological assessment (Turk & Flor, 1984). A patient may display initially elevated baselines and delay in returning to baseline after a stressful situation. This pattern is indicative of autonomic overrresponsivity. Another common pattern is that the patient shows overreactivity in a particular physiological response (e.g., heart rate), but not in others. In this case, a "diathesis stress" model (Turk & Flor, 1984), in which the structurally weak organ becomes the primary pathway for physiological responses to stress, would be supported.

Psychophysiological assessment may also be made under real-life stressful conditions, such as portable monitoring of digital temperature for Raynaud's disease patients during external cold-temperature situations (e.g., in an air-conditioned office).

Self-Report

Assessments for stress management may also include questionnaire measures of life events and daily hassles. Major life changes, as measured by the Life Event Scale, can be important sources of psychosocial stress and precursors of somatic illness (Holmes & Rahe, 1967), presumably because they challenge the person's capacity to adapt to change (Wickramasekera,

1988). Retrospective and prospective studies, however, have shown only modest correlations ($r = .15–.3$) between increases in life change and the onset of physical or mental illness (Depue & Monroe, 1986; Rabkin & Struening, 1976).

The Hassles Scale (Kanner, Coyne, Schaefer, & Lazarus, 1981) assesses stressful everyday events. Hassles are considered to be irritating and frustrating daily demands and include such things as traffic noise, preparing meals, having to wait, and unexpected company. Consistent with the emphasis on perception of an event rather than its mere occurrence, the Hassles Scale allows for recording perceived intensity of daily life events as well as their frequency. It has been demonstrated that frequency and intensity of daily hassles is related to somatic health outcomes ($r = .3–.45$), and this effect remains even after the effects of major life events are statistically removed (DeLongis, Coyne, Dakor, et al., 1982; Kanner, Coyne, Schaefer, & Lazarus, 1981; Lazarus, DeLongis, Folkman, & Gruen, 1985). Given the measurement of daily events over a shorter retrospective period (one month) and assessment of the perceived intensity of the daily events, the Hassles Scale is probably a more sensitive instrument than Life Event Scale in detecting pre to post changes in frequency and intensity of life stress, especially over short time periods (Beckham, Gustafson, May, & Annis, 1987).

STRESS MANAGEMENT TRAINING (SMT)

SMT generally involves three components: treatment rationale, relaxation training, and cognitive intervention. Providing the patient with a rationale is considered to be a crucial component of stress management treatment and is believed to promote a sense of control and responsibility and feelings of hope in the patient that will lead to enhanced compliance with specific behavioral interventions (Meichenbaum, 1986).

The rationale component of treatment often involves using learning concepts to explain the etiology and occurrence of the condition, how stress can affect the symptoms, and how skills learned in SMT can result in prevention and alleviation of presenting problems. Maladaptive responses are described as ineffectual habits, and new ways of coping are presented as skills that can be learned to replace old ways of thinking and behaving.

Relaxation Training

Relaxation is a major target skill in stress management interventions. Relaxation can provide the patient with a competing response to psychophysiological arousal when confronted with stressful situations. Relaxation training is often presented in the form of progressive muscle relaxation in which the patient alternately tenses and relaxes muscle groups (Bernstein & Borkovec, 1973). After relaxation has been practiced by the patient under nonstressful conditions, systematic desensitization may be used to assist the patient in decreasing anxiety during threatening situations. For example, the patient may find conversations about promotion with his employer highly stressful, and symptoms of his disorder (e.g., peptic ulcer disease) flare when he anticipates or has such conversations. In systematic desensitization, the patient imagines a hierarchy of progressively anxiety-provoking aspects of the situation and practices relaxation while imagining these scenes.

Although relaxation procedures are usually viewed as a physiological self-control component, they can also have positive cognitive and emotional effects. Practice provides the patient an opportunity to focus attention away from daily activities, increase feelings of calm, and decrease worry. Having relaxation available as a coping skill may also enhance self-efficacy and encourage individuals to attempt changes in other maladaptive habitual coping styles or life-styles (Godaert, 1982).

Cognitive Interventions

Cognitive interventions emphasize the mediating role of cognitive processes in eliminating or sustaining maladaptive patterns. Faulty reasoning may lead to erroneous beliefs and cognitive distortions. For example, a genital herpes patient may erroneously think, "No one will ever want me as a partner because of my condition. I am not fit to be anyone's boyfriend." These thoughts can contribute to the patient's perception of stress in potentially difficult situations. The patient in this example may desire an intimate relationship but find that his faulty thinking makes him feel anxious and uncomfortable in situations in which he has the chance to meet attractive females.

As a first step in cognitive intervention, patients are taught to identify negative thoughts associated with stressful situations. Then patients are taught cognitive coping skills such as calming self-statements to reframe the overly negative perception of events, in order to decrease the impact of the stressor. For example, a peptic ulcer disease patient might have an argument with his wife and begin to feel stomach pain. He might think to himself, "She's killing me. This relationship is over and I'll never be able to control this horrible pain." In response to this situation, the patient may be trained to make calming self-statements such as: "Arguments are part of marriage. We have some problems, but we are trying to work them out. This stomach pain is a signal for me to take steps to take care of myself. I'm going to practice relaxation now."

In cognitive interventions, the emphasis is on self-control and regulation. First, patients are taught to recognize situations that trigger their symptoms and to use relaxation to prevent physiological arousal from reaching the point at which symptoms occur. Second, once symptoms occur, patients are taught to use their relaxation and cognitive coping skills to reduce the impact of their symptoms. Cognitive interventions may be particularly important to patients who have significant self-control deficits, such as those who are extremely anxious or depressed (Holroyd, 1986).

FUTURE DIRECTIONS IN SMT

Although substantial empirical progress has been made regarding the effect of SMT on stress-related disorders, several important areas deserve further investigation.

First, it would be useful to conduct additional controlled studies of SMT. The effectiveness of SMT for peptic ulcer disease, for example, has only been investigated in a single controlled study which is now out of date (Chappell, Stefan, Rogerson, & Pike, 1936). There have been few controlled studies of SMT with other disorders that may have stress-related components such as atopic dermatitis, premenstrual syndrome, cancer, or fibromyalgia. Controlled studies can identify the stress-related disorders that are most likely to respond to SMT. There is also a clear need for controlled studies that compare SMT to attention placebo and routine medical treatment and that evaluate the effects of specific treatment components (e.g., relaxation training, biofeedback, cognitive interventions). Experimental demonstrations of the effectiveness of SMT are likely to lead to greater acceptance of this cognitive-behavioral intervention by health care professionals.

A second important area for future investigation is the comparison of individual versus group SMT and evaluation of the length and frequency of SMT sessions. For some clinical problems, such as coronary heart disease, intensive treatment (up to 3 years) in a small group format is believed to be crucial to treatment success (Powell & Thoresen, 1987). For other clinical problems, such as Raynaud's disease (Freedman, Lynn, Ianni, & Hale, 1981), treatment in a series of 8 to 12 weekly individual sessions appears to be sufficient.

A third important area for future research is the tailoring of treatment procedures to the specific needs of the patient. As we have seen, SMT typically involves a combination of cognitive and behavioral treatment components. Some of these components may be more salient for a particular patient than others. SMT programs, indeed, have been criticized for failing to use comprehensive behavioral assessment procedures. Such an assessment would enable the therapist to tailor treatment so as to address target behaviors and controlling variables unique to each patient (Hillenberg & DiLorenzo, 1987). Tailoring treatment would enable therapists to streamline treatment and reduce costs, thereby making SMT more readily available to a greater number of patients.

One of the most challenging aspects of SMT is teaching patients how to apply the skills they have learned to a variety of stressful situations. Psychophysiological methods potentially can be quite useful in generalizing the effects of SMT. Psychophysiological assessments can provide objective data on a patient's ability to relax in different stressful situations (e.g., during stressful imagery or public speaking). Problem situations can be identified and biofeedback provided to teach the patient to relax when he or she needs it most. Some patients may need to learn to relax while they are in particular postures or activities such as standing or walking. Research shows that training in arousal reduction in one position (e.g., reclining) does not generalize well to other positions (Cram, 1987).

Spouse training and family interventions may also be helpful in the behavioral management of stress-related disorders. Involving spouses in treatments for agoraphobia and alcohol abuse has led to significant and lasting treatment gains (Cerny, Barlow, Craske, & Himadi, 1987; McCrady et al., 1986). Training family members to decrease patient illness behaviors through extinction procedures and to reinforce behaviors incompatible with illness behaviors has been shown to be effective in a number of chronic, stress-related disorders (Wooley, Blackwell, & Winget, 1978).

In the past decade, training in stress management has become more available to the general population. SMT is offered in community colleges, adult education centers, and as an employee benefit in many corporate settings. The benefits of SMT are widely publicized in the media, and this has led to an increased demand for SMT services. Patients having stress-related disorders are now, in some cases, requesting that their physicians refer them for SMT. It is possible that the growing popularity of SMT may lead to a reduction in the incidence and prevalence of stress-related disorders. Epidemiologic studies are needed to determine whether SMT can, in fact, have such broad effects in the general population.

CONCLUSIONS

In the past decade, behavioral medicine researchers have demonstrated that cognitive-behavioral interventions can play an important role in the management of a wide range of disease conditions. There is also growing recognition that these interventions can potentially be used as a behavioral means of promoting health and preventing disease.

As the field of behavioral medicine advances, we can expect to see continued growth in the use of cognitive-behavioral interventions. The emphasis on empiricism and methodological rigor that is characteristic of cognitive-behavioral research is likely to have an ongoing influence on the development of behavioral medicine interventions. With further development and refinement, cognitive-behavioral intervention is likely to emerge as the treatment of choice for many behavioral medicine applications.

TREATMENT RESOURCES

Blanchard, E. B. & Andrasik, F. A. (1985). *Management of chronic headaches: A psychological approach.* New York: Pergamon. A practical guide to biofeedback and relaxation approaches to headache treatment. The authors have validated the approaches outlined in numerous controlled studies.

Fordyce, W. E. (1976). *Behavioral methods for chronic pain and illness.* St. Louis: Mosby. Best introduction to operant behavioral treatment of chronic pain; written by the pioneer in the field.

Turk, D. C., Meichenbaum, D., & Genest, M. (1983). *Pain and behavioral medicine: A cognitive behavioral perspective.* New York: Guildford. Best overview of cognitive-behavioral treatment approaches for chronic pain management. Contains step-by-step outline of treatment process.

Woolfolk, R. L., & Lehrer, P. M. (1984). *Principles and practice of stress management.* New York: Guilford. Edited book that provides a practical guide to all facets of stress management.

CHAPTER 14

Management of Classroom Disruptive Behavior and Academic Performance Problems

Dale Walker
Charles R. Greenwood
Barbara Terry

Some of the earliest successful applications of the behavioral approach and applied behavior analysis occurred in public school settings (Becker, Madsen, Arnold, & Thomas, 1967; Hall, Lund, & Jackson, 1968; Patterson, 1965; Walker & Buckley, 1968). These school applications were important as demonstrations of the effective use of behavioral principles within the school. Furthermore, they could be systematically learned and applied by principals, teachers, parents, and students. However, because these studies focused on only a few specific behaviors over short periods of time, they did not serve as a demonstration of a technology that would be practical to handle the daily behavior management tasks facing teachers.

The seventies saw the emergence of an in-

The preparation of this manuscript was supported by grants from the National Institute of Child Health and Human Development (HD 03144) and the Office of Special Education Programs (G008730085) to the Juniper Gardens Childrens' Project, Schiefelbush Institute for Life Span Studies, University of Kansas.

creasing number of specific behavior management procedures, applications to an increasingly sophisticated set of problems, and an increased focus on methods of teacher training and the quality of implementation (Becker, Engelmann, & Thomas, 1971; Hall & Copeland, 1972; Hops, Walker et al., 1978). Throughout the eighties, there was an increased effort to employ behavior management strategies on a broader scale: over longer periods of the school day, focused on groups of students as well as individual students, integrated within the academic curriculum, and focused school- and community-wide (Becker, 1986; Greenwood, Delquadri, & Hall, 1984; Mayer, Butterworth, Nafpaktitis, & Sulzer-Azaroff, 1983). In addition to the criteria of effectiveness, seen as the hallmark of applied behavioral procedures, research in classroom behavior management began to address the factors that affect its use and acceptability in schools. These factors include cost, efficiency, teacher and pupil acceptability, and consumer satisfaction (Schwartz & Baer, 1991; Wolf, 1978).

Over the past 30 years, an effective classroom behavior management technology has emerged and is still developing, only partially adopted by schools. The goal in this chapter is to cover these procedures that represent current knowledge and best practice.

THE NEED FOR BEHAVIORAL MANAGEMENT IN THE SCHOOL

The demands for effective behavior management procedures are widespread and at times highly dramatic (See Table 14.1). When asked to rate their most difficult problems related to schooling and public education, teachers and the public at large consistently rank discipline as problem number one or two (Gallup & Clark, 1987; Menacker, Hurwitz, & Weldon, 1988; Ritter, 1989; Rose, 1988). There has also been widespread dissatisfaction and concern with the quality of the national educational product. Media reports regularly discuss the problem of low academic achievement and the lowering of basic skills among the nation's work force (Anderson, Hiebert, Scott, & Wilkinson, 1985; Bernick, 1986; US Department of Labor, 1988). Additional evidence for the magnitude and long-standing nature of the problem of low academic achievement is contained in the numerous national legislative and regulatory mandates that address this problem (Chapter I of the Educational Consolidation and Improvement Act of 1981, Public Law 94-142; Public Education of All Handicapped Children Act of 1975 and its amended version, Public Law 99-457), and the huge costs associated with such mandates.

Those working in education face a persistent, long-term problem because of the number of students who are at risk for school failure and the obvious difficulty in finding and implement-ing instructional and behavior management solutions for this problem (Carnine, 1988; Carta, 1991; Levin, 1986; Smith & Lincoln, 1988). The practical importance of solving this national problem, even in part, may be appreciated by considering the consequences of raising a person's academic skills just one grade level in terms of tested academic achievement. Gaining a single grade level has the potential of increasing a person's lifetime earnings by 3.6% and decreasing the probability of future welfare dependency, unplanned pregnancies, and arrests (Smith & Lincoln, 1988).

IS PUNISHMENT A SOLUTION?

Traditionally, the national response to discipline in the schools has been reactive, in the form of punitive measures instead of preventive or effective practices. Punitive measures have ranged from those with a long-standing tradition, such as *corporal punishment*, *suspension*, and *expulsion* (Cryan, 1987; Rose, 1988); referral and placement in segregated special-education programs (Bartlett, 1989); *school building security*, including locked doors and law enforcement in the form of guards and police; to *classroom interactions with teachers* that routinely show rates of disapproval higher than rates of approval (White, 1975). The typical approach to discipline has been to get tough and use punitive measures (Canter & Canter, 1976), which have been associated with numerous serious side-effects including physical injury, bruising, aggression, humiliation, decreased academic performance, increased truancy, and school dropout (Bongiovanni & Hyman, 1978; Rose, 1988).

Although empirical evidence exists to support the effectiveness of a number of punishment procedures in reducing unwanted behaviors (Foxx & Azrin, 1972; Luce, Delquadri, & Hall, 1980), many practical, ethical, legal, and emotional issues enter into the decision whether punishment is an acceptable treatment choice

TABLE 14.1 Ecobehavioral analysis of school-wide behavior management goals

Ecological Setting	Student Behavior Goals	Student Behavior Problems	Illustrative Citation
1. To/from school	In seat, seat belts, safe behavior, peer social interaction, pedestrian skills, preparedness, attendence	Dangerous behavior, hitting, fighting, disruption, tardiness, threatening, teasing, stealing, smoking, drugs, vandalism	Green, Bailey, & Barber (1981)
2. Playground/recreational	Appropriate game play, recreational behavior, peer social interaction, compliance with school rules	Dangerous behavior, hitting, fighting, rule breaking, teasing, stealing, smoking, drugs, isolate play, self-stimulation, vandalism	Friman, Barnard, Altman, & Wolf (1986)
3. Transition/hallways	Compliance with school rules, safe behavior, peer social interaction	Rule breaking, dangerous behavior, running, tripping, hitting, fighting, threatening, smoking, drugs	Carden-Smith & Fowler (1984)
4. Classroom instruction	Attention, task participation, academic responding, classroom rules, appropriate social interaction, appropriate locale, compliance	Rule breaking, inappropriate locale, disruption, fighting, damaging property, off-task, disrespect, noncompliance, competing behavior, self-stimulation	Delquadri, Greenwood, Stretton, & Hall (1983)
5. Special education services	Attention, task participation, manners, compliance with rules and teacher instructions	Late, rule breaking, noncompliance, competing behavior, self-stimulation, off-task	Smith, Young, West, Morgan, & Rhode (1988)
6. Lunch room	Compliance with school rules, table manners, safe behavior, peer social interaction	Rule breaking, dangerous behavior, problems handling food, noise level, verbal abuse, hitting, teasing,	LaRowe, Tucker, & McGuire (1980)

(Continues)

TABLE 14.1 (Continued)

Ecological Setting	Student Behavior Goals	Student Behavior Problems	Illustrative Citation
		fighting, self-stimulation, noncompliance	
7. Library/assembly room	Attention, compliance with school rules, manners, safe behavior, quiet social interaction	Off-task, noise level, rule breaking, teasing, fighting, disruption, verbal abuse	Fishbein & Wasik (1981)
8. Home	Home study/ homework, school attendance, parent-child review of school goals and progress	Work not taken home, lack of effort, refusal, noncompliance, rule breaking, no effort, limited or inappropriate social interactions with parents	Schumaker, Hovell, & Sherman (1977)

(LaVigna, 1987; Martin, 1981; Newsom, Favell, & Rincover, 1983; Schroeder, Oldenquist, & Rojahn, 1990). Punishment procedures that have been experimentally validated (e.g., timeout) have also been associated with negative side-effects such as crying, retaliation, school vandalism, and avoidance that may greatly undermine their value relative to the problem—prevention and reduction of unwanted behavior.

Although claims regarding side-effects associated with punishment have not always been substantiated through empirical evidence (Axelrod, 1990; Johnston, 1985; Newsom et al., 1983) there is a general preference for the use of procedures that do not include punishment (Horner et al., 1990). Due to the concerns about the use of punishment, the field of behavior analysis in education has been challenged to develop alternatives to punishment. Current research emphasizes the identification of factors thought to maintain unwanted behaviors, in an effort to decrease their probability of occurrence (Carr, Newsom, & Binkoff, 1980) and to focus on increasing engagement in academic behaviors rather than emphasizing reduction of misbehavior (Greenwood, Delquadri, & Hall, 1989; Haring & Kennedy, 1990; LeLaurin & Risley, 1972).

THE CONCEPTUAL BASIS FOR SCHOOL BEHAVIOR MANAGEMENT PROCEDURES

Currently, effective behavior management approaches in schools are based on the principles of operant conditioning (Kazdin, 1980; Skinner, 1953, 1984). These principles demonstrate that environmental events such as rules and teacher praise may influence student behavior(s) that they precede as antecedents or follow as consequences. To affect student behavior(s) reliably, antecedents or consequences must be contingently associated with the behavior in question (Kazdin, 1980). For example, teacher's attention will not increase a student's study behavior if it only follows occasions of nonstudy (Hall, Lund, & Jackson, 1968).

The principles of operant conditioning, then, affect behavior(s) at school by the systematic, contingent application or removal of classroom antecedent and consequent events. These principles include: (1) reinforcement, as in the contingent presentation of a positive stimulus or removal of a negative stimulus, resulting in an *increase* in the behavior; (2) punishment, as in the contingent application of an aversive stimulus or the removal of a positive stimulus, resulting in the *decrease* in the target behavior; (3) extinction, using the termination of a positive stimulus or the removal of reinforcement contingent on a target behavior, resulting in a decrease in the behavior; and (4) stimulus control, by the manipulation of antecedent events that either increase or decrease the probability of occurrence of the target behavior.

The goal of behavior management procedures based on the operant model is to bring desired adaptive skills under *stimulus control:* to bring desired adaptive skills under the control of appropriate relevant stimuli (Albin & Horner, 1988). In simple terms, teaching and behavior management are the processes through which new behaviors are established in situations where they did not previously occur. When behaviors do not occur in the classroom in the presence of the appropriate stimuli, antecedent/consequence processes are needed to increase the frequency of the desired response. Similarly, when inappropriate behaviors occur in the presence of these stimuli, antecedent/consequence processes are needed to reduce the occurrence of these responses. When stimulus control is achieved, desired behaviors have a much higher probability of occurring in the classroom, to the exclusion of undesired behaviors.

As a result of the process of stimulus control

being utilized in the practices of the school and classroom, students will learn what is expected of them as desired behaviors, and there will be more opportunities for successful performance of these behaviors because students will find that these behaviors are frequently reinforced. The results of this process are that teachers will find the majority of their interactions with students to be concerned with students' appropriate behaviors, academic goals, and accomplishments, and that students will have more opportunities for learning and more positive experiences with their teachers and the school environment (Greenwood, 1991; Mayer et al., 1983; Wahler & Fox, 1981).

ESTABLISHING SPECIFIC BEHAVIORAL GOALS

A major issue in behavior management is the identification and selection of target behaviors and the situations in which they are expected to occur.

Behavioral Response Definitions

Behavioral response specification ensures that the specific behaviors targeted for change within a content domain or response class are defined in terms of explicit, observable, and measurable terms. Behavioral objectives include descriptions of: (1) the behavior that will be changed, (2) the conditions under which the behavior is expected, and (3) the standards or criteria that are used to determine the success of the change (Sobsey & Ludlow, 1984). Because behavioral and academic change goals are framed as observable behaviors, they can be reliably measured and can be changed by the application of behavioral management procedures. Behavioral definitions ensure that teachers can accurately discriminate the presence or absence of the response and thus manipulate the antecedents occasioning it or provide/remove the consequences related to the behavior.

For example, a behavioral objective might be: "On the playground, when his name is called by the teacher, Jim will acknowledge by waving his hand, on 80% or more opportunities." The response, acknowledging the teacher's call, has been defined in specific terms and with a set criterion level (e.g., 80% of opportunities). A hallmark of behavioral approaches to classroom behavior management has been the use of target behavior measurement as a means of assessing progress toward change goals (Baer, Wolf, & Risley, 1986; Shapiro & Lentz, 1985). Some important methods of behavioral assessment in classrooms and schools have been continuous observational and product measures of performance, in which behavioral definitions have provided the focal point (Greenwood, Carta, & Atwater, 1991; Rusch, Rose, & Greenwood, 1988; West & Young, 1990).

When used as the targets of behavior change programming efforts, behavioral definitions become central units within contingency statements. Contingency statements specify the relationship between the antecedent stimuli, the response, and the consequence. For example, the teacher might state the following contingency: "During reading, if you raise your hand each time you need my help, I will let you select the next story we will read." As we will see shortly, contingency statements become the core of most behavior management programs.

Task Analysis

The procedure of task analysis ensures that target responses within a content domain are optimally defined within a response class for purposes of change (Becker, 1986; Rusch, Rose, & Greenwood, 1988). The procedure recognizes that behavior change is an orderly process that proceeds most effectively in terms of small, rather than large, ordered steps. In a traditional task analysis, this progression is a series of steps in hierarchical order from least to most complex, which are taught in order. For example, a task analysis of completing a dictionary assignment would begin with obtaining a dictionary, looking for key words beginning with the beginning letter of interest, looking for the page containing the word, reading the definition, writing its definition, and looking for the next word. As can be seen, the analysis is a sequence of steps involved in the entire performance of the behavior from beginning to end.

General Case Programming

The tenet of general case programming is that teaching with *some members* of a stimulus class can result in correct responding to *all members* of the stimulus class, and thus generalization may be achieved without additional training (Horner, McDonnell, & Bellamy, 1986). General case programming is a task analysis in which the universe of stimulus conditions that should control a response are identified. From this universe, the general features of these stimuli are identified and taught. The goal is to assure that the response will occur reliably under a range of appropriate stimuli and situations, through training that directly includes some of these stimulus features (Albin & Horner, 1988; Becker, 1986, 1988).

The procedures employed to produce change in target behaviors generally include establishing contingencies of reinforcement or punishment and/or rearranging behavioral antecedent conditions (Favell & Reid, 1988).

CHANGING BEHAVIOR THROUGH CONTINGENCY MANAGEMENT

Positive and Negative Contingencies of Reinforcement

Positive reinforcement procedures in schools have ranged from those using primary reinforcers or unconditioned reinforcers, such as food, to secondary reinforcers or conditioned reinforcers, such as praise, good grades, and points that have become reinforcing, based on the history of reinforcement associated with them. For a stimulus to be a reinforcer it *must* result in an increase or strenghthening of the target behavior. For example, when students earn points for correct spelling of words that contribute to a winning team effort, their spelling accuracy tends to increase (Delquadri, Greenwood, Stretton, & Hall, 1983).

Procedures based on negative reinforcement used in schools refer to the contingent termination or removal of a stimulus that results in the *increase* of the target behavior. For example, if a student is required to stay after school to complete assignments but is allowed to leave once the assignments are completed, and the student would rather be elsewhere, he or she will probably complete the assignments so as to leave school and engage in preferred activities. Negative reinforcement, however, is not a recommended teaching strategy, because it requires the presence of an aversive or unpleasant situation and may be prone to some unpredictable negative side-effects.

There are few negative side-effects to the use of positive reinforcement to manage behavior. As a result, researchers have productively explored a number of contingency arrangements that apply to students individually and in groups (Greenwood & Hops, 1981; Kalfus, 1984).

Individualized Contingencies

Individualized contingencies are those in which each student has a completely idiosyncratic program. Each student has a unique set of target behaviors, point-earning strategy, and set of back-up reinforcers. For example, it may be determined that one student in a classroom has the entry skills to use a point-based reinforcement system, contingency contract, or self-management program (Browder & Shapiro, 1985; Hughes & Hendrickson, 1987; Kelley & Stokes, 1982; Murphy, 1988), whereas another

may be best served by using a program based initially on edible or physical reinforcement procedures.

Standardized Contingencies

Standardized contingencies are those commonly employed in classroom token economy systems. Typically, all students in the classroom are involved in the program. The behavioral requirements are specified in terms of conduct rules and academic performance that are uniform for all class members, but reinforcement is applied separately to each student depending on individual performance (Greenwood & Hops, 1981; Kalfus, 1984).

Group-Oriented Contingencies

In contrast, group-oriented contingencies involve all students in response requirements, point earning, and/or backup reinforcement so that group dependencies or interdependencies are formed. In these cases, each student's reinforcement depends in part on his or her own performance and on that of a peer or peers. For example, students may be reinforced on the basis of the class-average score or a team score, rather than their own performance. Greenwood and his colleagues reported the use of a clock light recording device for just this purpose (Greenwood, Hops, Delquadri, & Guild, 1974; Greenwood, Hops, & Walker, 1977; Greenwood et al., 1979). The device enabled a teacher to record the amount of time all students were engaged in appropriate classroom behavior. When even one student was not engaged, the teacher turned off the clock. At the end of the session, the total time that all students had collectively engaged in the desired behaviors was made available. If this score was high enough to meet the criterion for reinforcement, then all students were allowed to engage in group activity. If the score was low, none of the students were able to engage in the activity. Thus, in this system, behavioral requirements were standardized, recording of behavior depended on the collective effort of the group, and reinforcement of each individual was dependent on his or her own behavior and that of the other group members.

The advantages of group-oriented contingencies, in addition to the fact that they enable a system that is applied to all students, is that they enlist the natural reinforcing properties of peer influence in support of the teacher's behavior change goals. Peers provide assistance, tutoring, help, and encouragement in group-oriented systems because they have a vested interest in how other class members perform (Greenwood, Carta, & Hall, 1988).

Reinforcer Effectiveness

The probability that a consequence will act in an optimal manner to increase the frequency of a response is in a constant state of variation. Teachers must therefore constantly seek to maintain the effectiveness of the consequences they use as reinforcers (Morgan & Jenson, 1988). Reinforcer effectiveness is dependent on a number of factors that act to increase or decrease effectiveness. These factors include timing, satiation, and selection (Rusch et al., 1988). Reinforcers are more effective when provided immediately following the response to be strengthened. Delays between response occurrence and onset of reinforcement decrease the probability of strengthening the target behavior. Repeated use of the same consequence over and over reduces its effectiveness as a reinforcer. This is known as satiation; repeated presentation of the same consequence such as edibles diminishes their ability to strengthen a response, due to the fact that the person may be full or the taste is no longer pleasing. Strong reinforcers should be selected and tested to assure effectiveness.

New reinforcers may be identified by observing what students do during free time. The activities or behaviors they select (high-probability behaviors) may be used to reinforce classroom behaviors (low-probability behaviors)

(Premack, 1959). New reinforcers may be identified by asking students what they would like to do, by having them select from a list of alternatives, or by observing what they choose and testing the function of those selected. Events that are not reinforcers may become reinforcers by allowing students to engage in these activities and observing their reaction to them (reinforcer sampling). In many cases, exposure and experience with a previously unknown event or activity will establish it for use as a reinforcer.

Schedules of Reinforcement

In classrooms and schools, the classic schedules of reinforcement, as described in the experimental analyses in behavior literature (Skinner, 1953), have not always been used, because they are difficult to implement in applied settings such as classrooms, due to the additional demands placed on teachers to monitor the reinforcement schedule. However, two helpful generalizations based on the reinforcement schedule literature apply to the classroom. These are the continuous versus intermittent reinforcement schedules and the behaviors associated with these schedules, which have an important impact on classroom behavior change.

Continuous Schedules

Because *continuous reinforcement* schedules rapidly accelerate the response that produces reinforcement, such schedules are frequently used to bring responses up to a desired level of occurrence. In this case, each occurrence of the response is reinforced. Once the response is established, the scheduling is shifted to an intermittent schedule.

Intermittent Schedules

Intermittent schedules tend to maintain a high frequency of responding even under the condition of greatly reduced reinforcement. In this case, a student may learn that a response will produce reinforcement only after some un-known period of responding. Consequently, in behavior management applications particularly, continuous reinforcement has been used first to establish a desired frequency of responding, fol-lowed by a gradual transition to an intermittent reinforcement schedule to maintain these levels over time (Wolery, Bailey, & Sugai, 1988). For example, in the *Program for Academic Survival Skills* (PASS), students earned reinforcement after each session in which they increased the level of classroom-appropriate behavior over the prior day's level. This continuous schedule re-mained in effect until students reached the 80% criterion. After this point, an intermittent schedule was employed in which students were required to meet the 80% criterion over several days in order to obtain the reinforcer (Green-wood et al., 1974). The intermittent schedule encouraged students to maintain the high level of responding and the teacher was gradually able to reduce the amount of reinforcement de-livered.

Differential Reinforcement Procedures

Differential reinforcement procedures are of the greatest relevance to school management pro-grams, because they are most often procedures that are acceptable to parents, teachers, students, and the general public. The basic premise of differential reinforcement is that through the reduction of opportunities to re-ceive reinforcement for a particular inappropri-ate behavior and the increase in opportunities to receive reinforcement for appropriate alterna-tive behavior(s), the unwanted behavior will de-crease.

The four most commonly utilized differential reinforcement procedures include: (1) shaping, (2) differential reinforcement of incompatible behavior (DRI), (3) differential reinforcement of low-rate behavior (DRL), and (4) differential re-inforcement of alternate behavior (DRA).

Shaping

Shaping is the systematic reinforcement of *only* those responses that approximate the target be-havior and the extinction of those that do not. Using shaping procedures, it is possible to in-crease a student's accuracy in writing a letter, for example, from a low level to a high level by differentially reinforcing only those responses that more than any others approximate the de-sired behavior. Thus, shaping of a behavior can result in the teaching of a specific response by using only reinforcement in the absence of rules, instructions, or prompts. However, it is more common to combine shaping with other procedures such as use of antecedent stimuli, to arrive at the target performance more quickly.

Incompatible Behavior

Differential reinforcement of incompatible be-havior (DRI) is a procedure whereby a response that is topographically incompatible with the target behavior is reinforced (Deitz & Repp, 1983). Incompatibility in this case refers to the physical impossibility of performing the un-wanted behavior and the appropriate behavior simultaneously. Incompatible behaviors that are reinforced during DRI procedures are those be-haviors that, when occurring, greatly reduce or inhibit the unwanted behavior because of their physical-functional incompatibility. For in-stance, appropriate toy play cannot occur si-multaneously with hand-flapping or body rock-ing (Eason, White, & Newsom, 1982), nor can disruptive behavior occur during the tallying of scores following peer tutoring if the disruptive student is given the responsibility of adding scores on a calculator that requires concen-tration.

Alternative Behavior

Although similar to DRI, differential reinforce-ment of alternative behavior (DRA) should be used in cases when a topographically incompat-ible behavior may not be identifiable or when

DRI would not be a functional or practical response to replace the target behavior. For example, Carr and Durand (1985) taught students to recruit adult attention instead of engaging in tantrums or self-injurious behaviors in situations where adult attention was often at low levels and task difficulty was high. Although not topographically dissimilar from the target behaviors, the replacement behavior (recruitment of adult attention) was a more appropriate and effective way of gaining adult assistance, one that would enable the students to communicate their needs in a socially appropriate manner.

The advantages to using DRI and DRA to prevent and manage behavior are that they focus on strengthening an appropriate alternative behavior that adds to the students' repertoire. Considerations when using DRI and DRA are: (1) that the communicative function of the target behavior be identifiable; (2) that the incompatible or replacement behaviors selected should include behaviors that the student already performs with ease, so that additional lessons are not required to teach the alternate behavior; and (3) that the incompatible or alternative behavior will be useful or functional for the student.

Low Rates of Behavior

Differential reinforcement of low rates of behavior (DRL) is a strategy whereby responses that occur below a predetermined rate or level are reinforced, and thus alternative behavior increases and reinforcement for undesired behavior is removed. During DRL, the student receives reinforcement for periods of time during which the target behavior occurs at a lower rate or frequency than during baseline observations (Deitz & Repp, 1973). DRL is an appropriate treatment choice for behaviors that may occur at excessive rates but that are appropriate at decreased rates (e.g., raising hand for help).

Rotholz and Luce (1983) applied DRL to reduce gazing at the ceiling and inappropriate vocalizations, respectively, by two students with autism. The DRL procedure for one student consisted of reinforcement for progressively lower rates of gazing, until gazing at lights ceased to conflict with the student's classwork. The reinforcing stimulus in this study was the opportunity to look through a gyroscope, contingent on ceiling-gazing that was below the criterion set for the session. For the second student, inappropriate vocalizations were gradually decreased and attainment of criterion levels was reinforced by using music, a preferred activity for the student.

To this point the chapter has discussed contingencies based on reinforcement procedures; next to be covered will be those based on punishment.

Punishment

It is preferable to manage unwanted classroom behaviors through preventive and proactive measures that emphasize the identification and manipulation of antecedents controlling the behavior and through the use of procedures that manipulate reinforcement. There will be occasions, however, when the behavior(s) in question will interfere with classroom activities and goals to an extent that requires an intervention plan that includes the use of punishment (Lahey & Drabman, 1981).

A procedure is a punisher if it involves the application of a stimulus event or removal of reinforcement, contingent on a given behavior, and results in reduction of the behavior (Favell, 1983; Johnston, 1972). The behavioral view of punishment does not imply that the recipient experiences any painful sensation, only that the punishing stimulus results in a decrease or elimination of the behavior it follows (Favell & Reid, 1988; Johnston, 1972).

Before deciding to use any management procedure that includes punishment, there should be agreement among teachers, parents, and other persons involved, including the student(s) whenever possible, that there is a legitimate need to manage the behavior(s). Several questions should be included in this decision-making process (Gaylord-Ross, 1980):

1. Does the behavior cause injury to the student or to others?
2. Does the behavior present a safety risk to the student or to others?
3. Does the behavior interfere with the student's or with other students' learning?
4. Does the behavior have serious social consequences for the student?
5. Have efforts to change the behavior using less restrictive procedures been tried and failed?

If these questions are answered affirmatively, then the use of punishment to manage behavior may be appropriate. Guidelines regarding the use of punishment have been developed and should be referred to when deciding on methods to manage classroom behavior (Schroeder, Oldenquist, & Rojahn, 1990).

As with positive reinforcement, contingencies based on punishment require the specification of the behavior to be punished, the identification of the antecedent conditions to the behavior, and the selection of the punishment procedure. Punishments employed in most classroom behavior management programs are typically mild and include temporary loss of reinforcers (e.g., loss of teacher attention, point loss, or suspension of point-earning privileges), and/or the presentation of mild reprimands.

Extinction

Extinction, sometimes referred to as planned ignoring in classroom behavior management, involves removing the teacher's attention contingent on the occurrence of an undesired behavior (Snell & Smith, 1978). Extinction has been effective for reducing disruptive classroom behaviors (Pinkston, Reese, LeBlanc & Baer, 1973), tantrums (Rolider & Van Houten, 1985), and self-stimulatory behaviors (Aiken & Salzberg, 1984).

Considerations when using extinction procedures include identifying the reinforcers that maintain the behavior and ensuring that reinforcement can be temporarily withheld. Extinction, although effective for managing many behaviors, may be slow-acting and occasionally results in a temporary increase in the behavior (extinction burst). Therefore, extinction may not be an appropriate treatment choice for managing behaviors that are dangerous (i.e., aggression and self-injury) or behaviors that are intolerable in classrooms (i.e., destruction of property or impeding other students' learning). Further, student behavior that is not attention-seeking can probably not be managed through the use of extinction, as the removal of attention will not be a punisher (Carr & Newsom, 1985; Kazdin, 1980).

Verbal Reprimands

Verbal reprimands or the expression of disapproval (Van Houten & Doleys, 1983) are used to manage behavior through the use of brief teacher statements: (1) to interrupt the unwanted behavior (e.g., by saying "No!"), (2) to redirect the student via reiteration of rules, or (3) to warn that a loss of points or privileges will follow if the behavior continues.

However, the literature regarding the effectiveness of verbal reprimands is somewhat inconclusive. For example, in an early study, Hall et al. (1971) reported that teacher reprimands consisting of pointing at the student and exclaiming "No!" were effective for reducing self-injurious and aggressive behaviors. On the other hand, Thomas, Becker, and Armstrong (1968) concluded that reprimands did not naturally serve as effective punishers when used in classrooms.

There are several considerations about using verbal reprimands as a classroom management technique. The effectiveness of reprimands may be influenced by: (1) nonverbal cues (e.g., eye contact, pointing) that often accompany reprimands; (2) the intensity (e.g., shouting, whispering) of the reprimand; (3) the behavioral control (e.g., history of being paired with reinforcing or unpleasant events) that the person delivering the reprimand has with regard to the person receiving the reprimand; (4) the proximity (distance) of the person who is delivering the reprimand to the student receiving disapproval; (5) whether the verbal reprimand is paired with any other management procedure (time-out); and (6) whether the reprimand is consistently paired with the misbehavior (Van Houten & Doleys, 1983; White, 1975).

Response Cost

Response cost procedures involve the removal of reinforcement such as point gain or loss (McLaughlin & Malaby, 1972; Phillips, 1968), or television viewing (Hall et al., 1972), contingent on misbehavior. Response cost has been effective for managing behavior in classrooms (Axelrod, 1973) and is often included as one component of token systems (Walker, Hops, & Greenwood, 1981).

Response cost relies on the contingent removal of reinforcers that have already been acquired but that do not necessarily maintain the behavior. When implementing a response cost program based on points, for example, the response cost should be applied after *every* instance when the target behavior occurs; the ratio of points earned to those lost should be monitored closely; the subtraction of points should be done in a manner that does not inadvertently reinforce the behavior producing the point loss; and, most importantly, the student's appropriate behavior(s) must be reinforced frequently (Walker, 1983). In general, response cost procedures are used throughout our everyday environment. For instance, traffic tickets, fines for sending bill payments in late, and losing minutes of recess are all response cost procedures (Wolery et al., 1988).

A disadvantage of response cost is that it will be effective only with persons who are reinforced by earning points or other items and can be punished through their loss. Further, response cost procedures involve the delivery of attention for misbehavior (e.g., the removal of points), which in some cases may result in increasing the behavior.

Overcorrection

Overcorrection is an application of response cost. Overcorrection requires that the student restore the environment to a condition as good as or better than prior to the misbehavior (restitution), and/or that he or she practice appropriate behavior (positive practice) (Foxx & Azrin, 1972). Overcorrection procedures requiring restitution are used, for example, in situations where a student or students have left a mess following an activity, and those students are required to clean up the entire classroom before they are allowed to go outside for recess. Positive practice overcorrection might be employed with students who run down the hall. In this case, the student(s) would be required to return to the location where they ran, and practice repeatedly walking appropriately back to their destination (Azrin & Powers, 1975).

Overcorrection has been reported to be most effective when paired with reinforcement of other behaviors (Measel & Alfieri, 1976) and with verbal warnings (Foxx & Azrin, 1973). An advantage of overcorrection is that it should be easy for the student to discriminate desired from undesired behaviors.

Time-out

Time-out is a procedure that reduces the occurrence of a behavior by removing access to reinforcement for a specified time and then reinstating access to reinforcement (e.g., 2 minutes away from peers on playground) (Porterfield, Herbert-Jackson, & Risley, 1976). Time-out is a procedure frequently utilized by teachers (Zabel, 1986) and has been used to manage tantrum behavior, aggression, and the destruction of property (Mace, Page, Ivancic, & O'Brien, 1986). The success of time-out depends entirely on the reinforcement available in the time-in situation (Solnick, Rincover, & Peterson, 1977). For time-out to be effective, students must have no access to reinforcement during the time-out or they may engage in the misbehavior to escape from a less reinforcing or boring situation (Solnick et al., 1977).

A disadvantage of time-out is that it may be negatively reinforcing for the teacher, as the misbehaving student is removed from the activity and sometimes, briefly, from the classroom. In other words, time-out procedures may be misused or overused because it is sometimes easier to have the misbehavior out of sight. Time-out may also provide the student with the opportunity for engaging in other unwanted behaviors such as playing with materials in the time-out area, singing, or in general being disruptive to obtain peer attention (Plummer, Baer, & LeBlanc, 1977). Therefore, when time-out is used to manage behavior in the classroom, it should be monitored very closely (Durand & Carr, 1987). Finally, time-out should be implemented only in conjunction with instructive techniques for increasing desired behaviors, as time-out does not teach alternate, more appropriate behaviors (Sulzer-Azaroff & Mayer, 1986).

In general, punishment procedures should be delivered consistently, immediately following the target behavior, to ensure that only the target behavior is decreased and to avoid gradually building up tolerance to the punisher (Azrin & Holz, 1966; Johnston, 1985). All punishment programs should be monitored by a review process, and careful records should be kept regarding the effects of the program on the target behavior(s). Most importantly, punishment procedures should *only* be used within an integrated program consisting of several methods to

manage behavior, particularly those in which functional alternative behaviors to the misbehavior are strengthened (Baer, 1970; Horner & Day, 1991; White & Haring, 1976).

CHANGING BEHAVIOR THROUGH ALTERING ANTECEDENTS

The goal of the procedures previously discussed and their contingencies is to ensure that behaviors either increase or decrease in frequency according to teachers' objectives. However, the exact contexts and situations in which these behaviors occur is another major element of classroom behavior management. The extent to which the antecedents are made explicit and unambiguous will determine much of the success of a behavior management system.

Behavior changes may be made by noting that in specific situations the desired response does/does not occur, and then introducing contingencies or reinforcement/punishment to strengthen or decrease the response in these situations. Alternatively, however, behavior change may also be made by directly changing the situational factors without introducing new contingencies.

Physical Arrangements

The physical arrangement of the classroom (or lunchroom, etc.) may dramatically facilitate or constrain the behaviors desired in these settings during some or all of the activities there (Krantz & Risley, 1977). For example, the classroom physical environment might be rearranged to maximize opportunities for student responding (e.g., having all students in equal proximity to the teacher), or desks might be arranged so that the necessary traffic pathways for moving in and out of the classroom efficiently are provided. It is also important that the classroom be arranged in a manner that gives the teacher an unobstructed view of all students, for purposes of tracking and reinforcing student behavior (Paine, Radicci, Rosellini, Deutchman, & Darch, 1983). Many behavior problems develop out of the sight of the teacher when the classroom is arranged in a manner that hinders the teacher's ability to observe and monitor students.

Daily Schedules

The daily and weekly schedule of instructional activities has a major impact on students' ability to comply with and engage in the subject-matter goals of the classroom (Hall, Delquadri, Greenwood, & Thurston, 1982). Schedules form the basis for the transitions between activities in and out of the classroom and the changes in behavior associated with each activity (e.g., reading, seatwork, recess, etc.). Schedules that are explicit, that publicly display listings of activities and the associated start and stop times, may be used as a continuing basis for teaching students when transitions are to be made. For example, the schedule can be used as a basis for prompting clean-up behaviors, giving instructions to move to a group or return to one's seat, requiring line-up to leave the classroom, and preparing for the next activity. Schedules may also be used as criteria for starting and stopping activities and evaluating the success of each transition, thus avoiding transitions that are too long or troublesome.

Classroom Behavior Rules

Classroom and school rules are another class of antecedent stimuli commonly employed in behavior management programs. Behavior rules posted in the classroom provide the basis for both prompting and reinforcing students for engaging in desired behaviors (Greenwood, Hops

TABLE 14.2   Sample set of general classroom rules

Be on time to class.

Enter the classroom quietly.

Go to your assigned area quickly.

Begin the entry task promptly.

Listen to the teacher's directions or explanations.

Raise your hand if you wish to talk.

Follow the teacher's directions.

Organize required materials promptly.

Start assigned work promptly.

Keep working.

Ask for help only after you have first tried by yourself.

SOURCE: Colvin, Lowe, & Clanton (1988), p. 32.

et al., 1974). For example, posted rules that have been discussed with and reviewed by students can be used as a basis for reinforcing students who arrive and enter the classroom correctly; for initiating work tasks, and remaining engaged and busy after tasks are completed; and for handling questions and requests for help (Joyce, Joyce, & Chase, 1989).

To be most effective, classroom rules must be stated in a positive manner, specifying the behavior *desired* rather than the undesired behavior (see Table 14.2). Rules should be stated simply, in terms referring to the behavior, and posted on charts in the classroom so they can function as continuous stimulus control for the desired behaviors.

Prompts

Prompts are stimuli that act to signal a student response. For example, teacher instructions and commands can act to direct students' attention to particular aspects of a lesson or task. Instructions can also provide the signals needed by students to begin a response or terminate a response. For example, an important behavior management strategy is to ensure that all students are attending to the teacher *before* instructions are given. Problems may develop if instructions are delivered and student responses begin before students are prepared to make the desired response (Greenwood, Carta, & Hall, 1988). When instructions about the activity that students are to do become confused with the signal to start the activity, behavior problems will probably occur, and teachers may find their instructions take overly long to complete.

Alternatively, many teachers will prompt and obtain student attention before giving a direction, such as saying, "Look at me students!" As students give eye contact, the teacher praises them and waits until all students are looking, then gives the directions and students are signaled to respond (e.g., "Please line up by tables—Table 1, Table 3, Table 2, etc.").

Antecedent Rearrangement

As indicated, antecedent stimuli can dramatically support the organization and efficiency of behavior management efforts. However, direct manipulation of antecedents can also be used to prevent or reduce problem behaviors. For example, when certain behavior problems are identified as occurring during specific times or activities and not during others, control of the problem may be obtained by altering or removing the activity from the schedule and replacing it with activities not associated with the problem. For some students, task demands and high error rates in math, for example, may precede behavior problems. A solution to the problem in the short term may be to remove the task from the schedule, and, in the long term, to reorganize the task by breaking it into smaller units and increasing the success rate, then gradually reintroducing the task into the student's schedule (Gardner, Cole, Davidson, & Karan, 1986; Touchette, McDonald, & Langer, 1985).

To this point the chapter has dealt with procedures for arranging and making explicit the antecedent stimuli and situational contexts for appropriate classroom behavior and for efficient teacher manipulation of antecedents.

EXAMPLES OF SCHOOL INTERVENTION

Direct Instruction Systems

Direct instruction is a well-established and empirically tested system that integrates academic instruction and behavior management goals and procedures (Gersten, Carnine, & Woodward, 1987; Stallings & Stipek, 1986). It has been replicated across numerous content areas (e.g., reading, mathematics, language, science, logic), across different populations (e.g., regular and special education students, including those with severe handicaps) (Horner & Albin, 1989), and across age levels (e.g., preschool through secondary-aged students) (Gersten, Keating, & Becker, 1988; Slavin & Madden, 1987; Weisberg, 1989). Comprehensive, longitudinal evaluations (Becker, 1977; Gersten et al., 1987) have demonstrated that gains on academic tests and in classroom behavior have resulted from the use of direct instruction in the elementary grades, and that these effects affect later success at high school and college levels.

Direct instruction is a methodology that can be readily applied to classroom instruction because of its implementation-ready curriculum packages. Direct instruction employs general case programming, antecedent arrangements within classrooms and within teacher-student interactions, and reinforcing consequences, including teacher approval and point systems. It is designed to prevent the occurrence of unwanted behaviors by its intensive promotion of alternative and incompatible academic responding through teacher prompting and differential reinforcement schedules (e.g., DRI and DRA).

The scope of influence of direct instruction has been in regular classrooms and special-education settings. Direct instruction has been used by teachers for its specific materials and programs, and its procedures have been generalized and applied to other content areas of instruction and behavior management (Colvin & Sugai, 1989). The quality of teacher implementation is supported by scripted materials that directly prompt teacher behavior during instruction. As a result, it is relatively easy to evaluate the fidelity of teacher implementation of direct instruction programs. In this entirely teacher-mediated program, students are taught in small groups, and standardized contingencies of reinforcement are followed.

Classwide Peer Tutoring Systems

A number of procedures employ group-oriented and peer-mediated contingencies to facilitate instruction, manage behavior, and teach cooperative social relationships (Greenwood, 1991; Greenwood, Carta, & Hall, 1988). Classwide peer tutoring (CWPT), for example, is one such system that has been extensively evaluated (Greenwood, Terry, Arreaga-Mayer, & Finney, 1992). CWPT has focused primarily on classroom and special-education instruction and the management of behavior in regular and special-education classrooms.

CWPT involves tutoring pairs, competing teams, point earning, and clearly specified instructions and guidelines (Greenwood, Maheady, & Carta, 1991). In some cases, these systems have received large-scale, longitudinal evaluations (Greenwood, Dinwiddie et al., 1984; Greenwood, Delquadri, & Hall, 1989). These systems have been an effective method for organizing instruction and managing behavior on a classwide basis. Similar systems based on group contingencies involve the use of several small teams rather than tutors (Maheady, Harper, & Sacca, 1988); other systems use teams and group contingencies (Slavin, Madden, & Leavy, 1984).

As with direct instruction, CWPT systems are focused on increasing students' academic responses and promoting appropriate classroom behaviors as alternatives to unwanted behaviors. However, because CWPT employs various group reinforcement contingencies and utilizes students as peer teachers, managers, and monitors, it simultaneously teaches specific aspects of peer social relations as well. Thus, it has the potential to integrate academic material, classroom conduct, and peer social-content goals as alternative behaviors that may result in the prevention of many unwanted, competing behaviors. CWPT addresses the generalization of academic and social responding because of the use of peer social interaction, peer prompting, and the delivery of consequences. Unlike direct instruction, however, CWPT is less sophisticated in its focus on content and general case programming.

Thus, programs based on direct instruction and group-oriented contingencies with peer mediation represent highly developed, evaluated, and adoption-ready applications of behavior management procedures that are currently available for use in classrooms.

One development in behavior management applications in the last several years has been their expansion through the entire school. This is evident in the development of leveled behavior management systems in some classrooms that interface with other classrooms (Sugai & Colvin, 1989) and with entire school systems.

Leveled Classroom Systems

One of the major problems of behavior change has been instituting behavior change and then transferring and maintaining changes in integrated classrooms (Anderson-Inman, Walker, & Purcell, 1984; Carta, Atwater, Schwartz, & Miller, 1990; Sailor, 1991). Leveled behavior management systems have most frequently been used as a means of bridging the gap between the behavior of students with initially severe problems and the behaviors expected in the

TABLE 14.3   Illustration of a single level

Level II — Name: Bronze Stars

GENERAL DESCRIPTION

The Bronze Star level falls between the White and Gold Star levels. It provides opportunities for students to experience greater independence and responsibility. Although academic and behavioral demands are increased, classroom and school privileges also are increased at this level. More opportunities for peer socialization are available. No more than 50% of day is spent in the regular classroom.

EXPECTATIONS AND TRANSITION CRITERIA

1. Model five classroom rule-following behaviors
2. Display five classroom rule-following behaviors with no more than three demerits.
3. Have performance monitoring sheet available at morning and afternoon performance evaluation meetings.
4. Participate in performance evaluation meeting appropriately with no more than 3 demerits.
5. Follow teacher directives the first time within 5 seconds (90% of opportunities).
6. Meet daily individualized goals.
7. Take, complete (50%), and return homework assignments.
8. Take time-outs on first request (75%); second request (100%).

CONSEQUENCES AND PRIVILEGES

1. Full participation in all in-class activities, but not in out-of-class privileges.
2. Free time in room alone or with others.
3. Breaks permitted with permission and hall pass.
4. Special contracts if teacher-developed.
5. Daily snack with second helpings on either drinks or crackers, no specials.

TRANSITION RULES

MOVE BACK a level if 3 consecutive days pass with five or fewer expectations fulfilled or if one major time-out or three minor time-outs earned in 1 day.

MOVE UP a level when all expectations are satisfied concurrently.

SOURCE: Sugai & Colvin (1989), p. 19. Reprinted by permission.

regular classroom setting. Leveled systems are designed as a progression of steps, from the first levels, representing the most control of a student's behavior, to the last level, in which the student's behavior must conform to the demands and schedules of reinforcement available in the regular classroom. Once the student reaches the final level, he or she begins spending time in the integrated classroom and is better prepared to make a successful transition. A single step in a leveled system is illustrated in Table 14.3. Notice that the student is in the process of returning to the regular classroom program (e.g., not less than 50% of time spent in the regular classroom). The level is organized according to expectations and transition criteria, consequences and privileges, and transition rules or movement across levels.

Entire Schoolwide Systems

Increasingly, behavior management programs have been applied to classrooms and programs in entire schools. Unified behavior management

TABLE 14.4   Topics and activities included in team training workshops

Behavioral Concepts That Teachers Were Taught

Conditions that engender school vandalism and disruption

Antivandalism programs

Positive reinforcement

Methods of identifying reinforcers

Negative reinforcement

Extinction

Reinforcing alternative responses

Modeling

Differential reinforcement of low rates

Differential reinforcement of other responses

Response cost

Time-out

Overcorrection

Punishment and its side effects

Practical Applications of These Concepts

Using certificates and rewards

Improving staff morale

Teaching students to get positive recognition

Teaching students to reinforce teachers

Readability assessment procedures

Adapting material to student reading levels

Positive reinforcement bombardment

Secret pal game

I spy game

Good behavior game

Slot machine game

Other group contingency games and programs

Token systems

Daily report cards

School discipline plans

SOURCE: Mayer, Butterworth, Nafpaktitis, & Sulzer-Azaroff (1983), p. 361.

systems are used to manage the behaviors of all students in a school building and are designed to be more or less standard in implementation across classrooms. An example of the content of a program taught by Mayer et al. (1983) is presented in Table 14.4.

Difficulties with this technology for school-wide use include limited empirical support

(Paine & Bellamy, 1982) and problems of fidelity or quality of teacher implementation. For example, an evaluation of a well-known approach based on the Hunter Model (the Napa evaluation) failed at least in part because of serious drift in levels of teacher implementation of the program from one year to the next (Slavin, 1986; Stallings & Krasavage, 1986). Thus, further research is needed to evaluate standard, schoolwide systems that focus not only on change in student behavior but also monitor the quality of teacher implementation of these systems.

CONCLUSIONS

This chapter has reviewed the well-established principles of behavior management and illustrated their use through a number of data-based applications. Most evident is that in addition to being effective, behavior management procedures are becoming increasingly preventive and comprehensive in scope and are integrated into the academic instruction goals of schools and community programs. The behavioral approach is the basis for many of the best practices used to manage behavior (Strain et al., 1992).

Classroom behavior management has become increasingly focused on group, as well as individual, behavior change in schools. It is evident from the applications reviewed that the principles of behavior are rarely applied singly. They are more usually employed in combination and over time, in order to orchestrate and coordinate the acquisition, generalization, and maintenance of desired behaviors while simultaneously preventing and reducing unwanted behaviors. These applications most readily fit three general strategies, including variations of: (1) analysis of and rearrangement of antecedent stimulus conditions that maintain behavior, (2) differential reinforcement of incompatible and alternative behaviors, and (3) arrangement of consequences for problem behaviors.

With a few notable exceptions (Mayer et al., 1987) data supporting the use of behavior management solutions in the entire range of school settings and behaviors as described in Table 14.1 are lacking in the literature. Thus, although substantial progress has been made in terms of increasing the breadth and scope of behavior management solutions by simultaneously addressing academic and competing behaviors (e.g., direct instruction) or academic and peer social interaction (e.g., classwide peer tutoring) in the classroom, much of behavior management appears to be a collection of procedures and practices for specific problems occurring in specific situations, with little continuity across behaviors, settings, time of day, or program implementation.

The continuing challenge of wide-scale acceptance for the developers of behavioral approaches to behavior management lies in the development of procedures that address relatively standard problems of the school. The successful adoption of these procedures by schools requires that they not only be effective for managing behavior, but must also decrease, not increase, teacher work load, and they must be procedures that will be preferred and utilized by teachers. These procedures should be designed to work well in conjunction with other procedures. Thus, effective behavior management should be inclusive of more than just behavior management principles or advice. Instead, behavior management in schools must include a body of effective practices that promote classroom instructional goals and effective behavior management.

TREATMENT RESOURCES

Becker, W. C. (1986). *Applied psychology for teachers: A behavioral cognitive approach.* Chicago: Science Research Associates.

Browder, D. M., & Shapiro, E. S. (1985). Applications of self-management to individuals with severe handicaps: A review. *Journal of the Association for Persons with Severe Handicaps, 10,* 200–208.

Carta, J. J., Atwater, J., Schwartz, I. S., & Miller, P. A. (1990). Applications of ecobehavioral analysis to the study of transitions across early education. *Education and Treatment of Children, 13,* 298–315.

Rusch, F. R., Rose, T., & Greenwood, C. R. (1988). *Introduction to behavior analysis in special education.* Engelwood Cliffs, NJ: Prentice-Hall.

CHAPTER 15

Attention-Deficit Hyperactivity Disorder

George J. DuPaul
David C. Guevremont
Russell A. Barkley

Attention-Deficit Hyperactivity Disorder (ADHD) is a common childhood disorder that represents developmentally inappropriate levels of inattention, impulsivity, and overactivity. It occurs in 3% to 5% of the school-age population or, stated differently, at least one child in every classroom (Barkley, 1981). As a result, ADHD is one of the most commonly referred and heavily studied psychological disorders of childhood. The purpose of this chapter is to review briefly several treatment interventions that have demonstrated effectiveness in the therapeutic management of ADHD and to provide an overview of current and future research endeavors into the important parameters and outcomes associated with these interventions.

HISTORY, DEFINITION, AND POSSIBLE CAUSES

The symptoms comprising what is currently known as ADHD were recognized as early as the 1860s, and formal discussion of the symptoms as a behavioral syndrome was published by Still in 1902 (Still, 1902). Over the years, researchers stressed the overactivity component of the disorder (Chess, 1960; Wender, 1971; Werry, 1968; Werry & Sprague, 1970), which resulted in the use of labels such as *hyperactivity* or *hyperkinesis*. At times, this emphasis on hyperactivity led to the exclusion of any other identifying problems (e.g., inattention) now believed to coexist with fidgetiness, restlessness, and gross motor overactivity.

In 1972, Douglas emphasized the need to consider the child's inattention and impulsivity as the more pervasive and chronic problems (Douglas, 1972), and follow-up research (Weiss & Hechtman, 1986) seems to have borne this out. For this and related reasons, the label of hyperactivity was replaced by the term Attention-Deficit Hyperactivity Disorder as espoused by the American Psychiatric Association in its DSM-III-R (American Psychiatric Association, 1987).

The essential features of ADHD are developmentally inappropriate degrees of inattention, impulsiveness, and hyperactivity. People with the disorder generally display some disturbance in each of these areas, but to varying degrees. Of the 14 criteria listed, therapists consider a criterion met only if the behavior is considerably more frequent than that of most people of the same mental age. The diagnostic features are:

1. **A disturbance of at least 6 months during which at least eight of the following criteria are present:**
   - Often fidgets with hands or feet or squirms in seat (In adolescents, this may be limited to subjective feelings of restlessness.)
   - Has difficulty remaining seated when required to do so
   - Is easily distracted by extraneous stimuli
   - Has difficulty awaiting turn in games or group situations
   - Often blurts out answers to questions before they have been completed
   - Has difficulty following through on instructions from others, fails to finish chores (not due to oppositional behavior or failure of comprehension)
   - Has difficulty sustaining attention in tasks or play activities
   - Often shifts from one uncompleted activity to another
   - Has difficulty playing quietly
   - Often talks excessively
   - Often interrupts or intrudes on others
   - Often does not seem to listen to what is being said to him or her
   - Often loses things necessary for tasks or activities at school or at home (e.g., toys, pencils, assignments)
   - Often engages in physically dangerous activities without considering possible consequences but not for the purpose of thrill-seeking

2. **Onset before the age of 7**

3. **Does not meet the criteria for a Pervasive Developmental Disorder**

Although some of the symptom descriptions may appear vague or ambiguous, these represent a vast improvement in objectivity over previous diagnostic schema. In addition, the cutoff score of 8 out of 14 symptoms was established in a national clinical field trial (Barkley, Spitzer, & Costello, 1989).

In addition to the core diagnostic symptoms, children with ADHD may exhibit a variety of associated behavioral and emotional problems (e.g., noncompliance, poor peer relations, academic underachievement). Although these occur more frequently among ADHD children than among their normal counterparts, there is a great deal of individual variability regarding symptom emergence and chronic status through the course of development. In fact, investigators have recently begun to attribute the adjustment difficulties of these children to basic deficits in behavioral self-regulation such as deficits in self-directed instruction (Kendall & Braswell, 1985), self-regulation of arousal to meet environmental demands (Douglas & Parry, 1983), or rule-governed behavior (Barkley, 1981, 1989b). Thus, treatment interventions must be designed to affect multiple targets with the underlying goal of improving self-regulation of behavior.

Numerous factors have been proposed as causes of ADHD, yet no single variable has been found to account fully for its genesis. In fact, it may be most prudent to view ADHD as the final common pathway of a number of possible causal events (Barkley, 1988). In general, the major causal variables that have been identified can be categorized as neurological factors, toxic reactions, genetic linkage, and environmental factors (see Anastopoulos & Barkley, 1988, for a more detailed review). Most of the available evidence would point towards neurological (e.g., neurotransmitter imbalance) and/or genetic variables as the primary causes of ADHD, with environmental events and neurotoxins (e.g., lead exposure, food additives) playing minimal roles. However, most investigators agree that environmental factors (e.g., presence of parental psychopathology) are among the best predictors of long-term outcome.

DEVELOPMENTAL COURSE OF ADHD

A plethora of empirical data has been gathered to suggest that temperament and behavior control difficulties begin in the ADHD child's early years and continue throughout the lifespan. Specifically, infants with difficult temperament who are excessively active, have poor sleeping and eating habits, and are prone to irritable moods are at greater risk for ADHD than children with more normal temperaments (see Ross & Ross, 1982, for a review). Further, the majority of children who will be identified as having ADHD begin to manifest significant overactivity, noncompliance, and short attention span by 3 years of age. Typically, complaints regarding these excessive behaviors are first brought to the parent's attention by other caretakers such as teachers, daycare personnel, or relatives. Toilet training may be difficult and occur later than normal, presumably due to the child's noncompliance (Hartsough & Lambert, 1985).

The stability of the ADHD child's behavioral excesses from the preschool years to early elementary grades has been well documented (Campbell, Schleifer, & Weiss, 1978). In fact, by first grade (i.e., 6 years old) greater than 90% of children with ADHD will have been identified as problematic by their parents or teachers. In addition to inattention, impulsivity, and excessive activity, other significant problems may emerge, including poor relationships with peers (Pelham & Bender, 1982), chronic underachievment, specific learning disabilities, conduct problems (e.g., lying, stealing), disruptive behavior in group situations, and, in later years, feelings of low self-esteem.

At home, ADHD children frequently evidence an inability to consistently complete routine chores and activities (e.g., preparing for school, completing homework, cleaning their rooms). In fact, this irresponsibility may cause parents to spend an inordinate amount of their time supervising their children's activities. Stress in the parental role as well as the risk for maternal depression may increase at this time (Breen & Barkley, 1988; Mash & Johnston, 1983).

Several distinct developmental patterns begin to emerge during adolescence. As many as 30% to 70% of children with ADHD will continue to exhibit the core symptoms of the disorder in adolescence, (Barkley, Fischer, Edelbrock, & Smallish, 1990; Gittelman, Manuzza, Shenker, & Bonagura, 1985; Lambert, Hartsough, Sassone, & Sandoval, 1987). Those children who do not display significant aggressiveness or peer relationship problems are likely to exhibit continued difficulties with inattention and impulsivity that primarily affect school performance (Paternite & Loney, 1980); they are typically described as underachieving. Once out of school and working, these teenagers appear to experience fewer adjustment problems than during their school years. Those exhibiting aggression and conduct problems remain at risk for more significant maladjustment, such as delinquent behavior in the community (Gittelman et al., 1985; Lambert et al., 1987; Satterfield, Hoppe, & Schell, 1982) and problematic peer relationships. There is some evidence to suggest that adolescents with ADHD, primarily those with co-existing conduct disorder, are more likely to use alcohol and cigarettes (Barkley, Fischer et al., 1990; Gittelman et al., 1985), although there are contradictory findings (Weiss, Hechtman, Perlman, Hopkins, & Wener, 1979). In addition, these teenagers are at higher risk for automobile accidents (Weiss et al., 1979); greater grade retentions, suspensions, and expulsions (Barkley, Fischer et al., 1990); dropping out of high school (Weiss et al., 1985); experiencing low self-esteem; and poor social acceptance (Weiss, Hechtman, & Perlman, 1978).

In general, the above behavior patterns may continue into adulthood; most follow-up studies indicate that individuals with childhood ADHD function less adequately in a number of spheres (e.g., socially, psychologically, occupationally) than do controls or their normal siblings (Loney, Whaley-Klahn, Cosier, & Conboy, 1981; Thorley, 1984; Weiss, Hechtman, Milroy, & Perlman, 1985). Specifically, there is a greater risk for adult antisocial personality disorder (Loney et al., 1981; Weiss et al., 1985), alcoholism, and complaints of interpersonal problems or psychological difficulties (Weiss et al., 1985). These findings may suggest that some adult psychiatric disorders are equivalent to or are residual forms of childhood ADHD (Wender, Reimherr, & Wood, 1981; Wood, Reimherr, Wender, & Johnson, 1976).

This poor prognosis is not evident for all ADHD children and is apparently mediated by several factors. The research literature indicates that a number of significant variables are associated with poorer outcome in this population, including low intelligence in childhood, aggressiveness and oppositional behavior, poor peer acceptance, emotional instability, and extent of parental psychopathology (Hechtman, Weiss, Perlman, & Amsel, 1984; Loney et al., 1981; Paternite & Loney, 1980). Although extensive, long-term treatment through adolescence may reduce the risk of maladjustment (Satterfield, Satterfield, & Schell, 1987), lesser degrees of treatment, including stimulant medication, have not been found to have a significant impact on adult outcome (Hechtman, Weiss, & Perlman, 1984; Paternite & Loney, 1980). Thus, clinicians have taken the approach that ADHD is a developmental disorder of self-control and social conduct that is chronic and without cure. An attitude of coping rather than curing is frequently communicated to the family by the clinician, intimating that treatment may lead to the reduction of problems but not necessarily completely eliminate them.

ASSESSMENT OF ADHD

A comprehensive evaluation of ADHD in children will include multiple assessment techniques conducted across sources (i.e., parents, teachers) and settings. The primary goals of the assessment are to: (1) gather information about the developmental deviance of ADHD symptoms or other problem behaviors; (2) rule out other psychiatric, learning, or emotional problems that may be causing inattention, impulsivity, and/or overactivity; (3) determine the degree of consistency between sources and across situations with respect to report of behaviors associated with ADHD; and (4) identify and prioritize targets for intervention. Typically, assessment techniques will include interviews with the parent(s), teacher, and child; parent and teacher rating scales of child behavior; self-report ratings of older children and adolescents; clinic-based measures of ADHD symptoms; direct observational techniques; and parent self-report measures of relevant psychiatric conditions (Barkley, 1988; Rapport, 1987). In addition, psychological testing, especially of intelligence and achievement, may be required for 30% to 40% of ADHD children because of co-existing learning disabilities (Safer & Allen, 1976).

Interviews

Parent and teacher interviews are indispensable components of the evaluation, as they provide an ideal forum to assess perceptions of the child's behavior in the home and school settings. Although interviews are often criticized for their lack of reliability and accuracy, this is often a function of the manner in which they are conducted. More reliable and valid information is provided in the context of a structured, functional-analytic interview approach. Specifically, data are gathered with respect to the nature, frequency, age of onset, antecedents, consequences, chronicity, and variation of problem behaviors across time and settings (see A. M. Gross, 1984, for more details regarding behavioral interviewing). The parent interview will also include a review of the child's developmental, medical, educational, and family history. Potential problems in myriad domains (e.g., social, intellectual, emotional) are also surveyed. Ultimately, the parent and teacher interviews will provide detailed information regarding the antecedents and consequences of child behavior across problematic settings.

Rating Scales

The completion of behavior rating scales by parents and teachers has become the most common method to determine the deviance of a child's behavior relative to his or her peers. Several comprehensive rating scales are currently available that include normative data across gender and age groups. Some of the more popular questionnaires include the Child Behavior Checklist (Achenbach & Edelbrock, 1983), Conners Rating Scales (Goyette, Conners, & Ulrich, 1978), and Revised Behavior Problem Checklist (Quay & Peterson, 1983). All of these scales include factors that quantify a child's relative status with respect to frequency of ADHD-related behaviors and thus provide valuable information about his or her diagnostic status. Rating scales also allow the clinician to survey the frequency of behaviors associated with other psychopathological conditions (e.g., depression, conduct problems). Although the above checklists provide information regarding the frequency or intensity of child behavior problems, additional measures, such as the Home and School Situations Questionnaires (Barkley & Edelbrock, 1987), document the pervasiveness or specificity of problem behaviors across situations (e.g., when asked to do chores, during independent seatwork).

Clinic-Based Tests

Clinic-based tests of attention span and impulse control are becoming more prevalent in the assessment of ADHD. These include tasks such as the Continuous Performance Test (Rosvold, Mirsky, Sarason, Bransome, & Beck, 1956) and Matching Familiar Figures Test (Kagan, 1966). Normative data are available for versions of these tasks, so an individual child's score can be compared to those of his or her age group. These measures have been found to differentiate between groups of ADHD and normal children and are sensitive to the effects of stimulant medication (see Ross & Ross, 1982, for a review). However, their diagnostic sensitivity at the individual case level and their relation to real-world (i.e., home and school) behavior has not been fully documented. Thus, caution is typically applied when interpreting the results of these measures.

Direct Observation

Direct observational methods offer some advantages relative to clinic-based tests, in that they involve recording behavior in the child's natural environment or in analogue settings structured to elicit behaviors representative of the problems occurring outside of the clinic. Thus, they offer a greater level of ecological validity than do tests of attention span and impulse control. Several observational coding systems have been developed specifically to delineate the frequency, intensity, and/or duration of behaviors (e.g., off-task, fidgets, vocalizations) associated with ADHD that may ultimately be targets for intervention as they occur in classroom or playroom settings (Abikoff, Gittelman-Klein, & Klein, 1977; Jacob, O'Leary, & Rosenblad, 1978; Milich, Loney, & Landau, 1982). Typically, children are observed while completing individual deskwork, interacting with their peers, or listening to teacher instructions, as these are frequently their most problematic situations. Coding systems have also been developed for observations of behavior in analogue settings (e.g., clinic playroom) where children are asked to complete academic tasks (Barkley, Fischer, Newby, & Breen, 1988) or to respond to parental commands (Mash & Barkley, 1986). Unfortunately, normative data are not available for most of these observational systems, thus limiting their utility in determining the statistical deviance of a child's behavior.

The assessment of ADHD will often include an evaluation of the psychological status of the child's parents, as there is some evidence to suggest a greater incidence of depression and other psychopathology among parents of ADHD children (Biederman et al., 1987; Cantwell, 1975). Self-report measures of psychiatric symptoms and parental stress are completed in an effort to investigate the reciprocal impact of parent and child characteristics. Finally, a pediatric exam may be indicated in those instances where treatable medical conditions are evident, as in allergies, enuresis, encopresis, and tic disorders that are more common in ADHD children. Medical evaluations will certainly be necessary where treatment with behavior-modifying drugs is to be considered. In summary, there are specific strengths and weaknesses associated with each of the components of an ADHD evaluation. Thus, multiple sources and procedures are necessary to obtain reliable and valid diagnostic information that will be useful for treatment planning.

GOALS OF
INTERVENTION FOR ADHD

Given the diversity, multiplicity, pervasiveness, and chronic nature of behavior problems associated with ADHD, a variety of treatments implemented across settings and by different service providers will often be required. As has been stated, there is no cure for ADHD in children. Even the most effective treatments available are typically short-term in nature and symptomatic in focus. Knowledge of the etiology of the disorder is minimal and provides little assistance in treatment selection. Recent evidence would suggest that long-term, multi-method therapy reduces the risk for poor adolescent and adult outcome (Satterfield et al., 1987), but the results of most treatment outcome studies do not indicate significant long-term improvements. However, if short-term reductions in problem severity are obtained, the degree of criticism, ostracism, and potential for abuse to which the child may be subjected is also likely to be reduced. That these interventions can also provide some relief to the families and teachers of these children further supports their use. Therefore, the goal of therapy is to cope with, not cure, the ADHD, and periodic intervention will almost certainly be needed to guide the child through the years.

The remainder of this chapter will review the behaviorally-based interventions that have shown the greatest promise for treating ADHD, including parent counseling/training in child management skills and classroom behavior-modification techniques. The major targets of intervention typically are the child's poor attention span, impulsivity or self-control, and non-compliance with caregivers' directives (e.g., rule-governed behavior). Pharmacological interventions will also be discussed, given their documented effectiveness and evidence that the combination of medication and behavior modification is superior to any single treatment (Gittelman et al., 1980). Alternative treatment methods with less well-documented efficacies (e.g., self-instructional strategies) will be briefly reviewed to point out their limitations. Given the variety and complexity of these techniques, it is not possible to describe their implementation in great detail. However, references to more thorough reviews are included in the section of treatment resources.

Behaviorally Based Interventions for ADHD

Parent Education and Counseling

Although determination of its actual efficacy awaits scientific scrutiny, many clinicians consider the education of parents to be a crucial initial step in the treatment of ADHD (Barkley 1981, 1989a). Inaccurate information about the disorder abounds in the media (e.g., Bacon, 1988) and so much popular lore about ADHD (e.g., that sugar causes ADHD) permeates our society that accurate information must be disseminated to parents to counteract these inaccuracies. Parents require a full depiction of the nature, course, outcome, causes, and treatments of ADHD if they are to fully appreciate the gravity of this handicapping condition. Particular emphasis is given to describing ADHD as a condition of biological origins wherein the underlying causal mechanisms are unlikely to be corrected by treatment. This requires the parents to accept that their child has an impairment and to adjust household and educational expectations accordingly. These adjustments are rarely easily made as they must be specifically defined according to the features of each child's family, community, and culture. The overall goal of such modifications would be to maximize the best fit between the unique characteristics of the child and the ever-changing demands made upon him or her by the environment.

Information about ADHD can be disseminated through ongoing discussions with the clinician, books written for parents about ADHD (Ingersoll, 1988; Wender, 1987), or audio/video cassettes prepared on the subject. When parents adopt the perspective that ADHD is a handicapping condition, other treatments are implemented more easily than when parental views are anchored in the belief that there is nothing permanently wrong with the child. Clearly, research is needed to document the utility of this educational approach in isolation and/or in combination with other interventions. Until then, at an intuitive level, parent education remains an essential component to treatment.

Parent Training in Child Behavior Management

Parent training in child behavior management is an essential component in the overall treatment of most families with an ADHD child. A variety of parent training programs have been designed over the years, each differing in philosophy, method, and effectiveness. Barkley (1981) initially described a parent training program for use specifically with children manifesting ADHD. Although bearing a resemblance to other parenting programs, several unique components are included so as to address the special needs of ADHD children and their families. The development of the program was based on several theoretical and empirical influences, the earliest of these being the two-stage program developed by Hanf (1969) and later refined and extensively researched by Forehand and his associates with noncompliant children (Forehand & McMahon, 1981; Wells & Forehand, 1985). The research conducted to date on its effectiveness with ADHD children is quite promising (Pisterman et al., 1988; Pollard, Ward, & Barkley, 1983). This program, as it is used specifically with ADHD children, is thoroughly discussed in Barkley (1981, 1987) and in Anastopoulos and Barkley (1989).

Like other behaviorally based parent training programs, the program described by Barkley (1981) for ADHD children emphasizes the control of behavior by its consequences and, more specifically, the components of positive reinforcement, extinction, and punishment. Unique is the emphasis on tailoring specific parenting methods to theoretically and empirically derived notions of ADHD. An especially prominent premise taught in the program is that ADHD is largely a biologically-based temperamental style that predisposes a youngster to be inattentive, impulsive, and restless, as well as deficient in his or her capacity for rule compliance (Barkley, 1989b). A variety of specialized parenting skills are emphasized to address these deficits. In a similar vein, data derived from years of laboratory research, showing fundamental differences in the performance of ADHD children under various reinforcement and punishment schedules are incorporated into disciplining strategies that parents are asked to introduce at home. Specifically, great emphasis is given to the need for immediate consequences and richer reinforcement schedules for ADHD children and to the consistency with which consequences are delivered over time and across caregivers. The use of more intensive motivational-incentive procedures and response cost techniques is also emphasized. Implicit in these methods is the premise that a different home environment has to be developed and, more explicitly, that parents must learn to cope with, rather than cure, what is likely to be a chronic problem.

The approach employed in this treatment of ADHD children comprises a core of nine sessions with the parents, which can be extended to cover additional problem areas other than noncompliance once the core sequence is completed. This program is quite similar to that discussed in detail by Forehand and McMahon (1981), except that certain core principles are given greater emphasis in response to empirical findings regarding the deficits that make up ADHD. Each session follows a similar sequence of events, including a review of the information covered in the previous week, a brief assessment of whether any critical events transpired since the last session, and a review of the relative success or failure of procedures that have been implemented. New information is then introduced by the therapist with respect to the particular method(s) parents are to employ during the next week. During sessions in which the child is included for practice of techniques, a playroom with observation facilities is used. The session then concludes

with feedback to the parent, and homework is assigned. Written handouts detailing the session's techniques and procedures are distributed to parents for review and practice during the coming week.

The parent training program is typically conducted in the following sequence: (1) information about the nature and implications of ADHD; (2) description of the parameters of parent-child interactions and general principles of behavior modification; (3) development of effective command strategies and promotion of positive attention to appropriate behavior; (4) establishment of a home token economy system; (5) implementation of response cost and time-out from positive reinforcement as punishment techniques; (6) management of problem behavior in public places; and (7) instruction in strategies to encourage maintenance and generalization of behavioral improvements.

Although the specific behaviors targeted for intervention will vary across individuals, they usually include compliance with chores, completion of homework, attention to commands or instruction, and appropriate social interactions with siblings or friends. Unfortunately, the consistent use of contingent social praise is rarely sufficient in prompting and maintaining behavioral change in children with attention and behavior problems (Pfiffner, Rosen, & O'Leary, 1985). Thus, the most crucial aspect of the program is parental implementation of a token economy system that includes clearcut rewards and penalties for child behavior. Although this type of intervention is not unique to ADHD, parents are instructed in several modifications that take into account the fact that ADHD children tend to get bored with a narrow range of rewards, can become overexcited by an exclusive reliance on highly stimulating reinforcement, and can be overwhelmed by commands that tax their attention span (e.g., multi-step chores).

Despite its substantial research record in the treatment of noncompliance in children (Forehand & McMahon, 1981), the child management program outlined above has not yet received extensive empirical evaluation in the treatment of ADHD children (Pollard, Ward, & Barkley, 1983). Drawing from the research findings with behavior problem children in general, a number of studies have attested to the efficacy of this training model in managing children's noncompliance, decreasing defiance, and increasing child compliance and cooperation (Eyberg & Robinson, 1982). Long-term outcome studies have reported favorable results as well, with treatment effects persisting for as long as 4 to 5 years after training (Baum & Forehand, 1981; Forehand, Rogers, McMahon, Wells, & Griest, 1981; Webster-Stratton, 1985).

Studies examining the generalization of treatment effects across settings have also reported positive outcomes in child compliance following parent training taught in the clinic (Forehand et al., 1979; Peed, Roberts, & Forehand, 1977; Webster-Stratton, 1985). More pervasive generalization following treatment, however, does not appear to be a natural outcome of parent training. When teachers do not receive comparable training in behavior management procedures, little change in child compliance is observed in the school setting (Breiner & Forehand, 1981; Forehand et al., 1979). The results suggest that increases in child compliance are specific to the adult trained in management techniques and to the settings in which they are actively applied.

Case Illustration

Rating scales and observational data on mothers interacting with their ADHD boys were used to evaluate the effects of the parent training program described above (Pollard, Ward, & Barkley, 1983). Four boys were observed interacting with their mothers in a clinic playroom while the boys were given tasks to accomplish (e.g., putting toys away, picking up clothes). Observations were conducted repeatedly during the period that the parents attended parent training sessions. The results (in the context of an A-B case study) of training for two boys with severe ADHD are discussed here.

Initial goals of training were to reduce the number of maternal commands necessary to achieve compliance from the child and to increase maternal positive attention for occurrences of compliance. These effects are seen in Figure 15.1, where baseline levels of commands ranged between 40% and 65% of all interaction during this task period. Although maternal attention to compliance was initially high for both boys, positive attention tended to decline over subsequent baseline observations. Once training was initiated, maternal commands fell below 50% of baseline levels and maternal positive attention to compliance increased approximately threefold above baseline levels for both boys.

Both boys displayed severely noncompliant behavior at home, yet, as Figure 15.2 shows, compliance with the clinic tasks ranged between 60% to 80% in baseline phases. Although this appears relatively high, normal boys in this playroom complied with approximately 95% or more of their mothers' commands (Cunningham & Barkley, 1979). Nonetheless, this result provides support for the caution often given to psychology students that initial clinic observations of parent-child interactions are not always representative of typical home behavior and may be skewed in the positive direction. This can probably be accounted for by the novelty of the situation and by limitations imposed by the behavior coding system, wherein initial obedience is scored as compliance. However, this same system does not make allowances for children who fail to maintain compliance long enough to complete the task: a deficit highly characteristic of ADHD children. Despite this state of affairs, as training proceeded, parental report indicated that home behavior began to improve to the levels seen in the clinic.

The results in Figure 15.2 show treatment-related improvements in both immediate compliance to requests and in sustained obedience over time (lower graphs) for both boys. Only after time-out procedures were implemented by mothers (following Session #12) did com-

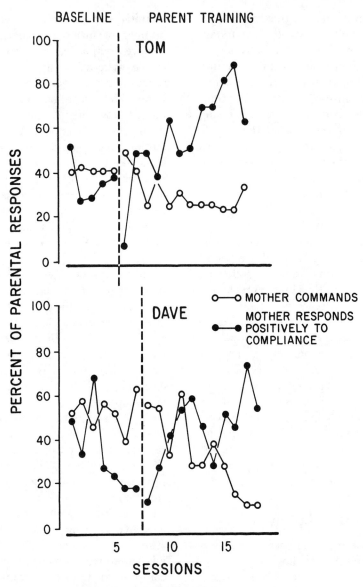

FIGURE 15.1

FIGURE 15.1

Percentages of maternal commands and of maternal positive responses to compliance for two ADHD boys measured using the Response Class Matrix during a parent-training program for noncompliance.

SOURCE: R. Barkley (1981). *Hyperactive children: A handbook for diagnosis and treatment.* New York: Guilford Press. Copyright by Guilford Press. Reprinted with permission.

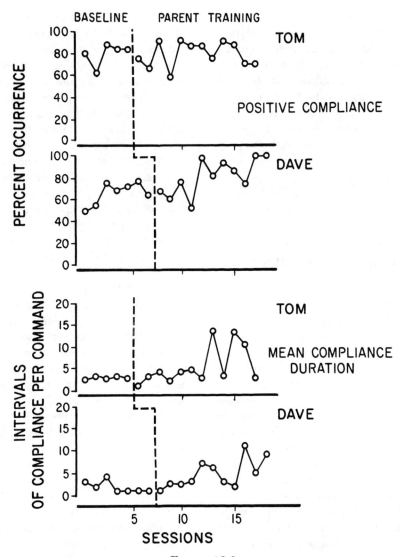

FIGURE 15.2

Percentage of child positive compliance to commands and mean compliance duration for two ADHD boys measured using the Response Class Matrix during a parent-training program for noncompliance.

SOURCE: R. Barkley (1981). *Hyperactive children: A handbook for diagnosis and treatment.* New York: Guilford Press. Copyright by Guilford Press. Reprinted with permission.

pliance begin to approach normal levels. Prior to treatment, parent ratings on several questionnaires indicated that both children were exhibiting developmentally inappropriate levels of overactivity, inattention, and noncompliance at home. Following treatment, both boys obtained ratings at least 50% below baseline levels. It should be noted that posttreatment ratings continued above the norm, underscoring the point that these programs teach parents to cope with, not cure, ADHD in children.

CLASSROOM BEHAVIOR MANAGEMENT

One of the most problematic situations for children with ADHD is their classroom. It is quite evident that the requirements (e.g., sit still, remain quiet, complete work) placed upon children's behavior in educational settings are quite difficult for the ADHD child to meet. These children typically exhibit out-of-seat or off-task behaviors wherein they may wander about the room, disturb others, play with objects irrelevant to the assigned task, or display excessive restlessness at their desks. Hence, academic assignments are rarely completed on time or are completed in a hasty, careless fashion. Accuracy on such tasks suffers as a result. On the playground, peer interaction problems are typical, owing to the child's immature, selfish, and often aggressive behavior. Thus, the school setting taxes the child with ADHD in precisely those areas of his or her greatest deficits— sustained attention, impulse control, overactivity, and compliance.

Numerous behavior modification procedures have been employed to enhance the classroom performance of children with ADHD, with the most salient and widely studied techniques including token reinforcement programs, contingency contracting, punishment procedures, and home-based contingency methods. As was the case for home-based behavior modification, little research has been conducted on the effectiveness of classroom behavioral interventions specifically with ADHD children. Rather, most empirical investigations have studied samples of children with nonspecific behavior disorders, some of whom display charactersitics associated with ADHD (e.g., inattention, excessive restlessness). Nevertheless, behavior modification procedures that have incorporated positive reinforcement (e.g., teacher praise, access to classroom privileges) contingent upon target behaviors have led to significant increases in attention to assigned work, task completion, and, in some cases, academic accuracy (see Ayllon & Rosenbaum, 1977, or Barkley, 1989a, for reviews).

One of the more established findings from the literature is that children with attention and impulse control problems tend to evidence greater improvement in classroom conduct and attention to task when behavioral interventions include mild punishment procedures. For example, negative reprimands following inattentive responding may be necessary, in addition to the provision of positive reinforcement, to maintain appropriate on-task behavior (Pfiffner & O'Leary, 1987). Further, to be most effective, verbal reprimands should be delivered immediately contingent upon the occurrence of disruptive behavior and delivered in a consistent, specific fashion so as to be audible only to the child who has committed the transgression (Rosen, O'Leary, Joyce, Conway, & Pfiffner, 1984). Since youngsters with attention and behavioral control problems respond less optimally to procedures that rely exclusively on social contingencies (e.g., praise or reprimands), greater gains in behavioral control and academic productivity are obtained when a combination of token reinforcement and response cost (loss of token) strategies is employed (Rapport, Murphy, & Bailey, 1982). An individualized system is developed wherein the child earns or loses tokens, based on his or her task-related performance. Tokens are then exchanged for back-up reinforcers such as classroom or home-based privileges. Many of the same factors (e.g., rotating back-up reinforcers to prevent boredom or satiation, programming for generalization) that were discussed for home token economies must also be considered when designing school interventions.

PHARMACOTHERAPY FOR ADHD

Although the prescription of stimulant medication is certainly not a behaviorally based intervention, it will be discussed briefly since it is the most extensively studied and widely used intervention for ADHD (Ross & Ross, 1982). Further, these medications are often combined with behavioral interventions to achieve effects that are frequently greater than those obtained with either treatment alone (Gittelman et al., 1980). Over 70% of children with ADHD who take these medications evidence behavioral improvements, based on parent/teacher judgements, laboratory task performance, and direct observations (Barkley, 1977).

The stimulant medications most commonly employed in the treatment of ADHD are methylphenidate (Ritalin), d-amphetamine (Dexedrine), and pemoline (Cylert). Ritalin is by far the most popular of these, presumably due to its ease of administration and relatively few side-effects (Barkley, 1981). A great deal of evidence has been gathered to indicate that Ritalin and other stimulants significantly enhance certain behavioral, cognitive, and academic processes. For example, it has been found to improve the performance of children with ADHD on laboratory tests of sustained attention (Rapport et al., 1987), impulsive-reflective responding (Brown & Sleator, 1979), short-term recall (Sprague & Sleator, 1979), and associative learning (Vyse & Rapport, 1989). Medication-induced enhancements of children's on-task and

academic accuracy rates in the classroom have also been obtained (Douglas, Barr, O'Neill, & Britton, 1986), along with associated reductions in disruptive, out-of-seat behavior (Werry & Conners, 1979). Further behavioral effects are found with respect to increased compliance, independent play, and responsiveness to social interactions with parents, teachers, and peers (Barkley, Karlsson, Strzelecki, & Murphy, 1984; Cunningham, Siegel, & Offord, 1985).

In contrast to the above, the results of several long-term follow-up studies investigating stimulant medication effects have been quite disappointing (Hechtman, Weiss, & Perlman, 1984). Children can apparently remain on these medications from 2 to 10 years with few additional improvements seen beyond those obtained at the outset of treatment. It should be pointed out, however, that there are many shortcomings to these investigations (e.g., poor outcome measures, inconsistent dosage procedures), thus minimizing the likelihood of obtaining reliable findings.

Contrary to recent media reports (e.g., Bacon, 1988) that have reported severe side-effects associated with psychostimulants, these drugs are quite mild relative to other classes of medications. The most frequent side-effects are decreased appetite and insomnia (Barkley, McMurray, Edelbrock, & Robbins, 1989). Several other side-effects may be associated with stimulant treatment in a minority of cases, including somatic symptoms (e.g., headaches or stomachaches), increased tension, growth inhibition, and increases in heart rate or blood pressure. In general, the frequency and severity of the above are apparently dose-related and may diminish with reductions in dosage and/or passage of time (Barkley, 1989a).

ALTERNATIVE TREATMENTS

The treatment modalities discussed above have proven effective in the treatment of ADHD and associated behavioral difficulties through years of research. These interventions are frequently augmented by individualized academic instruction, social skills training (Pelham & Bender, 1982), or cognitive-behavioral strategies (Hinshaw, Henker, & Whalen, 1984; Kendall & Braswell, 1985). The latter are of particular interest because they involve direct instruction in self-control strategies that would presumably increase the likelihood of generalization and maintenance of treatment gains, as the presence of external stimuli (e.g., parents, teachers, medication) are not necessary across time and settings (Zentall, 1989). Typically, children will be trained to instruct themselves to pay attention and behave more reflectively (i.e., stop, look, and listen) in task situations. In addition, they may be taught to reinforce themselves (e.g., self-praise, administer token reinforcer) following accurate compliance with self-control strategies. Although these techniques sound promising, most of the well-controlled investigations conducted to date have found little evidence for the effectiveness of cognitive strategies with this population, either in isolation or combination with other treatments (see Abikoff, 1985, for a review). Nevertheless, more empirical data need to be collected regarding the effects of these supplementary strategies before their value in treating ADHD can be fully determined (Whalen & Henker, 1986).

In addition to the treatments reviewed above, a plethora of interventions that are not supported by empirical data have been proposed for treating ADHD. These include the provision of talk or play therapies, administration of megavitamins, and dietary management. In general, well-controlled research investigating the effects of these treatments indicates little improvement in the behavior of all but a small minority of children with ADHD (Conners, 1980). This is not surprising, as most are based on faulty causal assumptions (e.g., that ADHD is caused by emotional trauma or ingestion of food additives). Unfortunately, many families are desperate to find a cure for ADHD and will zealously pursue treatments that may be unproven. In many cases, this wastes valuable time and resources that could be devoted to the implementation of more appropriate therapeutic strategies.

FUTURE DIRECTIONS

Although an impressive amount of work has been done to improve our knowledge about ADHD and the treatment strategies that effectively manage it, investigations over the next several years will continue to focus on defining the process and outcome variables that have the greatest impact on intervention outcome. Some brief examples of current and future research endeavors will provide the reader with a feel for the diversity of this area. Three major lines of study will be discussed, to address the following questions: (1) What treatments will be most effective in ameliorating the unique difficulties of the ADHD adolescent; (2) What are the necessary and sufficient components of a program to train parents of ADHD children in behavior modification strategies; and (3) How do we promote the long-term maintenance of treatment-related gains in the school performance of children with ADHD?

Historically, the prevailing clinical lore maintained that the symptoms of ADHD diminished significantly during adolescence, presumably due to maturational processes. As summarized earlier in this chapter, most children continue to exhibit significant symptoms of ADHD and related disturbances during their teen years (Weiss & Hechtman, 1986). Additional significant family issues typically arise, including acceptance of responsibility (e.g., homework, chores), disagreements over the teenager's rights and privileges, and social activities in which the adolescent engages. Therefore, the adjustment difficulties potentially encountered by ADHD teenagers are more varied and complex than during their childhood years, necessitating a modification of treatment goals and target behaviors.

Although teenagers with ADHD exhibit a high rate of positive response to stimulant medications (Klorman, Coons, & Borgstedt, 1987), little is known about the effects of behaviorally-based interventions with this population. In fact, parent training in behavior modification procedures has been almost exclusively applied and studied with ADHD children between the ages of 2 and 11 years. What components of parent training must be modified to account for the critical developmental differences summarized above? In addition to changes in target behaviors, it may be important to include the adolescent in therapy sessions, to promote greater acceptance of and cooperation about responsibilities. Training in negotiation skills and use of privileges in a contractual framework may be needed. Alternatively, perhaps a therapeutic approach that supplements contingency management procedures is necessary to address the myriad changes in the parent-child relationship that are associated with adolescence. For instance, Problem-Solving Communication Training (PSCT) (Foster & Robin, 1989) is a highly directive, skill-oriented therapy program that involves an integration of behavioral, cognitive, and family systems models. It is comprised of four interrelated components: (1) teaching problem-solving skills; (2) modifying problematic communication patterns; (3) changing faulty cognitions (e.g., irrational thoughts) that may precipitate or maintain problematic interactions; and (4) altering structural patterns (e.g., nonparticipation of the parent) within the family. Although PSCT has been shown to be effective in reducing family conflict in distressed parent-adolescent pairs (Foster, Prinz, & O'Leary, 1983), its effects with the ADHD population are just beginning to be studied. Continued research will be necessary to delineate the relative success of alternative therapeutic procedures (i.e., contingency management, PSCT) in addressing the difficulties of adolescents with ADHD.

A second area of burgeoning research involves identifying the components of parent training in contingency-management procedures that are necessary and sufficient to bring about behavioral change in children with ADHD. Although strong evidence has been gathered regarding the general success of this treatment approach for children with disruptive behavior disorders, including ADHD, it is unclear which treatment components (e.g., token reinforcement, response cost, time-out from positive reinforcement) are necessary and/or sufficient to produce therapeutic effects. Further, is it crucial, as Barkley (1981) suggested, to tailor the parent training procedures (e.g., by providing information on the nature and implications of ADHD) to meet more specifically the needs of children with ADHD? Finally, what role could cognitive strategies play in enhancing the effectiveness of parental use of behavioral techniques? It has been suggested that the former could be used to identify and change faulty beliefs about parenting skills and child behavior, as well as to clarify and modify parental expectations for success (Anastopoulos & Barkley, 1989). Given the need for treatments that are time- and cost-efficient, investigations delineating the differential effectiveness of parent training components are clearly warranted.

A final area of inquiry to be reviewed involves the maintenance over time of changes in a child's classroom performance following short-term behavioral intervention. Surprisingly few investigations to date have investigated this important issue specifically with ADHD children. Even less attention has been paid to systematically examining techniques for withdrawing treatment while maintaining obtained behavioral change. When contingencies are withdrawn abruptly (as is typically the case in the busy world of the classroom), the frequency of the target behavior usually returns to baseline levels quite rapidly (Walker, Mattson, & Buckley, 1971). Further, several researchers have suggested that children with ADHD exhibit motivational deficits (Barkely, 1989a), have an elevated reward threshold (Haenlein & Caul, 1987), and respond poorly to partial reward schedules (Douglas, 1984). All of the above would imply that it is crucial to study effective maintenance strategies when treating ADHD children, as their characteristic response to reinforcement would suggest that they are unlikely to sustain behavioral improvement when contingencies are withdrawn abruptly. Although a variety of techniques have been identified to promote maintenance, including employing natural contingencies, expanding stimulus control, and gradually fading contingencies (Kazdin, 1984), the relative success of these has not been studied specifically with ADHD children.

CONCLUSION

A multimodal intervention approach is usually necessary to address the many adjustment difficulties of children with ADHD. The two treatment modalities that have proven effective in ameliorating the symptoms of ADHD are psychostimulant medications and behavior-modification techniques applied at home and/or in the classroom. A number of investigations have demonstrated that their combination is superior to either treatment alone in producing short-term academic and behavioral improvements (see Pelham & Murphy, 1986, for a review). The combination of stimulant medication and behavior modification is frequently supplemented with special-education instruction, social skills and self-control training programs, and, to a lesser extent, residential placement to address associated behavioral or emotional difficulties. Despite a rather impressive research literature attesting to the success of behavior-modification procedures over the

short-term, further work is necessary to delineate more specifically the necessary and sufficient components of contingency management, how these procedures must be adjusted to meet the needs of adolescents with ADHD, and what techniques will promote maintenance of behavioral improvements over time. Behaviorally based interventions must continue to be refined through well-controlled research, to meet the overall goal of engineering a best fit between the characteristics of the ADHD child and the demands of the social environment.

TREATMENT RESOURCES

Barkley, R. A. (1981). *Hyperactive children: A handbook for diagnosis and treatment.* New York: Guilford. An excellent resource for detailed descriptions of diagnostic procedures, behavior management strategies, and pharmacological interventions for ADHD.

Barkley, R. A. (1987). *Defiant children: A clinician's manual for parent training.* New York: Guilford. A practical guide to parent training in behavior modification techniques. Although the target population is not specifically children with ADHD, the procedures are applicable to this group, since many children with this disorder are also defiant and excessively noncompliant.

Kendall, P. C., & Braswell, L. (1985). *Cognitive-behavioral therapy for impulsive children.* New York: Guilford. A step-by-step guide to the theoretical underpinnings and implementation of cognitive-behavioral procedures with specific emphasis on classroom applications.

Rapport, M. D. (1987). Attention deficit disorder with hyperactivity. In M. Hersen, & V. B. Van Hasselt (Eds.), *Behavior therapy with children and adolescents: A clinical approach.* New York: Wiley. A review and description of the impact of classroom-based response cost procedures and pharmacological interventions on the academic performance of children with ADHD.

Ross, D. M., & Ross, S. A. (1982). *Hyperactivity: Current issues, research, and theory* (2nd ed.). New York: Wiley. A comprehensive review of the research literature that includes several chapters devoted to intervention strategies.

CHAPTER 16

Parent and Family Management Training

Karen C. Wells

The origins of the development of parent training as an important, viable, scientifically sound treatment modality for children can be traced to the late 1950s and early 1960s when two reviews appeared that noted the relative ineffectiveness of traditional forms of psychotherapy with children, especially children with acting out or aggressive behavior disorders (Levitt, 1957, 1963). A number of researchers, notably Gerald Patterson, took note of these reviews, especially because they coincided with their own accumulating clinical experience. For example, in his book, *Coercive Family Process*, Patterson (1982) relates that at the time the Levitt reviews appeared, he (Patterson) was in training at one of the best psychoanalytically oriented outpatient facilities in the country, learning the fundamental child treatment techniques existing at that time (i.e., intensive individual analytic therapy; nondirective play therapy). Like many therapists, Patterson was initially satisfied with occasional successes and with parental reports of some improvement. Shortly,

however, he noticed that even the most highly trained therapists failed to effect permanent objective changes in most aggressive child disorders. The Levitt reviews reinforced the belief that his experiences were not unique.

In seeking an explanation for these facts, Patterson first looked to the existing theories of child aggression. Perhaps the treatment strategies being used did not address accurately enough the putative causes of the child's aggression (i.e., the inadequacies of the child's defenses against underlying anxiety and, secondarily, a reflection of parental neuroses). However, the answer did not seem to be there. Staff therapists were doing a competent job of administering treatments based on the traditional child theories. Student therapists were carefully supervised. However, their aggressive child patients continued to engage in aggressive behavior.

As a result of these observations, Patterson devoted his clinical and research career to the description, understanding, and, most important to the purposes of this chapter, treatment of child aggressive disorders by using parent training strategies. Concurrently, other clinician/researchers such as Robert Wahler, Rex Forehand, and a host of colleagues have also conducted work that advanced theory development and treatment progress in the area of parent training. This chapter will provide an update on the current state of the art of empirically based parent training. Other approaches to parent counseling that have little empirical basis (e.g., parent effectiveness training or systematic training for effective parenting) will not be considered here.

CONCEPTUAL BASES FOR PARENT TRAINING

Parent training first developed as a treatment approach for children who display disruptive behavior and aggressive disorders. Such children represent the most common referrals to mental health centers for treatment, with fully $\frac{1}{2}$ to $\frac{3}{4}$ of all child and adolescent referrals representing these kinds of problems (for a review, see Wells & Forehand, 1985). Empirically based parent training treatment strategies are a direct outgrowth of studies examining the clinical and behavioral characteristics of these children who are referred to as oppositional, socially aggressive, and conduct disordered by various authors and diagnostic schema. This literature has been reviewed in detail by Patterson (1982), Wells and Forehand (1981, 1985), and Wells (1984).

Specific definitions of antisocial behavior conduct disorders and descriptions of interventions specifically designed to treat those disorders are presented in the next chapter. Although parent training is used in the treatment of conduct disorder, the major focus of the present chapter is on treating children who demonstrate primarily less severe forms of socially aggressive behavior. Most of these chil-

dren and adolescents would be diagnosed as having oppositional defiant disorder. The behaviors used to define this disorder include losing one's temper, arguing, refusing and/or defying adult rules/requests, deliberately annoying others and being easily annoyed oneself, externalizing blame, swearing, and frequently feeling angry, resentful, or vindictive.

Aggressive children begin their careers with the same aversive behaviors displayed by normal children (e.g., whining, yelling, noncompliance, hitting). Furthermore, these behaviors often are displayed in the context of interactions with other people and frequently occur in bursts. What characterizes the aggressive child is the frequency and duration of these chains or bursts of aversive social interaction. Aggressive children display more frequent chains, and their chains have longer duration. Their aversive behaviors are not random but contingent; that is, they are more likely to occur in the presence of specific behaviors from other family members. Furthermore, the child's aversive behaviors are used contingently to produce a reliable impact on the victim (i.e., to control his or her behavior).

At the level of single behaviors, the aversive behaviors that the aggressive child displays at a high rate and that affect others contingently are negative commands, disapproval, humiliating statements, noncompliance, negativism, physically negative acts, and yelling (Patterson, 1976, 1982). These children also display a significantly lower proportion than normal children of positively valenced behavior such as approval expressed to others, positive attention, independent play, laughing, and talking. More important from the perspective of developing parent training strategies, the parents of aggressive children also display a number of behavioral characteristics that differentiate them from the parents of normal children. Aggressive children's parents display a significantly higher rate of poorly formulated and delivered commands to their children (Forehand, King, Peed, & Yoder, 1975). A significantly higher proportion of their commands are delivered in a threatening, angry, or nagging manner. They criticise their children more frequently and supply more negative and ineffective consequences for deviant as well as nondeviant behavior. These parents also display a significantly lower rate of positive attention and rewards to their children's prosocial behavior and confront deviant child behavior with effective consequences less frequently than parents of normal children (Forehand et al., 1975; Patterson, 1982).

In summarizing the results of studies such as those mentioned above, Patterson (1982) called attention to an essential theme: The parents of aggressive children cannot or do not punish well. Instead of applying effective consequences for aggressive behavior, they engage in other behaviors such as scolding, threatening, nagging, and repeating commands that do not effectively confront the behavior. Patterson (1982) has referred to this ineffective parent behavior as *nattering* or irritable aggression: negative verbal interchange that is not backed up by effective punishment. Patterson (1982) provided analyses from sequential observation data that empirically demonstrated this frequently lamented clinical observation: Parents of aggressive children seldom follow through effectively on their threats and scolding. The more important contribution of Patterson's analyses, however, was the finding that the parents' irritable aggression has a paradoxical effect, in that it actually serves to *escalate* the child's aggressive behavior. Thus, it has an effect exactly the opposite of that intended by the parent. After repeated interactions of this type, the child learns that nattering signifies irritation with no intention to follow through. This state of affairs, combined with the relatively low rate of positive attention to prosocial child behaviors, results in a motivational environment in which the child has relatively little negative incentive to decrease aggressive behavior and relatively little positive incentive to increase prosocial behavior.

Lest the above analysis sound too much like

an indictment of parents, it is essential to point out that direction of causation is not implied by these findings; that is, it is not necessarily the case that the parent behaviors mentioned above cause aggressive disorders in children. Rather, it appears that the process of coercion between family members is a reciprocal influence process in which aggressive behavior on the part of both parent and child is escalated and maintained by the behavior of the other member of the interacting dyad. In addition, Patterson (1982) reviewed evidence that the propensity to behave aggressively on the part of both parent and child is also affected by the temperaments and psychological states of children and parents. Temperamentally difficult children, he asserts, require greater skill to deal with and are more likely to elicit irritable reactions in even the most well-meaning parents. Depressed or maritally conflicted parents may experience disruptions in their ability to parent their children effectively.

As can be seen, the answer to the question of what causes social aggression in families is clearly complex. It appears that aggression in both parents and children is a joint function of what they bring to the situation in terms of their own psychological, constitutional, or temperamental states; their past learning histories; the social systems in which they find themselves; and the way their behaviors reciprocally influence each other in the present. This complex social learning analysis must be kept in mind when conceptualizing and implementing parent training programs, lest parents feel isolated and blamed by the approach being taken.

Given that the analysis of social aggression in families is complex, why parent training? Although it can be demonstrated that children exert behavioral effects on parents (Emery, Binkoff, Houts, & Carr, 1983), in our culture, families tend to be hierarchically ordered, with parents wielding most of the power and authority in the family. There are certainly many individual and subcultural exceptions or variations to this rule, but the general assumption in parent training models has been that parents, by virtue of their parenthood, have the moral, legal, and ethical responsibility to care for young children, and not vice versa. In addition, it has been assumed that parents, by virtue of their adult status, have greater capacity than children for maturity of judgment and greater ability to exert self-control in changing overlearned and highly reinforced patterns of behavior. The assumption has been that by entering the complex system of mutually interrelated family influence processes at the level of the parents, changes will occur in the child's behavior that in the long run will feed back to the parents, so that irritable aggression and negative verbal interchange will no longer be elicited from parents at such a high rate, thereby reducing further the child's display of aggressive behavior. Thus, the system should eventually become one that perpetuates low rates of mutual coercion rather than high rates of mutual coercion.

Empirically based parent training cannot be properly understood and should not be undertaken in clinical settings without an understanding of the theoretical model (and supporting empirical data) that is briefly presented above. Many clinical situations arise that are not covered by even the most thorough therapy cookbooks. Only an understanding of the conceptual model will enable the clinician to address these situations properly. Likewise, many nuances of treatment dictated by an understanding of the model will be missed by technicians who are not also theoreticians. Because the above review cannot do justice to the rich literature in this area, the reader is referred to Patterson (1982, 1986), McMahon and Wells (1989), Wells and Forehand (1985), and Wells (1984) for more thorough presentations. With this background in mind, parent training therapy models and an update of the empirical work in this area will next be covered.

Many eminent clinician/researchers have been involved in the development and evaluation of parent training programs, among them Robert Wahler, K. Daniel O'Leary, Elaine Blechman, and others. This review will focus on programs developed at the two major centers that have produced the most extensive and systematic research: Rex Forehand and his colleagues at the University of Georgia, and Gerald Patterson, John Reid and their colleagues at the Oregon Social Learning Center (OSLC).

HANF-FOREHAND PARENT TRAINING PROGRAM

Description of Program

Rex Forehand and his colleagues developed a line of research based on a treatment program developed by Connie Hanf for use with $2\frac{1}{2}$- to 8-year-old children. The program has been explicated in detail by Forehand and McMahon (1981). Briefly, the program is divided into two phases. In Phase I, parents learn a specific set of skills for improving their child's prosocial behaviors. The rationale is that whenever a disruptive behavior (e.g., noncompliance) can be identified, its prosocial opposite (e.g., compliance) can almost always be specified. Efforts should be directed to improving prosocial behaviors prior to the introduction of punishment strategies. In Phase II, parents learn to deliver clear, direct, developmentally appropriate instructions to their children and to punish noncompliance with an effective procedure that minimizes nattering and irritable verbal interchange during the disciplinary process.

Specifically, in the First phase parents learn to be more effective reinforcing agents by increasing the frequency and range of social rewards delivered to their child. To accomplish this the parents learn to attend to and describe the child's appropriate, prosocial behavior. In addition, the parents learn to reduce their use of commands, questions, and criticisms directed to the child (i.e., nattering). After training in attending and describing, parents learn to use verbal and physical rewards contingent on compliance and other prosocial behaviors that the parents consider desirable. Furthermore, the parents learn to ignore minor inappropriate behavior.

Daily homework assignments are given to require the parents to spend at least one 15-minute period (each) per day attending and rewarding appropriate behavior. The parents are also required to use these skills outside the clinic to increase at least two prosocial child behaviors. All of these skills are taught with modeling, behavior rehearsal, and feedback from the therapist.

In Phase II, parents learn to decrease the noncompliance displayed by their child. First, parents are taught to give clear, direct, age-appropriate commands (instructions) to their children. If the child does not comply with the initial command, parents learn to give a warning followed by a time-out (TO) procedure if the warning does not result in compliance; the TO procedure consists of placing the child in a chair in a corner. The child must remain in the chair for 3 to 10 minutes (depending on child's age) and must be quiet for the last 15 to 30 seconds. The child is then returned to the uncompleted task and the initial command is restated. The procedure continues until the child eventually complies.

Once parents learn this fundamental set of skills, additional strategies may be used to promote generalization of treatment effects to activities outside of home and to other behaviors. For example, once parents learn to apply a time-out procedure for noncompliance, they may establish a set of house rules that, if violated, result in immediate time-out (e.g., no fighting; no name-calling). This procedure is especially helpful for behaviors over which parents expect children to learn self-control. Likewise, parents learn how to implement time-out procedures outside the home or, in situations in which immediate time-out is not feasible, to use a marked time-out procedure. As with punish-

ment inside the home, parents are always guided to accompany any punishment plan outside the home with a positive reinforcement plan for encouraging prosocial behavior.

Evaluation of Treatment Outcome

Forehand and his colleagues conducted an extensive program of research to evaluate the efficacy and the generalization of treatment effects that use this model of parent training and to identify factors that predict or moderate treatment outcome. Some of this research is reviewed in detail in Wells and Forehand (1981, 1985).

As is often the case in the first wave of research on a treatment program, the first several studies evaluating the efficacy of this approach to parent training were pre/post analyses with no control group (Forehand & King, 1974; Forehand, Cheney, & Yoder, 1974; Hanf & Kling, 1973). Each of these studies demonstrated significant improvement from pre- to posttreatment with oppositional children. Subsequently, Forehand and King (1977) applied the program to 11 oppositional children and compared this to a *normal comparison* group. Results showed that after treatment, treated children were actually more compliant than normal controls on behavioral measures and reached normal levels in parent-perceived adjustment on parent report measures.

The first true experimental evaluation of this program to address some of the methodological problems inherent in the use of quasi-experimental designs and normal comparison groups was conducted by Peed, Roberts, and Forehand (1977). In this study, behavioral observations were conducted by trained, reliable observers in the clinic and in homes of oppositional children at pre- and posttreatment. A number of parent report inventories of child adjustment also were used. Subjects were randomly assigned to either an immediate treatment group or a wait-list control group.

Mothers and children in the treatment group showed significant improvement in their respective dysfunctional behaviors, whereas families in the control group did not. Interestingly, improvement in parent perception measures was noted in both groups, even though behavioral improvement only occurred in the treated group, suggesting that some relief was experienced by parents because of the knowledge that they would soon be entering a treatment program. (Wait-listed subjects received treatment subsequent to the completion of the research.)

In the only study that has compared the Hanf-Forehand program to an active, viable treatment alternative, Wells and Egan (1988) recently treated 19 children meeting DSM-III criteria for oppositional disorder and their families, using either parent training or systems family therapy. Families were randomly assigned to treatments and measures included behavioral observations conducted in the clinic as well as several parent report inventories to assess aspects of parent adjustment empirically related to child disorders (Griest & Wells, 1983). Results of this study showed that parent training was more effective than family therapy in reducing the primary symptom of oppositional disorder, noncompliance with parental instructions. No differences were noted on secondary measures of parent adjustment (i.e. parent depression, anxiety, and marital adjustment). Although this study suggests that parent training is more effective than systems family therapy for oppositional disorder, it says nothing about family therapy's efficacy for other childhood disorders such as anxiety disorders or psychosomatic disorders. Indeed, some quasi-experimental research suggests that systems family therapy may be very helpful in the treatment of psychosomatic disorders in children (Liebman, Minuchin, & Baker, 1974a, 1974b, 1974c).

The studies reviewed above showed that parent training is an effective treatment approach for problems of social aggression in young children and is more effective than another frequently used treatment strategy. Its efficacy having been demonstrated, a line of research was conducted to evaluate the generalization of treatment effects obtained with parent training. Generalization refers to the extent to which treatment effects obtained in the clinic maintain over time (temporal generalization); generalize to other behaviors not targeted in treatment (behavioral generalization); generalize to other situations such as home and school (setting generalization); and generalize to other persons such as siblings or classmates (subject generalization).

Maintenance of Treatment Effects

Regarding temporal generalization, Forehand and Long (1988) recently reviewed most of the published literature pertaining to maintenance of treatment effects and conducted the longest follow-up of children treated with parent training to date (up to 10 years posttreatment). They reviewed 12 studies that collected long-term follow-up data from 1 to 9 years posttreatment. Of these 12 studies, 8 showed evidence of maintenance of treatment effects on all measures, 3 showed maintenance on some measures and not others, and 1 showed lack of maintenance of treatment effects at 1 year follow-up. In the latter study and also one study not reviewed by Forehand and Long (1988) that failed to show maintenance of treatment effects, mothers had very low income, had low educational attainment, lived in high-crime areas, and presented multiple problems in addition to their children's aggressive conduct (e.g., depression, marital violence, chronic maternal illness) (Wahler, 1980; Wahler & Dumas, 1987). Wahler (1980) referred to these mothers as insular, i.e., mothers who are cut off from positive social contact and experience high rates of negatively valenced social contact. Wahler and his colleagues repeatedly demonstrated that insular mothers fail to maintain treatment-acquired gains after a parent training program. Contrast this with the results of Baum and Forehand

(1981), who reported maintenance of treatment effects at 1 to 4.5 years on all measures. In that sample, only 1 of the 34 families studied was receiving welfare.

It appears from the research summarized that, in general, treatment effects obtained with parent training do generalize across time. Insular mothers represent a notable exception to this general statement. In discussing the insular mother's special problems in parenting, Wahler and his colleagues noted that it is not simply low socioeconomic status (SES) that results in disrupted parenting and child behavior problems, but rather the process of insularity that is at least one of the direct controlling influences. For example, Wahler (1980) and Wahler and Graves (1983) showed that aversive contacts by insular mothers with other adults (i.e., social workers, family members) were correlated with aversive behavior directed by the mother to her children on the same day. Insularity may not be the only process contributing to the poor treatment maintenance of low SES mothers, but it is at least one important influence that has been systematically identified in empirical research. Treatment of these families needs to incorporate special attention to these factors.

Long-Term Effects on Overall Functioning

Treatment effects may in general be demonstrated to maintain over extended periods of time, but this does not necessarily suggest that treated subjects are functioning normally in all areas at long-term follow-up. Forehand and Long (1988) studied 21 families who had participated in parent training treatment of oppositional and aggressive child behavior $4\frac{1}{2}$ to $10\frac{1}{2}$ years earlier and compared these families with 21 matched normal controls. The families were assessed from multiple perspectives, although the measures used necessarily differed from those used in the original studies as many of the children had now reached adolescence.

On some measures of child and parent functioning there were no differences between treated families and normal comparison families. For example, no significant differences emerged for the adolescents on the conduct disorder and socialized aggressive dimensions of the Revised Behavior Problem Checklist, as rated by mothers, fathers, and teachers. This is heartening, since parent training is directly targeted toward treatment of conduct problems. There were no differences between the samples on a measure of issues disagreement or on measures of child depression or anxiety/withdrawal as rated by parents. Likewise, there were no differences between the two samples with respect to prosocial competencies of the adolescent or parenting competencies of the parents. Treated mothers actually reported *better* marital adjustment than nontreated mothers, and treated fathers reported less interparental conflict than nontreated fathers. No differences between the two groups existed in parents' self-reports of their own functioning. These latter findings are also heartening because parent depression and marital conflict have repeatedly been noted in families of children with conduct problems (Griest & Wells, 1983).

On the other hand, treated adolescents were functioning more poorly than nontreated normal adolescents on a number of variables. Mothers and fathers of treated adolescents reported more problems with family communication and conflict. Teachers reported treated adolescents as having more attention problems and more anxiety/withdrawal. Fathers reported treated adolescents to have lower cognitive competence, and the grade point averages (GPAs) of treated adolescents were lower than those of nontreated adolescents. Of the children in the parent training group, 35% had received additional therapy subsequent to the parent training treatment.

The results of Forehand and Long's study (1988) do not directly address the maintenance question, as there is no comparison group of clinic-referred subjects who did not receive treatment and since the posttreatment and follow-up measures were necessarily different. Nevertheless, it is encouraging that many of the measures directly assessing children's aggression and conduct problems and parent factors associated with conduct problems were within normal limits, because these are the variables that parent training is designed to address. Nevertheless, adolescents continue to experience (or acquire) difficulties in other areas, suggesting that an expanded parent training model may be needed.

Generalization Effects

Generalization Across Settings

A few studies have looked at the setting generalization of the Hanf-Forehand parent training program. In the Peed et al. study (1977) reported earlier, generalization from the clinic to the home was examined by conducting pre- and posttreatment observations in clinic and home settings and conducting treatment in the clinic. Results showed that positive changes obtained in the clinic did generalize to the home, in that home improvements were noted in critical parenting skills and in target child behaviors. No changes occurred in the control group in home observational measures.

Two studies evaluated generalization of treatment effects to school by using behavioral observations in both home and school (Forehand, Sturgis et al., 1979; Breiner & Forehand, 1981). Both studies showed no statistically significant changes in school behavior following treatment in the clinic. Inspection of the individual data in both studies showed that some children increased their levels of noncompliance in the school and some children decreased their levels of noncompliance; the two groups, in effect, canceled each other out.

These studies revealed that generalization from clinic to home does occur, probably due to similar stimulus conditions in both of these set-

tings (i.e., parents displaying similar behaviors toward their children in the clinic and at home). However, generalization to the school, where there is a different set of adult caregivers interacting with the child, does not necessarily occur. In fact, although some children improve, others may become worse in school, indicating that an idiosyncratic assessment of school behavior needs to occur during or following clinic treatment for home-referred behavior problems.

Generalization to Untreated Behaviors

One study directly examined behavioral generalization of the Hanf-Forehand parent training program (Wells, Forehand, & Griest, 1980). In this study, the effects of treatment for noncompliance were examined on related but untreated disruptive behaviors (i.e., tantrums, hitting, crying) by examining changes in a code category (other deviant behavior) collected during behavioral observations. Results showed that the other deviant behaviors decreased significantly from pre- to posttreatment, even though they were not targeted for treatment. These data would indicate that behavioral generalization does occur, at least for coercive behaviors in the same response class as noncompliance. However, this conclusion is somewhat equivocal, as Patterson's research group has reported nonsignificant decreases in nontargeted deviant behaviors following their treatment program (Patterson, 1974; Patterson, Cobb, & Ray, 1973; Patterson & Reid, 1973). Therefore, as with generalization to school, behavioral generalization should probably be assessed on a case-by-case basis if the clinician and parents wish to see changes in other deviant behaviors. If generalization does not spontaneously occur, then treatment efforts need to be directed to those behaviors.

Generalization to Nontargeted Siblings

One study examined generalization of parenting skills and treatment effects to untreated siblings, following treatment of a referred child (Humphreys, Forehand, McMahon, & Roberts, 1978). Results showed that without any prompting from the therapist, mothers did generalize positive parenting skills and siblings did improve their noncompliance following treatment of a target child. These results indicate that behavioral improvement can be seen in nontargeted children even without specific instructions to mothers to generalize the use of their skills.

Based on the studies reviewed in this section, a general statement can be made, based on group outcome data that temporal, behavioral, and subject (sibling) generalization of the effects of parent training using the Hanf-Forehand program does occur; setting generalization does not reliably occur. However, because the results are based on group statistics, they do not predict generalization effects with 100% accuracy for every individual. For example, in Patterson's work, although treatment effects generally maintain (based on group statistics), up to $\frac{1}{3}$ of the sample does not maintain treatment-acquired gains at follow-up, and booster sessions are required during posttreatment follow-up to bolster treatment effects (Patterson, 1974). For these reasons, clinicians should assess for the presence of generalization and provide adjunctive treatment strategies when necessary. Examples of such strategies are discussed in the next section.

Adjunctive Treatment Strategies

Because of the recognition that all children do not maintain treatment-acquired gains, a series of studies examined adjunctive treatment strategies designed to promote and enhance the treatment effects obtained with parent training. Wells, Griest, and Forehand (1980) designed a self-control program that involved instructing parents in self-monitoring, self-evaluation, and self-reinforcement of parenting skills they learned during parent training. Results of an ex-

perimental evaluation of this program showed that treatment effects for children of parents who received parent training and self-control training were significantly enhanced at follow-up, compared to children whose parents received only parent training.

Likewise, McMahon, Forehand, and Griest (1981) showed that formal training in social learning principles during the course of therapy results in enhanced maintenance of treatment effects. In addition, parents who received such formal training reported greater satisfaction with treatment.

Finally, Griest et al. (1982) investigated the effects of parent enhancement therapy on temporal generalization. This study was based on a growing body of literature suggesting that other aspects of parent functioning besides parenting skills are related to child aggressive disorders, to success in therapy, to maintenance of treatment effects, and to parents' perceptions of their children (Griest & Wells, 1983). In this study, some parents received parent training plus an adjunctive treatment strategy that included attention to marital satisfaction, parent depression, and parent knowledge of child development. Another group of parents received parent training alone. Once again, the adjunctive treatment strategy enhanced maintenance of treatment effects at follow-up, compared to parent training alone. Similar results were reported by Dadds, Schwartz, and Sanders (1987), who showed that the addition of an adjunctive partner support therapy program (brief marital therapy) to parent training produced significant gains over parent training alone in maritally discordant parents at 6-month follow-up.

These studies all indicate that adjunctive treatment strategies can enhance the effects of parent training, especially in families experiencing areas of dysfunction other than child-conduct problems alone (such as marital distress). Formal training in social learning principles should probably be incorporated into all parent training therapy plans. Other adjunctive strategies can be used whenever the idiosyncratic assessment reveals high levels of parent distress in other areas of functioning. Without such intervention, any positive effects obtained with parent training in the short run may be absent at follow-up.

OREGON SOCIAL LEARNING CENTER PARENT TRAINING AND FAMILY MANAGEMENT PROGRAMS

Description of Program

The parent training approaches of Patterson, Reid, and their collegues have been used with older children, up to 16 years of age. The basic treatment program can be loosely divided into three stages, with progression to each successive stage contingent on successful completion of the one before.

The first phase focuses on teaching parents the language and concepts of social learning theory by using programmed texts. Parents must pass a test that assesses knowledge of concepts before they pass on to the next stage of treatment.

In the next stage, parents learn to define, track, and record behavior and are asked to delineate two deviant and two prosocial behaviors of their child. The parents then record these behaviors for a 3-day period at home.

In the third phase, parents learn to develop intervention programs, beginning with two or three easily tracked behaviors. A point system is set up, whereby the child earns and loses points, contingent on positive and negative behavior, respectively. Points are exchanged *daily* for back-up rewards selected by the child. In addition, parents learn to use social reinforcers, such as verbal labelled rewards for positive behavior, and to implement a time-out procedure for negative behaviors. Thus, the child or young adolescent earns multiple reinforcers for

positive behavior and multiple negative consequences for deviant behavior.

In more recent discussions of treatment procedures, Patterson has emphasized the addition of problem-solving skills training as part of basic parent training. Problem solving involves training parents to generate solutions to problematic situations that arise, using the concepts and skills they have learned earlier, with decreasing amounts of input from the therapist. This training is designed to assist the parents in coping with children on their own as children present new behaviors or as new developmental issues arise. (For a complete presentation of Patterson's treatment approach see Patterson, Reid, Jones, & Conger, 1975.)

Evaluation of Treatment Program

Patterson and his colleagues conducted a number of studies early in the development of their clinical procedures, to demonstrate the efficacy of this approach to parent training. These studies demonstrated that treated families showed improvements equal to or greater than 30% reduction from baseline in scored deviant behavior (home observations) following treatment (Patterson, 1974; Patterson & Reid, 1973; Patterson, Cobb, & Ray, 1973). Data demonstrating generalization across time and siblings also were reported (Arnold, Levine, & Patterson, 1975; Patterson, 1974). In addition, this clinical program has been compared to both wait-list controls (Wiltz & Patterson, 1974) and to attention-placebo controls (Walter & Gilmore, 1973). In each case, parent training led to greater improvement in deviant child behavior than did control conditions. However, in both of these studies, there were differences in baseline data for the experimental and control groups, suggesting possible selection bias in group assignment. In addition, the treatment time was abbreviated in both studies.

Because of these flaws, Patterson, Chamberlain, and Reid (1982) conducted a third controlled study, in which cases were randomly assigned to parent training or community control conditions. In the community control group, families were referred to local mental health practitioners who employed treatments based on their own standards of care. All families submitted to a standardized assessment battery before and after treatment.

Results showed that the group receiving parent training experienced a 63% reduction from baseline level in the rate of deviant child behavior in the home, whereas the community control group showed a 17% reduction. The group by time interaction was significant. At termination, 70% of the parent training subjects had scores within the normal range, and 33% of the community control subjects had scores within the normal range. Both groups experienced a decrease in parent-reported problem behaviors. Differences between the groups in parent daily report data were not significant. This study corrected many of the design flaws in earlier studies employing control groups. The conclusion that parent training, when applied in an open-ended, time-unlimited fashion by relatively experienced therapists, is more effective than standard treatment procedures available in the community would appear to be a valid one.

Since the early demonstrations of efficacy, research on the clinical procedures of Patterson, Reid, and their colleagues have turned to questions of replication and community dissemination, adjunctive treatment procedures relating to therapist clinical skills, and development of specialized approaches for different diagnostic groups.

Replication and Community Dissemination

Fleischman (1981) conducted a systematic replication of the procedures developed by Patterson. Although some attempt was made to conduct the study without input from Patterson and his senior colleagues, the clinic where the treatment was conducted was established by the research center directed by Patterson. Fleishman was a student of Patterson's, and therapists had 2 to 6 years of experience in parent training, presumably at Patterson's research center, prior to their work in this study. However, neither Patterson nor his senior colleagues served as supervisors of the treatment or the methods. Treatment was open-ended and conducted by experienced therapists. No control group was employed. Results of this study showed that child misbehavior showed significant reductions by termination, as measured by objective home observations, parent daily report of symptoms, parental attitudinal descriptions of the child, and parents' own counts of problematic behavior. Improvements were maintained at 1-year follow-up.

In another replication study, Fleishman and Szykula (1981) evaluated Patterson's procedures in a true community setting, funded by Title XX funds. Again, therapists initially were trained by staff at Patterson's research center. Results of this study were comparable to those reported earlier from studies conducted in research facilities; that is, significant treatment effects were found for Total Aversive Behavior measured in the home by trained, objective observers; parent-collected daily behavior data; and global ratings of improvement by parents. The cost of treatment per family was $776 in the third year of the clinic and referrals to the clinic were steadily increasing. Thus, it appears that the results of Patterson's research on parent training can be replicated by others. In addition, the procedures can be implemented effectively in clinical settings in an efficient and cost-effective manner.

Coping with Client Noncompliance

In spite of the positive results obtained by Patterson and others affiliated with his research center, a number of studies conducted in the

1970s failed to show unequivocal, significant treatment effects from using parent training procedures (Bernal, Klinnert, & Shultz, 1980; Eyberg & Johnson, 1974; Ferber, Keeley, & Shemberg, 1974). Two factors differentiated these studies from those obtaining positive results: the use of a session-limited format and the use of relatively inexperienced therapists who had been taught to administer the treatment in a standardized, educative format.

These observations have prompted a line of research that looks at clinical skills displayed by experienced therapists, which may assist therapists in dealing with client resistance or non-cooperativeness with treatment procedures. Studies examining therapy process have shown that client resistance is systematically related to the phase of parent training therapy, and to therapist's ratings of treatment outcome (Chamberlain, Patterson, Reid, Kavanagh, & Forgatch, 1984). In addition, Patterson and Forgatch (1985) have shown that therapists' efforts to teach and confront are significantly related to client noncompliance. This effect was also demonstrated in an experimental study in which therapist behaviors of teaching and confronting were manipulated, and increases in client resistance were systematically observed (Patterson & Forgatch, 1985). These findings represent a considerable paradox for the parent trainer who must teach a systematic set of parent training procedures but who confronts increases in client noncooperativeness when she or he does so.

These studies and other observations have led Patterson and his colleagues to postulate three components of effective treatment: (1) parent training techniques to alter ineffective parent management practices; (2) therapist clinical skills for dealing with parent noncooperativeness; and (3) a therapist support system for maintaining effective therapist performance (Patterson, 1985).

Although therapist clinical skills as they relate to parent training have not been systematically identified by Patterson and his colleagues to date, preliminary analyses of therapy process data show that therapist behaviors such as supporting and facilitating are accompanied by a decrease in client noncooperativeness. In addition, skilled therapists have been shown to engage in a higher rate of *joining* behavior than novice therapists (as reported in Patterson, 1985). Joining has to do with therapist behaviors that establish a relationship with the client and engage him or her in the therapy process. These and other preliminary analyses have prompted Patterson to propose three critical therapist skills for reducing client noncooperativeness: (1) skills for joining with or engaging the client in the therapy process; (2) skills for reframing in a supportive way the problems or obstacles that the parents bring up in therapy; and (3) persistence of the therapist in teaching and confronting parents. Although clinical examples of the use of these skills are beyond the scope of this chapter, such examples can be found in Chamberlain and Baldwin (1988). The work of Patterson and his colleagues has been increasingly concerned with the identification, evaluation, and training of skills such as these, to enhance the likelihood that parent training strategies will be accepted and carried forward by parents.

Treatment Approaches for Predelinquent Behavior

In early parent training research, all children referred for treatment received the same treatment, regardless of differences in their characteristics or presenting problems. However, a study by Moore, Chamberlain, and Mukai (1979) found that of children treated at Patterson's center, those who were referred for stealing had a much poorer long-term outcome than children for whom stealing was not part of the presenting problem.

Studies such as this prompted Reid to develop additions to standard parent training when the target child is displaying covert, predelinquent, antisocial behavior such as stealing. The changes in treatment are based on the notion that stealing is a behavior that is normally concealed from parents and is less likely to be monitored by them. Therefore, after learning standard parenting skills, parents of stealers are taught to apply specific negative consequences whenever a *suspicion* of stealing has occurred. The actual behavior does not have to be observed. Thus, it becomes the child's responsibility not only to refrain from stealing but also to remain above suspicion. Finally, in order to improve monitoring and parental supervision of the child, a check-in system is negotiated. Daily phone calls are made to the home by the therapist to support the parents and to remind them to apply consequences for each and every suspected stealing event, no matter how minor or insignificant.

Reid, Hinjosa-Rivera, and Lorber (1980) evaluated the effectiveness of this enhanced approach to parent training for parents of young stealers. Parent reports of stealing and of other referral problems decreased significantly. Total Aversive Behavior, measured during home observations, decreased nonsignificantly but had not been high at baseline for this group of children, whose aggressive behaviors were primarily low-frequency and covert.

However, in order to conclude that the enhanced treatment program results in significant improvements over standard parent training, a control group of stealers receiving standard treatment should be employed and assessments outside the family system, such as court and police records, should be included. Until then, the results of Reid et al. (1980) are encouraging but not confirmed.

In a more recent study that further extends and enhances the basic treatment program of Patterson, Reid and their associates, Bank, Marlow, Reid, Patterson, and Weinrott (1991) treated delinquent adolescents and compared their treatment to that provided by other community agencies that normally offer services for such cases. In order to be accepted into the study, boys had to be repeat offenders with at least two offenses recorded in police files. One of these had to be a nonstatus offense. Thus, there can be no doubt that this was a seriously aggressive subject population.

For this group, treatment was modified so that not only were prosocial and antisocial behaviors targeted for treatment, but also other behaviors believed to put the child at risk for further delinquency (such as curfew violations, congregating with delinquent friends, etc.). Parents learned to track and monitor these behaviors in order to facilitate supervision. In addition, families were involved as a unit in developing behavioral contracts. Instead of time-out procedures, parents were taught to use more age-appropriate punishment procedures such as work details and point loss or restitution. Parental monitoring of the child's whereabouts and activities was emphasized, since lack of monitoring has been strongly related to delinquency.

Results of this study showed that the family management and community control groups were comparable at baseline on all categories of official offenses. By the end of the first year all offense categories (i.e., nonstatus offenses, index offenses, total offenses) except status offenses had been significantly lowered for the family management group; in the community control group, offenses had increased minimally. By the end of the second year, offenses in the family management group remained low and offenses in the community control group had also reduced. In each category, the offense rate was still higher in the community control group, but it is not clear from the analyses whether the differences at the end of the second year were significant. The striking finding of the study is the difference in time required for the respective approaches to have an effect on offense rates, with family management therapy being clearly superior in this regard.

Another notable finding of the study had to do with the savings to the community due to the treatment approach. There was a significant difference in institution time between the two groups in both the first and second years after treatment. Adolescents in the family management group spent 2,241 fewer days in institutional confinement than did community-treated adolescents, with a savings to the community of $135,000 over the 3-year period. This means that although the family management group had about 14% more time available to commit offenses during the treatment and follow-up years, they nevertheless committed 24% fewer offenses.

These results offer strong support that family management therapy may be one of the most viable treatments available for outpatient care of delinquent youths. It seems to be more effective than treatment that is available from typical community resources on an outpatient basis. This is not to say that the approach is a panacea for delinquency, since only 18% of subjects in the family management group completely dropped out of the delinquency process. (Only one of the community-control subjects did so.) Once adolescents reach the point of delinquency, family management training may slow the path to chronic-offender status rather than reversing it. Nevertheless, the study did demonstrate that this approach was more effective than other available treatments and showed that parent training can be enhanced and extended to a family management approach for this difficult client population.

MAJOR ISSUES IN CURRENT AND FUTURE RESEARCH

The clinical and empirical work reviewed so far in this chapter reveals that parent training and family management strategies can bring about reliable changes in children's behavior and appear to do so more effectively than a variety of other approaches to treatment. However, the field is still in need of basic studies to address

treatment outcome and long-term maintenance. Many of the existing studies suffer from conceptual and design flaws such as inadequate and poorly defined samples; truncated treatment provided by inexperienced therapists; failure to assess long-term maintenance against normal and untreated clinical samples; lack of attention to issues of treatment specificity and treatment integrity; and use of weak treatments in which there is a failure to address all variables potentially contributing to the child's problematic behavior. In other words, research should address several questions: For what types and subtypes of children are parent training strategies suitable? Does parent training truly affect the long-term course of aggressive behavior in children? What characteristics of treatments and therapists are related to short- and long-term behavior change? How should parent training treatments be enhanced to respond to the idiosyncratic characteristics of families that potentially affect aggressive behavior (e.g., parent depression, marital conflict, insularity, etc.).

Subject Types and Subtypes

Categorical models of classification in use in this country (typified by DSM-III-R) specify several types and subtypes of children who display disruptive behavior disorders. DSM-III-R identifies two major syndromes of aggressive behavior, conduct disorder and oppositional defiant disorder. The conduct disorder category has three subtypes: group subtype, solitary subtype, and undifferentiated subtype. DSM-III-R also identifies another major category of disruptive behavior, attention-deficit hyperactivity disorder. These children frequently display aggressive behavior as a secondary component of their behavioral syndrome.

Dimensional and other empirical approaches to classification of aggression reliably identify at least two subtypes and sometimes more (for a review, see Wells & Forehand, 1985). Likewise,

Conners and Wells (1986) have proposed that there are not one but several syndromes of hyperactivity, another diagnostic category to which parent training approaches have been applied. With the exception of one study by Moore, Chamberlain, and Mukai (1979), we do not know how parent training approaches interact with type or subtype of behavior disorder in children; that is, for which subtypes are parent training approaches more or less effective? Patterson and his colleagues speculated that different subtypes of behavior disorder may arise from different etiologic patterns in the family and may have different prognoses and responses to treatment (Lorber & Patterson, 1981; Patterson, 1982). However, there has been relatively little empirical follow-up to these hypotheses. More work is needed on the classification of disruptive behavior disorders and whether some classes of children are more amenable to parent training therapy than others.

Related to the issue of classification are studies on predictors of treatment outcome after using parent training therapies. Reviews of this research (Griest & Wells, 1983; Lochman, 1993) have identified several family characteristics that appear to be related to the outcome and/or long-term maintenance of treatment effects obtained with parent training. Among these are socioeconomic disadvantage, social insularity, maternal depression, marital discord, and sibling aggression. Children who display aggression in more than one setting may be less amenable to parent training than children whose aggression is displayed only in the home (Horne & Van Dyke, 1983) and children who are stealers have a poorer outcome (Moore et al., 1979). However, there is little other work on child characteristics that may predict treatment outcome. With the exception of the work by Griest et al. (1982) and Dadds et al. (1987), little effort has been made to incorporate the findings on predictor variables into revisions of the treatment models. More research is clearly needed in these areas.

Long-Term Impact

Several reviews have demonstrated that childhood aggressive behavior is extremely stable across time (Loeber, 1982; Olweus, 1979). In fact, Kazdin (1987) proposed that aggressive, antisocial behavior should be considered a chronic disorder requiring regular intervention over a period of years rather than a one-shot, supposedly curative treatment. In spite of this, parent training is often offered in an abbreviated or time-limited fashion. Evidence that one-shot parent training may not be sufficient comes from the work of Forehand and Long (1988), who found that, even for relatively mild aggressive disorders, children and their families were still not functioning normally in all areas at adolescent follow-up, and a substantial percentage of those receiving parent training had sought additional treatment subsequently. Long-term follow-up of treatment, provided over a period of several years, is needed to assess the full impact of parent training on the true course of aggressive behavior disorders. In addition, such a model should be compared against the long-term impact of treatments that continue to be provided in the community (e.g., hospitalization, traditional outpatient therapy, etc.).

Treatment and Therapist Characteristics

A few studies have examined characteristics of treatment that may differentially affect outcome; for example, group versus individual treatment (Eyberg & Matarazzo, 1980) and mother versus father versus couple treatment (Adesso & Lipson, 1981). In addition, Patterson has speculated in recent writings that open-ended treatment provided by experienced therapists is more effective than time-limited therapy provided by inexperienced therapists. Also, the Oregon group has made a number of additions and changes to treatment, based on clinical observations and theoretical speculations.

However, component analyses of parent training programs are practically nonexistent. No one really knows which components are essential for a positive outcome or if the addition of new components substantially alters outcome. Also, such basic questions as the impact of inclusion of fathers in therapy have not conclusively been addressed.

Two research studies do seem to indicate that therapist behaviors are important with respect to the receptiveness and compliance of parents to the therapy process. Much more work is needed in this area, both in terms of identifying relevant therapist behaviors and in training therapists in skills that affect the process of therapy, compliance of parents with homework assignments, dropout rates, and ultimately the outcome of treatment. Studies looking at the range of skills that differentiate experienced from inexperienced therapists would be helpful in this regard. This work, as it applies to parent training, is in its infancy.

CONCLUSIONS

Evidence of the potential need for enhancement of the basic parent training model comes from two lines of research. First, as mentioned earlier, a growing body of work has identified areas of family dysfunction other than parenting skills deficits that may be related to aggressive behavior disturbances in children. These include maternal depression, marital dysfunction, social insularity, and parent attributions, among others (Griest & Wells, 1983; Patterson, 1982). When attention to one or more of these factors has been incorporated into treatment,

short- or long-term outcome has been enhanced (Dadds et al., 1987; Griest et al., 1982). Likewise, the addition of treatment ingredients such as self-control training (Wells, Griest, & Forehand, 1980) and training in social learning theory (McMahon, Forehand, & Griest, 1981) had also been shown to enhance the maintenance of treatment effects.

Further evidence of the need for enhancement of treatment comes from the long-term follow-up study by Forehand and Long (1988), showing that adolescents were still functioning abnormally in some areas at long-term follow-up. The parent training model may not go far enough in assessment and treatment of multiple areas of dysfunction for children presenting with primary symptoms of aggression.

Both lines of research suggest that there may be a need for expansion of the basic parent training model to incorporate attention to other areas of family and child dysfunction if there is to be a clinically significant impact on the course of aggressive disorders. Griest and Wells (1983) proposed such an expanded behavioral family therapy model years ago, but little attention has been paid to developing and evaluating an expanded model. There is clearly much work remaining to be done in parent training research and development.

TREATMENT RESOURCES

Forehand, R., & McMahon, R. J. (1981). *Helping the noncompliant child: A clinician's guide to parent training*. New York: Guilford.

Patterson, G. R. (1982). *Coercive family process*. Eugene, OR: Castalia.

CHAPTER 17

Antisocial Behavior and Conduct Disorder

Alan E. Kazdin

Antisocial behavior in childhood includes a variety of acts such as fighting, destroying property, stealing, lying, and running away, among others. These behaviors occur in varying degrees over the course of normal development (Achenbach & Edelbrock, 1981; MacFarlane, Allen, & Honzik, 1954). For most children, antisocial behaviors diminish over time, do not interfere with everyday functioning, and do not appear to have untoward consequences in adulthood. However, for a significant number of children, these behaviors are relatively extreme and do not attenuate over the course of childhood. Conduct disorder refers to instances when the children or adolescents evince a *pattern of antisocial behavior*, when there is *significant impairment* in everyday functioning at home or school, or when the behaviors are *regarded as unmanageable by significant others* (Kazdin, 1987a). Thus, the term conduct disorder is reserved for

Completion of this research was supported by a Research Scientist Award (MH00353) and by a grant (MH35408) from the National Institute of Mental Health.

antisocial behavior that is clinically significant and clearly beyond the realm of normal functioning.

As conduct disorder emerges, a wide range of consequences are evident, including disruptive relations with parents, teachers, and peers; poor school performance; and corrective efforts to intervene in ways that themselves may be disruptive (e.g., transfer to new classrooms, schools, and neighborhoods). Clinically severe antisocial behavior is likely to bring the youth into contact with various social agencies. Mental health services (clinics, hospitals) and the criminal justice system (police, courts) are the major sources of contact for youths whose behaviors are identified as severely antisocial. Within the educational system, special services, teachers, and classes are often provided to manage such children on a daily basis.

This chapter focuses on the treatment of antisocial and aggressive behavior among children and adolescents. The chapter examines the nature of antisocial behavior and characteristics of children and their families. Current assessment modalities in use, including behavioral measures, are also presented. Finally, behavioral and cognitively based treatments are highlighted to convey the scope of interventions in use and the current status of outcome evidence.

DESCRIPTION OF THE DYSFUNCTION

Central Features

The overriding feature of conduct disorder is a persistent pattern of behavior in which the rights of others and age-appropriate social norms are violated. Isolated acts of physical aggression, destruction of property, stealing, and firesetting are sufficiently severe to warrant concern and attention in their own right. Although these behaviors may occur in isolation, several of these are likely to appear together as a constellation or syndrome.

Antisocial behavior that is clinically severe, interferes with functioning in everyday life, and entails several symptoms that co-occur is recognized in contemporary diagnosis as a specific disorder, referred to as Conduct Disorder.[1] In the *Diagnostic and Statistical Manual of Mental Disorders* (DSM-III-R) (American Psychiatric Association, 1987), the diagnosis is reached if the child or adolescent shows any three of the following symptoms:

1. Stealing without confrontation of a victim
2. Running away
3. Lying
4. Deliberate firesetting
5. Truancy

[1] For the present chapter, conduct disorder will be used to refer to clinically severe levels of antisocial behavior. Conduct Disorder, as a proper noun, will refer specifically to the diagnostic category, as defined by DSM-III-R (APA, 1987).

6. Breaking into someone's house, building, or car
7. Destroying property
8. Cruelty to animals
9. Sexual activity forced on another person
10. Use of a weapon
11. Frequently initiated fights
12. Stealing with confrontation of a victim
13. Physical cruelty to people

The symptoms must be present for at least six months for the diagnosis to apply. Any given individual is not likely to show all of the symptoms specified in the diagnostic criteria. However, the symptoms reflect core features of the disorder.

Merely listing the symptoms does not adequately convey the features that distinguish clinically referred youths. First, among youths with a diagnosis of Conduct Disorder many of the behaviors such as fighting, temper tantrums, stealing, and others are relatively *frequent*. In some cases, the behaviors may be of a low frequency (e.g., firesetting), in which case *intensity* or *severity* is the central characteristic. Second, *repetitiveness* and *chronic nature* of the behaviors are critical features. The behaviors are not likely to be isolated events or to be restricted to a brief period during which other influences or stressors (e.g., change in residence, divorce) are operative. Third, the *breadth of the deviant behaviors* is central as well. Rather than an individual *symptom* or target behavior, there are usually several behaviors that occur together and form a *syndrome* or constellation of symptoms. It is common for such youths to evince several symptoms beyond the minimal number required for the diagnosis. Fourth, included with the diagnosis is the criterion that the individual suffers *impairment* in everyday life. This is usually reflected in significant problems in interpersonal relations with others (e.g., parents, teachers, siblings, peers) and deficiencies in meeting role expectations (e.g., academic dysfunction, deportment problems at school).

The symptoms of Conduct Disorder bring to mind a related designation, juvenile delinquency. Delinquency also includes many behaviors that are antisocial. However, delinquency is a legal designation. Youths are designated as delinquent when they are adjudicated because they commit illegal acts. Conduct Disorder and delinquency overlap; in the course of a youth's life he or she may meet criteria for both and be involved in both mental health and juvenile justice systems.

Conduct Disorder requires a pattern of symptoms for a particular duration, as already mentioned. Conduct-disordered youth do not necessarily violate a law. For example, an 8-year-old boy with a diagnosis of Conduct Disorder may get into frequent fights at school, lie, steal from his parents, and destroy toys of his siblings and peers. With the pattern lasting several months, the boy would meet criteria for the diagnosis, although none of the behaviors was delinquent in the sense that a law was violated. In contrast, another child might engage in acts not included in the list of symptoms for Conduct Disorder (e.g., prostitution, selling drugs) and be designated as delinquent. Isolated acts that break the law are sufficient for delinquency. Thus, although there is overlap between Conduct Disorder and delinquency, they often represent different acts and paths. Although a distinction can be drawn, many of the behaviors of delinquents and conduct-disordered youths overlap and fall under the general rubric of antisocial behavior. Both Conduct Disorder and delinquency encompass a variety of constituent antisocial behaviors and are treated here together.

Associated Features

The core features of Conduct Disorder do not convey the full scope of impairment of children and adolescents who meet the diagnostic criteria. Apart from the antisocial, aggressive, and defiant behaviors, there are several correlates or associated features as well. Among alternate symptoms of antisocial children, those related to *hyperactivity* have been the most frequently identified. These symptoms include excessive motor activity, restlessness, impulsiveness, and inattentiveness. Several other behaviors have been identified as problematic among antisocial youths, such as noncompliance, boisterousness, showing off, and blaming others (Quay, 1986). Many of these appear to be relatively mild forms of obstreperous behavior in comparison to aggression, theft, vandalism, or other acts that cause damage to persons or property.

Children with conduct disorder are also likely to suffer from *academic deficiencies*, as reflected in achievement level, grades, and specific skill areas, especially reading (Ledingham & Schwartzman, 1984; Sturge, 1982). Such children are often seen by their teachers as uninterested in school, unenthusiastic toward academic pursuits, and careless in their work (Glueck & Glueck, 1950). They are more likely to be left behind in grades and to end their schooling sooner than their peers matched in age, socioeconomic status, and other demographic variables (Bachman, Johnston, & O'Malley, 1978; Glueck & Glueck, 1968). The core symptoms of the dysfunction appear to begin a sequence of events that fosters continued dysfunction. Thus, failure to complete homework and possible truancy or lying are likely to decrease the efforts of teachers to aid the student. Consequently, the initial dysfunctions at school are likely to portend further deterioration.

Poor interpersonal relations are likely to correlate with antisocial behavior. Children high in aggressiveness or other antisocial behaviors are rejected by their peers and show poor social skills (Behar & Stewart, 1982; Carlson, Lahey, & Neeper, 1984). Such youths are socially ineffective in their interactions with an array of adults (e.g., parents, teachers, community members). Specifically, antisocial youths are less likely to defer to adult authority, show politeness, and promote further positive interactions (Freedman, Rosenthal, Donahoe,

Schlundt, & McFall, 1978; Gaffney & McFall, 1981).

The correlates of antisocial behavior involve not only overt behaviors but also a variety of *cognitive and attributional processes*. Antisocial youths are deficient in the cognitive problem-solving skills that underlie social interaction (Dodge, 1985; Kendall & Braswell, 1985). For example, such youths are more likely than their peers to interpret gestures of others as hostile and are less able to identify solutions to interpersonal problem situations or to take the perspective of others.

Parent and Family Features

A variety of parent and family characteristics are associated with conduct disorder (Kazdin, 1987a; US Congress, 1991). Parents of antisocial youths are more likely to suffer from various psychiatric disorders than parents of children in the general population (Rutter, Tizard, & Whitmore, 1970). Criminal behavior and alcoholism, particularly of the father, are two of the stronger and more consistently demonstrated parental characteristics of youths with severe antisocial behavior (Robins, 1966; Rutter & Giller, 1983; West, 1982).

Several features related to the interaction of parents with their children characterize families of conduct-disordered youths. Parent disciplinary practices and attitudes have been especially well studied. Parents of conduct-disordered youths tend to be harsh in their attitudes and disciplinary practices with their children (Farrington, 1978; Glueck & Glueck, 1968; McCord, McCord, & Howard, 1961). These children are more likely than nonreferred children and clinical referrals without antisocial behavior to be victims of child abuse and to be in homes where spouse abuse is evident (Behar & Stewart, 1982; Lewis, Shanok, Pincus, & Glaser, 1979). Lax, erratic, and inconsistent discipline practices by a given parent and between the parents also characterize families of children

with conduct disorder. For example, severity of punishment on the part of the father and lax discipline on the part of the mother have been implicated in delinquent behavior (Glueck & Glueck, 1950; McCord, McCord, & Zola, 1959). When parents are consistent in their discipline practices, even if they are punitive, children are less likely to be at risk for antisocial behavior (McCord, McCord, & Zola 1959).

Parents of antisocial children are more likely to give commands to their children, to reward deviant behavior directly through attention and compliance, and to ignore or provide aversive consequences for prosocial behavior (Patterson, 1982). Fine-grained analyses of parent-child interaction suggest that antisocial behavior, particularly aggression, is systematically albeit unwittingly trained in the homes of antisocial children.

Supervision of the child, as another aspect of parent-child contact, has frequently been implicated in conduct disorder (Glueck & Glueck, 1968; Goldstein, 1984; Robins, 1966). Parents of antisocial or delinquent children are less likely to monitor their children's whereabouts, to make arrangements for the children's care when parents are temporarily away from the home, or to provide rules in the home stating where the children can go and when they must return home (Wilson, 1980).

Dysfunctional family relations are manifested in several ways. Parents of antisocial youths, compared with parents of normal youths, show less acceptance of their children; demonstrate less warmth, affection, and emotional support; and report less attachment (Loeber & Dishion, 1983; McCord et al., 1959; West & Farrington, 1973). At the level of family relations, less supportive and more defensive communications among family members, less participation in activities as a family, and more clear dominance of one family member are also evident (Alexander, 1973; Hanson, Henggeler, Haefele, & Rodick, 1984; West & Farrington, 1973). In addition, unhappy marital relations, interpersonal conflict, and aggression characterize the parental relations of delinquent and antisocial children (Hetherington & Martin, 1979; Rutter & Giller, 1983). Whether or not the parents are separated or divorced, it is the extent of their discord that is associated with antisocial behavior and childhood dysfunction.

The present discussion does not exhaust the range of characteristics of parents and families of conduct-disordered youths. Other characteristics such as mental retardation of the parent, early marriage of the parents, lack of parent interest in the child's school performance, and lack of participation of the family in religious or recreational activities have also been found (Glueck & Glueck, 1968; Wadsworth, 1979). Many of the factors come in clusters. For example, family size, overcrowding, poor housing, poor parental supervision, parent criminality, and marital discord are likely to be related. Thus, although research often can identify the influence of individual components, in practice they are invariably intertwined.

ASSESSMENT OF ANTISOCIAL BEHAVIOR

The diverse features of conduct disorder are germane to assessment and treatment decisions. The central characteristics of the child's dysfunction need to be carefully delineated. At the same time, associated features (e.g., hyperactivity, school performance) and contextual factors (e.g., parent psychopathology, child-rearing practices) make relevant an extremely broad set of constructs, each with manifold measurement strategies. The present discussion focuses on assessment of child antisocial behavior to convey progress and prospects within this domain. Several measures developed specifically to assess antisocial behavior are enumerated in Table 17.1 with their salient characteristics. A few measures are highlighted below for illustrative purposes.

Self-Report Measures

Self-report measures are frequently used in clinical work with adult patient samples. There is a greater reluctance to rely on self-report in children and adolescents. Children occasionally are found to have underestimated the presence and severity of their symptoms if parallel information is obtained from other sources (Kazdin, French, Unis, & Esveldt-Dawson, 1983; Orvaschel, Puig-Antich, Chambers, Tabrizi, & Johnson, 1982). Underreporting of antisocial behaviors might be expected because children may not perceive their behaviors as unusual or problematic, or they may hide the behaviors from adults to avoid punishment. Actually, antisocial behaviors have been readily identified through self-report (Herjanic & Reich, 1982). Indeed, information regarding antisocial behaviors is often more readily reported by children and adolescents than by others or by institutional records (Elliott & Ageton, 1980; Williams & Gold, 1972). The validity has been attested to by studies showing that self-reported antisocial behaviors predict subsequent arrest and convictions as well as educational, employment, and marital adjustment (Bachman et al., 1978; Farrington, 1984).

Relatively few self-report measures of conduct problems are available (see Table 17.1). Among those listed, no single measure enjoys widespread use or has been the focus of large-scale psychometric research. As an illustration, the *Children's Action Tendency Scale* (CATS) (Deluty, 1979) presents the child with 13 situations that reflect conflict situations. The child is asked to choose how he or she would respond from among alternative answers presented in a forced-choice format. The responses and the resulting scores reflect aggression, assertiveness, and submissiveness. The aggressiveness scale directly reflects characteristics of conduct disorder. This subscale has been shown to possess adequate internal consistency and test-retest reliability (over 4 months). Validity evidence has derived from demonstrations that CATS

TABLE 17.1   Selected measures of antisocial behaviors for children and adolescents

Measure	Response Format	Age[a] Range	Special Features
		SELF-REPORT	
Children's Action Tendency Scale (Deluty, 1979)	30 items in forced-choice format; child selects what he or she would do in interpersonal situations.	6–15 years	Scores for response dimensions: aggressiveness, assertiveness, and submissiveness.
Adolescent Antisocial Self-Report Behavior Checklist (Kulik, Stein, & Sarbin, 1968)	52 items, each of which is rated by the child on a 5-point scale (from "never" to "very often").	Adolescence	The measure samples a broad range of behaviors from mild misbehavior to serious antisocial acts. The items load 4 factors: delinquency, drug usage, parental defiance, and assaultiveness.
Self-Report Delinquency Scale (Elliott & Ageton, 1980)	47 items that measure frequency with which individual has performed offences included in the Uniform Crime Reports. Responses provide frequency with which behavior was performed over the last year.	11–21 years	Measure has been developed as part of the National Youth Survey, an extensive longitudinal study of delinquent behavior, alcohol and drug use, and related problems in American youths.
Minnesota Multiphasic Personality Inventory Scales (Lefkowitz, Eron, Walder, & Huesmann, 1977)	True-false items derived from Scales F (test-taking attitude), 4 (psychopathic deviate), and 9 (hypomania) are summed to yield an aggression/delinquency score.	Adolescence	Part of more general measure that assesses multiple areas of psychopathology.
Interview for Aggression[b] (Kazdin & Esveldt-Dawson, 1986)	Semistructured interview; 30 items pertaining to aggression, such as getting into fights, starting arguments. Each item rated on a 5-point scale for severity and a 3-point scale for duration.	6–13 years	Yields scores for severity, duration, and total (severity + duration) aggression. Separate factors assess overt and covert behaviors.
Children's Hostility Inventory[b] (Kazdin, Rodgers, Colbus, & Siegel, 1987)	38 true-false statements assessing different facets of aggression and hostility.	6–13 years	Derived from Buss-Durke Hostility Guilt Inventory. A priori subscales from that scale comprise factors that relate to overt acts

TABLE 17.1 (Continued)

Measure	Response Format	Ageª Range	Special Features
			(aggression) and aggressive thoughts and feelings (hostility).

REPORTS OF OTHERS

Measure	Response Format	Ageª Range	Special Features
Eyberg Child Behavior Inventory (Eyberg & Robinson, 1983a)	36 items rated on 1- to 7-point scale for frequency and whether the behavior is a problem.	2–17 years	Designed to measure wide range of conduct problems in the home.
Sutter-Eyberg Student Behavior Inventory (Funderburk & Eyberg, 1989)	36 items identical in format but not content to the Eyberg Child Behavior Inventory.	2–17 years	Measures a range of conduct problem behaviors at school.
Peer Nomination of Aggression (Lefkowitz et al., 1977)	Items that ask children to nominate others who show the characteristics (e.g., "Who starts a fight over nothing"?).	3rd through 13th grade	Items reflect the child's peer reputation regarding overall aggression. Different versions of peer nominations have been used.

DIRECT OBSERVATIONS

Measure	Response Format	Ageª Range	Special Features
Adolescent Antisocial Behavior Checklist (Curtiss et al., 1983)	57 items to measure antisocial behavior during hospitalization. Behaviors are rated as having occurred or not, based on staff observations.	Adolescence	The items can be scored by using different sets of subscales; one set focuses on the form of the problem (e.g., physical versus verbal harm); another set focuses on the objects of aggression (e.g., toward self, others, property). Different versions are available and differ in scoring.
Family Interaction Coding System (Reid, 1978)	Direct observational system to measure occurrence of nonoccurrence of 29 specific parent-child behaviors in the home. Each behavior is scored within small intervals for an hour each day over a period of several days.	3–12 years	Individual behaviors are observed but usually summarized with a total aversive behavior score. The general procedure can be adopted, using some or all of the behaviors of the FICS.

273

(Continues)

TABLE 17.1 (Continued)

Measure	Response Format	Age[a] Range	Special Features
Parent Daily Report (Chamberlain & Reid, 1987)	Parents identify symptoms of antisocial behavior. After symptoms are identified, the parent is called daily for several days. Each day the parent is asked if each behavior has or has not occurred in previous 24-hour period.	3–12 years	Measure does not reflect a standardized set of items but refers more to an assessment approach for collecting data on behaviors at home.

[a] The age ranges are tentative and are derived from age of cases reported rather than inherent restrictions of the measure.
[b] This measure has separate versions: (1) a self-report measure for children, and (2) a parent-report measure to evaluate children's behavior.

aggressiveness correlates with teacher and peer measures of the same construct, differentiates aggressive from nonaggressive school children, and reflects change after treatment of antisocial behavior (Deluty, 1979, 1983; Groot & Prins, 1989; Kazdin, Bass, Siegel, & Thomas 1989). Notwithstanding the initial evidence in behalf of the measure, the CATS is not in widespread use. Further work is needed to provide larger-scale evaluation of normative data and to examine the measure in relation to other strategies that assess antisocial behavior.

Reports of Significant Others

Reports of significant others (parents, teachers, therapists) are the most widely used measures of childhood disorders in general. As an assessment modality, measures completed by significant others have major advantages. Many rating scales are available that can be completed relatively quickly and can cover a wide range of symptom areas (Barkley, 1988). There may be a partial bias in the types of conduct problems that rating scales can assess. Behaviors such as

teasing, fighting, yelling, arguing, and other overt acts are likely to be easily detected by parents and teachers. More covert acts such as stealing, substance abuse, and gang behavior may be more difficult to detect. Parents are the most frequently relied-upon source of information because they usually are readily available, are knowledgeable about the child's behavior over time and across situations, and play a central role in the referral of children for treatment.

Measures completed by significant others have received more attention than self-report measures. A prime example is the frequently used and extensively evaluated *Eyberg Child Behavior Inventory* (ECBI) (Eyberg & Robinson, 1983a; Robinson, Eyberg, & Ross, 1980). The measure is used to assess child behavior problems that parents report at home. Sample items include: verbally fighting with friends one's own age, refusing to do chores when asked, poor table manners, and yelling or screaming. Most of the items reflect refusal and other oppositional behaviors that are annoying to parents, rather than serious antisocial acts, although there are exceptions (e.g., stealing, destroying objects). Each item is rated by the parent as to whether it is a problem (yes, no) and how often it occurs (Likert scale; 1=never, 7=always). The measure yields two scores that reflect the number of problems (items endorsed affirmatively) and the intensity of the problem (total score of the Likert-scale scores summed for all items).

The ECBI stands apart from other measures devoted to conduct problems, by virtue of the scope of available evidence. The measure has been used in studies to evaluate the instrument and concurrent validity of other measures, to characterize child dysfunction and family adjustment, and to evaluate alternative treatments. Psychometric evaluation has indicated that the ECBI has adequate reliability (e.g., internal consistency and test-retest reliability) and validity (e.g., criterion, convergent, and discriminant) (Boggs, Eyberg, & Reynolds, 1990; Eyberg & Robinson, 1983a; Eyberg & Ross, 1978; Robinson et al., 1980). Also, the measure reflects change associated with treatment of conduct problems (Eyberg & Robinson, 1982; Webster-Stratton, Kolpacoff, & Hollinsworth, 1988). Normative data are also available for children and adolescents (Eyberg & Robinson, 1983a; Robinson et al., 1980), including recent data spanning grades 1–12 (Burns & Patterson, 1990). Clearly, among available measures for antisocial behavior, the measure has achieved substantial attention.

Teacher evaluations of child behavior also play a role in identification of conduct disorder. Teachers observe children for protracted amounts of time and across a wide range of situations (e.g, structured versus unstructured classroom activities; academic, social, and recreational settings). Moreover, the teacher can evaluate children in the context of their peers. A given child's departure from his or her peers provides a perspective that may not be available to parents.

As an illustration, the *Sutter-Eyberg Student Behavior Inventory* (SESBI) (Funderburk & Eyberg, 1989) has been developed as a teacher rating scale to assess conduct problems at school. The measure closely parallels the ECBI in items and scoring format. However, several items were modified or replaced to reflect behavior at school (e.g., makes noises in class, sasses teacher, demands teacher attention). As with the ECBI, the behaviors tend to focus on annoying problems rather than the more severe forms of antisocial acts. The measure has been subjected to considerable psychometric evaluation with nonreferred and clinic samples. Data recently reported have demonstrated internal consistency, test-retest reliability (1 and 3 weeks), interrator reliability, and convergent validity with ratings completed by others (Funderburk, Eyberg, & Behar, 1989; Ladish, Sosna, Warner, & Burns, 1989; Schaughency, Hurley, Yano, Seeley, & Talarico, 1989). The close relation to the ECBI and the relative ease with which each is administered make the SESBI attractive for school assessment of conduct problems.

Antisocial behavior is often included in multidimensional rating scales completed by parents and teachers. The measures include diverse symptom areas designed to cover a broad spectrum of dysfunctions, one or more of which address antisocial behavior (e.g., aggression, delinquency). Typically these scales present a large number of items that the parent or teacher rates in terms of presence or absence or severity of dysfunction. The measures do not focus primarily on antisocial behavior and hence are not included in Table 17.1. However, the measures warrant mention because of their breadth and level of development.

The *Child Behavior Checklist* (CBCL) (Achenbach & Edelbrock, 1983) exemplifies this type of instrument in which parents complete items to convey characteristics of their children. There are separate versions of the measure for parents, teachers, and children of different age groups spanning 2–16 years of age. The most commonly used version is the parent form, which includes 118 items that refer to behavior problems, each of which is rated on a 3-point scale (0 = not true, 2 = very or often true). Three sample items related to conduct disorder include: cruelty, bullying, or meanness to others; argues a lot; sets fires. The scale yields several different factors or constellations of symptoms including aggression, delinquency, hyperactivity, anxiety, depression, uncommunicativeness, schizophrenia, and others. The scale has been evaluated separately for boys and girls in different age groups from nonclinic samples. Consequently, with the CBCL one can evaluate an individual child's standing relative to same-age and gender peers who have not been referred for treatment. Many other rating scales and checklists have been administered to parents. Prominent samples include the *Revised Behavior Problem Checklist* (Quay & Peterson, 1983), the *Parent Symptom Questionnaire* (Conners, 1970), the *Louisville Behavior Checklist* (Miller, Hampe, Barrett, & Noble, 1971), the *Institute for Juvenile Research Behavior Checklist* (Lessing, Williams, & Revelle, 1981), and the (*Personality Inventory for Children* (Wirt, Lachar, Klinedinst, & Seat, 1977).

Several multidimensional scales are also available for teachers. These measures do not differ in structure or format. Indeed, many scales such as the *Revised Behavior Problem Checklist* have been administered to parents, teachers, and other adults (e.g., clinic staff). For several measures, parallel forms exist for teacher and parents. Examples include the *CBCL-Teacher Report Form* (Achenbach & Edelbrock, 1986), the *Conners Teachers Questionnaire* (Conners, 1969), and the *School Behavior Checklist* (Miller, 1972), which are parallel to the forms mentioned above for parents.

As an assessment modality, multidimensional parent and teacher rating scales have been widely used. Their value derives from sampling a wide spectrum of symptom areas and from their ease of administration. Considerable data have been generated on their use and psychometric properties (reliability and validity). Also, normative data are available for many measures that permit comparison of clinic and nonclinic samples and variations in symptom areas as a function of age, gender, social class, and other subject or demographic variables.

Peer Evaluations

Ratings by peers are worth distinguishing, even though peers qualify as significant others. Also, peer measures reflect an assessment and methodology that departs from the rating scales used for parent and teacher assessments. Peer-based measures usually consist of different ways of soliciting peer nominations of persons who evince particular characteristics such as aggressiveness (Banta & Walder, 1961; Pekarik, Prinz, Liebert, Weintraub, & Neale, 1976). For example, peers may be asked to nominate children in class to answer such questions as, "Who gets into most fights?" or "Who starts a fight over nothing?" (Huesmann, Lefkowitz, & Eron, 1978; Lochman & Lampron, 1985). A child's score usually is the proportion of nominations in which he or she has been selected. The consensus of the peer group is likely to reflect consistencies in performance and stable characteristics. Indeed, elementary school peer evaluations of aggressive behavior correlate with antisocial behavior years later (Huesmann, Eron, Lefkowitz, & Walder, 1984; Tremblay, LeBlanc, & Schwartzman, 1988).

Peer sociometric ratings are often used to assess such characteristics as popularity, likeability, acceptance, rejection, and social competence. Such characteristics are quite relevant, given the difficulties that antisocial children usually evince in each of these areas. Peer evaluations of social dimensions are correlated with independent evaluations of adjustment. Although the perspective of peers is clearly unique and important, the clinical utility of peer ratings is limited. The measures have enjoyed use in situations in which one has access to a peer group, such as in a classroom. Studies of antisocial behavior and intervention projects in school settings have been able to utilize peer-based measures.

Direct Observation

The youth's specific behaviors at home, at school, or at a clinic can be observed directly. The key ingredients of direct observations are: defining behavior carefully, identifying the situations in which behavior will be observed, using trained observers to record the behaviors, and ensuring that behavior is observed accurately and reliably. The requirements for direct observation vary as a function of the complexity of the assessment procedures. Several observation systems are available (Eyberg & Robinson, 1983b; Forehand & McMahon, 1981; Patterson, 1982; Wahler, House, & Stambaugh, 1976). They differ in the specific behavioral codes for various conduct problems, the setting in which they are usually completed (e.g., home, clinic, school), and the extent to which the situation and tasks are structured for the parent and child (e.g., specific tasks such as playing a game, or everyday interaction) (Reid, Baldwin, Patterson, & Dishion, 1988). Typically, a given measure has been designed for one setting such as the home or clinic. However, the codes can be adapted for use across settings. In each situation, highly trained observers usually are required to observe behavior.

An advantage of direct observations is they provide samples of the actual frequency or occurrences of particular antisocial or prosocial behaviors. Direct observations have their own liabilities. Many behaviors, especially covert acts (theft, drug use, firesetting, sexual promiscuity), are not readily observed directly. Also, when behaviors are observed directly and obtrusively, the act of observation can influence their performance. Nevertheless, observations contribute unique information by sampling behavior directly.

As an illustration of direct observational methods, the *Family Interaction Coding System* (FICS) warrants special mention (Patterson, 1982). The FICS has been used to record behaviors of antisocial children as they interact with their parents and siblings at home (Patterson, Reid, Jones, & Conger, 1975; Reid, 1978). More specifically, the measure is designed to assess aggressive behaviors and the antecedents and consequences (family interactions) with which they are associated. Among direct observation systems, the FICS is relatively elaborate; 29 different behaviors are coded by observers as present or absent in each of several brief time intervals (e.g., 30 seconds) over a period of approximately 1 hour. Prosocial and deviant child behaviors (e.g., complying with requests, attacking someone, yelling) and parent behaviors (e.g., providing approval, playing with the child, humiliating the child) are included.

The FICS has several important requirements. To begin with, observers must be carefully trained and monitored closely to ensure that the codes are scored reliably. In addition, the situations in which observers complete their assessment need to be partially controlled to limit the variability in the setting. For example, when the FICS is used in the home, families are instructed to remain in a small number of rooms during the period in which observations are obtained and not to watch television or to make outgoing phone calls; all of these restrictions help observers score child-parent interactions.

The FICS and other observational systems, beyond those included in Table 17.1, have been used in several studies (McMahon & Forehand, 1988; Reid et al., 1988). However, individual measures have been largely restricted to the specific research programs for which they were designed. The methods are somewhat complex, require well-trained observers, and are not easily disseminated for widespread use. Direct observational systems need not involve such well-developed and formalized systems as the FICS. Occasionally observational codes are devised for individual cases, to observe one or more behaviors at home or at school (Kazdin, 1989a). With relatively simple definitions and only one or a few codes, parents and teachers can be used in place of trained observers. The ease of implementation in such cases, relative to more complex systems, bears a commensurate reduction in the scope of information. The more complex codes evaluate multiple child behaviors and usually provide information about parent-child interchanges; more simplified codes tend to focus on one or two target behaviors of the child.

Not all observational procedures that include multiple behaviors of the child require trained observers at home. A unique measure designed to assess behaviors at home is the *Parent Daily Report* (PDR) (Patterson, 1982; Chamberlain & Reid, 1987). This measure is completed by the parent, who is called each day for a period covering several days (e.g., 6–10 days). Each day a list of conduct problem behaviors is reviewed with the parent. The parent is asked whether any of several behaviors has occurred in the preceding 24-hour period. From the replies, two scores usually are delineated, namely, the total number of conduct problem behaviors and the total number of target behaviors. The total problem behavior score is the sum of the behaviors that were noted to have occurred that day. The target behavior score is the sum of occurrences of a subset of the behaviors that the parents previously identified as problematic.

The PDR embraces the advantages of direct observations, including specification of the behaviors and observations restricted to a specific time period. Also, the measure samples behaviors in everyday situations without artificial constraints that direct observations by observers can impose. Finally, the PDR can assess low-rate behaviors (stealing, firesetting) that are less likely to be evident in the usual observational systems. However, the measure relies on impressions and is not invariably based on what actually occurred. Correspondence between what the parent says the child did and what the child has actually done may vary widely.

The PDR has been shown to be reliable as reflected in measures of interjudge (caller) agreement, internal consistency, and test-retest reliability (over periods of 2–4 weeks). The measure correlates moderately with direct observations (FICS) and reflects change associated with interventions designed to reduce antisocial behavior (Chamberlain & Reid, 1987; Kazdin et al., 1989; Patterson, 1982; Webster-Stratton et al., 1988). Some data are available on normative samples to facilitate interpretation of the results (Chamberlain & Reid, 1987). Low interparent agreement, occasionally low correlations with direct observations, and different conclusions for total behavior versus target behavior scores raise ambiguities with the measure. Also, at this point, the measure has not been standardized; different versions are in use, varying in the number and content of behavioral categories (Chamberlain & Reid, 1987; McMahon & Forehand, 1988). As such, the measure refers more to a procedure than to a specific scale.

Institutional and Societal Records

Evaluation of antisocial youths frequently relies on institutional records such as school attendance, grades, graduation, school suspensions and expulsions, contact with the police, or arrest records. Institutional records are exceedingly important because they represent socially significant measures of the impact of the problem. Governmental agencies at the state and national level monitor such events as the number of juvenile arrests or juvenile court cases. Such information can plot important social trends and facilitate decision making about allocation of resources and services for a particular problem.

There are many problems with institutional and societal records as measures of antisocial behavior. Most antisocial and delinquent acts are not observed or recorded. In fact, research has suggested that 9 of 10 illegal acts are not detected or not acted on officially (Empey, 1982). This conclusion has been supported by studies that ask children and adolescents to report on their delinquent and antisocial behaviors (Elliott & Ageton, 1980; Williams & Gold, 1972). Official records can greatly underestimate the occurrence of antisocial behaviors because of imperfect and often discretionary recording of the act in some archival record. Nevertheless, institutional records are critical measures for the evaluation of antisocial behavior. Antisocial behavior by its very nature often leaves its mark on society (e.g., vandalism, firesetting, crime statistics). Institutional records have been used to measure the behavior of juveniles and to evaluate interventions designed to reduce antisocial behavior (Kirigin, Braukman, Atwater, & Wolf, 1982; Offord et al., 1985).

Projective Techniques

Projective tests present ambiguous or relatively unstructured material to the child. Responses are considered to reflect underlying psychological processes, depending on the specific assessment device and the theoretical position from which the device or scoring system has been derived. Several different measures have been used to examine constructs directly relevant to conduct disorder, including aggression, anger, and hostility, as well as the psychic processes such as defense mechanisms, ego development, and fantasy through which these constructs may be manifest. Prominent among the measures are the Rorschach, Thematic Apperception Test or Children's Apperception Test, Figure Drawings, and others (Lochman, 1984). Individual measures often include a number of scoring systems and stimulus configurations (e.g., subsets of TAT cards). Reviews and critiques have questioned the validity of such measures and the unclear relation of projective test performance to overt antisocial acts (Gittelman, 1980; Lochman, 1984). Research can be cited to demonstrate that alternative projective tests distinguish aggressive from nonaggressive individuals or correlate significantly with other measures of antisocial behavior (Koppitz, 1966; Purcell, 1956). However, as an assessment modality, projective techniques do not enjoy widespread use for conduct disorders. Infrequent use may be due in part to fact that the measures by design do not attempt to access directly the core phenomenological symptoms of the disorder and do not aid in achieving a psychiatric diagnosis based on current phenomenological approaches.

Multimodal Assessment

Each of the above modalities has its own strengths, methodological weaknesses, and sources of bias. For example, parent evaluations of deviant child behavior provide an obviously important and unique perspective, given that parents usually are in an excellent position to comment on the child's functioning. However, parent ratings of child deviance are influenced by parent psychopathology, stress, and marital discord (Forehand, Lautenschlager, Faust, & Graziano, 1986; Mash & Johnston, 1983). Also, parents occasionally fail to detect problems identified through child report or direct observation. Similarly, direct observation reflects performance of a particular behavior free from the global judgments and recollections of parents and teachers. Unfortunately, critical behaviors of interest may be too low in frequency, covert, or performed when observers are not present, so direct observation may miss many behaviors of interest.

No single measure has been shown to assess the multiple facets of dysfunction that conduct disorder reflects. Consequently, the assessment of conduct disorder should include multiple measures that encompass different methods of assessment (e.g., interviews, direct observations), perspectives (e.g., child, parent, teacher), domains (e.g., affect, cognition, behavior), and settings (at home, at school, in the community). The importance of multichannel assessment strategies is also accentuated by findings on several substantive methodological and substantive questions about child performance.

Cross-Situational Performance

Children with conduct problems are likely to evince dysfunction across diverse situations such as home and school. Assessment of child behavior in one of these settings cannot be assumed to represent performance in other settings. For example, in a treatment study with antisocial children, ratings of child behavior were obtained from parents and teachers to assess a broad range of symptoms at home and at school (Kazdin et al., 1989). Correlations before treatment indicated that total symptom scores at home (Child Behavior Checklist) and at school (School Behavior Checklist) were not significantly correlated ($r = .08$). This low correlation suggests considerable specificity of performance for conduct problem behavior and/or large discrepancies in the perspectives of parents and teachers. After treatment, pre- to posttreatment change at home was significantly correlated with change at school ($r = .26$, $p < .05$). Although improvements in performance in one setting were related to improvements in the other setting, the magnitude of the correlation was low. These data as well as other studies indicate the relative independence in level of conduct problems and other dysfunctions across different settings (Achenbach, McConaughy, & Howell, 1987; Kazdin, 1989b; Kazdin & Bass, 1988). Thus, multimodal assessment is essential to characterize performance across different settings.

Symptoms and Prosocial Functioning

The impetus for seeking evaluation or treatment usually is the presence of maladaptive, disturbing, or disruptive behaviors. Naturally, the effects of treatment would be measured by the extent to which the problems identified at the outset of treatment are reduced when treatment is completed. Often assessment includes other symptom areas to see if treatment reduces dysfunction in other domains than those initially identified as problematic. The reduction of symptoms is obviously central to the evaluation of outcome.

In addition to symptom reduction, it is important to assess the prosocial functioning or adaptive skills of the child. Prosocial functioning refers to the presence of positive adaptive behaviors and experiences, such as participating in social activities, socially interacting, and making friends. With children and adolescents, adjustment may depend heavily on the positive adaptive behaviors or skills, given the significance of the peer group and prosocial experiences outside the home.

Reducing symptoms no doubt can improve a child's functioning. However, the overlap of symptom reduction and positive prosocial functioning may not be great (Kazdin, 1989b; Kazdin et al., 1989). For example, in the latter study, parents rated antisocial children on the CBCL, which yielded scores for overall symptoms (total behavior problems) and prosocial functioning (total social competence). Scores on these measures were correlated significantly, and as would be expected, negatively ($r = .31$, $p < .001$). The magnitude of the correlation is relatively low, indicating approximately 9% shared variance. Changes in symptoms and prosocial functioning from pre- to posttreatment also showed a very low correlation ($r = -.17$, ns). Similar findings were evident when symptoms and prosocial functioning were examined at school. Thus, reductions in symptoms were not strongly associated with improvements in prosocial functioning.

These findings suggest that *antisocial* behavior is not merely the opposite of *prosocial* behavior. Thus, multiple measures are essential to examine the positive adaptive functioning of children as well as target symptoms of interest. In the case of treatment evaluation, such assessment may be particularly critical. Quite possibly, treatments that appear equally effective in reducing symptoms may vary in the extent to which they promote and develop pro-social behaviors. In addition, for children whose symptom reduction is equivalent, the long-term prognosis may vary as a function of prosocial behaviors evident at treatment outcome. For these reasons, assessment of prosocial behavior remains important.

Method Variance

The assessment of childhood disorders has shown that method factors can contribute significantly to the information yielded. The role of the rater (child, parent) has received special attention (Achenbach et al., 1987). Results have shown across diverse areas of functioning that measures of the same construct (e.g., aggression or depression) completed by different raters often show low-magnitude correlations (Kazdin, Esveldt-Dawson, Unis, & Rancurello, 1983; Kazdin, French, & Unis, 1983; Kazdin, French, Unis, & Esveldt-Dawson, 1983). Measures that are completed by the same rater, even if they are of different constructs, occasionally correlate as well as or more highly than measures of the same construct by different raters. Multimethod, multitrait evaluations indicate that both trait (construct) variance and method variance contribute to the results (Kazdin, Esveldt-Dawson, Unis, & Rancurello, 1983; Reynolds, Anderson, & Bartell, 1985; Wolfe, Braukmann, & Ramp, 1987). The strong method component indicates that conclusions reached about performance with one method of assessment may differ from those reached in relation to another measure. The contribution of raters as one method factor is yet another reason to include multiple methods of assessment.

Limitations of Current Assessment Techniques

Assessment of antisocial behavior is an area in which further research is clearly needed. A battery of assessment devices should be developed

to sample the full range of antisocial behaviors and to evaluate performance across settings (e.g., school, home, community). Few well-validated measures exist to assess performance in any one setting. Of the currently available measures, standardization and normative data are the exception rather than the rule. General checklists that assess the full range of psychopathology, including antisocial behavior, provide excellent psychometric data. Understandably, the measures do not provide a fine-grained evaluation of antisocial behaviors. Thus, the general checklists do not substitute for scales designed specifically for antisocial behavior.

Direct observational measures represent highly refined methods for scrutinizing specific antisocial behaviors. A difficulty with behavioral measures has been the lack of standardization. The measures have been restricted to individual research programs, often require extensive training to complete, and are difficult to interpret, given the absence of normative data. Development of direct observational measures that include some of the advantages of self-report scales (e.g., ease of use, transferability across settings and research programs) would greatly add to assessment tools in this area.

BEHAVIORAL TREATMENTS

A wide range of treatment techniques has been applied to antisocial behavior and conduct disorder, including diverse forms of individual, group, family, behavioral, and cognitive therapy as well as alternative medications, inpatient therapy, day-treatment, and community programs (Brandt & Zlotnick, 1988; Kazdin, 1985; McMahon & Wells, 1989; US Congress, 1991). As yet, no clearly effective intervention has controverted the course of clinically referred antisocial behavior. Behavioral approaches have offered considerable promise. Before alternative approaches are highlighted, the relevant literature will be discussed. Antisocial behavior, conduct disorder, and conduct problems have no uniform definition within behavior modification. The terms are often used to embrace the full range of disruptive behaviors including antisocial, aggressive, and oppositional behaviors, and tantrums, excessive whining, overactivity, teasing, and others. Although psychiatric diagnosis represents one way of delineating various constellations of behavior such as Conduct Disorder, most treatment studies, whether or not they focus on behavior modification, do not use diagnostic categories (Kazdin, Bass, Ayers, & Rodgers, 1990). Such a diagnosis is not particularly informative for developing treatment strategies. The presence or absence of a diagnosis does not specify the severity of dysfunction in quantifiable terms, nor does it by itself illuminate the specific symptoms or symptom pattern that the individuals show.

Aggressive and oppositional behaviors have served as a focus of different behavioral techniques. The assessment of these behaviors serves as the basis for identifying youth for treatment and then for evaluating the extent to which changes have been achieved. Five classes of treatment are highlighted here to illustrate the approaches and their promise, including operant-conditioning-based interventions, social skills training, cognitively based treatments, and parent- and family-based treatments. The literature in these areas is vast and hence the present discussion is only illustrative.

Operant Conditioning Techniques

The principles of operant conditioning have generated a large number of interventions (Cooper, Heron, & Heward, 1987; Kazdin, 1989a). The techniques can be distinguished on the basis of whether they attempt to increase the frequency of appropriate (e.g., nonaggressive) behavior or to decrease the frequency of inappropriate behavior. A large number of demonstrations are available in which positive reinforcement is used to increase specific behaviors. Obviously, merely

providing incentives for behavior is not likely to be very effective. Several parameters of administration (e.g., frequency, immediacy, contingent delivery, and schedule of delivery) are critically important and directly influence effectiveness. Variation of these parameters has provided an extraordinary range of methods of delivering reinforcement (Kazdin, 1989a).

Punishment procedures are also used in behavioral programs to suppress or eliminate conduct problem behaviors. The punishment procedures differ from the usual consequences applied to behavior in everyday life; they are also implemented somewhat differently. Punishment procedures in the context of treatment typically consist of the withdrawal of reinforcers. Procedures such as time-out from reinforcement (removal of positive reinforcers for a brief period of time), response cost (the loss of a positive reinforcer such as a token or privilege), and overcorrection (correcting the environmental effects of the inappropriate behavior and practicing appropriate performance) are three commonly used methods. There are many examples in which variations of reinforcement and punishment techniques are used to reduce conduct problems in children and adolescents at home and at school (Kazdin, 1989a).

Illustrations

Large-scale programs combine several reinforcement and punishment contingencies to change behavior. Perhaps the best-known of these is the program at Achievement Place (in Kansas), which is conducted for youths (ages 10 to 16) who have been adjudicated for a variety of offenses, primarily felonies. Diverse psychiatric diagnoses have been applied to the population, including personality disorder, adjustment reaction, and conduct disorder. The program is conducted in a home-style situation in which a small number of boys or girls (usually six to eight) live with a specially trained married couple. The children participate in a token economy in which a variety of self-care (e.g., room cleaning), social (e.g., communicating with peers, participating in group activity), and academic behaviors (e.g., reading, completing homework) are reinforced with points. The points can be exchanged for rewards and privileges such as allowance, access to TV, games and tools, and permission to go downtown or to stay up late. Points can be lost for failure to meet particular responsibilities (e.g., to maintain passing grades in school) or violation of rules (e.g., being late in returning home, lying, stealing). The program is managed by the "teaching parents" who complete special training in the general principles and practical skills needed to administer the program effectively. In addition to reinforcement and punishment techniques, several other procedures are included, such as training children in specific skill areas (e.g., vocational training), self-government in which children decide many of the consequences for their behavior, a close interpersonal relationship with the teaching parents, and a structured family situation (Wolf et al., 1976). Several studies have demonstrated the effects of reinforcement and punishment contingencies on such behaviors as aggressive statements, completion of homework and chores, keeping up on current events, and communication skills (Phillips, Phillips, Wolf, & Fixsen, 1973; Werner et al., 1975). In addition, while the youths were in the program, the gains were reflected in a reduction in criminal offenses in the community and significantly fewer criminal offenses by residents than by others in community-based or more traditional institutional programs (Kirigin et al., 1982).

The teaching-family model has been extended to over 200 group homes throughout the United States and in a few foreign countries (Jones, Weinrott, & Howard, 1981; Wolf, Braukmann, & Ramp, 1987). Evaluations of these extensions across multiple settings have not supported the efficacy of the procedures on community measures. Measures of offenses and reinstitutionalization from 1 to 3 years after participation in the program are no different for youths who complete the program from those who participate in

more traditional programs (Jones et al., 1981; Kirigin et al., 1982; Kirigin, Wolf, Braukmann, Fixsen, & Phillips, 1979). Thus, the evidence has been relatively consistent in showing gains during treatment but not thereafter. Reliable changes while the program is in effect are quite important. The results suggest that continued treatment, perhaps on an intermittent basis, may be required to achieve sustained improvements.

Evaluation

Many other operant conditioning programs have been evaluated for a wide range of youths with conduct problems. The work has encompassed different settings, age groups, and levels of severity of conduct problems, as reflected in programs in correctional institutions (Hobbs & Holt, 1976), schools (Kolvin et al., 1981; Walker, Hops, & Greenwood, 1981), summer camps (Hughes, 1979), and the community (O'Donnell, Lydgate, & Fo, 1979), to mention a few. These and other operant-conditioning-based interventions can reduce aggressive behavior and increase prosocial behavior.

There are limitations in what the studies have shown. First the programs tend to focus on one or a few target behaviors, rather than the larger constellation of behaviors in which the individual behavior may be embedded. Thus, the often dramatic effects achieved with a particular behavior are tempered by the absence of information on related behaviors that may not have been addressed. Second, long-term follow-up is rarely assessed. Because of the recalcitrance of severe conduct problem behaviors to change, return and continuation of the behaviors are likely. Consequently, demonstrations of long-term impact are greatly needed.

Social Skills Training

Social skills training (SST) refers to a behavioral treatment approach that has been widely applied to children, adolescents, and adults (Kelly, 1982;

Michelson, Sugai, Wood, & Kazdin, 1983). Training focuses on the verbal and nonverbal behaviors that affect social interactions. Specific behaviors are developed to enhance the child's ability to influence his or her environment, to obtain appropriate outcomes, and to respond appropriately to demands of others.

The underlying rationale for SST is drawn from the notion that conduct problems in children are basically interpersonal problems. Children are often identified as in need of treatment because their behaviors have a deleterious impact on others, as evident in aggressive acts, property destruction, noncompliant behavior, negativism, and tantrums. Several maladaptive patterns of social interaction among children have been implicated in clinical dysfunction. For example, asocial behavior, social isolation, and unpopularity in childhood are risk factors for childhood psychopathology, delinquency and conduct problems, dropping out of school, and antisocial behavior in adulthood (Kazdin, 1987a).

SST develops a variety of interpersonal skills, usually in the context of individual treatment sessions. Typically, training includes several procedures such as instructions, modeling by the therapist, practice by the child, corrective feedback, and social reinforcement (praise) for appropriate performance. The sequence of these procedures is enacted with several interpersonal situations, as in interactions with parents, siblings, and peers. In each situation, the child and therapist role-play the appropriate behaviors. Instructions convey what the child is to do, the overall purpose (e.g., "It is important to be positive when interacting with others. Look at the other person when talking"), and the salient features of the behavior. Modeling by the therapist shows exactly how the behavior should be performed. Feedback from the therapist conveys how the child's responses might be improved. The therapist may model what the child has done and show the child how the action might be done differently. The child again enacts the desired behaviors. If they are appropriate, the therapist provides social reinforcement. The general

sequence is continued until the child's responses are appropriate in particular situations and across a large number of different situations.

Illustration

As an example, Elder, Edelstein, and Narick (1979) used SST with four adolescents who had been hospitalized (from 2 months to 5 years). Each had a history of verbal and physical aggressiveness. Based on the behavior checklist ratings and interviews with the youths, the following behaviors were selected for treatment: interrupting others, responding to negative provocation, and making requests of others. Role-play situations were devised in which training was conducted. Training was carried out in a group in which each person had an opportunity to role-play and to observe others enacting the situation. Treatment was evaluated in a multiple-baseline design in which the behaviors were trained in sequence by using instructions, modeling, practice, and feedback, as highlighted earlier. SST altered the specific skills that were trained; improvements were also associated with increases in social behaviors on the ward and with decreases in the frequency of seclusion for inappropriate behavior. Three of the four subjects were discharged and maintained their gains up to 9 months later.

Evaluation

Several studies have demonstrated that social skills can be developed in aggressive and conduct problem children and adolescents (Kazdin, 1985). In such studies, the focus is usually on specific behaviors in simulated social situations. These behaviors include hostile tone of voice, eye contact, content of verbal statements, making appropriate requests of others, and responding appropriately to unreasonable requests. Evidence for effectiveness of training with conduct problem children comes mainly from studies with small samples of only one or a few children. Also, the effects of SST on ad-

TABLE 17.2   Interpersonal cognitive problem-solving skills

1. **Alternative solution thinking**—the ability to generate different options (solutions) that can solve problems in interpersonal situations.

2. **Means-end thinking**—the awareness of the intermediate steps required to achieve a particular goal.

3. **Consequential thinking**—the ability to identify what might happen as a direct result of acting in a particular way or choosing a particular solution.

4. **Causal thinking**—the ability to relate one event to another over time and to understand why one event led to a particular action from another person.

5. **Sensitivity to interpersonal problems**—the ability to perceive a problem when it exists and to identify the interpersonal aspects of the confrontation that may emerge.

SOURCE: adapted from Spivack, Platt, & Shure (1976).

justment in the community and over the course of follow-up have infrequently been evaluated (Gross, Brigham, Hopper, & Bologna, 1980). Thus, apart from changes in highly specific behaviors within the treatment setting, the therapeutic impact is difficult to evaluate. It is generally accepted that conduct-disordered youths have limited social skills. However, the identification of a small set of circumscribed behaviors may be insufficient to address the breadth of dysfunction that such youths show, as outlined earlier in the chapter.

Problem-Solving Skills Training

Several interventions have focused on the child's cognitive processes (perceptions, self-statements, attributions, and problem-solving skills) that are presumed to underlie maladaptive behavior. Cognitive processes are frequently accorded a major role in aggressive behavior (Rubin, Bream, & Rose-Krasnor, 1991; Shirk, 1988). Aggression is not merely triggered by environmental events, but rather through the way in which these events are perceived and processed. The processing refers to the child's appraisals of the situation, anticipated reactions of others, and self-statements in response to particular events. Clinic and nonreferred children

identified as aggressive have shown a predisposition to attribute hostile intent to others, especially in social situations where the cues of actual intent are ambiguous (Dodge, 1985). Understandably, when situations are initially perceived as hostile, children are more likely to react aggressively. The ability to take the perspective of, or to empathize with, other persons is also related to aggressive behavior (Ellis, 1982; Feshbach, 1975).

The relation between cognitive processes and behavioral adjustment has been evaluated extensively by Spivack and Shure (1982; Shure & Spivack, 1978; Spivack, Platt, & Shure, 1976). These investigators have identified different cognitive processes or interpersonal cognitive problem-solving skills that underlie social behavior (see Table 17.2). The ability to engage in these processes is related to behavioral adjustment, as measured, for example, in teacher ratings of disruptive behavior and social withdrawal. Disturbed children tend to generate fewer alternative solutions to interpersonal problems; focus on ends or goals rather than the intermediate steps to obtain them; see fewer consequences associated with their behavior; fail to recognize the causes of other people's behavior; and be less sensitive to interpersonal conflict.

Problem-solving skills training (PSST) consists of developing interpersonal problem-solving skills in which conduct problem children are considered to be deficient. Many variations of PSST have been applied to conduct problem children (Camp & Bash, 1985; Kendall & Braswell, 1985; Spivack et al., 1976). The variations share many characteristics. First, the emphasis is on *how* children approach situations. Although it is obviously important that children ultimately select appropriate means of behaving in everyday life, the primary focus is on the thought *processes* rather than the *outcome* or specific behavioral acts that result. Second, children are taught to engage in a step-by-step approach to solve interpersonal problems. They make statements to themselves that direct attention to certain aspects of the problem or tasks that lead to effective solutions. Third, treatment utilizes structured tasks involving games, academic activities, and stories. Over the course of treatment, the cognitive problem-solving skills are increasingly applied to real-life situations. Fourth, the therapist usually plays an active role in treatment. He or she models the cognitive processes by making verbal self-statements, applies the sequence of statements to particular problems, provides cues to prompt use of the skills, and delivers feedback and praise to develop correct use of the skills. Finally, treatment usually combines several different procedures, including modeling and practice, role-playing, and reinforcement and mild punishment (loss of points or tokens).

Case Study

The application of PSST can be illustrated more concretely in a case application. Cory was a 10-year-old boy who was hospitalized on a short-term children's inpatient unit. He was hospitalized to begin a treatment regimen designed to control his aggressive and disruptive behavior at home and at school. At home, Cory constantly fought with his siblings, stole personal possessions of all family members, swore,

disobeyed family rules, and refused to participate in family activities. He had been caught on three occasions playing with matches and setting fires in his room. At school, Cory had been in fights with several of his peers in class. He threatened peers, ran around the classroom throwing crayons and pencils as if they were darts, and hit the teacher with various toys and supplies. Before coming for treatment, he was suspended from school for assaulting a classmate and choking him to the point that the child almost passed out.

PSST was begun and completed while Cory was in the hospital, because his parents said they could not return for treatment on an outpatient basis once hospitalization ended. Cory received 20 individual sessions of PSST with 2–3 sessions each week. The treatment was administered by a social worker with special training in PSST. The treatment sessions began by teaching Cory the problem-solving steps. These consist of specific self-statements, with each statement representing a step for solving a problem. The steps or self-statements include:

1. What am I supposed to do?
2. I have to look at all my possibilities.
3. I have to concentrate and focus.
4. I need to make a choice and select a solution.
5. I need to find out how I did.

In the first session, Cory was taught the steps so they could be recalled without special reminders or cues from the therapist. In the next several sessions, the steps were applied to simple problems involving various academic tasks (e.g., arithmetic problems) and board games (e.g., checkers). In each of these sessions, Cory's task was to identify the goal, the alternative choices or options and their consequences, the best choice in light of these consequences, and so on. In the sessions, Cory and the therapist took turns using the steps to work on the task. In these early sessions, the focus was on teaching the steps and training Cory to become facile in applying them to diverse but relatively simple situations. After Session 8, the games were withdrawn, and the steps were applied to problems that were related to interactions with parents, teachers, siblings, peers, and others.

Cory was also given assignments outside of treatment. The assignments initially were to identify "real" problems (e.g., with another child on the inpatient service) where he could use the steps. When he brought one of these situations to the session, he described how the steps could have been used. He earned points for bringing in such a situation and these points could be exchanged for small prizes. As the sessions progressed, he received points not only for thinking of situations outside of treatment but also for using the steps in the actual situations. His use of the steps was checked by asking him exactly what he did, role-playing the situation within the session, and asking other staff on the ward if the events were accurate.

The majority of treatment consisted of applying the steps in the session to situations where Cory's aggressive and antisocial behaviors have emerged. To illustrate how this proceeds, a portion of Session 17 follows:

Therapist: Well, Cory today we are going to act out some more problem situations by using the steps. You have been doing so well with this that I think we can use the steps today in a way that will make it even easier to use them in everyday life. When you use the steps today, I want you to think in your mind what the first steps are. When you get to Step 4, say that one out loud before you do it. This will let us see what the solution is that you have chosen. Then, Step 5, when you evaluate how you did, can also be thought in your mind. We are going to do the steps in our heads today like this so that it will be easier to use them in everyday life without drawing attention to what we are doing. The same rules apply as in our other sessions. We still want to go slowly in using the steps and we want to select good solutions.

OK, today I brought in a lot of difficult situations. I think it is going to be hard to use the steps. Let's see how each of us does. I have six stacks of cards here. You can see the stacks are numbered from 1 to 6. We will take turns rolling the die and take a card from the stack with the same number. As we did in the last session, we are going to solve the problem as we sit here, then we will get up and act it out as if it is really happening. OK, why don't you go first and roll the die.

Cory: (rolls the die) I got a 4.

Therapist: O.K. Read the top card in that stack (therapist points to fourth stack).

Cory: (reads the card) "The principal of your school is walking past you in the hall between classes when he notices some candy wrappers that someone has dropped on the floor. The principal turns to you and says in a pretty tough voice, "Cory, we don't litter in the halls at this school! Now pick up the trash!'"

Therapist: This is a tough one—how are you going to handle this?

Cory: Well, here goes with the steps. (Cory holds his first finger up and appears to be saying Step 1 to himself; he does this with Steps 2 and 3 as well. When he gets to Step 4 he speaks out loud.) I would say to him that I did not throw the wrappers down and I would keep walking.

Therapist: Well, it was *great* that you did not get mad and talk back to him. He was sort of accusing you and you hadn't really thrown the papers down. But, if you just say, "I didn't do it," and walk away, what might happen?

Cory: Nothing. Because I *didn't* do it.

Therapist: Yeah, but he may not believe you—maybe especially because you got into trouble before with him. Also, he asked you for a favor and you could help a lot by doing what he asked. Try going through the steps again and see if you can turn your pretty good solution into a great one.

Cory: (goes through Steps 1, 2, and 3 again; at Step 4 he speaks) I would say to him that I did not throw the wrappers down, but that I would gladly pick 'em up and toss them in the trash.

Therapist: (with great enthusiasm) That's great—that's a wonderful solution! O.K. Go to Step 5, how do you think you did.

Cory: I did good because I used the steps.

Therapist: That's right but you did more than that. You nicely told the principal that you did not do it *and* you did the favor he asked. What do you think he will think of you in the future? Very nicely done. O.K. Now let's both get up and act this out. I am the principal. Why don't you stand over there (pointing to the opposite corner of the treatment room). O.K. let's start. "Hey, Cory, pick up those wrappers on the floor. You are not supposed to litter in the halls. You know better than that."

Cory: (carries out Steps 1, 2, and 3 in his head. At Step 4 he acts out the step directly in face-to-face interaction with the principal [therapist] and speaks.) "Mr. Putnam, I didn't throw these on the floor, but if you want I will pick them up and toss them in the trash."

Therapist: (acting as principal) Yeah, that would be great. Thanks for helping out; these kids make a mess of this place.

Therapist: (as herself). Well, Cory how do you think you did?

Cory: Pretty good, because I used the steps and got a good solution.

Therapist: (as herself). I think you did great! The treatment session continues like this with a variety of situations. When the child does especially well, the situation may be made a little more difficult or provocative to help him apply the steps under more challenging circumstances.

Evaluation

Several studies have shown that cognitively based interventions can alter the behavior of aggressive and antisocial youths (see Baer & Nietzel, 1991; Durlak, Fuhrman, & Lampman, 1991, for reviews). In several studies with impulsive or aggressive children and adolescents, cognitively based treatment has led to significant changes in behavior at home, at school, and in the community, with gains evident up to 1 year later (Arbuthnot & Gordon, 1986; Kazdin, Esveldt-Dawson, French, & Unis, 1987, Kazdin et al., 1989; Kendall & Braswell, 1982; Lochman, Burch, Curry, & Lampron, 1984). However, the magnitude of the changes needs to be greater than those currently achieved to return children to normative or adaptive levels of functioning at home and at school. Some evidence has suggested that older children may respond better than younger children, possibly due to the higher level of cognitive development of older children (Durlak et al., 1991). Duration of treatment has influenced outcome in one study with longer treatment (more than 18 sessions) leading to greater change than shorter treatment (Lochman, 1985). In general, the factors that contribute to treatment outcome have been infrequently studied in the treatment of aggressive children.

Parent Management Training

Parent management training (PMT) refers to procedures in which a parent or parents are trained to interact differently with their children. Research has shown that parents of conduct problem children, particularly those with aggressive behavior, engage in several practices that promote antisocial behavior and suppress prosocial behavior (Patterson, 1982). These practices include the inadvertent and direct reinforcement of aggressive behavior, frequent use of commands, nonreinforcement of prosocial behaviors, and others. PMT alters the pattern of interchanges between parent and child so that prosocial, rather than aggressive, behavior is directly fostered within the family.

Although many variations of PMT exist, several common characteristics can be identified. First, treatment is conducted primarily with the parent(s) who directly implement several procedures in the home. There usually is no direct intervention of the therapist with the child. Second, parents are trained to identify, define, and observe problem behavior in new ways. The careful specification of the problem is essential for the delivery of reinforcing or punishing consequences and for evaluating whether the program is achieving the desired goals. Third, the treatment sessions cover social learning principles and the procedures that follow from them, including positive reinforcement (e.g., the use of social praise and tokens or points for prosocial behavior), mild punishment (e.g., use of time-out from reinforcement, loss of privileges), negotiation, and contingency contracting. Fourth, the sessions provide opportunities for parents to see how the techniques are implemented, to practice using the techniques, and to review the behavior-change programs in the home.

The immediate goal of the program is to develop specific skills in the parents. This is usually achieved by having parents apply their skills to relatively simple behaviors that can be easily observed and that are not enmeshed with more provoking interactions (e.g., punishment, battles of the will, coercive interchanges). As the parents become more proficient, the program can address the child's most severely problematic behaviors and encompass other problem areas (e.g., school behavior).

Case Illustration

The application of PMT can be illustrated by a case of a 7-year-old boy named Shawn, who was referred for treatment because of his aggressive outbursts toward his two younger sisters at home and his peers at school. He argued and had severe tantrums at home, stayed out late at night, and occasionally stole from his mother's live-in boyfriend. At school, his behavior in class was difficult to control. He fought with peers, argued with the teacher, and disrupted the class. PMT was provided to the mother. The boyfriend was unable to attend the meetings regularly, due to his work as a trucker and his extended periods away from the home. Training began by discussing Shawn's behavior and describing child-rearing practices that might be useful in developing prosocial behavior as well as reducing or eliminating the problems for which he was referred.

A clinician with a master's degree, trained in PMT for over 2 years, met with the parents once each week for approximately 16 sessions. The overall goal of treatment was to train the parents to behave differently in relation to Shawn and their other children. Specifically, they were to be trained to identify concrete behaviors to target, to observe these behaviors systematically, to implement positive reinforcement programs, to provide mild punishment as needed, and to negotiate such programs directly with the child.

The contents of the 16 sessions provided to the parent(s) are highlighted in the box below. Each session lasted about 2 hours. In each session, the therapist reviewed the previous week's observations and implementation of the program. The purpose was to identify how the parents behaved in relation to their children. Queries were made to review precisely what the parents did (e.g., praise, administer points or tokens, send the child to time-out) in response to the child's behavior. Although the mother would invariably focus on the behavior of the child and how well or poorly the child was doing, the therapist directed the conversation toward the behaviors that she performed in relation to the child. The therapist and parent(s) role-played situations at home in which the parent might have responded more effectively. Parents practiced delivering the consequences and received feedback and reinforcement for this behavior from the therapist. Any problems in the programs, ambiguity of the observation procedures, or other facets were discussed. Thus, each session began with a review of practical issues and applications of the previous week. After the program was reviewed, new material was taught, as indicated in the box that follows.

Parent Management Training
Sessions for the Case of Shawn

Session Number, Topic, and Brief Description

1. Introduction and overview. This session provides the parents with an overview of the program and outlines the demands placed upon them and the focus of the intervention.

2. Defining and observing. Parents are trained to pinpoint, define, and observe behavior. The parents and trainer define specific problems that can be observed and develop a specific plan to begin observations.

3. Positive reinforcement. The focus is on learning the concept of positive reinforcement, factors that contribute to the effective application, and rehearsal of applications in relation to the target child. Specific programs are outlined for praise and points to be provided for the behaviors observed during the week.

4. Review of the program and data. Observations of the previous week and application of the reinforcement program are reviewed. Details about the administration of praise, points, and back-up reinforcers are discussed and enacted as needed, so the trainer can identify how to improve parent performance. Changes are made in the program as needed.

5. Time-out from reinforcement. Parents learn about time-out and the factors related to its effective application. The use of time-out is planned for the next week for specific behaviors.

6. Shaping. Parents are trained to develop behaviors by reinforcement of successive approximations and to use prompts and fading of prompts to develop terminal behaviors.

7. Review and problem solving. The concepts discussed in all prior sessions are thoroughly reviewed. The parent is asked to apply these concepts to hypothetical situations presented in the session. Areas of weakness in understanding the concepts or their execution in practice serve as the focus.

8. Attending and ignoring. Parents learn about attending and ignoring, and chose undesirable behavior that they will ignore and a positive opposite behavior to which they will attend. These procedures are practiced in the session.

9. School intervention. Plans are made to implement a home-based reinforcement program to develop school-related behaviors. Prior to this session, discussions with the teachers and parents have identified specific behaviors to focus on in class (e.g., deportment) and at home (e.g., homework completion). These behaviors are incorporated into the reinforcement system.

10. Reprimands. Parents are trained in effective use of reprimands.

11. Family meeting. The child and parent(s) are brought into the session. The programs are discussed, along with any problems. Revisions are made as needed to correct misunderstandings or to alter facets that may not have been implemented in a way that is likely to be effective.

12. Review of skills. Here the programs are reviewed along with all concepts about the principles. Parents are asked to develop programs for a variety of hypothetical everyday problems at home and at school. Feedback is provided about program options and applications.

13. Negotiating and contracting. The child and parent meet together to negotiate new behavioral programs and to place these in contractual form.

14. **Low-rate behaviors.** Parents are trained to deal with low-rate behaviors such as firesetting, stealing, or truancy. Specific punishment programs are planned and presented to the child as needed for behaviors characteristic of the case.

15, 16, & 17. **Review, problem solving, and practice.** Material from other sessions is reviewed in theory and practice. Special emphasis is given to role-playing application of individual principles as they are enacted with the trainer. Parents practice designing new programs, revising ailing programs, and responding to a complex array of situations in which principles and practices discussed in prior sessions are reviewed.

Between the weekly sessions, the therapist called the parents on two occasions to find out how the programs were working and to handle problems that arose. The calls between sessions were designed to correct problems immediately instead of waiting until a week elapsed. Shawn's mother and the therapist developed a program to increase Shawn's compliance with requests. Simple chores were requested (e.g., cleaning his room, setting the table) in the first few weeks of the program, to help the parents apply what they had learned. Time-out from reinforcement was introduced to provide mild punishment for fighting. Any fights in the home resulted in Shawn going to an isolated place in the hall near the kitchen of his home for a period of 5 minutes. If he went to time-out immediately upon instructions from his mother or her boyfriend, the duration of time-out was automatically reduced to 2 minutes. This immediate reduction was designed to reinforce compliance with the request to go to time-out.

Over time, several behaviors were incorporated into a program where Shawn earned points that could purchase special privileges (e.g., staying up 15 minutes beyond bedtime, having a friend sleep over, small prizes, time to play his video game). About halfway through treatment, a home-based reinforcement program was developed to alter behaviors at school. Two teachers at the school were contacted and asked to identify behaviors to be developed in class. The program was explained and they were asked to initial cards that Shawn carried to indicate how well he behaved in class and whether he completed his homework. Based on daily teacher evaluations, Shawn earned additional points at home.

After approximately 5 months, Shawn had improved greatly in his behavior at home. He argued very little with his mother and sisters. His parents felt they were much better able to manage him. At school, Shawn's teachers reported that he could remain in class like other children. Occasionally, he would not listen to the teacher or precipitated heated arguments with his peers. However, he was less physically aggressive than he had been prior to treatment.

Evaluation

The effectiveness of PMT has been evaluated extensively with behavior problem children varying in age and degree of severity of dysfunction (Kazdin, 1987b; McMahon & Wells, 1989; Miller & Prinz, 1990). Several controlled studies have demonstrated improvements in child behavior at home and at school over the course of treatment. Moreover, these changes surpass those achieved with variations of family-based psychotherapy, attention-placebo (discussion), and no-treatment conditions. PMT has brought the problematic behaviors of treated children within normative levels of their peers who are functioning adequately. Improvements often remain evident a year after treatment (Fleischman & Szykula, 1981); the continued benefits of treatment have been evident with noncompliant children up to 4.5 years (Baum & Forehand, 1981) and 10 years later (Forehand & Long, 1988). The impact of PMT has also been reflected beyond the target child. Siblings improve, even though they are not directly focused on during treatment. In addition, maternal psychopathology, particularly depression, decreases systematically following PMT. These changes suggest that PMT can alter multiple aspects of dysfunctional families (Kazdin, 1985).

Several characteristics of treatment administration contribute to outcome, including the duration of treatment, providing parents with indepth knowledge of social-learning principles, and utilizing time-out from reinforcement in the home (Kazdin, 1987b). Parent and family characteristics also relate to treatment outcome. As might be expected, families characterized by multiple risk factors associated with childhood dysfunction (e.g., marital discord, parent psychopathology, social isolation, and socioeconomic disadvantage) tend to show fewer gains in treatment and are less likely to maintain therapeutic gains (Dumas & Wahler, 1983; Strain, Young, & Horowitz, 1981). Thus, variables beyond the specific parent-child interactions must be considered in treatment.

Many issues regarding the effects of PMT remain. The treatment cannot be applied to many cases of conduct problem children in need of treatment. The requirement of active participation on the part of a parent makes the treatment inapplicable to some cases where parent dysfunction and unwillingness cannot be surmounted. In cases where treatment can be applied, further follow-up data are needed. With antisocial youths referred for aggressive behavior, follow-up typically has been completed up to one year. Given the recalcitrance of severe antisocial behavior, evidence is needed to assess the long-term impact. Notwithstanding the potential limitations, PMT is one of the better-developed and researched therapies for aggressive child behavior.

Functional Family Therapy

Functional family therapy (FFT) reflects an integrative approach to treatment that has relied on a systems and behavioral view of dysfunction. Clinical problems are conceptualized from the standpoint of the functions they serve in the family as a system, as well as for individual family members. The assumption is made that problem behavior evident in the child is the only way some interpersonal functions (e.g., intimacy, distancing, support) can be met among family members. Maladaptive processes within the family are considered to preclude a more direct means of fulfilling these functions. The goal of treatment is to alter interaction and communication patterns in such a way as to foster more adaptive functioning. Treatment is also based on learning theory and focuses on specific stimuli and responses that can be used to produce change. Identification of specific target behaviors, reinforcement of new, adaptive ways of responding, and empirical evaluation and monitoring of change are included in this perspective. More recent formulations of FFT have added cognitive processes to broaden the focus (Morris, Alexander, & Waldron, 1990). This perspective focuses on the attributions, attitudes, assumptions, expectations, and emotions of the family. Family members may begin treatment with attributions that focus on blaming others or themselves. New perspectives may be needed to serve as the basis for developing new ways of behaving.

FFT requires that the family see the clinical problem from the relational functions it serves within the family. The therapist points out interdependencies and contingencies between family members in their day-to-day functioning, with specific reference to the problem that has served as the basis for seeking treatment. Once the family sees alternative ways of viewing the problem, the incentive for interacting more constructively is increased.

The main goals of treatment are to increase

reciprocity and positive reinforcement among family members, establish clear communication, specify behaviors that family members desire from each other, teach family members to negotiate constructively, and help identify solutions to interpersonal problems. The family members read a manual that describes social learning principles, to develop familiarity with the concepts used in treatment. In therapy, family members identify behaviors they would like others to perform. Responses are incorporated into a reinforcement system in the home, to promote adaptive behavior in exchange for privileges. However, the primary focus is within the treatment sessions where family communication patterns are altered directly. During the sessions, the therapist provides social reinforcement (verbal and nonverbal praise) for communications that suggest solutions to problems, clarify problems, or offer feedback to other family members.

Illustration

The technique requires understanding of several types of functions that behaviors can serve within the family.[2] These include behaviors that family members perform to sustain contact and closeness (merging), to decrease psychological intensity and dependence (separating), and to provide a mixture of merging and separating (midpointing). These processes are intricate because they usually involve the relations of all family members with each other. Also, the behaviors of a given family member may serve multiple and opposing functions in relation to different individuals within the family. Thus, a behavior that draws one family member close

may distance another member. Finally, several different behaviors (e.g., a child fighting with a sibling, getting into trouble at school, running away from home overnight) may serve similar functions (e.g., bringing the mother and father together).

During the course of treatment, all family members meet. The focus of treatment is to identify consistent patterns of behavior, the range of functions they serve, and messages they send. A number of specific techniques that can be used to focus on relations in therapy are used. The specific techniques, goals, and illustrations are presented in Table 17.3.

A number of other strategies are employed during the course of treatment. These include not blaming individuals; relabeling thoughts, feelings, and behaviors to take into account relational components; discussing the implications of symptom removal; changing the context of the symptom to help alter the functions it may have served; and shifting the focus from one problem or person to another. FFT is not designed merely to identify functional relations but also to build new and more adaptive ways of functioning. Communication patterns are altered and efforts are made to provide families with concrete ways of behaving differently, both in the sessions and at home (Alexander & Parsons, 1982).

Evaluation

The few available outcome studies of FFT have shown relatively clear effects. The initial study included male and female delinquent adolescents referred to juvenile court for such behaviors as running away, truancy, theft, and unmanageability (Alexander & Parsons, 1973). Cases were assigned to FFT, an attention-placebo condition (group discussion and expression of feeling), or a no-treatment control group. Posttreatment evaluation, following 8 treatment sessions, revealed that FFT led to greater discussion among family members, more equitable

---

[2] An illustration of the entire process of FFT is difficult to convey because of the complex set of techniques, their relation to the nature of family functioning, and their dependence on individual features of the family. The technique is well illustrated elsewhere and guidelines are provided for therapists (Alexander & Parsons, 1982). Selected features of the techniques can be described and illustrated to convey the manner in which the technique operates.

TABLE 17.3   Selected therapy techniques in functional family therapy

Technique	Goal

Asking questions—To help focus on the relationship raised by the issue or problem.

Example: After a description of an event involving the child (named Ginger) and the mother, the therapist may ask the father, "How do you fit into all of this?"

Making comments—To help identify and clarify relationships.

Example: The therapist may say to the father, "So you are drawn into this argument when your wife gets upset?"

Offering interpretations—To go beyond the obvious observations by inferring possible motivational states, effects on others, and antecedents.

Example: The therapist may say, "So when you have an argument, you believe that this is a message that you are needed, but at the same time, you feel pushed away."

Identifying sequences—To point to the relations among sequences or patterns of behavior so as to see more complex effects of interactions, such as several functional relations over time.

Example: The therapist says (to mother), "It seems to me that the argument between Ginger and you makes both you and your husband upset. This leads to everyone arguing for awhile about who did what and what has to be done, and no one agrees;" (to mother and father), "After the dust settles, you both have something to talk about and to work on. This brings you both together at least for a little while;" (to Ginger) This may help you a lot, too, Ginger, because you don't get to see your mother and father talking together like this very often."

Using the therapist as a direct tool—To have the therapist refer to his or her relation to the family within the session and speculate on what functions this could serve.

Example: The therapist says, "I feel as if I am still being asked to choose sides here because I may serve a function similar to the one that Ginger serves: to help bring you two together. That's not good or bad, but we need to see how we can get you two together when there is no argument or battle with a third party.

Stopping and starting interaction—To intervene to alter interactions between or among family members. The purpose may be to induce new lines of communication, to develop relations between members not initiating contact, or to point out functions evident at the moment.

Example: The therapist says to Ginger and father, "What do you two have to say about the effect that this has on each of you?" (The mother is not asked to comment here).

---

speaking, and more spontaneous speech than did the attention-placebo and no-treatment conditions.

In an extension of the program, Alexander and Parsons (1973) compared FFT, client-centered family groups, psychodynamically oriented family therapy, and no treatment. The FFT group showed greater improvement on family interaction measures and lower recidivism rates from juvenile court records up to 18 months after treatment. Follow-up data obtained $2\frac{1}{2}$ years later indicated that the siblings of those who received FFT showed significantly lower rates of referral to juvenile courts (Klein, Alexander, & Parsons, 1977). Thus, the results suggest significant changes in both target children and their siblings.

FFT shows obvious promise, notwithstanding the paucity of studies and independent replication attempts. From the few available studies, several statements can be supported. First, the effectiveness of treatment is influenced by the relationship (e.g., warmth, integration of affect and behavior) and structuring (e.g., directiveness) skills of the therapist (Alexander, Barton, Schiavo, & Parsons, 1976). Second, process measures of family interactions at posttreatment are related to subsequent recidivism (Alexander & Parsons, 1973). This finding lends credence to the model from which treatment was derived. Finally, in the outcome studies, client-centered and psychodynamically oriented forms of family-based therapies have not achieved the positive effects of FFT. Thus, treatment of the clinical problem at the level of the family does not appear to be sufficient per se to alter antisocial behavior.

Combined Treatments

The discussion has highlighted selected treatments for conduct problems, to illustrate behavioral interventions and their effects. The focus on specific, concrete behaviors (social skills training) or cognitive processes that underlie behavior (problem-solving skills training) illustrates treatment that is usually conducted in individual treatment sessions with the child. The approach with parents (parent management training) or families as a whole (functional family therapy) conveys a broader focus in which the child may or may not play a major part. Finally, other interventions (operant conditioning techniques) often make an effort to restructure contingencies in diverse settings in which the child functions, including home, school, community, and institutional settings.

Individual treatment techniques address specific facets of conduct disorder. It is possible that altering one area of functioning (e.g., social skills, problem-solving skills) has extended effects. However, conduct disorder is a pervasive dysfunction in the sense that for many children a variety of domains are deleteriously affected. Deviant behavior (aggression), poor peer relations (rejection from peers), academic dysfunction, maladaptive child-rearing practices of the families, and so on are commonly associated with conduct disorder. This has led investiga-

tors to ponder the value of combining various treatments that have shown promise as individual treatment techniques.

For example, as highlighted previously, problem-solving skills training and parent management training have reduced aggression and antisocial behavior in conduct problem children. Among the concerns is that the impact of treatment should be augmented in terms of greater change for individuals and to affect a larger proportion of treated individuals. The combination of problem-solving skills training and parent management training is a viable option because the treatments address different facets of conduct disorder. Recent evidence suggests that the combination of these treatments surpasses the impact of the individual treatments (Kazdin, Siegel, & Bass, 1992). Combinations of treatments known to affect different facets of conduct disorder may be primary candidates for research. However, insufficient research is available at present to argue for particular combinations or to suggest that they genuinely improve long-term outcomes.

ISSUES AND LIMITATIONS

Behavior modification encompasses a variety of treatments applied to many different clinical problems. The strength of the outcome evidence cannot be captured by general statements regarding individual or combined techniques. The accretion of a body of evidence and continued focus on research are critical features that will help to generate the types of impact needed in clinical care. A number of issues are noteworthy in relation to the development of effective treatments. Already mentioned was the need for long-term follow-up evaluation of treatments that have been shown to produce change. Several other issues can be identified as critical to further development of behavioral treatments.

Understanding Dysfunction

Behavioral treatments begin with the assumption that many dysfunctions and problematic behaviors can be altered by providing learning experiences. The amenability to change of many clinical dysfunctions supports this assumption as a general point of departure. However, a long-term investment in developing effective treatments requires understanding of the determinants of disorder and the points at which intervention is likely to be effective. Theoretical views and alternative models of dysfunction should be developed and tested. Broad views of disorder derived from a single conceptual model (e.g., psychodynamic, learning) focus attention on important levels of understanding. However, their breadth has often limited the ability to generate testable hypotheses regarding the development of specific disorders.

Within contemporary research, there is an effort to develop models of dysfunction that address the relation of specific influences and how these influences may operate to produce clinical dysfunction. These efforts might be referred to as mini-models because they consider a circumscribed set of influences and their effects. Because they are restricted in scope, such models are more likely to provide testable hypotheses to illuminate the emergence, course, and influences of specific types of disorders. The development of mini-models of dysfunction has profited from the use of alternative statistical techniques such as path analysis and structural equation modeling. The analyses provide useful tools to test hypotheses about concurrent and longitudinal influences and the interrelations among diverse domains of influence that might be operating simultaneously (Newcomb & Bentler, 1988).

For example, family influences on the development of antisocial behavior have been elaborated by Patterson and his colleagues (Patterson, 1986; Patterson, Capaldi, & Bank, 1991). Models have been developed to explain how parents unwittingly train antisocial behavior in the home; the impact of the child's coercive interactions and noncompliance on self-esteem, peer relations, and academic performance; and the impact of stressors on maternal discipline practices. Evaluation of one of the models, for example, has suggested that inept discipline practices and coercive parent-child interactions escalate and foster increasingly aggressive child behavior. The model has had direct implications for intervention by suggesting ways of altering coercive processes in the home to reduce aggressive child behavior.

Other researchers have evaluated models to identify factors that contribute to antisocial behavior. For example, to identify critical paths toward deviance, Newcomb and Bentler (1988) examined the consequences of drug use during adolescence on young adulthood. Several domains of functioning were assessed (e.g., drug use, social conformity, criminal activity, deviant peer networks). During adolescence, teen drug use was related to lower social conformity, greater criminal activity, and a deviant friendship network. Early drug use was related in later years to reduction in academic pursuits (less involvement in college), job instability (unemployment, being fired), and increased psychoticism (e.g., disorganized thought processes). Evaluating the relations among different domains and their paths leading to deviance has implications for designing interventions. For example, for many youths an intervention devoted to drug use alone might not be optimally effective because drug use often reflects a life-style that involves deviant attitudes and behavior in other areas.

These illustrations convey the importance of basic research on the characteristics and development of antisocial behavior. Antecedents of antisocial behavior and the constellation of characteristics that accompanies antisocial behavior provide leads for treatment. Treatments can focus on the central characteristics that predict long-term consequences. Also, early antecedents of antisocial behavior might be altered in an effort to prevent antisocial behavior among adolescents. Hence, basic research aids both treatment and prevention efforts.

Classification of Dysfunction

Behavior modification focuses primarily on the presenting problems, often at the level of individual symptoms. A limitation resulting from this approach has been the absence of a consistent way of delineating and diagnosing child and adolescent dysfunction. This limitation has led to the accumulation of the kind of research in which the sample to whom treatment has been applied is not always clear. Ironically, the assessment of child dysfunction before, during, and after treatment is often exemplary in terms of the usual assessment desiderata (e.g., the use of multiple measures from multiple domains, assessment over time) (Mash & Terdal, 1988). At the same time, no uniform methods of diagnostic assessment are systematically used to permit communication of characteristics in a consistent way.

Proponents of behavioral techniques have eschewed psychiatric diagnosis, due in large part to the conceptual models on which early versions of contemporary diagnosis (e.g., DSM-I, DSM-II) were based. Contemporary diagnosis (e.g., DSM-III, DSM-III-R) emphasizes the presenting symptoms rather than presumed etiologies and would make the use of diagnosis compatible with behavioral methods (Kazdin, 1983). Nevertheless, there has been reluctance to draw upon contemporary diagnosis as a way of describing samples included in treatment research or to develop an alternative diagnostic system that could serve as a way to compare samples across studies.

The failure of behavioral research to adopt a standard method of defining child populations and to assess the range of their dysfunction (e.g., across multiple axes) has had consequences for developing the knowledge base on the treatment of child and adolescent disorders.

The accumulation of a knowledge base has been hampered by difficulties in discerning the nature of the sample and the characteristics of their clinical dysfunction. For example, in much of the literature, behavioral treatments focus on emotional and disruptive behavior disorders. The terms used to describe the sample are often varied (e.g., social skills deficits, impulsive children, conduct problems). The same term used in different studies has little consistent meaning; within a study the level of impairment is often unclear. In such cases, the absence of diagnostic information or standardized assessment raises ambiguities regarding the range, severity, and duration of clinical impairment.

Psychiatric diagnosis is only one means to convey the level, type, and severity of clinical dysfunction. Diagnosis does not resolve many issues in the search for consistencies in delineating dysfunction, because the diagnostic criteria have undergone periodic revisions. An alternative is to use standardized measures such as parent and teacher checklists. For example, the Child Behavior Checklist (Achenbach & Edelbrock, 1983) assesses multiple symptom domains, broad scales (internalizing, externalizing), and prosocial behavior (participation in activities, social interaction, progress at school). The measure permits evaluation of these characteristics in relation to same-age peers functioning adequately in everyday life. The normative basis of this and similar measures also would be helpful for better definition of the treated population. At this time, a basic priority is the need to specify operationally and in more detail the nature of the child's dysfunction. Better specification may help identify the children for whom treatments will be effective.

Focusing on the Constellation of Behaviors

An important issue for many behavioral interventions is the focus of treatment. Often one or two salient behaviors serve as the target. A demonstration that behavior such as fighting in the classroom or obeying parents at home is altered dramatically is noteworthy. Decreases in classroom fighting are important. However, additional assessment is needed to evaluate functioning in class (e.g., deportment or other measures, academic functioning), at home (e.g., compliance with parents, interactions with others), and in the community (e.g., staying out over night, stealing with peers). Effectively altering one or a few behaviors, although impressive, may have no clear impact on the overall functioning of the child in other relevant behaviors and situations.

The matter of constellations of behavior raises questions for research. There is broad agreement on the findings that clinical problems (symptoms) come in packages. The co-occurrence of symptoms is part of a broader phenomenon in which behaviors, whether or not they are symptoms, tend to occur in clusters (Kazdin, 1982; Voeltz & Evans, 1982). The organization of behaviors, how they emerge as clusters, how these clusters change across situations and over time, and where to intervene to optimize behavior change remain to be evaluated. The focus on clusters of behavior has been an important topic of research within behavior modification. For example, Wahler (1975) carefully observed children over extended periods in the home and at school and elaborated the nature of clusters of behaviors. In a number of studies, he found that groups of specific behaviors consistently occur together. As an illustration, for one child, behaviors such as engaging in self-stimulation, socially interacting with adults, and complying with adult instructions tended to go together. Treatment that focused on one of the behaviors that was part of the cluster altered other behaviors as well. The spread of treatment effects to different behaviors could not be explained by similarity of the behaviors.

The tendency of responses to change together or as a cluster has been referred to as *response co-variation*. The responses co-vary (are correlated and change together). A number of studies have demonstrated that behaviors cluster together and that changing one of the behaviors in the cluster alters other behaviors as well (Kazdin, 1982). At this point, the applied implications of broad clusters have yet to be exploited in the development or application of treatment. However, one study noted that aggressive behavior in a child could be reduced by increasing another behavior (solitary play) with which it was negatively correlated (Wahler & Fox, 1980b). Thus, preliminary evidence suggests that once the correlational patterns of behavior are identified, they can be exploited to produce therapeutic change. Constellations and clusters of behavior are in need of greater attention in general. The focus may be particularly important within behavior modification, where the treatment of concrete and isolated behaviors can neglect broader domains of functioning.

CONCLUSIONS

Behavior modification represents a broad approach to treatment, one that encompasses diverse conceptual views, techniques, and applications. Behavioral treatments share a common commitment to operationalization, assessment, and evaluation. The present chapter has highlighted variations of operant conditioning, social skills training, problem-solving skills training, parent management training, and functional family therapy. These techniques convey the diverse foci in the context of conduct problems.

Each of the techniques has generated reliable changes in child functioning. Interpretation of the effects is obscured in part by issues related to the nature of dysfunction and the current status of the assessment of antisocial behavior. As for the nature of dysfunction, antisocial behavior in children represents a broad complex of behaviors. Many of these relate specifically to conduct disorder (e.g., aggression, truancy). Others are associated features (e.g., academic performance). Evaluation of an intervention requires assessment of manifold domains. Measures of antisocial behavior are not well developed, although progress can be readily identified.

Treatments, behavioral and nonbehavioral, often focus on a particular domain made salient by an approach or narrow conceptual model (e.g., family interaction, cognitive processes). Research on individual models is needed to further the understanding of dysfunction. However, at the level of treatment, clinically referred cases often experience dysfunction in many areas. The focus on domains from one or two models might be expected to effect minimal change. Further work is needed to identify the intervention foci that can affect change for the full scope of the dysfunction.

TREATMENT RESOURCES

Camp, B. W., & Bash, M. A. S. (1985). *Think aloud: Increasing social and cognitive skills—a problem solving program for children*. Champaign, IL: Research Press.

Feindler, E. L., & Ecton, R. B. (1986). *Adolescent anger control: Cognitive-behavioral techniques*. Elmsford, NY: Pergamon.

Forehand, R., & McMahon, R. J. (1981). *Helping the noncompliant child: A clinician's guide to parent training*. New York: Guilford.

Horne, A. M., & Sayger, T. V. (1990). *Treating conduct and oppositional disorders in children*. Elmsford, NY: Pergamon.

Kendall, P. C., & Braswell, L. (1992). *Cognitive-behavioral therapy for impulsive children* (2nd ed). New York: Guilford.

King, C. A., & Kirschenbaum, D. S. (1992). *Helping young children develop social skills*. Pacific Grove, CA: Brooks/Cole.

Michelson, L., Sugai, D. P., Wood, R. P., & Kazdin, A. E. (1983). *Social skills assessment and training with children*. New York: Plenum.

CHAPTER 18

Childhood and Adolescent Depression

W. Edward Craighead
John F. Curry
Donna K. McMillan

Although Spitz described depression among institutionalized infants as early as 1946, little was subsequently written about childhood and adolescent depression until about 1970. This may be attributed to several factors, the most important of which was the prevailing psychoanalytic stance that depression could not occur in an individual who had not developed a mature superego.

During the 1960s, the understanding of the nature and treatment of adult depression advanced enormously as biological psychiatry focused heavily on this topic (Ballenger, 1988). This was followed by the development during the 1970s of several cognitive-behavioral models of adult depression (Craighead, 1980). Both empirical and conceptual advances from these two developments, in contrast to the psychoanalytic viewpoint, allowed for the possible occurrence of depression among children and adolescents. This led to considerable interest in the study of depression among youngsters during the 1970s and especially in the 1980s. Angold (1988) re-

cently concluded that research conducted during the latter time period "has demonstrated without doubt that all of the symptoms of adult depression can and do occur in childhood and adolescence, and . . . they occur quite commonly" (p. 482).

This chapter will review the recent and ongoing research regarding the psychopathology of childhood and adolescent depression. It will also present a description and review of the currently available intervention programs designed to alleviate or ameliorate depression in these age groups.

DEFINING DEPRESSION

The term *depression* can refer to several different but related conditions. As Carlson and Cantwell (1980a) delineated, depression may refer to: (1) a single *symptom* or mood state that in itself must be differentiated from low normal mood or sadness; (2) a set of symptoms or signs that regularly co-occur, which in clinical areas is called a *syndrome;* or (3) a diagnosed, clinical mood *disorder*. The child presenting to an outpatient clinic with persistently sad mood may have the symptom of depression. However, unless that symptom is accompanied by other cognitive (thoughts), affective (feelings), and/or somatic symptoms, which tend to cluster together in a subset of emotionally disturbed children, the child's condition does not imply syndromal depression. To meet diagnostic criteria for a mood disorder, syndromal depression must be part of a broader pattern, involving severity, duration, and course or natural history; in some diagnostic systems there must also be some degree of practical or functional impairment (e.g., the Research Diagnostic Criteria of Spitzer, Endicott, & Robins, 1978). Finally, a condition hypothesized to be a disorder must itself be validated by studies of external criteria. These critieria include family history of the disorder, response to specific treatments, and the specific psychological and/or biological correlates of the disorder.

As Carlson and Cantwell (1980a) reported, these increasingly stringent definitions of what is meant by depression lead to decreasing numbers of children considered to be depressed. In their study of 210 children or adolescents referred for psychiatric treatment, 60% had the symptom of depression, 47% had a significant number of depressive symptoms (syndromal depression), but only 28% met DSM-III criteria for a depressive disorder (American Psychiatric Association [APA], 1980). In the well-known Isle of Wight community epidemiological study, Rutter and his colleagues (Rutter, Tizard, & Whitmore, 1970/1978; Rutter, Graham, Chadwick, & Yule, 1976) reported that 40% of the adolescents at age 14–15 reported substantial feelings of misery and depression and 20% expressed feelings of self-deprecation, but less than 2% received a diagnosis of clinical depression. Although sadness and misery have long been seen in some children referred for

mental health intervention, as noted earlier the existence of syndromal depression and depressive disorders has only recently been recognized, and mood disorders among youths are still in need of considerable validating research (Quay, Routh, & Shapiro, 1987).

Conceptual Viewpoints of Depression

There have been a number of viewpoints about depression, including the view that depression does not even exist among children and adolescents. Carlson and Garber (1986) have outlined five schools of thought regarding the nature of depressive disorders in childhood. The clinician who seeks to study depression in young people and to communicate findings to other mental health professionals should be aware of his or her own view on these issues, as well as that of colleagues to whom findings will be communicated.

Carlson and Garber (1986) noted two schools of thought that have been prominent in the past. The first, based on psychoanalytic theories of personality development, denied the existence of full-syndrome mood disorders prior to the completion of superego development during adolescence. In the 1960s and 1970s, this view gave way to the theory of masked depression.

According to masked depression theory, such diverse presenting complaints as delinquent behavior, somatic complaints, or being out of parental control could be signs or symptoms of an underlying, dynamically motivated depressive state. Although this theory brought with it the advantage of sensitizing clinicians to affective disturbances in children and adolescents who otherwise were not diagnosed with a mood disorder, the theory has gradually given way to more direct models of depression in young people. One criticism of the masked depression theory was that virtually all childhood psychopathology could be seen as originating in, or reflecting, a depressive state (Kovacs & Beck, 1977), and therefore, no one could be proven nondepressed. At a more pragmatic level, careful inquiry about depressive symptoms showed that many of the masking behaviors were rather "thin masks", and that the presence of depressive syndromes could be determined directly by interview (Carlson & Cantwell, 1980b). This led to the current view that other disorders often accompany depression, but are more accurately conceptualized as co-morbid conditions than as depressive sequelae or defensive masks.

The more recent schools of thought outlined by Carlson and Garber (1986) accept childhood and adolescent depression as a clinical entity but disagree on its essential features. The third school of thought was identified with Weinberg and colleagues (Weinberg, Rutman, Sullivan, Penick, & Dietz, 1973), who described the depressive syndrome in children as composed of several symptoms identical to those of adult depression and some symptoms developmentally specific to childhood. The most influential school of thought, however, and the one that underlies most recent research has been the fourth view: that depressive disorders are essentially similar in adulthood and in childhood, although associated features may vary (Puig-Antich & Weston, 1983). This point of view has enabled researchers to use a common set of criteria, such as DSM-III-R, to define depressive disorders across the life span. Although this approach has led to unparalleled productivity in the study of early-onset depressive disorders, it has been criticized by proponents of a fifth point of view for failing to take into account the impact of developmental tasks, abilities, and limitations on symptomatology (Cicchetti & Schneider-Rosen, 1986). This fifth viewpoint, largely identified with the title *developmental psychopathology*, will continue to examine age-related variables in depressive symptomatology and to clarify the issue of essential versus associated symptoms during development. Several efforts to address this question will be noted in the subsequent material in this chapter.

Classification of Depression

The current descriptions of depressive disorders outlined in the Research Diagnostic Criteria (Spitzer et al., 1978), DSM-III (APA, 1980), or DSM-III-R (APA, 1987) are used by most investigators to define depressed children and adolescents. Both DSM-III and DSM-III-R list three nonbipolar (non-manic-depressive) depressive disorders: 1) major depression; 2) dysthymia; 3) adjustment disorder with depressed mood.

Major depressive disorder (MDD) is a full-syndrome episode lasting at least two weeks, marked by a persistently depressed mood (or irritable mood in children or adolescents) or significant loss of interest or pleasure in usual activities. In addition, at least five symptoms (including one of the symptoms just noted) must be present nearly every day. These symptoms may include significant weight or appetite loss or gain; insomnia or hypersomnia; psychomotor agitation or retardation; fatigue or loss of energy; feelings of worthlessness or excessive guilt; loss of ability to think, concentrate, or make decisions; recurrent thoughts of death or suicide, or a suicide plan or attempt. Major depression itself ranges from relatively mild episodes to severe episodes with psychotic features such as delusions. It may occur only once or it can be a recurrent disorder.

Dysthymia (DD) is a less severe form of depression. Depressed or irritable mood must be present most of the time, on more days than not, for at least 1 year (2 years in adults). Depressed mood must be accompanied by at least two of the following symptoms: poor or excessive appetite; insomnia or hypersomnia; fatigue; low self-esteem; concentration difficulties; or hopelessness.

An adjustment disorder with depressed mood (ADDM) is, by definition, a reaction to an identifiable stressor, marked predominantly (in this case) by depressed mood. It lasts no more than 6 months and does not meet criteria for MDD.

Prevalence of Symptoms and Disorders

Studies using a variety of self-report measures suggest that approximately 20% of American adolescents report mild to more severe levels of depressive symptomatology (Kandel & Davies, 1982; Kaplan, Hong, & Weinhold, 1984; Peterson & Craighead, 1986). The Isle of Wight study found a marked increase in depressive feelings between ages 10–11 and ages 14–15, as well as a large increase in cases of depressive disorder, going from 3 to 35 cases among approximately 2,000 youngsters (Rutter, 1986). Kashani, McGee, Clarkson et al. (1983) reported a prevalence rate of 1.8% for major depression in a community sample of 9-year-olds. In an adolescent community sample, prevalence rose to 4.7%, with an additional 3.3% meeting criteria for dysthymia (Kashani, Carlson et al., 1987). Recently, Whitaker, Johnson, Shaffer et al. (1990) studied lifetime prevalence rates of various psychiatric disorders among 9th to 12th graders (largely 14–17 years old) in an entire county in New Jersey. Based on a two-step diagnostic procedure (self-report followed by interviews), they found that 4.0% of the students suffered from major depression and 4.9% were dysthymic. The diagnostic procedure allowed for individuals to receive both diagnoses, so the rates are not independent. Such dysthymic individuals who also currently suffer from major depression are diagnosed as having double depression. Between 80% and 90% of these students were rated as impaired by their disorder(s), but only slightly over half of them had sought treatment for their problems.

Based on these epidemiological data, it is clear that depressed symptoms and disorders exist during childhood and increase dramatically during adolescence.

Age-Related Differences in Depression

In one of two studies that directly compared two age groups, Ryan and colleagues (1987) studied two clinically referred samples of 95 prepubertal children and 92 adolescents with MDD. On most symptoms, there was no significant difference between age groups. However, prepubertal children with MDD were more likely to show depressed appearance, psychomotor agitation, hallucinations, and the associated features of somatic complaints, separation anxiety, and phobias. Adolescents were more likely to demonstrate anhedonia (lack or loss of ability to experience pleasure), hypersomnia, weight change, and hopelessness; to have made more lethal suicide attempts; and to have more associated alcohol or drug use.

The other direct developmental comparison study was conducted by Kashani, Rosenberg, and Reid (1989), with 8-, 12-, and 17-year-olds in a nonreferred community sample. Overall depression scores increased with age, with depression more frequent in adolescence than in childhood or pre-adolescence. Fatigue, agitation, irritability, and passive suicidal thoughts also increased with age. Crying was more frequent in younger children. Few of the subjects in this study were depressed by DSM-III criteria, and different diagnostic interviews were used in the two studies, so the results unfortunately are not directly comparable to those of Ryan et al. (1987).

At the other end of the developmental spectrum, two studies have compared adolescents and adults diagnosed with MDD. Both studies involved small samples of inpatients. Strober, Green, and Carlson (1981) reported that psychotic, endogenous, and psychomotor-retarded depressions occurred in adolescent inpatients but were less prevalent than among adult depressed inpatients. However, Friedman, Hurt, Clarkin, Corn, & Aronoff (1983) reported higher rates of these severe depressions among their adolescent inpatients than did Strober and colleagues; they reported virtually no symptomatic differences between adults and adolescents with MDD in their setting. Differences in application of diagnostic threshold, referral patterns, or definitions of criteria could account for the different findings in these two studies. Considerably more research involving direct comparison of large samples evaluated at a single center is needed before conclusions can be drawn about developmental differences in the phenomenology of MDD or milder types of depression. To date, there are relatively few *reliable* differences across developmental stages.

Course of Depressive Disorders

Kovacs and her colleagues (Kovacs, Feinberg, Crouse-Novak, Paulauskas, & Finkelstein, 1984; Kovacs, Feinberg, Crouse-Novak, Paulauskas, Pollock, & Finkelstein, 1984; Kovacs, Paulauskas, Gatsonis, & Richards, 1988) have studied the course of the three DSM-III nonbipolar depressive disorders with children who had prepubertal onset. Both dysthymia (DD) and adjustment disorder with depressed mood (ADDM) had earlier onsets than major depressive disorder (MDD). The latter had a mean duration of 32 weeks, and DD had a mean episode length of over 3 years. Children with ADDM recovered the fastest, on the average by 21 weeks and did not have a relapse. Development of a subsequent episode of MDD within 5 years was equally high for DD and MDD groups (69% versus 72%) and clearly demonstrated the seriousness of these disorders in childhood. These percentages of depressive disorders are similar to the findings from another follow-up study among depressed children of parents with depressive disorder; the study reported that 58% of the children initially diagnosed as depressed (at a mean age of 10) were still depressed at 4-year follow-up (mean age 14) (Apter et al., 1982). Similarly, Poznanski, Krahenbuhl, and Zrull (1976) also reported that 50% of their depressed children in a

long-term follow-up study were still depressed as young adults. Harrington, Fudge, Rutter, Pickles, and Hill (1990), reporting on an 18-year adult follow-up of 80 depressed English children who had been treated at Maudsley Hospital in London, found that about 60% had had a depressive episode by the time of the follow-up assessment.

Finally, a proportion of seriously depressed adolescents go on to develop bipolar affective disorder or other disorders. Strober and Carlson (1982) found that 20% of a sample of 60 adolescent inpatients diagnosed with MDD during hospitalization had a bipolar (manic-depression) outcome by follow-up 4 years later. Akiskal and his colleagues (1983) reported similar findings for outpatient adolescents and adults. Kovac and colleagues (1988) recently reported that, within their longitudinal study of children with prepubertal-onset depression, there was an estimated time-dependent risk of 36% of developing a conduct disorder by age 19.

In summary, studies to date suggest that depressive disorders of early onset carry a high risk for subsequent depression or certain other serious disorders.

Co-Morbidity and Associated Disorders

Childhood and adolescent depression is complicated by the frequency with which the disorder is accompanied by other symptoms or disorders. The most common co-existing disorders appear to be anxiety disorder and conduct disorder (Geller, Chestnut, Miller, Price, & Yates, 1985). It appears that about one-third of MDD adolescents suffer from a co-morbid conduct disorder and vice versa (Puig-Antich, 1982; Chiles, Miller, & Cox, 1980). Kovacs, Feinberg, Crouse-Novak, Paulauskas, and Finkelstein (1984) also found co-occurrence of attention-deficit disorder and dysthymia in some children.

In a small study (N=21) of suicide completers aged 11 to 19, Shafii and colleagues (Shafti, Steltz-Lenarsky, Derrick, Beckner, & Whittinghill, 1988) found a combination of mood disorder and another diagnosable disorder, especially substance abuse or conduct disorders, in 76% of the victims, compared to 24% of matched controls. Shaffer (1974) had similarly found that about 70% of adolescent suicide completers were diagnosed as depressed or depressed and antisocial (oppositional and/or conduct disorder).

The implications of these findings for clinicians assessing and treating depression include the need to evaluate for a variety of other commonly co-existing conditions, including anxiety disorders, substance abuse, conduct disorder, oppositional disorder, and attention deficit disorder. Specific assessment of suicidal ideation, intent, and risk are always required, and inquiry should be made about possible manic or hypomanic symptoms.

ASSESSMENT

The diagnosis of depressive clinical disorders requires the gathering of adequate information from the child or adolescent and his or her family to determine the presence and chronicity of the symptoms of the disorders. In clinical situations this information can be accumulated over time from various professional and interpersonal interactions. In order to arrive at a reliable and valid diagnosis in a clinical or research setting, it is best to engage the individual (and a family member, especially with children) in a standard clinical interview. Additional sources of information regarding the nature, severity, and consequences of the disorders can be obtained from self-report scales and parent, peer, and clinician rating scales. Curry and Craighead (in press) and Kendall, Cantwell, and Kazdin (1989) recently provided a summary and critique of these various assessment instruments and procedures.

Diagnostic Interviews

There are two highly structured interviews: Diagnostic Interview for Children and Adolescents (Welner, Reich, Herjanic, Jung, & Amado, 1987) and Diagnostic Interview Schedule for Children (Costello, Edelbrock, Dulcan, Kulas, & Klaric, 1984). There are three semistructured interviews: Interview Schedule for Children (Kovacs, 1985b); Child Assessment Schedule (CAS) (Hodges, McKnew, Cytryn, Stern, & Kline, 1982); and Schedule for Affective Disorders and Schizophrenia for School Age Children (K-SADS) (Puig-Antich & Chambers, 1978).

In order to evaluate the presence and severity of core depressive symptoms in children and adolescents, the interview should include the child and a parent. None of the listed interviews is a gold standard for defining depression, but the K-SADS and CAS have adequate psychometric properties and allow the clinician sufficient flexibility to determine the presence of DSM-III-R symptomatology.

Self-Report

The self-report instruments are measures of depressive severity and do not provide adequate information for a diagnosis. These measures include among others: Children's Depression Inventory (CDI) (Kovacs & Beck, 1977; Kovacs, 1985a); Beck Depression Inventory (BDI) (Beck, Ward, Mendelson, Mock, & Erbaugh, 1961); and Children's Depression Scale (Tischer & Lang, 1983). The CDI is the most widely used scale and has been demonstrated to have adequate psychometric properties. However, the BDI may be a better choice for older adolescents. The reader is referred to Curry and Craighead (1992) and Kendall et al. (1989) for a detailed review of these scales and a description and critique of the various other approaches to assessing depression.

TREATMENTS

Three therapies have demonstrated effectiveness in the treatment of adult MDD (Craighead, Evans, & Robins, in press); these treatments are antidepressant medications, cognitive-behavioral therapy, and interpersonal psychotherapy. Largely because childhood and adolescent depression are now considered to be similar to adult depression, downward extensions of these three treatments have been developed for use with younger people. The appropriateness and effectiveness of these downward extensions have begun to be investigated.

Antidepressant Medications

Tricyclic antidepressant medications (e.g., nortriptyline, amitriptyline, imipramine, desipramine) are extensively used as effective medications for adult MDD. This class of medications is also widely administered to depressed children and adolescents. Reports of controlled placebo trials, however, report no significant differences between these medications and placebo response among younger patients (Geller, Cooper, Graham, Marsteller, & Bryant, 1990; Geller, Cooper, McCombs, Graham, Wells, 1989; Kashani, Shekim, & Reid, 1984; Klein & Koplewitz, 1986; Kramer & Feiguine, 1981; Puig-Antich, Perel, Lupatkin et al., 1987; Ryan, Puig-Antich, Cooper et al., 1986). For example, in a study of 38 prepubertal children, 68% were found to respond to placebo but only 56% responded to imipramine (Puig-Antich et al., 1987). Similar negative results (i.e., no significant differences between placebo and drug effectiveness) were found in studies of amitriptyline (Kashani et al., 1984; Kramer & Feiguine, 1981; Ryan, 1990). Geller et al. (1989; 1990) tested the efficacy of nortriptyline with

depressed children ranging in age from 6 to 17; they also found no evidence for increased effectiveness of medication over placebo.

Given the lack of evidence for the effectiveness of tricyclic antidepressants, Ryan (1990) and others have suggested that investigators begin to evaluate other antidepressant medications. Simeon, Dinicola, Ferguson, and Copping (1990) conducted a placebo-controlled double-blind study of the effectiveness of fluoxetine (Prozac) with 40 depressed adolescents. They found no significant difference between the effectiveness of the drug and a pill-placebo.

It should be kept in mind that the effectiveness rates of these medications among adolescents with MDD are fairly comparable to rates among adult MDD patients. However, the placebo response rate (about $\frac{2}{3}$ of adolescent patients get better) is much larger than that among adults and essentially precludes that any treatment will exceed placebo in effectiveness. As Conners (1990) has noted, the sample sizes were so small that the investigators had little chance of demonstrating significant differences between the pharmacologic treatments and the placebo condition. Unfortunately, the Geller et al. (1990) trial with nortriptyline seems to indicate that antidepressant medications may be particularly ineffective with non-placebo-responder adolescents with MDD.

Cognitive-Behavioral Treatments

Although Beck (1976) is generally credited with the development of cognitive-behavior therapy for the treatment of adult MDD, a number of additional influences affected the emergence of cognitive-behavioral interventions with children (Craighead, 1982). These included Bandura's (1977) social learning theory developed from his research on modeling, self-control research, problem-solving research; Meichenbaum's (1977) research on self-instructional training; and Ellis' Rational-Emotive Therapy (1962). The procedures described below have emerged from a clinical and conceptual background that was a mixture of all these influences. These conceptual developments were described in Chapters 1 and 2 in this book.

Petti, Bornstein, Delamater, and Conners (1980) described the treatment of a depressed 10-year-old girl who received a multifaceted therapy package that included behavioral and cognitive-behavioral interventions, and also supportive family therapy and antidepressant drug treatment. This treatment was reportedly effective, but it was impossible to determine what element(s) of the treatment actually produced the clinical changes.

Frame, Matson, Sonis, Fialkov, and Kazdin (1982) reported a case study in which a 10-year-old boy received behavioral treatment for MDD. The diagnosis was determined from information provided by a psychiatric interview, independent ratings of a videotape of the child, and completion by the child's mother of the Children's Depression Inventory, the Child Behavior Problem Checklist, and the Bellevue Index of Depression. After assessment of problems in the boy's social interaction, Frame and colleagues implemented "a behavioral training package designed to alter the specific responses which characterized (his) social interactions." Specifically, they used instructions, modeling, role-play, and feedback to modify four behaviors: inappropriate body position (e.g., turning away from others); lack of eye contact; poor speech quality (e.g., mumbling); and bland affect ("lack of emotional tone in the voice and failure to employ facial, hand, or arm gestures while speaking"). Within a multiple baseline design and using objective measures of change, the researchers found that treatment produced substantial changes in the targeted behaviors. This study, like the Petti et al. study (1980), is based on a single subject without replication. Although the treatment resulted in specific behavioral changes, there was no report of its impact on the more global measures of depression.

Butler, Miezitis, Friedman, and Cole (1980) used several self-report measures (the Piers-Harris Self-Concept Scale, the Children's Depression Inventory, the Moyal-Miezitis Stimulus Appraisal Questionnaire, and the Nowicki-Strickland Locus of Control Scale for Children) as well as teacher interviews to assess depression in fifth and sixth grade children. Following identification of 56 depressed youngsters by use of self-report and teacher judgements, Butler et al. (1980) randomly assigned these children to one of three groups: Role-Play, Cognitive Restructuring, or Attention-Placebo. All three conditions consisted of 10 one-hour weekly small-group sessions. The role-playing treatment focused on problems relevant to depressed children; the cognitive restructuring treatment sought to teach such skills as recognition of irrational thoughts; and the attention-placebo control group was taught to solve problems in a cooperative manner. Butler et al. (1980) reported that statistically significant differences were found on the CDI and on the Locus of Control measure at posttest. Both the role-playing and cognitive restructuring treatments appeared to be effective, with the role-playing treatment showing the greatest improvement on each dependent measure.

More recently, Reynolds and Coats (1986) assessed depression in a high school population by using the Beck Depression Inventory (BDI), the Reynolds Adolescent Depression Scale (RADS), and the Bellevue Index of Depression (BID). These investigators then randomly assigned 30 moderately depressed (but not diagnosed) students to one of three treatment conditions: cognitive-behavioral therapy, relaxation training, or wait-list control group. Each of the two active-treatment conditions met in small groups for ten 50-minute sessions over a 5-week time span. The *cognitive-behavioral* treatment consisted primarily of training in self-control skills. Subjects were shown the importance of accurate self-monitoring and its ability to influence mood. Subjects were further educated as to the depressive tendencies of over-attending to unpleasant events and emphasizing short-term rather than long-term consequences. They were shown the need to monitor and increase the number of positive activities in which they engaged. The role of accurate self-evaluation was discussed, and faulty assumptions about their responsibility for events (i.e., negative attributional style) were pointed out. The importance of setting realistic and attainable goals was emphasized, and self-reinforcement was encouraged. The *relaxation training* condition emphasized the relation between stress, muscle tension, and depression. Subjects in this condition learned to relax major muscle groups and independently practiced this at home. They were then taught to utilize these relaxation skills to offset anxiety in situations that they identified as tension-producing.

Following treatment, members of both treatment groups exhibited significantly lower levels of depression as assessed by the BDI, the RADS, and the BID. Comparison of the cognitive-behavioral and relaxation groups revealed no significant differences in effectiveness between the two groups. The two treatment groups differed significantly from the control group on the BDI and BID, and these differences were still evident at a 5-week follow-up.

Stark, Reynolds, and Kaslow (1987) reported similar results in a study of 29 prepubertal school children who were moderately to severely depressed, as indicated by scores on the CDI. Subjects in this study were randomly assigned to one of three conditions: self-control training, behavioral problem solving, or wait-list (control group). Each treatment consisted of twelve 50-minute sessions spread over a 5-week period. Both the self-control and behavioral problem-solving groups received training in self-monitoring, including the need to monitor and increase the number of pleasant activities. The self-control condition additionally emphasized self-monitoring of thoughts and moods, long-term rather than short-term consequences of behavior, more adaptive attributional styles, more realistic standards for self-evaluation, in-

creased self-reinforcement, and decreased self-punishment. The behavioral problem-solving treatment, in contrast, focused largely on problem-solving skills. In addition, it provided a forum for expression of feelings and encouraged subjects to learn about their feelings and to evaluate the ways in which their behavior affected social relationships.

Results from this study indicated that subjects in both treatment conditions showed significantly reduced depressive symptomatology both on self-report measures (the CDI and the Child Depression Scale (CDS) and on an interview measure (the Children's Depression Rating Scale - Revised (CDRS-R)) from pre- to posttreatment. These gains were maintained at an 8-week follow-up. Neither intervention appeared to be superior to the other. Stark et al. (1987) pointed out that the comparable effectiveness of these two treatments may be due to the substantial overlap of the techniques used in the two treatments. Although this study provides evidence to support the use of such interventions, Stark et al. (1987) suggested that incorporating the family into treatment may be beneficial, since family difficulties are often associated with childhood depression.

Cognitive-Behavioral Combined with Family and School Interventions

Three groups of researchers have reported attempts to combine cognitive-behavioral techniques with family intervention. Lewinsohn and colleagues (1987) developed a "Coping with Depression" course, which they administered separately to adolescents and their parents. Gotlib and Colby (1987) described "interpersonal systems therapy," a combination of family systems therapy and individual cognitive-behavioral therapy. Stark and colleagues (Stark & Brookman, in press; Stark, Rouse, & Livingston, in press) described a similar combination with an additional school-based intervention.

The "Coping with Depression" Course

Lewinsohn, Hoberman, and Clarke (1989) developed a "psychoeducational" approach to the treatment of depression and have reported successful treatment of a variety of adult depressed populations. Lewinsohn et al. (Lewinsohn, Hops, Williams, Clarke, & Andrews, 1987) reported on a 7-week, 14-session adaptation of the Coping with Depression course in which groups of adolescents were taught techniques to: (1) control their depressed mood through relaxation; (2) increase pleasant events; (3) control negative thoughts; (4) develop effective communication, problem-solving and negotiation skills; and (5) increase social skills. In addition, a similar, 7-week, 7-session course for parents was developed. It presented an overview of the information taught in the adolescent group sessions.

Lewinsohn et al. (1987) studied 61 depressed high school students who were interviewed with the K-SADS and met the criteria for a depressive disorder (either major, minor, or intermittent). These subjects were randomly assigned to one of three conditions: adolescent group in conjunction with parent group, adolescent group only, or a wait-list control. At the end of the 7-week treatment, BDI scores and DSM-III diagnoses had significantly improved for both treatment conditions, compared with the control group. Following treatment, the percentages of subjects who no longer met criteria for a depressive disorder were as follows: 47.4% of the combined adolescent-parent group, 42.9% of the adolescent-only group, and 5.3% of the wait-list control group. Although there was no significant difference between the two treatment groups, the combined adolescent and parent group condition tended to show greater improvement than the adolescent-only group.

Kahn, Kehle, Jenson, and Clark (1990) tested the effectiveness of the "Coping with Depression" course (but did not include treatment with parents) with 68 moderately to severely depressed 10- to 14-year-olds. Following a multi-stage gating assessment procedure (which included use of the Reynolds Adolescent Depression Scale [RADS], BDI, CDI, Piers-Harris Self-Concept Scale, parent-reported RADS and CDI, as well as clinical interview), subjects were randomly assigned to one of four conditions: the "Coping with Depression" course, relaxation training, self-modeling, or wait-list control. Both the "Coping with Depression" and relaxation conditions met in small groups for twelve 50-minute sessions over a 6- to 8-week period. The self-modeling condition consisted of 10–12 minute sessions that were held twice weekly over a 6- to 8-week period. In the latter condition, subjects watched videotapes of themselves engaging in desirable, nondepressive behaviors.

Analysis showed that at posttest all three treatment groups were statistically significantly different from the control group and that these gains were maintained at 1-month follow-up. However, the treatment groups tended to have different levels of *clinical* significance. In the cognitive-behavioral "Coping with Depression" group 76% to 88% of subjects moved from the dysfunctional to functional range, but only 65% to 76% of the relaxation group, 59% to 70% of the self-modeling group, and 12% to 18% of the control group reached that level of change.

The Interpersonal Systems Approach

As described by Gotlib and Colby (1987), the interpersonal systems approach to the treatment of depression is family systems therapy modified to take into account intrapsychic (i.e., cognitive), as well as interpersonal factors. This treatment somewhat resembles a downward extension of interpersonal psychotherapy applied in a family context. This approach assumes that depression is at least in part caused and maintained by the relationships between family members. For example, a depressed individual frequently will engage in behaviors that are aversive to others, leading family members to become annoyed and frustrated. The depressed individual may become aware of these reactions to him, feel more needy, and then inadvertently increase the annoying depressive behaviors.

The interpersonal systems approach also assumes that depression serves some function within the family (e.g., a child's depression may help to reduce marital conflict between the parents). The entire family is seen in therapy, since it is assumed that all family members share responsibility for the depression.

Interpersonal systems therapy is generally short-term, action-oriented, and present-focused. In therapy, family interactions that maintain the depression are explored, and the focus is thus shifted from the identified depressed individual to the family. Family sessions are often supplemented with individual sessions in which the depressed patients are encouraged to understand their own negative cognitive style and the effects of their depression on others. In addition, patients are urged to increase the number of pleasurable activities in which they engage. For Gotlib and Colby (1987), interpersonal systems therapy is the treatment of choice, particularly when a child is the identified patient. They presented a case-study description of the successful treatment of a depressed adolescent.

Although the interpersonal systems approach appears to be a promising treatment alternative, no controlled comparison studies have been reported. Evaluation of the efficacy of such an approach awaits empirical testing. As described below, however, Stark, Rouse, and Livingston (in press) have evaluated a similar model of intervention.

Evaluations of Family Therapy Additions to Treatment

Stark, Rouse, and Livingston (in press) used a multiple gate assessment procedure to identify depressed children. They screened subjects twice with the CDI and then with a semi-structured interview; 24 depressed children were randomly assigned to one of two experimental conditions: cognitive-behavioral treatment with a family component or traditional counseling with a somewhat similar family component. Cognitive-behavioral treatment included training in self-control skills, social skills, cognitive restructuring, assertiveness, and relaxation. Parents were urged to increase the number of pleasant family activities and to encourage their children's use of their new skills. The traditional-counseling group focused more on group interactions as well as emotions and self-esteem. In this treatment, parents were taught to increase the number of pleasant family activities and to improve communication.

Results of this study showed significantly less depression at posttest in comparison with pretest for both conditions, and these improvements were maintained at follow-up 7 months later. At posttest there was a significant difference in the effectiveness of the two interventions: the cognitive-behavioral group exhibited significantly less depression and fewer depressive cognitions at posttest than did the traditional-counseling group. Primarily because of attrition and the resultant loss of statistical power, these significant differences were no longer present at a 7-month follow-up assessment. Therefore, this study provides some support for the combined use of cognitive-behavioral and family therapy techniques.

Stark and Brookman (in press) also examined family interactions important in the development and maintenance of depression. They broadened this focus on interpersonal difficulties to include social difficulties with peers, and they suggested that intervention in both family and school situations can be beneficial. Their case study of a depressed 11-year-old girl (assessed via the CDI and the K-SADS-P) suggested that the combination of family systems and school-based intervention was effective in the treatment of childhood depression.

The studies reviewed suggest that cognitive-behavioral interventions have been successful in the treatment of childhood depression, and that addition of family systems therapy (and perhaps school-based intervention) to cognitive-behavioral treatment can be therapeutically beneficial. Although the best of these treatments have proven superior to wait-list conditions, in the main they have all been equally effective. This suggests the possibility that these psychotherapeutic interventions are working because of their placebo or demand effects. The equivalent of a pill-placebo psychotherapy control is a difficult condition to achieve. It should be noted, however, that in the Stark, Rouse, and Livingston study (in press), the cognitive-behavioral treatment with a family component was superior to another treatment that should have had equal placebo and experimental-demand effects. Furthermore, at a practical level it appears that these treatments work and there are no known side effects from participating in the intervention programs.

CONCLUSIONS

Although the existence of depression among children and adolescents was questioned before the 1970s, its presence is now widely acknowledged. It appears that major depression exists in childhood and increases to about 4% among ad-olescents. It is best diagnosed by a clinical interview with the patient and a parent; additional information can be reliably obtained about the nature and severity of the disorder from various self-report, teacher, parent, clinician, and peer ratings. The outcome of treating depressed children and adolescents with antidepressant medications has been disappointing, but because published research on this topic is still fairly limited, firm conclusions cannot be drawn. Treatment of depressed youngsters with cognitive-behavioral interventions, especially when the family is included, has been fairly successful. Although it is also too soon to conclude that this is the treatment of choice for MDD, the demonstrated effectiveness of the treatment to date is encouraging.

TREATMENT RESOURCES

Gotlib, I. H., & Colby, C. A. (1987). *Treatment of depression: An interpersonal systems approach.* New York: Pergamon.

Lewinsohn, P. M., Antonuccio, P. O., Steinmetz, J. L., & Teri, L. (1984). *The coping with depression course.* Eugene, OR: Castalia.

Pope, A. W., McHale, S. M., & Craighead, W. E. (1988). *Self-esteem Enhancement with Children and Adolescents.* New York: Pergamon Press.

Stark, K. D., & Brookman, C. S. (In press). Childhood depression: Theory and family-school intervention. In M. J. Fine and C. Carlson (Eds.), *Handbook of family-school intervention: A systems perspective.* New York: Grove & Stratton.

CHAPTER 19

Mental Retardation

Thomas L. Whitman

In recent years the histories of behavior modification and mental retardation have been closely linked. In the 1950s and 1960s, a growing emphasis on educating and training persons with mental retardation developed as a result of parent movements; the emergence of the National Association for Retarded Children; a change in the ethical, legal, and political climates; and especially the emergence of new teaching technologies (Rosen, Clark & Kivitz, 1976). As a consequence of the efforts of early behavior modifiers, effective techniques were developed for use in institutions serving persons with mental retardation in the 1960s and 1970s (Whitman, Scibak, & Reid, 1983). More recently, catalyzed by the elaboration of the cognitive paradigm, cognitive-behavioral programs have begun to be introduced into school and community settings (Reid, 1988). In this chapter, the nature of mental retardation will be briefly discussed, along with pro-

The writing of this chapter was supported in part by a training grant from the National Institute of Child Development (5T32 HD07184-10)

cedures for assessing this developmental disorder. Then a more elaborate description of behavioral and cognitive-behavioral interventions that have been employed with the mentally retarded will be presented. Finally, current issues and challenges confronting behavioral educators and researchers will be described.

DEFINITION AND THEORY

A current and widely accepted definition of mental retardation put forth by the American Association on Mental Retardation describes this disorder as occurring during the developmental period and involving "significantly subaverage general intellectual functioning existing concurrently with deficits in adaptive behavior" (Grossman, 1983, p. 11). According to this definition, a person is mentally retarded only if *both* intellectual and behavioral deficiencies are present. Thus, individuals who are intellectually subaverage but whose adaptive behavior is adequate, and individuals who manifest behavior deficiencies but intellectually are not subaverage, are not labeled as mentally retarded. Although specific adaptive behavior deficiencies vary depending on the level of mental retardation, deficits in adaptive behavior generally occur in several or all of the following domains: sensorimotor, communication, self-help, socialization, academic, reasoning, judgment, and vocational.

In most classification systems, retarded individuals are categorized in terms of the severity of their intellectual and/or behavior deficiencies. For example, the American Association on Mental Retardation places individuals into four categories of retardation: mild, moderate, severe, and profound (Grossman, 1983). Some classification schema emphasize level of expected learning capabilities and categorize individuals as educable mentally retarded (EMR) or trainable mentally retarded (TMR) (Robinson & Robinson, 1976). Still other classification systems categorize mentally retarded individuals on the basis of etiology, such as disorders associated with either genetic or chromosomal abnormalities, disease, injury, toxic agents, malnutrition, and/or social-economic disadvantages. Advocates of a behavioral approach to assessment are generally cautious when it comes to using classification systems, preferring to emphasize the uniqueness of individuals with mental retardation. They warn that general labels often have little scientific or educational value and can facilitate a dangerous stereotyped response on the part of the clinical-educational community (Bellack & Hersen, 1977).

Although there is a fairly general consensus concerning how mental retardation should be defined, a considerable difference of opinion exists regarding the major causes that produce the cognitive and behavioral deficiencies in mentally retarded persons. Within a behavioral framework, the development of mental retardation is associated with environmental conditions including: a restricted physical-stimulus environment, inappropriate reinforcement patterns, a

history of aversive experiences, and absence of appropriate models (Bijou, 1966). Zigler and Balla (1982) also emphasized within their motivational theory the importance of social-environmental influences, in particular the role of factors such as "a lack of continuity of care by parents or other caretakers, an excessive desire by parents to institutionalize their child, impoverished economic circumstances, and a family history of marital discord, mental illness, abuse and/or neglect" (p. 11). From a cognitive perspective, a wide variety of defects and problems has been proposed to account for the deficiencies of persons with mental retardation. These characteristics include: smaller memory capacities, inefficient working memory processes, small and disorganized knowledge bases, limited and passive encoding strategies, metacognitive deficiencies, and poorly developed executive processes for controlling thinking. In general, disagreements between cognitive theorists regarding the nature of mental retardation are related to which of the deficiencies are primary. Butterfield and Ferretti (1987) emphasize that our present knowledge is limited concerning how these factors interact and specifically distinguish low and higher intelligence persons. It seems probable, however, because considerable individual differences exist among mentally retarded persons, that different theories are needed to explain their deficiencies.

There are also numerous opinions regarding the role that genetic-organic and environmental factors play in producing these cognitive deficiencies (Zigler & Balla, 1982). Campione and Brown's theory of intelligence (1978) describes two interacting systems that affect complex cognitive functioning: a biologically based architectural system that influences efficiency and speed of processing, and an environmentally developed system that controls retrieval of knowledge from long-term memory. Mentally retarded individuals are sometimes viewed as including two distinct but overlapping populations (Zigler, 1967). The members of one group typically show evidence of central nervous system pathology, often have physical handicaps and stigmata, and usually have IQs in the moderate range or below (Grossman, 1983). In contrast, the members of the other group, who are often from the lowest socioeconomic strata, manifest no signs of neurological dysfunction or other readily detectable physical or clinical signs of mental retardation and generally have IQs in the mild range. For further information concerning specific theories of mental retardation, the reader is referred to edited books by Borkowski and Day (1987); Brooks, Sperber, and McCauley (1984); Day and Borkowski (1987); and Ellis (1963, 1979).

ASSESSMENT

Assessment of mentally retarded persons serves multiple purposes. It is employed to diagnose formally the condition of mental retardation and to classify individuals as mildly, moderately, severely, or profoundly retarded. Assessment is also used to identify a person's behavioral deficits and excesses, along with the variables that control their occurrence, and to assess an individual's assets and resources (Nelson & Hayes, 1979). Moreover, assessment is employed to identify the presence of psychological disorders existing concurrently with mental retardation (Matson & Barrett, 1982; Matson & Frame, 1983). Finally, assessment is utilized to evaluate the ongoing and long-range effectiveness of treatment (Kazdin & Straw, 1976; Shapiro & Barrett, 1983). Readers are referred to Reschley (1982) for a discussion of diagnostic and classification issues, to Matson and Barrett (1982) and Matson and Frame (1983) for information about psychopathology in mentally retarded persons, and to Bates and Hanson (1983) and Poling and Parker (1983) for information about techniques used to monitor treatment effectiveness.

Because mental retardation is defined by the presence of both intellectual and behavioral deficiencies, psychometricians have emphasized the development of instruments for evaluating these problems. Although intelligence tests have been used successfully to predict school performance and to identify individuals who will benefit from special educational placements, there is widespread agreement that they do not measure ability to learn in specific situations, provide useful instructional information about what and how to teach, or reflect changing conceptions about the nature of intelligence (Robinson & Janos, 1987). Intelligence tests have been particularly criticized for underestimating what a person can achieve as a result of intensive training. Kaufman (1979) suggested, however, that intelligence tests, if used *intelligently*, can provide useful information about a person's strengths and weaknesses and what should be emphasized in an educational program. Although more specific cognitive assessment procedures for evaluating mentally retarded persons have not yet been developed, it is clear that progress is being made in this regard. For example, Feuerstein and his colleagues have developed, as part of their instrumental enrichment program, a promising learning potential assessment device that allows the processes and functions that constitute mental acts to be cognitively mapped (Feuerstein, 1980; Feuerstein, Rand, Hoffman, Hoffman, & Miller, 1979). More recently, Reid (1988) has described specific assessment procedures that can be utilized in developing math, reading, writing, and spelling programs.

In contrast to traditional intelligence tests, behavioral assessment involves multiple methods (interviews, checklists, standardized tests, and formal observation) and multiple informants (mentally retarded persons, their parents, teachers, and/or other caretakers) to assess an individual's overt behaviors, cognitions, affect, and physiological status across a range of situations (family, school, neighborhood, and work). Behavioral assessments have been particularly useful in developing individualized educational programs by providing teachers with information concerning specific adaptive behaviors and behavior deficiencies in need of remediation, data about the response requirements of a task to be performed, and hypotheses concerning specific environmental stimuli that promote or inhibit behavioral growth.

Because of the widespread use of intellectual and behavior assessment procedures by professionals working with persons, particularly children, with mental retardation, some of the more commonly employed instruments will be briefly described.

Standardized Intelligence and Achievement Tests

The Stanford-Binet intelligence scale (Terman & Merrill, 1973), now revised, has been the most widely employed intelligence test because it can be used with children as young as 2 years old and children with relatively low levels of ability, and because its format is appealing to mentally retarded children (Robinson & Robinson, 1976). The WPPSI (Wechsler, 1967), also revised, and the WISC-R (Wechsler, 1974) have been the most popular alternatives to the Stanford-Binet. The WISC-R, which covers the ages from 6 through 18, is used for the identification of mental retardation in school settings. Although its usefulness is limited because it is not normed for children under 6 and does not accurately reflect IQ scores below the mild range, Kaufman (1979) argues that it gives the fairest assessment of children labeled mentally retarded due to psychosocial disadvantage. The System of Multicultural Pluralistic Assessment (SOMPA) (Mercer & Lewis, 1977), a battery of measures incorporating medical and social information, is also recommended for use with socially disadvantaged minority children. The Kaufman Assessment Battery for Children (K-ABC) (Kaufman & Kaufman, 1983), which measures mental processing (sequential processing and simultaneous processing) and achievement in children aged 2 through 12, also has several characteristics that recommend its use with mentally retarded children, including its

appeal to young children, the availability of sociocultural norms, and the availability of a nonverbal scale to assess mental processing in hearing-impaired and language-deficient children (Kaufman, Kamphaus, & Kaufman, 1985). For a review of methods for assessing intelligence with mentally retarded children, the reader is referred to Barrett and Bruening (1983).

Achievement tests are commonly used adjuncts to intelligence tests. The Wide Range Achievement Test-Revised (WRAT-R) (Jastak & Wilkinson, 1984); the Kaufman Test of Educational Achievement (K-TEA) (Kaufman & Kaufman, 1985); the Woodcock-Johnson Psychoeducational Battery (Woodcock & Johnson, 1978); and the Peabody Individual Achievement Test (PIAT) (Dunn & Markwardt, 1970), currently being restandardized, are achievement tests routinely used to assess the academic skills of school-age children. They assess current skill in such areas as spelling, math, and reading. Once general areas of weakness are identified, additional assessment, typically based on a task analysis of the deficient skills, is utilized.

Adaptive Behavior Scales

Behavioral checklists are widely used in the behavioral assessment of persons with mental retardation. The AAMD Adaptive Behavior Scale—School Version (Lambert, Windmiller, Cole, & Figuerra, 1981); the Adaptive Behavior Inventory for Children (Mercer & Lewis, 1977); and the AAMD Adaptive Behavior Scale—Clinical version (Nihira, Foster, Shellhaas, & Leland, 1974) are frequently used methods of assessing the adaptive behavior of mentally retarded children. The Vineland Adaptive Behavior Scales (VABS) (Sparrow, Balla, & Cicchetti, 1984), a revision of the original Vineland Social Maturity Scale (Doll, 1935, 1965), assess the personal and social sufficiency of individuals from birth to adulthood. Like other adaptive behavior measures, the VABS requires that the respondent (a parent, teacher, or primary caretaker) be familiar with the individual's behavior. Three versions are available: an interview edition, survey form; an interview edition, expanded form; and a classroom edition. Each version measures adaptive behavior in four domains: communication, daily living skills, social skills, and motor skills. Interview editions also assess maladaptive behaviors such as sleep disturbance, temper tantrums, poor eye contact, self-injurious behaviors, and so forth. Although adaptive behavior scales involve rating behavior retrospectively (Cone, 1977) and do not provide information sufficiently specific to design effective interventions, they are economical in cost, effort, and therapist time; provide a comprehensive view of a child's repertoire of adaptive and maladaptive behavior, including some behavior that might be missed with other assessment procedures; and facilitate the selection of behaviors for closer scrutiny in the analysis and treatment design stages (Ciminero & Drabman, 1977). The reader is referred to reviews by Meyers, Nihira, and Zetlin (1979); Reschley (1982); and Shapiro and Barrett (1983) for further information about instruments for assessing adaptive behavior.

TECHNIQUES AND AREAS OF APPLICATION

When the application of behavior therapy to persons with mental retardation is contrasted with its use with individuals with other disorders, one is struck by both the diversity of the technologies employed and the range of deficiencies and problems addressed. Because mental retardation is a developmental disorder, programming is directed toward developing the broad array of skills necessary for successful adaption during both childhood and adulthood. As behavior therapy emerged as a discipline in

the 1960s, special attention was given to persons with severe and profound mental retardation, who then resided almost exclusively in large public institutions. When behavior therapists entered these institutions, the severely and profoundly retarded were often considered by staff to be both uneducable and untrainable. During the next several decades, an array of techniques, many of which were derived from operant-learning principles, were developed and successfully applied to teach a range of basic responses, including self-help skills, receptive and expressive language skills, and social, academic, and vocational skills. In addition, programs directed at dealing with a range of maladaptive behaviors were formulated. Gradually, more attention was paid by behavior therapists to the problems of persons with mild and moderate mental retardation. With this broadening focus, techniques based on cognitive and social learning were also developed for use with this population, and emphasis was placed on the development of self-regulated behavior in community settings.

To give the reader a better idea of the broad range of training techniques that have been formulated for use with persons with mental retardation, examples of techniques drawn from classic and more recent research will be presented. Specifically, contingency management, behavior deceleration, verbal instruction, self-regulation, cognitive and metacognitive training, and visual instruction procedures will be described.

Contingency Management Programs

A basic tenet of operant theory is that behavior is developed and maintained by its reinforcing consequences. The process of isolating reinforcers becomes particularly important when working with severely and profounded retarded individuals, who often are difficult to motivate. Moreover, in order to create new behavioral repertoires, a variety of response induction procedures is employed, including shaping, verbal instruction, modeling, and physical guidance. Examples of the applications of operant techniques for training self-help, communication, social-leisure, and community living skills are provided in this section. For a more extended discussion of these technologies and their application with mentally retarded persons, the reader is referred to books by Repp (1983) and Whitman, Scibak, and Reid (1983).

Self-Help Skills

Behavioral programs have been employed to develop a range of self-help behaviors, including feeding, dressing, personal hygiene, and toileting. One of the prime characteristics of behavior modification programs has been the emphasis on defining response goals in a clear and comprehensive fashion, specifically on breaking down complex behaviors into their separate response components and identifying the total chain of behaviors that make up a self-help skill. For example, Matson, Marchetti, and Adkins (1980) task-analyzed the self-help skill of showering. They broke this skill into a chain of 29 responses, which included components such as placing towel and washcloth on stand by shower; adjusting water temperature; washing; rinsing and then drying the various parts of the body; and putting towel and washcloth in a dirty-clothes hamper. (See Matson, Ollendick, & Adkins, 1980, for a task analysis of mealtime behavior.) Typically, in most self-help training programs, increasingly directive prompts (telling, showing, and then physically guiding) are introduced as necessary to initiate responses, and then subsequently faded as the learner becomes proficient. In teaching profoundly multihandicapped persons self-help skills, physical guidance often needs to be employed. For example, in self-feeding programs the trainer may physically guide a client's hand through the entire feeding sequence, then gradually reduce the

amount of guidance as the client demonstrates progress (O'Brien & Azrin, 1972).

In teaching a sequence of responses, such as those involved in self-feeding, either a forward-chaining procedure (in which the first response in a chain is taught first and then the next response, until all the responses in the chain are learned) or a backward-chaining procedure (in which the last response in a chain is taught first, then the next to last, etc.) is employed (Horner & Keilitz, 1975; O'Brien, Bugle, & Azrin, 1972). Self-feeding is relatively easy to teach, perhaps because of the inherent reinforcer (food) involved. One obstacle in teaching self-feeding skills relates to the infrequency of meals and thus of learning opportunities. Furthermore, because of satiation, food ceases to be a reinforcer in training. To circumvent these problems, Azrin and Armstrong (1973) divided each meal into three mini-meals; as a consequence, training sessions were shorter but more intensive and frequent. Training consisted of faded guidance and positive (repeated) practice. Their research indicated that the 11 mentally retarded adults who participated in the treatment were successfully trained within 12 days.

Another self-help area in which behavior modifiers have made a significant contribution is toilet training. Work in this area has been characterized by both procedural and technological innovation. Many applied research programs incorporate electronic signaling devices as part of the treatment regimens. For example, Azrin and Foxx (1971) employed a pants alarm and a toilet bowl alert device to signal the trainer when toileting accidents and appropriate elimination occurred. Azrin and Foxx (1971), as well as Azrin, Bugle, and O'Brien (1971), utilized these devices in conjunction with procedures for increasing subjects' fluid intake (and thereby the frequency of toileting) and monitoring accidents (pants checks). Reinforcement was provided for both appropriate elimination and dry pants. Time-out from reinforcement was employed for toileting accidents. A correction procedure was also used. This procedure required subjects to clean themselves, their clothes, and the affected environment (floor, chair). Azrin and Foxx (1971) successfully used this approach with nine profoundly mentally retarded adults. Their program differed from a forward-moving technique described by Van Wagenen, Meyerson, Kerr and Mahoney (1969), in that no attempt was made to interrupt the clients' inappropriate elimination and take them to the toilet.

Van Wagenen and Murdock (1966) also developed a transistorized signal device that sounded when urination in pants occurred. Van Wagenen et al. (1969) used this apparatus to train nine profoundly mentally retarded children. Their program involved increasing fluid intake to increase the number of target responses, a forward-training procedure, and positive reinforcement for appropriate elimination at the commode. When an accident was in the process of occurring (signaled by the transistorized device) the child was told to stop and was immediately taken to the toilet. The objective was to get the child to turn off and eventually inhibit the inappropriate response (urination in pants) and to turn on the appropriate response (urination in toilet). All subjects were trained in independent toileting within 5 to 22 days.

Nocturnal enuresis in mentally retarded persons has also been targeted by behavior modifiers. Although early research focused on this problem with normal children (Mowrer & Mowrer, 1938), it was not until the late 1960s that investigators began treating enuresis in mentally retarded individuals. Azrin, Sneed, and Foxx (1973) developed a rapid method of decreasing bedwetting for a group of profoundly mentally retarded adults. Their dry-bed procedure entailed use of a urine alarm, increased fluid intake, and hourly toileting trips during the night. Accidents were followed by reprimand, a toilet trip, and an overcorrection procedure (the client cleaned the bed and practiced getting up and going to the toilet for a

45-minute period). The authors reported that the average time to train clients was 1.4 nights.

Communication Skills

Receptive and expressive language deficiencies are common among mentally retarded individuals. Garcia and De Haven (1974) estimated that speech is absent or nearly absent in 75% to 85% of individuals with IQs less than 50. Training of receptive skills has emphasized verbal control of motor behavior (i.e., instruction-following behavior). For example, Whitman, Zakaras, and Chardos (1971) employed physical guidance, fading, and positive reinforcement procedures to increase severely mentally retarded children's compliance to both trained and untrained (generalization) instructions. The training parameters controlling generalized instruction-following have been systematically analyzed by Striefel and his colleagues (Striefel, Wetherby, and Karlan, 1976).

The expressive language of mentally retarded individuals, including both speech and nonvocal communication behaviors, has also been examined frequently by behavioral researchers. For children without any expressive skills, imitative verbal behavior has been focused on as a first step in a speech training program. In an excellent early study, Risley and Wolf (1967) illustrated how imitative behavior can be developed and lead to functional speech in echolalic children. Other studies have focused training on developing basic syntax (emission of sentences with a noun, verb, and object) (Stremal, 1972). More recent social-skill-training programs have focused on conversational skills. Treatment packages, typically consisting of instructions, modeling, behavior rehearsal, and reinforcement, have resulted in changes in such skills as asking and answering questions and extending social invitations (Kelly, Furman, Phillips, Hathorn, & Wilson, 1979).

Although some children are unable to develop functional speech, they are still able to learn to communicate by nonvocal means. For this reason, applied researchers have evaluated a variety of programs for teaching signing. For example, Faw, Reid, Schepis, Fitzgerald, and Welty (1981), using verbal instruction, modeling, manual guidance, contingent reinforcement, and verbal feedback, taught six profoundly mentally retarded adolescents to respond to picture objects with manual signs and to use these signs subsequently in the presence of the objects in their natural environment. Signing skills were found to be maintained over a 33- to 49-week period. In a subsequent study, Schepis et al. (1982) developed an interesting and successful incidental signing program for five profoundly retarded and four autistic children. The incidental program involved rearranging the natural physical environment to prompt signing; altering routine staff-resident interactions so that the staff prompted, manually guided, and reinforced signing; and conducting minitraining sessions.

Social-Leisure and Community Skills

Since the early 1970s, there has been increasing emphasis on the community placement of mentally retarded individuals. With this trend has come the realization that there are a number of skills that facilitate adaptation in community settings. Initially, investigators working with persons with mental retardation emphasized the training of simple social skills such as toy contact or toy manipulation (Wehman & Marchant, 1978) and social interactions among children in a play situation (Strain, 1975). Keogh, Faw, Whitman, and Reid (1984) employed a treatment package, consisting of modeling, verbal and physical prompts, and corrective feedback, to train severely retarded adolescent boys to play with commercial games. Increasingly, more developmentally advanced skills, such as telephone usage (Risley & Cuvo, 1980), money management (Cuvo, Veitch, Trace, & Konke, 1978), pedestrian behavior (Page, Iwata, &

Neef, 1976), clothing-selection (Nutter & Reid, 1978), cooking (Johnson & Cuvo, 1981), use of fast food restaurants and buses (McDonnell & Ferguson, 1988; Marholin, O'Toole, Touchette, Berger, & Doyle, 1979), and mending clothes (Cronin & Cuvo, 1979) have been focused upon in behavioral training programs. For example, in an innovative study, Page et al. (1976) taught basic pedestrian skills to retarded students in a classroom environment that was built to simulate city traffic conditions. The specific responses taught included sequential street crossing, intersection recognition, pedestrian-light skills, traffic-light skills, and stop-sign skills. After training, subjects demonstrated the targeted pedestrian skills under actual city traffic conditions.

With the emphasis on sheltered and supported employment, an increasing number of studies have concentrated on developing work and work-related skills in mildly, moderately, and even severely retarded individuals. Training programs have focused on teaching a variety of simple and more complex job skills, such as sorting different sized bolts and assembling bicycle brakes (Gold, 1972). Particular emphasis in the training literature has been placed on task-analyzing jobs. A comprehensive description of a task analysis is provided by Gold (1976), who distinguished between a content task analysis, in which a task is broken down into teachable behaviors, and a process task analysis, in which the strategies for teaching these behaviors are provided. The training strategies used in vocational programs also differ from those in other skill areas by their emphasis on the use of stimulus prompts, such as jigs and pictorial stimuli. A jig, as described by Gold and Barclay (1973), is a stimulus discrimination aid, such as color-coding different nuts and bolts, to facilitate their being accurately sorted into different storage compartments. In contrast, pictorial prompts cue the responses by showing the trainee how to perform. For example, Wacker and Berg (1984) used pictorial prompts, in conjunction with modeling, feedback, and reinforcement procedures, to facilitate the work performance of severely mentally retarded adolescents on several complex assembly tasks.

In addition to teaching specific job skills, research has focused on maintaining and increasing work output. A variety of procedures has been evaluated in past studies, including differentially reinforcing higher rates of work (Bellamy, Inman, & Yeates, 1978); changing the latency of reinforcement by decreasing pay periods from one month to one week (Martin & Morris, 1980); increasing the amount of money per task (Bates, Renzagalia, & Clees, 1980); and manipulating antecedent stimuli, such as providing specific job information and reducing environmental distractions through use of partitions (Martin, Pallotta-Cornick, Johnston, & Goyos, 1980). (For a further description of procedures for teaching job-related skills, the reader is referred to reviews by Martin, Burger, Burger-Elias, and Mithaug, 1988; and Rusch & Schutz, 1981).

Deceleration Procedures

Although mental retardation is a developmental disorder characterized by the absence of critical adaptive behaviors, mentally retarded persons, particularly the severely and profoundly retarded individuals in institutional settings, also frequently display maladaptive responses (e.g., stereotyped, self-injurious, and aggressive behaviors). Deceleration programs have been employed to prevent clients from hurting themselves or others, to reduce behaviors that interfere with the implementation of adaptive training programs, and to decrease bizarre-appearing behaviors that serve to stigmatize mentally retarded persons in society. A variety of deceleration procedures have been evaluated in past research, including extinction, differential reinforcement, time-out, response cost, aversive stimulation, and overcorrection.

Extinction

Extinction involves the withholding of reinforcement to decrease a maladaptive behavior that presumably developed as a result of being reinforced. Because the extinction process can be very gradual, extinction procedures are commonly employed as one component of a differential reinforcement program. Differential reinforcement programs typically involve putting an inappropriate behavior on extinction and reinforcing either any behavior other than the inappropriate response (DRO), or reinforcing a particular desirable response that inhibits the occurrence of the undesirable behavior. In an example of this type of program, Zlutnick, Mayville, and Moffat (1975) successfully employed differential reinforcement in conjunction with a physical guidance procedure to reduce seizure-like behavior in a 17-year-old boy diagnosed as mentally retarded. Specifically, the boy was guided at the onset of a seizure-like behavior to make an alternative response and then reinforced for this response.

Time-Out and Response Cost

Two procedures that bear some similarity to extinction are time-out from reinforcement and response cost. Time-out involves the loss of opportunity to receive positive reinforcers for a certain period of time. For example, during time-out a child may be placed in a corner of a room or removed from an environment where positive reinforcers are immediately available (e.g., from a playroom where toys and friends are present) and placed in another room where these stimuli are not present. There are several problems with the more radical types of exclusionary procedures, such as those that involve removal of a person from one room to another. These procedures are cumbersome and time-consuming to administer. In addition, exclusionary procedures have been objected to by some who view them as unethical and inhumane and associate them with cruel and unwarranted punishment. To address these problems, Foxx and Shapiro (1978) developed an interesting nonexclusionary procedure, involving a ribbon, for use in a classroom situation. When worn by a child, the ribbon cued teacher reinforcement; however, when misbehavior occurred, the ribbon was removed from the offender, thereby signalling that reinforcement was no longer to be given. After applying this procedure with five retarded children, Foxx and Shapiro found a general reduction in disruptive behaviors from a baseline condition and also from treatment condition during which reinforcement alone was given. Response cost, although similar to time-out, does not involve loss of the opportunity for reinforcement for a period of time but rather the loss of a specific positive reinforcer in an individual's possession. Frequently, response cost procedures are used in conjunction with token economies and involve the loss of tokens or money.

Applying Aversive Stimuli

In contrast to time-out and response cost, some punishment procedures do not withdraw positive reinforcers but involve the administration of aversive stimuli. Certainly, the most recognizable and the most notorious example of this procedure is shock. However, a variety of other aversive stimuli have been used in punishment programs, including lemon juice, aromatic ammonia, water mist, hairtugging, and spanking. In a dramatic example of an effective use of aversive stimuli, Sajwaj, Libet, and Agras (1974) eliminated a chronic, life-threatening rumination response in a 6-month-old child by squirting lemon juice into the child's mouth whenever ruminative tongue movements were observed. Results indicated not only a marked decrease in rumination but also an increase in the child's weight.

Overcorrection

Another commonly employed deceleration procedure is overcorrection. Overcorrection in-

volves one and sometimes two procedures that require an offender either to restore an environment disturbed by his or her deviant behavior, not only to its original state but to an improved state, and/or to practice more appropriate modes of responding. These two general types of procedures have been referred to, respectively, as *restitutional* and *positive-practice* overcorrection. Examples of restitutional overcorrection procedures that have been successfully employed in institutional situations include: having a profoundly retarded, physically aggressive client straighten furniture disturbed during an aggressive episode, as well as straightening other furniture on the ward (Foxx & Azrin, 1972); and requiring retarded adults who stole food from a commissary to return the food and also to purchase additional food for the commissary (Azrin & Wesolowski, 1974). Positive-practice procedures, which also vary considerably in their specific structure, have been used to decrease a variety of behaviors, including stereotypy and self-injurious behavior (Foxx & Azrin, 1973a). Both types of overcorrection procedure have been effectively employed in toilet-training programs with retarded children (Azrin & Foxx, 1971; Foxx & Azrin, 1973b). Children who had accidents were required to clean themselves (restitution) and then to practice repeatedly going to the toilet: specifically, pulling their pants down, sitting down, getting up, and pulling up their pants (positive practice).

Ethical Issues

Society's perception and acceptance of a punishment technique has and will undoubtedly continue to determine the extent of the employment of that technique. At present, therapists are reluctant to use the more restrictive and aversive punishment programs, even when less restrictive procedures have been unsuccessful. The reasons for this position are complex, relating to the association of punishment with cruel and inhumane treatment, production of unnecessary pain, and physical abuse. Society has tended to perceive punishment as a means of dealing with more criminal and delinquent types of behavior. In psychiatric circles, punishment has been linked with engendering anxiety, which in turn is seen as precipitating maladaptive avoidance responses and defense mechanisms. Ultimately, if behavior modifiers are to use punishment procedures, they must empirically document that these procedures are effective and do not produce undesirable side effects, and educate the public concerning the appropriate educative use of these techniques.

Verbal Instruction

Traditional behavioral education programs have focused on the manipulation of consequences to modify responding. However, with the growing interest in cognitive variables within the field of mental retardation, more attention has been directed by behaviorists toward examining and manipulating the antecedents of behavior to achieve desired outcomes. One of the most-utilized educational techniques is verbal instruction. Although the vast majority of cognitive and behavioral training programs for persons with mental retardation contain a verbal component, surprisingly little research has been directed toward examining the relative efficacy of verbal instructional methods versus other methods. In a revealing study, Repp, Barton, and Brulle (1981) evaluated the effectiveness of five different types of staff instruction with severely mentally retarded students: (1) verbal instruction, (2) gestural instruction, (3) verbal instruction with physical assistance, (4) nonverbal instruction with physical assistance, and (5) physical assistance. Data were collected on the instruction-following behavior of the clients in several naturalistic settings. The authors reported that verbal instruction, the most commonly utilized instruction, was one of the least effective methods of obtaining an appro-

priate response, whereas some type of physical assistance, either administered alone or with a gestural instruction, was the least utilized and yet most effective instructional technique. Extrapolating from research suggesting that persons with mental retardation have attentional and associational problems (Luria, 1961; Zeaman & House, 1963, 1979), Whitman (1987) has theorized that this population may also have difficulty focusing on the pertinent cues contained in verbal instructions, and as a consequence have difficulties using speech to control motor behavior. In the next sections, two methods for developing verbal control will be briefly described: correspondence training and self-instruction.

Correspondence Training

Correspondence training has been employed to increase various academic, social, and personal behaviors, such as listening and appropriate sitting, sharing, appropriate posture, and choosing nutritious snacks (Baer, Blount, Detrich, & Stokes, 1987; Keogh Burgio, Whitman, & Johnson, 1983; Whitman, Scibak, Butler, Richter, & Johnson, 1982). In applying this training procedure, the assumption is made that there should be a relationship between what people say and what they do. Past research has indicated that persons with mental retardation often fail to self-regulate verbally and are excessively dependent on others for guidance and direction (Whitman, 1987; Zigler, 1966). Thus, the establishment of correspondence between verbal and non-verbal behavior in persons with mental retardation appears to be an especially appropriate endeavor, specifically because it establishes the individual as the locus of control through developing verbal self-regulation. Correspondence training can proceed in one of two basic sequences: (1) reinforcing an individual for doing what he or she says (say-do) or (2) reinforcing a person for truth-telling or accurately reporting (saying) what he or she actually did (do-say). Although it has been argued that both of these procedures facilitate verbal control of nonverbal behavior (Rogers-Warren & Baer, 1976), research suggests that the say-do procedure may be more effective in accomplishing this goal (Paniagna, Pumariega, and Black, 1988).

To date, only a handful of studies have explored the utility of correspondence training with mentally retarded persons. In an example of research in this area, Keogh, Burgio, Whitman, and Johnson (1983) used a combined say-do and do-say treatment package to increase listening skills in moderately and mildly mentally retarded individuals in an instructional situation. During correspondence training, the subjects were required to state what they had to do to be good listeners. The subjects were then videotaped during a listening task and the appropriateness of listening behavior was rated. Following this session, subjects were asked a series of questions concerning their behavior during the task (e.g., Were you quiet? Did you look at the teacher?) Reinforcement was provided when correspondence occurred *both* between what the children said they would do and what they actually did (say-do), *and* between what they actually did and what they said they did (do-say). Results indicated that all children increased their listening skills in the training situation and that several of the subjects showed generalization of their appropriate listening to two different settings.

Self-Instruction

In addition to correspondence training and external (e.g., teacher-administered) instructional procedures, a third verbal training technique, self-instruction, has been employed with persons with mental retardation. Self-instruction, although similar to external instruction, requires individuals to cue themselves verbally during the training process. Self-instruction is also similar to correspondence training, in that emphasis is placed on developing self-regulatory speech. However, self-instruction typically involves a more complex set of verbal

cues to be learned by the student, as well as a more complex teaching algorithm. Based on the fact that past research has shown that persons with mental retardation have difficulties attending to and organizing stimulus input (House & Zeaman, 1963; Spitz, 1973), self-instruction appears to be particularly suited for use with this population, in that it focuses attention on relevant verbal cues, facilitates organization of nonverbal stimuli, and encourages verbal self-regulation of action.

Self-instructional training has been successfully used to increase a variety of behaviors in persons with mental retardation, including general and specific academic skills such as attending and math skills (Burgio, Whitman & Johnson, 1980; Johnston, Whitman, & Johnson, 1980); social-leisure skills (Keogh, Faw, Whitman, & Reid, 1984); and vocational skills (Whitman, Spence, & Maxwell, 1987; Rusch, Morgan, Martin, Riva, & Agran, 1985). From a content perspective, the instructions employed in past research typically included several statements focusing upon: (1) task definition, (2) behavioral strategies for approaching a task, (3) the need for self-evaluation, (4) the use of self-coping strategies, and (5) self-reinforcement. Burgio et al. (1980) utilized this type of self-instructional package to increase attending behavior with highly distractible mildly and moderately mentally retarded children. Strategic self-instructions were introduced to assist students in completing printing and math assignments, ignoring distractions, and dealing with task failure. After the children were taught to self-instruct through modeling, behavioral rehearsal, and fading procedures, distracting auditory and visual stimuli were introduced into the training situation to simulate natural conditions in the classroom. Children were requested to verbalize distraction-ignoring self-statements (e.g., I am not going to look. I'm going to keep doing my work). The results indicated that mentally retarded children could be taught to use a relatively complex set of self-instructions and that the use of these self-instructions was associated with reductions in off-task behavior and distractibility. Although changes in the rate and accuracy in printing and math did not occur, the authors suggested that performance improvements might have been observed if the program had been continued over a longer period of time.

Self-Management Techniques

A variety of rationales have been given for using self-management techniques with mentally retarded individuals. This approach is consistent with the philosophical notion that this population should be allowed to participate in their own programming, make choices, and become as independent as possible (Litrownik, 1982). From a practical perspective, it has also been suggested that self-management programs will promote maintenance and generalization of behavior change, and require less instructional time and effort than traditional behavior management methods (Cole, Gardner, & Karan, 1985). Whereas the essential feature of self-instruction is its emphasis on client self-verbalization, self-management programs are distinguished by their provision of specific strategies to enable children to self-regulate. Although self-instructional training programs often incorporate specific self-management strategies, self-management training programs may or may not be enacted through use of a self-instructional training format. A three-stage model of self-regulation, proposed by Kanfer (1970) and Kanfer and Karoly (1972), has had considerable impact on the development of self-management programs. This model suggests that for individuals to regulate their own behavior independently, they must learn to set appropriate standards or criteria for their performance, to self-monitor their actions, and to self-administer contingencies to their behavior. These procedures, which have been examined in past research with mentally retarded persons, will be summarized briefly here. For more extensive discussion of this self-management literature the reader is referred to Litrownik (1982); Martin, Burger, Burger-Elias, and Mithaug (1988); and Whitman, Burgio, and Johnston (1984).

Setting Standards

Litrownik, Cleary, Lecklitner, and Franzini (1978) suggest that for mentally retarded persons, the ability to set appropriate self-imposed standards is crucial to independent functioning. These authors investigated whether moderately mentally retarded children were capable of developing this skill in the context of a bowling game. After observing a videotape of clown models who set and subsequently met their own criteria for the number of pins to be knocked down during a frame, the children were able to establish and meet the same performance standards as the clown models. Litrownick et al. subsequently, employing a similar modeling procedure, trained the children to develop standards based on their own past bowling performance. After training, the children learned to set and maintain appropriate personal standards for themselves not only on the bowling task, but also on two (pinball and picture-matching) generalization tasks. Although this study suggests that persons who are mentally retarded can learn to set standards, research is needed to assess the extent to which standard-setting interventions facilitate behavioral productivity (e.g., quality and quantity of output in the academic or work arena). Snow, Mercatoris, Beal, and Weber (1982) suggest that this type of intervention would be particularly useful in workshop settings, where tasks are manual and concrete.

Self-Monitoring

A second self-management procedure, self-monitoring, was originally used as a means of obtaining baseline data outside of a formal treatment environment. Recognition of the reactive effects of self-monitoring has led clinicians to employ this technique as an intervention in its own right with a variety of populations, including individuals who are mentally retarded. For example, Zegiob, Klukas, and Junginger (1978) found that self-monitoring could be successfully employed to decrease nose and mouth picking and stereotypic behavior in mildly and moderately retarded adolescents. Intervention focused on teaching the trainees to identify the occurrence of these target behaviors and record them on an index card. These self-monitoring procedures were explained, modeled, and prompted during an initial session. In subsequent sessions, subjects were given the materials necessary to self-record without further instruction. Results indicated that training produced dramatic decreases in target behaviors, gains that were maintained at a 6-month follow-up. Findings from this study further suggested that for some individuals, delivering noncontingent social praise for involvement in the self-management program led to further decreases in target behaviors over and above those produced by the initial self-monitoring intervention. Although subjects were found to lack accuracy in their self-recording, this fact did not appear to influence the effectiveness of the intervention. Litrownik, Freitas, and Franzini (1978) demonstrated that moderately and even severely retarded children can be taught to accurately self-monitor in a bowling situation through the use of a modeling procedure.

Self-Reinforcement

A third self-management procedure, self-reinforcement, has typically been used in conjunction with self-monitoring techniques. Individuals with mental retardation have been able to learn to self-reinforce and, as a consequence, effect other changes in their own behavior. For example, Shapiro and his colleagues conducted several studies with mildly mentally retarded

children who were off-task in a classroom situation. Shapiro and Klein (1980) taught four moderately mentally retarded children to self-monitor and self-reinforce their on-task behavior through the use of a multiphase intervention program. During treatment, the teacher initially awarded tokens for a child's on-task behavior. After the token program had been in effect for two sessions, a self-assessment phase occurred in which children learned to self-monitor their own on-task behavior accurately. The teacher introduced and gradually faded verbal prompts, instructions, and direction, and initiated a questioning procedure. During questioning, children were asked after a timer went off, "Do you get a token? Why?" In the next phase, children were first verbally prompted by the teacher to take a token, then nonverbally prompted to take a token, and finally were expected to take a token without teacher prompts. In a final phase, children were required to perform all steps of the self-management program independently. Large gains in on-task behavior, which occurred during the initial token program, were maintained throughout the self-management training phases and at a 2-month follow-up. Shapiro, McGonigle, and Ollendick (1980) subsequently examined the utility of a simple versus a more intensive training procedure for teaching moderately and mildly retarded children to self-manage (self-monitor and self-reinforce) their on-task behavior. Results demonstrated that a more elaborate self-management program, similar to that used by Shapiro and Klein (1980), was needed to maintain high levels of on-task responses. Although both of these studies provide suggestive evidence concerning the effectiveness of self-reinforcement procedures, the relative contribution of self-reinforcement and self-assessment to the treatment effect remains unclear and needs to be examined. Shapiro et al. (1980) suggest that the effect of self-reinforcement over and above self-monitoring may vary across individuals.

Cognitive and Metacognitive Interventions

Mentally retarded individuals have been found to use fewer, simpler, and more passive cognitive strategies than nonretarded individuals do in memory and learning-task situations (Butterfield & Ferretti, 1987). Research has also documented that mentally retarded persons have problem-solving deficits (Turnure & Zigler, 1964); lack logical foresight (Spitz & Winters, 1977); and have a limited search capacity (Borys, Spitz, & Donans, 1982). Although a fundamental and irreversible inability to produce and use specific task-relevant strategies was thought at one time to account for the poor performance exhibited by mentally retarded individuals, a decade of research has established that mentally retarded individuals are capable of acquiring and using such strategies to mediate performance on a variety of memory and learning tasks (Campione, 1987). For example, Ross and Ross (1973, 1978) conducted a series of studies to demonstrate that retarded children can develop complex problem-solving skills. In one study having particular applied significance (Ross & Ross, 1978), educable mentally retarded children were trained to choose the best alternative from a number of solutions to familiar social or environmental problems. Training took place in discussion groups of four or five participants. The following issues were discussed: the concept of choice and an order criteria for choosing one of several attractive or unattractive alternatives, choices in emergency situations, and choices based on logic. Choices were taught in the context of game situations, and subjects were given tallies on a score card for good answers or for trying hard. Results showed that the training group was superior to the control group in selecting the best choice and in providing reasons for their choices. Although the subjects required 40 training sessions to acquire these cognitive skills, the authors stressed that the length of time spent in training was justified by the long-term social benefits for these children.

A main focus of strategy training research has been on developing instructional methods for promoting strategy maintenance and transfer. For example, Burger, Blackman, Holmes, and Zetlin (1978) developed a training program to teach mildly retarded children the use of a sorting and retrieval strategy in a memory task situation. Subjects were asked to recall pictures of common items that belonged to several superordinate categories. The strategy taught to facilitate recall involved asking subjects to group together pictures that seemed to go together, to identify the superordinate category to which the items belonged, and to count the number of pictures in each category. Results indicated that the performance of subjects given this training was superior to a control group on measures of short- and long-term recall. Burger, Blackman, and Tan (1980) found at a 6-month follow-up of subjects in this study that the children had maintained use of the instructed strategy. These authors cited the following training conditions as critical for achieving maintenance: (1) active participation by the children, (2) multiple training sessions over several days, (3) analysis of important task components, (4) systematic introduction of the relevant strategies, (5) employment of fading techniques, and (6) provision of information to the children regarding the value of strategy use.

Although specific strategy training research has produced a general optimism that many cognitive deficiencies of persons with mental retardation can be remediated, the inability of this population to employ instructed strategies effectively across situations has led researchers to postulate that mentally retarded persons possess a metacognitive deficiency. Metacognition refers to the knowledge an individual possesses about his cognitive process and products (Flavell, 1976). Closely linked to the concept of metacognition is that of executive functioning, which refers to the actual use of metacognitive knowledge in regulating strategic deployment. Mentally retarded children have been found to be deficient in both metacognitive knowledge and executive processing skills (Borkowski & Kurtz, 1987; Campione, 1987). In general, research in this area suggests that both general strategic knowledge and executive routines should be provided during instructional efforts, to promote flexible use of specific strategies. Although metacognitive training programs for individuals with mental retardation vary considerably, these programs typically contain one or more of the following components.

1. Active involvement is encouraged. The child is sensitized concerning the relationship of personal effort and successful performance.
2. Self-awareness is promoted. The child is encouraged to analyze and examine in a learning situation what he or she knows about a task and how it might be approached.
3. In addition to being given specific instruction about strategy employment, information concerning the general utility of a strategy in other situations is provided.
4. Self-monitoring, planning and, checking skills are taught, to ensure that strategies are deployed effectively.

For specific examples of how such programs have been structured with persons with mental retardation, the reader is referred to the work of Brown, Campione, and their colleagues (Brown & Barclay, 1976; Campione & Brown, 1978; Brown, Campione, & Murphy, 1977).

Visual Instruction and Imagery

Although programs for teaching behavioral and cognitive skills to persons with mental retardation typically rely on the use of verbal and/or nonverbal visual cues, inspection of these programs reveals the primary role of verbal instruc-

tion. The appropriateness of this emphasis on verbal instruction, however, has been questioned because of the pronounced language deficiencies of individuals with mental retardation (Matthews, 1971; Yoder & Miller, 1972). Because the perceptual system of children with mental retardation seems to be relatively better-developed than their verbal representational system (Inhelder, 1968), a number of investigators have suggested that visually-oriented techniques might be more effectively employed than verbal procedures in teaching children with mental retardation (Mansdorf, 1977; Pressley, 1990; Whitman, 1990). A variety of visual cuing procedures has been evaluated in past research, including modeling, picture cueing, and imagery induction (Cullinan, 1976; Greeson, & Jens, 1977; Groden & Cautela, 1984; Mansdorf, 1977; Martin, Rusch, James, Decker, & Trtol, 1982; Pressley, Cariglia-Bull, Deane, & Schneider, 1987; Smith & Meyers, 1979; Wacker & Berg, 1983). Of these procedures, imagery induction relies most heavily on the use of verbal cues to elicit visual mediators, and picture cueing relies almost exclusively on concrete visual cues. The latter procedure has been found to be particularly effective in developing complex skills in training programs with severely handicapped individuals.

For example, Wacker & Berg (1984) used picture prompts to teach three severely/moderately mentally retarded individuals a valve assembly task. The task involved collecting a specified number of parts and placing them in compartments at three different work stations. A book was created with pictures depicting each of 18 different pieces involved in the task. Pictures were sequentially arranged in the book, corresponding to the order they were to be placed at the work station. At the bottom of each picture was a number specifying the number of pieces to be placed in a compartment. During training, students were taught to turn the pages in order, select the objects depicted by the pictures, count the correct number of objects, and place the objects on the assembly tray. Minimal training was required to teach the students to use the picture prompts. Performance increased from an average of 4% accuracy during baseline to 100% accuracy at posttest. Additionally, the participants generalized their behavior to a task on which they had received no training, performing at 96% accuracy. When the pictures were removed during a second baseline, accuracy dropped to 50%. Martin et al. (1982) also employed picture prompts to teach severely mentally retarded individuals to prepare a complex meal. Martin and colleagues suggested that picture prompts can be used to establish a look-do behavioral sequence similar to the say-do sequence used in correspondence training. Although previous research suggests that picture prompts are effective in directly controlling behavior, it is not clear to what extent picture prompts can be faded to promote greater independent functioning..

FUTURE RESEARCH DIRECTIONS

In this section, a variety of areas that should be addressed in future research are described. For a more extensive discussion of these areas the reader is referred to Whitman, Hantula, and Spence (1990).

The Development of Self-Regulation

Because of the mentally retarded individual's dependency on others, it is not surprising that behavior modifiers have progressively turned their attention to the development of technologies that teach self-control and self-management skills. In general, the research reviewed in this chapter suggests that a variety of self-management skills, including standard setting, self-monitoring, self-reinforcement, problem

solving, and specific cognitive and general metacognitive strategies, can be taught to individuals with mental retardation. Research also suggests that such skills not only can be taught, but also, when utilized, can result in more appropriate academic, job-related, and community living behaviors (Shapiro, 1981, 1986; Whitman, 1987; Whitman, Burgio, & Johnston, 1984). Shapiro (1986) concludes that although it is unlikely that mentally retarded individuals will acquire self-control skills without instruction, they are often capable of learning these skills with a minimum of effort.

In their review of research in the self-management area, Martin et al. (1988) found that self-management procedures generally produce durable and generalizable behavior changes. In studies where comparison data were available, they also observed that self-management instruction appeared to be more successful in achieving these effects than traditional trainer-based programs. Martin et al. (1988) suggested that future research on self-management procedures should examine the relative contributions of the different self-management components (e.g., self-monitoring and self-reinforcement) to the total self-management process, the specific circumstances in which these components are most effective, and the questions of whether multicomponent procedures are more effective than a single approach and to what extent these procedures, once learned, are employed in other situations. Special attention should be given by researchers to assessing the characteristics of individuals who benefit most from self-management training and to examining how this type of training can be structured to serve a greater number of individuals. For example, future research needs to examine how the linguistic abilities of retarded individuals determine the amount of benefit they derive from self-management programs delivered through a self-instructional format and how this format can best be arranged to facilitate learning for individuals who are less verbally skilled. At present, it appears that verbal self-regulation will more readily develop in individuals who have better language skills and that individuals who are less linguistically proficient may require more extensive training before verbal control of motor behavior is established (Whitman, 1987).

Behavioral Pharmacology

Although pharmacological interventions have been effectively employed to increase adaptive behavior and to decrease maladaptive behavior, these interventions can be problematic. Drugs affect the entire biochemical as well as the behavioral system of the individual. For example, tranquilizers that inhibit maladaptive behavior may also interfere with the acquisition and maintenance of adaptive behaviors, and long-term use of tranquilizers may cause a variety of physiological side effects, such as tardive dyskinesia and other Parkinsonian-like syndromes (Burgio, Page, & Capriotti, 1985; Gualtieri & Hawk, 1980; Marholin, Touchette, & Stewart, 1979). For these reasons, researchers have investigated the viability of other treatment options. A variety of studies suggests that contingency management procedures work as well as or better than pharmacological programs in reducing the frequency of inappropriate behaviors (Burgio, et al., 1985; Durand, 1982; Luiselli, 1986; Rapport, Murphy, & Bailey, 1982; Shafto & Sulzbacher, 1977; Singh & Winton, 1984). Research also indicates that once sufficient stimulus control over behavior is obtained, the need for drugs is reduced (Laties, Wood, & Cooper, 1981). Given the efficacy of non-drug behavioral treatments and the fact that therapeutic drug usage may expose an individual to a host of potential undesirable and sometimes permanent side effects, it would seem that pharmacological agents should be employed only as a temporary means to gain environmental control over behavior. Before such a conclusion is drawn, however, research should address more systematically the issue of behav-

ioral co-variation, more specifically to evaluate nontargeted behaviors that might be adversely or positively affected by pharmacotherapy in addition to those that the drug was intended to change (Schroeder, Gualtieri, & Van Bourgondien, 1986). Research is also needed to examine the relative efficacy of behavioral and pharmacological approaches and the utility of these approaches in combination for controlling various types of maladaptive behavior.

Electromechanical Aids and Microcomputers

Until recently, behavioral educators have not stressed the development of electromechanical aids and modified environments. However, the integration of such aids with behavior management seems to have much to offer severely and profoundly handicapped individuals. In instances where behavior modification programs cannot effect direct changes in adaptive behavior, the behavioral programmer may be able to teach retarded persons how to use devices such as wheelchairs and canes, alternative communication systems, artificial limbs, hearing aids, and eyeglasses that in turn enable them to interact more effectively with their living environments. Moreover, behavior modifiers should be able to assist in designing and evaluating new living environments that are less behaviorally demanding, more accessible, and more usable by multihandicapped persons (Jones, Lattimore, Ulicny, & Risley, 1986). In general, the outlook for the development and utilization of such technology is bright. The rapidly expanding availability of microcomputers and electromechanical equipment may signal a new era in the development of aids for the multihandicapped individual (Coker, 1984; Pfadt & Tryon, 1983). Electromechanical devices are relatively inexpensive, easily constructed and maintained, and may be adapted to a wide variety of client needs (Mulick, Scott, Gaines, & Campbell, 1983). When interfaced with a microcomputer, electromechanical devices allow minute responses, such as wrist turns or head nods, to control significant environmental events. At present, research is needed to examine the use of behavioral techniques to help handicapped persons employ existing and newly developed aids, and to assess how modified living environments can increase the frequency of adaptive responses and reduce maladaptive behavior.

The microcomputer can also serve functions besides that of an aid to coping with the environment. For example, it can be employed as an individualized tutor. Because training and education with the mentally retarded are often highly individualized, computer-assisted instruction (CAI) provides a means of delivering individualized instruction without focusing all of the teacher's time on one student. Applications of CAI with the mentally retarded can be used to teach academic skills, such as reading and mathematics, or to teach more basic discrimination and conceptual skills. (See Ager, 1985; Conners, Caruso, & Detterman, 1986; and Tighe & Groeneweg, 1985 for reviews, and Lally, 1981, 1982, for CAI applications of minicomputers.) Although existing CAI systems cannot always be employed with mentally retarded individuals, these systems can be adapted and modified to meet the specific physical and behavioral needs of retarded individuals, such as by providing other input devices than the usual keyboard (see Wood, 1986, for a review). Clearly the effectiveness of CAI systems for teaching persons with varying levels of mental retardation also should be evaluated and compared with more traditional forms of instruction.

Programs for Elderly Mentally Retarded Individuals

Although individuals with mental retardation are living longer (Lubin & Kiely, 1985), research directed at developing and evaluating behavior modification programs for the elderly members of this population has been sparse (Foxx, McMorrow, Bittle, & Ness, 1986; Kleitsch, Whitman, & Santos, 1983; Schleien, Weyman, & Kiernan, 1981). The reason for this lack of empirical study is unclear. It seems likely that applied researchers do not view elderly mentally retarded people as distinct from younger mentally retarded individuals and tacitly assume that the needs of older retarded individuals can be met through the same types of programs developed for younger populations. Available evidence suggests, however, that the needs of the aging mentally retarded individuals are different from those of younger mentally retarded people, as well as from aging individuals of normal intellectual capacity (Heller, 1985; Puccio, Janicki, Otis, & Rettig, 1983).

From a therapeutic perspective, a variety of programs seem mandated. Programs are needed to teach the aged mentally retarded how to cope with and adapt to the aging process and to live independently for a longer period of time; for example, programs could teach them new behaviors, such as being responsible for taking their medication, using community medical facilities, and employing devices such as a cane or walker. Programs are also needed to help retarded individuals adapt to new living arrangements. Older retarded individuals, dependent on elderly parents, may suddenly be placed in nursing homes when a parent becomes ill or dies. Elderly group-home residents who are unable to participate in existing day programs may also be relocated. Such relocations in the nonretarded elderly are often associated with increases in stress, illness, and mortality rates (Heller, 1985). Transition for retarded individuals might be eased by appropriate behavioral training programs that allow for a gradual transition into a new setting. Cognitive-behavioral programming may also assist retarded individuals in coping with personal loss, particularly loss due to the death of parents, relatives, and friends. The challenge that behavior modifiers must confront is to recognize when existing behavioral interventions are adequate with this population, when these programs should be revised and tailored to the changing needs of the aging retarded individuals, and when new programs must be developed. To ensure proper program selection, behavioral practitioners must evaluate the efficacy of both existing and new programs.

Family Interventions

Research suggests that the presence of a mentally retarded child in a family may increase stress and lead to family schism (Reed & Reed, 1965). Bristol (1979) found that one variable differentiating high-stress from low-stress mothers of autistic children was the adequacy of the informal social supports provided by the nuclear family, extended family, friends, neighbors, and parents of other developmentally delayed children. Although in the past, behavioral training programs have typically involved only mothers of retarded children, Parke (1986) has argued that conceptualizations concerning the parenting unit must be expanded to include the father-child unit and mother-father-child relationships. Research indicates, however, that fathers of mentally retarded children show more signs of stress, are less effective copers, and are less involved with their handicapped child than are mothers (Bristol & Gallagher, 1986; Cummings, 1976; Gallagher, Scharfman, & Bristol, 1984). Results by Stoneman and Brody (1982) indicate that despite the fact that a developmentally delayed child puts increased demands on the family, fathers of these children do not help mothers any more than do fathers of nonhandicapped children. In combination, these studies suggest that inclusion of fathers of mentally retarded children in parent training programs may have positive effects on the children's development, maternal well-being, the marital relationship, and general family functioning. A broader family-systems conceptualization suggests that inclusion of nonhandicapped siblings in intervention programs may

also be advisable. Farber (1975) contends that families of severely retarded children are better able to cope when siblings are able to assume helping roles in the family. In support of this contention, a variety of studies indicates the positive effects of sibling interaction on child development (see Brody & Stoneman, 1986, for a review). In a more general vein, the influence of social support systems, extrafamilial as well as intrafamilial, on family stability should be examined. Data from Wahler's (1980) study indicate that a mother's successful implementation of a behavioral intervention program is directly related to the availability of social supports.

Thus, both research and theory indicates that behavior modifiers could benefit considerably from taking a broader family-systems perspective as they structure home intervention programs for retarded children. Particular attention should be given to the development of early intervention programs to be implemented when the handicapped individual first shows signs of delay. More emphasis also should be placed on structuring and evaluating training programs that include the fathers and siblings of retarded family members as well as the mothers. It seems likely that inclusion of multiple family members in a training program should reduce family conflict and stress, improve the family's perception of its retarded member, and facilitate both enduring and generalized behavioral changes. A family-systems perspective suggests that in addition to the direct and indirect effects of the program on each family member, the status of various family relationships, such as the marital relationship and nonhandicapped sibling-parent relationships, should be assessed.

TREATMENT RESOURCES

Cipani, E. (Ed.). (1989). *The treatment of severe behavior disorders.* Washington, DC: American Association on Mental Retardation. (A monograph describing recent promising developments for treating the severe behavior problems of persons with mental retardation and other developmental disorders.)

Dever, R. B. (1988).*Community living skills*. Washington, DC: American Association on Mental Retardation. (Identifies the skills needed for independence in everyday life.)

The following texts describe the principles and procedures of applied behavior analysis, along with examples of specific training programs for persons with mental retardation.

Repp, A. C. (1983). *Teaching the mentally retarded*. Englewood Cliffs, NJ: Prentice-Hall.

Rusch, F. R., Rose, T., & Greenwood, C. R. (1988). *Introduction to behavior analysis in special education*. Englewood Cliffs, NJ: Prentice Hall.

Whitman, T. L., Scibak, J. W., & Reid, D. H. (1983). *Behavior modification with the severely and profoundly retarded: Research and application*. San Diego: Academic Press.

Wolery, M., Bailey, D. B., & Sugai, G. M. (1988). *Effective teaching: Principles and procedures of applied behavior analysis with exceptional students*. Boston: Allyn & Bacon.

CHAPTER 20

Autism

Laura Schreibman

Few professionals would dispute that children with autism present one of the most interesting, frustrating, and important challenges with which researchers and clinicians must deal. The intriguing and sometimes bizarre behavioral excesses and deficits exhibited by these severely handicapped children have stimulated substantial research interest somewhat out of proportion to the relative rarity of the disorder (approximately 1 in 2,500 births). Despite numerical infrequency, however, the impact of an autistic child on the family, schools, community, and society is substantial. It is not surprising that efforts to understand the disorder and develop effective treatments have remained in the forefront of research.

Nothing about autism seems to be simple, and this can certainly be said about its treatment. The first treatment model for autism was based on the concept that the disorder was

Preparation of this chapter was supported by U.S. Public Health Service Research Grants MH 39434 and 28210 from the National Institute of Mental Health.

caused by psychopathology in the parents and that the way to treat the children was to remove them from the parents and place them in another environment with totally accepting and nurturing surrogate parents (Bettelheim, 1967). Systematic investigation of both the theory of etiology and the treatment has led to the conclusion that both the parent-causation hypothesis of etiology and the psychodynamic treatment approach based on this hypothesis are incorrect (Cantwell, Baker, & Rutter, 1978; Cox, Rutter, Newman, & Bartak, 1975; De-Myer, 1979; Koegel, Schreibman, O'Neill, & Burke, 1983; McAdoo & DeMyer, 1978; Pitfield & Oppenheim, 1964; Schopler & Reichler, 1971). Thus, we now know that autism is an organically-based disorder, not caused by the parents, and that a completely different approach to treatment is warranted.

Because of the failure of the psychodynamic approach to provide effective treatment for children with autism, the behavioral model of treatment was attempted (Lovaas, 1979). Fortunately, the behavioral model, with its strong foundation in the experimental analysis of behavior, has proven to be an effective treatment approach. In fact, behavioral treatment has been the only treatment model empirically determined to be effective with autistic children.

DESCRIPTION OF AUTISM

Autism was first described as a distinct clinical disorder by Leo Kanner in 1943. Kanner noted a group of children that he determined were qualitatively different from other child clinical populations. He specified several behavioral characteristics that he considered important in differentiating autistic children from other disordered youngsters. Over the years there has been some controversy as to which behaviors are indeed requisite for the diagnosis of autism, but most of Kanner's original criteria remain. What follows is a description of the behavioral characteristics that are most often associated with the diagnosis of autism.

Specific Behavioral Characteristics

Deficits in Social Behavior

Probably the hallmark feature of autism is severe and pervasive *deficits in social attachment and behavior*. Many professionals have indicated that abnormal social behavior is primary to the diagnosis (Fein, Pennington, Markowitz, Braverman, & Waterhouse, 1986; Rimland, 1964; Rutter, 1978; Schreibman, 1988a; L. Wing, 1976). Typically, these children show little or no attachment to their parents, fail to establish eye contact, prefer to be alone, and do not interact with peers. As infants, they may stiffen or go limp when held and fail to raise their arms in anticipation of being picked up from the crib. When older, they may actively avoid affection,

do not come to their parents when hurt or frightened, are not unhappy to see their parents leave, and show no emotion when the parents return after an absence. Indeed, it is quite dramatic to see a child who is not genuinely attached to his or her parents, and it is equally dramatic to hear a mother lament that her child does not need her. Autistic children are true loners in the complex social environment that is so important to the development of normal children (Schreibman, 1988a).

Language Deficits

Another important behavioral characteristic of autistic children is their failure to acquire communicative *language* (Ornitz & Ritvo, 1976; Rutter, 1978; Schreibman, 1988a; J. K. Wing, 1966; L. Wing, 1976). Approximately half of children with autism do not develop functional speech (Rutter, 1978), and those who do, characteristically exhibit speech that is qualitatively different than the speech of normal children or children with other disorders (Bartak, Bartolucci, & Pierce, 1977; Ricks & Wing, 1975; Rutter, 1965, 1978; L. Wing, 1976). Those autistic children who do acquire speech typically exhibit a speech anomaly known as *echolalia*, the repetition of the speech of others (Fay, 1969). *Immediate echolalia* occurs when the child repeats something just heard (Carr, Schreibman, & Lovaas, 1975; Fay, 1969; Schreibman & Carr, 1978). For example, the child answers, "Are you a good boy?" when asked, "Are you a good boy?" *Delayed echolalia* occurs when the child repeats something he or she has heard in the past. For example, a child sitting at the dinner table might begin to repeat a television commercial heard several hours (days, months, etc.) ago.

Speaking autistic children also frequently exhibit *pronominal reversal*, wherein pronouns are used incorrectly. The most common problem being that the child uses "you" instead of "I." Thus, the child may say to the parent, "*You* want to go outside" rather than, "*I* want to go outside." In addition, the speech of these children is often characterized by *dysprosody*, where the melodic features of speech are inaccurate, making it sound abnormal (Baltaxe, 1981; Baltaxe & Simmons, 1975; Schreibman, Kohlenberg, & Britten, 1986; Simon, 1976). In such cases the speech tends to be inaccurate in pitch, rhythm, inflection, intonation, pace, and/or articulation.

Ritualistic Behavior

Another of Kanner's original criteria that is still considered important in the diagnosis of autism is the children's *ritualistic behavior and insistence on sameness in their environment* (Schreibman, 1988a). The children may be particularly compulsive, ritualistically lining up objects such as blocks or toy cars in neat rows, perhaps by color or size. They may insist on wearing particular items of clothing or eating only particular foods, to the exclusion of others. Such children often have unusual fixations with such things as numbers, letters, bus routes, geometric shapes, or schedules. For example, one child was so concerned with vacuum cleaners that he insisted on taking a Dust Buster to bed with him at night; another was so obsessed with newsman Dan Rather that he wanted to talk about little else. These children may insist on collecting certain objects that they must carry with them at all times. They may display a marked resistance to changes in their environment, noticing even minute changes such as the altered position of a chair in the living room. They may resist changes in daily routine or routes of travel. In all of these cases the children may become extremely upset if their rituals or compulsions are interrupted or violated.

Sensory Responsiveness

Individuals with autism frequently appear to possess a sensory deficit, and indeed many of the children have histories of suspected but unconfirmed deafness or blindness. They display an *unusual responsiveness to their sensory environment* (Lovaas, Koegel, & Schreibman, 1979; Ornitz & Ritvo, 1976; Rimland, 1964; Schreibman & Charlop, 1989; Schreibman & Koegel, 1981, 1982). A child might seem not to see a person walking into the room but on another occasion could be fascinated by watching particles of dust fall in a beam of light. Similarly, a child may not respond to his or her name but can repeat a television commercial heard several hours previously. This unusual responsiveness is often referred to as *apparent* sensory deficit because the deficit is more apparent than real (Schreibman, 1988a).

Self-Stimulation

Another behavior frequently seen in children with autism is *self-stimulation* (Lovaas, Newsom, & Hickman, 1987; Ornitz & Ritvo, 1976; Rimland, 1964). This is repetitive, stereotyped behavior whose primary function seems to be to provide the child with sensory feedback. The most common forms of self-stimulation (also called stereotypy or disturbances of motility) are rhythmic body rocking, rocking from foot to foot, waving or flapping of the arms and/or hands (often in front of the eyes), spinning in circles, quick darting movements, and body posturing. Other common forms of self-stimulation are toe walking, head rolling, repetitive vocalizations, spinning objects, gazing at lights, and repeatedly rubbing textured surfaces. This behavior is significant in that it not only makes the child look bizarre and abnormal, but it also has been shown to interfere with the child's responsiveness and learning (Koegel & Covert, 1972; Lovaas, Litrownik, & Mann, 1971; Ornitz & Ritvo, 1976; Schreibman & Koegel, 1982).

Related to the occurrence of self-stimulation is the autistic child's lack of appropriate play (Koegel, Firestone, Kramme, & Dunlap, 1974). These children seldom play with toys in the manner in which normal children do but usually manipulate them in a self-stimulatory fashion. For example, rather than rolling a toy car along the floor while making motor noises, an autistic child might merely pick up the car and spin a wheel in front of his eyes, perhaps for hours.

Self-Injurious Behavior

Possibly the most dramatic behavior seen in many autistic children is *self-injurious behavior* (SIB). This behavior occurs when the individual inflicts physical damage on his or her own body (Carr, 1977; Tate & Baroff, 1966). The most common forms of SIB are headbanging and self-biting of hands or wrists (Rutter & Lockyer, 1967). Other frequent SIBs are elbow or leg banging, hair pulling, face scratching, and self-slapping of the face or sides. The intensity of SIB can range from relatively benign, such as gently hitting the head on a soft surface, to life-threatening, such as forceful striking of the head on a concrete wall (Carr, 1977; Lovaas & Simmons, 1969; Schreibman, 1988a).

Inappropriate Affect

Autistic children frequently display *inappropriate affect*. Their emotional responses may be flattened, excessive, or otherwise inappropriate (Rimland, 1964, American Psychiatric Association [APA], 1987). Some children have tantrums or laugh hysterically for no reason that is apparent to the observer. Others show little emotion at all. They may not fear dangerous situations but display intense fear of objects or events that are harmless (L. Wing, 1976). For example, the author of this chapter has seen autistic children show intense fear of such non-threatening objects as tortillas, ferns, balloons, Bill Cosby, and ketchup.

Associated Features

In addition to these major characteristics, children with autism tend to be *physically healthy* and have none of the physical stigmata characteristic of children with other disorders (Dun-

lap, Koegel, & Egel, 1979; Kanner, 1943; Rimland, 1964; Schreibman, 1988a). Although normal or above-normal intelligence was once thought to characterize these youngsters (Eisenberg & Kanner, 1956; Kanner, 1943), it is now known that the majority of them suffer some degree of *mental retardation* (Rutter, 1978; Schreibman, 1988a; Schreibman & Koegel, 1981, 1982). Research estimates indicate that approximately 80% of autistic children score below 70 on IQ tests (Ritvo & Freeman, 1978). Although most of these children score within the retarded range on intellectual assessments, many of them do display isolated areas of skilled performance, especially in the areas of musical, mechanical, or mathematical skills (Applebaum, Egel, Koegel, & Imhoff, 1979; Rimland, 1978). In rare cases these isolated skills are truly exceptional so that the individual is considered to be a savant (Rimland, 1978).

ASSESSMENT

Diagnostic Issues

It is hoped that the above discussion of the behavioral characteristics of autistic children has given the reader a clear picture of a complex disorder. Given the unusual nature of the syndrome and the fact that autistic children share several behavioral characteristics with other disordered children (e.g., retarded, aphasic), it should not be surprising that issues in diagnosis have always been at the forefront of autism research. As a matter of fact, there has been an extended history of controversy over which behaviors are essential for the diagnosis of autism. The emphasis on arriving at a clear consensus on diagnosis may be particularly important for two reasons. First, it is useful for the determination of comparable populations for research. Thus, if one is doing research on autism, it is helpful to know that your population of subjects is comparable (i.e., shares behavioral characteristics) to the populations in other research. In this way, autism research can be cumulative and move forward. A second reason for reaching consensus on diagnosis is that the autism label may be useful for purposes of referrals for services, educational placements, or other reasons. (Although in principle the diagnostic label is useful, its actual utility may be questionable, as will be shown below.)

At present, there are two major sets of diagnostic criteria used in determining the appropriateness of an autism diagnosis. One is the set of criteria put forth in the revision of the third edition of the American Psychiatric Association's *Diagnostic and Statistical Manual of Mental Disorders* (APA, 1987). The other is the set of diagnostic criteria defined by the National Society for Autistic Children (Ritvo & Freeman, 1978). These two sets of criteria are similar in terms of the essential characteristics needed for the diagnosis but do not overlap completely.

To assess children for the diagnosis, a number of measures are typically used. Traditionally, assessments include a battery of tests designed to measure the child's functioning in several areas (Schreibman & Charlop, 1987). Usually these include tests of intellectual ability (e.g., the Wechsler or Stanford-Binet IQ tests), language skills (e.g., Peabody Picture Vocabulary Test), emotional adjustment (e.g., Draw-a-Person Test), and other assessments. However, such tests are often inappropriate for autistic children, since certain behavioral characteristics such as lack of motivation, noncompliance, speech anomalies, tantrums, attentional deficits, and withdrawal from environmental stimulation interfere with obtaining test scores that accurately reflect the child's level of functioning.

To supplement these more traditional assessments, other methods have been developed to assist in the determination of diagnosis. These methods include clinical interviews with the parents, informal observations of the child, checklists, observational schemes, and behavioral assessments (Newsom & Rincover, 1982; Schreibman & Charlop, 1987). Clinical interviews allow the examiner to obtain a thorough behavioral history from the parents and to observe the child in structured and/or unstructured situations. Behavior checklists specifically designed for the autistic population have been derived to aid in diagnosis as well as to provide information regarding the characteristics of a specific child. Both clinical interviews and the use of these behavior checklists are useful in helping to determine if autism is an appropriate diagnosis according to the established diagnostic schemes (APA, 1987; Ritvo & Freeman, 1978).

As alluded to above, however, pinning a label on a child may be of use for purposes of general autism research or referrals but may have little utility otherwise (Schreibman, 1988a). When one is concerned with designing an intervention strategy for a child with autism, it becomes immediately and painfully obvious that the label is of little help, for several reasons. First, a diagnosis of autism does not specify the behaviors of a particular child, because of the heterogeneity implicit in the syndrome. Thus a mute, severely retarded child who engages in a great deal of self-stimulation and an echolalic, nonretarded child who engages in very little self-stimulation may both receive a diagnosis of autism. However, it is obvious that these are very different children and appropriate treatments for them may likewise be very different. Second, a diagnosis of autism does not automatically imply a specific treatment program. Language training might take different forms for a child who is mute and a child who is echolalic. Third, a label of autism does not provide information regarding prognosis. Some children may improve a great deal in treatment and others very little (Lovaas, 1987).

Behavioral assessment was developed out of the need to obtain information that would avoid the limitations cited above and allow for the design of effective treatments tailored to the needs of an individual child with autism. With behavioral assessment, the researcher or clinician has a specific picture of the behaviors of a given child and this information is then used to design a treatment plan that is most appropriate for this child. Information for the behavioral assessment is obtained from parents and teachers and, most important, from direct structured observations of the child (for detailed descriptions of structured observation, see Lovaas, Koegel, Simmons, & Long, 1973; Newsom & Rincover, 1982; Schreibman & Charlop, 1987).

When considering the specific behaviors of a child, the behavior therapist typically identifies the behavior excesses and deficits that need attention. Behavioral *excesses* are behaviors that occur at an intensity or frequency that is inappropriate (e.g., tantrums), or those that are inappropriate at any intensity (e.g., selfstimulation, SIB). Behavioral *deficits* are behaviors that are not exhibited but whose absence is inappropriate (e.g., speech, social behavior). Once specific behavioral excesses and deficits are identified, the treatment provider then chooses from an arsenal of behavioral techniques available the ones that will decrease or eliminate behavioral excesses and will establish or increase deficient behaviors. Thus, once individual behaviors are identified and specific procedures are chosen, the treatment provider has a treatment plan.

Role of Assessment in Treatment

Designing a treatment program for a child with autism consists of three main steps (Dunlap, Koegel, & O'Neill, 1985). First, one must carefully and precisely define the behavioral excesses and deficits targeted for change. Second, the behaviors must be accurately measured. Third, based on the first two steps, a treatment intervention is designed and implemented. More recently, a fourth step, adding provisions in the treatment program for the maintenance and generalization of behavior change, has been added (Schreibman, 1988b).

Defining the target behaviors typically involves a description of the topography of the response, relative frequency of occurrence, duration, and occasion for occurrence. For example, if the therapist decides to target SIB in a particular child then he or she must behaviorally define SIB for the specific child to be treated. Although SIB shares some features across children (e.g., it causes injury), any one child will show a specific, perhaps idiosyncratic, set of responses. Thus, one child's SIB may be defined in these terms: forcibly striking side of head with closed fists, striking head on floor, striking head on furniture, biting outside of wrist leading to redness or broken skin. The therapist might also determine that these behaviors are likely to occur when the child is not otherwise engaged in a task, is in the presence of other children, and/or is presented with an instruction. This information gives a rather clear picture of potentially controlling variables of the behavior targeted for change.

It should be apparent that much of the accuracy of the definitions of target behaviors depends upon the measurement of these behaviors. Accurate and careful measurement allows for the quantification of the initial severity of the behavior, identification of environmental controlling variables, and the continuous assessment of treatment effects. Discrete events, such as echolalic vocalizations or SIB acts, can be tallied to provide a frequency count. The therapist can also record responses on a trial-by-trial basis or count permanent products of behavior (e.g., number of math problems completed). Behaviors that occur with variable duration or intermittently, such as selfstimulation, can be quantified on an interval or time-sampling basis. Basically, the idea is to utilize assessment procedures that will allow for an objective, observable, accurate record of the behavior(s) of interest. However, the process of assessment is an ongoing one. Although it is necessary to assess the behavior targets carefully, in order to develop a treatment plan (see below), it is equally important to continue the assessment, to evaluate the effectiveness of the treatment program. Continual assessment allows the researcher or treatment provider to determine whether or not a particular intervention is having an effect and to note the nature of that effect. It may be necessary to alter the treatment plan if assessment shows that the current procedures are not having the desired effect.

After carefully defining the target behaviors and establishing appropriate assessment procedures, the treatment provider moves to the third step, the development of a treatment plan. The researcher or treatment provider now seeks to relate the occurrence of the target behaviors to environmental conditions that support them. As the environmental determinants of a behavior are identified and understood, the environment can be manipulated to alter the behavior in the desired direction (Schreibman & Koegel, 1981). Fortunately, an extensive existing literature describes many of the behaviors seen in children with autism, and this knowledge can be used to identify potentially successful treatent procedures. For example, a good understanding of environmental determinants of SIB has been established (Carr, 1977); this existing knowledge can be used and related to the specific case at hand. Thus, treatment procedures that have already been identified and developed can be utilized. Unfortunately, sometimes the literature does not isolate the variables controlling a particular behavior, and it may be that multiple determining variables are functions. In such cases, the clinician must attempt to uncover the controlling variable(s) in the specific case. The usual approach to this problem is to observe the events immediately preceding the behavior (i.e., the antecedents) and the events immediately following the behavior (i.e., consequences) and see if a pattern becomes apparent. Take, for example, the situation where an autistic child engages in SIB. Perhaps the clinician notices that when a teacher asks the child to participate in an educational activity (antecedent), the child hits himself (response), which results in the teacher terminating the demands (consequence). If this appears to be a pattern,

the clinician might speculate that the teacher's demands are a cue for the child to engage in SIB and that this behavior is reinforced by the cessation of demands. This is an example of negative reinforcement of SIB—the child escapes or avoids an aversive event (teacher demands) by engaging in SIB. Once the relationship between the behavior and the environment is determined, this will suggest a particular treatment. In this example, the clinician might arrange the environment so that the child's SIB does not lead to cessation of the demands, thus removing the reinforcer that has been maintaining the behavior.

This process of identifying controlling variables for the specific behaviors associated with autism may allow for the development of more efficient treatments. As the environmental determinants of behavior are understood, behaviors that have similar controlling variables may be grouped together and manipulation of these variables may affect multiple behaviors (Dunlap, Koegel, & O'Neill, 1985).

Once the treatment provider has carefully defined the target behavior(s), settled on appropriate assessment, determined the environmental variable(s) that may be supporting inappropriate behavior and/or that may be required to strengthen a deficient behavior, it is time to implement the behavioral treatment. What follows below is a brief description of some of the specific treatment procedures that have been successfully employed with autistic children.

TREATMENT OF BEHAVIORAL EXCESSES

Decreasing behavioral excesses has understandably been of high priority from the beginning of behavioral work with these children. Severe SIB, tantrums, aggression, and self-stimulatory behavior are disruptive, interfere with the children's ability to benefit from the social and educational environment, and may serve to stigmatize the children by virtue of their intense and/or bizarre appearance. Although these behaviors may decrease as the child increases his or her repertoire of appropriate behaviors, it is still the case that inappropriate behavioral excesses often remain an enduring obstacle to treatment.

The most common behavioral procedures used to reduce behavioral excesses have been minimally intrusive procedures such as extinction, verbal reprimands, and time-out. More intrusive procedures such as contingent presentation of physical aversives (e.g., water mist spray, spanking, and localized electric shock) have also been used for particularly severe behaviors. Recent research has focused increasingly on the development of technologies to decrease disruptive behavioral excesses by using nonaversive procedures. Some examples of the procedures that have proven effective with these behaviors are discussed below.

Extinction

Extinction has been shown to be effective in reducing such interfering behaviors as tantrums, aggression, and SIB (Schreibman, 1988a). This procedure generally consists of withholding or removing a reinforcer that was maintaining the disruptive behavior (e.g., attention). As with any operant behavior, identification of the maintaining reinforcer and the subsequent failure to deliver this reinforcer when the behavior occurs results in extinction of the behavior. Some examples of how extinction has been successfully utilized with disruptive behaviors in children with autism should be helpful.

Based on earlier research suggesting that in many cases SIB was maintained by social attention (Lovaas, Freitag, Gold, & Kassorla, 1965), Lovaas and Simmons (1969) demonstrated how the self-injury of two children was significantly reduced or eliminated by withdrawal of positive reinforcement (in the form of social attention) that had been maintaining the behavior in the past. Basically, these investigators removed the restraints the children were wearing and allowed them to engage in the SIB. No one came to the children nor was any social attention available while the children engaged in the behavior. (Arrangements were made so the children could not cause any significant damage during these extinction sessions.) As expected, the children's behavior showed the predictable extinction curve. For some individuals, SIB is maintained by *negative* reinforcement (Carr, 1977). Carr, Newsom, and Binkoff (1976) demonstrated that one child's SIB was maintained by the escape or avoidance of aversive stimuli. This child had learned that if he hit himself when presented with a demand (e.g., a teacher's instruction), the demand situation would be terminated or avoided. In such cases, extinction would involve continuing to make demands despite the SIB so that the reinforcement for SIB (avoidance or escape from task demands) would no longer be presented and the behavior would extinguish. Rincover, Cook, Peoples, and Packard (1979) used extinction to reduce self-stimulation in several autistic children. These investigators identified the sensory reinforcers for individual children's self-stimulatory behavior. When this sensory consequence was removed, the children's self-stimulation decreased. Thus, for one child, self-stimulatory plate-spinning was maintained by the sound of the spinning plate on a table. Rincover et al. (1979) eliminated the sound of the plate by placing a carpet on the table. When this was done, the child's self-stimulatory spinning extinguished.

Punishment

Punishment in various forms has been effectively used to eliminate disruptive behaviors exhibited by autistic children. Usually, and ideally, punishment procedures are employed only when alternative, less intrusive, procedures have been tried. Punishment is also more likely to be applied in situations where the target behavior is such that an extinction procedure would be ethically indefensible. Thus, in cases of life-threatening SIB or dangerous aggression, one would need to consider the potential risks presented by an extinction burst or by a slow, gradual decrease in the behavior. Also, as with any use of punishment, it is essential to program positive consequences for alternative behaviors.

The types of punishment procedures utilized with children with autism have varied considerably. For example, in the Lovaas and Simmons study (1969) cited above, the investigators also demonstrated how punishment in the form of brief, localized, contingent electric shock rapidly suppressed SIB in three children who had extensive histories of self-abuse and who had not responded to other treatments. Immediately upon the occurrence of an SIB act, a therapist said "No!" and the child received a brief shock to the leg. It took only one or two of these shocks to completely suppress the behavior. The suppressive effect of the shock did not generalize across people or environments and the investigators had to program shock in different environments and by different people, but the suppression of the SIB allowed these children to learn alternative, appropriate behaviors with which to manipulate their environment.

Overcorrection

Another form of punishment, *overcorrection*, has been successfully employed with autistic children. This procedure also involves presentation of a contingent aversive stimulus, although it avoids physical aversives. Briefly, this procedure involves having the child engage in effortful behavior (aversive stimulus) contingent upon the target behavior excess. For example, Azrin,

Gottlieb, Hughart, Wesolowski, and Rahn (1975) report using overcorrection to reduce SIB. Treatment included a combination of procedures including: (1) positive reinforcement of incompatible behaviors (e.g., playing ball); (2) required relaxation where, contingent on SIB, the client was required to stay in bed for 2 hours while maintaining his arms in an extended downward position by his sides (a position incompatible with striking his head); (3) requiring the client to spend 20 minutes practicing holding his hands away from his body in several positions whenever an SIB occurred; and (4) requiring the client to do other things with his hands, such as clasp them behind his back or hold onto armrests.

Time-Out

Time-out is an effective but relatively mild punishment technique for dealing with disruptive behavior. White, Nielsen, and Johnson (1972) have defined time-out as a situation in which the occurrence of a response is followed by a period of time during which a variety of reinforcers is no longer available. Wolf, Risley, and Mees (1964) provided an early example of the use of time-out. They used the procedure with an autistic child who exhibited tantrums and SIB. These behaviors were effectively reduced by placing the child alone in a room each time the behavior occurred. Two things are important to remember when using time-out. First, one must consider the duration of time-out. Although durations of 2 minutes (Bostow & Bailey, 1969) to 3 hours (Burchard & Tyler, 1965) have been used successfully, durations in the range of 5 to 20 minutes are used most often. Second, time-out is only likely to be effective if the time-in setting is more reinforcing than the time-out setting (Solnick, Rincover, & Peterson, 1977). Thus, placing a school child in time-out for disruptive behavior might not be an effective punishment procedure if the classroom situation is unpleasant; the child might want to escape the classroom by going to time-out.

Ethical Issues with Punishment

The use of punishment raises several general concerns. First, punishment serves only to suppress, not eliminate, a behavior. It is therefore important to teach the child another behavior to replace the disruptive behavior if the suppression is to be maintained. For example, if a child has been engaging in SIB because of the positive attention it provides, the clinician might consider using punishment to gain control over the behavior temporarily and during this period teach the child another, more appropriate, behavior for gaining attention (e.g., talking, play). Second, there has been an increasing emphasis in recent years on the promotion of nonaversive interventions in treatment of autistic and other individuals (Horner et al., 1990). When considering punishment procedures, nothing inherent in the technical definition of punishment denotes pain. As discussed earlier in this book, punishment must be functionally defined so that whether a stimulus is aversive or not is determined by its effect on the behavior upon which it is contingent. Thus punishers may be as mild as a frown or a gentle "No." When considering interventions, the rule of thumb is that the least intrusive effective treatment should be employed. Clinicians need to respect the dignity of the client and choose procedures that will facilitate the person's integration into society, as opposed to segregating him or her by instituting an aversive procedure that serves to stigmatize or to reduce the opportunities to participate in society. Third, although punishment procedures have been documented as effective, the issues relating to the use of such procedures in community settings have not been adequately addressed.

Nonaversive Interventions

Although a technology of totally nonaversive interventions has yet to be achieved, some promising strides have been made in the right direction. The recent identification and discussion of two nonaversive interventions, *stimulus control manipulation* and *functional equivalence*, have prompted the design of treatments that have been shown to be effective in many situations where past treatments were limited to punishment procedures.

Stimulus Control Manipulation

Touchette, MacDonald, and Langer (1985) presented some important data indicating that the severely aggressive and self-injurious behavior of autistic individuals could be effectively controlled and eliminated by manipulating the antecedent (rather than consequence) of the behavior. Looking at the behavior of these individuals makes apparent that the disruptive behavior occurs under some stimulus conditions but not under others. For example, a child might engage in aggression or SIB when demands are placed upon him but almost never while watching television, eating, or taking a bath. Touchette et al. (1985) propose that certain stimulus conditions become discriminative for disruptive behavior and other stimulus conditions do not. Given this information, the clinician can immediately reduce the frequency of the disruptive behaviors to zero or near zero by programming the child's day so that none of the stimuli discriminative for the behaviors are presented. Thus, to continue the example, the child's day could be filled with watching television, eating meals, and taking baths. In addition, no demands would be placed on him. Such a program should lead to long periods of no disruptive behavior. Situations that once led to SIB and aggression (e.g., demands) are then gradually reintroduced in such a way that they no longer evoke the behavior. The obvious advantage of this treatment approach is that it may be possible to gain control immediately over severely disruptive behavior without the use of a contingent aversive stimulus. The only potential limitation to this stimulus control treatment is that it might not always be feasible to program an individual's environment so as to completely eliminate all discriminative stimuli for disruptive behavior. However, it is likely that the therapeutic use of manipulating the stimulus control of these behaviors will be a technique receiving much research and clinical attention in the future.

Functional Equivalence

In a particularly imaginative analysis and conceptualization, Carr and his colleagues have emphasized looking at the function of aggressive and other disruptive behavior in the child's environment (Carr, 1988). These investigators speculated that the behavioral excesses may serve a communicative function for autistic (and other severely language-impaired) individuals. Some children apparently use echolalia (a behavioral excess) to communicate that they do not understand what is being said to them (Carr, Schreibman, & Lovaas, 1975). Apparently a person can communicate needs and desires in a number of ways, and only some of these involve language as we normally consider it. Carr and Durand (1985b) posit that there is a relationship between disruptive behaviors and a person's ability to communicate. These investigators suggest that it may be useful to view behavior problems as a primitive form of communication and, following a functional analysis of the behavior, proceed to teach verbal skills designed to communicate the same meaning as the problem behavior does. For example, Schreibman and Carr (1978) taught children a verbal skill (saying, "I don't know") to replace echolalia. Carr and Durand (1985a), in a remarkable demonstration, showed that an autistic child's aggressive behavior could be conceptualized as the child's means of communicating that he did not wish to engage in a particular activity, that the activity was too difficult, and so forth. By teaching the child to say, "Help me," the child's communicative intent was achieved in a more appropriate manner and the reinforcement he received for this behavior maintained the language skill. Thus the problem behavior and communicative intent were functionally equivalent and one response could be replaced with another. In this instance, language replaced aggression.

TREATMENT FOR BEHAVIORAL DEFICITS

Although the behavioral excesses exhibited by many children with autism are usually treated by using the same procedures, efforts to remediate behavioral deficits typically are much more behavior-specific, and different behaviors are attacked with different procedures. Thus, when discussing behavioral interventions for deficits, it makes sense to address each behavior separately. Since space limitations prevent exhaustive coverage of this area, discussion will focus on training procedures to increase speech, breadth of attention, and motivation.

Speech and Language Training

Possibly the most serious behavioral deficit in autism is the failure to acquire appropriate language. Since language plays such a pivotal role in the acquisition of so much of human behavior, it is not surprising that severe deficits in this area would have a profound impact on many areas of functioning. This would, of course, include difficulties in social behavior, as so much of the social environment is verbal.

Imitation Training

Prior to the late 1960s, no one had come up with an effective program to teach vocal speech to autistic children. Lovaas, Berberich, Perloff, and Schaeffer (1966) provided the first empirically derived, replicable, effective program for teaching vocal speech to children with autism.

These investigators, after initially attempting to teach speech to the children by shaping individual vocal responses through the method of successive approximations, developed a more effective and efficient method based on imitation training. Imitation can be conceptualized as a discrimination in which the response resembles its discriminative stimulus. These experimenters taught imitation by using a series of systematic steps in which the child's vocal responses were reinforced (with food and praise) when they matched those of the therapist and were not reinforced if they did not. Once imitation was established, it served as a cornerstone in building more complex language functions such as semantics and grammar (Lovaas, 1966, 1977; Risley & Wolf, 1967). Thus, once a child has learned to say "candy" imitatively, the meaning of the word can be taught by associating the label with the referent. To teach the child to say "candy" when candy was presented, the therapist might hold up a piece of candy, say, "What is this?" and prompt the child to say "candy" by providing the vocal model for the child to imitate. When the child imitates and says "candy" he or she is reinforced. This is repeated over several trials with the therapist gradually fading out the imitative prompt until the child says "candy" when asked "What is this?" and a piece of candy is presented. Thus, if reinforcement is associated with saying "candy" in the presence of candy (as opposed to other items) the child will acquire the discrimination that "candy" is the label for this food.

Teaching basic language forms is a necessary step in any language program, but this must be supplemented with training in more complex language skills. Because it is known that autistic children often have difficulty in learning language skills involving abstract concepts (Hermelin & O'Connor, 1970; Rutter, 1968), one may question whether operant procedures such as those described above can be effective in teaching these more difficult language skills. There is ample evidence in the literature to support the contention that indeed operant techniques are effective in teaching concepts such as prepositions, pronouns, concepts of time, yes/no, similarities and differences, compound sentence structures, and many other complex and sophisticated language skills (Fay & Schuler, 1980; Lovaas, 1977; Schreibman, 1988a). In fact, a longitudinal look at the literature in the area of language training for nonverbal autistic children (and other severely language-handicapped children) provides an interesting view of the cumulative nature of research in this area. Research has provided the building blocks of our extensive knowledge about how to teach speech and language to these children.

Spontaneous Language

An example of the cumulative nature of research in this area is provided by the training of spontaneity of language. Once therapists were able to build a linguistic repertoire in these children, they began to notice that although the children could talk, they rarely did so unless spoken to first. That is, their speech remained under the control of the verbal discriminative stimulus of another speaker and not usually under the control of other, nonverbal, features in the environment (Charlop, Schreibman, & Thibodeau, 1985). For example, they would answer, "Ben," when asked, "What is your name?" but rarely or never volunteered, "My name is Ben," if not asked first. Using a procedure designed to teach autistic children to request items in their environment, Charlop et al. (1985) gradually transferred stimulus control of an appropriate verbal response (e.g., "I want cookie") from a therapist's imitative model to the presentation of the object (e.g., cookie). Thus, the children learned to make requests without verbal cues. Schreibman, Charlop, and Tryon (1981) further transferred stimulus control of verbal responses (e.g., "I want cookie") from the object to a general situation or environment where such a verbal response would be appropriate. Thus, the children learned to say,

"I want cookie," when they were in a kitchen or a grocery store, although a cookie was not directly visible.

Echolalic Speech

When working with a child who is mute, one must teach not only language functions but also the vocal repertoire required. In contrast, language training with children who exhibit echolalia requires a different set of techniques. Echolalic children already imitate; in fact, that is their main problem—they imitate too much. Their echoing not only serves to stigmatize them socially, but it interferes with their acquisition of normal language. With these children, language training involves teaching them to use speech in appropriate contexts.

The behavioral literature has provided a variety of successful procedures for reducing or eliminating echolalic speech. One way to reduce echolalia is to increase the child's repertoire of appropriate speech. Prompting procedures have been successfully employed to teach appropriate responses (Lovaas et al., 1973; Risley & Wolf, 1967). To illustrate the use of this procedure, suppose the clinician wishes to teach an echolalic autistic child to label a dog when asked to do so. At first when shown a picture of a dog and asked, "What is this?" the child will probably echo, "What is this?" instead of correctly labeling "dog." Using prompts, the therapist might present a picture of a dog, and very softly (almost inaudibly) say, "What is this?" and then loudly say "dog" and wait for the child to echo "dog." During the fading of the prompts, the therapist would gradually increase the volume of the question and decrease the prompt for the response "dog." Finally, upon presentation of the picture, the therapist would say, "What is this?" and the child would say "dog."

Although such procedures have proved useful for decreasing instances of immediate echolalic speech and increasing appropriate language, a more effective and efficient technology became available once we understood more about the environmental determinants supporting immediate echolalia. The generalized, durable suppression of the behavior required an analysis of these variables. Carr et al. (1975) found that one variable (but not the only one, as noted by Prizant & Duchan, 1981) related to immediate echolalia was the comprehensibility of the verbal stimulus. Thus, if an echolalic child was presented with a verbal stimulus for which he or she had an appropriate response, the child would give the correct response. However, when presented with a verbal stimulus for which he or she did not have a response, the stimulus was echoed. For example, if asked to "touch your head," and the child understood the command, he or she would probably comply without echoing. In contrast, if asked to "indicate your cranium," the child would probably echo the command. To substantiate their conclusion that incomprehensibility (i.e., lack of appropriate response) was associated with echolalia, Carr et al. (1975) demonstrated that training of a response to a previously incomprehensible stimulus eliminated echoing of that stimulus. Since it would be impossible to teach a child appropriate responses to any incomprehensible stimulus that might be encountered, Schreibman and Carr (1978) taught echolalic children a generalized verbal response that would be functional in any situation where they were confronted with a stimulus they did not understand. These investigators taught echolalic children to say, "I don't know," when presented with a question for which they had no response. By saying, "I don't know," instead of echoing, the children sounded less deviant and communicated to the speaker the need to teach the appropriate response. This line of research provides an illustration of the contributions of rigorous behavior analysis to the development of successful intervention strategies.

The research just reported deals with immediate echolalia. It is probable that the environmental variables controlling the occurrence of delayed echolalia and other speech anomalies are different. Understanding of these variables awaits future systematic analyses. With such understanding should come the development of effective treatment interventions.

Natural Language Paradigm

One promising approach to teaching speech incorporates procedures that in some ways are very different from those discussed thus far. The natural language paradigm (NLP) consists of a set of procedures for language training that focus not just on teaching specific verbal responses, or imitation, but rather teach language by incorporating procedures to enhance motivation and promote generalization, issues to be discussed later. NLP was designed to incorporate procedures to increase motivation (e.g., initiation by the child, taking turns, interspersing previously-mastered tasks, reinforcing the child's attempts to respond) with procedures for promoting generalization (loose structure, common stimuli, natural environment). During NLP training, the child and therapist interact in a play setting with a variety of play materials. The child is initially allowed to choose which toy or activity he or she would like to talk about and play with. The therapist then models an appropriate verbalization for the child to imitate (e.g., "car"). When the child makes a communicative attempt (imitates word, phrase, or part of phrase; gestures toward toy), the toy is given to the child as a reinforcer. Then it is the therapist's turn to play with the toy and the therapist either models a different verbalization (e.g., "car goes fast") or provides a new referent for the initial verbalization. Koegel, O'Dell, and Koegel (1987) demonstrated that this type of speech training resulted in better acquisition and generalization of language as compared to the more traditional behavioral training. In fact, it has also been demonstrated that parents can effectively utilize this procedure to teach language to their children (Laski, Charlop, & Schreibman, 1988).

Although the language training interventions discussed above offer an overview of procedures that have been successfully employed, this discussion is by no means exhaustive. Language intervention is typically one of the most researched areas in the field of autism, testimony to both its importance in treating children and its difficulty.

Remediating Attentional Deficits

Perhaps nowhere in the field of autism is the cumulative nature of research and practice as clearly evident as in the study of attentional deficits and their remediation. As mentioned earlier in the description of the disorder, deficits in responsivity and attention are common with this population. Many of these children have histories of suspected deafness or blindness because they seem oblivious to their surroundings, although on other occasions they may be very attentive to some irrelevant aspect of their environment such as the pattern in floor tile or dust in a light beam. Similarly, they may not pick up behaviors that are modeled in their social environment. Obviously, failure to use environmental stimulation effectively would have a profound and devastating effect on the individual's ability to learn new behaviors.

Because the behavioral model of treatment emphasizes the identification of controlling environmental variables, the attentional patterns of autistic individuals have been analyzed by using the principles of experimental psychology, particularly discrimination learning. It was reasoned that identification and description of a specific attentional deficit in these youngsters would then allow for the study of effective treatments. If effective procedures for remediating the deficit were found, then one could predict that widespread areas of functioning would be affected. Indeed, this is exactly what has happened.

Stimulus Overselectivity

Lovaas, Schreibman, Koegel, and Rehm (1971) used a discrimination task to investigate how autistic, retarded, and normal children responded to simultaneous multiple cues. The children were taught to press a lever when presented with a compound stimulus consisting of three components: a visual stimulus (red floodlight), an auditory stimulus (noise from a speaker), and a tactile stimulus (slight pressure on the leg). Once this discrimination was established, the individual components were presented singly, to determine which had acquired control over the child's lever presses. When this was done, it was found that the children with autism typically responded on the basis of only one of the three components. Thus, for example, the child might press the lever when the auditory cue was presented but not when the visual or the tactile cue was presented. This was in contrast to the normal children who typically responded to all of the individual components and the retarded children who typically responded to two of the components. It was subsequently determined that the autistic children could learn to respond to the other single cues. The problem was not one of responding to a particular cue. Rather, it was in responding to the cue in the context of other cues. These investigators referred to this attentional pattern as *stimulus overselectivity*, suggesting the over-restricted nature of the responsiveness to the sensory environment. Stimulus overselectivity has also been demonstrated when only two cross-model cues are used (Lovaas & Schreibman, 1971) and if the multiple cues fall within the same modality (Koegal & Wilhelm, 1973; Reynolds, Newsom, & Lovaas, 1974; Rincover, 1978; Schreibman, 1975; Schreibman et al., 1986).

The implications of stimulus overselectivity for the functioning of these children become apparent when one considers the number of learning situations that require response to multiple cues. Most learning requires response to contiguous or near-contiguous association of cues, and a deficit in this ability bodes ill for the ability to learn. Consider, for example, the case where someone holds up an apple and says "apple." If the child hears the label but does not see the referent (apple) then the label for the object

will not be learned. Similarly, if the child sees the apple but does not hear the word, the label for the object will not be learned. This example indeed sounds like what appears in many autistic children. In fact, stimulus overselectivity has been implicated as a variable influencing language acquisition, social behavior, observational learning, the use of prompts, and generalization (see Lovaas et al., 1979, and Schreibman, 1988a, for reviews of this literature).

Within-Stimulus Prompts

Once stimulus overselectivity was identified and its parameters more precisely defined, the task became one of using the information to assist in the design of effective treatments. Work in this area took two directions. The first was to develop teaching strategies that allowed the child to *learn despite the overselective attention*. Schreibman (1975) demonstrated prompting procedures that allowed overselective autistic children to learn difficult discriminations that they could not learn previously. Briefly, this procedure ensured that the child could respond to the discrimination without having to attend to simultaneous multiple cues. To illustrate, if one wished to teach the child to discriminate the letter E from F, a traditional prompting procedure would employ an added cue to prompt the child to the right answer. The teacher might print each letter on a small card, present the two cards to the child, say "E" (or "F"), and then point to the correct choice as a prompt. This is called an extra-stimulus prompt, to denote that a stimulus was added to the situation. The child must respond to the pointing prompt (previously established as functional) and to the letter. Although this is an effective type of prompt for most children, one can see how it might be problematic for an overselective child. As Schreibman (1975) found, the children tend to respond only to the pointing prompt and learn nothing about the training stimulus (letter). However, such a discrimination could be learned by these children if a different type of prompt was used. Specifically, they were able to learn if a prompt was used that did not require response to simultaneous multiple cues. For example, if trying to teach discrimination of E from F, the only relevant cue is the bottom line of the E. In this case, the child might first be trained to respond to the bottom line (__) when told to point to E (versus a blank card). Once this is established, the redundant lines could be faded in for both letters. This is called a within-stimulus prompt to denote that the prompt is presented within the training stimulus and the child never has to respond to multiple cues. By using this type of prompt, difficult discrimination can be taught to children who are overselective in their attention (Rincover, 1978; Schreibman, 1988a,b).

Although the use of within-stimulus prompts allows the child to learn even though he or she is overselective, some discriminations are not amenable to this type of training, and setting up such prompts can be difficult and tedious. The applicability of such training in classroom situations might be limited. Because of the limitations of this type of prompting, researchers turned to another intervention direction. This involved attempting to *remediate the stimulus overselectivity* so that the children could learn in a manner more like normal children and thus benefit from the same teaching techniques that work for nonautistic children.

Conditional Discriminations

The first question that needed to be asked was whether or not these children could respond to simultaneous multiple cues. Since the overselectivity research had revealed that under some conditions the overselectivity effect disappeared (Schreibman, Koegel, & Craig, 1977), it seemed hopeful that the attentional deficit was amenable to remediation. In subsequent research, Koegel and Schreibman (1977) and Schreibman, Charlop, and Koegel (1982) demonstrated that overselective autistic children could learn to respond to multiple cues if they were trained on a conditional discrimination. A

conditional discrimination is one that must be solved on the basis of multiple cues. For example, a mother asks her daughter to get her *red sweater*. Assuming that the child has sweaters of different colors and several items of red clothing, the child must respond to *both* the object (sweater) and the color (red) in order to bring the correct item. Further, it was demonstrated that if an overselective child was trained on a series of conditional discriminations, he or she learned a *set* to respond to multiple cues and approached new conditional discriminations without showing the overselectivity pattern. These results are indeed encouraging, in that they show that stimulus overselectivity is amenable to reduction. Since this is the case, it remained to be determined whether the predicted widespread positive changes in the children's behavior would follow the reduction of overselectivity.

As predicted, research has demonstrated that training on successive conditional discriminations remediates overselectivity and that this in turn leads to improvements in the children's functioning. Schreibman et al (1982) demonstrated that after overselectivity had been remediated via the conditional discrimination training, autistic children who previously had been unable to learn with extra-stimulus (pointing) prompts were now able to do so. Further, Burke and Koegel (1987) found that after overselective attention was reduced, autistic children demonstrated both increased social responsiveness and increased utilization of incidental language cues. Research in this area is still in its infancy, but it is safe to assume that continuation of the directed line of research in this area will yield more effective and efficient interventions.

Enhancing Motivation

As noted above, attention is fundamental to the learning of specific behaviors, and changes in attention are associated with improved learning, social responsiveness, and so forth. Similarly, motivation to respond, and thus to learn, is fundamental to learning behaviors and is notoriously deficient in children with autism. Because of this deficit and its important implications, researchers and clinicians have focused a good deal of effort in this area. In initial work with this population, professionals depended on primary reinforcers such as food to motivate the children to respond. This is because these children typically are unresponsive to the social reinforcers (e.g., "Good boy!") that normally serve to strengthen and maintain the behavior of non-autistic children (Ferster, 1961; Lovaas & Newsom, 1976). However, the use of food as a reinforcer posed several problems. First, children may become satiated with reinforcers such as food, and once they are satiated, the reinforcers stop working. Second, primary reinforcers are artificial, particularly for older individuals. Third, food reinforcers exist in only limited settings such as treatment settings and thus interfere with generalization of behavior to other settings where food is not available.

Novelty of Stimuli

In an attempt to remedy some of the above problems, researchers embarked on investigations to increase the effectiveness of reinforcers. One procedure has involved manipulating the novelty of reinforcing stimuli. Thus, satiation might be prevented by merely changing or varying the reinforcing stimuli. For example, Egel (1981) demonstrated that the satiation typically found when using food reinforcers could be reduced if the reinforcer was varied instead of being held constant. He compared autistic children's behavior during conditions when one (of three) highly preferred edible reinforcers at a time was available contingent upon correct responses (constant condition), to conditions when all three of the preferred foods were varied across trials. Results indicated that satiation occurred more rapidly when each of the reinforcers was individually presented than when a

reinforcer was presented from a pool of several reinforcers.

Relating Reinforcer to Response

Another approach to increasing reinforcer effectiveness has been to investigate the relationship between the reinforcer and the response upon which it is contingent. Litt and Schreibman (1981) demonstrated that when response to a particular task stimulus is associated with one particular reinforcer, performance is better than if varied reinforcers are associated with the same response or if a single reinforcer is associated with all responses. Koegel and Williams (1980) and Williams, Koegel, and Egel (1981) demonstrated that when the acquisition of the reinforcer is a natural part of the response requirement, it is more effective than when a reinforcer is obtained in a task-independent manner. To illustrate, if a therapist wishes to teach the child the preposition "under," it is more effective to have the child reach under a box and find an edible reinforcer in that location than it would be to have the child reach under the box and then be handed an edible reinforcer. Both are examples of reinforcing correct responses but in the former situation obtaining the reinforcer is *directly* related to performing the correct response (reaching "under"), and in the latter situation the reinforcer is not directly related to the response. In sum, therapists can sustain a relatively high level of motivation by systematically varying the mode of presentation of previously functional reinforcers.

Choice of Task and Reinforcer

Discovering more effective ways to deliver primary reinforcers has proven useful in motivating children with autism, but most researchers agree that it is probably more important to develop procedures for establishing functional secondary reinforcers, or social reinforcers, such as praise, hugs, smiles, and approval. Since these secondary reinforcers serve to establish and maintain so much behavior in normal individuals, and since these are the type of reinforcer most likely to be available in nontreatment settings, it is important to establish them as functional reinforcers for these children. A few early investigations had some success along these lines (Lovaas, Schaeffer, & Simmons, 1965; Lovaas, Freitag, et al., 1966), but the techniques used had limited generalization and were impractical as regular clinical interventions. More recent work by Dyer (1987) and Koegel, Dyer, and Bell (1987) suggests that social responsiveness may be enhanced by allowing the child to take a more active role in choosing the reinforcers and the specific tasks of instruction. For example, instead of the therapist deciding that the task is prepositions and the reinforcer is candy, motivation to respond is increased if the child is allowed to choose the nature of the task, the task materials, and the reinforcer.

Use of Maintenance Tasks

The instructional setting in which autistic children are taught has also been the focus of investigations into motivation. In the past, a typical behavior-modification learning environment consisted of a structured setting in which several trials of the same task were presented. Although such settings are designed to decrease off-task and disruptive behavior such as tantrums and self-stimulation, such environments may have led to a decrease in motivation and an increase in boredom (Dunlap, 1984). To resolve this problem, several researchers have investigated the effects on motivation of varying the instructional tasks. This generally involves designing the learning environment so that overall reinforcement and success remain high, by including previously mastered (maintenance) tasks along with new target behaviors. Under such conditions, motivation remains high (Dunlap, 1984; Koegel & Koegel, 1986; Neef, Iwata, & Page, 1980). Significant increases in motivation have also occurred when researchers have

reinforced the child's attempts at correct responses, rather than waiting for exactly correct responses before delivering a reinforcer (Koegel, O'Dell, & Dunlap, 1988; Koegel, O'Dell, Koegel, 1987).

This research suggests that there is much we can do to enhance the motivation of autistic children. It is apparent that although establishing powerful, and more natural, reinforcers remains a problem area for this population, research is on the right track in developing procedures to increase reinforcer effectiveness and thus motivate these children to respond and learn.

GENERALIZATION OF BEHAVIOR CHANGE

Work with autistic children has taught clinicians two things. First, it is difficult to teach new behaviors to these children. Fortunately, systematic research such as that described above has helped immensely in allowing researchers to design effective ways to teach them. Second, teaching new behaviors is only half the battle—the other half is to obtain generalization of the new behaviors. Children with autism are notorious for displaying difficulties in generalization; one need only ask a teacher or parent for examples of this failure to generalize. Typically, the child will learn a behavior (e.g., sitting appropriately at a table for a meal) in one setting (classroom) but will jump up from the table and throw utensils in another setting (home). Sometimes the parent and teacher cannot believe they are talking about the same child. All types of generalization are affected. The child fails to show *stimulus generalization* in a situation when a behavior (i.e., eating appropriately at the table) was learned at school but failed to generalize to the home. Failure of *response generalization* is evident when the child learns a specific behavior (e.g., do not walk across the street when the signal is red) but fails to generalize to another related behavior (e.g., do not ride a bike across the street when the signal is red). Problems in *temporal generalization*, or maintenance, are evident when the child learns a behavior but will not exhibit the behavior after a period of time.

In an effort to enhance generalization of learned behaviors, researchers have adopted strategies used with all populations as well as strategies specifically developed for children with autism (Schreibman, 1990). Many specific strategies have been developed to facilitate and promote generalization, and all cannot be described here. The following are examples of frequently used techniques and some of the newer strategies that are showing great promise in increasing the generalization of behavior change.

Training Procedures That Enhance Generalization

Intermittent Schedules of Reinforcement

As mentioned, several generalization strategies that are employed with all individuals are used with autistic children (Stokes & Baer, 1977). One approach to facilitating generalization of behavior change is to make the treatment environment similar to the natural environment (Stokes & Baer, 1977). A way to do this is to use intermittent schedules of reinforcement during the treatment. This presents an atmosphere that is more like the natural environment, in which behaviors are seldom reinforced on a continuous (CRF) schedule. In such cases, the new behavior is established via CRF but then is gradually shifted to an intermittent schedule so that it is more difficult for the child to discriminate the treatment situation from a different (generalization) setting. This enhances stimulus generalization (Koegel & Rincover, 1977; Rincover & Koegel, 1975). In addition, intermittent schedules have served to increase

the maintenance of treatment gains, allowing naturally occurring intermittent reinforcers to take over in natural environments.

Naturally Maintaining Contingencies

The use of naturally maintaining contingencies (natural reinforcers) during treatment will also make the treatment resemble nontreatment settings (Stokes & Baer, 1977). When using this strategy, it is important that the reinforcers used in the treatment setting be similar to those that are likely to be available in natural settings, and behaviors should be taught that are likely to earn such reinforcers. Several studies along these lines have provided encouraging results from employing this strategy with autistic children. For example, Carr, Binkoff, Kologinsky, and Eddy (1980) taught autistic youngsters to use sign language to request items that were likely to be found outside the treatment environment and that had reinforcing value for them (e.g., food and toys). This led to generalization of the spontaneous signing for these items, as signing was reinforced in the natural environment because it was followed by presentation of the preferred items.

Sequential Modification

Another strategy to enhance generalization is to use procedures that directly train generalized responding. Sequential modification is such a procedure, in which generalization is programmed in every situation where it does not spontaneously generalize. For example, if the child learned to speak in speech therapy class but did not speak in other settings (e.g., home and school) or to other people (e.g., teachers, parents, siblings), then he or she would be trained in each of the desired settings and in the presence of each of the other people. Nordquist and Wahler (1973) trained the parents of an autistic child in a clinic setting to increase the child's compliance and to teach imitative skills. Once the treatment gains were established, the parents implemented their trained skills in the home. Treatment gains then generalized from the clinic to the home.

Pivotal Target Behaviors

The generalization strategies described above and others commonly used (Stokes & Baer, 1977) have proven to be extremely useful in achieving and enhancing generalization with this population. However, a relatively new approach may hold promise for much more extensive and effective generalization. Some researchers have been evaluating the generalized effects of *teaching pivotal target behaviors.* Pivotal behaviors are ones that affect widespread changes in other behaviors. It is obvious that treatment would be more effective and efficient if it focused on a few of these pivotal behaviors instead of on many individual target behaviors. A substantial body of research (Koegel & Mentis, 1985; Lovaas et al., 1979) has implicated two such central behaviors in the failure of autistic children to generalize treatment gains. These two behaviors are *motivation* and *responsivity to multiple cues.*

Motivation

Autistic children are notorious for not being motivated to learn new behaviors or to generalize acquired behaviors. Because of this motivation problem and the failure to respond to such motivators as affection and approval from others, researchers have had to resort to artificial reinforcers such as food and avoidance of pain (Schreibman, 1988b). If motivation is increased (even by using artificial reinforcers), increased learning and performance are evident. Thus, it seems reasonable to assume that if motivation can be increased, there should be an improvement over a broad range of collateral behaviors.

Responsivity to Multiple Cues

Responsivity to multiple cues is another area, as noted, in which autistic children have been shown to have severe deficits (Schreibman, 1988a; Lovaas et al., 1979). Many of these children exhibit stimulus overselectivity and respond to restricted range of cues in their environment. Stimulus overselectivity obviously interferes with the acquisition of new behaviors, and its effects on generalization are also apparent. A vivid demonstration of this was provided by Rincover and Koegel (1975). These investigators had therapists teach children to perform simple responses (e.g., touch the nose when so directed). After the children learned the responses, a different therapist was brought in and asked the child to perform the same behavior. Several of the children failed to perform the behavior with this new therapist. Subsequent analysis showed that these children's responses had come under the control of a very limited and usually irrelevant stimulus in the original training situation. For example, one child's responses came under the control of an idiosyncratic hand movement of the original therapist. Since the new therapist did not use this hand movement, the cue for the child's response was not present and the child did not respond.

Issues of Generalization and Maintenance

Based on the findings described above, a treatment package of procedures previously identified as effective in increasing motivation and normalizing responsivity might lead to widespread generalization and maintenance of treatment effects. Recent research has indeed focused on training in these pivotal behaviors.

In a demonstration indicating that this approach to generalization may be effective, Koegel, O'Dell, & Koegel (1987) devised the natural language paradigm (described earlier in this chapter) for nonverbal autistic children. This treatment program incorporates several motivation-enhancing procedures previously identified in the literature (Koegel & Koegel, 1988). These include allowing the child a good deal of control over the activities involved in training, frequent variation of the learning tasks, using direct (as opposed to indirect) reinforcers, varying the reinforcers, and reinforcing the child's attempts to respond. Koegel, O'Dell, & Koegel, (1987) found that this language training paradigm was superior to a more structured, repetitive-practice, language training program in several dimensions of generalization, including increased use of appropriate, spontaneous, and generalized speech. In addition, incorporating procedures known to increase responsivity (Koegel & Schreibman, 1977; Schreibman et al., 1982) has led to the development of a revised pivotal response training package (Koegel, Schreibman, Good, et al., 1989) that focuses on both increasing motivation and increasing responsivity to multiple cues. Preliminary data suggest that the training of these pivotal target behaviors leads to positive behavior change and generalization (Koegel, O'Dell, & Koegel, 1987; Laski et al., 1988).

Another important approach to enhancing generalization is to extend the treatment beyond the clinic environment. The rationale for such an extension is that generalization and maintenance of treatment effects may be enhanced if treatment allows the child to benefit from the treatment environments most functional for normal children: the home and classroom. Thus, research has focused on *classroom programs*, *parent training programs*, and training in *self-management*. It is important to emphasize here that these programs utilize the same behavioral principles discussed earlier. What characterizes these programs is who provides the treatment and the setting(s) where the treatment is provided.

Classroom Instruction

Several strategies have been utilized to enhance the generalization of learned behaviors, only a few of which can be presented here. One strategy that has recently received attention is the focus on providing a functional curriculum (Brown et al., 1979; Dunlap et al., 1979) to handicapped students. A functional curriculum includes behaviors that are frequently required in the individual's everyday environments (e.g., home, school, community), are longitudinal, and are age-appropriate (Johnson & Koegel, 1982). This curriculum requires that the educator assess the behaviors and environment of the student, and target for instruction those behaviors that will be the most useful (and thus reinforced) in the individual's natural environment (i.e., generalization settings). Thus, the student might be taught to use public transportation, kitchen appliances, and vending machines. A functional curriculum also requires teaching behaviors that are age-appropriate. Since many autistic and other handicapped students function at a lower level than their chronological age, the tendency is to have them work on tasks that are really appropriate for younger individuals. For example, an 18-year-old girl who is severely retarded might be taught to sort colored pencils. Such a skill might be important and age-appropriate for a preschooler but it is stigmatizing for an 18-year-old. It might be better to have this student sort cutlery or clothing. Such skills would be more functional and age-appropriate for her. A functional curriculum should also be longitudinal in that the specific skills taught should be ones whose form and content can be shifted as the student becomes older but for which the basic skill required will remain relatively the same. For example, one might teach a younger child to use a simple vending machine. At first, the child might use the machine to get a candy bar. However, the same basic skill would be functional when the child grows up and might wish to use vending machines to obtain more age-appropriate items such as postage stamps. In short, the functional curriculum ensures training in generalizable skills.

Another important research emphasis has provided information on how to ensure that children with autism benefit from the educational situation. Koegel and his colleagues (Koegel & Rincover, 1974; Rincover & Koegel, 1977) identified two main requisite skills that these children often lack. One is the ability to learn while in a large group and the other is to work independently on tasks without constant teacher supervision. Research by these investigators has demonstrated that with special training, autistic children can be taught to learn in a group teaching situation when a single teacher is providing information or instructions to a large group (Koegel & Rincover, 1974), and that the children can be taught to work on individualized instructional materials for long periods of time without constant teacher supervision and reinforcement (Rincover & Koegel, 1977). The acquisition of these important classroom skills ensures that the child will be able to learn in a variety of classrooms and benefit from the instructional routines used in classrooms. Again, this should serve to enhance generalization by allowing effective instruction in a variety of situations.

Parent Training

Parent training as a generalization strategy is appropriate, as the parents are around the child most of the time and in most of the child's environments, so parents can provide training in the child's natural environment. In addition, parents can ensure that the child's school gains are transferred to the home and can expand on the child's repertoire by teaching additional behaviors.

The fact that parents can learn and implement the principles of behavioral interventions has been well established (Freeman & Ritvo, 1976; Koegel Glahn, & Nieminen, 1978; Koegel, Schreibman, Britten, Burke, & O'Neill, 1982; Laski et al., 1988; Schopler & Reichler, 1971). What has also been demonstrated (Koegel et al., 1978) is that parents must be taught *general behavioral principles* (as opposed to specific strategies for specific behaviors) in order to generalize parenting skills to the home and/or to teach a wide range of behaviors. Thus, for example, one must teach the parents about positive reinforcement or extinction rather than a

particular procedure for reducing this specific child's noncompliance in a particular situation. Procedures used to train parents have included lectures, written instructions, live and videotape modeling, direct prompting, shaping, behavioral rehearsal, feedback from a parent trainer, and telephone contacts (Schreibman & Britten, 1984). Many programs have utilized a combination of these procedures. O'Dell (1974) concluded that the form of the parent training is not important in determining outcome. What is essential is the inclusion of training in basic behavioral principles.

Koegel et al. (1982) compared a parent training program to a program in which the children were treated in a clinic setting and parents were not trained. In both conditions the treatment consisted of a structured format, the identification of specific target behaviors and the delivery of clear antecedents (S^Ds), application of clear consequences, use of prompts, and use of shaping. The basic goals, sequence, and content of the treatment were the same for both the parent training group and the clinic treatment group. The only difference was in who provided the treatment: the parent or the clinician. Dependent measures included (among others) generalization measures of the child's behavior, such as behavioral observations in a free play setting with parents, therapists, and strangers. The results of this investigation showed that on almost every individual measure there was as much initial improvement and more durable improvement with 25 to 50 hours of parent training as compared with 225 hours of direct clinic treatment. In addition, the children whose parents were trained showed greater generalization of behavior gains than did the children who were trained in the clinic and whose parents had not been trained. This was undoubtedly due to the fact that the parents were present in many different settings and situations that served to promote generalization, and the clinician was not. However, although generalization was superior in the parent training condition, it appeared that problems in generalization still existed, as the children did not tend to generalize their gains in the absence of the trained parent (i.e., in the presence of a stranger).

One set of procedures that holds promise for enhancing generalization with parent training is the procedures discussed above as related to training in pivotal behaviors. For example, Laski et al. (1988) implemented a parent training package consisting of the motivation-enhancing procedures discussed above. The program focused on teaching language skills; the procedures included shared control, reinforcing attempts to speak, frequent task variation, and direct response-related reinforcement (e.g., contingent access to preferred toy or activity). Parents of four nonverbal and four verbal/echolalic autistic children were taught to use these motivation-enhancing procedures. It was found that after training, all parents increased the frequency with which they modeled appropriate words and phrases for their child to imitate, prompted verbal responses, and required the child to respond verbally. Importantly, verbal imitation increased for all the children, as did answers to questions and spontaneous speech. In addition, these improvements generalized across three nontreatment settings. These data suggest that parents can learn the teaching techniques and that their use can produce generalization of speech gains in their children.

Self-Management Training

Training in self-management is a means of further achieving generalized treatment effects, in that it gives the child a means of providing his or her own treatment in different settings and for different target behaviors. Self-management typically involves self-selection of treatment targets, self-evaluation of performance, self-monitoring, and self-reinforcement. Self-management, although commonly used by nonhandicapped individuals, has only recently been used with individuals with handicaps (see reviews by Browder & Shapiro, 1985, and

O'Leary & Dubey, 1979). Directly relevant to the present discussion are three studies involving children with autism. Sainato, Strain, Lefebvre, and Rapp (1990) found that preschool children with autism could use a self-evaluation treatment package to increase their independent work skills. Koegel and Koegel (1990) demonstrated that autistic children could use self-management to reduce their own self-stimulatory behavior. Stahmer and Schreibman (1992) demonstrated that autistic children could use a self-management program to play appropriately with toys for long periods of time without supervision. Both of these latter studies utilized the same self-management training program (Koegel, Koegel, & Parks, 1992). This program involves selection of a target behavior, having the child discriminate the target behavior (e.g., playing appropriately versus inappropriately), and teaching the child to record whether he or she had engaged in the appropriate behavior (i.e., self-evaluate and self-monitor) and, if so, to obtain a previously selected reinforcer (self-reinforcement). The children are required to engage in the target behavior gradually for longer and longer periods of time (duration) or to engage in the behavior more often (frequency).

Self-management holds potential for turning more of the child's treatment over to the child him- or herself. Such an approach serves to make the child more independent, increase generalization, increase the child's responsibility for treatment, and reduce the burden on other caretakers (e.g., parents). Although it remains to be determined what limitations are placed on self-management instruction by the child's functioning level, treatment targets, and other factors, the area is receiving increased attention.

CONCLUSION

As should be apparent from this description of the behavioral treatment of autism, much has been accomplished. The systematic application of the experimental analysis of behavior to the problems associated with treating these children has allowed clinicians to be far more effective then they were even a few years ago. This forward progress has been possible only because of the symbiotic relationship between the laboratory and the clinical arenas. Thus, as clinicians identified important treatment targets, the researchers have gone to the laboratory to develop an understanding of the target behaviors and how the systematic application of behavioral principles might change the behavior. This information is then brought back into the clinic setting for testing. Sometimes the clinic itself serves as the laboratory. The important point is that by basing its development on a firm foundation of empirical self-evaluation, the field has been able to undergo continual refinement and improvement.

Since behaviorists are good at self-evaluation, their failures are as apparent as their successes. They have certainly been extremely effective and successful in dealing with behaviors associated with autism. Self-injury, attentional deficits, disruptive behaviors, and even language have been effectively treated with behavioral methods. However, success is lacking in other areas. The field is still a long way from completely resolving all the issues in language training and many problems remain. For example, while therapists are relatively good at establishing language skills, many of the more

subtle aspects of language remain problematic. Thus, many speaking autistic children still have odd inflection and pacing, do not look at their listener, over-concentrate on topics, and do not pay attention to the subtle social cues of others to control their language. Probably the most important failure is that researchers have not yet been able to crack the "nut" of autism—the deficits in social behavior and attachment. Thus, therapy has not resolved the problem of teaching these children to be social. Treatment can teach them social behaviors but still has not determined how to make people important to them.

One should look upon these limitations not as failures but as challenges. They challenge researchers to continue their systematic analyses and to understand these behaviors as they have understood others. The goals may be more difficult but are not impossible. This is where future efforts must be, and are, directed.

TREATMENT RESOURCES

Koegel, R. L., Koegel, L. K., & Parks, D. R. (1992). *How to teach self-management skills to individuals with severe handicaps: A training manual.* University of California, Santa Barbara. Unpublished manuscript.

Koegel, R. L., Schreibman, L., Good, A. B., Cerniglia, L., Murphy, L., & Koegel, L. K. (1989). *How to teach pivotal behaviors to autistic children.* University of California, Santa Barbara. Unpublished manuscript.

CHAPTER 21

Applications to Pediatric Psychology

Lizette Peterson

Daniel D. Sherman

Michelle Zink

Three factors characterize pediatric psychology: the treatment of medically ill and injured children, a focus on developmental issues, and the use of behavioral intervention strategies (Peterson & Harbeck, 1988). Each of these factors is essential in defining the field. Early descriptions of pediatric psychology relied on the population served; pediatric psychology served children hospitalized by acute or chronic illness and trauma (Wright, 1967). Other descriptions highlighted the importance of assuming a developmental orientation and the need for child-specific clinical skills (Tuma, 1975). Reliance on behavioral conceptualizations and treatment methods has typified descriptions of pediatric psychology (Walker, 1979).

This chapter will serve as an overview of some of the different challenges within pediatric psychology and will present a sample of the behavioral interventions that have been created to meet these challenges. The potential arena is very broad (Drotar et al., 1989). For instance, one focus of pediatric psychologists has been

the development of skills necessary to treat physical disease and the skills and motivation that are required for compliance with medical regimens. Both kinds of skills can directly influence the course of medical illness. Another focus has yielded interventions that diminish children's acute and chronic pain and reduce manifestations of disease such as seizure activity. The majority of the chapter focuses on these activities. However, brief attention will also be directed to another focus—efforts to limit pain and anxiety that accompany various diagnostic and corrective medical procedures. Finally, the chapter will conclude with a relatively new focus within pediatric psychology— the long-term prevention of medical disorders and trauma, prevention that can be attained through promoting behaviors that enhance health and avoid injury and substance abuse.

The range of these disparate interventions is great. However, the extent of children's needs, abilities, and past experiences across differing developmental levels is even greater. When focusing on a given problem requiring intervention, it is essential for the pediatric psychologist to consider the differences in approaches dictated by the age, life experiences, and the cognitive, affective, and social maturity of the child. Unlike many of the interventions within behavioral medicine that serve adults, interventions with medically ill and injured children must occur within and be evaluated against a rapidly changing background of growth and development. Further, even extensive knowledge of normal developmental abilities is not always a sufficient basis for intervention, because chronic illness may alter the developmental course of many skills (Karoly, 1982). Moreover, acute illness may result in the temporary loss of previously attained skills (Willis, Elliott, & Jay, 1982) and a reduction in the desire and ability to acquire new skills (Magrab & Calcagno, 1978). Some medical treatments may even cause permanent decreases in certain areas such as cognitive ability (Soni, Morten, Pitner, Owens, & Powazek, 1975). Thus, recognizing the complex interweavings of prior developmental competencies and current abilities on the one hand, with each medical disorder and its treatment on the other, is the crucial and formidable assignment accepted by those who practice pediatric psychology.

No wonder that when presented with such challenges, the field has relied on behavioral principles to dictate interventions. With such complexity, it is important to be able to depend on conceptualizations that clearly identify the target for intervention and specify the changes that are desirable. Furthermore, the time demands inherent in medical settings require the use of potent interventions that yield demonstrable results in the same short time typically allocated to medical interventions (Roberts, Quevillon, & Wright, 1979).

The rest of the chapter will sample from the abundance of behavioral interventions that have been used successfully with pediatric patients. The chapter is organized around major target areas for pediatric psychologists. Each section

considers a small number of examples of intervention strategies paired with different child disorders. Although many techniques are actually applicable to a variety of different medical problems, for simplicity, each target for intervention is referred to only once in the chapter. In addition, many of the problem areas (such as medical compliance) overlap with other topic areas (such as skill-building approaches). For the sake of clarity, the chapter will discuss each area separately. Nevertheless, in actuality both the problem areas and the methods for intervention overlap in clinical practice.

The overview presented here is issue and application oriented; it does not address conceptual concerns or provide methodological critiques of the work conducted thus far in each area. Finally, this brief chapter cannot begin to provide a comprehensive overview of the field that has been described in several recent texts (Peterson & Harbeck, 1988; Roberts, 1986; Routh, 1988; Tuma, 1982; Varni, 1983). Instead, the chapter attempts to provide an illustration of the potential for behavioral interventions with child medical patients.

INTERVENTIONS FOR CHILDREN WITH CHRONIC DISEASES

The life expectancy for children with chronic illness has improved steadily over the last two decades. New medical diagnostic and treatment techniques have altered the previously fatal course of many diseases. However, with these changes have come a new set of demands on chronically ill children and their families. Adjustment to the disease and to the often arduous and demanding medical interventions can be difficult. This portion of the chapter will focus on three areas of adjustment facilitated by behavioral intervention: building normal developmental and medical intervention skills, increasing compliance with medical regimens, and alleviating disease symptoms.

Interventions to Teach Specific Skills

Two types of skills are often targeted by pediatric psychologists. First, some children do not spontaneously acquire developmentally appropriate behaviors because of their disease, and teaching these behaviors often becomes the goal of intervention programs. Also, for many types of chronic illness, the parents and the child him- or herself assume the bulk of the medical care. It thus becomes essential that the appropriate family members acquire the necessary medical skills to administer testing and treatment effectively.

Increasing Age-Appropriate Motor Behavior

Some childhood diseases slow or even prevent the normal development of behaviors such as standing, walking, skipping, and fine motor control. Physical therapy sometimes assists such children in attaining the muscular control necessary for self-care, play, and locomotion. However, not all children cooperate with the effortful and sometimes painful program of physical therapy. For example, Manella and Varni (1981) describe an intervention for a 4-year-old child with myelomeningocele (spina bifida). Despite 6 months of physical therapy designed to teach her to stand and walk, the child refused to walk and continued to crawl, scoot, or demand to remain in a stroller. When the physical therapist insisted that the child attempt to acquire some muscular control, the girl would cry and tantrum. Manella and Varni began a program of successive approximation to walking by rewarding the girl for complying with instructions to simply stand while using her crutches. When she did so, she was allowed to play briefly with colorful stuffed animals and

was praised. Gradually, the animals were moved away from the child and she was required to stand erect and eventually to walk a few feet. The program was terminated when the child was willing to walk 160 feet. The mother continued the program and at last report the child was walking to all school functions. This combination of small steps, praise, readily attainable reinforcers, and parental support typifies interventions that are successful in increasing normal developmental skills such as language, self-feeding, and toileting skills in chronically ill children.

Medical Treatment Skills for Children

Chronically ill children often must be responsible for some aspects of their own care. For example, insulin-dependent diabetes mellitus is a demanding disorder in which the child must regularly test his or her urine or blood to check the balance between energy expenditure, food intake, and injected insulin. This is a complicated regimen, and some authors have described the use of structured educational interventions such as teaching machines to educate young diabetics about necessary diet, testing, and injecting (Collier & Etzwiler, 1971).

One of the aspects requiring special skill is the injecting of insulin. The syringe must be prepared so that no air is injected, the injection must be appropriately placed, and the injection site needs to be changed from injection to injection. Modeling appears to be a useful addition to the use of small steps described in teaching children how to inject. Gilbert et al. (1982) used a modeling film in which children observed a peer acquiring self-injection skills, after which they were taught to self-inject. In comparison to children who viewed a nutrition film, older girls who viewed the modeling film showed enhanced self-injection skills. The authors suggest that the older girls may have been the most developmentally ready to acquire self-injection skills.

Although such single-component interventions are often successful, children who are initially resistant to skill acquisition or who can benefit from additional family support may require additional intervention. Epstein et al. (1981) suggest that the most effective interventions use combinations of intensive education, modeling, parental involvement, rewards, and self-monitoring.

Medical Treatment Skills for Parents

Some medical treatments that have historically only been accomplished within the hospital setting are gradually being shifted to outpatient use by the ill child's parents. Home therapy allows the child fewer disruptions in his or her regular routine and a more normal life. On the other hand, there is an inherent danger if the medical procedure is performed incorrectly. Thus, the method of instruction of such skills is critical.

In one such program, Sergis-Deavenport and Varni (1982, 1983) taught parents of children with hemophilia to administer factor replacement therapy. Hemophilia is a chronic illness in which the blood lacks the ability to clot and excessive bleeding can result from a small bump or cut. Internal bleeding, particularly into primary body cavities or into the joints, is a special problem. Factor replacement therapy involves the intravenous administration of a clotting substance. When bleeding begins, factor replacement therapy can avoid a prolonged bleeding episode. However, the administration of factor replacement therapy is a demanding procedure. Sergis-Deavenport and Varni describe a three-stage training program for parents who wish to administer the factor replacement therapy at home. In the first stage, 20 discrete behaviors were modeled and rehearsed to reconstitute the factor replacement under sterile conditions. In the second, 20 steps were involved in preparing the syringe. In the third stage, 36 steps were used to complete the infusion. Parents receiving this training program observed and rehearsed the skills until they

could reliably complete the criteria for training established by Sergis-Deavenport and Varni (80% of the steps correctly). At follow-up, parents demonstrated 97% accuracy in carrying out this demanding medical procedure.

The same techniques, such as small steps, modeling, and praise, used successfully for children can thus teach adults to administer even very complex medical treatments successfully. Similar behavioral techniques have focused on teaching parents and children to administer postural drainage therapy for children with cystic fibrosis (Stabler, Fernald, Johnson, Johnson, & Ryan, 1981) and to complete physical therapy for children with hemophilia (Varni, 1981a).

At times, skill alone fails to establish child and parent compliance with the suggested medical regimen. The more complex the regimen, the less immediate feedback for noncompliance; and the more costly the compliance behaviors, the less compliance may be expected. Fortunately, behavioral interventions can not only increase skill levels but can affect other aspects of compliance as well, as can be seen in the next section.

Interventions to Enhance Medical Compliance

Many individuals prefer the term *adherence* to the term *compliance*. They argue that adherence denotes patients acting in concert with the physician rather than passively complying. This chapter uses the more traditional term compliance but still emphasizes the child's and family's proactive interaction with the treatment protocol suggested by the physician. Medical compliance necessitates not only skills but also the structure and motivation to carry through appropriately. Compliance demands run the gamut from requiring individuals to perform certain behaviors (e.g., pill ingestion, urine testing, or painful exercise) to asking that they decrease behaviors (e.g., eating certain foods or exposing themselves to allergens). Compliance involves all of the challenges implicit in the behavioral literature on enhancing self-control. The discussion begins by considering direct interventions to enhance compliance and then considers systems influences from the family and beyond that affect compliance.

Reinforcing Dietary Compliance

There are many medical conditions in which a special diet is necessary. For example, children with kidney dysfunction must regularly undergo hemodialysis, a procedure in which their blood is shunted through a machine that duplicates (although imperfectly) the removal of waste products ordinarily assumed by the kidneys. Dialysis patients are typically maintained on a special diet that limits the amount of products that must be removed from the body during dialysis. The rigidity of such a diet often poses adherence problems for children.

An early study in this area demonstrated that a reinforcement system could improve dietary compliance for hemodialysis patients. Magrab and Papadopoulou (1977) created a point system they called "Specially for You" for dialysis patients aged 11 to 18. The subjects were allowed to select prizes like model car kits, earrings, comic books, and puzzles at the exchange rate of 18 points for $2 value of the merchandise. When the subjects underwent dialysis, their weight, potassium level, and BUN (a measure of protein breakdown) level was measured and subjects were rewarded 2 to 3 points for maintaining appropriate levels. This intervention resulted in lower BUN and potassium levels in subjects who had experienced problems with their levels previously, and diminished weight fluctuation in all subjects. When the points were withdrawn, weight fluctuation increased, demonstrating that it was the contingent reinforcement and not merely additional skill in recognizing appropriate foods that influenced compliance. Similar programs targeting diabetic children's adherence in blood glu-

cose testing (Carney, Schechter, & Davis 1983), and dietary adherence (Lowe & Lutzker, 1979), as well as calorie consumption in children with cystic fibrosis (Stark, Bowen, Tyc, Evans, & Passero, 1990), support the utility of this approach.

Reinforcing Difficult or Painful Aspects of the Medical Regimen

Generally speaking, compliance with a medical regimen is time-consuming and effortful. It is even more difficult to establish compliance with a medical regimen that is painful and for which the rewards are to be received in the distant future. JRA (juvenile rheumatoid arthritis) is a disease that typically begins in children under 10 years of age. It is manifested by painful swelling and stiffness in major joints, and primarily affects the knees and elbows. In many instances, JRA can be crippling. Intervention typically involves a combination of medication, exercise, and the wearing of splints to maintain joint mobility (Jette, 1980). However, the splints are not only time-consuming to put on, but they actually decrease mobility while in use, and they can be painful to wear. Rapoff, Lindsley, and Christophersen (1984) reported on the treatment of a 7-year-old child with systemic-onset JRA. These clinicians used a token system to increase the use of wrist and knee splints at night. Appropriate splint use rose from around 0% to around 80%, demonstrating sizeable increases in compliance with the regimen when reinforcement was used.

Problem Solving in Parents of Chronically Ill Children

The influences of reinforcement programs and other interventions for medically ill and injured children are likely to be enhanced in situations where the parent is invested in complying. For many types of regimen compliance, the parent has primary responsibility for dispensing the medication, coordinating a special diet, and promoting activities such as exercise or urine testing. As noted earlier, some training programs have directly focused on the parents. Additionally, the parents' ability to deal with the demands of the medical regimen may have an indirect but decided influence on compliance. Recent research suggests the importance of behaviorally assessing this ability.

Fehrenbach and Peterson (1989) examined the disease-specific problem-solving ability of parents with children who had been diagnosed early in life with phenylketonuria. This disease results in an inability to metabolize certain dietary substances (phenylalanine), and if left untreated, it can result in severe neurological impairment and mental retardation. However, the use of a special diet can avoid such negative outcomes. Unfortunately, the diet is quite complex and there are no immediately discernible symptoms resulting from failure to adhere to the diet. Thus, it is difficult for children to completely avoid all substances forbidden by the diet. Fehrenbach and Peterson found that parents who showed good ability to report effective solutions to vignettes involving the child's dietary habits had children who showed more appropriate levels of phenylalanine than parents who suggested poor solutions. Although temporal stress (i.e., having to make a decision quickly) decreased the problem-solving effectiveness of all parents, those parents with children in good dietary control remained superior in their problem-solving ability to parents of children in poor dietary control, even when temporally stressed. Other researchers have similarly underscored the importance of problem-solving abilities in families of chronically ill children. For example, Kucia et al. (1979) showed that disease management in children with cystic fibrosis was positively influenced by good problem-solving abilities in the parents of these chronically ill children.

Recently, Graves, Meyers, and Clark (1988) described a problem-solving training intervention for 6- to 12-year-old obese children and their parents. Training focused on problem identification, selection of alternatives, evaluation of the success of the alternative, and identification of a method of implementing changes in eating patterns. In comparison to families receiving standard treatment, families in the problem-solving group had children who lost more weight and maintained these losses better through 3- and 6-month follow-up. Both this intervention study and the preceding descriptive studies suggest the utility of focusing on parental problem-solving skills when intervening to improve compliance.

In addition to focusing directly on parental skills to increase compliance, other, more interactive qualities can influence compliance. A discussion of some of these systems-based factors follows.

Family Systems Factors

The single-variable applications for children and for parents that have successfully increased compliance illustrate the importance of a systematic, structured approach combined with reinforcement. However, compliance must take place within the context of many other factors that may strongly influence the child, including school systems that may or may not make allowance for the child's relatively unseen disease and peer systems in which activity limitations and side effects of a painful disease may be disruptive.

Probably no system has a more profound impact on the chronically ill child than the family system (Kazak, 1989). In some cases, the system that functioned well when the child was younger may break down as the parent shifts responsibility to a child not yet ready to take responsibility. When this happens in families of diabetic children, for example, metabolic control is compromised (Anderson, Auslander, Jung, Miller, & Santiago, 1990). In other cases, the child's illness and dysfunction may play a necessary role in the family, creating what Minuchin (1974) termed a system-maintaining symptom. For example, by directing the parents' attention away from their marital difficulties and toward his or her own behavior, the ill child may unintentionally function to decrease family strife. Such a role within the family is sometimes more influential than the external rewards that can be brought to bear.

Not only does the parent influence the child and the child influence the parent, but higher-order family variables may have direct or indirect influence on both parent and child. Ultimately, the manner in which the family functions as a whole can form the basis for good or poor compliance. For example, family conflict has been clearly related to lowered diabetic adherence, and family cohesion was found to be related to improved adherence in diabetic children (Hauser et al., 1990). Heightened family conflict and enmeshment has also been found to be associated with behavioral disorders in children with gastrointestinal anomalies (Tarnowski, King, Green, & Ginn-Pease, 1991).

Similarly, Chaney and Peterson (1989) found that families who were either very high (showing rigid, enmeshed patterns) or low (showing disengaged, chaotic patterns) in family cohesion and adaptability showed lower medication compliance than did families with intermediate levels of closeness and flexibility. When administering a reinforcement program or any other compliance-enhancing intervention, it thus seems sensible to consider the system in which the program must function.

When discussing programs designed to build skills or increase compliance, motivation to implement and maintain the program becomes a central component. In the final section addressing the treatment of chronic disease, symptom alleviation will be considered. Here, families and children typically appear highly motivated for change and yet unwanted symptoms continue. Behavioral interventions can make a unique contribution to this area as well.

Interventions to Alleviate Symptoms

This section will consider two types of programming to reduce unwanted symptoms: programs to reduce pain and interventions to reduce seizure frequency. These serve only as examples of successful behavioral programming to reduce unwanted symptoms. There are many others, including disparate targets such as joint immobility in JRA, hair pulling, pica, fecal incontinence, and psychogenic vomiting (Peterson & Harbeck, 1988, 1990).

Chronic Headache

Over a dozen studies using several different treatment methods have been conducted to show that behavioral techniques can reduce recurrent headache in children (Hoelscher & Lichstein, 1984). One of the simplest interventions is the use of differential reinforcement of other behavior (DRO) in which the child is rewarded for withholding reports of headache pain for progressively longer periods of time. Ramsden, Friedman, and Williamson (1983) relied on such an intervention with a 6-year-old girl who repeatedly had reported severe headaches over a period of 3 years, despite the absence of any medically documented reason for headache. Initially, the program was school-based and consisted of the girl earning a preferred activity at the end of each day in which no report of headache pain had occurred. Further, her participation in Monday recess was contingent on a specified number of headache-free days the week before, and this number was gradually increased over time. Several weeks later, a home program was instituted with participation in a preferred mother-daughter activity contingent on no headache reports. Weekend bonuses were then offered. At posttreatment and 10-month follow-up, the child remained headache-free.

Other investigators have used behavior therapy techniques such as biofeedback and relaxation (see review by Vieyra, Hoag, & Masek, 1991). For example, Labbé and Williamson (1983) treated three children with migraine headache by using finger temperature biofeedback. Children were taught to increase the temperature of their fingers twice daily and at the first sign of a migraine. This is thought to redirect excessive blood flow away from the brain. At 2-year follow-up, the children had experienced no further headaches.

McGrath (1990) reported on a cognitive-behavioral program used to treat children's pain. It flexibly applied different components to the children that needed them. Education was given to all children; psychological methods of controlling pain (e.g., exercise, relaxation, hypnosis) were taught. Parents were taught to assist children in alternative ways of coping with stress and were instructed not to attend to pain cues. This program has successfully reduced headache in elementary and secondary school children. In addition to treating headaches, techniques such as biofeedback, relaxation, and parental rewards for the absence of pain have also been successful with other forms of chronic pain, as will be seen in the next section.

Muscle and Joint Pain

A variety of childhood medical disorders can cause muscle contraction and joint degeneration, often resulting in pain and decreases in limb use that can ultimately be crippling (Walco & Varni, 1991, provide a detailed overview of this area). Juvenile rheumatoid arthritis has already been discussed. A similar phenomenon occurs in children with hemophilia, wherein repeated bleeding into the joints results in hemarthroses (i.e., destruction of the cartilage and pathological bone formation). LaBaw (1970) used deep muscle relaxation and self-hypnosis to reduce chronic joint pain in children with hemophilia and found that the children not only reported reduced pain but also that fewer factor replacement products were needed to promote blood clotting. Similarly, Varni (1981a, 1981b)

used progressive muscle relaxation and guided imagery focusing on warming the affected joints of children with hemophilia. Then thermal biofeedback was used to give the subjects feedback on their success. Children receiving this treatment reported decreased pain after treatment and at 8-month follow-up and provided physiological evidence of treatment effectiveness with an impressive average increase of 5.6° from baseline in the temperature of the afflicted joint. Similarly, relaxation has been shown to be a helpful component for children with cerebral palsy who avoid physical therapy due to muscular pain (LaGreca & Ottinger, 1979), and relaxation and imagery associated with joint warming have been shown to assist children with juvenile rheumatoid arthritis (McGrath, 1990).

Unlike muscle and joint pain that often has a demonstrable physical basis, as many as 10% to 15% of school-age children report abdominal pain that cannot be linked to a distinct physical problem (Barr & Feuerstein, 1983). Behavioral interventions can successfully treat this kind of pain as well.

Recurrent Nonspecific Abdominal Pain

The syndrome of recurrent nonspecific abdominal pain includes paroxysmal pain that interrupts daily life activities and at minimum involves at least 3 episodes in 3 months (Apley, 1975). Typically such children are assessed first by a gastroenterologist to exclude the possibility of an organic cause and only in the absence of physical findings are treated by a psychologist. Initial treatment may involve improved toileting habits, dietary fiber supplement, and relaxation. Edwards, Finney, and Bonner (1991) found fiber therapy to be helpful with children who had recurrent abdominal pain with constipation, but did not find that relaxation was helpful. They suggested that this may have been because they did not alter family contingencies for using the relaxation or dealing with pain. In contrast, Sanders et al. (1989) described the multimodal relaxation plus parental contingency management treatment of a group of such children, ages 6–12. These children were taught to cope with pain by using relaxation procedures, self-coping statements, and distraction. Their parents were taught to ignore pain-relevant behavior (e.g., sighing, rubbing the abdomen) and to redirect the child to an enjoyable activity whenever the child complained of pain. A DRO schedule was used to reward days free from pain complaints. Following treatment, in comparison to a no-treatment control, treated children reported decreased pain and more pain-free days, had fewer maternal reports of pain, and demonstrated improved behavior as reported by the children's teachers on a behavior problem checklist. Finney, Lemanek, Cataldo, Katz, and Fugua (1989) found similar success with children reporting recurrent abdominal pain who were treated with self-monitoring, parental extinction, relaxation, fiber, and mandatory school attendance.

The successful use of interventions like DRO and distraction in the treatment of a subjective phenomenon such as pain often suggests to the naive reader that the pain is not "real" and that the child is merely malingering. This is definitely not the interpretation of the clinicians who treat these children. Further, treatments similar to those used for pain are successful in alleviating symptoms that (unlike pain) are clearly observable. The next section presents several examples of programming to remove unwanted, observable symptoms as it describes behavioral interventions for seizure disorders.

Seizure Activity

The major medical intervention to control seizures is the use of anticonvulsant medications, and the majority (70% to 80%) of seizures in children can be controlled through appropriate use of such medication (Johnston & Freeman, 1981). However, because such medication does not control all seizures and has a variety of neg-

ative side effects (Gordon, 1978), behavioral treatment of seizures provides an important alternative.

Some authors have relied on basic behavior modification procedures for seizure control in children. For example, Zlutnick, Mayville, and Moffat (1975) described a simple interruption technique for children with discernible preseizure behavior. When the children exhibited preseizure behaviors, the intervention agent grasped the child by the shoulders, gave a little shake, and shouted "No." This technique was effective in reducing seizures for 4 of the 5 children tested. The fifth child did not demonstrate discernible preseizure behavior.

Gardner (1967) described the successful treatment of a 10-year-old girl by ignoring seizures and rewarding seizure-incompatible behavior. Lane and Samples (1984) outlined the use of a DRO procedure to decrease severe seizures in a 3-year-old girl. Balaschak (1976) similarly reported a reduction in seizures from 60% of school days to 21% of school days, when an 11-year-old child was treated with a token system. The child was rewarded with points toward social interactions and candy bars, contingent on the absence of seizures.

Other clinicians have relied on relaxation and cognitive behavioral techniques. For example, Ince (1976) treated a 12-year-old boy for both grand mal and petit mal seizures by teaching the child to use deep muscle relaxation whenever he experienced a preseizure aura and also whenever he felt very anxious. Next, Ince used systematic desensitization to decrease the child's reaction to anxiety-provoking events such as peer teasing and concern over having a seizure in public. Following treatment, the child's seizures decreased from 10 grand mal and 25 petit mal seizures per week to no seizures at 6-month follow-up.

Several researchers have utilized EEG feedback to decrease the high amplitude/low frequency waveforms characteristic of seizures and have reported that this treatment decreased seizure activity in adults (Kuhlman, 1978; Lubar & Bahler, 1976). Finley (1976) demonstrated that

EEG feedback reduced seizure activity in one adolescent patient. However, this promising technique has yet to receive wide application to children.

It is noteworthy that both chronic pain and seizure activity can be successfully treated in children by using techniques originally designed for purposes of anxiety reduction. The next major section of this paper addresses interventions for acutely ill and injured children, and for children undergoing elective surgery. The same behavioral techniques used to diminish pain, anxiety, and movement disorders in children with chronic pain or seizure problems are also effective interventions for children whose pain and anxiety stems from invasive medical procedures.

INTERVENTIONS TO REDUCE DISTRESS DURING COMMON MEDICAL PROCEDURES

There are a variety of factors that contribute to children's distress during diagnostic procedures such as venipunctures, lumbar punctures, and bone marrow aspirations; discrete medical interventions such as burn debridement or cancer chemotherapy; and multicomponent medical experiences such as surgery. More specifically, the intensity of discomfort, the length of the procedure, and the presence of frightening visual stimuli are important environmental contributors to a child's distress. Further, the child's age, history of similar procedures, characteristic way of coping, and current expectations for the procedure also may influence the distress experienced. Parents also influence their children's responses. Finally, as outlined below, behavioral techniques used prior to the procedure can reduce children's anxiety and discomfort in many of these procedures.

Venipunctures and Injections

Needle-based procedures are often cited by children as among the most fear-provoking of medical events (Eland & Anderson, 1977) and thus it is surprising that there has not been more research focused on preparing children for such events. Some authors have reported that the use of firm instruction (e.g., "Stand on your feet and do not be silly"), in contrast to no instructions, results in less vomiting or fainting during mass immunizations (Hedberg & Schlong, 1973). However, other clinicians have found that a more empathetic and descriptive narration of what is about to happen, from the coldness of the alcohol to the stick of the needle, resulted in less crying, wincing, anger, and refusing to comply than did stern instructions to, "Act big and brave. Remain very still" (Fernald & Corry, 1981). Timing of explanations by parents to coincide with children's distress level also appears to be effective in reducing distress (Jacobson et al., 1990). The effectiveness of simple instructions concerning what is likely to happen can also be amplified by relabeling the sensations that will be experienced in an accurate but positive fashion (Eland, 1981).

Behavioral coping techniques have also been shown to reduce distress during injections. Ayer (1973) reported that having children focus on vivid mental images reduced the distress of needle-phobic child patients. Manne, Redd, Jacobsen, Gorfinkle, Schorr, and Rapkin (1990) used a unique distraction technique in the form of a party blower. Children were taught to control their breathing and attention by slowing unfolding the party blower with their breath while the parent counted out loud. Children who previously required restraint demonstrated greatly reduced pain and distress following training with this simple device.

Peterson and Shigetomi (1981) employed in-depth training, cue-controlled deep muscle relaxation, self-instruction, and imagery prompted by the parent directly before the medical procedure began. They found that the combination of a modeling film with training in coping techniques was most effective during venipunctures and injections in diminishing observable distress and increasing compliance. In addition to their effectiveness for brief medical interventions, such as injections and venipunctures, such techniques are also used successfully within more invasive medical procedures, as seen in the next section.

Diagnostic Oncology Procedures

Lumbar punctures (sometimes called spinal taps) and bone marrow aspirations are needle-based procedures used to determine the stage of disease and the success of intervention for childhood cancer. Because the results literally are a life-or-death matter, these procedures are emotionally charged for both parent and child. Both procedures are accomplished in the child's back, and the resultant inability of the child to observe what is going on adds to the anxiety-provoking nature of these procedures. Although this section focuses on treatment for these children, the parents are also beginning to be successfully targeted as recipients for stress inoculation procedures (Jay & Elliott, 1990).

Hypnosis and relaxation techniques (LaBaw, Holton, Tewell, & Eccles, 1975; Zeltzer & LeBaron, 1982) were among the most successful early intervention procedures used to help children cope with these diagnostic procedures. More recently, relaxation techniques have formed the central core of multicomponent procedures such as controlled breathing, positive imagery, reinforcement for complying with requests, and self-instruction (Jay, Elliott, Ozolins, & Olson, 1983). The availability of several different multicomponent interventions allows children to select their preferred coping techniques and to individualize the intervention program to fit their own abilities and needs.

The most common medical intervention for reducing distress due to diagnostic procedures is sedation, which can range from mild to heavy. Any amount of sedation may reduce the child's sense of ability to control events and results in carry-over symptoms such as drowsiness and nausea following the procedure. Jay, Elliot, Katz, and Seigel (1987) contrasted a multicomponent program of relaxation, distraction, and goal setting for reward with the use of mild sedation (valium) and found that compared to a no-treatment control group, the behaviorally prepared children were significantly less behaviorally distressed, reported less pain, and had lower pulse rates than control children. The children who received valium were at an intermediate level, not differing greatly from either the controls or the behaviorally prepared children. Thus, behavioral preparation appears to be at least as effective as sedation and in contrast to sedation, might be expected to have positive rather than negative side effects. This finding is particularly important for medical conditions in which sedation must be limited, as is the case with the treatment of child burn victims, discussed in the following section.

Burn Hydrotherapy

Although the procedures discussed to this point are very anxiety-provoking, none involves the substantial, sustained pain resulting from the treatment of child burn victims. It is necessary when treating children's burns to remove old medication and dead tissue by scrubbing it away with sterile gauze as clean water circulates around the child. Children's screaming, crying, and noncompliance often extend the painful procedure (Varni, Bessman, Russo, & Cataldo, 1980). Because it is essential that children ingest fluids and move about to prevent pneumonia, sedation must be minimized.

Like the oncology procedures just discussed, early interventions to assist child burn victims involved hypnosis (Bernstein, 1965) and meditation (Weinstein, 1976). More recent programs involve multicomponent interventions that rely on relaxation, deep breathing, attention distraction, rewards, and elaborate emotive imagery. Elliott and Olson (1983) described one example of a powerful imagery treatment in which children were taught to imagine a scene involving a favorite storybook hero who asked them to heroically endure the treatment. This use of imagery, in combination with coaching in relaxation and deep breathing, increased the children's compliance and reduced their reported pain during tanking and debridement.

Elective Surgeries

Unlike the discrete procedures (venipuncture, injections, diagnostic procedures, and burn hydrotherapy) just considered, elective surgeries involve a wide range of events, each carrying a diverse array of stimulus characteristics. As examples, admission to the hospital, with the attaching of an ID bracelet and the donning of strange hospital attire, forms one experience, and venipuncture or finger-prick blood tests form another. Spending the night in the hospital is rated by many parents as the most fear-provoking event of their child's surgery (Peterson & Shigetomi, 1982). Preoperative sedation often involves an injection or inserting an intravenous line into the child's hand or arm. Anesthesia, particularly if a mask is used, can be very threatening. After surgery, postoperative vomiting and pain require additional coping.

Information and Modeling

A variety of differing interventions have been used in the preparation for surgery, most based on the premise that children and parents can benefit from information about what is to happen. In fact, one early study showed that children were less distressed even in the absence of preparation if their mothers had received preparatory information (Skipper & Leonard, 1968). Later, Wolfer and Visintainer (1975) de-

scribed *stress point preparation* in which a nurse was present to buffer the occurrence of any major stressors. The nurse described to the child what would happen during each stress point, using a doll as a model. The nurse was also available to reassure the mother and to answer questions. This combination of information and emotional support resulted in children who were more cooperative, less distressed, and who recovered from surgery, in terms of fluid intake and voiding, more rapidly than children who did not receive such preparation.

The majority of well-controlled research on preparation for surgery has used a model to dispense information and demonstrate adaptive functioning. Cassell (1965) successfully employed a puppet model to reduce children's concern about cardiac catheterization. Melamed and Siegel (1975) described a filmed model for children and noted that child surgery patients exposed to the modeling film, in contrast to child patients viewing a control film, had lower observational ratings of behavioral distress and reported less fear. Pinto and Hollandsworth (1989) found that allowing the parent to view a modeling film with the child further reduced child distress in comparison with children who viewed the film alone, which in turn was more effective than no film at all. Pinto and Hollandsworth also documented that the costs of hospitalization for the patients who viewed the film were less than for those who did not, for a dollar savings of $183.17 on the average for each child, after film costs were considered. It is not possible to estimate the monetary value of the lowered physical arousal, reduced self-reported anxiety, and diminished signs of behavioral distress that Pinto and Hollandsworth reported, but the financial savings alone should be sufficient to persuade even the most cost-conscious hospital administrator of the value of modeling preparations for children.

Coping Skills

The impact of a model may be improved by the use of the kind of coping techniques described earlier. For instance, Peterson and Shigetomi (1981) found that cue-controlled relaxation, self-instruction, and imagery were effective auxiliary tools in preparing children for elective surgery. Similarly, Zastowny, Kirschenbaum, and Meng (1986) used stress inoculation techniques to prepare parents to assist their children in coping with elective surgery. Children whose parents received this preparation were more cooperative prior to surgery and received higher ratings of behavioral adjustment after surgery. The prepared parents were also less anxious than parents not receiving the preparation. Later, Robinson and Kobayashi (1991) attempted to replicate these findings and cautioned against trying to teach coping skills by using a prerecorded videotape procedure. Interactive teaching may be necessary.

Treatment Matching

Children have been shown to have differing characteristic styles of information gathering prior to an invasive procedure, and children who seek out information are typically better adjusted and experience less distress than children who avoid information (Peterson & Toler, 1986). Although few data exist on treatment-to-subject matching, it appears as if complementing rather than matching children's typical mode of seeking out information may be preferred (Smith, Ackerson, & Blotcky, 1989).

The techniques used for preparing children and their parents for an elective surgery share the conceptual base of primary prevention. That is, rather than waiting until the child is distressed and then attempting to mitigate that distress, these techniques attempt to prevent at least a portion of the distress before it occurs. The final segment in this chapter extends the concept of prevention to the area of health promotion. Health promotion interventions focus on establishing behaviors that are linked to long-term health and avoiding behaviors that are related in the long run to illness. Interventions for chronically and acutely ill and injured children

are important, but preventing illness and injury results in even more benefit to children and their families.

HEALTH PROMOTION INTERVENTIONS

There are a wide variety of differing areas of health promotion that rely on behavioral techniques (see Peterson, Chaney, and Harbeck, 1989, for details). This discussion will focus on establishing healthy daily habits such as toothbrushing, diet, and aerobic activity; avoiding substance abuse; and preventing injuries.

Daily Habits

Dental Hygiene

A third of the population of this country over age 45 have no teeth left at all, due to advanced periodontal disease that is largely preventable if early dental hygiene habits are acquired (Albino, 1984). One early study in this area demonstrated that instruction in oral hygiene (even when only given if requested by the child) and tokens contingent upon reductions in plaque resulted in substantial and maintained reductions in plaque in second-grade children (Martens, Frazier, Hirt, Meskin, & Proshek, 1973). Subsequent research has confirmed the value of using both intense instruction and rewards for reduced plaque in school settings (Albino, Tedesco, & Lee, 1980, Lund & Kegeles, 1982) and summer camps (Lattal, 1969).

Dietary Habits

Diet has a wide-ranging impact on diverse aspects of health. For example, diet directly affects dental health through controlling microbial growth (Stamm, 1980), and is linked through increased fiber intake to reductions of both many forms of cancer and childhood encopresis (Houts & Peterson, 1986). Diet also influences cardiovascular disease in adults (Perry, Klepp, & Schultz, 1988). It is clear, for example, that blood lipid levels in adults relate directly to atherosclerosis and that childhood levels are highly predictive of adult levels (Berenson & Epstein, 1983).

Behavioral techniques that assist obese children in altering their dietary habits are well-developed and quite successful, at least in effecting initial weight loss. Using structured rules such as those outlined in the "Traffic Light Diet" (Epstein, Masek, & Marshall, 1978); involving the family (Epstein, Wing, Steranchak, Dickson, & Michelson, 1980), especially when both parent and child utilize self-monitoring and altered eating habits (Epstein, McCurley, Wing, & Valoski, 1990); working within the school systems (Epstein, Masek, & Marshall, 1978); making plans; and using self-instruction (Coates, Jeffrey, Slinkard, Killen & Danaher, 1982) all are techniques that have had a positive impact on obese children. These interventions also show promise with normal-weight children. For example, recent research suggests that even preschoolers can learn to select healthy snacks if appropriate structure and reinforcement are used (Stark, Collins, Osnes, & Stokes, 1986).

At a different level of analysis, community-wide intervention programs have recently shown positive preventive effects. The North Karelia Youth Project (Walters, Hofman, Connelly, Barrett, & Kost, 1985) used instruction and personal contact for the children highest in cholesterol levels. A 2-year follow-up revealed decreased cholesterol levels in treated girls (but not boys) (Puska et al., 1982). Similarly, the Minnesota Heart Health Youth Program used peer leaders and home nutrition kits. Pilot study results from this program suggest clear reductions in children's dietary fat (Perry, Murray, & Klepp, 1987). Similar reductions in children's blood lipids have been reported in community interventions in other countries as well (Alexandrov et al., 1988).

Changes in dietary sodium, a major contributor to high blood pressure, may be more difficult to obtain. Luepker, Perry, Murray, and Mullis (1988) noted that increases in knowledge about sodium are easy to achieve but because most (93%) ingested sodium is already contained within processed foods, interventions focusing on salt added during cooking or at the table are unlikely to be effective. Instead, teaching a method by which high sodium foods can be avoided, similar to the methods used for high calorie foods that were noted earlier, may be necessary.

Activity Levels

In addition to diet, activity levels have a profound effect on health, especially cardiovascular health. Tuckman and Hinkle (1986) documented that adding only 30 minutes of aerobic activity three times a week resulted in demonstrable increases in aerobic fitness in normal-weight children. Similarly, Danforth et al. (1990) demonstrated significant decreases in diastolic and systolic blood pressure on low-SES African-American children identified as above the 95th percentile in blood pressure. Their program relied on vigorous exercise over a 12-week period and resulted in improved cardiovascular fitness as well as decreased hypertension. Alpert, Field, Goldstein, and Perry (1990) demonstrated that aerobic exercise even had demonstrable cardiovascular effects on preschool children, in addition to improving their agility.

As was the case with dietary changes, the most extensive literature on increasing aerobic activity has taken place in the weight-loss area. To illustrate, expanding the existing physical education requirements at school (Epstein, Woodall, Goreczny, Wing, & Robertson, 1984) and creating lifestyle changes in daily aerobic activity (e.g., walking, rather than using the elevator or bus) have been particularly successful (Epstein, Wing, Koeske, Ossip, & Beck, 1982). The importance of lifestyle changes rather than brief interventions to temporarily elevate levels of aerobic activity is clear. For example, Epstein, Wing, Koeske, and Valoski (1985) compared life-style changes in activity to both a running/biking regimen and a structured exercise program, and found the most consistent and maintained changes in fitness in the lifestyle exercise group. Similarly, Kleges, Eck, Haddock, and Kleges (1990) demonstrated that even in preschoolers, children at risk for obesity had lower activity rates than children not at risk. However, simply being out of doors increased activity rates for the children, regardless of risk status. The conclusion from all of these studies suggests that increased exercise relevant to cardiovascular health can be obtained in child subjects.

Avoiding Substance Abuse

The third factor most relevant to cardiovascular health is cigarette smoking. Smoking is also linked to a variety of types of cancer. Because cigarettes are exceptionally addictive, preventing smoking onset seems the preferred way to avoid these risks. A number of programs have evolved in recent years to prevent smoking onset. Educational programs often result in improved attitudes about smoking but without concomitant decreases in smoking onset (Iammarino, Heit, & Kaplan, 1980; Rabinowitz & Zimmerli, 1974).

In contrast, behavioral prevention programs have been quite successful, at least in reducing smoking initiation in the short run. One of the earliest and best-known interventions was conducted by Evans et al. (1978). They used not only education focused on the dangers of smoking but also information on the immediate attractiveness and fitness advantages of smoking abstinence. Small groups of students practiced active problem solving to deal with pressures to begin smoking. Feedback on number of classmates smoking was given throughout the study. This intervention method resulted in decreased smoking onset in comparison to a control group.

Subsequent programs have yielded similar success in reducing smoking initiation through the use of peer models (McAlister, Perry, & Maccoby, 1979), focused attempts to develop social refusal skills (Botvin & Eng, 1982), and family involvement (Flay, Johnson, & Hansen, 1984). The most effective programs in the future are likely to involve multiple components such as health education, social skills training, and peer pressure intervention (Johnson, Hansen, Collins, & Graham, 1985).

Fewer studies have addressed prevention of illegal drug use (Evans, 1988). Descriptive studies suggest that parent modeling, disrupted family functioning, peer drug use and peer approval, and general social skills influence early alcohol use (Cronkite & Moos, 1980; Kline, Canter, & Robin, 1987), and that prior use predicts current use, even in pregnant adolescents (Gilchrist, Gillmore, & Lohr, 1990). These studies seem to suggest the utility of continuing approaches similar to those that have already been proven effective in smoking prevention.

The few outcome studies that currently exist support such extensions. For example, Botvin, Baker, Dusenbury, Tortu, and Botvin (1990) described their drug abuse prevention program, labeled "Life Skills Training." This 12-unit curriculum was taught to nearly 5,000 high school students and focused on drug knowledge and on personal and social skills, specifically those necessary for peer and advertising resistance. Prevention effects for the program included lower use of cigarettes, marijuana, and excessive alcohol.

Other projects have expanded the school-based components to include interventions from parents and community as well. Johnson et al. (1990) described what they termed a "comprehensive community-based drug prevention" program. The components of this program included 10 school sessions focused on drug-use resistance skills, a parent organization to train parents in prevention and communication skills, community action such as a drug abuse prevention task force, and mass media coverage. Lowered use of tobacco and marijuana resulted. Many scientists foresee prevention efforts in the future that rely on intervention at the individual, home, school, community, and nationwide levels, including substantial media intervention based on social learning theory (Schilling & McAlister, 1990) to maximize preventive effects.

Injury Prevention

Although covered last, injury prevention is far from the least important activity for pediatric psychologists. Injuries are the leading killer of children in this country, accounting for more deaths than the next six leading causes of death (Derschewitz & Williamson, 1977) and necessitating medical care for one in every three children each year (Starfield, 1977). Tragically, the majority of these injuries can be prevented. Although this section will deal with unintentional (or "accidental") injury, behavioral programs to combat deliberate parental injury of children are also beginning to be evaluated (Wolfe, Edwards, Manion, & Koverola, 1988).

The single largest cause of death and disability in childhood is motor vehicle collisions, and the bulk of injuries (up to 70% of serious injuries and up to 90% of child fatalities) can be avoided by the use of child safety devices (Roberts, Layfield, & Fanurik, 1988). Behaviorists have recently demonstrated the utility of teaching and rewarding parents (Roberts & Turner, 1986) and preschoolers (Roberts & Layfield, 1987) when arriving at school with safety restraints in use. Subsequent research confirmed that direct observation was unnecessary and that a highly intermittent reinforcement schedule was sufficient to keep rates of safety restraint use at a relatively high level (Roberts & Broadbent, 1989).

Other researchers have successfully targeted specific child-based skills for avoiding various kinds of injuries. For example, Yeaton and Bailey (1978) used modeling and reinforcement for successive approximations to teach preschoolers to cross the street safely. Jones, Kazdin, and Haney (1981) described a program to teach a complex set of skills that allowed children

to escape a variety of situations during a fire and later noted that teaching children to elaborate the rationale for each step further improved their skills (Jones, Ollendick, & Schinske, 1989). The Child Research Laboratory at the University of Missouri-Columbia has used after-school programs (Peterson, 1984b), weekly outings with undergraduate volunteers (Peterson, 1984a), summer school classes (Peterson & Thiele, 1987), and parents in their own homes (Peterson, Mori, Selby, & Rosen, 1988) to teach children to deal with a variety of threats to their safety including severe weather, food preparation, first aid for cuts or burns, fires, and threatening strangers. Most of these studies have targeted community children, but recent programs have begun to focus on children at special risk (e.g., psychiatric patients with a history of firesetting and aggression were taught fire-safety skills by Kolko, Watson, & Faust, 1991). By using modeling, problem solving, and extensive behavioral rehearsal, these programs demonstrate that children can effectively acquire skills that may prevent their own injury.

Other behaviorists have targeted the parents by offering structure and reinforcement for removing safety hazards from the home. However, the most successful strategies have involved environmental changes such as window guards to reduce children's falls in urban areas (Spiegel & Lindaman, 1977) and child-proof medical closures (Walton, 1982). Behavioral analyses of the process by which children are injured may in the future reveal additional avenues for both environmental and individual intervention (Garling & Valsinger, 1986; Peterson, Farmer, & Mori, 1987).

CONCLUSIONS AND ISSUES FOR THE FUTURE

The literature presented in this chapter provides a mere sampling of the possible applications of behavioral techniques to children who are ill or injured. Relatively simple techniques such as systematic reinforcement can be used to teach skills (e.g., pill swallowing), increase compliance (e.g., blood testing in children with diabetes), and assist the child in performing difficult or painful motor tasks. Modeling can teach complex skills to prevent disease (e.g., periodontal disease) or injury (e.g., fire escape), and to treat a disorder (e.g., insulin injection). Modeling can also decrease anxiety and enhance compliance with stressful medical interventions. Relaxation procedures can limit anxiety, pain, headache, and even seizure activity. DRO procedures use positive consequences to reduce unwanted behaviors and sensations, such as pain and seizure activity. The use of all of these techniques, however, requires a clear set of operationalized goals that are tailored to the child's developmental needs (Peterson & Harbeck, 1988).

This chapter made early reference to the relatively greater demands that medical illness place on children than on adults, because children must also negotiate developmental challenges. For instance, the child's ability to discriminate and recall complicated chains of behavior is strongly influenced by his or her developmental level. Although the use of fading and overrehearsal are useful here, an awareness of young children's limitations in perceiving, interpreting, and remembering earlier events must also be considered (Peterson & Harbeck, 1990).

It is also essential to be aware of normal developmental competencies and their vulnerability to the disruptive impact of illness and stressful medical procedures. For instance, a preschool child who is just beginning to establish social skills may experience a greater loss in developing peer interaction competencies because of prolonged hospitalization than would an older child who had already developed and practiced a set of interactional skills. A preadolescent who is just beginning to wish for independence from family rules may have more difficulty with a rigid medical regimen than would a younger child. Clearly,

the interaction of the ill child's medical condition with his or her developmental competencies requires special interventions that combine all three of the essential components of pediatric psychology—a medical population, developmental sensitivity, and behavioral interventions.

This chapter has addressed one aspect of each disorder at one point in time. However, the practitioner needs to consider the ill child in the context of his or her family, peer system, school, and even community, and to align these systems and subsystems with the goals of the child.

Finally, the importance of health promotion in preventing childhood illness and injury should be emphasized. Many experts believe that future improvements in morbidity and mortality rates will result from changes in lifestyle habits rather than biologically based medical advances (Matarazzo, 1980). There now exits a compelling literature that clearly demonstrates the effectiveness of behavioral techniques in remediating pediatric problems. The future should see an equally strong literature on behavioral contributions to the prevention of childhood illness and injury.

TREATMENT RESOURCES

Jay, S. M., & Elliott, C. H. (1990). A stress inoculation program for parents whose children are undergoing painful medical procedures. *Journal of Consulting and Clinical Psychology, 58,* 799–804.

Luepker, R. V., Perry, C. L., Murray, D. M., & Mullis, R. (1988). Hypertension prevention through nutrition education in youth: A school-based program involving parents. *Health Psychology, 7,* 233–245.

Peterson, L. (1984). Teaching home safety and survival skills to latchkey children: A comparison of two manuals and methods. *Journal of Applied Behavior Analysis, 17,* 279–293.

Peterson, L., & Shigetomi, C. (1981). The use of coping techniques to minimize anxiety in hospitalized children. *Behavior Therapy, 12,* 1–14.

Varni, J. W. (1981). Self-regulation techniques in the management of chronic arthritic pain in hemophilia. *Behavior Therapy, 12,* 185–194.

CHAPTER 22

Future Directions

From an historical perspective, behaviorally based approaches to mental health problems, which only began to receive widespread evaluation and application in the 1960s and 1970s, would still be considered newcomers. Due in part, however, to increased demands for shorter, more cost-effective treatments and in part to the flexibility and adaptability of a model based on empiricism, behavioral and cognitive-behavioral approaches have become mainstream therapies. In some areas, such as the treatment of mental retardation, autism, and chronic schizophrenia, the use of behavioral techniques, which were once considered controversial, is now standard fare. Further, although behavior therapy was once seen as limited to fairly circumscribed areas or to mild problems such as phobias, there is now essentially no disorder for which behavioral intervention is considered inappropriate. This state of affairs has dramatically changed the major issues that need to be addressed by behavior therapists. Initially, behavior therapists had to jus-

tify the use of an approach that was, at best, considered superficially effective and, at worst, manipulative and dehumanizing. However, as the evidence mounted that behavioral interventions were at least as effective as traditional therapies and could be used to achieve humanitarian goals, ethical issues became less salient. Ethical guidelines have been made clearer and more specific, but they apply equally to interventions derived from any theoretical orientation and typically do not single out behavioral procedures. Thus, although behaviorists and cognitive-behaviorists continue to be sensitive to ethical issues, the central focus of the last decade has been the refinement of interventions and vigorous evaluation of their efficacy.

The disorders addressed in the previous chapters of this book were chosen to reflect problem areas in which the utility of behavioral intervention has been well established. For each of these areas, the authors have highlighted current achievements, discussed issues that have not yet been satisfactorily addressed, and suggested ways in which researchers might work in the future to improve treatment of those disorders. The present chapter will describe some additional areas in which behavioral research is currently making a strong, positive impact, as a way to illustrate some important trends for the next decade of behavioral research.

First, behavioral interventions are likely to become increasingly influential in traditional mental health arenas, through their application to additional psychiatric disorders that were once considered too complex or difficult for a behavioral approach. Second, behavioral interventions will be used increasingly to address public health problems and social issues that are related to mental health. Third, behavioral interventions and experimental methodology will expand to outside the traditional fields of mental health and education to address related aspects of human behavior.

APPLICATIONS WITH COMPLEX DISORDERS

Post-Traumatic Stress Disorder

Behaviorally oriented researchers have been involved in investigations of post-traumatic stress disorder (PTSD) since the early 1980s, when this disorder first gained recognition as an official diagnostic category in DSM-III. PTSD is characterized by the following symptoms: subjective distress (i.e., anxiety, guilt, depression), re-experiencing symptoms (i.e., flashbacks, dreams), numbing (lack of positive emotions), social avoidance or avoidance of trauma-related situations, and high physiological arousal associated with trauma memories. Early behavioral researchers focused on ways to adapt and refine behavioral techniques that had been developed to treat phobias and generalized anxiety: exposure treatments (e.g., systematic desensitization

and flooding) and anxiety/stress management techniques. Most of the research has been conducted with two specific populations in which PTSD frequently occurs; war veterans and rape survivors. Fortunately, the conclusions drawn from studies of both populations have been consistent suggesting that PTSD resulting from other traumas, such as accidents or natural disasters, is likely to respond as well.

Directed Therapeutic Exposure

Directed therapeutic exposure (DTE) is the term that has been used to describe a type of flooding or implosive therapy developed for PTSD (Lyons and Keane, 1989). Although it is often quite effective, undergoing the treatment procedure can be distressing for the client. Thus, DTE is always conducted within the context of a strong, supportive therapeutic relationship, and often in conjunction with techniques designed to enhance coping skills. Sessions are usually 2 to $2\frac{1}{2}$ hours twice a week, so that progress will be made quickly. A hierarchy of intrusive memories is developed and the client learns relaxation skills. The therapist then guides the client in vividly imagining each scene until that scene no longer elicits intense anxiety. The goal is not to erase the memories but to reduce the intrusive quality of the memories. It is assumed that a person naturally tries to forget or to distract himself or herself from the most aversive aspect of the memories, so the intense anxiety associated with those memories does not extinguish naturally. Thus, DTE is designed to provide a more systematic, intense, and thorough type of exposure than might occur, for example, in a support group where clients discussed their memories.

Evaluation of DTE

Three outcome studies supporting the use of DTE have been reported. Keane, Fairbank, Caddell, and Zimering (1989) randomly assigned 24 veterans (inpatients and outpatients)

379

diagnosed with PTSD to either 14 sessions of DTE or a wait-list control. DTE was more effective in reducing re-experiencing symptoms, anxiety, guilt, and depression, but it did not significantly diminish the numbing and social avoidance symptoms. Despite successful maintenance of therapeutic effects at 6-month follow-up, social adjustment still had not improved. The authors suggested that specific skills training might be needed to improve social adjustment.

Two other studies found that DTE enhanced overall treatment effectiveness when it was added to more traditional treatment programs, one an outpatient program (Cooper & Clum, 1989) and one an inpatient program (Boudewyns & Hyer, 1990). Both studies included assessment of physiological arousal during a behavioral avoidance test in which the subject was asked to imagine his or her traumatic scenes. In Cooper and Clum's study, neither DTE nor standard treatment resulted in significant reductions of physiological arousal at posttest. However, in Boudewyns & Hyer's study, reductions in physiological responding were associated with improvement on psychological measures, regardless of treatment condition. Thus, physiological arousal in response to trauma memories appears to be quite resistant to extinction even with DTE, but decreased physiological arousal was associated with more positive outcome.

Exposure-Based Treatments for Rape Survivors

Research on PTSD among rape survivors also supports the importance of dealing directly with the trauma memories. Initially, case studies demonstrated that both systematic desensitization and anxiety-management techniques could successfully reduce rape-related fears, anxiety, and depression. However, in the first controlled study, Resnick, Jordan, Girelli, Hatter, and Marhoefer-Doorah (1988) found

that neither assertive training nor anxiety-management techniques (both of which included some exposure) were more effective than supportive psychotherapy, although all three groups improved relative to a group of wait-list controls.

A more recent study by Foa, Rothbaum, Riggs, and Murdock (in press) on rape survivors meeting PTSD criteria (averaging 6 years after assault) supports the conclusion that intensive exposure, such as that found in DTE, is the most specifically effective aspect of behavioral treatment. In that study, subjects receiving only anxiety management were more improved at posttest than those receiving prolonged exposure (intensive imaginal and *in vivo* exposure sessions with no anxiety-management instructions). Both treatments were more effective than supportive psychotherapy or a wait-list. However, only subjects in the prolonged exposure group continued to improve after treatment, sufficiently that by 3-month follow-up the prolonged exposure group was superior. Foa and colleagues hypothesized that the anxiety-management procedures produced more immediate relief, and exposure procedures led to more permanent changes in the trauma memories through the emotional processing that occurred as subjects repeatedly confronted such memories. If so, both treatments may be useful but in different ways. Anxiety management may be more useful in relieving initial, acute distress and may reduce the number of survivors with prolonged distress; intensive exposure may be necessary for those with prolonged distress. Another interesting point is that Foa's procedures included *in vivo* exposure to avoided situations, and her study found more substantial improvement in avoidance symptoms than did the studies utilizing DTE. Thus, investigators in this area will probably continue to refine exposure methods so they will be more effective in reducing both avoidance and the physiological arousal associated with the distressing memories.

Personality Disorders

Historically, behavior therapists have been unwilling to use the psychiatric classification system to label a person as having a "personality disorder" (known also as Axis II diagnosis). Psychiatric diagnoses in general were seen as less useful than simply identifying specific dysfunctional behaviors, thoughts, or emotional responses. Personality disorder diagnoses were seen as especially problematic, as they were notably unreliable, with a great deal of overlap among the various diagnostic categories. However, the development of structured and semi-structured diagnostic interviews (Standage, 1989) has alleviated many of the reliability concerns and has facilitated research by allowing investigators to set clear selection criteria for samples of subjects.

A number of factors suggest that interventions for personality disorders will become increasingly important for the future of behavior therapy. Personality disorders are not generally seen as responding well to medications, so psychological interventions are likely to remain the treatment of choice. Clients with personality disorders are also seen by therapists of all orientations as the most difficult to treat. No current therapies are highly effective for such clients, so there is much interest in developing new ways to address these chronic problems. It has also been noted that the major disorders already discussed (Axis I disorders such as depression and bulimia) are more difficult to treat when the person has a co-existing personality disorder. Thus, development of effective treatments for personality disorders may enhance treatment effectiveness for Axis I disorders.

Interventions for
Avoidant Personality Disorder

The treatment of avoidant personality disorder (AVPD) provides an example of the extension of behavioral approaches to the treatment of personality disorders. Behavior therapists have

successfully treated circumscribed social anxiety or social phobias for some time, but subjects who would meet criteria for AVPD were usually excluded from experimental studies. Recently Alden (1989) hypothesized that additional skills-oriented components might be needed for subjects with AVPD. Two variations of a standard 10-week graduated exposure treatment for social anxiety were compared; one included social skills training and one included skills for developing intimacy. Neither variation was more effective than simple exposure, but all subjects improved relative to a no-treatment group. However, subjects were still not functioning at the level of normative comparison samples at posttest, suggesting that longer treatment periods might be needed. Similarly, in a study of social skills training for AVPD, Stravynski, Grey, and Elie (1987) reported that anxiety reduction supposedly due to the exposure component of treatment appeared to be more important than skills acquisition.

Renneberg, Goldstein, Phillips, & Chambless (1990) reported on a clinical replication series with 17 AVPD subjects. Significant pre to post changes were found after a 4-day intensive group treatment that included systematic desensitization, behavioral rehearsal, and self-image work. Improvements were maintained at 1-year follow-up, but Renneberg and colleagues noted that most subjects had continued in individual therapy during that time. These studies indicate that traditional exposure treatment is appropriate for AVPD, but more intensive or longer treatment may be needed.

Applications of Cognitive
Therapy to Personality Disorders

Cognitive therapy is another intervention that is now being applied to personality disorders. As cognitive techniques, initially designed for fairly short-term interventions, came to be used more widely, therapists began to treat more clients with chronic problems and to note that cognitive therapy was often not as effective for those clients. In two recent books (Beck & Freeman, 1990; Young, 1990), cognitive therapists describe how they have modified cognitive techniques when treating personality disorders. These approaches, developed out of extensive clinical practice, have not yet been empirically validated, but the tremendous need for effective therapy for personality disorders suggests that such interventions will be an important focus of research in the future.

Young (1990) explains why short-term cognitive therapy may be inadequate for personality-disordered clients. Such clients are described as not having easy access to their feelings, thoughts, and images; and having vague and hard-to-define problems, less motivation to do homework and learn strategies to help themselves, interpersonal difficulties such that a collaborative relationship with the therapist is quite difficult, and entrenched beliefs and behavior patterns that are resistant to a purely logical, empirical approach. Young's approach is focused on identifying, confronting, and changing early maladaptive schemas (stable patterns of thinking developed in childhood). Although it retains most of the important elements of Beck's cognitive therapy, schema-focused therapy is viewed by Young as an extension, integrating techniques from other approaches. The most notable differences are the greater focus on childhood origins of problems, the therapeutic relationship, and the greater use of emotive and confrontational techniques.

Since personality disorders cover a wide range of behaviors, it is not possible to evaluate the use of cognitive therapy for personality disorders in general. Researchers must evaluate its utility for each diagnosis separately, as the measures used to assess change depend on the problematic behaviors, thoughts, and feelings associated with each specific disorder. At the present time, the only empirical data evaluating cognitive approaches is related to the treatment of borderline personality disorder (BPD).

Interventions for Borderline Personality Disorder

Individuals diagnosed with borderline personality disorder are characterized by difficulties in four areas: (1) disturbances in *emotional functioning*, as evidenced by emotional lability and/or problems with anger; (2) *interpersonal problems*, as evidenced by disruptive and chaotic relationships and excessive fear of being alone; (3) problems in *self-schema*, as evidenced by difficulties with self-identity and/or a pervasive sense of emptiness; (4) problems in *impulse control and distress tolerance*, as evidenced by patterns of extremely problematic impulsive behaviors and/or parasuicidal behaviors (attempts to hurt, mutilate, or kill oneself). Parasuicide is the most prominent overt or specific behavior problem associated with this disorder, and it is perhaps the single most dysfunctional aspect, as it makes it difficult for professionals to help such clients with their other problems when so much effort is expended on just keeping them safe. In addition, due to their interpersonal difficulties, BPD clients frequently change therapists or quit treatment, disrupting any progress that has been made and further reducing any professional's ability to help them develop a more stable support system.

Turner (1989) reported on four cases of BPD in which intensive cognitive-behavior therapy was utilized over a period of a year. Cognitive-behavioral treatment significantly decreased specific problem behaviors such as self-injury, and no hospitalization was required in three of the four patients. The introduction of Alprazolam, a minor tranquilizer, demonstrated some positive effects on mood. Improvements were maintained at 1-year follow-up, although two of the patients required some additional therapy during the year.

The only controlled outcome study of a cognitive-behavioral approach has evaluated Linehan's dialectical behavior therapy (DBT) (Linehan, 1989), which was developed specifically to reduce parasuicidal behaviors. DBT incorporates cognitive and behavioral techniques, but a strong emphasis is placed on building a positive, collaborative therapist-client relationship and using that relationship to address and change dysfunctional interaction problems. The primary focus is on the emotional system, a system that is seen as not always readily accessed or changed by modifying the cognitive system. In addition to the empirical reasoning characteristic of more traditional cognitive therapies, a dialectical way of reasoning is modeled by the therapist. Dialectical reasoning is used to achieve synthesis of oppositions rather than focusing on verifying either side of an oppositional argument. This type of reasoning is considered particularly useful to counter extreme and absolute thinking, to foster nonevaluative thinking, to draw attention to the differences between feelings and facts, and to increase tolerance for ambiguity.

Specific skills in three domains are taught in a fairly didactic fashion. *Interpersonal effectiveness training* includes assertive and social skills and interpersonal problem solving. *Emotional control training* includes cognitive and behavioral techniques to reduce emotional distress (e.g., depression, anxiety, anger). *Distress tolerance* involves training in self-observation, meditation, mindfulness, and other methods to help accept and tolerate realities if they cannot be changed or at least until they can be changed. In addition, six behavioral patterns characteristic of borderline personality disorder are explicitly used to help clients label, understand, and then change their own behavior. For example, the *apparently competent person syndrome* is used to explain the fact that BPD individuals usually have areas in which they are quite competent and thus appear more generally competent than they really are. Other people, then tend to think they need less help, encouragement, advice, support, or training than they actually do. The client's response is both intense guilt over his or her failures and inability to live up to others' expectations, and intense anger at others for their lack of support and unrealistic expectations.

In the Linehan (1989) study, women who met borderline personality disorder criteria and had multiple recent parasuicidal episodes were randomly assigned to DBT (one year of individual and group treatment) or to treatment as usual in the community. DBT was more effective in reducing the number and medical severity of parasuicidal episodes and days in the hospital. However, subjects continued to report fluctuating but often high levels of subjective distress (i.e., anxiety and depression). No patient dropped out of DBT, as compared with the control group in which only 50% of the patients were still with the same community therapist at the end of the year. Thus, the initial success of cognitive-behavioral treatment in keeping BPD clients in treatment and reducing costly and disruptive hospital stays is very promising. However, considerable work remains to be done.

Research in both these areas highlights the fact that techniques designed to address emotions more directly are becoming an important aspect of the cognitive-behavioral approach. Such an expansion of the behavioral model may prove quite a challenge, since emotions are even less easily fit into the rigorous traditions of operational definition and empirical validation than are cognitions. However, the addition of cognitions has proved useful in many areas, as noted in chapters throughout this book, and, by staying closely tied to specifying the behaviors that are associated with cognitions and emotions, behaviorists are likely to find a useful role for emotions without sacrificing the progress that has been made.

Obsessive-Compulsive Disorder

A number of chapters in this book have mentioned that psychopharmacology is the standard comparison, i.e., the most effective alternative treatment available for a particular disorder. Although there are always people who are unwilling or unable (due to side effects or other medical problems) to take a particular medication, a psychological therapy must usually do at least as well as medication treatment in order to be considered a better alternative. Medication is often seen as easier, faster, and more cost-effective. Although many investigations comparing behavioral treatments to medication are still underway, the studies mentioned throughout this book have demonstrated that behavioral or cognitive-behavioral treatment has been demonstrated to be at least as effective as medication in the treatment of depression, bulimia, obesity, and panic attacks. In all of these disorders, except perhaps depression, it also appears that behavior therapy may have the advantage of lower relapse rates. Many medications are effective while they are being used, but the problems often return when the patient stops taking the medication. In contrast, many people are able to maintain their progress after behavioral treatment is terminated.

Many investigators have hoped that these two powerful modalities might be combined in some way so that their effects would be complementary or additive, as there is still room for improvement in treating all these disorders and since some clients do not respond completely to either medication or behavioral intervention alone. Unfortunately, combined treatments have generally not been significantly more effective than a single modality. In some cases, adding the medication has actually detracted from the long-term effectiveness of the behavior therapy. Nonetheless, the fact that new medications are constantly being developed and the possibility that more effective ways to combine or sequence these treatments might be found, suggests that increasingly sophisticated investigations of combined approaches will be an important aspect of behavioral research in the future.

The treatment of obsessive-compulsive disorder (OCD) is an area of anxiety treatment (not discussed in Chapter 5), which serves as an example of the possibilities of combined treatment. OCD is classified as an anxiety disorder,

but it is also considered to be closely linked to depressive disorders. OCD is a relatively rare disorder in its most severe form, and in the past it was considered to be essentially unresponsive to traditional verbal psychotherapies. Although roughly two-thirds of those with OCD demonstrate at least some improvement within five years, there is little evidence that this improvement is related to any form of treatment they have received (Rachman & Wilson, 1980). The majority of OCD patients report having problems with both obsessions (intrusive repetitive thoughts, images, or impulses that are unacceptable and unwanted) and compulsions (repetitive, stereotyped acts that may be partly acceptable but are considered excessive or exaggerated). The most common obsessions, in descending order of frequency, involve dirt, contamination, aggression, orderliness of inanimate objects, sex, and religion (Akhtar, Wig, Verma, Pershod, & Verma 1975), and the most common compulsions are cleaning rituals and checking rituals. The experience of subjective compulsion, the report of internal resistance (trying hard not to do or think it), and the presence of insight (person can acknowledge the senselessness of the impulse or idea but cannot resist it) are considered to be the three major indicators of OCD (Rachman, 1982).

Exposure and Response Prevention Treatment (ERP)

Initially, behavioral procedures (systematic desensitization) that were developed to treat phobias were applied to OCD but were not very effective. However, by 1980 an effective behavioral treatment based on exposure and response prevention (ERP) had been developed and evaluated. Such a program is described in Foa et al. (1992). That treatment program consists of 15 daily 2-hour sessions (plus 2 hours daily of homework assignment), conducted over a 3-week period, followed by 2 home sessions (4 hours each) during the fourth week to facilitate generalization of treatment effects. Each session consists of an hour of imaginal exposure in which increasingly disturbing scenes from the patient's hierarchy are presented, followed by an hour of *in vivo* exposure in which the objects or situations evoking anxiety are introduced in a gradual manner (e.g. touching floors, driving in a car). Response prevention consists of prohibiting all ritualistic behavior (even imagining doing the rituals) during the entire 3-week period; for example, no washing or cleaning (except a brief shower every fifth day), and no retracing steps, checking, or counting are allowed. Compliance is monitored by nursing staff if treatment is done in a hospital or by a designated friend/relative, but compliance is not enforced by physical restraint.

Due to the initial aversiveness of the program, about 30% of patients refuse to consider such a treatment. Of those who enter treatment, about 65% to 75% are substantially improved at the end of treatment, with 20% to 40% demonstrating some degree of relapse by follow-up (Foa, Steketee, & Ozarow, 1985). The most common reason for failure in the program is the inability or unwillingness to tolerate the distress evoked by the sessions and/or to refrain from the rituals during and between sessions.

Comparison of ERP and Pharmacotherapy

Pharmacotherapy is the only other available treatment that has been shown to be effective. Several antidepressants have been somewhat effective but the most consistently effective results have been reported for clomipramine. However, the effect size of clomipramine alone is generally smaller than that of behavior therapy (Marks et al., 1988) and relapse after discontinuation is generally high (90% reported in Pato, Zohar-Kadouch, Zohar, & Murphy, 1988).

To determine whether clomipramine would enhance behavioral treatment, Marks et al. (1988) compared conditions in which clomipramine was combined with different types of exposure. Clomipramine given in tandem with self-exposure instructions was much more effective than when given with anti-exposure instructions (i.e. instructions to avoid exposure to anxiety-provoking stimuli and to use rituals as much as needed to feel comfortable). In addition, by the end of treatment those receiving placebo and exposure were as much improved as those receiving clomipramine and exposure. Thus, the authors concluded that exposure was a stronger factor than the clomipramine.

Results from Foa, Kozak, Steketee & McCarthy (1992), in a study utilizing the antidepressant imipramine, also support the conclusion that behavioral treatment alone may be all that is necessary. This study compared OCD patients with mild depressive symptoms to those with severe depressive symptoms. Imipramine alone did reduce depression, particularly among the more severely depressed, but did not reduce OCD symptoms. Once all patients had received exposure treatment, those receiving imipramine and those receiving placebo demonstrated comparable improvement on both depression and OCD symptoms. Thus, as in the Marks study, medication did not add significantly to results achieved with behavioral treatment alone. As the exposure treatment improved both the OCD symptoms and the depression (whether or not antidepressants were used), Foa and colleagues concluded that the depression associated with OCD is probably a result of distress over the OCD symptoms rather than a separate problem.

In the same study, Foa and her colleagues added 12 weekly sessions of supportive psychotherapy as a follow-up to the typical 3-week intensive exposure treatment. They felt this addition was responsible for their exceptionally low relapse rate (15%). Thus, longer-term follow-up or supportive therapy may be yet another way to enhance maintenance effects of behavior therapy in a cost-efficient way.

APPLICATIONS TO
LARGER SOCIAL PROBLEMS

Child Abuse and Neglect

Child maltreatment has long been recognized as a serious social problem, but it has been difficult to develop interventions for such a complex problem. Evaluation is even more problematic in light of the legal and ethical issues that are raised by assessments. Several behaviorally based treatments have been developed for parents who physically abuse their children, but much less work has been done on neglect, despite the fact that neglect is more commonly reported than physical abuse and that many parents are both abusive and neglectful. Azar and Siegel (1990) present a behavioral conceptualization of child abuse, outlining five areas in which abusive parents have deficits: (1) maladaptive interpretive processes, including unrealistic expectations of children, poor problem solving, and negative interpretations of children's misbehavior; (2) poor parenting skills; (3) poor impulse control; (4) poor stress-coping skills; and (5) poor social skills.

Parent Training

Empirical research has focused primarily on parents of children in early and middle childhood. The most common intervention has been training the parents to use more appropriate methods of child management (such as those described in Chapter 16). Additional strategies are often added to address specific issues of abusive parents, such as anger-control training, stress-management training, communication training, relaxation techniques, marital counseling, and interventions for depression. Single-case studies (Azar & Wolfe, 1980; Isaacs, 1982) have provided some initial support, and several group designs have verified that such treatment packages are more effective than no treatment (Azar & Twentyman, 1984; Egan, 1983; Wolfe, Sand-

ler, & Kaufman, 1981). The only comparison to other interventions is reported by Brunk, Henggeler, and Whelan (1987), who compared two short-term treatments: standard behavioral group parent training and a multisystem approach (individualized for each family). The approach included components such as techniques from family-systems therapy to change interaction patterns, education about child-management strategies and appropriate expectations, methods for improving social-perspective-taking abilities, marital therapy, and skills training to deal with the extended family and outside agencies. Both treatments were equally effective in reducing overall stress of the parent, the severity of identified parent problems, and parental psychiatric symptomatology. Unfortunately, no measures of the children's wellbeing were included.

Two studies of large, community-based programs are quite promising and suggest that behaviorally based programs can be implemented on a large scale and that such programs enhance the outcome of standard social services. Reductions in multiple incidents of maltreatment (Lutzker & Rice, 1984) and out-of-home placements have been reported (Szykula & Fleishman, 1985). More specific effects of such programs on children's well-being or their long-term development have not been documented.

Prevention of Abuse and Re-Abuse

The severity of the physical and emotional consequences of abuse and the fact that 30% to 70% of abused children are re-abused has focused attention on early identification (treating abuse in parents of infants and toddlers) and prevention of abuse among parents considered to be at risk. Barth, Blythe, Schinke, Stevens, and Schilling (1983) describe a self-control training program for parents of infants and toddlers, using videotaped scenarios to elicit dysfunctional self-statements associated with losing control, followed by generation of possible alternative actions. Other studies have focused on increasing positive and responsive parent-infant interactions in at-risk or maltreating parents through the use of role-modeling, visual and verbal prompts, and behavioral rehearsal (Lutzker, Lutzker, Braunling-McMorrow, & Eddleman, 1987; Wolfe, Edwards, Manion, & Koverola, 1988). Such interventions can be carried out in the parents' home by trained paraprofessionals, making them more cost-effective than traditional therapy. Similarly, behavioral training has been used to teach parents to identify and reduce common household safety hazards that have been noted as especially common among abusive families (Barone, Greene, & Lutzker, 1986).

Interventions for Child Neglect

Lutzker (1990) considers child neglect more difficult to treat than abuse because parents often do not recognize their deficiencies and may be less willing to cooperate with treatment. In addition, neglect is usually chronic and more difficult to define and substantiate. In the Brunk et al. (1987) study, therapists reported a greater reduction of family problems in the abusive families than in those that were only neglectful. Lutzker describes a number of innovative single-case studies in which behavioral programs were designed to remediate specific problems in families referred for child neglect. For example, a program was devised to increase personal cleanliness of two children; the program included counselor visits, laundry service, and reinforcement of an older sibling contingent on the younger child's appearance. Menu-planning and grocery-shopping skills were taught to a mentally retarded mother so her children would receive adequate nutrition. Monitoring, feedback, and reinforcement for the mother were used in another case to insure that children were bathed regularly and that bathrooms and other rooms were cleaned and clothes washed. Lutzer acknowledges that these interventions were intensive and somewhat invasive, but the conditions were sufficiently severe to warrant such intervention, as it was the only way to avoid having to remove the children.

Emotional neglect is a more difficult problem to address than abuse. Lutzker, Megran, Dachman, & Webb (1985) documented that parents could be trained to increase their affective skills (e.g., congruence between verbal and nonverbal messages, initiating positive physical contact with child, improved eye contact) when they interacted with a child. Trained mothers maintained their improved performance during follow-up and showed generalization of skills toward other children in the family.

Treating Child Victims

Interventions have demonstrated that specific parenting behaviors can be altered, but treatment for the child victims has often been overlooked. The serious long-term problems caused by these disruptions in normal developmental processes, especially at early ages, have been clearly documented (Cicchetti, in press). Although counseling/therapy for the child victim is often recommended or even mandated by social services, parents often do not comply and there is little empirical evidence to indicate whether such interventions are effective.

A series of studies reported by Fantuzzo and his associates (Fantuzzo, 1990) illustrate how behavioral interventions can be used to improve the social interactions of withdrawn, maltreated (primarily neglected) preschoolers. These studies indicate that such children responded well to programmed play initiations by peers but not by adults. Aggressive, abused preschoolers preferred to interact with adults rather than peers and responded better when an adult was responsive to them than when the adult initiated play. Thus, the specific problems of children who have been abused or neglected must be clearly identified so that practical, accessible treatment programs can be developed and evaluated.

Interventions Focused on the Elderly

Behavioral techniques have been applied to many problems of the elderly. In fact, the behavioral perspective has become so pervasive in work with the elderly that the term *behavioral gerontology* is used to designate this specialty area that brings together professionals from many different disciplines to address the specific physical, mental, and social problems of the elderly.

Enhancing Self-Care Skills

Much of the behavioral literature has reported on interventions for the elderly in institutional settings. Baltes and her colleagues (Baltes & Reisenzein, 1986) have demonstrated that institutional staff are more likely to reinforce dependent rather than independent behaviors. Numerous studies, reviewed by Smyer, Zarit, and Qualls (1990), have demonstrated ways in which behavioral interventions have been effective in increasing activity levels, exercise, self-care, and social interaction in both the institutionalized elderly and those at risk for institutionalization.

Effective behavioral treatments have also been developed to reduce urinary incontinence, one of the most prevalent health problems of elderly nursing-home residents. Hu et al. (1989) and Schnelle et al. (1989) reported on two sites of a large clinical trial to evaluate a program that consisted of prompting patients to toilet, assisting to toilet, praise and staff social interaction for successful toileting, and social reinforcement for being dry at regular checks. This program produced significant reductions in incontinence, compared to baseline and compared to a control group that received standard incontinence-related care. Maintenance of treatment effects during a 22-week follow-up period was reported (Hu et al., 1989). Outpatient programs, including self-monitoring, exercise, scheduled toileting, and biofeedback, have also been reported to be effective (Burgio & Engle, 1987).

Coping with Alzheimer's Disease

Another specific disorder affecting large numbers of the elderly is Alzheimer's disease (AD), a progressive, degenerative brain disease for which there is no known cause or cure. Cognitive deterioration may be accompanied by a variety of additional behavior problems including depressive behaviors and more severely disruptive behaviors. Hussian (1987) describes how basic behavior management techniques, originally developed and evaluated for similar behavioral problems in other populations, have been used by institutional staff to modify the severe behavioral problems often demonstrated by AD patients. For example, extinction, time-out, response cost, differential reinforcement for other behavior, and many stimulus enhancement (cueing) or control techniques are used to handle problems with verbal abuse, complaining, demanding, aggression, noncompliance, wandering, and inappropriate sexual behavior. These disruptive behaviors are particularly distressing and difficult for family caregivers. Teri & Logsdan (1990) describe how family caregivers can be trained to use basic behavior management strategies similar to those employed by parents who have been trained to manage their children's behaviors.

Teri and Gallagher (1991) have described strategies for alleviating depression in AD patients. For patients whose cognitive impairment is still relatively mild, cognitive therapy (adapted from Beck's CBT) has been used to challenge dysfunctional thoughts and help patients revise their "should" rules and develop more adaptive attitudes toward their disabilities. For patients with moderate to severe cognitive impairment, behavioral strategies adapted from Lewinsohn's work (Lewinsohn, Antonuccio, Steinmetz, & Teri, 1984) have been used successfully. Both patient and caregiver are involved in this process, which focuses on identifying and increasing pleasant activities. Preliminary reports in this promising new area are positive, but rigorous controlled trials will be needed to document the specific effectiveness of these techniques.

Coping with Anxiety/Depression

The problems of the institutionalized elderly have been extensively described, but the mental health needs of the elderly in the community have often been neglected. Deberry, Davis, and

Reinhard (1989) reported on a 10-week program designed to reduce anxiety and depression in geriatric outpatients. A relaxation/meditation program was more effective in reducing anxiety than was cognitive restructuring and assertion training, but neither intervention effectively reduced anxiety or depression. Thompson, Gallagher, and Czirr (1989) reported more positive results. Short-term cognitive and behavioral treatments were both as effective as short-term psychodynamic therapy, and all were significantly better than no treatment. Gains were maintained at 1-year follow-up. These short-term therapies were found to be less effective with subjects who initially reported more endogenous depressive symptoms as well as those with evidence of a pre-existing personality disorder. Beutler et al. (1987) found group cognitive therapy somewhat more effective than supportive therapy or medication with a minor tranquilizer.

Smyer et al. (1990) concluded that short-term structured cognitive and behavioral therapies clearly can be effective with the elderly, many of whom are not receiving adequate treatment for their mental health problems. Given the limited resources of the elderly, psychoeducational programs may well be the most effective way to reach a large segment of the elderly population. Scogin et al. (1989) demonstrated positive results of two cognitive-behavioral self-help books (as "bibliotherapy") for mildly to moderately depressed adults.

Interventions to Prevent/Cope with AIDS

Since its discovery in 1981, acquired immune deficiency syndrome (AIDS) has emerged as perhaps the most serious and troubling infectious disease epidemic of the twentieth century. Until (and probably even after) effective medical treatments are developed, psychological interventions are essential in both preventing the spread of the disease and slowing the progression of the disease in those infected. Preventive programs are designed to decrease high-risk sexual behav-

iors (e.g., not using condoms) and needle-sharing among IV drug users.

Uncontrolled large-scale community education and prevention programs appear to have resulted in significant decreases in high-risk sexual behaviors among homosexuals (Ekstrand and Coates, 1990). In the report cited, episodes of unprotected intercourse decreased from 34% in 1985 to 3% in 1988. As Kelly and St. Lawrence (1988) noted, however, high-risk sexual practices continue in gay communities other than in the AIDS epidemic epicenters of New York, San Francisco, and Los Angeles, and additional controlled trials of prevention efforts that can be widely applied are needed.

Two specific behavioral and cognitive-behavioral programs designed to reduce high-risk behaviors related to AIDS have been reported. Kelly, St. Lawrence, Hood, & Brasfield (1989), working in medium-sized communities, randomly assigned 104 homosexual men who were engaging in high-risk sexual behavior to experimental or wait-list control treatment. The experimental condition, which consisted of 12 weekly group sessions, was composed of AIDS-risk education, cognitive-behavioral self-management training, sexual-assertion training, and social skills development designed to enhance social support. The group format allowed modeling and social reinforcement for behavioral change and cognitive problem solving. Following intervention, experimental group subjects reported greater decreases in unprotected sex and used condoms more frequently than did the control group. These behavioral changes were maintained at an 8-month follow-up. Experimental subjects also reported being more capable of refusing casual propositions and coercions to engage in high-risk sexual activities. The groups did not differ on other, lower-risk sexual practices.

Coates, McKusick, Stites, & Kuno (1989) evaluated the effects of a behaviorally oriented stress management program on sexual behaviors and levels of immune functioning; 64 men were randomly assigned to either an experimental treatment or wait-list condition. The experimental program, which consisted of 8 weekly meetings and 1 retreat, focused on medication education, relaxation training, behavioral changes in positive health habits, and coping skills to offset the stress of having AIDS. The program, relative to the control condition, resulted in a significant decrease in the number of sexual partners, but did not produce differential change in immune functioning.

The importance of the topic and the urgency of the need for prevention of AIDS-risk behaviors warrant further application of these intervention procedures. In addition, research on AIDS prevention may ultimately help in developing interventions to decrease other high-risk sexual behaviors that result in sexually transmitted diseases and unwanted pregnancies (Coates, 1990).

APPLICATIONS TO SPORTS PSYCHOLOGY

Sports psychology is an example of how important behavioral strategies have become important in areas outside the traditional mental health context. In a recent review of this area, Whelan, Mahoney, and Meyers (1991) concluded that the cognitive-behavioral perspective largely dominates the field of applied sports psychology. Sports psychology is a relatively new area of specialization, in which psychological factors are studied in an effort to determine their effects on performance in all levels of sports, from the purely recreational to elite, world-class athletics.

Enhancing Performance

Research on elite athletes has indicated that they differ from non-elite collegiate athletes in certain psychological skills, particularly in their handling of performance anxiety, level of confidence, ability to concentrate, and use of mental preparation and imaginal rehearsal strategies (Mahoney, Gabriel, & Perkins, 1987). Various techniques derived primarily from cognitive-

behavioral work on anxiety and stress management have been adapted to help other athletes develop these important psychological skills. Over 100 published empirical evaluations support the conclusion that such interventions do improve physical performance. The usual targets are specific skills for individual sports such as golf, handball, swimming, bowling, karate, archery, ice skating, weight lifting, gymnastics, and tennis; however, individual skills used in team sports such as volleyball or basketball have also been studied.

Whelan, Meyers, & Berman (1989) reported a statistically significant effect size in a meta-analysis of 56 studies in which cognitive strategies were used to enhance the skills of inexperienced or moderately competent college students. In addition, Greenspan and Feltz (1989) evaluated 19 other studies done with competitive athletes and concluded that certain psychological interventions enhanced performance of already highly skilled athletes in competition. Both reviewers noted that more rigorous methodology and more follow-up assessments (to see if effects persist after the intervention is over) are needed to evaluate the utility of the procedures more carefully. This area remains an active and promising field for behavioral applications.

Cognitive strategies involving mental rehearsal and/or some type of arousal management have been the most extensively evaluated. A specific example of such a sports psychology package is visuo-motor behavior rehearsal (VMBR) (Suinn, 1983). This program was designed to assist competent athletes in coping with competitive stress and performance errors. After learning relaxation, positive thought control, energy control strategies, and imagery skills, the athletes apply these skills as they visualize slow-motion images. Gradually the difficulty and speed of the images is increased and coping with performance errors is included in the imaginal rehearsal. Eventually the cognitive strategies are practiced *in vivo*. Hall and Erffmeyer (1983) effectively combined VMBR with videotape modeling. Self-regulatory strategies (e.g. self-monitoring) and goal-setting strategies have also been used in many studies, but their utility appears to vary, depending on type of task and initial skill level. For example, Kirschenbaum, Ordman, Tomarken, and Holtzbauer (1982) reported that novice bowlers improved more after positive self-monitoring (successes) than after negative self-monitoring, traditional instruction, or no instruction. However, type of monitoring made no difference with more experienced bowlers. Tu and Tothstein (1979) found that independently motivated junior high females improved their running performance more when they set their own goals, and extrinsically motivated subjects improved more under goals set by an instructor.

Enhancing Coaching Skills

Smith and his colleagues (Smith & Smoll, 1991) have provided an interesting example of how behavioral strategies can be used to affect the athlete's social environment. They studied specific coaching behaviors and found that certain behaviors had predictable effects on child athletes. They then used this information to develop a cognitive-behavioral training program to teach coaches how to provide a more positive sports environment for young athletes. Using a combination of instruction, modeling, role-playing, self-monitoring, and behavioral observation and feedback, coaches were trained to follow specific behavioral coaching guidelines. Compared with untrained coaches, trained coaches gave more reinforcement in response to good performance and effort, and they responded to mistakes with more encouragement and technical instruction and with fewer punitive responses. Players liked the trained coaches better and thought they were better teachers. Although their win-loss records were the same, the players of trained coaches reported higher self-esteem, liking their teammates more, and enjoying their experience more. Thus, it appears that with relatively brief training, coaches can establish a more socially supportive environment in a system that plays an important role in the lives of many children.

Reducing Injury Risk

The importance of the entire social system within which athletics are carried out is supported by research indicating that psychosocial factors contribute to injury risk. For example, Smith, Smoll, and Ptacek (1990) found that negative life events (stressors) were correlated with days of practice and competition missed due to injuries, but only among the athletes low in social support and psychological coping skills. In this way, intervention programs designed to provide a positive supportive system and enhance coping skills should increase an athlete's resiliency.

Thus, behavioral principles are being used in sports psychology not only to enhance performance skills but to reduce injury risk, enhance enjoyment, and increase participation in sports. Since participation in exercise has already been shown to be important in enhancing mental health (e.g., a more adaptive way to control weight and moderate negative affect) as well as physical health (e.g., improved immune functions and reduction of cardiovascular risk), sports psychology applications are likely to play an important role in the future by improving overall quality of life. In addition, research in sports psychology will probably lead to refinements of cognitive-behavioral techniques that may make them more effective when used for mental health problems as well.

CONCLUSIONS

Interventions derived from the behavioral model have, in a sense, come of age. Behavior therapists are no longer the new kids on the block, struggling to establish a reputation. Behavioral and cognitive therapists/researchers have generated more experimental data to substantiate claims for the effectiveness of their interventions than ever available in the history of clinical psychology. Three decades of research represent a continuous process of developing and testing interventions to change behavior, celebrating the positive results, and, just as important, learning from the negative results. A model in which hypotheses can be stated and confirmed or refuted is open to revision, and this flexibility is a major reason that behavioral and cognitive models continue to generate viable new applications.

This chapter has outlined several important directions in which behavioral and cognitive researchers may turn in the next decade. The shift will probably continue toward addressing more complex, long-standing clinical problems that are considered difficult to treat. The treatment of post-traumatic stress disorder is an area in which intensive behavioral procedures may be used as part of a multifaceted treatment program. When such a disorder includes many diverse symptoms (i.e., the re-experiencing symptoms and the social avoidance), interventions may be needed to target each area. In the treatment of PTSD and personality disorders, behavioral researchers have taken the lead in specifying the behaviors or lack of behaviors that constitute these more complex disorders that defy the notion of a single outcome variable. Fortunately, a behavioral approach is well-suited to the idea of multiple measures and interventions targeting several variables. Preliminary evidence suggests that cognitive interventions, with their focus on the personal schemas that influence behavior, may be particularly helpful in understanding long-standing maladaptive behavior patterns such as personality disorders, which seem to be self-perpetuating and do not respond well to more straightforward behavioral interventions.

The trend toward integration with other schools of therapy and models of human behavior is likely to accelerate. Sophisticated research designed to evaluate separate and combined approaches will let the data answer questions about the relative merits of alternative approaches and whether effectiveness is enhanced or diminished by combined treatments. The interactional model presented in Chapter 2 provides a framework for developing and understanding such work. As evidenced by the work on obsessive-compulsive disorder, combination treatments are not always better than single treatments, and it is important to take a close look at the mechanisms for change associated with each approach.

The trend toward using established behavioral and cognitive approaches to address pressing social problems will probably accelerate. Child abuse/neglect and AIDS prevention are areas in which behavioral principles have suggested useful alternatives to traditional approaches. Large-scale, proactive educational efforts based on learning principles may help reduce the impact of these problems. Behavioral methods, proven effective for other institutionalized populations, have also provided cost-effective and humane ways to manage the behavioral problems of the elderly.

One final note, to show how far the application of behavioral principles has gone from its early use with chronic psychiatric inpatients and snake phobics, is a quick look at sports psychology. Clearly, behavioral principles are being used to enhance our lives, not just to ameliorate behavior problems. When brief behavioral approaches can be used to help Little League coaches learn to help children feel better about themselves, enjoy sports, and reduce injuries, the possibilities for widespread applications in many areas, to improve the quality of life for all of us, are quite exciting.

REFERENCES

Abikoff, H. (1985). Efficacy of cognitive training interventions in hyperactive children: A critical review. *Clinical Psychology Review, 5*, 479–512.

Abikoff, H. Gittelman-Klein, R., & Klein, D. (1977). Validation of a classroom observation code for hyperactive children. *Journal of Consulting and Clinical Psychology, 45*, 772–783.

Abramson, L. Y., Seligman, M. E. P., & Teasdale, J. (1978). Learned helplessness in humans: Critique and reformulation. *Journal of Abnormal Psychology, 87*, 49–74.

Achenbach T. M., & Edelbrock, C. (1981). Behavioral problems and competencies reported by parents of normal and disturbed children aged four through sixteen. *Monographs of the Society for Research in Child Development, 46*, (188.)

Achenbach T. M., & Edelbrock, C. (1983). *Manual for the Child Behavior Checklist and Revised Child Behavior Profile.* Burlington, VT: University Associates in Psychiatry.

Achenbach, T. M., & Edelbrock, C. S. (1986). *Manual for the Teacher's Report Form and teacher version of the Child Behavior Profile.* Burlington, VT: University of Vermont.

Achenbach, T. M., McConaughy, S. H., & Howell, C. T. (1987). Child/adolescent behaviors and emotional problems: Implications of cross-informant correlations for situational specificity. *Psychological Bulletin, 101*, 214–232.

Adams, H. E., Malatesta, V., Brantley, P. J., & Turkat, I. D. (1981). Modification of cognitive processes: A case study of schizophrenia. *Journal of Consulting and Clinical Psychology, 49*, 460–464.

Adesso, V. J., & Lipson, J. W. (1981). Group training of parents as therapists for their children. *Behavior Therapy, 12*, 625–633.

Adler, C. M., Craske, M. G., & Barlow, D. H. (1987). Relaxation-induced panic (RIP): When resting isn't peaceful. *Integrative Psychiatry, 5*, 94–112.

Ager, A. (1985). The role of microcomputers in teaching mentally retarded individuals. In J. M. Berg (Ed.), *Science and service in mental retardation* (pp. 224–231). New York: Methuen.

Agras, W. S. (1987). *Eating disorders.* New York: Pergamon.

Agras, W. S., Dorian, B., Kirkley, B. G., Arnow, B., & Bachman, J. (1987). Imipramine in the treatment of bulimia: A double-blind controlled study. *International Journal of Eating Disorders, 6*, 29–38.

Agras, W. S., & Kraemer, H. C. (1983). The treatment of anorexia nervosa: Do different treatments have different outcomes? In A. J. Stunkard & E. Stellar (Eds.), *Eating and its disorders* (pp. 286–302). New York: Raven.

Agras, W. S., Leitenberg, H., & Barlow, D. H. (1968). Social reinforcement in the modification of agoraphobia. *Archives of General Psychiatry, 19*, 423–427.

Agras, W. S., Schneider, J. A., Arnow, B., Raeburn, S. D., & Telch, C. F. (1989). Cognitive-behavioral and response-prevention treatments for bulimia nervosa. *Journal of Consulting and Clinical Psychology, 57*, 215–221.

Aiken, J. M., & Saltzberg, C. L. (1984). The effects of a sensory extinction procedure on sterotypic sounds of two autistic children. *Journal of Autism and Developmental Disorders, 14*, 291–299.

Aiken, R. C. B. (1969). Measurement of feeling using visual analogue scales. *Proceedings of the Royal Society of Medicine, 62*, 989–993.

Akhtar, S., Wig, N. H., Verma, V. K., Pershod, D., & Verma, S. K. (1975). A phenomenological analysis of symptoms in obsessive-compulsive neuroses. *British Journal of Psychiatry, 127*, 342–348.

Akiskal, H. S., Walker, P., Puzantian, V. R., King, D., Rosenthal, T. L., & Dranon, M. (1983). Bipolar outcome in the course of depressive illness: Phenomenologic, familial, and pharmacologic predictors. *Journal of Affective Disorders, 5*, 115–128.

Albin, R. W., & Horner, R. H. (1988). Generalization with precision. In R. H. Horner, G. Dunlap, & R. L. Koegel (Eds.), *Generalization and maintenance: Lifestyle changes in applied settings* (pp. 99–120). Baltimore: Paul H. Brookes.

Albino, J. E. (1984). Prevention by acquiring health-enhancing habits. In M. C. Roberts & L. Peterson (Eds.), *Prevention of problems in childhood: Psychological research and applications* (pp. 200–231). New York: Wiley.

Albino, J. E. , Tedesco, L. A., & Lee, C. Z. (1980). Peer leadership and health status: Factors moderating response to a children's dental health program. *Journal of Clinical Preventive Dentistry, 2*, 18–20.

Alden, L. (1989). Short-term structured treatment for avoidant personality disorder. *Journal of Consulting and Clinical Psychology, 57*, 756–764.

Alexander, B. K., & Hadaway, P. F. (1982). Opiate addiction: The case for adaptive orientation. *Psychological Bulletin, 92*, 367–381.

Alexander, J. F. (1973). Defensive and supportive communications in normal and deviant families. *Journal of Consulting and Clinical Psychology, 40*, 233–231.

Alexander, J. F., Barton, C., Schiavo, R. S., & Parsons, B. V. (1976). Systems-behavioral intervention with families of delinquents: Therapist characteristics, family behavior, and outcome. *Journal of Consulting and Clinical Psychology, 44*, 656–664.

Alexander, J. F., & Parsons, B. V. (1973). Short-term behavioral intervention with delinquent families: Impact on family process and recidivism. *Journal of Abnormal Psychology, 81*, 219–225.

Alexander, J. F., & Parsons, B. V. (1982). *Functional family therapy*. Monterey, CA: Brooks/Cole.

Alexandrov, A., Isakova, G., Maslennikova, G., Shugaeva, E., Prokhorov, A., Olferiev, A., & Kulikov, S. (1988). Presentation of atherosclerosis among 11-year-old school children in two Moscow administrative districts. *Health Psychology, 7*, 247–252.

Allport, G. W. (1961). *Pattern and growth in personality*. New York: Holt, Rinehart, & Winston.

Almy, T. P. (1977). Therapeutic strategy in stress-related digestive disorders. *Clinics in Gastroenterology, 6*, 709–622.

Alpert, B., Field, T., Goldstein, S., & Perry, S. (1990). Aerobics enhances cardiovascular fitness and agility in preschoolers. *Health Psychology, 9*, 48–56.

American Psychiatric Association. (1980). *Diagnostic and statistical manual of mental disorders (DSM-III)*. Washington, DC: American Psychiatric Press.

American Psychiatric Association. (1987). *Diagnostic and statistical manual of mental disorders* (3rd ed., rev.). Washington, DC: American Psychiatric Press.

Anastopoulus, A. D., & Barkley, R. A. (1988). Biological factors in attention deficit-hyperactivity disorder. *The Behavior Therapist, 11*, 47–53.

Anastopoulus, A. D., & Barkley, R. A. (1989). A training program for parents of children with Attention Deficit-Hyperactivity Disorder. In C. E. Shaefer, & J. Briesmeister (Eds.), *Handbook of parent training: Parents as co-therapists for children's behavior problems*. New York: Wiley.

Anderson, B. J., Auslander, W. F., Jung, K. C., Miller, J. P., & Santiago, J. V. (1990). Assessing family sharing of diabetes responsibilities. *Journal of Pediatric Psychology, 15*, 477–492.

Anderson, K. O., Bradley, L. A., McDaniel, L. K., Young, L. D., Turner, R. A., Agudelo, C. A., Keefe, F. J., Pisko, E. J., Snyder, R. M., & Semble, E. L. (1987). The assessment of pain in rheumatoid arthritis: Validity of a behavioral observation method. *Arthritis and Rheumatism, 30*, 36–43.

Anderson, R. C., Hiebert, E. H., Scott, J. A., & Wilkinson, I. A. (1985). *Becoming a nation of readers: The report of the Commission on Reading*. Champaign, IL: The Center for the Study of Reading.

Anderson-Inman, L, Walker, H. M., & Purcell, J. (1984). Promoting transfer of skills across settings: Transenvironmental programming for handicapped students in the mainstream. In W. Heward, T. Heron, D. Hill, & J. Trap-Porter (Eds.), *Focus on behavior analysis in education* (pp. 17–37). Columbus, OH: Charles E. Merrill.

Andreasen, N. C. (1988). *Schizophrenia*. Kalamazoo, MI: Upjohn.

Andreasen, N. C., & Olsen, S. (1982). Negative vs. positive schizophrenia: Definition and validation. *Archives of General Psychiatry, 39*, 789–794.

Angold, A. (1988). Childhood and adolescent depression II: Research in clinical populations. *British Journal of Psychiatry, 153*, 476–492.

Anthony, W. A., & Nemec, P. B. (1984). Psychiatric rehabilitation. In A.S. Bellack (Ed.), *Schizophrenia: Treatment, management, and rehabilitation*. Orlando, FL: Grune & Stratton.

Apley, J. (1975). *The child with abdominal pains*. London: Blackwell Scientific Publications.

Appel, M. A. (1986). Hypertension. In K. A. Holroyd & R. L. Creer (Eds.), *Self-management of chronic disease: Handbook of clinical interventions and research*. Orlando, FL: Academic Press.

Applebaum, E., Egel, A. L., Koegel, R. L., & Imhoff, B. (1979). Measuring musical abilities of autistic children. *Journal of Autism and Developmental Disorders, 9*, 279–285.

Apter, A., Borengasser, M. A., Hamovit, J., Bartko, J. J., Cytryn, L., & McKnew, D. H. (1982). A four-year follow-up of depressed children. *Journal of Preventive Psychiatry, 1*, 331–335.

Arbuthnot, J. & Gordon, D. A. (1986). Behavioral and cognitive effects of a moral reasoning development intervention for high-risk behavior-disordered adolescents. *Journal of Consulting and Clinical Psychology, 54*, 208–216.

Argyle, M., & Kendon, A. (1967). The experimental analysis of social performance. In L. Berkowitz (Ed.), *Advances in experimental social psychology* (Vol. 3). New York: Academic Press.

Arkowitz, H. (1981). The assessment of social skills. In M.

Hersen & A. S. Bellack (Eds.), *Behavioral assessment: A practical handbook*. New York: Pergamon.

Arkowitz, H., Lichtenstein, E., McGovern, K., & Hines, P. (1975). The behavioral assessment of social competence in males. *Behavior Therapy, 6*, 3–13.

Arnold, J., Levine, A., & Patterson, G. R. (1975). Changes in sibling behavior following family intervention. *Journal of Consulting and Clinical Psychology, 43*, 683–688.

Arnow, B. A., Taylor, D. B., Agras, W. S., & Telch, M. J. (1985). Enhancing agoraphobia treatment outcome by changing couple communication patterns. *Behavior Therapy, 16*, 452–467.

Ash, M.G., & Woodward, W.R. (Eds.). (1988). *Psychology in twentieth-century thought*. New York: Cambridge University Press.

Atkinson, R. L., Atkinson, R. C, Smith, E. E., & Hilgard, E. R. (1987). *Introduction to Psychology* (9th ed.). San Diego: Harcourt Brace Jovanovich.

Auslander, W. F., Haire-Joshu, D., Rogge, M., & Santiago, J. V. (1991). Predictors of diabetes knowledge in newly diagnosed children and parents. *Journal of Pediatric Psychology, 16*, 221–228.

Avery, D., & Winokur, G. (1976). Mortality in depressed patients treated with electroconvulsive therapy. *Archives of General Psychiatry, 33*, 1029–1037.

Axelrod, S. (1973). Comparison of individual and group contingencies in two special classes. *Behavior Therapy, 4*, 89–90.

Axelrod, S. (1990). Myths that (mis) guide our profession. In A. C. Repp & N. N. Singh (Eds.), *Perspectives on the use of nonaversive and aversive interventions for persons with developmental disabilities* (pp. 59–72). Sycamore, IL: Sycamore.

Ayer, W. A. (1973). Use of visual imagery n needle phobic children. *Journal of Dentistry for Children, 28*, 41–43.

Ayllon, T., & Azrin, N. (1968). The token economy: A motivational system for psychotherapy and rehabilitation. New York: Appleton-Century-Crofts.

Ayllon, T. & Rosenbaum, M. (1977). The behavioral treatment of disruption and hyperactivity in school settings. In B. Lahey & A. Kazdin (Eds.), *Advances in clinical child psychology*, (Vol. 1, pp. 83–118). New York: Plenum.

Azar, S. T. (1989). Training parents of abused children. In C. E. Schaefer & J. M. Briesmester (Eds.), *Handbook of parent training: Parents as cotherapists for children's behavior problems* (pp. 414–441). New York: Wiley.

Azar, S. T., & Seigel, B. R. (1990). Behavioral treatment of child abuse: A developmental perspective. *Behavior Modification, 14*, 279–300.

Azar, S. T., & Twentyman, C. T. (1984, November). *An evaluation of the effectiveness of behaviorally versus insight oriented group treatments with maltreating mothers*. Paper presented at the annual meeting of the Association for Advancement of Behavior Therapy, Philadelphia.

Azar, S. T., & Wolfe, D. A. (1989). Child abuse and neglect. In E. J. Mash & R. A. Barkley (Eds.), *Treatment of childhood disorders* (pp. 451–489). New York: Guilford.

Azrin, N. H., & Armstrong, P. M. (1973). The "mini-meal": A method for teaching eating skills to the profoundly retarded. *Mental Retardation, 11*, 9–13.

Azrin, N. H. Besalel, V. A., Bechtel, R., Michalicek, A., Mancera, M., Carroll, D., Shuford, D., & Cox, J. (1980). Comparison of reciprocity and discussion-type counseling for marital problems. *American Journal of Family Therapy, 8*, 21–28.

Azrin, N. H., Bugle, C., & O'Brien, F. (1971). Behavioral engineering: Two apparatuses for toilet training retarded children. *Journal of Applied Behavior Analysis, 4*, 249–253.

Azrin, N. H., & Foxx, R. (1971). A rapid method of toilet training the institutionalized retarded. *Journal of Applied Behavior Analysis, 4*, 89–99.

Azrin, N. H., & Holtz, W. C. (1966). Punishment. In W. K. Honig (Ed.), *Operant behavior: Areas of research and application*. New York: Appleton-Century-Crofts.

Azrin, N. H., Gottlieb, L., Hughart, L., Wesolowski, M. D., & Rahn, T. (1975). Eliminating self-injurious behavior by educative procedures. *Behavior Research and Therapy, 13*, 101–111.

Azrin, N. H., & Powers, M. (1975). Eliminating classroom disturbances of emotional disturbed children by positive practice procedure. *Behavior Therapy, 6*, 525–534.

Azrin, N. H., Sneed, J. J., & Foxx, R. M. (1973). Dry bed: A rapid method eliminating bed-wetting (enuresis) of the retarded. *Behaviour Research and Therapy*, 427–434.

Azrin, N. H., & Wesolowski, M. D. (1974). Theft reversal: An overcorrection procedure for eliminating stealing by retarded persons. *Journal of Applied Behavior Analysis, 7*, 577–581.

Babor, T. F., Stephens, R. S., & Marlatt, G. A. (1987). Verbal report methods in clinical research on alcoholism: Response bias and its elimination. *Journal of Studies on Alcohol, 48*, 410–424.

Bachman, J. G., Johnston, L. D., & O'Malley, P. M. (1978). Delinquent behavior linked to educational attainment and post-high school experiences. In L. Otten (Ed.), *Colloquium on the correlates of crime and the determinants of criminal behavior* (pp. 1–43). Arlington, VA: The MITRE Corp.

Bacon, J. (1988). What's the best medicine for hyperactive kids? *USA Today*, February 17, D, p. 4.

Baer, D. M. (1970). A case for the selective reinforcement of punishment. In C. Neuringer & J. L. Michael (Eds.), *Behavior modification in clinical psychology*, (pp. 243–249). New York: Appleton-Century-Crofts.

Baer, D. M., Wolf, M. M., & Risley, T. R. (1968). Current dimensions of applied behavior analysis. *Journal of Applied Behavior Analysis, 1*, 91–97.

Baer, J. S., Kivlahan, D. R., Fromme, K., & Marlatt, G. A. (1991). Secondary prevention of alcohol abuse with college student populations: A skills training approach. In N. Haxher, W. R. Miller, & C. T. Greeley, *Self-control and the addictive behaviors* (pp. 339–356). Botony, Australia: Maxwell MacMillon.

Baer, R. A., Blount, R. L., Detrich, R., & Stokes, T. F. (1987). Using intermittent reinforcement to program maintenance of verbal/nonverbal correspondence. *Journal of Applied Behavior Analysis, 20*, 179–184.

Baer, R. A., & Nietzel, M. T. (1991). Cognitive and behavioral treatment of impulsivity in children: A meta-analytic review of the outcome literature. *Journal of Clinical Child Psychology, 20*, 400–412.

Balaschak, B. A. (1976). Teacher-implemented behavior modification in a case of organically based epilepsy. *Journal of Consulting and Clinical Psychology, 44*, 218–223.

Bales, J. (1990). Skinner gets award, ovations at APA talk. *APA Monitor, 21*(10), 1–6.

Ballenger, J. C. (1988). Biological aspects of depression: Implications for clinical practice. In A. J. Frances & R. E. Hales (Eds.), *Review of Psychiatry* (pp. 169–187). Washington, DC: American Psychiatric Press.

Baltaxe, C. A. (1981). Acoustic characteristics of prosody in autism. In P. Mittler (Ed.), *Frontiers of knowledge in mental retardation*. Baltimore: University Park Press.

Baltaxe, C. A. & Simmons, J. Q. (1975). Language in childhood psychosis: A review. *Journal of Speech and Hearing Disorders, 30*, 439–458.

Baltes, M. M., & Reisenzein, R. (1986). The social world in long-term care institutions: Psychosocial control toward dependency? In M. M. Baltes and P. B. Baltes (Eds.), *The psychology of control and aging* (pp. 315–343). Hillsdale, NJ: Erlbaum.

Ban, T. A., & Freyhan, F. A. (1980). *Drug treatment of sexual dysfunction*. New York: Karger.

Bandura, A. (1965). Influence of models' reinforcement contingencies on the acquisition of imitative responses. *Journal of Personality and Social Psychology, 1*, 589–595.

Bandura, A. (1969). *Principles of behavior modification*. New York: Holt, Rinehart, & Winston.

Bandura, A. (1971). Psychotherapy based upon modeling principles. In A. E. Bergin & S. L. Garfield (Eds.), *Handbook of psychotherapy and behavior change: An empirical analysis*. New York: Wiley.

Bandura, A. (1977). *Social learning theory*. Englewood Cliffs, NJ: Prentice-Hall.

Bandura, A. (1977). Self-efficacy: Toward a unifying theory of behavioral change. *Psychological Review, 84*, 191–215.

Bandura, A. (1986). *Social foundations of thought and action: A social cognitive theory*. Englewood Cliffs, NJ: Prentice-Hall.

Bandura, A., & Walters, R. H. (1963). *Social learning and personality development*. New York: Holt, Rinehart & Winston.

Bank, L., Marlowe, J. H., Reid, J. B., Patterson, G. R., & Weinrott, M. R. (1991). A comparative evaluation of parent-training interventions for families of chronic delinquents. *Journal of Abnormal Child Psychology, 19*, 15–33.

Banta, T. J., & Walder, L. O. (1961). Discriminant validity of a peer-rating measure. *Psychological Reports, 9*, 573–582.

Barkley R. A. (1977). A review of stimulant drug research with hyperactive children. *Journal of Child Psychology and Psychiatry, 18*, 137–165.

Barkley, R. A. (1981). *Hyperactive children: A handbook for diagnosis and treatment*. New York: Guilford.

Barkley, R. A. (1987). *Defiant children: A clinician's manual for parent training*. New York: Guilford.

Barkley, R. A. (1988a). Attention deficit-hyperactivity disorder. In E. Mash & L. Terdal (Eds.), *Behavioral assessment of childhood disorders* (2nd ed., pp. 69–104). New York: Guilford.

Barkley, R. A. (1988b). Child behavior rating scales and checklists. In M. Rutter, A. H. Tuma, & I. S. Lann (Eds.), *Assessment and diagnosis in child psychopathology* (pp. 113–155). New York: Guilford.

Barkley, R. A. (1989a). Attention deficit-hyperactivity disorder. In E. Mash & R. Barkley (Eds.), *Treatment of childhood disorders* (pp. 39–72). New York: Guilford.

Barkley, R. A. (1989b). The problem of stimulus control and rule-governed behavior in children with attention deficit disorder with hyperactivity. In J. Swanson, & L. Bloomingdale (Eds.), *Attention deficit disorders* (Vol. 4). New York: Pergamon.

Barkley, R. A., Edelbrock, C. S. (1987). Assessing situational variation in children's behavior problems: The Home and School Situations Questionnaries. In R. Prinz (Ed.), *Advances in behavioral assessment of children and families* (Vol. 3, pp. 157–176). Greenwich, CT: JAI Press.

Barkley, R. A., Fischer, M., Edelbrock, C. S., & Smallish, L. (1990). The adolescent outcome of hyperactive children diagnosed by research criteria I: An 8-year prospective follow-up study. *Journal of the American Academy of Child and Adolescent Psychiatry, 29*, 546–557.

Barkley, R. A., Fischer, M., Newby, R., & Breen, M. (1988). Development of a multi-method clinical protocol for assessing stimulant drug responses to ADHD children. *Journal of Clinical Child Psychology, 17,* 14–24.

Barkley, R. A., Karlsson, J., Strzelecki, E., & Murphy, J. (1984). Effects of age and Ritalin dosage on the mother-child interactions of hyperactive children. *Journal of Consulting and Clinical Psychology, 52,* 750–758.

Barkley, R. A., McMurray, M. B., Edelbrock, C. S., & Robbins, K. (1989). The response of agressive and non-agressive ADHD children to two doses of methylphenidate. *Journal of the American Academy of Child and Adolescent Psychiatry, 28,* 873–881.

Barkley, R. A., Spitzer, R., & Costello, A. (1989). *The development of the DSM-III-R criteria for the disruptive behavior disorders.* Manuscript submitted for publication.

Barlow, D. H. (1981). *Behavioral assessment of adult disorders.* New York: Guilford.

Barlow, D. H. (1988). *Anxiety and its disorders: The nature and treatment of anxiety and panic.* New York: Guilford.

Barlow, D. H., & Cerny, J. A. (1988). *Psychological treatment of panic.* New York: Guilford.

Barlow, D. H., Cohen, A. S., Waddell, M., Vermilyea, J. A., Klosko, J. S, Blanchard, E. B., & Di Nardo, P. A. (1984). Panic and generalized anxiety disorders: Nature and treatment. *Behavior Therapy, 15,* 431–449.

Barlow, D. H., Craske, M. G., Cerny, J. A., & Klosko, J. S. (1989). Behavioral treatment of panic disorder. *Behavior Therapy, 20,* 261–282.

Barlow, D. H., O'Brien, G. T., & Last, C. G. (1984). Couples treatment of agoraphobia. *Behavior Therapy, 15,* 41–58.

Barlow, D. H., O'Brien, G. T., Last, C. G., & Holden, A. E. (1983). Couples treatment of agoraphobia: Initial outcome. In K. D. Craig & R. J. McMahon (Eds.), *Advances in clinical behavior therapy.* New York: Brunner/Mazel.

Barlow, D. H., Sakheim, D. K., & Beck, J. G. (1983). Anxiety increases sexual arousal. *Journal of Abnormal Psychology, 92,* 49–54.

Barlow, D. H., Vermilyea, J. A., Blanchard, E. B., Vermilyea, B. B., Di Nardo, P. A., & Cerny, J. A. (1985). The phenomenon of panic. *Journal of Abnormal Psychology, 94,* 320–328.

Barlow, D. H., & Wolfe, B. E. (1981). Behavioral approaches to anxiety disorders: A report on the NIMH-SUNY Albany research conference. *Journal of Consulting and Clinical Psychology, 49,* 448–454.

Barone, V. J., Greene, B. F., & Lutzker, J. R. (1986). Home safety with families being treated for child abuse and neglect. *Behavior Modification, 10,* 95–114.

Barr, R. C., & Feuerstein, M. (1983). Recurrent abdominal pain syndrome: How appropriate are our basic clinical assumptions? In P. J. McGrath & P. Firestone (Eds.), *Pediatric and adolescent behavioral medicine: Issues in treatment* (pp. 457–476). New York: Springer.

Barrett, R. P., & Bruening, S. E. (1983). Assessing intelligence. In J. L. Matson, & S. E. Breuning (Eds.), *Assessing the mentally retarded. New York: Grune & Stratton.*

Barrowclough, C., & Tarrier, N. (1987). A behavioural family intervention with a schizophrenic patient: A case study. *Behavioural Psychotherapy, 15,* 252–271.

Barrowclough, C., & Tarrier, N. (1990). Social functioning in schizophrenic patients: The effects of expressed emotion and family intervention. *Social Psychiatry and Psychiatric Epidemiology, 25,* 125–129.

Bartak, L., Bartolucci, G., & Pierce, S. J. (1977). A preliminary comparison of phonological development in autistic, normal, and mentally retarded subjects. *British Journal of Disorders of Communication, 12,* 137–147.

Barth, R. P., Blythe, B. J., Schinke, S. P., Stevens, P., & Schilling, R. E. (1983). Self control training with maltreating parents. *Child Welfare, 62,* 313–323.

Bartlett, L. (1989). Disciplining handicapped students: Legal issues in light of Honig V. Doe. *Exceptional Children, 55,* 357–366.

Bates, P. E., & Hanson, H. B. (1983) Behavioral Assessment. In J. L. Matson, & S. E. Breuning (Eds.), *Assessing the mentally retarded.* New York: Grune & Stratton.

Bates, P. E., Renzaglia, A., & Clees, T. (1980). Improving the work performance of severely/profoundly retarded young adults: The use of a changing criterion procedural design. *Education and Training of the Mentally Retarded, 15,* 95–104.

Bateson, G., Jackson, D. D., Haley, J., & Weakland, J. (1956). Toward a theory of schizophrenia. *Behavioral Science, 1,* 251–264.

Baucom, D. H. (1982). A comparison of behavioral contracting and problem-solving/communications training in behavioral martial therapy. *Behavior Therapy, 13,* 162–174.

Baucom, D. H. (1984). The active ingredients of behavioral marital therapy: The effectiveness of problem-solving/communication training, contingency, contracting, and their combination. In K. Hahlweg & N. S. Jacobson (Eds.), *Marital interaction: Analysis and modification.* New York: Guilford.

Baucom, D. H., & Epstein, N. (1989). *Cognitive behavioral marital therapy.* New York: Brunner/Mazel.

Baucom, D. H., & Hoffman, J. A. (1986). The effectiveness of marital therapy: Current status and application to the clinical setting. In N. S. Jacobson & A. S. Gurman (Eds.), *Clinical handbook of marital therapy.* New York: Guilford.

Baucom, D. H., & Lester, G. W. (1986). The usefulness of cognitive restructuring as an adjunct to behavioral marital therapy. *Behavior Therapy, 17*, 385–403.

Baum, C. G., & Forehand, R. (1981). Long term follow-up of parent training by use of multiple outcome measures. *Behavior Therapy, 12*, 643–652.

Beach, S. R. H., & O'Leary, K. D. (1986). The treatment of depression occurring in the context of marital discord. *Behavior Therapy, 17*, 43–49.

Beck, A. T. (1963). Thinking and depression: I. Idiosyncratic content and cognitive distortions. *Archives of General Psychiatry, 9*, 324–333.

Beck, A. T. (1964). Thinking and depression: II. Theory and therapy. *Archives of General Psychiatry, 10*, 561–571.

Beck, A. T. (1967). *Depression: Clinical, experimental, and theoretical aspects.* New York: Harper & Row.

Beck, A. T. (1970). Cognitive therapy: Nature and relation to behavior therapy. *Behavior Therapy 1*, 184–200.

Beck, A. T. (1973). *Depression: Causes and treatment.* Philadelphia: University of Pennsylvania Press.

Beck, A. T. (1976). *Cognitive therapy and the emotional disorders.* New York: International Universities Press.

Beck, A. T. (1984). Cognition and therapy. *Archives of General Psychiatry, 41*, 1112–1114.

Beck, A. T. (1985). Theoretical perspectives on clinical anxiety. In A. H. Tuma & J. D. Maser (Eds.), *Anxiety and the anxiety disorders.* Hillsdale, NJ: Laurence Erlbaum.

Beck, A. T., & Emery, G. (1985). Anxiety *disorders and phobias: A cognitive perspective.* New York: Basic Books.

Beck, A. T., & Freeman, A. (1990). *Cognitive therapy for personality disorders.* New York: Guilford.

Beck, A. T., Rush, A. J., Shaw, B. F., & Emery, G. (1979). *Cognitive therapy of depression: A treatment manual.* New York: Guilford.

Beck, A., Ward, C., Mendelson, M., Mock, J., & Erbaugh, J. (1961). An inventory for measuring depression. *Archives of General Psychiatry, 4*, 53–63.

Becker, R. E., Heimberg, R. G., & Bellack, A. S. (1987). *Social skills training treatment for depression.* New York: Pergamon.

Becker, W. C. (1977). Teaching reading and language to the disadvantaged: What we have learned from field research. *Harvard Education Review, 47*, 518–543.

Becker, W. C. (1986). *Applied psychology for teachers: A behavioral cognitive approach.* Chicago: Science Research Associates.

Becker, W. C. (Ed.) (1988). Direct instruction: A general case for teaching the general case. *Education and Treatment of Children, 11*, 301–401.

Becker, W. C., Engelmann, S., & Thomas, D. R. (1971). *Teaching: A course in applied psychology.* Chicago: Science Research Associates.

Becker, W. C., Madsen, C. H., Arnold, C. R., & Thomas, D. R. (1967). The contingent use of teacher attention and praise in reducing classroom behavior problems. *Journal of Special Education, 1*, 287–307.

Beckham, J. C., Gustafson, D. J., May, J. G., & Annis, L. V. (1987). Stress and rheumatoid arthritis: Can a cognitive coping model help explain a link? *Seminars in Arthritis and Rheumatism, 17*, 81–89.

Bedrosian, R. C., & Beck, A. T. (1980). Principles of cognitive therapy. In M. J. Mahoney (Ed.), *Psychotherapy process: Current issues and future directions.* New York: Plenum.

Behar, D., & Stewart, M. A. (1982). Aggressive conduct disorder of children. *Acta Psychiatrica Scandinavica, 65*, 210–220.

Beidel, D. C., Turner, S. M., Stanley, M. A., & Dancu, C. V. (1989). The Social Phobia and Anxiety Inventory: Concurrent and external validity. *Behavior Therapy, 20*, 417–427.

Beier, E. G., & Sternberg, D. P. (1977). Marital communication. *Journal of Communication, 27*, 92–97.

Beier, E. G., & Sternberg, D. P. (1979, Summer). Subtle cues between newlyweds. *Journal of Communication*, pp. 92–97.

Belcher, J. R. (1988). Are jails replacing the mental health system for the homeless mentally ill? *Community Mental Health Journal, 24*, 185–195.

Bellack, A. S. (1979). A critical appraisal of strategies for assessing social skills. *Behavioral Assessment, 1*, 157–176.

Bellack, A. S. (1983). Recurrent problems in the behavioral assessment of social skills. *Behavior Research Therapy, 21*, 29–42.

Bellack, A. S. (1986). Schizophrenia: Behavior therapy's forgotten child. *Behavior Therapy, 17*, 199–214.

Bellack, A. S. (1989). A comprehensive model for treatment of schizophrenia. In A. S. Bellack (Ed.), *A clinical guide for the treatment of schizophrenia* (pp. 1–22). New York: Plenum.

Bellack, A. S. (1992). Cognitive rehabilitation for schizophrenia: Is it possible? Is it necessary? *Schizophrenia Bulletin, 18*, 43–50.

Bellack, A., & Hersen, M. (1977). *Behavior modification: An introductory textbook.* Baltimore, MD: Williams & Wilkins.

Bellack, A. S., & Hersen, M. (1977). The use of self-report inventories in behavioral assessment. In J. D. Cone & R. P. Hawkins (Eds.), *Behavioral assessment: New directions in clinical psychology*, (pp. 52–76). New York: Brunner-Mazel.

Bellack, A. S., Hersen, M., & Himmelhoch, J. (1981). Social skills training compared with pharmacotherapy and psychotherapy in the treatment of unipolar depression. *American Journal of Psychiatry, 138,* 1562–1566.

Bellack, A. S., Hersen, M., & Himmelhoch, J. (1983). A comparison of social skills training, pharmacotherapy and psychotherapy for depression. *Behavior Research and Therapy, 21,* 101–107.

Bellack, A. S., Hersen, M., & Lamparski, D. (1979). Role-play tests for assessing social skill: Are they valid? Are they useful? *Journal of Consulting and Clinical Psychology, 47,* 335–342.

Bellack, A. S., Hersen, M., & Turner, S. M. (1976). Generalization effects of social skills training in chronic schizophrenics: An experimental analysis. *Behavior Research and Therapy, 14,* 391–398.

Bellack, A. S., Hersen, M., & Turner, S. M. (1978). Role-play tests for assessing social skill: Are they valid? *Behavior Therapy, 9,* 448–461.

Bellack, A. S., Hersen, M., & Turner, S. M. (1979). Relationship of roleplaying and knowledge of appropriate behavior to assertion in the natural environment. *Journal of Consulting and Clinical Psychology, 47,* 670–678.

Bellack, A. S., Morrison, R. L., & Mueser, R. T. (1989). Social problem solving in schizophrenia. *Schizophrenia Bulletin, 15,* 101–116.

Bellack, A. S., Morrison, R. L., Wixted, J. T., & Mueser, K. T. (1990). An analysis of social competence in schizophrenia. *British Journal of Psychiatry, 156,* 809–818.

Bellack, A. S., Morrison, R. L., Mueser, R. T., & Wade, J. H. (1989). Social competence in schizoaffective disorder, schizophrenia, and bipolar disorder. *Schizophrenia Research, 2,* 391–401.

Bellack, A. S., & Mueser, R. T. (1991). Social skills training for schizophrenia? *Archives of General Psychiatry, 49,* 76.

Bellack, A. S., Turner, S. M., Hersen, M., & Luber, R. F. (1984). An examination of the efficacy of social skills training for chronic schizophrenic patients. *Hospital and Community Psychiatry, 35,* 1023–1028.

Bellamy, G. T., Inman, D. P., & Yeates J. (1978). Workshop supervision: Evaluation of a procedure for production management with the severely retarded. *Mental Retardation, 16,* 317–319.

Belles, D., & Bradlyn, A. S. (1987). The use of the changing criterion design in achieving controlled smoking in a heavy smoker: A controlled case study. *Journal of Behavior Therapy and Experimental Psychiatry, 18,* 77–82.

Bennett, G. A. (1986). Behavior therapy for obesity: A quantitative review of the effects of selected treatment characteristics on outcome. *Behavior Therapy, 17,* 554–562.

Bentall, R. P., Higson, P. J., & Lowe, C. F. (1987). Teaching self-instructions to chronic schizophrenic patients: Efficacy and generalization. *Behavioral Psychotherapy, 15,* 58–76.

Benton, M. R. & Schroeder, H. E. (1990). Social skills training with schizophrenia: A meta-analytic evaluation. *Journal of Consulting and Clinical Psychology, 58,* 741–747.

Berenson, G. S., & Epstein, F. H. (1983). Conference on blood lipids in children: Optimal levels for early prevention of coronary artery disease: Workshop report. Epidemiologic section. *Preventive Medicine, 12,* 741–797.

Bernal, M. E., Klinnert, M. D., & Schultz, L. A. (1980). Outcome evaluation of behavioral parent training and client centered parent counseling for children with conduct problems. *Journal of Applied Behavior Analysis, 13,* 677–691.

Bernick, M. (1986, January). Illiteracy and inner-city unemployment. *Phi Delta Kappan,* pp. 364–367.

Bernstein, D. A., & Borkovec, T. D. (1973). *Progressive relaxation training.* Champaign, IL: Research Press.

Bernstein, N. R. (1965). Observations on the use of hypnosis with burned children on a pediatric ward. *The International Journal of Clinical and Experimental hypnosis, 13,* 1–10.

Bertelsen, A., Harvald, B., & Hauge, M. (1977). A Danish twin study of manic-depressive disorders. *British Journal of Psychiatry, 130,* 330–335.

Bettelheim, B. (1967). *The empty fortress.* New York: Free Press.

Beutler, L. E., Scogin, F., Kirkish, P., Schretlen, D., Corbishley, A., Hamblin, D., Meredith, K., Potter, R., Bamford, C. R., & Levenson, A. I. (1987). Group cognitive therapy and alprazolam in the treatment of depression in older adults. *Journal of Consulting and Clinical Psychology, 55,* 550–556.

Bhatt, R. S., Wasserman, E. A., Reynolds, W. F., & Knauss, K. S. (1988). Conceptual behavior in pigeons: Categorization of both familiar and novel examples from four classes of natural and artificial stimuli. *Journal of Experimental Psychology: Animal Behavior Processes, 14,* 219–234.

Biglan, A., Hops, H., Sherman, L., Friedman, L. S., Arthur, J., & Osteen, V. (1985). Problem-solving interactions of depressed women and their husbands. *Behavior Therapy, 16,* 431–451.

Biederman, J., Munir, K., Knee, D., Habelow, W., Armentano, M., Autor, S., Watermaux, C., & Tsuang, M. (1987). High rate of affective disorders in probands with attention deficit disorders and in their relatives: A controlled family study. *American Journal of Psychiatry, 144,* 330–333.

Bijou, S. W. (1966). A functional analysis of retarded development. In N. Ellis (Ed.), *International review of research in mental retardation* (Vol 1, pp. 1–19). New York: Academic Press.

Billings, A. (1979). Conflict resolution in distressed and nondistressed married couples. *Journal of Consulting and Clinical Psychology*, 47, 368–376.

Billings, A. G., & Moos, R. H. (1984). Coping, stress, and social resources among adults with unipolar depression. *Journal of Personality and Social Psychology*, 46, 877–891.

Bjorvell, H., & Rosner, S. (1985). Long term treatment of severe obesity: Four year follow-up of results of combined behavioural modification programme. *British Medical Journal*, 291, 379–382.

Black, D. R., & Threlfall, W. E. (1988). Partner weight status and subject weight loss: Implications for cost-effective programs and public health. *Addictive Behaviors*, 14, 279–289.

Blackburn, I. M., Bishop, S., Glen, A. I. M., Whalley, L. J., & Christie, J. E. (1981). The efficacy of cognitive therapy in depression: A treatment trial using cognitive therapy and pharmacotherapy, each alone and in combination. *British Journal of Psychiatry*, 139, 181–189.

Blackburn, I. M., Eunson, K M., & Bishop, S. (1986). A two-year naturalistic follow-up of depressed patients treated with cognitive therapy, pharmacotherapy and a combination of both. *Journal of Affective Disorders*, 10, 67–75.

Blakely, R., & Baker, R. (1980). An exposure approach to alcohol abuse. *Behavior Research and Therapy*, 84, 319–325.

Blanchard, E. B., & Andrasik, F. (1985). *Management of chronic headaches: A psychological approach*. New York: Pergamon.

Blanchard, E. B., Andrasik, F., Neff, D. F., Arena, J. G., Ahles, T. A., Jurish, S. E., Pallmeyer, T. P., Saunders, N. L., Teders, S. J., Barron, K. D., & Rodichok, L. D. (1982). Biofeedback and relaxation training with three kinds of headache: Treatment effects and their prediction. *Journal of Consulting and Clinical Psychology*, 50, 562–575.

Blanchard, E. B., Andrasik, F., Neff, D. F., Jurish, S. E., & O'Keefe, D. M. (1981). Social validation of the headache diary. *Behavior Therapy*, 12, 711–715.

Blanchard, J. B., Mueser, R. T., & Bellack, A. S. (1992). Self- and interview-rated negative mood states in schizophrenia: Their convergence and prediction of thought disturbance. *Journal of Psychopathology and Behavioral Assessment*, 14, 277–291.

Blumenthal, J. A., & McKee, D. C. (1987). *Applications in behavioral medicine and health psychology: A clinician's source book*. Sarasota, FL: Professional Resource Exchange.

Bockoven, J. S. (1963). *Moral Treatment in American Psychiatry*. New York: Springer.

Boggs, S. R., Eyberg, S., & Reynolds, L. A. (1990). Concurrent validity of the Eyberg Child Behavior Inventory. *Journal of Clinical Child Psychology*, 19, 75–78.

Bongiovanni, A. F., & Hyman, I. A. (1978). Corporal punishment: Normative data and sociological and psychological correlates in a community college population. *Journal of Youth and Adolescence*, 11, 77–97.

Bonica, J. J. (1977). Neurophysiological and pathologic aspects of acute and chronic pain. *Archives of surgery*, 112, 750–761.

Bonn, J. A., Harrison, J., & Rees, W. L. (1973). Lactate infusion in the treatment of "free-floating" anxiety. *Canadian Psychiatric Association Journal*, 18, 41–46.

Borkovec, T. D., Stone, N. M., O'Brien, G. T., & Kaloupek, D. G. (1974). Evaluation of a clinically relevant target behavior for analog outcome research. *Behavior Therapy*, 5, 503–513.

Borkowski, J. G., & Day, J. D. (Eds.). (1987). *Cognition in special children: Comparative approaches to retardation, learning disabilities, and giftedness*. Norwood, NJ: Ablex.

Borkowski, J. G., & Kurtz, B. E. (1987). Metacognition and executive control. In J. G. Borkowski & J. D. Day (Eds.), *Cognition in special children: Comparative approaches to retardation, learning disabilities, and giftedness*. Norwood, NJ: Ablex.

Borys, S. V., Spitz, H. H., & Donans, B. A. (1982). Tower of Hanoi performance of retarded young adults and nonretarded children as a function of solution length and goal state. *Journal of Experimental Child Psychology*, 33, 87–110.

Bostow, D. E., & Bailey, J. B. (1969). Modification of severe disruptive and aggressive behavior using brief timeout and reinforcement procedures. *Journal of Applied Behavior Analysis*, 2, 31–38.

Botvin, G. J., Baker, E., Dusenbury, L., Tortu, S., & Botvin, E. M. (1990). Preventing adolescent drug abuse through a multimodal cognitive-behavioral approach: Results of a 3-year study. *Journal of Consulting and Clinical Psychology*, 58, 437–446.

Botvin, G. J., Baker, E., Renick, N. L., Filazzola, A. D., & Botvin, E. M. (1984). A cognitive-behavioral approach to alcohol abuse prevention. *Addictive Behavior*, 9, 137–147.

Botvin, G. J., & Eng, A. (1982). The efficacy of a multicomponent approach to the prevention of cigarette smoking. *Preventive Medicine*, 11, 199–211.

Boudewyns, P. A., and Hyer, L. (1990). Physiological response to combat memories and preliminary treatment outcome in Vietnam Veteran PTSD patients treated with direct therapeutic exposure. *Behavior Therapy*, 21, 63–87.

Boudewyns, P. A., & Shipley, R. H. (1983). *Flooding and implosive therapy*. New York: Plenum.

Bowen, M. (1961). The family as a unit of study and treatment. *American Journal of Orthopsychiatry*, 31, 40–60.

Bradley, L. A., Prokop, C. K., Margolis, R., & Gentry, W. D. (1978). Multivariate analyses of the MMPI profiles of low back pain patients. *Journal of Behavioral Medicine, 1,* 253–272.

Bradley, L. A., Young, L. D., Anderson, K. O., Turner, R. A., Agudelo, C. A., McDaniel, L. K., Pisko, E. J., Semble, E. L., & Morgan, T. M. (1987). Effects of psychological therapy on pain behavior or rheumatoid arthritis patients: Treatment outcome and six-month follow-up. *Arthritis and Rheumatism, 30,* 1105–1114.

Brady, M. P., McDougall, D., & Dennis, H. F. (1989). The schools, the courts, and the integration of students with severe handicaps. *The Journal of Special Education, 23,* 43–58.

Braff, D. L. (1992). Reply to cognitive therapy and schizophrenia. *Schizophrenia Bulletin, 18,* 37–38.

Brandt, D. E., & Zlotnick, S. J. (1988). *The psychology and treatment of the youthful offender.* Springfield, IL: Charles C. Thomas.

Breen, M., and Barkley, R. A. (1988). Child psychopathology and parenting stress in girls and boys having ADHD. *Journal of Pediatric Psychology, 13,* 265–280.

Breiner, J. L., & Forehand, R. (1981). An assessment of the effects of parent training on clinic-referred children's school behavior. *Behavioral Assessment, 3,* 31–42.

Brenner, H. D., Hodel, B., Roder, V. & Corrigan, P. (1992). Treatment of cognitive dysfunctions and behavioral deficits in schizophrenia. *Schizophrenia Bulletin, 18,* 21–26.

Bristol, M. M. (1979). *Maternal coping with autistic children: The effect of child characteristics and interpersonal support.* Unpublished doctoral dissertation, University of North Carolina at Chapel Hill.

Bristol, M. M., & Gallagher, J. (1986). Research on fathers of young handicapped children. In J. J. Gallagher & P. M. Vietze (Eds.), *Families of handicapped persons* (pp. 81–100). Baltimore: Brookes.

Brody, G. H., & Stoneman, Z. (1986). Contextual issues in the study of sibling socialization. In J. J. Gallagher & P. M. Vietze (Eds.), *Families of handicapped persons* (pp. 197–217). Baltimore: Brookes.

Brooks, P. H., Sperber, R., & McCauley, C. (1984). *Learning and cognition in the mentally retarded.* Hillsdale, NJ: Erlbaum.

Browder, D. M., & Shapiro, E. S. (1985). Applications of self-management to individuals with severe handicaps: A review. *Journal of the Association for Persons with Severe Handicaps, 4,* 200–208.

Brown, A. L., & Barclay, C. R. (1976). The effects of training specific mnemonics on the metamnemonic efficiency of retarded children. *Child Development, 47,* 70–80.

Brown, A. L. Campione, J. C., & Murphy, M. D. (1977). Maintenance and generalization of trained metamnemonic awareness by educable retarded children. *Journal of Experimental Child Psychology, 24,* 191–211.

Brown, G. W., & Harris, T. O. (1978). *Social origins of depression: A study of psychiatric disorder in women.* New York: Free Press.

Brown, L., Braston, M. B., Hamre-Nietupski, S., Pumpian, I., Certo, N., & Gruenwald, L. (1979). A strategy for developing chronological age appropriate and functional curricular content for severely handicapped adolescents and young adults. *Journal of Special Education, 13,* 81–90.

Brown, M. A., & Munford, A. M. (1983). Life skills training for chronic schizophrenics. *Journal of Nervous and Mental Disease, 171,* 466–470.

Brown, R., & Lewinsohn, P. M. (1984). A psychoeducational approach to the treatment of depression: Comparison of group, individual, and minimal contact procedures. *Journal of Consulting and Clinical Psychology, 52,* 774–783.

Brown, R. T., & Quay, L. C. (1977). Reflection—impulsivity of normal and behavior disordered children. *Journal of Abnormal Child Psychology, 5,* 457–462.

Brown, R. T., & Sleator, E. K. (1979). Methylphenidate in hyperkinetic children: Differences in dose effects on impulsive behavior. *Pediatrics, 64,* 408–411.

Brownell, K. D. (1986). Public health approaches to obesity and its management. *Annual Review of Public Health. 7,* 521–533.

Brownell, K. D. (1989). *Learn to eat.* Dallas, TX: Brownell & Hager.

Brownell, K. D., Heckerman, C. L., & Westlake, R. J. (1979). The behavioral control of obesity: A descriptive analysis of a large scale program. *Journal of Clinical Psychology, 35,* 864–869.

Brownell, K. D., & Jeffrey, R. W. (1987). Improving long-term weight loss: Pushing the limits of treatment. *Behavior Therapy, 18,* 353–374.

Brownell, K. D., Marlatt, G. A., Lichtenstein, E., & Wilson, G. T. (1986). Understanding and preventing relapse. *American Psychologist, 41,* 765–782.

Brownell, K. D., & Wadden, T. A. (1986). Behavior therapy for obesity: Modern approaches and better results. In K. D. Brownell & J. P. Foreyt (Eds.), *Handbook of eating disorders: Physiology, psychology, and treatment of obesity, anorexia, and bulimia* (pp. 180–197). New York: Basic Books.

Bruch, M. A. (1981). A task analysis of assertive behavior revisited: Replication and extension. *Behavior Therapy, 12,* 217–230.

Brunk, M., Henggeler, S. W., & Whelan, J. P. (1987).

Comparison of multisystemic therapy and parent training in the brief treatment of child abuse and neglect. *Journal of Consulting and Clinical Psychology, 55*, 171–178.

Bryant, B., & Trower, P. E. (1974). Social difficulty in a student sample. *British Journal of Educational Psychology, 44*, 13–21.

Bryant, B., Trower, P. E., Yardley, K., Urbieta, H., & Letemendia, F. J. J. (1976). A survey of social inadequacy among psychiatric outpatients. *Psychological Medicine, 6*, 101–112.

Buglass, P., Clarke, J., Henderson, A. S., Kreitman, D. N., & Presley, A. S. (1977). A study of agoraphobic housewives. *Psychological Medicine, 7*, 73–86.

Burchard, J. D., & Tyler, V. O. (1965). The modification of delinquent behavior through operant conditioning. *Behaviour Research and Therapy, 2*, 245–250.

Burger, A. L., Blackman, L. S., Holmes, M., & Zetlin, A. (1978). Use of active sorting and retrieval strategies as a facilitation of recall, clustering, and sorting by EMR and nonretarded children. *American Journal of Mental Deficiency, 83*, 253–261.

Burger, A. L., Blackman, L. S., & Tan, N. (1980). Maintenance and generalization of a sorting and retrieval strategy by EMR and nonretarded individuals. *American Journal of Mental Retardation, 84*, 373–389.

Burgio, K. L., & Engle, B. T. (1987). Urinary incontinence: Behavioral assessment and treatment. In L. L. Carstensen & B. A. Edelstein (Eds.), *Handbook of Clinical Gerontology* (pp. 252–266). New York: Pergamon.

Burgio, L. D., Page, T. J., & Capriotti, R. M. (1985). Clinical behavioral pharmacology: Methods for evaluating medication and contingency management. *Journal of Applied Behavior Analysis, 18*, 45–59.

Burgio, L. D., Whitman, T. L., & Johnson, M. R. (1980). A self-instructional package for increasing attending behavior in educable mentally retarded children. *Journal of Applied Behavior Analysis, 13*, 443–459.

Burke, J. C., Koegel, R. L. (1987). Some generalized effects of multiple cue training: A longitudinal assessment. Paper presented at the convention of the Association for Behavior Analysis, Nashville, TN.

Burns, G. L., & Patterson, D. R. (1990). Conduct problem behaviors in a stratified random sample of children and adolescents. *Psychological Assessment, 2*, 391–397.

Buss, A. H. (1966). *Psychopathology*. New York: Wiley.

Buss, A. R. (1978). The structure of psychological revolutions. *Journal of the History of the Behavioral Sciences, 14*, 57–64.

Butler, L., Miezitis, S., Friedman, R., & Cole, E. (1980). The effect of two school-based intervention programs on depressive symptoms in preadolescents. *American Educational Research Journal, 17*, 111–119.

Butterfield, E. C., & Ferretti, R. P. (1987). Hypotheses about intellectual differences among children. In J. G. Borkowski & J. D. Day (Eds.), *Cognition in special children: Comparative approaches to retardation, learning disabilities, and giftedness* (pp. 195–233). Norwood, NJ: Ablex.

Camp, B. W., & Bash, M. A. S. (1985). *Think aloud: Increasing social and cognitive skills—a problem solving program for children*. Champaign, IL: Research Press.

Campbell, S. B., Schleifer, M., & Weiss, G. (1978). Continuities in maternal reports and child behaviors over time in hyperactive and comparison groups. *Journal of Abnormal Child Psychology, 6*, 33–45.

Campione, J. C. (1987). Metacognitive components of instructional research with problem learners. In F. E. Weinert & R. H. Klewe (Eds.), *Metacognition, motivation, and understanding* (pp. 117–140). Hillsdale, NJ: Erlbaum.

Campione, J. D., & Brown, A. L. (1978). Toward a theory of intelligence: Contributions from research with retarded children. *Intelligence, 2*, 279–304.

Canter, L., & Canter, M. (1976). *Assertive Discipline: A take charge approach for today's educator*. Los Angeles, CA: Canter and Associates.

Cantwell, D. (1975). *The hyperactive child*. New York: Spectrum.

Cantwell, D. P., Baker, L., & Rutter, M. (1978). Family factors. In M. Rutter & E. Schopler (Eds.), *Autism: A reappraisal of concepts and treatment*. New York: Plenum Press.

Carden-Smith, L. K., & Fowler, S. A. (1984). Positive peer pressure: The effects of peer monitoring on children's disruptive behavior. *Journal of Applied Behavior Analysis, 17*, 213–227.

Carlson, C. L., Lahey, B. B., & Neeper, R. (1984). Peer assessment of the social behavior of accepted, rejected, and neglected children. *Journal of Abnormal Child Psychology, 12*, 189–198.

Carlson, G. A., & Cantwell, D. P. (1980a). A survey of depressive symptoms, syndrome and disorder in a child psychiatric population. *Journal of Child Psychology and Psychiatry, 21*, 19–25.

Carlson, G. A., & Cantwell, D. P. (1980b). Unmasking masked depression in children and adolescents. *American Journal of Psychiatry, 137*, 445–449.

Carlson, G. A., & Garber, J. (1986). Developmental issues in the classification of depression in children. In M. Rutter, C. Izard, & P. Read (Eds.), *Depression in young people*. New York: Guilford.

Carney, R. M., Schechter, K., & Davis, T. (1983). Improving adherence to blood glucose testing in insulin-dependent diabetic children. *Behavior Therapy, 14,* 247–254.

Carnine, D. (1988). Breaking the cycle of school failure. *Youth Policy, 10,* 22–25.

Carpenter, W. T., Heinrichs, D. W., & Alphs, L. D. (1985). Treatment of negative symptoms. *Schizophrenia Bulletin, 11,* 440–452.

Carpenter, W. T., Heinrichs, D. W., & Wagman, A. M. I. (1988). Deficit and nondeficit forms of schizophrenia. *American Journal of Psychiatry, 145,* 578–583.

Carr, E. G. (1977). The motivation of self-injurious behavior: A review of some hypotheses: *Psychological Bulletin, 84,* 800–816.

Carr, E. G. (1988). Functional equivalence as a mechanism of response generalization. In R. H. Horner, G. Dunlap, & R. L. Koegel (Eds.), *Generalization and maintenance: Life-style changes in applied settings.* Baltimore: Brooks.

Carr, E. G., Binkoff, J. A., Kologinsky, E., & Eddy, M. (1978). Acquisition of sign language by autistic children: I. Expressive labelling. *Journal of Applied Behavior Analysis, 11,* 489–501.

Carr, E. G., & Durand, V. M. (1985a). Reducing behavior problems through functional communication training. *Journal of Applied Behavior Analysis, 18,* 111–126.

Carr, E. G., & Durand, V. M. (1985b). The social-communicative basis of severe behavior problems in children. In S. Reiss & R. Bootzin (Eds.), *Theoretical issues in behavior therapy.* New York: Academic Press.

Carr, E. G., & Newson, C. D. (1985). Demand-related tantrums: Conceptualization and treatment. *Behavior Modification, 9,* 403–426.

Carr, E. G., Newsom, C. D., & Binkoff, J. A. (1976). Stimulus control of self-destructive behavior in a psychotic child. *Journal of Abnormal Child Psychology, 4,* 139–153.

Carr, E. G, Newson, C. D., & Binkoff, J. A. (1980). Escape as a factor in the aggressive behavior of two retarded children: *Journal of Applied Behavior Analysis, 13,* 101–117.

Carr, E. G., Schreibman, L., & Lovaas, O. I. (1975). Control of echolalic speech in psychotic children. *Journal of Abnormal Psychology, 3,* 331–351.

Carta, J. J. (1991). Education for young children in inner-city classrooms. *American Behavioral Scientist, 34,* 440–453.

Carta, J. J., Atwater J., Schwartz, I. S., & Miller, P. A. (1990). Applications of echobehavioral analysis to the study of transitions across early education. *Education and Treatment of Children, 13,* 298–315.

Cassell, S. (1965). Effects of brief puppet therapy upon the emotional response of children undergoing cardiac catheterization. *Journal of Consulting and Clinical Psychology, 29,* 1–8.

Cerny, J. A., Barlow, D. H., Craske, M., & Himadi, W. G. (1987). Couples treatment of agoraphobia: A two-year follow-up. *Behavior Therapy, 18,* 401–415.

Chamberlain, P. & Baldwin, D. V. (1988). Client resistance to parent training: Its therapeutic management. In T. R. Kratchowill (Ed.), *Advances in school psychology,* (Vol. 6, pp. 131–171). Hillsdale, NJ: Laurence Erlbaum.

Chamberlain, P., Patterson, G. R., Reid, J., Kavanagh, K., & Forgatch, M. (1984). Observation of client resistance. *Behavior Therapy, 15,* 144–155.

Chamberlain, P., & Reid, J. B. (1987). Parent observation and report of child symptoms. *Behavioral Assessment, 9,* 97–109.

Chambless, D. L., Caputo, G. C., Bright, P., & Gallagher, R. (1984). Assessment of fear in agoraphobics: The Body Sensations Questionnaire and the Agoraphobic Cognitions Questionnaire. *Journal of Consulting and Clinical Psychology, 52,* 1090–1097.

Chambless, D. L., Caputo, G. C., Jasin, S. E., Gracely, E. J., & Williams, C. (1985). The Mobility Inventory for Agoraphobia. *Behaviour Research and Therapy, 23,* 35–44.

Chaney, E. F., O'Leary, M. R., & Marlatt, G. A. (1978). Skill training with alcoholics. *Journal of Consulting and Clinical Psychology, 46,* 1092–1104.

Chaney, J. M., & Peterson, L. (1989). Family variables and disease management in juvenile rheumatoid arthritis. *Journal of Pediatric Psychology, 14,* 389–403.

Chapman, C. R. (1978). Pain: The perception of noxious events. In R. A. Sternbach (Ed.), *The psychology of pain* (pp. 169–202). New York: Raven.

Chappell, M. N., Stefan, J. J., Rogerson, J. S., & Pike, F. H. (1936). The value of group psychological procedures in the treatment of peptic ulcer. *American Journal of Digestive Diseases and Nutrition, 3,* 813–817.

Charlop, M. H., Schreibman, L., & Thibodeau, M. G. (1985). Increasing spontaneous verbal responding in autistic children using a time delay procedure. *Journal of Applied Behavior Analysis, 18,* 155–166.

Chess, S. (1960). Diagnosis and treatment of the hyperactive child. *New York State Journal of Medicine, 60,* 2379–2385.

Chiles, J. A., Miller, M. L., & Cox, G. B. (1980). Depression in an adolescent delinquent population. *Archives of General Psychiatry, 37,* 1179–1184.

Chow, S. L. (1988). Significance test or effect size? *Psychological Bulletin, 103,* 105–110.

Cicchetti, D. (in press). The organization and coherence of a socioemotional, cognitive, and representative development: Illustrations through a developmental psychopathology perspective on Down syndrome and child maltreatment. In R. Thompson (Ed.), *Nebraska Symposium on*

Motivation (Vol. 36). Lincoln, NE: University of Nebraska Press.

Cicchetti, D., & Schneider-Rosen, K. (1986). An organizational approach to childhood depression. In M. Rutter, C. Izard, & P. Read (Eds.), *Depression in young people*. New York: Guilford.

Ciminero, A. R., Calhoun, K. S., & Adams, H. E. (Eds.). (1986). *Handbook of behavioral assessment* (2nd ed.). New York: Wiley.

Ciminero, A. R., & Drabman, R. S. (1977). Current developments in the behavioral assessment of children. In B. B. Lahey & A. E. Kazdin (Eds.), *Advances in clinical child psychology* (Vol. 1). New York: Plenum.

Clark, D. M., Salkovskis, P. M., Hackmann, A., Middleton, H., Anastasiades, P., & Gelder, M. (1992). *A comparison of cognitive therapy, applied relaxation, and imipramine in the treatment of panic disorder*. Unpublished manuscript.

Clark, J. V., & Arkowitz, H. (1975). Social anxiety and self-evaluation of interpersonal performance. *Psychological Reports, 36*, 211–221.

Clarke, G., & Lewinsohn, P. M. (1989). The Coping with Depression Course: A group psychoeducational intervention for unipolar depression. *Behavior Change, 6*, 54–69.

Coates, T. J. (1990). Strategies for modifying sexual behavior for primary and secondary prevention of HIV disease. *Journal of Consulting and Clinical Psychology, 58*, 57–69.

Coates, T. J., Jeffrey, R. W.,, Slinkard, L. A., Killen, J. D., & Danaher, B. G. (1982). Frequency of contact and contingent reinforcement in weight loss, lipid change, and blood pressure reduction in adolescents. *Behavior Therapy, 13*, 175–185.

Coates, T. J., McKusick, L., Stites, D. P., & Kuno, R. (1989). Stress management training reduced number of sexual partners but did not improve immune function in men infected with HIV. *American Journal of Public Health, 79*, 885–887.

Cohen, L. J., Test, M. A., & Brown, R. L. (1990). Suicide and schizophrenia: Data from a prospective community treatment study. *American Journal of Psychiatry, 147*, 602–607.

Cohen, S. I., & Reed, J. L. (1968). The treatment of "nervous diarrhea"and other conditioned autonomic disorders by desensitization. *British Journal of Psychiatry, 114*, 275–280.

Coker, W. B. (1984). Homemade switches and toy adaptation for early training with nonspeaking persons. *Language, Speech, and Hearing Services in the Schools, 15*, 32–36.

Cole, C. L., Gardner, W. I., & Karan, O. C. (1985). Self-management training of mentally retarded adults: Preventing severe conduct difficulties. *Applied Research in Mental Retardation, 6*, 337–347.

Collier, B. N., & Etzwiler, D. D. (1971). Comparative study of diabetes knowledge among juvenile diabetics and their parents. *Diabetes, 20*, 51–57.

Collins, R. L., & Marlatt, G. A. (1981). Social modelling as a determinant of drinking behavior: Implications for prevention and treatment. *Addictive Behaviors, 6*, 233–239.

Collins, R. L., Rothblum, E. D., & Wilson, G. T. (1986). The comparative efficacy of cognitive and behavioral approaches to the treatment of obesity. *Cognitive Therapy and Research, 10*, 299–318.

Colvin, G., Lowe, R., & Clanton, B. (1988). School-wide discipline plan: A management primer for teachers and principals. *Direct Instruction News, 7*, 31–36.

Colvin, G., & Sugai, G. (1989). Proactive strategies for managing social behavior problems: An instructional approach. *Education and treatment of Children, 11*, 341–348.

Comfort, A. (1965). *The anxiety makers*. Camden, NJ: T. Nelson.

Cone, J. D. (1977). The relevance of reliability for behavioral assessment. *Behavior Therapy, 8*, 411–426.

Conger, A. J., Wallander, J. L., Mariotto, M. J., & Ward, D. (1980). Peer judgements of heterosexual-social anxiety and skill: What do they pay attention to anyhow? *Behavioral Assessment, 2*, 243–259.

Conners, C.K. (1969). A teacher rating scale for use in drug studies with children. *American Journal of Psychiatry, 126*, 884–888.

Conners, C. K. (1970). Symptoms patterns in hyperkinetic, neurotic, and normal children. *Child Development, 41*, 667–782.

Conners, C. K. (1980). *Food additives and hyperactive children*. New York: Plenum.

Conners, C. K. (1990, June). *Methodology of antidepressant drug trials with adolescents*. Paper presented at an NIMH workshop on tricyclic antidepressants in adolescence. Unpublished manuscript. (Available from C. K. Conners, Ph.D., Box 3362, Duke University Medical Center, Durham, NC 27710.)

Conners, C. K., & Wells, K. C. (1986). *Hyperkinetic children: A neuropsychosocial approach*. Beverly Hills, CA: Sage.

Conners, F. A., Caruso, D. R., & Detterman, D. K. (1986). Computer-assisted instruction for the mentally retarded. In N. R. Ellis & N. W. Bray (Eds.), *International review of research in mental retardation* (Vol. 14, pp. 105–129). Orlando, FL; Academic Press.

Cook, T. D., & Campbell, D. T. (Eds.). (1979). *Quasi-experimentation: Design and analysis issues for field settings*. Chicago: Rand McNally.

Cooper, A., Furst, J. B., & Bridger, W. H. (1969). A brief commentary on the usefulness of studying fear of snakes. *Journal of Abnormal Psychology, 74*, 413–414.

Cooper, J. O., Heron, T. E., & Heward, W. L. (1987). *Applied behavior analysis.* Columbus, OH: Merrill.

Cooper, N. A., & Clum, G. A. (1989). Imaginal flooding as a supplementary treatment for PTSD in combat veterans: A controlled study. *Behavior Therapy, 20,* 381–391.

Cooper, P. J., & Fairburn, C. G. (1983). Binge-eating and self-induced vomiting in the community. *British Journal of Psychiatry, 142,* 139.

Corah, N. L., Gale, E. N., & Illig, S. J. (1979). Psychological stress reduction during dental procedures. *Journal of Dental Research, 58,* 1347–1351.

Cordes, C. (1984). The plight of the homeless mentally ill. *APA Monitor, 15,* 1–13.

Corrigan, P. W. (1990, April). *A meta-analysis of social skills training in adult psychiatric populations.* Paper presented at the Annual Meeting of the Western Psychological Association, Los Angeles, CA.

Costello, A. J., Edelbrock, C. S., Dulcan, M. K., Kulas, R., & Klaric, S. R. (1984). *Development and testing of the NIMH Diagnostic Interview Schedule for Children in a clinic population.* First report (Contract No. REP-DB-81–0027). Rockville, MD: Center for Epidemiological Studies, National Institute of Mental Health.

Costello, C. G. (1982). Social factors associated with depression: A retrospective community study. *Psychological Medicine, 12,* 329–339.

Cox, A., Rutter, M., Newman, S., & Bartak, L. (1975). A comparative study of infantile autism and specific developmental receptive language disorder: II. Parental characteristics. *British Journal of Psychiatry, 126,* 146–159.

Coyne, J. C. (1976a). Depression and the response of others. *Journal of Abnormal Psychology, 85,* 186–193.

Coyne, J. C. (1976b). Toward an interactional description of depression. *Psychiatry, 39,* 28–40.

Coyne, J. C., Kahn, J. & Gotlib, I. H. (1987). Depression. In T. Jacob (Ed.), *Family interaction and psychopathology: Theories, methods, and findings.* NY: Plenum.

Craighead, L. W., & Agras, W. S. (1991). Mechanisms of action in cognitive-behavioral and pharmacological interventions for obesity and bulimia nervosa. *Journal of Consulting and Clinical Psychology, 59,* 115–125.

Craighead, L. W., & Blum, M. D. (1989). Supervised exercise in behavioral treatment for moderate obesity. *Behavior Therapy, 20,* 49–59.

Craighead, L. W., & Craighead, W. E. (1980). Implications of persuasive communication research for the modification of self-statements. *Cognitive Therapy and Research, 4,* 117–134.

Craighead, W. E. (1980). Away from a unitary model of depression. *Behavior Therapy, 11,* 122–128.

Craighead, W. E. (1982). A brief clinical history of cognitive-behavior therapy with children. *School Psychology Review, 11,* 5–13.

Craighead, W. E. (1990). There's a place for us: All of us. *Behavior Therapy, 21,* 3–23.

Craighead, W. E., Evans, D. D., & Robins, C. J. (In press). Unipolar depression. In S. M. Turner, K. S. Calhoun, & H. E. Adams (Eds.), *Handbook of clinical behavior therapy* (2nd ed.). New York: John Wiley & Sons.

Craighead, W. E., Kazdin, A. E., & Mahoney, M. J. (1981). *Behavior modification: Principles, issues and applications* (2nd ed.). Boston: Houghton Mifflin.

Craighead, W. E., Meyers, A. W., & Craighead, L. W. (1985). Conceptual issues in cognitive behavior therapy for children. *Journal of Abnormal Child Psychology, 13,* 331–342.

Cram, J. R. (1987). Surface EMG recordings and pain-related disorders: A diagnostic framework. *Biofeedback and Self-Regulation, 13,* 123–138.

Craske, M. G., Brown, T. A., & Barlow, D. H. (1991). Behavioral treatment of panic disorder: A two-year follow up. *Behavior Therapy, 22,* 289–304.

Cronbach, L. J., Gleser, G. C., Nanda, H., & Rajaratnam, N. (1972). *The dependability of behavioral measurements: Theory of generalizability for scores and profiles.* New York: Wiley.

Cronkite, R. C., & Moos, R. H. (1980). Determinants of the posttreatment functioning of alcoholic patients: A conceptual framework. *Journal of Consulting and Clinical Psychology, 48,* 305–316.

Cronin, K. A., & Cuvo, A. J. (1979). Teaching mending skills to mentally retarded adolescents. *Journal of Applied Behavior Analysis, 12,* 401–406.

Crowe, M. J. (1978). Conjoint marital therapy: A controlled outcome study. *Psychological Medicine, 8,* 623–636.

Crowther, J. H. (1983). Stress management training and relaxation imagery in the treatment of essential hypertension. *Journal of Behavioral Medicine, 6,* 169–187.

Cryan, J. R. (1987). The banning of corporal punishment: In child care, school and other educative settings in the United States. Position Paper. *Childhood Education, 63,* 146–153.

Cullinan, D. (1976). Verbalization in EMR children's observational learning. *American Journal of Mental Deficiency, 81,* 65–72.

Cummings, S. T. (1976). The impact of the handicapped child on the father: A study of fathers of mentally retarded and chronically ill children. *American Journal of Orthopsychiatry, 36,* 246–255.

Cunningham, C. E., & Barkley, R. A. (1979). The interactions of hyperactive and normal children with their mothers during free play and structured task. *Child Development, 50,* 217–224.

Cunningham, C. E., Siegel, L. S., & Offord, D. R. (1985). A developmental dose response analysis of the effects of methylphenidate on the peer interactions of attention deficit disordered boys. *Journal of Child Psychology and Psychiatry, 26,* 955–971.

Curran, J. P. (1977). Skills training as an approach to the treatment of heterosexual-social anxiety: A review. *Psychological Bulletin, 84,* 149–157.

Curran, J. P. (1979a). Pandora's box reopened? The assessment of social skills. *Journal of Behavioral Assessment, 1,* 55–71.

Curran, J. P. (1979b). Social skills: Methodological issues and future directions. In A. S. Bellack & M. Hersen (Eds.), *Research and practice in social skills training.* New York: Plenum.

Curran, J. P., Miller, I. W., Zwick, W. R., Monti, P. M., & Stout, R. L. (1980). The socially inadequate patient: Incidence rate, demographic and clinical features, and hospital and posthospital functioning. *Journal of Consulting and Clinical Psychology, 48,* 375–382.

Curran, J. P., Monti, P. M., & Corriveau, D. P. (1982). Treatment of schizophrenia. In A. S. Bellack, M. Hersen, & A. E. Kazdin (Eds.), *International handbook of behavior modification and therapy.* New York: Plenum.

Curran, J. P., & Wessberg, H. W. (1981). Assessment of social inadequacy. In D. H. Barlow (Ed.), *Behavioral assessment of adult disorders* (pp.405–438). New York: Guilford.

Curry, J. F., & Craighead, W. E. (1992). Assessment of childhood and adolescent depression. In T. M. Ollendick & M. Hersen (Eds.), *Handbook of child and adolescent assessment.* New York: Pergamon.

Curtiss, G., Rosenthal, R. H., Marohn, R. C., Ostro, E., Offer, D., & Trujillo, J. (1983). Measuring delinquent behavior in inpatient treatment settings: Revision and validation of the Adolescent Antisocial Behavior Checklist. *Journal of the American Academy of Child Psychiatry, 22,* 459–466.

Cuvo, A. J., Veitch, V. C., Trace, M. W., & Konke, J. L. (1978). Teaching change computation to the mentally retarded. *Behavior Modification, 2,* 531–548.

Dadds, M. R., Schwartz, S., & Saunders, M. R. (1987). Marital discord and treatment outcome in behavior treatment of child conduct disorders. *Journal of Consulting and Clinical Psychology, 55,* 396–403.

Dahlkoetter, J., Callahan, E. J., & Linton, J. (1979). Obesity and the unbalanced energy equation: Exercise versus eating habit change. *Journal of Consulting and Clinical Psychology, 47,* 898–905.

Danforth, J. S., Allen, K. D., Fitterling, J. M., Danforth, J. A., Farrar, D., Brown, M., & Drabman, R. S. (1990). Exercise as a treatment for hypertension in low socio-economic-status black children. *Journal of Consulting and Clinical Psychology, 58,* 237–239.

Darley, J. M., & Fazio, R. (1980). Expectancy confirmation process arising in the social interaction sequence. *American Psychologist, 35,* 867–881.

Darwin, C. R. (1872). *The expression of the emotions in man and animals.* London: John Murray.

Davison, G. C., & Valins, S. (1969). Maintenance of self-attributed and drug-attributed behavior change. *Journal of Personality and Social Psychology, 11,* 25–33.

Dawson, B., de Armas, A., McGrath, M. L., & Kelly, J. A. (1986). Cognitive problem-solving training to improve the child-care judgement of child neglectful parents. *Journal of Family Violence, 1,* 209–221.

Day, J. D. & Borkowski, J. D. (Eds.). (1987). *Intelligence and exceptionality: New directions for theory, assessment, and instructional practices.* Norwood, NJ: Albex.

de Silva, P., & Rachman, S. (1984). Does escape behaviour strengthen agoraphobic avoidance? A preliminary study. *Behaviour Research and Therapy, 22,* 87–91.

Dearth, N., Labenski, B. J., Mott, M. E., & Pellegrini, L. M. (1986). *Families helping families: Living with schizophrenia.* New York: Norton.

Deberry, S., Davis, S., & Reinhard, K. E. (1989). A comparison of meditation-relaxation and cognitive behavioral techniques for reducing anxiety and depression in a geriatric population. *Journal of Geriatric Psychiatry, 22,* 231–247.

DeGossely, M., Konicky, N., & Lenfant, H. (1975). La rectocolite hemorragique: Training autogene. A propos de quelques cas graves. *Acta Gastro-Enterologica Belgica, 38,* 454–462.

Deitz, D. E. D., & Repp, A. C. (1983). Reducing behavior through reinforcement. *Exceptional Education Quarterly, 3,* 34–46.

Deitz, S. M., & Repp, A. C. (1973). Decreasing classroom misbehavior through the use of DRL schedules of reinforcement. *Journal of Applied Behavior Analysis, 6,* 457–463.

DeLongis, A., Coyne, J. C., Dakof, G., Folkman, S. & Lazarus, R. S. et al. (1982). Relationships of daily hassles, uplifts and major life events to health status. *Health Psychology, 1,* 119–136.

Delquadri, J., Greenwood, C. R., Stretton, K., & Hall, R. V. (1983). The peer tutoring game: A classroom procedure for increasing opportunity to respond and spelling performance. *Education and Treatment of Children, 6,* 225–239.

Deluty, R. H. (1979). Children's Action Tendency Scale: A self-report measure of aggressiveness, assertiveness, and submissiveness in children. *Journal of Consulting and Clinical Psychology, 47,* 1061–1071.

Deluty, R. H. (1983). Children's evaluations of aggressive, assertive, and submissive responses. *Journal of Clinical Child Psychology, 12,* 124–129.

DeMyer, M. K. (1979). *Parents and children in autism*. Toronto: Wiley.

DePue, R. A., & Monroe, S. M. (1986). Conceptualization and measurement of human disorder in life stress research: The problem of chronic disturbance. *Psychology Bulletin, 99*, 36–51.

DeProspero, A., & Cohen, S. (1979). Inconsistent visual analysis of intrasubject data. *Journal of Applied Behavior Analysis, 12*, 573–579.

Derschewitz, R. A., & Williamson, J. W. (1977). Prevention of childhood household injuries: A controlled clinical trial. *American Journal of Public Health, 67*, 1148–1153.

Di Nardo, P. A., Barlow, D. H. (1988). *Anxiety Disorders Interview Schedule—Revised (ADIS-R)*. Albany, NY: State University of New York at Albany, Phobia and Anxiety Disorders Clinic.

Diamond, R. (1985). Drugs and the quality of life: The patient's point of view. *Journal of Clinical Psychiatry, 46*, 29–35.

Doane, J. A., Falloon, I. R. H., Goldstein, M. J., & Mintz, J. (1985). Parental affective style and the treatment of schizophrenia. *Archives of General Psychiatry, 42*, 34–42.

Dodge, K. A. (1985). Attributional bias in aggressive children. In P. C. Kendall (Ed.), *Advances in cognitive-behavioral research and therapy* (Vol. 4, pp. 73–110). Orlando, FL: Academic Press.

Doerfler, L. A., & Chaplin, W. F. (1985). Type III error in research on interpersonal models of depression. *Journal of Abnormal Psychology, 94*, 227–230.

Dolce, J. J., & Raczynski, J. M. (1985). Neuromuscular activity and electromyography in painful backs: Psychological and biomechanical models in assessment and treatment. *Psychological Bulletin, 97*, 502–520.

Doll, E. A. (1935). A genetic scale of social maturity. *The American Journal of Orthopsychiatry, 5*, 180–188.

Doll, E. A. (1965). *Vineland social maturity scale*. Circle Pines, MN: American Guidance Service.

Donahoe, C. P., Jr., & Driesenga, S. A. (1988). A review of social skills training with chronic mental patients. In M. Hersen, R. M. Eisler, & P. M. Miller (Eds.), *Progress in behavior modification* (pp. 131–164). Newbury Park, CA: Sage.

Donovan, D. M. (1988). Assessment of addictive behaviors: Implications of an emerging biopsychosocial model. In D. M. Donovan & G. A. Marlatt (Eds.), *Assessment of addictive behaviors*, (pp. 3–48). New York: Guilford.

Donovan, D. M., & Marlatt, G. A. (1988). *Assessment of addictive behaviors*. New York: Guilford.

Dore, F. Y., & Dumas, C. (1987). Psychology of animal cognition: Piagetian studies. *Psychological Bulletin, 102*, 219–233.

Douglas, V. I. (1972). Stop, look, and listen: The problem of sustained attention and impulse control in hyperactive and normal children. *Canadian Journal of Behavioural Science. 4*, 259–282.

Douglas, V. I. (1984). The psychological processes implicated in ADD. In L. M. Bloomingdale (Ed.), *Attention deficit disorder: Diagnostic, cognitive, and therapeutic understanding*. New York: Spectrum.

Douglas, V. I., Barr, R. G., O'Neill, M. E., & Britton, B. G. (1986). *Journal of Child Psychology and Psychiatry, 27*, 191–211.

Douglas, V. I., & Parry, P. A. (1983). Effects of reward on delayed reaction time task performance of hyperactive children. *Journal of Abnormal Child Psychology, 11*, 313–326.

Dow, M. G. (1985). Peer validation and idiographic analysis of social skill deficits. *Behavior Therapy, 16*, 76–86.

Dow, M. G., Biglan, A., & Glaser, S. R. (1985). Multimethod assessment of socially anxious and socially non-anxious women. *Behavioral Assessment, 7*, 273–282.

Dow, M. G., & Craighead, W. E. (1984). Cognition and social inadequacy: Relevance in clinical populations. In P. Trower (Ed.), *Radical approaches to social skills training*. New York: Methuen.

Dow, M. G., & Craighead, W. E. (1987). Social inadequacy and depression: Overt behavior and self-evaluation processes. *Journal of Social and Clinical Psychology, 5*, 99–113.

Dow, S. (1981). Retarded ejaculation. *Journal of Sex and Marital Therapy, 7*, 49–53.

Drake, R. E., & Ehrlich, J. (1985). Suicide attempts associated with akathisia. *American Journal of Psychiatry, 142*, 499–501.

Drazen, M., Nevid, J. S., Pace, N., & O'Brien, R. M. (1982). Work-site-based behavioral treatment of mild hypertension. *Journal of Occupational Medicine, 24*, 511–514.

Drewnowski, A., & Greenwood, M. R. C. (1983). Cream and sugar: Human preferences for high-fat foods. *Physiology and Behavior, 30*, 629–633.

Drotar, D., Johnson, S., Iannotti, R., Krasnegor, N., Matthews, K., Melamed, B., Millstein, S., Peterson, R., Popiel, D., & Routh, D. (1989). Child health psychology. *Health Psychology, 8*, 781–784.

Dumas, J. E., & Wahler, R. G. (1983). Predictors of treatment outcome in parent training: Mother insularity and socioeneconimic disadvantage. *Behavioral Assessment, 5*, 301–313.

Dunlap, G. (1984). The influence of task variation and maintenance tasks on the learning and affect of autistic children. *Journal of Experimental Child psychology, 37* 41–46.

Dunlap, G., Koegel, R. L., & Egel, A. L. (1979). Autistic children in school. *Exceptional Children, 45*, 552–558.

Dunlap, G., Koegel, R. L., & O'Neill, R. O. (1985). Pervasive developmental disorders. In Ph.D. Borstein & A. E. Kazdin (Eds.), *Handbook of clinical behavior therapy with children.* Homewood, IL: Dorsey.

Dunn, L. M., & Markwardt, F. C. (1970). *Peabody individual achievement test.* Circle Pines, MN: American Guidance Service.

Durand, V. M. (1982). A behavioral/pharmacological intervention for the treatment of severe self-injurious behavior. *Journal of Autism and Developmental Disabilities, 12*, 243–251.

Durand, V. M., & Carr, E. G. (1987). Social influences on "self-stimulatory" behavior: Analysis and treatment application. *Journal of Applied Behavior Analysis, 20*, 119–132.

Durlak, J. A., Fuhrman, T., & Lampman, C. (1991). Effectiveness of cognitive-behavioral therapy for maladapting children: A meta-analysis. *Psychological Bulletin, 110*, 204–214.

Dyer, K. (1987). The competition of autistic stereotyped behavior with usual and specially assessed reinforcers. *Research in Developmental Disabilities, 8*, 607–626.

D'Zurilla, T. J., & Goldfried, M. R. (1971). Problem solving and behavior modification. *Journal of Abnormal Psychology, 78*, 107–126.

Eason, J. J., White, M. J., & Newsom, C. D. (1982). Generalized reduction of self-stimulatory behavior: An effect of teaching appropriate play to autistic children. *Analysis and Intervention in Developmental Disabilities, 2*, 157–169.

Eckert, E. D., Goldberg, S. C. Casper, R. C., & Halmi, K. A. (1979). Cyproheptadine in anorexia nervosa. *British Journal of Psychiatry, 134*, 67–70.

Edelstein, B. A., & Eisler, R. M. (1976). Effects of modeling and modeling with instructions and feedback on the behavioral components of social skills. *Behavior Therapy, 7*, 382–389.

Education for All Handicapped Children Act, 20, U.S.C. 1401–1461 (1975).

Edwards, M. C., Finney, J. W., & Bonner, W. (1991). Matching treatment with recurrent abdominal pain symptoms: An evaluation of dietary fiber and relaxation treatments. *Behavior Therapy, 22*, 257–267.

Egan, K. (1983). Stress management and child management with abusive parents. *Journal of Child Psychology, 12*, 292–299.

Egel, A. L. (1981). Reinforcer variation: Implications for motivating developmentally disabled children. *Journal of Applied Behavior Analysis, 14*, 345–350.

Ehlers, A., & Margraf, J. (1989). The psychophysiological model of panic attacks. In P. M. G. Emmelkamp (Ed.), *Anxiety disorders. Annual series of European research in behaviour therapy.* (Vol. 4). Amsterdam: Swets.

Eisenberg, L., & Kanner, L. (1956). Early infantile autism: 1943–1955. *American Journal of Orthopsychiatry, 26*, 55–65.

Eisler, R. M., Blanchard, E. B., Fitts, H., & Williams, J. G. (1978). Social skill training with and without modeling for schizophrenic and non-psychotic hospitalized psychiatric patients. *Behavior Modification, 2*, 147–172.

Eisler, R. M., Hersen, M., & Miller, P. M. (1973). Effects of modeling on components of assertive behavior. *Journal of Behavior Therapy and Experimental Psychiatry, 4*, 1–6.

Eisler, R. M., Frederiksen, L. W., & Peterson, G. L. (1978). The relationship of cognitive variables to the expression of assertiveness. *Behavior Therapy, 9*, 419–427.

Ekstrand, M., & Coates, T. J. (1990). Maintenance of safer sexual behaviors and predictors of risky sex: The San Francisco Men's Health Study. *American Journal of Public Health, 80*, 973–977.

Eland, J. M. (1981). Minimizing pain associated with prekindergarten intramuscular injections. *Issues in Comprehensive Pediatric Nursing, 5*, 361–372.

Eland, J. M., & Anderson, J. E. (1977). The experience of pain in children. In A. Jacox (Ed.), *Pain: A source book for nurses and other professionals* (pp. 453–473). Boston: Little, Brown.

Elder, J. P., Edelstein, B. A., & Narick, M. M. (1979). Adolescent psychiatric patients: Modifying aggressive behavior with social skills training. *Behavior Modification, 3*, 161–178.

Elkin, I., Parloff, M. B., Hadley, S. W., & Autry, J. H. (1985). NIMH Treatment of Depression Collaborative Research Program. *Archives of General Psychiatry, 42*, 305–316.

Elkin, I., Shea, M. T., Watkins, J. T., Imber, S. D., Sotsky, S. M., Collins, J. F., Glass, D. R. Pilkonis, P. A., Leber, W. R., Docherty, J. P., Fiester, S. J., & Parloff, M. B. (1989). NIMH Treatment of Depression Collaborative Research Program: General effectiveness of treatments. *Archives of General Psychiatry. 46*, 971–983.

Elkins, R. L. (1980). Covert sensitization treatment of alcoholism: Contributions of successful conditioning to subsequent abstinence maintenance. *Addictive Behaviors, 5*, 67–89.

Elliott, C. H., & Olson, R. A. (1983). The management of children's distress in response to painful medical treatment for burn injuries. *Behavior Research and Therapy, 21*, 675–683.

Elliott, D. S., & Ageton, S. S. (1980). Reconciling race and class differences in self-reported and official estimates of delinquency. *American Sociological Review, 45*, 95–110.

Ellis, A. (1958). Rational psychotherapy. *Journal of General Psychology, 59*, 34–49.

Ellis, A. (1962). *Reason and emotion in psychotherapy.* New York: Lyle Stuart.

Ellis, N. R. (1963). *Handbook of mental deficiency.* New York: McGraw Hill.

Ellis, N. R. (1979). *Handbook of mental deficiency, psychological theory, and research* (2nd ed.). Hillsdale, NJ: Erlbaum.

Ellis, P. L. (1982). Empathy: A factor in antisocial behavior. *Journal of Abnormal Child Psychology, 10,* 123–134.

Emery, R. E., Binkoff, J. A., Houts, A. C., & Carr, E. G. (1983). Children as independent variables: Some clinical implications of child effects. *Behavior Therapy, 14,* 398–412.

Emmelkamp, P. M. G., Kuipers, A. C. M., & Eggeraat, J. G. (1978). Cognitive modification versus prolonged exposure in vivo: A comparison with agoraphobics as subjects. *Behaviour Research and Therapy, 16,* 33–41.

Emmelkamp, P. M. G., & Mersch, P. P. (1982). Cognition and exposure in vivo in the treatment of agoraphobia: Short term and delayed effects. *Cognitive Therapy and Research, 6,* 77–90.

Emmelkamp, P. M. G., & Wessels, H. (1975). Flooding in imagination vs. flooding in vivo: A comparison with agoraphobics. *Behaviour Research and Therapy, 13,* 7–15.

Empey, L. T. (1982). *American delinquency: Its meaning and construction.* Homewood, IL: Dorsey.

Endicott, J., & Spitzer, R. L. (1978). A diagnostic interview: The Schedule for Affective Disorders and Schizophrenia. *Archives of General Psychiatry, 35,* 837–844.

Epstein, L. H. (1985). Family-based treatment for preadolescent obesity. *Advances in Developmental and Behavioral Pediatrics, 6,* 1–39.

Epstein, L. H., Beck, S., Figueroa, J., Farkas, G., Kazdin, A. E., Daneman, D., & Becker, D. (1981). The effects of targeting improvements in urine glucose on metabolic control in children with insulin dependent diabetes. *Journal of Applied Behavior Analysis, 14,* 365–375.

Epstein, L. H., Masek, B. J., & Marshall, W. R. (1978). A nutritionally based school program for control of eating in obese children. *Behavior Therapy, 9,* 766–788.

Epstein, L. H., McCurley, J., Wing, R. R., & Valoski, A. (1990). Five-year follow-up of family-based behavioral treatments for childhood obesity. *Journal of Consulting and Clinical Psychology, 58,* 661–664.

Epstein, L. H. Wing, R. R., Koeske, R., Ossip, D., & Beck, S. (1982). A comparison of lifestyle change and programmed aerobic exercise on weight and fitness changes in obese children. *Behavior Therapy, 13,* 651–665.

Epstein, L. H., Wing, R. R., Koeske, R., & Valoski, A. (1985). A comparison of lifestyle exercise, aerobic exercise, and calisthenics on weight loss in obese children. *Behavior Therapy, 16,* 345–356.

Epstein, L. H., Wing, R. R., Steranchak, L., Dickson, B., & Michelson, J. (1980). Comparison of family-based behavior modification and nutrition education for childhood obesity. *Journal of Pediatric Psychology, 5,* 25–36.

Epstein, L. H., Woodall, K., Goreczny, A. J., Wing, R. R., & Robertson, R. J. (1984). The modification of activity patterns and energy expenditure in obese young girls. *Behavior Therapy, 15,* 101–108.

Epstein, N. (1982). Cognitive therapy with couples. *American Journal of Family Therapy, 10,* 5–16.

Erickson, L. M., Tiffany, S. T., Martin, E., & Baker, T. B. (1983). Aversive smoking therapies: A conditioning analysis of therapeutic effectiveness. *Behavior Research and Therapy, 21,* 595–611.

Evans, M. D., Hollon, S. D., DeRubeis, R. J., Piasecki, J. M., Grove, W. M., Garvey, M. J., & Tuason, V. B. (1992). Differential relapse following cognitive therapy and pharmacotherapy for depression. *Archives of General Psychiatry, 49,* 802–808.

Evans, R. I. (1988). Health promotion—Science or ideology. *Health Psychology, 7,* 203–219.

Evans, R. I., Rozelle, R. M., Mittelmark, M. B., Hansen, W. B., Bane, A. L., & Havis, J. (1978). Deterring the onset of smoking in children: Knowledge of immediate physiological effects and coping with peer pressure, media pressure, and parent modeling. *Journal of Applied Social Psychology, 8,* 126–135.

Eyberg, S. M., & Johnson, S. M. (1974). Multiple assessment of behavior modification with families: Effects of contingency contracting and order of treated problems. *Journal of Consulting and Clinical Psychology, 42,* 594–606.

Eyberg, S. M., & Matarazzo, R. G. (1980). Training parents as therapists: A comparison between individual parent-child interaction training and parent group didactic training. *Journal of Clinical Psychology, 36,* 492–499.

Eyberg, S. M., & Robinson, E. A. (1982). Parent-child interaction training: Effects on family functioning. *Journal of Clinical Child Psychology, 11,* 130–137.

Eyberg, S. M., & Robinson, E. A. (1983a). Conduct problem behavior: Standardization of a behavioral rating scale with adolescents. *Journal of Clinical Child Psychology, 12,* 347–354.

Eyberg, S. M., & Robinson, E. A. (1983b). Dyadic Parent-Child Interaction Coding System: A manual. *Psychological Documents, 13,* 24 (No. 2582).

Eyberg, S. M., & Ross, A. W. (1978). Assessment of child behavior problems: The validation of a new inventory. *Journal of Clinical Child Psychology, 7,* 113–116.

Fairburn, C. G. (1984). Cognitive behavioral treatment for bulimia. In D. M. Garner and P. E. Garfinkel (Eds.), *The handbook of psychotherapy for anorexia nervosa and bulimia*. New York: Guilford.

Fairburn, C. G. (1988a). The current status of the psychological treatments for bulimia nervosa. *Journal of Psychosomatic Research, 32*, 635–645.

Fairburn, C. G. (1988b). The uncertain status of the cognitive approach to bulimia nervosa. In K. M. Pirke, W. Vandereycken, & D. Ploog (Eds.), *The psychobiology of bulimia nervosa*. Berlin: Springer-Verlag.

Fairburn, C. G., Kirk, J., O'Connor, M., & Cooper, P. J. (1986). A comparison of two psychological treatments for bulimia nervosa. *Behavior Research and Therapy, 24*, 629–643.

Falkner, B., Onesti, G., & Angelakos, E. (1981). Effect of saltloading on the cardiovascular response to stress in adolescents. *Hypertension, 3* (Suppl. 2), 195–199.

Falloon, I. R. H. (1985). *Family management of schizophrenia: A study of clinical, social, family, and economic benefits*. Baltimore: John Hopkins University Press.

Falloon, I. R. H., Boyd, J. L., & McGill, C. W. (1984). *Family care of schizophrenia: A problem-solving approach to the treatment of mental illness*. New York: Guilford.

Falloon, I. R. H., Boyd, J. L., McGill, C. W., Williamson, M., Razani, J., Moss, H. B., Gilderman, A. M., & Simpson, G. M. (1985). Family management in the prevention of morbidity of schizophrenia: Clinical outcome of a two year longitudinal study. *Archives of General Psychiatry, 42*, 887–896.

Falloon, I. R. H., McGill, C. W., Boyd, J., & Pedersen, J. (1987). Family management in the prevention of morbidity of schizophrenia: social outcome of a two-year longitudinal study. *Psychological Medicine, 17*, 59–66.

Falloon, I. R. H., Mueser, K. T., Gingerich, S., Rappaport, S., McGill, C., & Hole, V. (1988). *Workbook for behavioural family therapy*. Buckingham, England: Buckingham Mental Health Service.

Fantuzzo, J. W. (1990). Behavioral treatment of the victims of child abuse and neglect. *Behavior Modification, 14*, 315–339.

Farber, B. (1975). Family adaption to severely mentally retarded children. In M. J. Begrab & S. A. Richardson (Eds.), *The mentally retarded and society: A social science perspective* (pp. 247–266). Baltimore: University Park Press.

Farrington, D. P. (1978). The family backgrounds of aggressive youths. In L.A. Hersov, M. Berger, & D. Shaffer (Ed.), *Aggression and antisocial behaviour in childhood and adolescence*. Oxford: Pergamon.

Farrington, D. P. (1984). Measuring the natural history of delinquency and crime. In R. A. Glow (Ed.), *Advances in the behavioral measurement of children* (Vol. 1). Greenwich, CT: JAI Press.

Favell, J. E. (1983). The management of aggressive behavior. In E. Schopler & G. B. Mesibov (Eds.), *Autism in adolescents and adults* (pp. 187–222). New York: Plenum.

Favell, J. E., & Reid, D. H. (1988). Generalizing and maintaining improvement in problem behavior. In R. H. Horner, G. Dunlap, & R. L. Koegel (Eds.), *Generalization and maintenance: Life-style changes in applied settings* (pp. 171–196). Baltimore: Paul H. Brookes.

Favell, J. E., McGimsey, J. F., & Schell, R. M. (1982). Treatment of self-injury by providing alternative sensory activities. *Analysis and Intervention in Development Disabilities, 2*, 83–104.

Faw, G. D. Reid, D. H., Schepis, M. J., Fitzgerald, J. R., & Welty, P. A. (1981). Involving institutional staff in the development and maintenance of sign language skills with profoundly retarded persons. *Journal of Applied Behavior Analysis, 14*, 411–423.

Fay, W. H. (1969). On the basis of autistic echolalia. *Journal of Communication Disorders, 2*, 38–47.

Fay, W. H., & Schuler, A. L. (1980). *Emerging language in autistic children*. Baltimore: University Park Press.

Fehrenbach, A. B., & Peterson, L. (1989). Parental problem solving skills, stress, and dietary compliance in phenylketonuria. *Journal of Consulting and Clinical Psychology, 57*, 237–241.

Fein, D., Pennington, B., Markowitz, P., Braverman, M., & Waterhouse, L. (1986). Towards a neuropsychological model of autism: Are the social deficits primary? *Journal of the American Academy of Child Psychiatry, 25*, 198–217.

Ferber, H., Keeley, S. M., & Shemberg, K. M. (1974). Training parents in behavior modification: Outcome of and problems encountered in a program after Patterson's work. *Behavior Therapy, 5*, 415–419.

Fernald, C. D., & Corry, J. J. (1981). Empathetic versus directive preparation of children for needles. *Journal of the Association for the Care of Children's Health, 10*, 44–47.

Ferster, C. B. (1961). Positive reinforcement and behavioral deficits of autistic children. *Child Development, 32*, 437–456.

Ferster, C. B. (1965). Classification of behavioral pathology. In L. Krasner & L. P. Ullmann (Eds.), *Research in behavior modification: New developments and implications*, (pp. 6–26). New York: Holt, Rinehart & Winston.

Ferster, C. B. (1973). A functional analysis of depression. *American Psychologist, 28*, 857–870.

Feshbach, N. (1975). Empathy in children: Some theoretical and empirical considerations. *Counseling Psychologist, 5*, 25–30.

Feuerstein, R. (1980). *Instrument enrichment: An intervention program for cognitive modifiability*. Baltimore: University Park Press.

Feuerstein, R., Rand, Y., Hoffman, M., Hoffman, M., & Miller, R. (1979). Cognitive modifiability in retarded adolescents: Effects of instrumental enrichment. *American Journal of Mental Deficiency, 83*, 539–550.

Fichter, M. M., Wallace, C. J., Liberman, R. P., & Davis, J. R. (1976). Improving social interaction in a chronic psychotic using discriminated avoidance ("nagging"): Experimental analysis and generalization. *Journal of Applied Behavior Analysis, 9*, 377–386.

Finch, A. J., & Eastman, E. S. (1983). A multimethod approach to measuring anger in children. *The Journal of Psychology, 115*, 55–60.

Finch, B. E., & Wallace, C. J. (1977). Successful interpersonal skills training with schizophrenic inpatients. *Journal of Consulting and Clinical Psychology, 45*, 885–890.

Fincham, F. D., Beach, S. R., & Baucom, D. H. (1987). Attribution processes in distressed and nondistressed couples: Self-partner attribution differences. *Journal of Personality and Social Psychology, 52*, 739–748.

Fincham, F. D., & Bradbury, T. N. (1987). The impact of attributions in marriage. A longitudinal analysis. *Journal of Personality and Social Psychology, 53*, 510–517.

Finley, W. W. (1976). Effects of sham feedback following successful SMR training in an epileptic: Follow-up study. *Biofeedback and Self-Regulation, 1*, 227–235.

Finney, J. W., Lemanek, K. L., Cataldo, M. F., Katz, H. P., & Fugua, R. W. (1989). Pediatric psychology in primary health care: Brief targeted therapy for recurrent abdominal pain. *Behavior Therapy, 20*, 283–291.

Fishbein, J. E., & Wasik, B. H. (1981). Effect of the good behavior game on disruptive library behavior. *Journal of Applied Behavior Analysis, 14*, 89–93.

Fisher, E. B., & Winkler, R. C. (1975). Self-control over intrusive experiences. *Journal of Consulting and Clinical Psychology, 6*, 911–916.

Flanders, J. (1968). A review of research on imitative behavior. *Psychological Bulletin, 69*, 316–337.

Flavell, J. H. (1976). Metacognitive aspects of problem-solving. In L. B. Resnick (Ed.), *The nature of intelligence*. Hillsdale, NJ: Lawrence Erlbaum.

Flay, B. R., Johnson, C. A., & Hansen, W. B. (1984). Evaluation of a mass media enhanced smoking prevention and cessation program. In J. P. Baggaley & J. Sharpe (Eds.), *Experimental research in TV instruction* (Vol. 5). Montreal, Canada: Concordia University.

Fleischman, M. J. (1981). A replication of Patterson's "Interventions for boys with conduct problems". *Journal of Consulting and Clinical Psychology, 49*, 342–351.

Fleischman, M. J., & Szykula, S. A. (1981). A community setting replication of a social learning treatment for aggressive children. *Behavior Therapy, 12*, 115–122.

Foa, E. B., Kozak, M. J., Steketee, G. S., & McCarthy, P. R. (1992). Treatment of depression and obsessive-compulsive symptoms in OCD by imipramine and behavior therapy. *British Journal of Clinical Psychology, 31*, 279–292.

Foa, E. B., Rothbaum, B. O., Riggs, D. S., & Murdock, T. B. (1991). Treatment of PTSD in rape victims: A comparison between cognitive-behavioral procedures and counseling. *Journal of Consulting and Clinical Psychology, 59*, 715–723.

Foa, E. G., & Steketee, G. A. (1979). Obsessive-compulsives: Conceptual issues and treatment interventions. In M. Hersen, R. M. Eisler, & P. M. Miller (Eds.), *Progress in behavior modification* (Vol. 8, pp. 1–53). New York: Academic Press.

Foa, E. B., Steketee, G. S., & Ozarow, B. (1985). Behavior therapy with obsessive-compulsives: From theory to treatment. In M. Mavissakalian (Ed.), *Obsessive-compulsive disorder: Psychological and pharmacologic treatment*. New York: Plenum.

Fordyce, W. E. (1976). *Behavioral methods for chronic pain and illness*. St Louis, MO: Mosby.

Fordyce, W. E., Brockway, J. A., Bergman, J. A., & Spengler, D. (1986). Acute back pain: A control-group comparison of behavioral vs. traditional management methods. *Journal of Behavioral Medicine, 9*, 209–217.

Forehand, R., Cheney, T., & Yoder, P. (1974). Parent behavior training: Effects on the noncompliance of a deaf child. *Journal of Behaviour Therapy and Experimental Psychiatry, 5*, 281–283.

Forehand, R., & King, H. E. (1974). Preschool children's noncompliance: Effects of short-term therapy. *Journal of Community Psychology, 2*, 42–44.

Forehand, R., & King, H. E. (1977). Noncompliant children: Effects of parent training on behavior and attitude. *Behavior Modification, 1*, 93–108.

Forehand, R., King, H. E., Peed, S., & Yoder, P. (1975). Mother-child interactions: Comparison of a noncompliant clinic group and a nonclinic group. *Behaviour Research and Therapy, 13*, 79–84.

Forehand, R., Lautenschlager, G. J., Faust, J., & Graziano, W. G. (1986). Parent perceptions and parent-child interactions in clinic-referred children: A preliminary investigation of the effects of maternal depressive moods. *Behaviour Research and Therapy, 24*, 73–75.

Forehand, R., & Long, N. (1988). Outpatient treatment of the acting out child: Procedures, long term follow-up data, and clinical problems. *Advances in Behaviour Research and Therapy 10*, 129–177.

Forehand, R., & McMahon, R. (1981). *Helping the noncompliant child: A clinician's guide to parent training*. New York: Guilford.

Forehand, R., Rogers, T., McMahon, R., Wells, K., & Griest, D. (1981). Teaching parents to modify child behavior problems: An examination of some follow-up data. *Journal of Pediatric Psychology, 6*, 313–322.

Forehand, R., Sturgis, E. T., McMahon, R. J., Aguar, D., Green, K., Wells, K., & Breiner, J. (1979). Parent behavioral training to modify child noncompliance: Treatment generalization across time and from home to school. *Behavior Modification, 3*, 3–25.

Forster, J. L., Jeffrey, R. W., Schmid, T. L., & Kramer, F. M. (1988). Preventing weight gain in adults: A pound of prevention. *Health Psychology, 7*, 515–525.

Foster, S., Prinz, R., & O'Leary, K. D. (1983). Impact of problem-solving communication training and generalization programming procedures on family conflict. *Child and Family Behavior Therapy, 5*, 1–23.

Foster, S. L., & Robin, A. L. (1989). Parent-adolescent conflict. In E. Mash & R. A. Barkley (Eds.), *Treatment of childhood disorders* (pp. 493–528). New York: Guilford.

Fowler, R. D. (1990). B. F. Skinner: Farewell, with admiration and affection. *APA Monitor, 21*(10), 2.

Foxx, R. M., & Azrin, N. H. (1972). Restitution: A method ofeliminating aggressive-disruptive behavior of mentally retarded and brain-damaged patients. *Behavior Research and Therapy, 10*, 15–27.

Foxx, R. M., & Azrin, N. H. (1973a). The elimination of self-stimulatory behavior of autistic and retarded children by overcorrection. *Journal of Applied Behavior Analysis, 6*, 1–14.

Foxx, R. M., & Azrin, N. H. (1973b). *Toilet training and the retarded: A rapid program for day and nighttime independent toileting.* Champaign, IL: Research Press.

Foxx, R. M., McMorrow, M. J., Bittle, R. C., & Ness, J. (1986). An analysis of social skills generalization in two settings. *Journal of Applied Behavior Analysis, 19*, 299–306.

Foxx, R. M., & Shapiro, S. T. (1978). The timeout ribbon: A non-exclusionary timeout procedure. *Journal of Applied Behavioral Analysis, 11*, 125–136.

Frame, C., Matson, J. L., Sonis, W. A., Fialkov, M. J., & Kazdin, A. E. (1982). Behavioral treatment of depression in a prepubertal child. *Journal of Behavioral Therapy and Experimental Psychiatry, 13*, 239–243.

Frederickson, L. W., Jenkins, J. O., Foy, D. W., & Eisler, R. M. (1976). Social skills training to modify abusive verbal outbursts in adults. *Journal of Applied Behavior Analysis, 9*, 117–127.

Freedman, B. J., Rosenthal, L., Donahoe, C. P., Schlundt, D. G., & McFall, R. (1978). A social-behavioral analysis of skill deficits in delinquent and nondelinquent adolescent boys. *Journal of Consulting and Clinical Psychology, 46*, 1448–1462.

Freedman, R. R., & Ianni, P. (1983). Role of cold and emotional stress in Raynaud's disease and scleroderma. *British Medical Journal, 287*, 1499–1502.

Freedman, R. R., Ianni, P., & Wenig, P. (1983). Behavioral treatment of Raynaud's disease. *Journal of Consulting and Clinical Psychology, 51*, 539–549.

Freedman, R., Lynn, S. J., Ianni, P., & Hale, P. A. (1981). Biofeedback treatment of Raynaud's disease and phenomenon. *Biofeedback and Self-Regulation, 6*, 355–365.

Freeman, B. J., & Ritvo, E. R. (1976). Parents as paraprofessionals. In E. R. Ritvo (Ed.), *Autism: Diagnosis, current research, and management.* New York: Spectrum.

Freeman, C. P. L., Barry, F., Dunkeld-Turnbull, J., & Henderson, A. (1988). Controlled trial of psychotherapy for bulimia nervosa. *British Medical Journal, 296*, 521–525.

Freud, S. (1962). *Three essays on the theory of female sexuality.* New York: (Work originally published in 1905).

Friday, N. (1973). *My secret garden.* New York: Pocket.

Friedman, J. (1983). *A treatment program for low sexual desire.* Unpublished doctoral dissertation, State University of New York at Stony Brook.

Friedman, R. C., Hurt, S. W., Clarkin, J. F., Corn, R., & Aronoff, M. S. (1983). Symptoms of depression among adolescents and young adults. *Journal of Affective Disorders, 5*, 37–43.

Friman, P., Barnard, J., Altman, K., & Wolf, M. (1986). Parent and teacher use of DRO and DRI to reduce aggressive behavior. *Analysis and Intervention in Developmental Disabilities, 6*, 319–330.

Fromm-Reichman, F. (1948). Notes on the development of treatment of schizophrenics by psychoanalytic psychotherapy. *Psychiatry, 11*, 263–273.

Fuchs, C. Z., & Rehm, L. P. (1977). A self-control behavior therapy program for depression. *Journal of Consulting and Clinical Psychology, 45*, 206–215.

Fuchs, K., Hoch, Z., & Paldi, E. (1978). Hypnodesensitization therapy of vaginismus: In vitro and in vivo methods. In J. LoPiccolo & L. LoPiccolo (Eds.), *Handbook of sex therapy.* New York: Plenum.

Funderburk, B. W., & Eyberg, S. M. (1989). Psychometric characteristics of the Sutter-Eyberg Student Behavior Inventory: A school behavior rating scale for use with preschool children. *Behavioral Assessment, 11*, 297–313.

Funderburk, B. W., Eyberg, S. M., & Behar, L. (1989, August). *Psychometric properties of the SESBI with high-SES Preschoolers.* Presented at the meeting of the American Psychological Association, New Orleans, LA.

Furman, W., Geller, M., Simon, S. J., & Kelly, J. A. (1979). The use of a behavioral rehearsal procedure for teaching job interview skills to psychiatric patients. *Behavior Therapy, 10,* 157–167.

Furomoto, L. (1989). The new history of psychology. In I. S. Cohen (Ed.), *The G. Stanley Hall Lecture Series,* (Vol. 9, pp. 3–34). Washington, D.C.: American Psychological Association.

Gaffney, L. R., & McFall, R. M. (1981). A comparison of social skills in delinquent and nondelinquent adolescent girls using a behavioral role-playing inventory. *Journal of Consulting and Clinical Psychology, 49,* 959–967.

Galassi, J. P., DeLo, J. S., Galassi, M. D., & Bastien, S. (1974). The College Self-Expression Scale: A measure of assertiveness. *Behavior Therapy, 5,* 165–171.

Gallagher, J. J., Scharfman, W., & Bristol, M. M. (1984). The division of responsibilities in families with preschool handicapped and nonhandicapped children. *Journal of the Division of Early Childhood, 8,* 3–11.

Gallup, A. M., & Clark, D. L. (1987). The 19th annual Gallup Poll of the public schools. *Phi Delta Kappan, 68,* 43–59,

Ganley, R. M. (1989). Emotion and eating in obesity: A review of the literature. *International Journal of Eating Disorders, 8,* 343–361.

Garcia, E., & DeHaven, E. D. (1974). Use of operant techniques in the establishment and generalization of language. A review and analysis. *American Journal of Mental Deficiency, 79,* 517–526.

Gardner, J. (1967). Behavior therapy treatment approach to a psychogenic seizure case. *Journal of Consulting and Clinical Psychology, 31,* 209–212.

Gardner, W. I., Cole, C. L., Davidson, D. P, & Karan, O. C. (1986). Reducing aggression in individuals with developmental disabilities. An expanded stimulus control, assessment, and intervention model. *Education and Training of the Mentally Retarded, 21,* 3–12.

Gardos, G., & Cole, J. O. (1976). Maintenance antipsychotic therapy: Is the cure worse than the disease? *American Journal of Psychiatry, 133,* 32–36.

Garling, T., & Valsinger, J. (1986). *Children within environments: Toward a psychology of accident prevention.* New York: Plenum.

Garn, S. M., & Clark, D. C. (1976). Trends in fatness and the origins of obesity. *Pediatrics, 57,* 443–456.

Garner, D. M., Fairburn, C. G., & Davis, R. (1987). Cognitive-behavioral treatment of bulimia nervosa: A critical appraisal. *Behavior Modification, 11,* 398–431.

Garner, D. M., Garfinkle, P. E., & Berris, K. M. (1982). A multidimensional psychotherapy for anorexia nervosa. *International Journal of Eating Disorders, 1,* 3–46.

Garner, D. M., Olmstead, M. P., & Polivy, J. (1983). De-

velopment and validation of a multidimensional eating disorder inventory for anorexia nervosa and bulimia. *International Journal of Eating Disorders, 2,* 15–34.

Gaylord-Ross, R. (1980). A decision model for the treatment of aberrant behavior in applied setting. In W. Sailor, B. Wilcox, & L. Brown (Eds.), *Methods of instruction for severely handicapped students* (pp. 135–158). Baltimore: Paul H. Brookes.

Geller, B., Chestnut, E. C., Miller, M. D., Price, D. T., & Yates, E. (1985). Preliminary data on DSM-III associated features of major depressive disorder in children and adolescents. *American Journal of Psychiatry, 142,* 643–644.

Geller, B., Cooper, T. B., Graham, D. L., Marsteller, F. A., & Bryant, D. M. (1990). Double-blind placebo-controlled study of nortriptyline in depressed adolescents using a "fixed plasma level" design. *Psychopharmacology Bulletin, 26,* 85–90.

Geller, B., Cooper, T. B., McCombs, H. G., Graham, D., & Wells, J. (1989). Double-blind placebo-controlled study of Nortriptyline in depressed children using a 'fixed plasma level' design. *Psychopharmacology Bulletin, 25,* 101–108.

Gersten, R. M., Carnine, D. W., & Woodward, J. (1987). Direct instruction research: The third decade. *Remedial and Special Education, 8,* 48–56.

Gersten, R. M., Keating, T., & Becker, W. C. (1988). The continued impact of the Direct Instruction model: Longitudinal studies of follow through students. *Education and Treatment of Children, 11,* 318–327.

Gersten, R., Woodward, J., & Darch, C. (1986). Direct instruction: A research-based approach to curriculum design and teaching. *Exceptional Children, 53,* 17–31.

George, W. H., & Marlatt, G. A. (1983). Alcoholism: The evolution of a behavioral perspective. In M. Galanter et al. (Eds.), *Recent advances in alcoholism* (Vol 1, pp. 105–138). New York: Plenum.

Gil, K. M., Ross, S. L., & Keefe, F. J. (1988). Behavioral treatment of chronic pain: Four pain management protocols. In R. D. France & K. R. R. Krishnan (Eds.), *Chronic pain* (pp. 376–413). Washington, DC: American Psychiatric Press.

Gilbert, B. A., Johnson, S. B., Spillar, R., McCallum, M., Silverstein, J. H., & Rosenbloom, A. (1982). The effects of a peer modeling film on children learning to self-inject insulin. *Behavior Therapy, 13,* 186–193.

Gilchrist, L. D., Gillmore, M. R., & Lohr, M. J. (1990). Drug use among pregnant adolescents. *Journal of Consulting and Clinical Psychology, 58,* 402–407.

Gilchrist, L. D., Schinke, P., Bobo, J. R., & Snow, W. H. (1986). Self-control skills for preventing smoking. *Addictive Behaviors, 11,* 169–174.

Giles, S. L. (1978). Separate and combined effects of biofeedback training and brief individual psychotherapy in the treatment of gastrointestinal disorders. *Dissertation Abstracts International, 39,* 2495B (University of Colorado—Boulder, University Micro-films No. 7820511).

Giles, T. R., Young, R. R., & Young, D. E. (1985). Behavioral treatment of severe bulimia. *Behavior Therapy, 16,* 393–405.

Gittleman, R. (1980). The role of psychological tests for differential diagnosis in child psychiatry. *Journal of the American Academy of Child Psychiatry, 19,* 413–438.

Gittleman, R. Mannuzza, S., Shenker, R., & Bonagura, N. (1985). Hyperactive boys almost grown up. *Archives of General Psychiatry, 42,* 937–947.

Gittleman-Klein, R., Abikoff, H., Pollack, E., Klein, D., Katz, S., Mattes, J. (1980). A controlled trial of behavior modification and methylphenidate in hyperactive children. In C. Whalen & B. Henker (Eds.), *Hyperactive children: The social ecology of identification and treatment.* New York: Academic Press.

Glaser, R., Rice, J., Sheridan, J., Fertel, R., Stout, J., Speicher, C., Pinsky, D., Kotur, M., Post, A., Beck, M., & Kiecolt-Glaser, J. (1986). Stress-related immune suppression: Health implications. *Brain, Behavior and Immunity, 1,* 7–20.

Glaser, R., Rice, J., Speicher, C. E., Stout, J. C., & Kiecolt-Glaser, J. (1987). Stress depresses interferon production by leukocytes concomitant with a decrease in natural killer cell activity. *Behavioral Neuroscience, 100,* 675–678.

Glasgow, R. E., & Arkowitz, H. (1975). The behavioral assessment of male and female social competence in dyadic heterosexual interactions. *Behavior Therapy, 6,* 488–498.

Glass, C. R., Gottman, J. M., & Shmurak, S. H. (1976). Response-acquisition and cognitive self-statement modification approaches to dating-skills training. *Journal of Counseling Psychology, 23,* 520–526.

Glasser, W. (1976). *Positive addiction.* New York: Harper & Row.

Glueck, S., & Glueck, E. (1950). *Unraveling juvenile delinquency.* Cambridge, MA: Harvard.

Glueck, S., & Glueck, E. (1968). *Delinquents and nonde-linquents in perspective.* Cambridge, MA: Harvard.

Glynn, S. M. (1990). Token economy approaches for psychiatric patients: Progress and pitfalls over 25 years. *Behavior Modification, 14,* 383–407.

Glynn, S. M., & Mueser, K. T. (1992). Social learning for the seriously mentally ill. In R.P. Liberman (Ed.), *Rehabilitation of the seriously mentally ill.* New York: Plenum.

Godaert, L. R. R. (1982). Relaxation treatment for hypertension. In R. S. Surwit, R. B. Williams, A. Steptoe, & R. Biersner (Eds.), *Behavioral treatment of disease.* New York: Plenum.

Gold, M. W. (1972). Stimulus factors in skill training of retarded adolescents on a complex assembly task: Acquisition, transfer, and retention. *American Journal of Mental Deficiency, 76,* 517–526.

Gold, M. W. (1976). Task analysis of a complex assembly task by the retarded blind. *Exceptional Children, 43,* 78–84.

Gold, M. W., & Barclay, C. R. (1973). The effects of verbal labels on the acquisition and retention of a complex assembly task. *The Training School Bulletin, 70,* 38–42.

Goldfried, M. R. (November, 1990). *Psychotherapy integration: A mid-life crisis for behavior therapy.* Invited address presented at the meeting of the Association for Advancement of Behavior Therapy, San Francisco.

Goldfried, M. R. & Goldfried, A. P. (1975). Cognitive change methods. In F. H. Kanfer & A. P. Goldstein (Eds.), *Helping people change* (pp. 89–116). London: MacMillan.

Goldman, H. H. (1982). Mental illness and family burden: A public health perspective. *Hospital and Community Psychiatry, 33,* 557–560.

Goldman, H. H. (1984). Epidemiology. In J. A. Talbott (Ed.), *The chronic mental patient: Five years later.* Orlando FL: Grune & Stratton.

Goldman, H. H., Adams, N. H., & Taube, C. A. (1983). Deinstitutionalization: The data demythologized. *Hospital and Community Psychiatry, 34,* 129–134.

Goldsmith, J. B., & McFall, R. M. (1975). Development and evaluation of an interpersonal skill-training program for psychiatric inpatients. *Journal of Abnormal Psychology, 84,* 51–58.

Goldstein, H. S. (1984). Parental composition, supervision, and conduct problems in youths 12 to 17 years old. *Journal of the American Academy of Child Psychiatry, 23,* 679–684.

Goldstein, J. M. (1988). Gender differences in the course of schizophrenia. *American Journal of Psychiatry, 145,* 684–689.

Goldstein, M. J., & Doane, J. A. (1982). Family factors in the onset, course, and treatment of schizophrenic spectrum disorders: An update on current research. *Journal of Nervous and Mental Disease, 170,* 692–700.

Goldstrom I. D., & Manderscheid R. W. (1981). The chronically mental ill: A descriptive analysis from the uniform client data instrument. *Community Support Service Journal, 2,* 4–9.

Gordon, N. (1978). Duration of treatment of childhood epilepsy. *Developmental Medicine and Child Neurology, 24,* 84–88.

Gormally, J., Black, S., Darton, S., & Rardin, D. (1982). The assessment of binge eating severity among obese persons. *Addictive Behaviors, 7,* 47–55.

Gorman, J. M., Fyer, M. R., Goetz, R., Askanazi, J., Liebowitz, M. R., Fyer, A. J., Kinney, J., & Klein, D. F. (1988). Ventilatory physiology of patients with panic disorder. *Archives of General Psychiatry, 45,* 31–39.

Gotlib, I. H., & Colby, C. A. (1987). *Treatment of depression: An interpersonal systems approach.* New York: Pergamon.

Gottman, J. M. (1979). *Marital interaction.* New York: Academic Press.

Gottman, J. M., & Krokoff, L. J. (1989). The relationship between marital interaction and material satisfaction: A longitudinal view. *Journal of Consulting and Clinical Psychology, 57,* 47–52.

Gottman, J. M., Notarius, C., Markman, H., Bank, S., Yoppi, B., & Rubin, M. E. (1976). Behavior exchange theory and marital decision making. *Journal of Personality and Social Psychology, 34,* 14–24.

Gottesman, I. I. (1968). Severity/concordance and diagnostic refinement in the Maudsley-Bethlem schizophrenic twin study. In D. Rosenthal & S. S. Kety (Eds.), *The transmission of schizophrenia.* New York: Pergamon.

Goyette, C. H, Conners, C. K., & Ulrich, R. F. (1978). Normative data for Revised Conners Parent and Teacher Rating Scales. *Journal of Abnormal Child Psychology, 6,* 221–236.

Graham, S. (1990). Skinner gave one last lesson in scholarship, human will. *APA Monitor, 21,* 3.

Graves, T., Meyers, A. W., & Clark, L. (1988). An evaluation of parental problem-solving training in the behavioral treatment of childhood obesity. *Journal of Consulting and Clinical Psychology, 56,* 246–250.

Green, B. G., Bailey, J. S., & Barber, F. (1981). An analysis and reduction of disruptive behavior on school buses. *Journal of Applied Behavior Analysis, 14,* 177–199.

Greenspan, M. J., & Feltz, D. L. (1989). Psychological interventions with athletes in competitive situations: A review. *The Sport Psychologist, 3,* 219–236.

Greenwald, D. P. (1977). The behavioral assessment of differences in social skill and social anxiety in female college students. *Behavior Therapy, 8,* 925–937.

Greenwood, C. R. (1981). Peer-oriented behavioral technology and ethical issues. In P. Strain (Ed.), *The utilization of peers as behavior change agents* (pp. 327–360). New York: Plenum.

Greenwood, C. R. (1991). Longitudinal analysis of time, engagement, and achievement in at-risk versus non-risk students. *Exceptional Children, 57,* 521–535.

Greenwood, C. R., Carta, J. J., & Atwater, J. (1991). Ecobehavioral analysis in the classroom: Review and implications. *Journal of Behavioral Education, 1,* 59–77.

Greenwood, C. R., Carta, J. J., & Hall, R. V. (1988). The use of tutoring strategies in classroom management and educational instruction. *School Psychology Review,* 258–275.

Greenwood, C. R., Delquadri, J., & Hall, R. V. (1984). Opportunity to respond and student academic performance. In W. Heward, T. Heron, D. Hill, & J. Trap-Porter

(Eds.), *Focus on behavior analysis in education* (pp. 58–88). Columbus, OH: Charles E. Merrill.

Greenwood, C. R., Delquadri, J., & Hall, R. V. (1989). The longitudinal effects of classwide peer tutoring. *Journal of Educational Psychology, 81,* 371–383.

Greenwood, C. R., Dinwiddie, G., Terry, B., Wade, L., Stanley, S., Thibadeau, S., & Delquadri, J. (1984). Teacher versus peer-mediated instruction: An ecobehavioral analysis of achievement outcomes. *Journal of Applied Behavior Analysis, 17,* 521–538.

Greenwood, C. R., & Hops, H. (1981). Group contingencies and peer behavior change. In P. Strain (Ed.), *The utilization of classroom peers as behavior change agents* (pp. 189–259). New York: Plenum.

Greenwood, C. R., Hops, H., Delquadri, J., & Guild (1974). Group contingencies for group consequences: A further analysis. *Journal of Applied Behavior Analysis, 7,* 413–425.

Greenwood, C. R., Hops, H., Walker, H. M., Guild, J. J., Stokes, J., Young, K., Keleman, K. S., & Willardson, M. (1979). Standardized classroom management program: Social validation and replication studies in Utah and Oregon. *Journal of Applied Behavior Analysis, 12,* 235–253.

Greenwood, C. R., Hops, H., & Walker, H. M. (1977). Program for academic survival skills (PASS): Effects on student behavior and achievement. *Journal of School Psychology, 15,* 25–35.

Greenwood, C. R., Maheady, L., & Carta, J. J. (1991). Peer tutoring in the regular education classroom. In G. Stoner, M. R. Shinn, & H. M. Walker (Eds.), *Intervention for achievement and behavior problems.* Washington, DC: National Association of School Psychologists.

Greenwood, C. R. Terry, B., Arreaga-Mayer, & Finney, R. (1992). The classwide peer tutoring program: Implementation factors moderating students' achievement. *Journal of Applied Behavior Analysis, 25,* 101–116.

Greeson, L. E., & Jens, K. G. (1977). Instructional modeling and the development of visual- and verbal-mediation skills by TMR children. *American Journal of Mental Deficiency, 82,* 58–64.

Griest, D. G., Forehand, R., Rogers, T., Breiner, J., Furey, W., & Williams, C. A. (1982). Effects of parent enhancement therapy on the treatment outcome and generalization of a parent training program. *Behaviour Research and Therapy, 20,* 429–436.

Griest, D. G., & Wells, K. C. (1983). Behavior family therapy for conduct disorders in children. *Behavior Therapy, 14,* 37–53.

Griez, E., & van den Hout, M. A. (1986). CO_2 inhalation in the treatment of panic attacks. *Behaviour Research and Therapy, 24,* 145–150.

Grilo, C. M., Shiffman, S., & Wing, R. R. (1989). Relapse crises and coping among dieters. *Journal of Consulting and Clinical Psychology, 57,* 488–495.

Groden, J., & Cautela, J. R. (1984). Use of imagery procedures with students labeled "trainable retarded". *Psychological Reports, 54,* 60–66.

Groot, M., & Prins, P. (1989). Children's social behavior: Reliability and concurrent validity of two self-report measures. *Journal of Psychopathology and Behavioral Assessment, 11,* 195–207.

Gross, A. M. (1984). Behavioral interviewing. In T. H. Ollendick & M. Hersen (Eds.), *Child behavioral assessment* (pp. 61–79). New York: Pergamon.

Gross, A. M., Brigham, T. A., Hopper, C., & Bologna, N. C. (1980). Self-management and social skills training: A study with predelinquent and delinquent youths. *Criminal Justice and Behavior, 7,* 161–184.

Grossman, H. (Ed.) (1983). *Classification in mental retardation* (Rev.). Washington, DC: American Association on Mental Deficiency.

Gualtieri, C. T., & Hawk, B. (1980). Tardive dyskinesia and other drug-induced movement disorders among handicapped children and youth. *Applied Research in Mental Retardation, 1,* 55–69.

Guthrie, E. R. (1952). *The psychology of learning.* New York: Harper.

Guy, W. (1976). *ECDEU assessment manual for Psychopharmacology.* Washington, DC: Department of Health, Education, and Welfare.

Haenlein, M., & Caul, W. F. (1987). Attention deficit disorder with hyperactivity: A specific hypothesis of reward dysfunction. *Journal of the American Academy of Child and Adolescent Psychiatry, 26,* 356–362.

Hahlweg, K., Helmes, B., Steffen, G., Schindler, L., Revenstorf, D., & Kunert, H. (1979). Beobachtungssstem für partnerschaftliche interaktion. *Diagnostica, 25,* 191–207.

Hahlweg, K., & Markman, H. J. (1988). Effectiveness of behavioral marital therapy: Empirical status of behavioral techniques in preventing and alleviating marital distress. *Journal of Consulting and Clinical Psychology, 56,* 440–447.

Hahlweg, K. Schindler, L., Revenstorf, D., & Brengelmann, J. C. (1984). The Munich marital therapy study. In K. Hahlweg & N. S. Jacobson (Eds.), *Marital interaction: Analysis and modification.* New York: Guilford.

Halford, W. R. (1991). Beyond Expressed Emotion: Behavioral assessment of family interaction associated with the course of schizophrenia. *Behavioral Assessment, 13,* 99–123.

Halford, W. R., & Hayes, R. (1991). Psychological rehabilitation of chronic schizophrenic patients: Recent findings on social skills training and family psychoeducation. *Clinical Psychology Review, 11,* 23–44.

Hall, C. S., & Lindzey, G. (1970). *Theories of personality.* New York: Wiley.

Hall, E. G., & Erffmeyer, E. S. (1983). The effects of visuo-motor behavior rehearsal with videotaped modeling on free throw accuracy of intercollegiate female basketball players. *Journal of Sport Psychology, 5,* 343–346.

Hall, R. G., Sachs, D. P. L., & Hall, S. M. (1979). Medical risk and therapeutic effectiveness of rapid smoking. *Behavior Therapy, 10,* 249–259.

Hall, R. V., Axelrod, S., Tyler, L., Grief, E., Jones, F. C., & Robertson, R. (1972). Modification of behavior problems in the home with a parent as observer and experimenter. *Journal of Applied Behavior Analysis, 5,* 53–64.

Hall, R. V., & Copeland, R. (1972). The responsive teaching model: A first step in shaping school personnel as behavior modification specialists. In F. W. Clark, D. R. Evans, & L. A. Hamerlynck (Eds.), *Implementing behavioral programs for schools and clinics* (pp. 125–150). Champaign, IL: Research Press.

Hall, R. V., Delquadri, J., Greenwood, C., & Thurston, L. (1982). The importance of opportunity to respond in children's academic success. In E. D. Edgar, N. Haring, J. R. Jenkins, & C. Pious (Eds.), *Serving young handicapped children: Issues and research* (pp. 107–149). Austin, TX: Pro-Ed.

Hall, R. V., Fox, R., Willard, D., Goldsmith, L., Emerson, M., Owen, M., Davis, F., & Porcia, E. (1971). The teacher as observer and experimenter in the modification of disputing and talking-out behaviors. *Journal of Applied Behavior Analysis, 4,* 141–149.

Hall, R.V., Lund, D., & Jackson, D. (1968). Effects of teacher attention on study behavior. *Journal of Applied Behavior Analysis, 1,* 1–12.

Halmi, K. A., Falk, J. R., & Schwartz, E. (1981). Binge-eating and vomiting: A survey of a college population. *Psychological Medicine, 11,* 697–796.

Hamilton, M. (1960). A rating scale for depression. *Journal of Neurology, Neurosurgery, and Psychiatry, 23,* 56–62.

Hanf, C. (1986 September). A two stage program for modifying maternal controlling during mother-child interaction. Paper presented at the Western Psychological Association Meeting. Vancouver, BC.

Hanf, C., & King, J. (1973). *Facilitating parent-child interaction: A two-stage training model.* Unpublished manuscript, University of Oregon Medical School.

Hanson, C. L., Henggeler, S. W., Haefele, W. F., & Rodick, J. D. (1984). Demographic, individual, and family relationship correlates of serious and repeated crime among adolescents and their siblings. *Journal of Consulting and Clinical Psychology, 52,* 528–538.

Haracz, J. L. (1982). The dopamine hypothesis: An overview of studies with schizophrenic patients. *Schizophrenia Bulletin*, *8*, 438–469.

Haring, T. G., & Kennedy, C. H. (1990). Contextual control of problem behavior in students with severe disabilities. *Journal of Applied Behavior Analysis*, *23*, 235–243.

Harrington, R., Fudge, H., Rutter, M., Pickles, A., & Hill, J. 1990). Adult outcomes of childhood and adolescent depression I: Psychiatric status. *Archives of General Psychiatry*, *47*, 465–473.

Harris, J. G. (1984). Prognosis in schizophrenia. In A. S. Bellack (Ed.), *Schizophrenia: Treatment, management and rehabilitation*. Orlando FL: Grune & Stratton.

Harris, R. T. (1983). Bulimarexia and related serious eating disorders with medical complications. *Annals of Internal Medicine*, *99* (Part 2), 800–807.

Harrison, R. (1986). Severe behavior problems. In L. Teri & P. Lewinsohn (Eds.), *Geropsychological assessment and treatment*, (pp. 125–140). New York: Springer.

Harrow, M., & Quinlan, D. M. (1985). *Disordered thinking and schizophrenic psychopathology*. New York: Gardner.

Hartman, W. E., & Fithian, M. A. (1972). *The treatment of sexual dysfunction*. Long Beach, CA: Center for Marital and Sexual Studies.

Hartsough, C. S., & Lambert, N. M. (1985). Medical factors in hyperactive and normal children: Prenatal, developmental, and health history findings. *American Journal of Orthopsychiatry*, *55*, 190–201.

Haslam, M. T. (1974). The relationship between the effect of lactate infusion on anxiety states and their amelioration by carbon dioxide inhalation. *British Journal of Psychiatry*, *125*, 88–90.

Hathaway, S. R., & McKinley, J. C. (1951). *The Minnesota Multiphasic Personality Inventory Manual*. New York: Psychological Corporation.

Hauser, S. T., Jacobson, A. M., Lavori, P., Wolfsdorf, J. I., Herskowitz, R., D., Milley, J. E., & Bliss, R. (1990). Adherence among children and adolescents with insulin-dependent diabetes mellitus over a four-year longitudinal follow-up: II. Immediate and long-term linkages with the family milieu. *Journal of Pediatric Psychology*, *15*, 527–542.

Hayes, S. C. (1987). A contextual approach to therapeutic change. In N. S. Jacobson (Ed.), *Psychotherapists in clinical practice: Cognitive and behavior perspectives* (pp. 327–387). New York: Guilford.

Hechtman, L., Weiss, G., & Perlman, T. (1984). Young adult outcome of hyperactive children who received long-term stimulant treatment. *Journal of the American Academy of Child Psychiatry*, *23*, 261–269.

Hechtman, L., Weiss, G., Perlman, R., & Amsel, R. (1984). Hyperactives as young adults: Initial predictors of outcome. *Journal of the American Academy of Child Psychiatry*, *23*, 250–260.

Hedberg, A. G. (1973). The treatment of chronic diarrhea by systematic desensitization: A case report. *Journal of Behaviour Therapy and Experimental Psychiatry*, *4*, 67–68.

Hedberg, A. G., & Schlong, A. (1973). Eliminating fainting by school children during mass inoculation clinics. *Nursing Research*, *22*, 352–353.

Heiman, J. R., Gladue, B. A., Roberts, C. W., & LoPiccolo, J. (1986). Historical and current factors discriminating sexually functional from sexually dysfunctional married couples. *Journal of Marital and Family Therapy*, *12*(2), 163–174.

Heiman, J. R., & LoPiccolo, J. (1988). *Becoming orgasmic: A personal and sexual growth program for women* (rev. ed.) Englewood Cliffs, NJ: Prentice-Hall.

Heiman, J. R., LoPiccolo, L., & LoPiccolo, J. (1976). *Becoming orgasmic: A sexual growth program for women*. Englewood Cliffs, NJ: Prentice Hall.

Heller, T. (1985). Residential relocation and reactions of elderly mentally retarded persons. In M. P. Janicki & H. M. Wisniewski (Eds.), *Aging and the developmental disabilities* (pp. 367–378). Baltimore: Brookes.

Henley, T. B., Johnson, M. G., & Jones, E. M. (1989). Definitions of psychology. *The Psychological Record*, *39*, 143–152.

Herjanic, B., & Reich, W. (1982). Development of a structured psychiatric interview for children: Agreement between child and parent on individual symptoms. *Journal of Abnormal Child Psychology*, *10*, 307–324.

Hermelin, B., & O'Connor, N. (1970). *Psychological experiments with autistic children*. Oxford: Pergamon.

Herrnstein, R. J., & Loveland, D. H. (1964). Complex visual concept in the pigeon. *Science*, *146*, 549–551.

Hersen, M., Bellack, A. S., & Turner, S. M. (1978). Assessment of assertiveness in female psychiatric patients: Motor and autonomic measures. *Journal of Behavior Therapy and Experimental Psychiatry*, *9*, 11–16.

Herz, M. I., & Melville, C. (1980). Relapse in schizophrenia. *American Journal of Psychiatry*, *137*, 801–805.

Hetherington, E. M., & Martin, B. (1979). Family interaction. In H. C. Quay & J. S. Werry (Eds.), *Psychopathological disorders of childhood* (2nd. ed.). New York: Wiley.

Higgins, R. L., & Marlatt, G. A. (1975). Fear of interpersonal evaluation as a determinant of alcohol consumption in male social drinkers. *Journal of Abnormal Psychology*, *84*, 644–651.

Hilford, N. G. (1975). Self-initiated behavior change by depressed women following verbal behavior therapy. *Behavior Therapy*, *6*, 703.

Hilgard, E. R. (1987). *Psychology in America: A historical survey*. New York: Harcourt Brace Jovanovich.

Hillenberg, J. B., & DiLorenzo, T. M. (1987). Stress management training in health psychology practice: Critical clinical issues. *Professional Psychology, 18*, 402–404.

Himadi, W. G., Cerny, J. A., Barlow, D. H., Cohen, S. L., & O'Brien, G. T. (1986). The relationship of marital adjustment to agoraphobia treatment outcome. *Behaviour Research and Therapy, 24*, 107–115.

Hinshaw, S. P., Henker, B., & Whalen, C. K. (1984). Cognitive-behavioral and pharmacologic interventions for hyperactive boys: Comparative and combined effects. *Journal of Consulting and Clinical Psychology, 52*, 739–749.

Hobbs, T. R., & Holt, M. D. (1976). The effects of token reinforcement on the behavior of delinquents in cottage settings. *Journal of Applied Behavior Analysis, 9*, 189–198.

Hodges, K., McKnew, D., Cytryn, L., Stern, L., & Kline, J. (1982). The Child Assessment Schedule (CAS) diagnostic interview: A report on reliability and validity. *Journal of the American Academy of Child Psychiatry, 21*, 468–473.

Hodgson, R. J., & Rankin, H. J. (1983). Cue exposure and relapse prevention. In W. M. Hay & P. E. Nathan (Eds.), *Clinical case studies in the behavioral treatment of alcoholism*, (pp. 207–226). New York: Plenum.

Hoelscher, T. J., & Lichstein, K. L. (1984). Behavioral assessment and treatment of child migraine: Implications for clinical reseach and practice. *Headache, 24*, 94–103.

Hogarty, G. E., Anderson, C. M., & Reiss, D. J. (1987). Family psychoeducation, social skills training, and medication in schizophrenia: The long and short of it. *Psychopharmacology Bulletin, 23*, 12–13.

Hogarty, G. E., Anderson, C. M., Reiss, D. J., Kornblith, S. J., Greenwald, D. P., Javna, C. D., & Madonia, M. J. (1986). Family psycho-education, social skills training, and maintenance chemotherapy: I. One year effects of a controlled study on relapse and expressed emotion. *Archives of General Psychiatry, 45*, 797–805.

Hogarty, G. E., Anderson, C. M., Reiss, D. J., Kornblith, S. J., Greenwald, D. P., Ulrich, R. F., & Carter, M. (1991). Family psychoeducation, social skills training, and maintenance chemotherapy in the aftercare treatment of schizophrenia. II. Two-year effects of a controlled study on relapse and adjustment. *Archives of General Psychiatry, 48*, 340–347.

Hogarty, G. E., & Flesher, S. (1992). Cognitive remediation in schizophrenia: Proceed . . . with caution! *Schizophrenia Bulletin, 18*, 51–58.

Hogarty, G. E., Schooler, N. R., Ulrich, R., Mussare, F., Ferro, P., & Herron, E. (1979). Fluphenazine and social therapy in the aftercare of schizophrenic patients: Relapse analyses of a two-year controlled study of fluphenazine decanoate and fluphenazine hydrochloride. *Archives of General Psychiatry, 36*, 1283–1294.

Hoiberg, A., Berard, S., Watten, R. H., & Caine, C. (1984). Correlates of weight loss in treatment and at follow-up. *International Journal of Obesity, 8*, 457–465.

Holden, A. E., & Barlow, D. H. (1986). Heart rate and heart rate variability recorded in vivo in agoraphobics and nonphobics. *Behavior Therapy, 17*, 26–42.

Hollon, S. D. (1981). Comparisons and combinations with alternative approaches. In L. P. Rehm (Ed.), *Behavior therapy for depression: Present status and future directions* (pp. 3–71). New York: Academic Press.

Hollon, S. D. (in press). Predicting outcome vs. differential response: Matching clients to treatments. In R. Pickens (Ed.), *Matching clients to treatments: A critical review*. Rockville, Maryland: National Institute on Drug Abuse.

Hollon, S. D., & Beck, A. T. (1978). Psychotherapy and drug therapy: Comparison and combinations. In S. L Garfield & A. E. Bergin (Eds.), *Handbook of psychotherapy and behavior change: An empirical analysis*, (2nd ed., pp. 437–490). New York: Wiley.

Hollon, S. D., & Beck, A. T. (1979). Cognitive therapy of depression. In P. C. Kendall and S. D. Hollon (Eds.), *Cognitive-behavioral interventions: Theory, research, and procedures* (pp. 153–203). New York: Academic Press.

Hollon, S. D., & Beck, A. T. (1986). Cognitive and cognitive-behavioral therapies. In S. L. Garfield & A. E. Bergin (Eds.), *Handbook of psychotherapy and behavior change: An empirical analysis*, (3rd ed., pp. 443–482). New York: Wiley.

Hollon, S. D., DeRubeis, R. J., & Evans, M. D. (1987). Causal mediation of change in treatment in depression: Discriminating between nonspecificity and noncausality. *Psychological Bulletin, 102*, 139–149.

Hollon, S. D., DeRubeis, R. J., Evans, M. D., Wiemer, M. J., Garvey, M. J., Grove, W. M., & Tuason, V. B. (1992). Cognitive therapy and pharmacotherapy for depression: Singly and in combination. *Archives of General Psychiatry, 49*, 774–781.

Hollon, S. D., DeRubeis, R. J., & Seligman, M. E. P. (1992). Cognitive therapy and the prevention of depression. *Applied and Preventive Psychology, 1*, 89–95.

Hollon, S. D., Evans, M. D., Elkin, I., & Lowery, A. (1984, May). *System for rating therapies for depression*. Paper presented at the Annual Meeting of the American Psychiatric Association, Los Angeles.

Hollon, S. D., & Garber, J. (1988). Cognitive therapy: A social-cognitive perspective. In L. Y. Abramson (Ed.), *Social-personal inferences in clinical psychology*. New York: Guilford.

Hollon, S. D., & Garber, J. (1990). Cognitive therapy of

depression: A social-cognitive perspective. *Personality and Social Psychology Bulletin, 16,* 58–73.

Hollon, S. D., Shelton, R. C., & Loosen, P. T. (1991). Cognitive therapy in relation to pharmacotherapy for depression. *Journal of Consulting and Clinical Psychology, 59,* 88–99.

Holmes, C. S., & Rahe, R. H. (1967). The social readjustment rating scale. *Journal of Psychosomatic Research, 11,* 213–218.

Holmes, M. R., Hansen, D. J., & St. Lawrence, J. S. (1984). Conversational skills training with aftercare patients in the community: Social validation and generalization. *Behavior Therapy, 15,* 84–100.

Holroyd, K. A. (1986). Recurrent headache. In K. A. Holroyd & R. L. Creer (Eds.), *Self-management of chronic disease: Handbook of clinical interventions and research.* Orlando FL: Academic Press.

Holtzworth-Munroe, A., & Jacobson, N. S. (1985). Causal attributions of married couples: When do they search for causes? What do they conclude when they do? *Journal of Personality and Social Psychology, 48,* 1398–1412.

Hooley, J. (1985). Expressed emotion: A review of the critical literature. *Clinical Psychology Review, 5,* 119–140.

Hoon, E. F., Hoon, P. W., & Wincze, J. (1976). The SAI: An inventory for the measurement of female sexual arousal. *Archives of Sexual Behavior, 5,* 208–215.

Hops, H., Walker, H. M., Fleischman, D. H., Nagoshi, J. T., Omura, R. T., Skindrud, K., & Taylor, J. (1978). CLASS: A standardized in-class program for acting out children. II: Field test evaluations. *Journal of Educational Psychology, 70,* 636–644.

Hops, H., Walker, H. M., & Greenwood, C. R. (1979). PEERS: A program for remediating social withdrawal in school. In L. A. Hamerlynck (Ed.), *Behavioral systems for the developmentally disabled: I. School and family environments* (pp. 48–66). New York: Brunner/Mazel.

Hops, H., Wills, T. A, Patterson, G. R., & Weiss, R. L. (1971). Marital interaction coding system. Unpublished manuscript, University of Oregon.

Horne, A. M., & Van Dyke, B. (1983). Treatment and maintenance of social learning family therapy. *Behavior Therapy, 14,* 606–613.

Horner, R. D., & Keilitz, I. (1975) Training mentally retarded adolescents to brush their teeth. *Journal of Applied Behavior Analysis, 8,* 301–309.

Horner, R. H., & Albin, R. W. (1989). Research on general-case procedures for learners with severe disabilities. *Education and Treatment of Children, 11,* 375–388.

Horner, R. H., & Day, M. H. (1991). The effects of response efficiency on functionally equivalent competing behaviors. *Journal of Applied Behavior Analysis, 24,* 719–732.

Horner, R. H., Dunlap, G., Koegel, R. L., Carr, E. G., Sailor, W., Anderson, J., Albin, R. W., & O'Neill, R. E. (1990). Toward a technology of "nonaversive" behavioral support. *Journal of the Association for Persons with Severe Handicaps, 15,* 125–132.

Horner, R. H., McDonnell, J. J., & Bellamy, G. T. (1986). Teaching generalized behaviors: General-case instruction in simulation and community settings. In R. H. Horner, L. H. Meyer, & H. D. Fredericks (Eds.), *Education of learners with severe handicaps: Exemplary service strategies* (pp. 289–315). Baltimore, MD: Paul H. Brookes.

Horowitz, M. J. (1986). *Stress response syndromes* (2nd ed.). Northvale, NJ: Jason Aronson.

House, B. J., & Zeaman, D. (1963). Miniature experiments in the discrimination learning of retardates. In L. P. Lipsitt & L. Spiker (Eds.), *Advances in child development and behavior* (Vol. 1), New York: Academic Press.

Houts, A. C., & Peterson, J. K. (1986). Treatment of a retentive encopretic child using contingency management and diet modification with stimulus control. *Journal of Pediatric Psychology, 11,* 375–383.

Hoy, E., Weiss, G., Minde, K., & Cohen, N. (1978). The hyperactive child at adolescence: Cognitive, emotional, and social functioning. *Journal of Abnormal Child Psychology, 6,* 311–324.

Hu, T., Igou, J. F., Kaltreider, L., Yu, L. C., Rohner, J. J., Dennis, P., Craighead, E., Hadley, E. C., & Ory, M. G. (1989). A clinical trial of behavior therapy to reduce urinary incontinence in nursing homes. *Journal of the American Medical Association, 261,* 2656–2662.

Huang, S., Plaut, S. M., Taylor, G., & Wareheim, L. E. (1981). Effect of stressful stimulation on the incidence of streptozotocin-induced diabetes in mice. *Psychosomatic Medicine, 43,* 5.

Huesmann, L. R., Eron, L. D., Lefkowitz, M. M., & Walder, L. O. (1984). Stability of aggression over time and generations. *Developmental Psychology, 20,* 1120–1134.

Huesmann, L. R., Lefkowitz, M. M., & Eron, L. D. (1978). Sum of MMPI Scales F, 4, and 9 as a measure of aggression. *Journal of Consulting and Clinical Psychology, 46,* 1071–1078.

Hughes, C. A., & Hendrickson, J. M. (1987). Self-monitoring with at-risk students in the regular class setting. *Education and Treatment of Children, 10,* 225–236.

Hughes, H. M. (1979). Behavior change in children at a therapeutic summer camp as a function of feedback and individual versus group contingencies. *Journal of Abnormal Child Psychology, 7,* 211–219.

Humphreys, L., Forehand, R., McMahon, R., & Roberts, M. (1978). Parent behavioral training to modify child noncompliance: Effects on untreated siblings. *Journal of Behavior Therapy and Experimental Psychiatry, 9,* 235–238.

Hunt, G. M., & Azrin, N. H. (1973). A community-reinforcement approach to alcoholism. *Behavioral Research and Therapy, 11*, 91–104.

Hunt, M. (1974). *Sexual behavior in the 1970's.* Chicago, IL: Playboy.

Huon, G. F., & Brown, L. B. (1985). Evaluating a group treatment for bulimia. *Journal of Psychiatric Research, 19*, 479–483.

Hurst, P. S., Lacey, J. H., & Crisp, A. H. (1977). Teeth, vomiting and diet: A study of the dental characteristics of 17 anorexia nervosa patients. *Postgraduate Medicine, 53*, 298.

Hussian, R. A. (1987). Wandering and disorientation. In L. L. Carstensen & B. A. Edelstein (Eds.), *Handbook of clinical gerontology* (pp. 177–188). New York: Pergamon.

Iammarino, N., Heit, P., & Kaplan, R. (1980). School health curriculum project: Long-term effects on student cigarette smoking and behavior change. *Health Education, 11*, 29–31.

Ince, L. D. (1976). The use of relaxation training and a conditioned stimulus in the elimination of epileptic seizures in a child: A case study. *Journal of Behavior Therapy and Experimental Psychiatry, 7*, 39–42.

Ingersoll, B. (1988). *Your hyperactive child: A parent's guide to coping with attention deficit disorder.* New York: Doubleday.

Ingram, J. A., & Salzberg, H. C. (1988). Cognitive-behavioral approaches to the treatment of alcoholic behavior. In M. Hersen, R. M. Eisler, & P. M. Miller (Eds.), *Progress in Behavior Modification.* Newbury Park, CA: Sage.

Inhelder, B. (1968). *The diagnosis of reasoning in the mentally retarded.* New York: John Day.

Isaacs, C. D. (1982). Treatment of child abuse: A review of the behavioral interventions. *Journal of Applied Behavioral Analysis, 15*, 273–294.

Izard, C. E., Kagan, J., & Zajonc, R. B. (1984). *Emotions, cognition, and behavior.* Cambridge UK: Cambridge University Press.

Izard, C. E., & Blumberg, M. A. (1985). Emotion theory and the role of emotions in anxiety in children and adults. In A. H. Tuma & J. D. Maser (Eds.), *Anxiety and the anxiety disorders.* Hillsdale, NJ: Laurence Erlbaum.

Jackson, P., & Oei, T. P. S. (1978). Social skills training and cognitive restructuring with alcoholics. *Drug and Alcohol Dependence, 3*, 369–374.

Jacob, R. G., O'Leary, K. d., & Rosenbald, C. (1978). Forman and informal classroom settings. Effects on hyperactivity. *Journal of Abnormal Child Psychology, 6*, 47–59.

Jacob, R. G., & Rapport, M. D. (1984). Panic disorder: Medical and psychological parameters. In S. M. Turner (Ed.), *Behavioral theories and treatment of anxiety.* New York: Plenum.

Jacobson, A. M., Hauser, S. T., Lavori, P., Wolfsdorf, J. I., Herskowitz, R. D., Milley, J. E., Bliss, R., Gelfand, E., Wertlieb, D., & Stein, J. (1990). Adherence among children and adolescents with insulin-dependent diabetes mellitus over a four-year longitudinal follow-up: I. The influence of patient coping and adjustment. *Journal of Pediatric Psychology, 15*, 511–526.

Jacobson, N. S. (1977). Problem-solving and contingency contracting in the treatment of marital discord. *Journal of Consulting and Clinical Psychology, 45*, 92–100.

Jacobson, N. S. (1978). Specific and nonspecific factors in the effectiveness of a behavioral approach to the treatment of marital discord. *Journal of Consulting and Clinical Psychology, 46*, 442–452.

Jacobson, N. S. (1981). The assessment of overt behavior. In L. P. Rehm (Ed.), *Behavior therapy for depression* (pp. 279–300). New York: Academic Press.

Jacobson, N. S. (1984). A component analysis of behavioral marital therapy: The relative effectiveness of behavior exchange and communication/problem-solving training. *Journal of Consulting and Clinical Psychology, 52*, 295–305.

Jacobson, N. S. (1989). The maintenance of treatment gains following social learning-based marital therapy. *Behavior Therapy, 20*, 325–336.

Jacobson, N. S., Dobson, K. S., Fruzetti, A. E., Schmaling, K. B., & Salusky, S. (1991). Marital therapy as a treatment for depression. *Journal of Consulting and Clinical Psychology, 59*, 547–557.

Jacobson, N. S., Follette, W. C., & McDonald, D. W. (1982). Reactivity to positive and negative behavior in distressed and nondistressed married couples. *Journal of Consulting and Clinical Psychology, 50*, 706–714.

Jacobson, N. S., Follette, W. C., & Revenstorf, D. (1984). Psychotherapy outcome research: Methods for reporting variability and evaluating clinical significance. *Behavior Therapy, 15*, 336–352.

Jacobson, N. S. Follette, W. C., Revenstorf, D., Baucom, D. H., Hahlweg, K., & Margolin, G. (1984). Variability in outcome and clinical significance of behavioral marital therapy: A reanalysis of outcome data. *Journal of Consulting and Clinical Psychology, 52*, 497–504.

Jacobson, N. S., Holtzworth-Munroe, A., & Schmaling, K. B. (1989). Spouse involvement in the treatment of depression, agoraphobia, and alcoholism. *Journal of Consulting and Clinical Psychology, 57*, 5–10.

Jacobson, N. S., & Margolin, G. (1979). *Marital therapy: Strategies based on social learning and behavior exchange principles.* New York: Brunner/Mazel.

Jacobson, N. S., & Revenstorf, D. (1988). Statistics for assessing the clinical significance of psychotherapy techniques: Issues, problems, and new developments. *Behavioral Assessment, 10*, 133–145.

Jacobson, N. S., Schmaling, K. B., & Holtzworth-Munroe, A. (1987). Component analysis of behavioral marital therapy: Two-year follow-up and prediction of relapse. *Journal of Marital and Family Therapy, 13*, 187–195.

Jacobson, N. S., Schmaling, K. B., Holtzwoth-Munroe, A., Katt, J. L., & Wood, L. F. (1989). Research-structured versus clinically flexible versions of social learning-based marital therapy. *Behaviour Research and Therapy, 27*, 173–180.

James, W. (1890). *The principles of psychology*, (2 Vols.). New York: Henry Holt & Co.

Jannoun, L., Munby, M., Catalan, J., & Gelder, M. (1980). A home-based treatment program for agoraphobia: Replication and controlled evaluation. *Behavior Therapy, 11*, 294–305.

Jansson, L., & 0st, L. G. (1982). Behavioral treatments for agoraphobia: An evaluative review. *Clinical Psychology Review, 2*, 311–336.

Jarrett, R. B., & Rush, A. J. (1985). Psychotherapeutic approaches for depression. In J. O. Cavenar (Ed.), *Psychiatry*, (vol. 1, pp. 1–35). Philadelphia: J. B. Lippincott.

Jastak, J. F., & Wilkinson, F. (1984). *The wide-range achievement test: Manual of instructions*. Wilmington, DE: Jastak.

Jay, S. M., & Elliott, C. H. (1983). Assessment and management of pain in pediatric cancer patients. In G. B. Humphreys, L. P. Dehne, B. G. Grindey, & R. T. Acten (Eds.), *Pediatric Oncology* (Vol. X). Boston: Martinus Nijhoff.

Jay, S. M., & Elliott, C. H. (1990). A stress inoculation program for parents whose children are undergoing painful medical procedures. *Journal of Consulting and Clinical Psychology, 58*, 799–804.

Jay, S. M., Elliott, C. H., Katz, E. R., & Siegel, S. E. (1987). Cognitive-behavioral and pharmacological interventions for children's distress during painful medical procedures. *Journal of Consulting and Clinical Psychology, 55*, 860–865.

Jay, S. M., Elliott, C. H., Ozolina, M., & Olson, R. (1983). *Behavioral management of children's distress during painful medical procedures*. Unpublished manuscript, University of Southern California—Los Angeles.

Jellinek, E. M. (1960). *The disease concept in alcoholism*. New Brunswick, NJ: Hill House.

Jemmott, J. B., & Locke, S. E. (1984). Psychological factors, immunologic mediation and human susceptibility to infectious diseases: How much do we know? *Psychological Bulletin, 95*, 78–108.

Jette, A. M. (1980). Functional status index: Reliability of a chronic disease evaluation instruction. *Archives of Physical Medicine and Rehabilitation, 61*, 395–401.

Johanson, C. E., & Schuster, C. R. (1982). Animal models of drug self-administration. In N. K. Mello (Ed.) *Behavioral and Biological Research* (Vol 2). Greenwich, CT: JAI Press.

Johnson, B. F. & Cuvo, A. J. (1981). Teaching mentally retarded adults to cook. *Behavior Modification, 5*, 187–202.

Johnson, C. A., Hansen, W. B., Collins, L. M., & Graham, J. W. (1985). High-school smoking prevention: Results of a three-year longitudinal study. *Journal of Behavioral Medicine, 9*, 439–452.

Johnson, C. A., Pentz, A. M., Weber, M. D., Dwyer, J. H., Baer, N., Mackinnon, D. P., Hansen, W. B., & Flay, B. R. (1990). Relative effectiveness of comprehensive community programming for drug abuse prevention with high-risk and low-risk adolescents. *Journal of Consulting and Clinical Psychology, 48*, 447–456.

Johnson, C. L., Stuckey, M. K., Lewis, L. D., & Schwartz, D. M. (1982). Bulimia: A descriptive survey of 316 cases. *International Journal of Eating Disorders, 2*, 3–16.

Johnson, J., & Koegel, R. L. (1982). Behavioral assessment and curriculum development. In R. L. Koegel, A. Rincover, & A. L. Egel (Eds.), *Educating and understanding autistic children*. San Diego, CA: College-Hill Press.

Johnson, M. B. Whitman, T. L., & Johnson, M. R. (1980). Teaching addition and substraction to mentally retarded children: A self-instruction program. *Applied Research in Mental Retardation, 1*, 141–160.

Johnston, J. M. (1972). Punishment of human behavior. *American Psychologist, 27*, 1033–1054.

Johnston, J. M. (1985). Controlling professional behavior [A review of *The effects of punishment on human behavior*]. *Behavior Analyst, 8*, 111–119.

Johnston, M. U., & Freeman, J. M. (1981). Pharmacologic advances in seizure control. *Pediatric Clinics of North America, 28*, 179–194.

Jones, M. C. (1924). A laboratory study of fear: The case of Peter. *Journal of Genetic Psychology, 31*, 308–315.

Jones, M. L., Lattimore, J., Ulicny, G. R., & Risley, T. R. (1986). Ecobehavioral design: Programming for engagement. In R. P. Barrett (Ed.), *Severe behavior disorders in the mentally retarded: Nondrug approaches to treatment*. New York: Plenum.

Jones, R. R., Weinrott, M. R., & Howard, J. R. (1981, June). *The national evaluation of the teaching family model*. Final report to the National Institute of Mental Health, Center for Studies in Crime and Delinquency.

Jones, R. T., Kazdin, A. E., & Haney, J. I. (1981). Social validation and training of emergency fire safety skills for potential injury prevention and eye saving. *Journal of Applied Behavior Analysis, 14*, 249–260.

Jones, R. T., Ollendick, T. H., & Shinske, F. K. (1989).

The role of behavioral versus cognitive variables in skill acquisition. *Behavior Therapy, 20,* 293–302.

Jordan, H. A., Canavan, A. J., & Steer, R. A. (1987). Long term follow-up of patients who lost weight in a cognitive behavioral treatment program. *Psychology of Addictive Behaviors, 1,* 14–21.

Joyce, B. G., Joyce, J. H., & Chase, P. N. (1989). Considerations for the use of rules in academic settings. *Education and Treatment of Children, 12,* 82–92.

Kabela, E., & Andrasik, F. (1988 November). *An analysis of thermal biofeedback and cognitive coping with pediatric migraineurs through 18 month follow-up.* Paper presented at the annual meeting of the Association for the Advancement of Behavior Therapy, Boston, MA.

Kadden, R. M., Cooney, N. L., Getter, H., & Litt, M. D. (1989). Matching alcoholics to coping skills or interactional therapies: Posttreatment results. *Journal of Consulting and Clinical Psychology, 57,* 698–704.

Kagan, J. (1966). Reflection-impulsivity: The generality and dynamics of conceptual tempo. *Journal of Abnormal Psychology, 71,* 17–24.

Kahn, J. S., Kehle, T. J., Jenson, W. R., & Clark, E. (1990). Comparison of cognitive-behavioral, relaxation, and self-modeling interventions for depression among middle-school students. *School Psychology Review, 19,* 196–211.

Kalfus, G. (1984). Peer mediated intervention: A critical review. *Child and Family Behavior Therapy, 6,* 17–43.

Kandel, D. B., & Davies, M. (1982). Epidemiology of depressive mood in adolescents. *Archives of General Psychiatry, 39,* 1205–1212.

Kane, J. M. (1989). Innovations in the psychopharmacologic treatment of schizophrenia. In A. S. Bellack (Ed.), *A clinical guide for the treatment of schizophrenia* (pp. 43–76). New York: Plenum.

Kane, J., Honigfeld, G., Singer, J., & Meltzer, H. (1988). Clozapine for the treatment-resistant schizophrenic. *Archives of General Psychiatry, 45,* 789–796.

Kanfer, F. H. (1970). Self-regulation: Research, issues, and speculation. In C. Neuringer & J. L. Michael (Eds.), *Behavior modification in clinical psychology,* New York: Apple-Century-Crofts.

Kanfer, F. H. (1971). The maintenance of behavior by self-generated stimuli and reinforcement. In A. Jacobs & L. B. Sachs (Eds.). *The psychology of private events: Perspectives on covert response systems,* (pp. 39–59). New York: Academic Press.

Kanfer, F. H. & Karoly, P. (1972). Self-control: A behaviorist excursion into the lion's den. *Behavior Therapy, 3,* 398–416.

Kanfer, F. H., & Saslow, G. (1969). Behavioral diagnosis.

In C. M. Franks (Ed.), *Behavior therapy: Appraisal and status,* (pp. 417–444).

Kanner, A. D., Coyne, J. C., Schaefer, C., & Lazarus, R. S. (1981). Comparison of two modes of stress measurement: Daily hassles and uplifts versus major life events. *Journal of Behavioral Medicine, 4,* 1–39.

Kanner, L. (1943) Autistic disturbances of affective contact. *The Nervous Child, 2,* 217–250.

Kaplan, H. S. (1974). *The new sex therapy.* New York: Brunner/Mazel.

Kaplan, H. S. (1977). Hypoactive sexual desire. *Journal of Sex and Marital Therapy, 3,* 3–9.

Kaplan, H. S. (1979). *Disorders of desire.* New York: Brunner/Mazel.

Kaplan, S. L., Hong, G. K., & Weinhold, C. (1984). Epidemiology of depressive symptomatology in adolescents. *Journal of the American Academy of Child Psychiatry, 23,* 91–98.

Karoly, P. (1982). Developmental pediatrics: A process oriented approach to the analysis of health competence. In P. Karoly, J. J. Steffen, & D. J. O'Grady (Eds.), *Child health psychology: Concepts and issues* (pp. 29–57). New York: Pergamon.

Karoly, P. (1985). The assessment of pain: Concepts and procedures. In P. Karoly (Ed.), *Measurement strategies in health psychology* (pp. 461–515). New York: Wiley

Kashani, J. H., Carlson, G. A., Beck, N. C., Hoeper, E. W., Corcoran, C. M., McAllister, J. A., Fallahi, C., Rosenberg, T. K., & Reid, J. C. (1987). Depression, depressive symptoms, and depressed mood among a community sample of adolescents. *American Journal of Psychiatry, 144,* 931–934.

Kashani, J. H., McGee, R. D., Clarkson, S. E., Anderson, J. C., Walton, L. E., William, S., Silva, P. A., Robins, A. J., Cytryn, L., & McKnew, D. H. (1983). Depression in a sample of nine year old children: Prevalence and associated characteristics. *Archives of General Psychiatry, 40,* 1217–1227.

Kashani, J. H., Rosenberg, T. K., & Reid, J. C. (1989). Developmental perspectives in child and adolescent depressive symptoms in a community sample. *American Journal of Psychiatry, 146,* 871–875.

Kashani, J. H., Shekim, W. O., & Reid, J. C. (1984). Amitriptyline in children with major depressive disorder: A double-blind crossover pilot study. *Journal of the American Academy of Child Psychiatry, 23,* 348–351.

Katahn, M., Pleas, J., Thackrey, M., & Wallston, K. A. (1982). Relationship of eating and activity self-reports to follow-up maintenance in the massively obese. *Behavior Therapy, 13,* 521–528.

Katz, M., & Lyerly, S. (1963). Methods of measuring adjustment and social behavior in the community: Rationale, description, discrimination validity and scale development. *Psychological Reports, 13,* 503–534.

Kaufman, A. S. (1979). *Intelligence testing with the WISC-R.* New York: Wiley.

Kaufman, A. S., Kamphaus, R. W., & Kaufman, N. L. (1985). The Kaufman assessment battery for children (K-ABC). In C. S. Newmark (Ed.), *Major psychological assessment instruments.* Newton, MA: Allyn & Bacon.

Kaufman, A. S., & Kaufman, N. L. (1983). *Kaufman assessment battery for children.* Circle Pines, MN: American Guidance Service.

Kaufman, A. S., & Kaufman, N. L. (1985). *Kaufman test of educational achievement.* Circle Pines, MN: American Guidance Service.

Kazak, A. E. (1989). Families of chronically ill children: A systems and social-ecological model of adaptation and challenge. *Journal of Consulting and Clinical Psychology, 57,* 25–30.

Kazdin, A. E. (1977). *The token economy: A review and evaluation.* New York: Plenum.

Kazdin, A. E. (1978). *History of behavior modification: Experimental foundations of contemporary research.* Baltimore, MD: University Park Press.

Kazdin, A. E. (1980a). *Behavior modification in applied settings* (2nd ed.). Homewood, IL: Dorsey.

Kazdin, A. E. (1980b). Acceptability of alternative treatments for deviant child behavior. *Journal of Applied Behavior Analysis, 13,* 259–273.

Kazdin, A. E. (1982a). Observer effects: Reactivity of direct observation. *New Directions for Methodology of Social and Behavioral Science, 14,* 5–19.

Kazdin, A. E. (1982b). Symptom substitution, generalization, and response covariation: Implications for psychotherapy outcome. *Psychological Bulletin, 91,* 349–365.

Kazdin, A. E. (1982c). *Single-case research designs: Methods for clinical and applied settings.* New York: Oxford University Press.

Kazdin, A. E. (1983). Failure of persons to respond to the token economy. In E. B. Foa, and P. M. G. Emmelkamp (Eds.), *Failures in behavior therapy* (pp. 335–354). New York: Wiley.

Kazdin, A. E. (1984). *Behavior modification in applied settings* (3rd ed.). Homewood, IL: Dorsey.

Kazdin, A. E. (1985). *Treatment of antisocial behavior in children and adolescents.* Homewood, IL: Dorsey.

Kazdin, A. E. (1987a). *Conduct disorder in children and adolescence.* Newbury Park, CA: Sage.

Kazdin, A. E. (1987b). Treatment of antisocial behavior in children: Current status and future directions. *Psychological Bulletin, 102,* 187–203.

Kazdin, A. E. (1989a). *Behavior modification in applied settings* (4th ed.). Pacific Grove, CA: Brooks/Cole.

Kazdin, A. E. (1989b). Hospitalization of antisocial children: Clinic course, follow-up status, and predictors of outcome. *Advanced in Behaviour Research and Therapy, 11,* 1–67.

Kazdin, A. E. (1992). *Research design in clinical psychology.* Needham Heights, MA: Allyn & Bacon.

Kazdin, A. E., & Bass, D. (1988). Parent, teacher, and hospital staff evaluations of severely disturbed children. *American Journal of Orthopsychiatry, 58,* 512–523.

Kazdin, A. E., & Bass, D. (1989). Power to detect differences between alternative treatments in comparative psychotherapy outcome research. *Journal of Consulting and Clinical Psychology, 57* 138–147.

Kazdin, A. E., Bass, D., Siegel, T., & Thomas, C. (1989). Cognitive-behavioral treatment and relationship therapy in the treatment of children referred for antisocial behavior. *Journal of Consulting and Clinical Psychology, 57,* 522–535.

Kazdin, A. E., & Esveldt-Dawson, K. (1986). The Interview for Antisocial Behavior: Psychometric characteristics and concurrent validity with child psychiatric inpatients. *Journal of Psychopathology and Behavioral Assessment. 8,* 289–303.

Kazdin, A. E., Esveldt-Dawson, K., French, N. H., & Unis, A. S. (1987). Problem-solving skills training and relationship therapy in the treatment of antisocial child behavior. *Journal of Consulting and Clinical Child Psychology, 55,* 76–85.

Kazdin, A. E., Esveldt-Dawson, K., Unis, A. S., & Rancurello, M. D. (1983). Child and parent evaluations of depression and aggression in psychiatric inpatient children. *Journal of Abnormal Child Psychology, 11,* 401–413.

Kazdin, A. E., French, N. H., & Unis, A. S. (1983). Child, mother, and father evaluations of depression in psychiatric inpatient children. *Journal of Abnormal Child Psychology, 11,* 167–180.

Kazdin, A. E, French, N. H., Unis, A. S., & Esveldt-Dawson, K. (1983). Assessment of childhood depression: Correspondence of child and parent ratings. *Journal of the American Academy of Child Psychiatry, 22,* 157–164.

Kazdin, A. E., Rodgers, A., Colbus, D., & Siegel, T. (1987). Children's Hostility Inventory: Measurement of aggression and hostility in psychiatric inpatient children. *Journal of Clinical Child Psychology, 16,* 320–328.

Kazdin, A. E., Siegel, T., & Bass, D. (1992). Cognitive problem-solving skills training and parent management training in the treatment of antisocial behavior in children. *Journal of Consulting and Clinical Psychology.*

Kazdin, A. E., & Straw, M. L. (1986). Assessment of behavior of the mentally retarded. In M. Hersen & A. S. Bellack (Eds.), *Behavioral assessment: A practical handbook.* New York: Pergamon.

Kazdin, A. E., & Wilson, G. T. (1978). *Evaluation of behavior therapy: Issues, evidence, and research strategies.* Cambridge, MA: Ballinger.

Keane, T. M., Fairbank, J. A., Caddell, J. M., & Zimering, R. T. (1989). Implosive (flooding) therapy reduces symptoms of PTSD in Vietnam Combat Veterans. *Behavior Therapy, 20,* 245–260.

Kedia, K. (1983). Ejaculation and emission: Normal physiology, dysfunction, and therapy. In R. J. Krane, M. B. Siroky, & I. Goldstein (Eds.), *Male sexual dysfunction* (pp. 37–54). Boston: Little, Brown.

Keefe, F. J. (1988). Behavioral assessment methods for chronic pain. In R. D. Frances & K. R. Krishnan (Eds.), *Chronic pain* (pp. 298–320). New York: American Psychiatric Press.

Keefe, F. J. (1989) Behavioral measurement of pain. In C. R. Chapman & J. D. Loeser (Eds.), *Pain measurement* (pp. 405–424). New York: Raven.

Keefe, F. J., & Block, A. R. (1982). Development of an observation method for assessing pain behavior in chronic low back pain patients. *Behavior Therapy, 13,* 363–375.

Keefe, F. J., Brown, C., Scott, D. S., & Ziesat, H. (1982). Behavioral assessment of chronic pain. In F. J. Keefe & J. A. Blumenthal (Eds.), *Assessment strategies in behavioral medicine* (pp. 321–350). New York: Grune & Stratton.

Keefe, F. J., Caldwell, D. S., Queen, K. T., Gil, K. M., Martinez, S., Crisson, J. E., Ogden, W., & Nunley, J. (1987a). Osteoarthritic knee pain: A behavioral analysis. *Pain, 28,* 309–321.

Keefe, F. J., Caldwell, D. S., Queen, K. T., Gil, K. M., Martinez, S., Crisson, J. E., Ogden, W., & Nunley, J. (1987b). Pain coping strategies in osteoarthritis patients. *Journal of Consulting and Clinical Psychology, 55,* 208–212.

Keefe, F. J., Caldwell, D. S., Williams, D. A., Gil, K. M., Mitchell, D., Robertson, C., Martinez, S., Nunley, J., Beckham, J. C., & Helms, M. (1990a). Pain coping skills training in the management of osteoarthritic knee pain: A comparative study. *Behavior Therapy, 21,* 49–62.

Keefe, F. J., Caldwell, D. S., Williams, D. A., Gil, K. M., Mitchell, D., Robertson, C., Martinez, S., Nunley, J., Beckham, J. C., & Helms, M. (1990b). Pain coping skills training in the management of osteoarthritic knee pain-II: Follow-up results. *Behavior Therapy, 21,* 435–447.

Keefe, F. J., Crisson, J. E., & Trainor, M. (1987). Observational methods for assessing pain: A practical guide. In J. A. Blumenthal & D. C. McKee (Eds.), *Applications in behavioral medicine and health psychology* (pp. 67–94). Sarasota, FL: Professional Resource Exchange.

Keefe, F. J., & Gil, K. M. (1986). Behavioral concepts in the analysis of chronic pain syndromes. *Journal of Consulting and Clinical Psychology, 54,* 776–783.

Keefe, F. J., & Gil, K. M., & Rose, S. C. (1986). Behavioral approaches in the multidisciplinary management of pain: Programs and issues. *Clinical Psychology Review, 6,* 87–113.

Keefe, F. J., & Hoelscher, T. (1987). Biofeedback in the management of chronic pain syndromes: Biofeedback Society of American task force report. In J. P. Hatch, J. G. Fisher, & J. D. Rugh (Eds.), *Biofeedback: Studies in clinical efficacy* (pp. 211–254). New York: Plenum.

Keefe, F. J., Kopel, S., & Gordon, S. B. (1978). *A practical guide to behavioral assessment.* New York: Springer.

Keefe, F. J., & Williams, D. C. (1989). New directions in pain assessment and treatment. *Clinical Psychology Review, 9,* 549–568.

Keefe, P. H., Wyshogrod, D., Weinberger, E., & Agras, W. S. (1984). Binge eating and outcome of behavioral treatment of obesity: A preliminary report. *Behavior Research and Therapy, 22,* 319–321.

Keith, S. J., & Matthews, S. M. (Eds.) (1988). A national plan for schizophrenia research: Panel recommendations—editors' introduction. *Schizophrenia Bulletin, 14,* 343–388.

Kelly, G. (1955). *The psychology of personal constructs.* New York: Norton.

Kelly, J. A. (1982). *Social skills training: A practical guide for interventions.* New York: Springer.

Kelly, J. A., Furman, W., Phillips, J., Hathorn, S., & Wilson, T. (1979). Teaching conversational skills to retarded adolescents. *Child Behavior Therapy, 1,* 84–97.

Kelly, J. A., Laughlin, C., Claiborne, M., & Patterson, J. (1979). A group procedure for teaching job interviewing skills to formerly hospitalized psychiatric patients. *Behavior Therapy, 10,* 79–83.

Kelly, J. A., & St. Lawrence, J. S. (1988). AIDS prevention and treatment: Psychology's role in the health crisis. *Clinical Psychology Review, 8,* 255–284.

Kelly, J. A., St. Lawrence, J. S., Hood, H. V., & Brasfield, T. L. (1989). Behavioral intervention to reduce AIDS risk activities. *Journal of Consulting and Clinical Psychology, 57,* 60–67.

Kelly, M., & Stokes, T. (1982). Contingency contracting with disadvantaged youths: Improving classroom performance. *Journal of Applied Behavior Analysis, 15,* 447–454.

Kendall, P. C., & Braswell, L. (1982). Cognitive-behavioral self-control therapy for children: A components analysis. *Journal of Consulting and Clinical Psychology, 50,* 672–689.

Kendall, P. C., & Braswell, L. (1985). *Cognitive-behavioral therapy for impulsive children.* New York: Guilford.

Kendall, P. C., Cantwell, D. P., & Kazdin, A. E. (1989).

Depression in children and adolescents: Assessment issues and recommendations. *Cognitive Therapy and Research, 13,* 109–146.

Kendall, P. C., & Hollon, S. D. (1979). Cognitive-behavioral interventions: Current status. In P. C. Kendall & S. D. Hollon (Eds.), *Cognitive-behavioral interventions: Theory, research, and procedures,* (pp. 1–9). New York: Academic Press.

Kennedy, S., Kiecolt-Glaser, J. K., & Glaser, R. (1988). Immunological consequences of acute and chronic stressors: Mediating role of interpersonal relationships. *British Journal of Medical Psychology, 61,* 77–85.

Keogh, D. A., Burgio, L., Whitman, T. L., & Johnson, M. (1983). Development of listening skills in retarded children: A correspondence training program. *Child and Family Behavior Therapy, 5,* 51–71.

Keogh, D. A., Faw, G. D., Whitman, T. L., & Reid, D. H. (1984). Enhancing leisure skills in severely retarded adolescents through a self-instructional treatment package. *Analysis and Intervention in Developmental Disabilities, 4,* 333–351.

Kessler, K. A., & Waletzky, J. P. (1981). Clinical use of the antipsychotics. *American Journal of Psychiatry, 138,* 202–209.

Kiecolt-Glaser, J. K., & Glaser, R. (1987). Psychosocial influences on herpes virus latency. In E. Kurstak, Z. J. Lipowski, & R. V. Moronzov (Eds.)., *Viruses, immunity and mental disorders* (pp. 403–411). New York: Plenum.

Kiecolt-Glaser, J. K., & Glaser, R. (1989). Psychoneuroimmunology: Past, present, and future. *Health Psychology, 8,* 677–682.

Killeen P. (1984). Emergent behaviorism. *Behaviorism, 12,* 25–39.

Kimble, G. A. (1961). *Hilgard and Marquis' conditioning and learning.* New York: Appleton-Century-Crofts.

Kimmell, H. D. (1967). Instrumental conditioning of autonomically mediated behavior. *Psychological Bulletin, 67,* 337–345.

Kimmell, H. D. (1974). Instrumental conditioning of autonomically mediated responses in human beings. *American Psychologist, 29,* 325–335.

Kinsey, A. C., Pomeroy, W. B., & Martin. C. E. (1948). *Sexual behavior in the human male.* Philadelphia: W. B. Saunders.

Kirigin, K. A., Braukmann, C. J., Atwater, J. D., & Wolf, M. M. (1982). An evaluation of teaching-family (Achievement Place) group homes for juvenile offenders. *Journal of Applied Behavior Analysis, 15,* 1–16.

Kirkley, B. G., & Fisher, E. B. (1988). Relapse as a model of nonadherence to dietary treatment of diabetes. *Health Psychology, 7,* 221–230.

Kirkley, B. G., Schneider, J. A., Agras, W. S., &

Bachman, J. A. (1985). Comparison of two group treatments for bulimia. *Journal of Consulting and Clinical Psychology, 53,* 43–48.

Kirschenbaum, D. S. (1988). Treating adult obesity 1988: Evolution of a modern program. *Behavior Therapist, 11,* 3–6.

Kirschenbaum, D. S., Ordman, A. M., Tomarken, A. J., & Holtzbauer, R. (1982). Effects of differential self-monitoring and level of mastery on sports performance: Brain power bowling. *Cognitive Therapy and Research, 6,* 335–342.

Kivlahan, D. R., Marlatt, G. A., Fromme, K., Coppel, D. B., & Williams, E. (1990). Secondary prevention with college drinkers: Evaluation of an alcohol skills training program. *Journal of Consulting and Clinical Psychology, 58,* 805–810.

Kleges, R., Eck, L., Haddock, C., & Kleges, L. (1990). Effects of obesity, social interactions, and physical environment on physical activity in preschoolers. *Health Psychology, 9(4),* 435–449.

Klein, D. F. (1980). Anxiety reconceptualized. *Comprehensive Psychiatry, 21,* 411–427.

Klein, D. F. (1993). False suffocation alarms, spontaneous panics, and related conditions: An integrative hypothesis. *Archives of General Psychiatry, 50,* 306–317.

Klein, D. F., & Davis, J. M. (1969). *Diagnosis and drug treatment of psychiatric disorders.* Baltimore, MD: Williams & Wilkins.

Klein, N. C., Alexander, J. F., & Parsons, B. V. (1977). Impact of family systems interventions on recidivism and sibling delinquency: A model of primary prevention and program evaluation. *Journal of Consulting and Clinical Psychology, 45,* 469–474.

Klein, R. G., & Koplewicz, H. S. (1986, October). *Tricyclic treatment of adolescent depression.* Unpublished manuscript. (Available from R. G. Klein, Long Island Jewish Medical Center, New Hyde Park, NY 11042.)

Kleinginna, P. R., & Kleinginna, A. M. (1988). Current trends toward the convergence of the behavioristic, functional, and cognitive perspectives in experimental psychology. *The Psychological Record, 38,* 369–392.

Kleitsch, E. D., Whitman, T. L., & Santos, J. (1983). Increasing verbal interaction among elderly socially isolated mentally retarded adults: A group language training procedure. *Journal of Applied Behavior Analysis, 16,* 217–233.

Klerman, G. L. (1977). Better but not well: Social and ethical issues in the deinstitutionalization of the mentally ill. *Schizophrenia Bulletin, 3,* 617–631.

Klerman, G. L, Weissman, M. M., Rounsaville, B. J., & Chevron, E. S. (1984). *Interpersonal psychotherapy of depression.* New York: Basic Books.

Kline, R. B., Canter, W. A., & Robin, A. (1987). Parameters of teenage alcohol use: A path analytic conceptual model. *Journal of Consulting and Clinical Psychology, 55,* 521–528.

Klorman, R., Coons, H. W., & Borgstedt, A. D. (1987). Effects of methylphenidate on adolescents with a childhood history of Attention Deficit Disorder: I. Clinical findings. *Journal of the American Academy of Child and Adolescent Psychiatry, 26,* 363–367.

Klosko, J. S., Barlow, D. H., Tassinari, R., & Cerny, J. A. (1990). A comparison of alprazolam and behavior therapy in treatment of panic disorder. *Journal of Consulting and Clinical Psychology, 58,* 77–84.

Koenigsberg, H. W., & Handley, R. (1986). Expressed emotion: From predictive index to clinical construct. *American Journal of Psychiatry, 143,* 1361–1373.

Kolko, D. J., Dorsett, P., & Milan, M. (1981). A total-assessment approach in the evaluation of social-skills training: The effectiveness of an anger control program for adolescent psychiatric patients. *Behavior Assessment, 3,* 383–402.

Kolko, D. J., Watson, S., & Faust, J. (1991). Fire safety prevention skills training to reduce involvement with fire in your psychiatric inpatients: Preliminary findings. *Behavior Therapy, 22,* 269–284.

Kolvin, I., Garside, R. F., Nicol, A. E., McMillan, A., Wolstenholme, F., & Leitch, I. M. (1981). *Help starts here: The maladjusted child in the ordinary school.* London: Tavistock.

Koegel, R. L. & Covert, A. (1972). The relationship of self-stimulation to learning in autistic children. *Journal of Applied Behavior Analysis 5,* 318–387.

Koegel, R. L., Dyer, K., & Bell, L. K. (1987). The influence of child preferred activities on autistic children's social behavior. *Journal of Applied Behavior Analysis, 20,* 243–252.

Koegel, R. L., Firestone, P. B., Kramme, K., W., & Dunlap, G. (1974). Increasing spontaneous play by suppressing self-stimulation in autistic children. *Journal of Applied Behavior Analysis, 7,* 521–528.

Koegel, R. L., Glahn, T. J., & Nieminen, G. S. (1978). Generalization of parent training results. *Journal of Applied Behavior Analysis, 11,* 95–109.

Koegel, R. L., & Koegel, L. K. (1986). Promoting generalized treatment gains through direct instruction of self-monitoring skills. *Direct Instruction News, 5,* 13–15.

Koegel, R. L., & Koegel, L. K. (1988). Generalized responsivity and pivotal behaviors. In R. H. Horner, G. Dunlap, & R. L. Koegel (Eds.), *Generalization and maintenance: Lifestyle changes in applied setting.* Baltimore: Paul H. Brookes.

Koegel, R. L., & Koegel, L. K. (1990). Extended reductions in sterotypic behavior through self-management in multiple community settings. *Journal of Applied Behavior Analysis, 23,* 119–128.

Koegel, R. L., Koegel, L. K., & Parks, D. R. (1989). *How to teach self-management skills to individuals with severe handicaps: A training manual.* Unpublished manuscript. University of California, Santa Barbara.

Koegel, R. L., & Mentis, M. (1985). Motivation in childhood autism: Can they or won't they? *Journal of Child Psychology and Psychiatry and Allied Disciplines, 26,* 185–191.

Koegel, R. L., O'Dell, M. C., & Dunlap, G. (1988). Producing speech use in nonverbal autistic children by reinforcing attempts. *Journal of Autism and Developmental Disorders, 18,* 525–538.

Koegel, R. L., O'Dell, M. C., & Koegel, L. K. (1987). A natural language teaching paradigm for nonverbal autistic children. *Journal of Autism and Developmental Disorders, 17,* 187–200.

Koegel, R. L., & Rincover, A. (1974). Treatment of psychotic children in a classroom environment: I. Learning in a large group. *Journal of Applied Behavior Analysis, 7,* 45–59.

Koegel, R. L., & Rincover, A. (1977). Research on the difference between generalization and maintenance in extratherapy responding. *Journal of Applied Behavior Analysis, 10,* 1–12.

Koegel, R. L., & Schreibman, L. (1977). Teaching autistic children to respond to simultaneous multiple cues. *Journal of Experimental Child Psychology, 24,* 299–311.

Koegel, R. L., Schreibman, L., Britten, K. R., Burke, J. C., & O'Neill, R. E. A comparison of parent training to direct clinic treatment. In R. L. Koegel, A. Rincover, & A. L. Egel (Eds.), *Educating and understanding autistic children.* San Diego: College Hill Press.

Koegel, R. L., Schreibman, L., Good, A. B., Cernigilia, L., Murphy, C., & Koegel, L. K. (1989). *How to teach pivotal behaviors to autistic children.* Unpublished manuscript. University of California, Santa Barbara.

Koegel, R. L., Schreibman, L., O'Neill, R. E., & Burke, J. C. (1983). The personality and family-interaction characteristics of parents of autistic children. *Journal of Consulting and Clinical Psychology, 51,* 683–692.

Koegel, R. L., & Wilhelm, H. (1973). Selective responding to the components of multiple visual cues by autistic children. *Journal of Experimental Child Psychology, 15,* 442–453.

Koegel, R. L., & Williams, J. (1980). Direct vs. indirect response-reinforcer relationships in teaching autistic children. *Journal of Abnormal Child Psychology, 4.* 536–547.

Kohlenberg, R. J. (1974). Directed masturbation and the treatment of primary orgasmic dysfunction. *Archives of Sexual Behavior, 3,* 349–356.

Koppitz, E. M. (1966). Emotional indicators on human figure drawings of shy and aggressive children. *Journal of Clinical Psychology, 22,* 466–469.

Kosteljanetz, M., Jensen, T. S., Nogard, B., Lunde, I., Jensen, P. B., & Johnson, S. G. (1981). Sexual and hypothalamic dysfunction in the post concussion syndrome. *Acta Nerologica Scandinavia*, *63*, 169–180.

Kovacs, M. (1985a). The Children's Depression Inventory (CDI). *Psychopharmacology Bulletin*, 21, 995–998.

Kovacs, M. (1985b). The Interview Schedule for Children. *Psychopharmacology Bulletin*, *21*, 991–994.

Kovacs, M., & Beck, A. T. (1977). An empirical clinical approach toward a definition of childhood depression. In J. G. Schulterbrantt & A. Raskin (Eds.), *Depression in childhood: Diagnosis, treatment, and conceptual models*. New York: Raven.

Kovacs, M., Feinberg, T. L., Crouse-Novak, M. A., Paulauskas, S. L., & Finkelstein, R. (1984). Depressive disorders in children: I. A longitudinal prospective study of characteristics and recovery. *Archives of General Psychiatry*, *41*, 229–237.

Kovacs, M., Feinberg, T. L., Crouse-Novak, M., Paulauskas, S. L., Pollock, M., & Finkelstein, R. (1984b). Depressive disorders in children: II. A longitudinal study of the risk for a subsequent major depression. *Archives of General Psychiatry*, *41*, 643–649.

Kovacs, M., Paulauskas, S., Gatsonis, C., & Richards, C. (1988). Depressive disorders in childhood (III): A longitudinal study of comorbidity with and risk for conduct disorders. *Journal of Affective Disorders*, *15*, 205–217.

Kovacs, M., Rush, A. T., Beck, A. T., & Hollon, S. D. (1981). Depressed outpatients treated with cognitive therapy or pharmacotherapy: A one-year follow-up. *Archives of General Psychiatry*, *38*, 33–39.

Kramer, A. D., & Feiguine, R. J. (1981). Clinical effects of amitriptyline in adolescent depression: A pilot study. *Journal of the American Academy of Child Psychiatry*, *20*, 636–644.

Kraepelin, E. (1913). Manic-depressive insanity and paranoia. In R. M. Barclay, *Textbook of psychiatry*. Edinburgh: Livingstone.

Krantz, P., & Risley, T. R. (1977). Behavioral ecology in the classroom. In K. D. O'Leary & S. G. O'Leary (Eds.), *Classroom management: The successful use of behavior modification* (pp. 349–366). New York: Pergamon.

Kreisman, D. E., Simmens, S. J., & Jay, V. D. (1979). Rejecting the patient: Preliminary validation of a self-report scale. *Schizophrenia Bulletin*, *5*, 220–222.

Kucia, C., Drotar, D., Doershuk, C. F., Stern, R. C., Boat, T. F., & Mathews, L. (1979). Home observation of family interaction and childhood adjustment to cystic fibrosis. *Journal of Pediatric Psychology*, *4*, 189–195.

Kuhlman, W. N. (1978). EEG feedback training of epileptic patients: Clinical and electroencephalographic analysis.

Electroencephalography and Clinical Neurophysioloty, *45*, 699–710.

Kulik, J. A., Stein, K. B., & Sarbin, T. R. (1968). Dimensions and patterns of adolescent antisocial behavior. *Journal of Consulting and Clinical Psychology*, *32*, 375–382.

LaBaw, W. L. (1970). Regular use of suggestibility by pediatric bleeders. *Haematologia*, *4*, 419–425.

LaBaw, W. L., Holton, C., Tewell, K., & Eccles, D. (1975). The use of self-hypnosis by children with cancer. *The American Journal of Clinical Hypnosis*, *17*, 233–238.

Labbé, E. E,. & Williamson, D. A. (1983). Temperature biofeedback in the treatment of children with migraine headaches. *Journal of Pediatric Psychology*, *8*, 317–325.

Lacey, J. H. (1983). Bulimia nervosa, binge eating, and psychogenic vomiting: A controlled treatment study and long-term outcome. *British Journal of Psychiatry*, *286*, 1609–1612.

Lader, M. H., & Mathews, A. M. (1968). A physiological model of phobic anxiety and desensitization. *Behaviour Research and Therapy*, *6*, 411–421.

Ladish, C., Sosna, T. D., Warner, D., & Burns, G. L. (1989, August). *Psychometric properties of the Sutter-Eyberg Student Behavior Inventory in a preschool sample*. Presented at the meetings of the American Psychological Association, New Orleans, LA.

LaGreca, A. M., & Ottinger, D. R. (1979). Self-monitoring and relaxation training in the treatment of medically ordered exercises in a 12-year-old female. *Journal of Pediatric Psychology*, *4*, 49–54.

Lahey, B. B., & Drabman, R. S. (1981). Behavior modification in the classroom. In W. E. Craighead, A. E. Kazdin, & M. J. Mahoney (Eds.), *Behavior modification: Principles, issues, and applications* (2nd ed., pp. 418–443). Boston: Houghton Mifflin.

Lally, M. (1981). Computer-assisted teaching of sight-word recognition for mentally retarded school children. *American Journal of Mental Deficiency*, *85*, 383–388.

Lally, M. (1982). Computer-assisted handwriting instruction and visual kinaesthetic feedback processes. *Applied Research in Mental Retardation*, *3*, 397–405.

Lambert, N. M., Hartsough, C. S., Sassone, D., & Sandoval, J. (1987). Persistence of hyperactive symptoms from childhood to adolescent and associated outcomes. *American Journal of Orthopsychiatry*, *57*, 22–32.

Lambert, N., Windmiller, M., Cole, L., & Figuerra, R. (1981). *AAMD adaptive behavior scale: Public school version*. Monterey, CA: Publishers Test Service.

Lane, V. W., & Samples, J. M. (1984). Tuberous sclerosis: Case study of early seizure control and subsequent normal development. *Journal of Autism and Developmental Disorders*, *14*, 423–427.

Lang, P. J. (1968). Fear reduction and fear behavior: Problems in treating a construct. In J. M. Shlien (Ed.), *Research in Psychotherapy* (Vol. 3). Washington, DC: American Psychological Association.

Lang, P. J. (1985). The cognitive psychophysiology of emotion: Fear and anxiety. In A. H. Tuma & J. D. Maser (Eds.), *Anxiety and the anxiety disorders*. Hillsdale, NJ: Laurence Erlbaum.

Lanyon, R. I., & Goodstein, L. D. (1971). *Personality assessment*. New York: Wiley.

LaRowe, L. N., Tucker, R. D., & McGuire, J. M. (1980). Lunchroom noise control using feedback and group contingent reinforcement. *Journal of School Psychology, 18*, 51–57.

Laski, E. K., Charlop, M. H., & Schreibman, L. (1988). Training parents to use the natural language paradigm to increase their autistic children's speech. *Journal of Applied Behavior Analysis, 21*, 391–400.

Last, C. G., Barlow, D. H., & O'Brien, G. T. (1984). Precipitants of agoraphobia: Role of stressful life events. *Psychological Reports, 54*, 567–570.

Laties, V. G., Wood, R. W., & Cooper, R. D. (1981). Stimulus control and the effect of drugs. *Psychopharmacology, 75*, 277–282.

Lattal, K. A. (1969). Contingency management of toothbrushing behavior in a summer camp for children. *Journal of Applied Behavior Analysis, 2*, 195–198.

LaVigna, G. W. (1987). Nonaversive strategies for managing behavior problems. In D. J. Cohen & A. M. Donnellan (Eds.), *Handbook of autism and pervasive developmental disorders* (pp. 418–429). New York: Irvington.

Lavine, R., Buchsbaum, M. S., & Poncy, M. (1976). Auditory analgesia: Somatosensory evoked response and subjective pain rating. *Psychophysiology, 13*, 140–146.

Lazarus, A. A. (1978). *In the mind's eye*. New York: Rawson.

Lazarus, R. S., DeLongis, A., Folkman, S., & Gruen, R. (1985). Stress and adaptational outcomes: The problem of confounding measures. *American Psychologist, 40*, 770–779.

Lazarus, R. S., & Folkman, S. (1984). *Stress, appraisal, and coping*. New York: Springer.

Ledingham, J. E., & Schwartzman, A. E. (1984). A 3-year follow-up of aggressive and withdrawn behavior in childhood. Preliminary findings. *Journal of Abnormal Child Psychology, 12*, 157–168.

Lee, N. F., & Rush, A. J. (1986). Cognitive behavioral group therapy for bulimia. *International Journal of Eating Disorders, 5*, 599–615.

Lefebvre, M. F. (1981). Cognition distortion and cognitive errors in depressed psychiatric and low back pain patients. *Journal of Consulting and Clinical Psychology, 49*, 517–525.

Leff, J., Kuipers, L., Berkowitz, R., & Sturgeon, D. (1985). A controlled trial of social intervention in the families of schizophrenic patients: Two-year follow-up. *British Journal of Psychiatry, 146*, 594–600.

Leff, J., & Vaughn, C. (1985). *Expressed emotion in families*. New York: Guilford.

Lefkowitz, M. M., Eron, L. D., Walder, L. O., & Huesmann, L. R. (1977). *Growing up to be violent: A longitudinal study of the development of aggression*. New York: Pergamon.

Lehman, A. (1983). The well-being of chronic mental patients. *Archives of General Psychiatry, 40*, 369–373.

Lehmann, H. E. (1959). Psychiatric concepts of depression: Nomenclature and classification. *Canadian Psychiatric Association Journal Supplement, 4*. S1–S12.

Leitenberg, H., Gross, J., Peterson, J., & Rosen, J. C. (1984). Analysis of an anxiety model and the process of change during exposure plus response prevention treatment of bulimia nervosa. *Behavior Therapy, 15*, 3–20.

Leitenberg, H., Rosen, J. C., Gross, J., Nudelman, S., & Vara, L. S. (1988). Exposure plus response-prevention treatment of bulimia nervosa. *Journal of Consulting and Clinical Psychology, 56*, 535–541.

LeLaurin, K., & Risley, T. R. (1972). The organization of daycare environments: "Zone" versus "man-to-man" staff assignments. *Journal of Applied Behavior Analysis, 5*, 225–232.

Lentz, R. J., Paul, G. L., & Calhoun, J. F. (1971). Reliability and validity of three measures of functioning with "hard core" chronic mental patients. *Journal of Abnormal Psychology, 77*, 313–323.

Lessing, E. E., Williams, V., & Revelle, W. (1981). Parallel forms of the IJR Behavior Checklist for parents, teachers, and clinicians. *Journal of Consulting and Clinical Psychology, 49*, 34–50.

Levenson, R. W, & Gottman, J. M. (1983). Marital interaction: Physiological linkage and affective exchange. *Journal of Personality and Social Psychology, 45*, 585–597.

Levin, H. M. (1986). *Educational reform for disadvantaged students: An emerging crisis*. Westhaven, CT: National Education Association.

Levine, J., & Zigler, E. (1973). The essential-reactive distinction in alcoholism: A developmental approach. *Journal of Abnormal Psychology, 81*, 242–249.

Levitt, E. E. (1957). The results of psychotherapy with children: An evaluation. *Journal of Consulting Psychology, 21*, 189–196.

Levitt, E. E. (1963). Psychotherapy with children: A further evaluation. *Behavior Research and Therapy, 1*, 45–51.

Levitt J. J., & Tsuang M. T. (1988). The heterogeneity of schizoaffective disorder: Implications for treatment. *American Journal of Psychiatry, 145*, 926–936.

Lewine, R. R. J., Watt, N. F., & Fryer, J. H. (1978). A study of childhood social competence, adult premorbid competence, and psychiatric outcome in three schizophrenic subtypes. *Journal of Abnormal Psychology, 87,* 294–302.

Lewinsohn, P. M. (1974). A behavioral approach to depression. In R. J. Friedman & M. M. Katz, (Eds.), *The psychology of depression: Contemporary theory and research,* (pp. 157–178). Washington, DC: Winston/Wiley.

Lewinsohn, P. M., Mischel, W., Chaplin, W., & Barton, R. (1980). Social competence and depression: The role of illusory self-perceptions. *Journal of Abnormal Psychology, 89,* 203–212.

Lewinsohn, P. M., Antonuccio, D. O., Steinmetz, J. L, & Teri, L. (1984). *The Coping with Depression Course.* Eugene, OR: Castalia.

Lewinsohn, P. M., & Atwood, G. E. (1969). Depression: A clinical-research approach. *Psychotherapy: Theory, Research and Practice, 6,* 166–171.

Lewinsohn, P. M., Biglan, A., & Zeiss, A. M. (1976). Behavioral treatment of depression. In P. O. Davidson (Ed.). *The behavioral management of anxiety depression, and pain,* (pp. 91–146). New York: Bruner/Mazel.

Lewinsohn, P. M., & Clarke, G. N. (1985). Group treatment of depressed individuals: The Coping with Depression Course. *Advances in Behavior Research and Therapy, 6,* 141–151.

Lewinsohn, P. M., Hoberman, H. M., & Clarke, G. N. (1989). The coping with depression course: Review and future directions. *Canadian Journal of Behavioral Science, 21,* 470–493.

Lewinsohn, P. M., Hops, H., Williams, J. A., Clarke, G. N., & Andrews, J. A. (1987, October). *Cognitive-behavioral treatment for depressed adolescents.* Paper presented at the annual meeting of the American Academy of Child and Adolescent Psychiatry, Washington, DC.

Lewinsohn, P. M., Lobitz, W. C., Wilson, S. (1973). "Sensitivity" of depressed individuals to aversive stimuli. *Journal of Abnormal Psychology, 81,* 259–263.

Lewinsohn, P. M., Mischel, W., Chaplin, W., & Barton, R. (1980). Social competence and depression: The role of illusory self-perceptions. *Journal of Abnormal Psychology, 89,* 203–212.

Lewinsohn, P. M., Munoz, R. F., Youngren, M. A., & Zeiss, A. M. (1986). *Control your depression* (2nd ed.). Englewood Cliffs, NJ: Prentice Hall.

Lewinsohn, P. M., Youngren, M. A., & Grosscup, S. J. (1979). Reinforcement and depression. In R. A. Depue (Ed.), *The psychobiology of depressive disorders: Implications for the effects of stress.* New York: Academic Press.

Lewis, D. O., Shanok, S. S., Pincus, J. H., & Glaser, G. H. (1979). Violent juvenile delinquents: Psychiatric, neurological, psychological, and abuse factors. *Journal of the American Academy of Child Psychiatry, 18,* 307–319.

Liberman, R. P., DeRisi, W. J., & Mueser, R. T. (1989). *Social skills training for psychiatric patients.* New York: Pergamon.

Liberman, R. P., & Green, M. F. (1992). Whither cognitive-behavioral therapy for schizophrenia? *Schizophrenia Bulletin, 18,* 27–36.

Liberman, R. P., Mueser, K. T., & Wallace, C. J. (1986). Social skills training for schizophrenics at risk for relapse. *American Journal of Psychiatry, 143,* 523–526.

Liberman, R. P., Wallace, C., Teigen, & Davis, J. (1974). Interventions with psychotic behaviors. In K. S. Calhoun, H. E. Adams, & K. M. Mitchell (Eds.), *Innovative treatment methods in psychopathology* (pp. 323–412). New York: Wiley.

Libet, J. M., & Lewinsohn, P. M. (1973). Concept of social skill with special reference to the behavior of depressed persons. *Journal of Consulting and Clinical Psychology, 40,* 304–312.

Lichtenstein, E., Harris, D. E., Birchler, G. R., Wahl, J. M., & Schmahl, D. P. (1973). Comparison of rapid smoking, warm, smoky air, and attention placebo in the modification of smoking behavior. *Journal of Consulting and Clinical Psychology, 40,* 92–98.

Lidz, T., Fleck, S., & Cornelison, A. (Eds.). (1965). *Schizophrenia and the family. New York:* International Universities Press.

Liebman, R., Minuchin, S., & Baker, L. (1974a). An integrated program for anorexia nervosa. *American Journal of Psychiatry, 131,* 432–436.

Liebman, R., Minuchin, S., & Baker, L. (1974b). The role of the family in the treatment of anorexia nervosa. *Journal of Child Psychiatary, 13,* 264–274.

Liebman, R., Minuchin, S., & Baker, L. (1974c). The use of structural family therapy in the treatment of intractable asthma. *American Journal of Psychiatary, 131,* 535–540.

Linehan, M. M. (1989). Cognitive and behavior therapy for borderline personality disorder. In A. Tasman, R. E. Hales, & A. J. Frances (Eds.), *American Psychiatric Press Review of Psychiatry* (Vol. 8, pp. 84–102). Washington, DC: American Psychiatric Press.

Lingswiler, V. M., Crowther, J. H., & Stephens, M. A. (1987). Emotional reactivity and eating in binge eating and obesity. *Journal of Behavioral Medicine, 10,* 287–299.

Linn, M. W., Klett, C. J., & Caffey, E. M., Jr. (1980). Foster home characteristics and psychiatric patient outcome: The wisdom of Gheel confirmed. *Archives of General Psychiatry, 37,* 129–132.

Litrownik, A. J. (1982). Special considerations in the self-management training of the developmentally disabled. In P. Karoly & F. Kanfer (Eds.), *Self-management and behavior change: From theory to practice* (pp. 315–352). New York: Pergamon.

Litrownik, A. J., Cleary, C. P., Lecklitner, G. L., & Franzini, O. R. (1978). Self-regulation in retarded persons: Acquisition of standards for performance. *American Journal of Mental Deficiency, 83,* 86–89.

Litrownik, A. J., Freitas, J. L., & Franzini, L. R. (1978). Self-regulation in mentally retarded children: Assessment and training of self-monitoring skills. *American Journal of Mental Deficiency, 82,* 499–506.

Litt, M. D., & Schreibman, L. (1981). Stimulus specific reinforcement in the acquisition of receptive labels by autistic children. *Analysis and Intervention in Developmental Disabilities, 1,* 171–186.

Lobitz, W. C., & LoPiccolo, J. (1972). New methods in the behavioral treatment of sexual dysfunction. *Journal of Behavior Therapy and Experimental Psychiatry, 3,* 265–271.

Lochman, J. E. (1984). Psychological characteristics and assessment of aggressive adolescents. In C. Keith (Ed.), *The aggressive adolescent: A clinical perspective* (pp. 17–62). New York: Free Press.

Lochman, J. E. (1985). Effects of different treatment lengths in cognitive behavioral interventions with aggressive boys. *Child Psychiatry and Human Development, 16,* 45–56.

Lochman, J. E. (1993). Modification of childhood aggression. In M. Hersen, R. M. Eisler, & P. M. Miller (Eds.), *Progress in behavior modification (Vol. 23).* Newbury Park, CA: Sage.

Lochman, J. E., Burch, P. R., Curry, J. F., & Lampron, L. B. (1984). Treatment and generalization effects of cognitive-behavioral and goal-setting interventions with aggressive boys. *Journal of Consulting and Clinical Psychology, 52,* 915–916.

Lochman, J. E., & Lampron, L. B. (1985). The usefulness of peer ratings of aggression and social acceptance in the identification of behavioral and subjective difficulties in aggressive boys. *Journal of Applied Developmental Psychology, 6,* 187–198.

Locke, H. J., & Wallace, K. M. (1959). Short-term marital adjustment and prediction tests: Their reliability and validity. *Journal of Marriage and Family Living, 21,* 251–255.

Loeber, R. (1982). The stability of antisocial and delinquent child behavior. A review. *Child Development, 53,* 1431–1446.

Loeber, R. & Dishion, T. J. (1983). Early predictors of male delinquency: A review. *Psychological Bulletin, 94,* 68–99.

Loney, J., Whaley-Klahn, M. A., Kosier, T., & Conboy, J. (1981, November). *Hyperactive boys and their brothers at 21: Predictors of aggressive and antisocial outcomes.* Paper presented at the meeting of the Society of Life History Research, Monterey, CA.

London, P. (1964). *The modes and morals of psychotherapy.* New York: Holt, Rinehart, & Winston.

Long, C. J., & Webb, W. L. (1980). Improving diagnostic strategies for pain patients. *Neurosurgery, 7,* 225–227.

Longo, D. J., Clum, G. A., & Yaeger, N. J. (1988). Psychosocial treatment for recurrent genital herpes. *Journal of Consulting and Clinical Psychology, 56,* 61–66.

Lonigan, C. J. (1990). Which behaviorism? A reply to Mahoney. *American Psychologist, 45,* 1179–1181.

LoPiccolo, J. (1977a). Direct treatment of sexual dysfunction in the couple. In J. Money & H. Musaph (Eds.), *Handbook of sexology.* New York: Elsevier/North Holland.

LoPiccolo, J. (1977b). From psychotherapy to sex therapy. *Society, 14,* 60–68.

LoPiccolo, J. (1980). Methodological issues in research on treatment of sexual dysfunction. In R. Green & J. Wiener (Eds.), *Methodological issues in sex research* (pp. 100–128). Washington, DC: U.S. Government Printing Office.

LoPiccolo, J. (1992). Post-modern sex therapy for erectile failure. In R. C. Rosen & S. R. Leiblum (Eds.), *Erectile failure: Assessment and Treatment.* New York: Guilford.

LoPiccolo, J., & Daiss, S. (1988). Management of psychogenic erectile failure. In E. Tanagho, T. Lue, & R. McClure (Eds.), *Contemporary management of impotence and infertility.* Baltimore: Williams & Wilkins.

LoPiccolo, & Friedman, J. (1988). Broad spectrum treatment of low sexual desire: Integration of cognitive, behavioral, and systemic therapy. In S. Leiblum & R. Rosen (Eds.), *Assessment and treatment of desire disorders.* New York: Guilford.

LoPiccolo, J., & Lobitz, W. C. (1972). The role of masturbation in the treatment of orgasmic dysfunction. *Archives of Sexual Behavior, 2,* 163–172.

LoPiccolo, J., & Steger, J. (1974). The sexual interaction inventory: A new instrument for assessment of sexual dysfunction. *Archives of Sexual Behavior, 3,* 585–595.

LoPiccolo, J., Stewart, R., & Watkins, B. (1972). Case study: Treatment of erectile failure and ejaculatory incompetence in a case with homosexual etiology. *Journal of Behavior Therapy and Experimental Psychiatry, 3,* 233–236.

LoPiccolo, J., & Stock, W. E. (1986). Treatment of sexual dysfunction. *Journal of Consulting and Clinical Psychology, 54*(2), 158–167.

LoPiccolo, J., & Stock, W. E. (1987). Sexual counseling in gynecological practice. In Z. Rosenwaks, F. Benjamin, & M. L. Stone (Eds.), *Basic gynecology.* New York: McMillan.

Lorber, R., & Patterson, G. R. (1981). The aggressive child: A concomitant of a coercive system. *Advances in Family Intervention, Assessment, and Theory, 2,* 47–87.

Lovaas, O. I. (1966). A program for the establishment of speech in psychotic children. In J. K. Wing (Ed.), *Early childhood autism.* London: Pergamon.

Lovaas, O. I. (1977). *The autistic child.* New York: Irvington.

Lovaas, O. I. (1979). Contrasting illness and behavioral models for the treatment of autistic children: A historical perspective. *Journal of Autism and Developmental Disorders, 9,* 315–323.

Lovaas, O. I. (1987). Behavioral treatment and normal educational and intellectual functioning in young autistic children. *Journal of Consulting and Clinical Psychology, 55,* 3–9.

Lovaas, O. I., Berberich, J. P., Perloff, B. F., & Schaeffer, B. (1966). Acquisition of imitative speech in schizophrenic children. *Science, 151,* 705–707.

Lovaas, O. I., Freitag, G., Gold, V. J., & Kassorla, I. C. (1965). Experimental studies in childhood schizophrenia: I. Analysis of self-destructive behavior. *Journal of Experimental Child Psychology, 2,* 67–84.

Lovaas, O. I., Freitag, G., Kinder, M. I., Rubenstein, B. D., Schaeffer, B., & Simmons, J. Q. (1966). Establishment of social reinforcers in two schizophrenic children on the basis of food. *Journal of Experimental Child Psychology, 4,* 109 –125.

Lovaas, O. I., Schaeffer, B., & Simmons, J. Q. (1965). Building social behavior in autistic children by the use of electric shock. *Journal of Experimental Research in Personality, 1,* 99–109.

Lovaas, O. I., Koegel, R. L., & Schreibman, L. (1979). Stimulus overselectivity in autism: A review of research. *Psychological Bulletin, 86,* 1236–1254.

Lovaas, O. I., Koegel, R. L., Simmons, J. Q., & Long, J. S. (1973). Some generalization and follow-up measurements in autistic children in behavior therapy. *Journal of Applied Behavior Analysis, 6,* 131–166.

Lovaas, O. I., Litrownik, A., & Mann, R. (1971). Response latencies to auditory stimuli in autistic children engaged in self-stimulatory behavior. *Behavior Research and Therapy, 9,* 39–49.

Lovaas, O. I., & Newsom, C. D. (1976). Behavior modification with psychotic children. In H. Leitenberg (Ed.), *Handbook of behavior modification and behavior therapy.* Englewood Cliffs, NJ: Prentice Hall.

Lovaas, O. I., Newsom, C., & Hickman, C. (1987). Self-stimulatory behavior and perceptual reinforcement. *Journal of Applied Behavior Analysis, 20,* 56–68.

Lovaas, O. I., Schaeffer, B., & Simmons, J. Q. (1965). Building social behavior in autistic children by use of electric shock. *Journal of Experimental Research and Personality, 1,* 99–109.

Lovaas, O. I., & Schreibman, L. (1971). Stimulus overselectivity of autistic children in a two stimulus situation. *Behaviour Research and Therapy, 9,* 305–310.

Lovaas, O. I., Schreibman, L., Koegel, R., & Rehm, R. (1971). Selective responding by autistic children to multiple sensory input. *Journal of Abnormal Psychology, 77,* 211–222.

Lovaas, O. I., & Simmons, J. Q. (1969). Manipulation of self-destruction in three retarded children. *Journal of Applied Behavior Analysis, 2,* 143–157.

Lowe, K., & Lutzker, J. R. (1979). Increasing compliance to a medical regimen with a juvenile diabetic. *Behavior Therapy, 10,* 57–64.

Lowe, M. R., & Cautela, J. R. (1978). A self-report measure of social skill. *Behavior Therapy, 9,* 535–544.

Lubar, J. F., & Bahler, W. W. (1976). Behavioral management of epileptic seizures following EEG biofeedback training of the sensorimotor rhythm. *Biofeedback and Self-Regulation, 1,* 77–104.

Lubin, B. (1967). *Manual for the Depression Adjective Check Lists.* San Diego: Educational and Industrial Testing Service.

Lubin, R. A., & Kiely, M. (1985). Epidemiology of aging in development disabilities. In M. P. Janicki & H. M. Wisniewski (Eds.), *Aging and the development disabilities* (pp. 95–113). Baltimore, MD: Brookes.

Luborsky, L., & Spense, D. P. (1978). Quantitative research on psychoanalytic therapy. In S. L. Garfield & A. E. Bergin (Eds.), *Handbook of psychotherapy and behavior change* (2nd ed.). New York: Wiley.

Luce, S., Delquadri, J., & Hall, R. V. (1980). Contingent exercise: A mild but powerful procedure for suppressing inappropriate verbal and aggressive behavior. *Journal of Applied Behavior Analysis, 13,* 583–594.

Luepker, R. V., Perry, C. L., Murray, D. M., & Mullis, R. (1988). Hypertension prevention through nutrition education in youth: A school-based program involving parents. *Health Psychology, 7,* 233–245.

Luiselli, J. K. (1986). Behavior analysis of pharmacological and contingency management interventions for self-injury. *Journal of Behavior Therapy and Experimental Psychiatry, 17,* 275–284.

Lund, A. K., & Kegeles, S. S. (1982). Increasing adolescents' acceptance of long-term personal health behavior. *Health Psychology, 1,* 27–43.

Luria, A. R. (1961). *The role of speech in the regulation of normal and abnormal behaviors.* New York: Liveright.

Lutzker, J. R. (1990). Behavioral treatment of child neglect. *Behavior Modification, 14,* 301–315.

Lutzker, J. R., Megran, D. A. Dachman, R. S., & Webb, M. E. (1985). Validating and training adult-child interaction skills to professionals and to parents indicated for child abuse and neglect. *Journal of Child and Adolescent Psychotherapy, 2,* 91–104.

Lutzker, J. R., & Rice, J. M. (1984). Project 12-Ways: Measuring outcome of a large in-home service for treatment and prevention of child abuse and neglect. *Child Abuse and Neglect, 8,* 519–524.

Lutzker, S. Z., Lutzker, J. R., Braunling-McMorrow, D., & Eddleman, J. (1987). Prompting to increase mother-baby stimulation with single mothers. *Journal of Child and Adolescent Psychotherapy, 4,* 3–12.

Lyons, J. A., & Keane, T. M. (1989). Implosive therapy for the treatment of combat-related PTSD. *Journal of Traumatic Stress, 2,* 137–152.

MacCorquodale, K., & Meehl, P. E. (1948). On a distinction between hypothetical constructs and intervening variables. *Psychological Review, 55,* 95–107.

MacDonald, M. L. (1978). Measuring assertion: A model and method. *Behavior Therapy, 9,* 889–899.

Mace, F. C., Page, T. J., Ivancic, M. T., & O'Brien, S. (1986). Effectiveness of brief time-out with and without contingent delays: A comparative analysis. *Journal of Applied Behavior Analysis, 19,* 79–86.

MacFarlane, J. W., Allen, L., & Honzik, M. P. (1954). *A developmental study of the behavior problems of normal children between 21 months and 14 years.* Berkeley, CA: University of California Press.

Madison, G. B. (1988). *The hermeneutics of postmodernity.* Bloomington, IN: Indiana University Press.

Madsen, C. H., Becker, W. C., Thomas, D. R., Koser, L., & Plager, E. (1970). An analysis of the reinforcing function of "sit down" commands. In R. K. Parker (Ed.), *Readings in educational psychology.* Boston: Allyn & Bacon.

Magana, A. B., Goldstein, M. J., Karno, M., Miklowitz, D. J., Jenkins, J., & Falloon, I. R. H. (1986). A brief method for assessing expressed emotion in relatives of psychiatric patients. *Psychiatry Research, 17,* 203–212.

Magrab, P. R., & Calcagno, P. L. (1978). Psychological impact of chronic pediatric conditions. In P. R. McGray (Ed.), *Psychological management of pediatric problems,* (Vol. 1, pp. 3–14). Baltimore: University Park.

Magrab, P. R., & Papadopoulou, Z. L. (1977). The effect of a token economy on dieting compliance for children on meodialysis. *Journal of Applied Behavior Analysis, 10,* 573–578.

Maheady, L., Harper, G. F., & Sacca, M. K. (1988). Classwide peer tutoring programs in secondary self-contained programs for the mildly handicapped. *Journal of Research and Development in Education, 21,* 76–83.

Mahoney, K., Rogers, T., Straw, M., & Mahoney, M. J. (December, 1977). Results and implications of a problem-solving treatment for obesity. Paper presented at the 11th Annual Convention of the Association for Advancement of Behavior Therapy, Atlanta, GA.

Mahoney, M. J. (1974). *Cognition and behavior modification.* Cambridge: Ballinger.

Mahoney, M. J. (1980). Psychotherapy and the structure of personal revolutions. In M. J. Mahoney (Ed.), *Psychotherapy process: Current issues and future directions* (pp. 157–180). New York: Plenum.

Mahoney, M. J. (1989). Scientific psychology and radical behaviorism: Important distinctions based in scientism and objectivism. *American Psychologist, 44,* 1372–1377.

Mahoney, M. J. (1990). Diatribe is not dialogue: On selected attempts to attack and defend behaviorism. *American Psychologist, 45,* 1183–1184.

Mahoney, M. J. (1991a). *Human change processes: The scientific foundations of psychotherapy.* New York: Basic Books.

Mahoney, M. J. (1991b). B. F. Skinner: A collective tribute. *Canadian Psychology, 32,* 628–635.

Mahoney, M. J., & Arnkoff, D. B. (1978). Cognitive and self-control therapies. In S. L. Garfield & A. E. Bergin (Eds.), *Handbook of psychotherapy and behavior change* (Vol. 2, pp. 689–722). New York: Wiley.

Mahoney, M. J., & Gabriel, T. J. (1990). Essential tensions in psychology: Longitudinal data on cognitive and behavioral ideologies. *Journal of Cognitive Psychotherapy: An International Quarterly, 4,* 5–21.

Mahoney, M. J., Gabriel, T. J., & Perkins, T. S. (1987). Psychological skills and exceptional athletic performance. *The Sport Psychologist, 1,* 181–199.

Mahoney, M. J., Kazdin, A. E., & Lesswing, W. J. (1974). Behavior modification: Delusion or deliverance? In C. M. Franks & G. T. Wilson (Eds.), *Annual review of behavior therapy: Theory and practice* (Vol. 2). New York: Brunner/Mazel.

Manella, K. J., & Varni, J. W. (1981). Behavior therapy in a gait training program for a child with myelomeningocele. *Physical Therapy, 61,* 1284–1287.

Manne, S. L., Redd, W. H., Jacobsen, P. B., Gorfinkle, K., Schorr, V., & Rapkin, B. (1990). Behavioral intervention to reduce child and parent distress during venipuncture. *Journal of Consulting and Clinical Psychology, 58,* 565–572.

Mansdorf, I. J. (1977). Learning concepts through modeling: Using different instructional procedures with institutionalized mentally retarded adults. *American Journal of Mental Deficiency, 82,* 287–291.

Marcus, M. D., Wing, R. R., Ewing, L., Kern, E., McDermott, M., & Gooding, W. (1990). A double-blind, placebo-controlled trial of fluoxetine plus behavior modification in the treatment of obese binge-eaters and non-binge eaters. *American Journal of Psychiatry, 147,* 876–881.

Marcus, M. D., Wing, R. R., & Hopkins, J. (1988). Obese binge eaters: Affect, cognitions and response to behavioral weight control. *Journal of Consulting and Clinical Psychology, 56,* 433–439.

Margolin, G. (1981). Behavior exchange in happy and unhappy marriages: A family cycle perspective. *Behavior Therapy, 12,* 329–343.

Marholin, D., O'Toole, K. M., Touchette, P. E., Berger, P. L., & Doyle, D. A. (1979). "I'll have a Big Mac, large fries, large Coke, and apple pie," . . . or teaching adaptive community skills. *Behavior Therapy, 10,* 236–248.

Marholin, D., Touchette, P. E., & Stewart, R. M. (1979). Withdrawal of chronic chlorpomazine medications: An experimental analysis. *Journal of Applied Behavior Analysis, 12,* 159–171.

Markman, H. J. (1979). Application of a behavioral model of marriage in predicting relationship satisfaction of couples planning marriage. *Journal of Consulting and Clinical Psychology, 47,* 743–749.

Markman, H. J. (1989, November). *Why is a 5 session communication training program associated with the prevention of divorce and marital distress?: Results from a 5-year follow-up.* Paper presented at the 23rd Convention of the Association for Advancement of Behavior Therapy, Washington, DC.

Markman, H. J., Floyd, F. J., Stanley, S. M., & Lewis, H. C. (1986). Prevention. In N. S. Jacobson & A. S. Gurman (Eds.), *Clinical handbook of marital therapy.* New York: Guilford.

Markman, H. J., Floyd, F. J., Stanley, S. M., & Storaasli, R. F. (1988). Prevention of marital distress: A longitudinal investigation. *Journal of Consulting and Clinical Psychology, 56,* 210–217.

Marks, I. M. (1987). *Fears, phobias, and rituals: Panic, anxiety, and their disorders.* New York: Oxford University Press.

Marks, I. M. Lelliott, P., Basoglu, M., Noshirvani, H., Monterio, W., Cohen, D., & Kasvikis, Y. (1988). Clomipramine, self-exposure and therapist-aided exposure for obsessive-compulsive rituals. *British Journal of Psychiatry, 152,* 522–534.

Marks, I. M., & Mathews, A. M. (1979). Brief standard self-rating for phobic patients. *Behaviour Research and Therapy, 17,* 263–267.

Marlatt, G. A., (1988, Spring). Research on behavioral strategies for the prevention of alcohol problems. *Contemporary Drug Problems,* pp. 31–45.

Marlatt, G. A., Demming, B., & Reid, J. B. (1973). Loss of control drinking in alcoholics: An experimental analogue. *Journal of Abnormal Psychology, 81,* 233–241.

Marlatt, G. A., & Donovan, D. M. (1980). Alcoholism and drug dependence: Cognitive social-learning factors in addictive behaviors. In W. E. Craighead, A. E. Kazdin, & M. J. Mahoney (Eds.), *Behavior modification: Principles, issues, and application,* (2nd ed., pp 264–285). Boston: Houghton Mifflin.

Marlatt, G. A., & George, W. H. (1990). Relapse prevention and the maintenance of optimal health. In S. Shumaker, E. Shron, & J. K. Ockene (Eds.) *The handbook of health behavior change* (pp. 44–63). New York: Springer.

Marlatt, G. A., & Gordon, J. R. (1980). Determinants of relapse: Implications for the maintenance of behavior change. In P. O. Davidson & S. M. Davidson (Eds.), *Behavioral medicine: Changing health lifestyles,* (pp. 410–452). New York: Brunner/Mazel.

Marlatt, G. A., & Gordon, J. R. (Eds.) (1985). *Relapse prevention: Maintenance strategies in the treatment of addictive behaviors.* New York: Guilford.

Marlatt, G. A., Kosturn, C. F., & Lang, A. R. (1975). Provocation to anger and opportunity for retaliation as determinants of alcohol consumption in social drinkers. *Journal of Abnormal Psychology, 84,* 652–659.

Marlatt, G. A., & Rohsenow, D. R. (1980). Cognitive processes in alcohol use: Expectancy and the balanced placebo design. In N. K. Mello (Ed.), *Advances in substance abuse* (Vol. 1, pp. 159–199). Greenwich, CT: JAI Press.

Marston, R., & Criss, J. (1984). Maintenance of successful weight loss: Incidence and prediction. *International Journal of Obesity, 8,* 435–439.

Martens, L. W., Frazier, P. J., Hirt, K. J., Meskin, L. H., & Proshek, J. (1973). Developing brushing performance in second-graders through behavior modification. *Health Services Reports, 88,* 818–823.

Martin, A. S., & Morris, J. L. (1980). Training a work ethic in severely mentally retarded workers—providing a context for maintenance of skill performance. *Mental Retardation, 18,* 67–71.

Martin, G., Pallotta-Cornick, A., Johnstone, G., & Goyos, A. C. (1980). A supervisory strategy to improve work performance for lower functioning retarded clients in a sheltered workshop. *Journal of Applied Behavior Analysis, 13,* 183–190.

Martin, I., & Levey, A. B. (1985). Conditioning, evaluations and cognitions: An axis of integration. *Behaviour Research and Therapy, 23,* 167–175.

Martin, J. E., Burger, D. L., Burger-Elias, S., & Mithaug, D. E. (1988). Applications of self-control strategies to facilitate independence in vocational and instructional settings. In N. W. Bray (Ed.), *International review of research in mental retardation.* (Vol. 16). San Diego: Academic Press.

Martin, J. E., & Dubbert, P. M. (1982). Exercise applications and promotion in behavioral medicine: Current status and future directions. *Journal of Consulting and Clinical Psychology, 50,* 1004–1017.

Martin, J. E., Rusch, F. R., James, V. L., Decker, P. J., & Trtol, K. A. (1982). The use of picture cues to establish self-control in the preparation of complex meals by mentally retarded adults. *Applied Research in Mental Retardation, 3,* 105–119.

Martin, R. (1981). Legal issues in preserving client rights. In G. T. Hannah, W. P. Christian, & H. B. Clark (Eds.), *Preservation of client rights* (pp. 3–13). New York: Free Press.

Martinson, W. D., & Zerface, J. P. (1970). Comparison of individual counseling and a social program with nondaters. *Journal of Counseling Psychology, 17,* 36–40.

Mash, E. J., & Barkley, R. A. (1986). Assessment of family interaction with the Response-Class Matrix. In R. Prinz (Ed.), *Advances in behavioral assessment of children and families* (Vol. 2, pp. 29–67). Greenwich, CT : JAI Press.

Mash, E. J., & Johnston, C. (1983). Parental perceptions of child behavior problems, parenting self-esteem, and mothers' reported stress in younger and older hyperactive and normal children. *Journal of Consulting and Clinical Psychology, 51,* 68–99.

Mash, E. J., & Terdal, L. G. (Eds.). (1988). *Behavioral assessment of childhood disorders* (2nd ed.). New York: Guilford.

Maslow, A. H. (1966). *The psychology of science: A reconnaissance.* Chicago: Henry Regnery.

Masters, W., & Johnson, V. (1966). *Human sexual response.* Boston: Little, Brown.

Masters, W., & Johnson, V. (1970). *Human sexual inadequacy.* Boston: Little, Brown.

Matarazzo, J. D. (1980). Behavioral health and behavior medicine: Frontiers for a new health psychology. *American Psychologist, 35,* 807–817.

Mathews, A. M., Johnston, D. W., Lancashire, M., Munby, M., Shaw, & Gelder, M. G. (1976). Imaginal flooding and exposure to real phobic situations: Treatment outcome with agoraphobic patients. *British Journal of Psychiatry, 129,* 362–371.

Mathews, A. M., Teasdale, J., Munby, M., Johnston, D., & Shaw, P. (1977). A home-based treatment program for agoraphobia. *Behavior Therapy, 8,* 915–924.

Matson, J. L., & Barrett, R. P. (Eds.). (1982). *Psychopathology in the mentally retarded.* New York: Grune & Stratton.

Matson, J. L., & Frame, C. (1983). Psychopathology. In J. L. Matson & S. E. Bruning (Eds.), *Assessing the mentally retarded.* New York: Grune & Stratton.

Matson, J. L., Marchetti, A., & Adkins, J. (1980). Comparison of operant- and independence-training procedures for mentally retarded adults. *American Journal of Mental Deficiency, 84,* 487–494.

Matson, J. L., Ollendick, T. A., & Adkins, J. (1980). A comprehensive dining program for mentally retarded adults. *Behavior Research and Therapy, 18,* 107–112.

Matthews, J. (1971). Communication disorders in the mentally retarded. In L. E. Travis (Ed.), *Handbook of speech pathology and audiology* (pp. 801–818). New York: Appleton-Century-Crofts.

Mayer, G. R., Butterworth, T., Nafpaktitis, M., & Sulzer-Azaroff, B. (1983). Preventing school vandalism and improving discipline. *Journal of Applied Behavior Analysis, 16,* 355–369.

Mayer, G. R., Nafpaktitis, M., Butterworth, T., & Hollingsworth, P. (1987). A search for the elusive setting events of school vandalism: A correlational study. *Education and Treatment of Children, 10,* 259–270.

McAdoo, G. W., & DeMyer, M. K. (1978). Personality characteristics of parents. In M. Rutter & E. Schopler (Eds.), *Autism: A reappraisal of concepts and treatment.* New York: Plenum.

McAlister, A., Perry, C., & Maccoby, N. (1979). Adolescent smoking: Onset and prevention. *Pediatrics, 63,* 650–658.

McCaul, K. D., & Malott, J. M. (1984). Distraction and coping with pain. *Psychological Bulletin, 95,* 516–533.

McCord, W., McCord, J., & Howard, A. (1961). Familial correlates of aggression in nondelinquent male children. *Journal of Abnormal and Social Psychology, 62,* 79–93.

McCord, W., McCord, J., & Zola, I. K. (1959). *Origins of crime.* New York: Columbia University Press.

McCrady, B. S., Noel, N. E., Abrams, D. B., Stout, R. L., Nelson, H. F., & Hay, W. N. (1986). Comparative effectiveness of three types of spouse involvement in outpatient behavioral alcoholism treatment. *Journal of Studies on Alcohol, 47,* 459–467.

McDonnell, J. J., & Ferguson, B. (1988). A comparison of general case in vivo and general case stimulation plus in vivo training. *Journal of the Association for Persons with Severe Handicaps, 13,* 116–124.

McEvoy, J. P. (1983). The clinical use of anticholinergic drugs as treatment for extrapyramidal side effects of neuroleptic drugs. *Journal of Clinical Psychopharmacology, 3,* 288–302.

McEwan, K. (1983). Perhaps it's time to leave minimal daters alone. *The Behavior Therapist, 6,* 100–101.

McFall, R. M. (1982). A review and reformulation of the concept of social skills. *Behavioral Assessment, 4,* 1–33.

McFall, R. M., & Lillesand, D. B. (1971). Behavior rehearsal with modeling and coaching in assertion training. *Journal of Abnormal Psychology, 77,* 313–323.

McFayden, M., & Presly, A. (1977). *Prolonged exposure for agoraphobia.* Unpublished manuscript.

McGrath, P. A. (1990). *Pain in children: Nature, assessment, and treatment.* New York: Guilford.

McLaughlin, T., & Malaby, J. (1972). Reducing and measuring inappropriate verbalizations in a token classroom. *Journal of Applied Behavior Analysis, 5,* 329–333.

McLean, P. D., & Hakstian, A. R. (1979). Clinical depression: Comparative efficacy of outpatient treatments. *Journal of Consulting and Clinical Psychology, 47,* 818–836.

McLellan, A. T., Childress, A. R., Ehrman, R., & O'Brien, C. P. (1986). Extinguishing conditioned responses during opiate treatment: Turning laboratory findings into clinical procedures. *Journal of Substance Abuse Treatment, 3,* 33–40.

McLellan, A. T., Luborsky, L., & O'Brien, C. P. (1980). Improved evaluation instrument for substance abuse patients. *Journal of Nervous and Mental Disease, 168,* 26–33.

McMahon, R. J., & Forehand, R. (1988). Conduct disorders. In E. J. Mash, & L. G. Terdal (Eds.), *Behavioral assessment of childhood disorders* (2nd ed., pp. 105–153). New York: Guilford.

McMahon, R. J., Forehand, R., & Griest, D. L. (1981). Effects of knowledge of social learning principles on enhancing treatment outcome and generalization in a parent training program. *Journal of Consulting and Clinical Psychology, 49,* 526–532.

McMahon, R. J., & Wells, K. C. (1989). Conduct disorders. In E. J. Mash & R. A. Barkley (Eds.), *Treatment of childhood disorders,* (pp. 73–132). New York: Guilford.

McNamara, K., & Horan, J. J., (1986). Experimental construct validity in the evaluation of cognitive and behavioral treatments for depression. *Journal of Counseling Psychology, 33,* 23–30.

Measel, C. J., & Alfieri, P. A. (1976). Treatment of self-injurious behavior by a combination of reinforcement for incompatible behavior and overcorrection. *American Journal of Mental Deficiency, 81,* 147–153.

Mehlman, S. K., Baucom, D. H., & Anderson, D. (1983). Effectiveness of cotherapists versus single therapists and immediate versus delayed treatment in behavioral marital therapy. *Journal of Consulting and Clinical Psychology, 51,* 258–266.

Meichenbaum, D. (1975). Self-instructional methods. In F. H. Kanfer & A. P. Goldstein (Eds.), *Helping people change.* New York: Pergamon.

Meichenbaum, D. (1977). *Cognitive behavior modification.* New York: Plenum.

Meichenbaum, D. (1986). Cognitive behavior modification. In F. H. Kanfer, & A. P. Goldstein (Eds.), *Helping people change: A textbook of methods* (pp. 346–380). New York: Pergamon.

Melamed, B. G., & Siegel, L. J. (1975). Reduction of anxiety in children facing hospitalization and surgery by use of filmed modeling. *Journal of Consulting and Clinical Psychology, 43,* 511–521.

Melamed, B. G., & Siegel, L. J. (1980). *Behavioral medicine: Practical applications in health care.* New York: Springer.

Melzack, R. (1988). The tragedy of needless pain: A call for social action. In R. Dubner, G. F. Gebhart & M. R. Bond (Eds.), *Proceedings of the Fifth World Congress on Pain.* New York: Elsevier.

Melzack, R., & Wall, P. D. (1965). Pain mechanisms: A new theory. *Science, 50,* 971–979.

Menacker, J. C., Hurwitz, E., & Weldon, W. (1988). Legislating school discipline: The application of a system-wide discipline code to schools in a large urban district. *Urban Education, 23,* 12–23.

Mercer, J. R., & Lewis, J. F. (1977). *System of Multicultural Pluralistic Assessment: SOMPA.* New York: Psychological Corporation.

Messer, S. B., Sass, L. A., & Woolfolk, R. L. (Eds.). (1988). *Hermeneutics and psychological theory: Interpretive perspectives on personality, psychotherapy, and psychopathology.* Brunswick, NJ: Rutgers University Press.

Meterissian, G. B., & Bradwejn, J. (1989). Comparative studies on the efficacy of psychotherapy, pharmacotherapy, and their combination in depression: Was adequate pharmacotherapy provided? *Journal of Clinical Psychopharmacology, 9,* 334–339.

Metropolitan Insurance Company. (1983). *Height and weight tables.* New York: Metropolitan Life Insurance Company.

Meyers, C. E., Nihira, K., & Zetlin, A. (1979). The measurement of adaptive behavior. In N. R. Ellis (Ed.), *Handbook of mental deficiency: Psychological theory and research* (2nd ed.). Hillsdale, NJ: Erlbaum.

Michelson, L., & Mavissakalian, M. (1985). Psychophysiological outcome of behavioral and pharmacological treatments of agoraphobia. *Journal of Consulting and Clinical Psychology, 53,* 229–236.

Michelson, L., Mavissakalian, M., & Marchione, K. (1985). Cognitive and behavioral treatments of agoraphobia: Clinical, behavioral, and psychophysiological outcomes. *Journal of Consulting and Clinical Psychology, 53,* 913–925.

Michelson, L., Mavissakalian, M., Marchione, K., Dancu, C., & Greenwald, M. (1986). The role of self-directed in vivo practice in cognitive, behavioral, and psychophysiological treatments of agoraphobia. *Behavior Therapy, 17,* 91–108.

Michelson, L., Sugai, D. P., Wood, R. P, & Kazdin, A. E. (1983). *Social skills assessment and training with children.* New York: Plenum.

Milich, R., Loney, J., & Landau, S. (1982). The independent dimensions of hyperactivity and aggression: A validation with playroom observation data. *Journal of Abnormal Psychology, 91,* 183–198.

Miklowitz, D. J., Goldstein, M. J., Falloon, I. R. H., & Doane, J. A. (1984). Interactional correlates of expressed emotion in the families of schizophrenics. *British Journal of Psychiatry, 144,* 482–487.

Miller, G. E., & Prinz, R. J. (1990). Enhancement of social learning family interventions for child conduct disorder. *Psychological Bulletin, 108,* 291–307.

Miller, L. C. (1972). School Behavior Checklist: An inventory of deviant behavior for elementary school children. *Journal of Consulting and Clinical Psychology, 38,* 138–144.

Miller, L. C., Hampe, E., Barrett, C., & Noble, H. (1971). Children's deviant behavior within the general population. *Journal of Consulting and Clinical Psychology, 37,* 16–22.

Milton, F., & Hafner, J. (1979). The outcome of behavior therapy for agoraphobia in relation to marital adjustment. *Archives of General Psychiatry, 36,* 807–811.

Minkoff, K. (1978). A map of chronic mental patients. In J. A. Talbot (Ed.), *The chronic mental patient.* Washington, DC: American Psychiatric Association.

Minuchin, S. (1975). *Families and family therapy.* Cambridge MA: Harvard.

Mischel, W. (1968). *Personality and assessment.* New York: Wiley.

Mischel, W. (1976). *Introduction to personality.* New York: Holt, Rinehart & Winston.

Mischel, W. (1979). On the interface of cognition and personality: Beyond the person-situation debate. *American Psychologist, 34,* 740–754.

Mitchell, J. E., & Groat, R. (1984). A placebo-controlled double-blind trial of amitriptyline in bulimia. *Journal of Clinical Psychopharmacology, 4,* 186–193.

Mitchell, J. E., Pyle, R. L., Eckert, E. D., Hatsukami, D., & Lentz, R. (1983). Electrolyte and other physiological abnormalities in patients with bulimia. *Psychological Medicine, 13,* 273–278.

Mitchell, J. E., Pyle, R. L., Eckert, E. D., Hatsukami, D., Pomeroy, C., & Zimmerman, R. (1990). A comparison study of antidepressants and structured intensive group psychotherapy in the treatment of bulimia nervosa. *Archives of General Psychiatry, 147,* 149–157.

Monti, P. M., Abrams, D. B., Binkoff, J. A., & Zwick, W. R. (1986). Social skills training and substance abuse. In C. R. Hollin & P. Trower (Eds.), *Handbook of social skills training* (pp. 111–142). Oxford: Pergamon.

Monti, P. M., Abrams, D. B., Kadden, R. M., & Cooney, N. L. (1989). *Treating alcohol dependence.* New York: Guilford.

Moore, D. R., Chamberlain, P., Mukai, L. H. (1979). Children at risk for delinquency: A follow-up comparison of aggressive children and children who steal. *Journal of Abnormal Child Psychology, 7,* 345–355.

Morgan, D. P., & Jensen, W. R. (1988). *Teaching behaviorally disordered students: Preferred practices.* Columbus, OH: Charles E. Merrill.

Morokoff, P., & LoPiccolo, J. (1986). A comparative evaluation of minimal therapist contact and fifteen session treatment for female orgasmic dysfunction. *Journal of Consulting and Clinical Psychology, 54,* 294–300.

Morris, J. B., & Beck, A. T. (1974). The efficiency of antidepressant drugs: A review of research (1958–1972). *Archives of General Psychiatry, 30,* 667–674.

Morris, S. B., Alexander, J. F., & Waldron, H. (1990). Functional family therapy: Issues in clinical practice. In I. R. H. Falloon (Ed.), *Handbook of behavior therapy.* New York: Guilford.

Morrison, R. L., (1988). Structured interviews and rating scales. In A. S. Bellack & M. Hersen (Eds.), *Behavioral assessment: A practical handbook* (3rd ed., pp. 252–278). New York: Pergamon.

Morrison, R. L., & Bellack, A. S. (1987). The social functioning of schizophrenic patients: Clinical and research issues. *Schizophrenia Bulletin, 13,* 715–725.

Morrison, R. L., Bellack, A. S., & Mueser, K. T. (1988). Facial affect recognition deficits and schizophrenia. *Schizophrenia Bulletin, 14,* 67–83.

Morrison, R. L., & Wixted, J. T. (1989). Social skills training. In A. S. Bellack (Ed.), *A clinical guide for the treatment of schizophrenia* (pp. 237–262). New York: Plenum.

Moser, A. J. (1974). Covert punishment of hallucinatory behavior in a psychotic male. *Journal of Behavior Therapy and Experimental Psychiatry, 5,* 297–299.

Mowrer, O. H. (1947). On the dual nature of learning: A reinterpretation of "conditioning" and "problem-solving." *Harvard Educational Review, 17,* 102–148.

Mowrer, O. H., & Mowrer, W. M. (1938). Enuresis: A method for its study and treatment. *American Journal of Orthopsychiatry, 8,* 436–459.

Muehlenhard, C. L., Koralewski, M. A., Andrews, S. L., & Burdick, C. A. (1986). Verbal and nonverbal cues that convey interest in dating: Two studies. *Behavior Therapy, 17,* 404–419.

Muehlenhard, C. L., & McFall, R. M. (1981). Dating initiation from a woman's perspective, *Behavior Therapy, 12,* 682–691.

Mueser, K. T. (1989). Behavioral family therapy. In A. S. Bellack (Ed.), *A clinical guide for the treatment of schizophrenia* (pp. 207–236). New York: Plenum.

Mueser, K. T., Bellack, A. S., Morrison, R. L., & Wade, J. H. (1990). Gender, social competence, and symptomatology in schizophrenia: A longitudinal analysis. *Journal of Abnormal Psychology, 99,* 138–147.

Mueser, K. T., Bellack, A. S., Morrison, R. L., & Wixted, J. T. (1990). Social competence in schizophrenia: Premorbid adjustment, social skill, and domains of functioning. *Journal of Psychiatric Research, 24,* 51–63.

Mueser, K. T., Bellack, A. S., & Wade, J. H. (1992). Validation of a short version of the Camberwell Family Interview. *Psychological Assessment, 4*, 424–429.

Mueser, K. T., & Berenbaum, H. (1990). Psychodynamic treatment of schizophrenia: Is there a future? *Psychological Medicine, 20*, 253–262.

Mueser, K. T., Foy, D. W., & Carter, M. J. (1986). Social skills training for job maintenance in a psychiatric patient. *Journal of Counseling Psychology, 33*, 360–362.

Mueser, K. T., Yarnold, P. R., Levinson, D. F., Singh, H., Bellack, A. S., Kee, K., Morrison, R. L., & Yadalam, K. G. (1990). Prevalence of substance abuse in schizophrenia: Demographic and clinical correlates. *Schizophrenia Bulletin, 16*, 31–56.

Mulick, J. A., Scott, F. D., Gaines, R. F., & Campbell, B. M. (1983). Devices and instrumentation for skill development and behavior change. In J. L. Matson & F. Andrasik (Eds.), *Treatment issues and innovations in mental retardation* (pp. 515–580). New York: Plenum.

Munby, J., & Johnston, D. W. (1980). Agoraphobia: The long-term follow-up of behavioural treatment. *British Journal of Psychiatry, 137*, 418–427.

Murphy, G. E., Simons, A. D., Wetzel, R. D. & Lustman, P. J. (1984). Cognitive therapy and pharmacotherapy, singly and together, in the treatment of depression. *Archives of General Psychiatry, 41*, 33–41.

Murphy, H. A., Hutchison, J. M., & Bailey, J. S. (1983). Behavioral school psychology goes outdoors: The effect of organized games on playground aggression. *Journal of Applied Behavior Analysis, 16*, 29–36.

Murphy, J. (1988). Contingency contracting in schools: A review. *Education and Treatment of Children, 11*, 257–269.

Murphy, J., & Lipshultz, L. (1988). Infertility in the paraplegic male. In E. Tanagho, T. Lue, & R. McClure (Eds.), *Contemporary management of impotence and infertility*. Baltimore, MD: Williams & Wilkins.

National Institute on Drug Abuse (1985). *National household survey on drug abuse*. Washington, D.C. : U.S. Department of Health and Human Services.

Neef, N. A., Iwata, B. A., & Page, T. J. (1980). The effects of interpersonal training versus high density reinforcement on spelling acquisition and retention. *Journal of Applied Behavior Analysis, 13*, 153–158.

Nelson, R. O. (1977). Methodological issues in assessment via self-monitoring. In J. D. Cone & R. P. Hawkins (Eds.), *Behavior assessment: New directions in clinical psychology*. New York: Brunner/Mazel.

Nelson, R., & Hayes, S. (1979) Some current dimensions of behavioral assessment. *Behavioral Assessment, 1*, 1–16.

Neuberger, O. W., Matarazzo, J. D., Schmitz, R. E., & Pratt, H. H. (1980). One-year follow-up of total abstinence in chronic alcoholic patients following emetic counterconditioning. *Alcoholism: Clinical and Experimental Research, 4*, 806–810.

Neuberger, O. W., Miller, S. I., Schmitz, R. E., Matarazzo, J. D., Pratt, H. H., & Hasha, N. (1982). Replicable abstinence rates in an alcoholism treatment program. *Journal of the American Medical Association, 248*, 960–963.

Newcomb, M. D., & Bentler, P. M. (1988). *Consequences of adolescent drug use: Impact on the lives of young adults*. Newbury Park, CA: Sage.

Newsom, C., Favell, J., & Rincover, A. (1983). The side-effects of punishment. In S. Axelrod & J. Apshe (Eds.), *The effects of punishment on human behavior* (pp. 285–316). New York: Academic Press.

Newsom, C., & Rincover, A. (1982). Autism. In E. J. Marsh & L. G. Terdal (Eds.), *Behavioral assessment of childhood disorders*. New York: Guilford.

Nihira, K., Foster, R., Shellhaas, N., & Leland, H. (1974). *AAMD adaptive behavior scale manual*. Washington, DC: American Association on Mental Deficiency.

Nordquist, V. M., & Whaler, R. G. (1973). Naturalistic treatment of an autistic child. *Journal of Applied Behavior Analysis, 6*, 79–87.

Norton, G. R., Harrison, B., Hauch, J., & Rhodes, L. (1985). Characteristics of people with infrequent panic attacks. *Journal of Abnormal Psychology, 94*, 216–221.

Nuechterlein, K. H., & Dawson, M. E. (1984). A heuristic vulnerability/stress model of schizophrenic episodes. *Schizophrenia Bulletin, 10*, 300–312.

Nutter, D., & Reid, D. H. (1978). Teaching retarded women a clothing selection skill using community norms. *Journal of Applied Behavior Analysis, 11*, 475–487.

O'Banion, K., & Arkowitz, H. (1977). Social anxiety and selective memory for affective information about the self. *Social Behavior and Personality, 5*, 321–328.

O'Brien, F., & Azrin, N. H. (1972). Developing proper mealtime behaviors of the institutionalized retarded. *Journal of Applied Behavior Analysis, 5*, 389–399.

O'Brien, F., Bugle, C., & Azrin, N. H. (1972). Training and maintaining a retarded child's proper eating. *Journal of Applied Behavior Analysis, 5*, 67–72.

O'Connor, J., & Dowrick, P. W. (1987). Cognitions in normal weight, overweight, and previously overweight adults. *Cognitive Therapy and Research, 11*, 315–326.

O'Dell, S. (1974). Training parents in behavior modification: A review. *Psychological Bulletin, 81*, 418–433.

O'Donnell, C. R., Lydgate, T., & Fo, W. S. O. (1979). The buddy system: Review and follow-up. *Child Behavior Therapy, 1*, 161–169.

O'Farrell, T. J., Cutter, H. S. G., & Floyd, F. J. (1985).

Evaluating behavioral marital therapy for male alcoholics: Effects on marital adjustment and communication from before to after treatment. *Behavior Therapy, 16,* 147–167.

O'Leary, K. D., & Borkovec, T. D. (1978). Conceptual, methodological, and ethical problems in placebo groups in psychotherapy research. *American Psychologist, 33,* 831–840.

O'Leary, S. G., & Dubey, D. R. (1979). Applications of self-control procedures by children: A review. *Journal of Applied Behavior Analysis, 12,* 449–465.

Oei, T. P. S., & Jackson, P. (1980). Long term effects of group and individual social skills training with alcoholics. *Addictive Behaviors, 5,* 129–136.

Oei, T. P. S., & Jackson, P. R. (1982). Social skills and cognitive behavioral approaches to the treatment of problem drinking. *Journal of Studies on Alcohol, 43,* 532–547.

Offord, D. R., Jones, M. B., Graham, A., Poushinsky, M., Sternerson, P., & Weaver, L. (1985). *Community skill-development programs for children: Rationale and steps in imple mentation.* Canada: Canadian Parks and Recreation Program.

Olweus, D. (1979). Stability of aggressive reaction patterns in males: A review. *Psychological Bulletin, 86,* 852–857.

Ornitz, E., & Ritvo, E. (1976). The syndrome of autism: A critical review. *The American Journal of Psychiatry, 133,* 609–621.

Orvaschel, H., Puig-Antich, J., Chambers, W. J., Tabrizi, M. A., & Johnson, R. (1982). Retrospective assessment of prepubertal major depression with the Kiddie-SADS-E. *Journal of the American Academy of Child Psychiatry, 21,* 392–397.

Orwin, A. (1973). The running treatment: A preliminary communication on a new use for an old therapy (physical activity) in the agoraphobic syndrome. *British Journal of Psychiatry, 122,* 175–179.

Ostrov, E., Marohn, R. C., Offer, D., Curtiss, G., & Feczko, M. (1980). The Adolescent Antisocial Behavior Check List. *Journal of Clinical Psychology, 36,* 594–601.

Overall, J. E., & Gorham, D. R. (1962). The Brief Psychiatric Rating scale. *Psychological Reports, 18,* 799–812.

Page, T. J., Iwata, B. A., & Neef, N. A. (1976). Teaching pedestrian skills to retarded persons: Generalization from the classroom to the natural environment. *Journal of Applied Behavior Analysis, 9,* 433–444.

Paine, S. C., & Bellamy, G. T. (1982). From innovation to standard practice: Developing and disseminating behavioral procedures. *The Behavior Analyst, 5,* 29–43.

Pain, S. C., Radicchi, J., Rosellini, L. C., Deutchman, L., & Darch, C. B. (1983). *Structuring your classroom for academic success.* Champaign, IL: Research Press.

Palmer, R. E. (1969). *Hermeneutics: Interpretation theory in Schlelermacker, Dilthey, Heidegger, and Gadamer.* Evanston, IL: Northwestern University Press.

Paniagna, F. A., Pumariega, A. J., & Black, S. A. (1988). Clinical effects of correspondence training in the management of hyperactive children. *Behavioral Residential Treatment, 3,* 19–40.

Parke, R. D. (1986). Fathers, families, and support systems: Their role in the development of at-risk and retarded infants and children. In J. J. Gallagher & P. M. Vietz (Eds.), *Families of handicapped persons* (pp. 101–113). Baltimore: Brookes.

Patel, C. H. (1977). Biofeedback-aided relaxation and meditation in the management of hypertension. *Biofeedback and Self-Regulation, 2,* 1–14.

Paternite, C., & Loney, J. (1980). Childhood hyperkinesis: Relationships between symptomatology and home environment. In C. K. Whalen & B. Henker (Eds.), *Hyperactive children: The social ecology of identification and treatment* (pp. 105–141). New York: Academic Press.

Pato, M. T., Zoka-Kadouch, R., Zohar, J., & Murphy, D. L. (1988). Return of symptoms after discontinuation of clomipramine: Inpatients with obsessive-compulsive disorder. *American Journal of Psychiatry, 145*(12), 1521–1525.

Patterson, G. R. (1965). An application of conditioning techniques to the control of a hyperactive child. In L. P. Ullman & L. Krasner (Eds.), *Case studies in behavior modification* (pp. 370–375). New York: Prentice-Hall.

Patterson, G. R. (1974). Interventions for boys with conduct problems: Multiple settings, treatments, and criteria. *Journal of Consulting and Clinical Psychology, 42,* 471–481.

Patterson, G. R. (1976). The aggressive child: Victim and architect of a coercive system. In L. A. Hamerlynck, L. C. Handy, and E. J. Mash (Eds.), *Behavior modification and families: Theory and research* (Vol 1, pp. 267–316). New York: Brunner/Mazel.

Patterson, G. R. (1982). *Coercive family process.* Eugene, OR: Castalia.

Patterson, G. R. (1985). Beyond technology: The next stage in developing an empirical base for parent training. In L. L'Abate (Ed.), *Handbook of family psychology and therapy* (Vol. 2), pp. 1344–1379. Homewood, IL: Dorsey.

Patterson, G. R. (1986). Performance models for antisocial boys. *American Psychologist, 41,* 432–444.

Patterson, G. R., Capaldi, D., & Bank, L. (1991). An early starter model for predicting delinquency. In D. J. Pepler & K. H. Rubin (Eds.), *The development and treatment of childhood aggression* (pp. 139–168). Hillsdale, NJ: Erlbaum.

Patterson, G. R., Chamberlain, P., & Reid, J. B. (1982). A comparative evaluation of a parent-training program. *Behavior Therapy, 13,* 638–650.

Patterson, G. R., Cobb, J. A., & Ray, R. S. (1973). A social engineering technology for retraining aggressive boys.

In H. E. Adams & P. Unikel (Eds.), *Issues and trends in behavior therapy.* Springfield, IL: Charles C. Thomas.

Patterson, G. R., & Forgatch, M. S. (1985). Therapist behavior as a determinant for client noncompliance: A paradox for the behavior modifier. *Journal of Consulting and Clinical Psychology, 53,* 846–851.

Patterson, G. R., & Reid, J. B. (1973). Interventions for families of aggressive boys: A replication study. *Behavior Research and Therapy, 11,* 383–394.

Patterson, G. R., Reid, J. B., Jones, R. R., & Conger, R. E. (1975). *A social learning approach to family intervention: Families with aggressive children.* Eugene, OR: Castalia.

Paul, G. L., & Lentz, R. J. (1977). *Psychosocial treatment of chronic mental patients: Milieu versus social-learning programs.* Cambridge, MA: Harvard University Press.

Paul, G. L., & Licht, M. H. (1988). Time-Sample Behavioral Checklist. In M. Hersen & A. S. Bellack (Eds.), *Dictionary of behavioral assessment techniques* (pp. 481–484). New York: Pergamon.

Peed, S., Roberts, M., & Forehand, R. (1977). Evaluation of the effectiveness of a standardized parent training program in altering the interaction of mothers and their noncompliant children. *Behavior Modification, 1,* 323–350.

Pekarik, E. G., Prinz, R. J., Liebert, D. E., Weintraub, S., & Neale, J. M. (1976). The Pupil Evaluation Inventory: A sociometric technique for assessing children's social behavior. *Journal of Abnormal Child Psychology, 4,* 83–97.

Pelham, W. E., & Bender, M. E. (1982). Peer relationships in hyperactive children: Description and treatment. In K. Gadow & E. Bialer (Eds.), *Advances in learning and behavioral disabilities* (Vol. 1, pp. 365–436). Greenwich, CT: JAI Press.

Pelham, W. E., & Murphy, H. A. (1986). Attention deficit and conduct disorders. In M. Hersen (Ed.), *Pharmacological and behavioral treatment.* New York: Wiley.

Pepper, S. C. (1942). *World hypotheses: A study in evidence.* Berkeley, CA: University of California Press.

Perri, M. G., McAllister, D. A., Gange, J. J., Jordan, R. C., McAdoo, W. G., & Nezu, A. M. (1988). Effects of four maintenance programs on the long-term management of obesity. *Journal of Consulting and Clinical Psychology, 56,* 529–534.

Perri, M. G., Nezu, A. M., Patti, E. T., McCann, K. L. (1989). Effect of length of treatment on weight loss. *Journal of Consulting and Clinical Psychology, 57,* 450–452.

Perris, C. (1966). A study of bipolar (manic-depressive) and unipolar recurrent depressive psychosis. *Acta Psychiatrica Scandinavia, 42,* (Suppl. No. 194), 1–189.

Perris, C. (1989). *Cognitive therapy with schizophrenic patients.* New York: Guilford.

Perry, C. L., Klepp, K. I, & Shultz, J. M. (1988). Primary prevention of cardiovascular disease: Communitywise strategies for youth. *Journal of Consulting and Clinical Psychology, 56(3),* 358–364.

Perry, C. L., Murray, D. M., & Klepp, K. I. (1987). Prediction of adolescent smoking and implications for prevention. *Morbidity and Mortality Weekly, 36,* 415–455.

Peters, M. N., & Richardson, C. T. (1983). Stressful life events, acid hypersecretion, and ulcer disease. *Gastroenterology, 84,* 114–119.

Peterson, A. C., & Craighead, W. E. (1986). Emotional and personality development in normal adolescents and young adults. In G. L. Klerman (Ed.), *Suicide and depression among adolescents and young adults* (pp. 19–52). Washington, DC: American Psychiatric Press.

Peterson, D. R. (1968). *The clinical study of social behavior.* New York: Appleton-Century-Crofts.

Peterson, L. (1984a). The "Safe at Home" game: Training comprehensive prevention skills in latchkey children. *Behavior Modification, 8,* 474–494.

Peterson, L. (1984b). Teaching home safety and survival skills to latchkey children: A comparison of two manuals and methods. *Journal of Applied Behavior Analysis, 17,* 279–293.

Peterson, L., Chaney, J., & Harbeck, C. (1989). Programming for healthy lifestyles in children. *The Behavior Therapist, 12(7),* 147–152.

Peterson, L., Farmer, J., & Mori, L. (1987). Process analysis of injury situations: A complement to epidemiological methods. *Journal of Social Issues, 43,* 33–44.

Peterson, L., & Harbeck, C. (1988). *The pediatric psychologist: Issues in professional development and practice.* Champaign, IL: Research Press.

Peterson, L., & Harbeck, C. (1990). Medical disorders. In S. Bellack, M. Hersen, & A. E. Kazdin (Eds.), *International handbook of behavior modification and therapy* (pp. 791–803). New York: Wiley.

Peterson, L., Mori, L., Selby, V., & Rosen, B. (1988). Community interventions in children's injury prevention: Differing costs and differing benefits. *Journal of Community Psychology, 16,* 62–73.

Peterson, L., & Shigetomi, C. (1981). The use of coping techniques to minimize anxiety in hospitalized children. *Behavior Therapy, 12,* 1–14.

Peterson, L., & Shigetomi, C. (1982). One-year follow-up of elective surgery child patients receiving preoperative preparation. *Journal of Pediatric Psychology, 7,* 43–48.

Peterson, L., & Thiele, C. (1987). Home safety at school. *Child and Family Behavior Therapy, 10,* 1–8.

Peterson, L., & Toler, S. M. (1986). An information seeking disposition in child surgery patients. *Health Psychology*, 5, 343–358.

Petti, T. A., Bornstein, M., Delamater, A., & Conners, C. K. (1980). Evaluation and multimodality treatment of a depressed prepubertal girl. *Journal of the American Academy of Child Psychiatry, 19*, 690–702.

Pfadt, A., & Tryon, W. W. (1983). Issues in the selection and use of mechanical transducers to directly measure motor activity in clinical setting. *Applied Research in Mental Retardation, 4*, 251–270.

Pfiffner, L. J., & O'Leary, S. G. (1987). The efficacy of all-positive management as a function of the prior use of negative consequences. *Journal of Applied Behavior Analysis, 20*, 265–271.

Pfiffner, L. J., Rosen, L. A., & O'Leary, S. G. (1985). The efficacy of an all-positive approach to classroom management. *Journal of Applied Behavior Analysis, 18*, 257–261.

Phillips, E. (1968). Achievement Place: Token reinforcement procedures in a home style rehabilitation setting for pre-delinquent boys. *Journal of Applied Behavior Analysis, 1*, 213–223.

Phillips, E. L., Phillips, E. A., Wolf, M. M., & Fixsen, D. L. (1973). Achievement Place: Development of the elected-manager system. *Journal of Applied Behavior Analysis, 6*, 541–561.

Piattelli-Palmarini, M. (1989). Evolution, selection and cognition: From "learning" to parameter setting in biology and in the study of language. *Cognition, 31*, 1–44.

Pinkston, E. M., Reese, N. M., LeBlanc, J. M., & Baer, D. M. (1973). Independent control of a preschool child's aggression and peer interaction by contingent teacher attention. *Journal of Applied Behavior Analysis, 6*, 115–124.

Pinto, R. P., & Hollandsworth, J. G. (1989). Evaluation of psychological preparation of pediatric surgery: The influence of parents on preparation and the cost vs. benefits of providing preparation services. *Heath Psychology, 8*(1), 79–95.

Pisterman, S., McGrath, P., Goodman, J. T., Webster, I., Mallory, R., & Firestone, P. (1988). Multimethod assessment of parent training outcome in the treatment of preschoolers with Attention Deficit Disorder with Hyperactivity. Paper presented at the 22nd annual meeting of the Association for the Advancement of Behavior Therapy, New York.

Pitfield, M., & Oppenheim, A. N. (1964). Child rearing attitudes of mothers of psychotic children. *Journal of Child Psychology and Psychiatry and Allied Disciplines, 5*, 51–57.

Platt, S. (1985). Measuring the burden of psychiatric illness on the family: An evaluation of some rating scales. *Psychological Medicine, 15*, 383–393.

Plummer, S., Baer, D. M., & LeBlanc, J. M. (1977). Func-

tional considerations in the use of procedural timeout and an effective alternative. *Journal of Applied Behavior Analysis, 10*, 689–705.

Poling, A. D., & Parker, C. (1983). Empirical strategies. In J. L. Matson & S. E. Bruening (Eds.), *Assessing the mentally retarded*. New York: Grune & Stratton.

Polivy, J., & Herman, C. P. (1985). Dieting and binging: A causal analysis. *American Psychologist, 40*, 193–201.

Pollard, S., Ward, E. M., & Barkley, R. A. (1983). The effects of parent training and Ritalin on the parent-child interactions of hyperactive boys. *Child and Family Behavior Therapy, 5*, 51–69.

Pope, H. G., Hudson, J. I., & Yurgelun-Todd, D. (1983). Bulimia treated with imipramine: A placebo controlled, double-blind study. *American Journal of Psychiatry, 140*, 554–558.

Porterfield, J. K., Herbert-Jackson, E., & Risley, T. R. (1976). Contingent observation: An effective and acceptable procedure for reducing disruptive behavior of young children in a group setting. *Journal of Applied Behavior Analysis 9*, 55–64.

Powell, L. H., & Thoresen, C. E. (1987). Modifying the type A behavior pattern: A small group treatment approach. In J. A. Blumenthal, & D. C. McKee (Eds.) *Applications in behavioral medicine and health psychology: A clinician's source book*. Sarasota FL: Professional Research Exchange.

Poznanski, E. O., Krahenbuhl, V., & Zrull, Z. P. (1976). Childhood depression: A longitudinal perspective. *Journal of the American Academy of Child Psychiatry, 15*, 491–501.

Premack, P. (1959). Toward empirical behavior laws: I. Positive reinforcement. *Psychological Review, 66*, 219–233.

Pressley, M. (1990). Four more considerations about self-regulation in the mentally retarded. *American Journal on Mental Retardation, 94*, 369–371.

Pressley, M., Cariglia-Bull, T., Deane, S., & Schneider, W. (1987). Short-term memory, verbal competence, and age as predictors of imagery instructional effectiveness. *Journal of Experimental Child Psychology, 43*, 194–211.

Pridal, C. G. & LoPiccolo, J. (1992). Brief treatment of vaginismus. In. R. A. Wells, & V. J. Giannetti (Eds.), *Casebook of the brief psychotherapies*. New York: Plenum.

Prizant, B. M., & Duchan, J. F. (1981). The functions of immediate echolalia in autistic children. *Journal of Speech and Hearing Disorders, 46*, 241–249.

Puccio, P., Janicki, M., Otis, J., & Rettig, J. (1983). Report of the Committee on Aging and the Developmentally Disabled. Albany, NY: Office of Mental Retardation and Developmental Disabilities.

Puig-Antich, J. (1982). Major depression and conduct disorder in prepuberty. *Journal of the American Academy of Child Psychiatry, 21*, 118–128.

Puig-Antich, J., & Chambers, W. (1978). The Schedule for Affective Disorders and Schizophrenia for School-Aged Children (K-SADS). New York: New York State Psychiatric Institute.

Puig-Antich, J., Perel, J. M., Lupatkin, W., Chambers, W. J., Tabrizi, M. A., King, J., Goetz, R., Davies, M., & Stiller, R. L. (1987). Imipramine in prepubertal major depressive disorders. *Archives of General Psychiatry, 44*, 81–89.

Puig-Antich, J., & Weston, B. (1983). The diagnosis and treatment of major depressive disorder in childhood. *Annual Review of Medicine, 34*, 231–245.

Purcell, K. (1956). The TAT and antisocial behavior. *Journal of Consulting Psychology, 20*, 449–456.

Puska, P., Vartiainen, E., Pallonen, V., Salonen, J. T., Poyhia, P., Koskela, K., & McAlister, A. (1982). The North Karelia Youth Project: Evaluation of two years of intervention on health behavior and DVD risk factors among 13–15 year old children. *Preventive Medicine, 11*, 550–570.

Pyle, R. L., Mitchell, J. E., Eckert, E. D., Halvorson, P. A., Neuman, P. A., and Goff, G. M. (1983). The incidence of bulimia in freshman college students. *International Journal of Eating Disorders, 2*, 75–85.

Quay, H. C. (1986). Classification. In H. C. Quay & J. S. Werry (Eds.), *Psychopathological disorders of childhood* (3rd ed., pp. 1–34). New York: Wiley.

Quay, H. C., & Peterson, D. (1983). *Manual for the Revised Behavior Problem Checklist.* Coral Gables, FL: Authors.

Quay, H. C., Routh, D. K., & Shapiro, S. K. (1987). Psychopathology of childhood: From description to validation. In M. R. Rosenzweig & L. W. Porter (Eds.), *Annual Review of Psychology, 38*, 491–532.

Rabinowitz, H. S., & Zimmerli, W. H. (1974). Effects of a health education program on junior high students' knowledge, attitudes, and behavior concerning tobacco use. *Journal of School Health, 44*, 324–330.

Rabkin, J. G. (1980). Stressful life events and schizophrenia: A review of the research literature. *Psychological Bulletin, 87*, 408–425.

Rabkin, J. G., & Struening, E. L. (1976). Life events, stress, and illness. *Science, 194*, 1013–1020.

Rachlin, H. (1989). *Judgement, decision, and choice: A cognitive/behavioral synthesis.* New York: W. H. Freeman.

Rachman, S. (1972). Clinical applications of observational learning, imitation, and modeling. *Behavior Therapy, 3*, 379–397.

Rachman, S. J. (1982). Obsessional-compulsive disorders. In A. S. Bellack, M. Hersen, & A. E. Kazdin (Eds.), *International handbook of behavior modification and therapy.* New York: Plenum.

Rachman, S., Craske, M., Tallman, K., & Solyom, C. (1986). Does escape behavior strengthen agoraphobic avoidance? A replication. *Behavior Therapy, 17*, 366–384.

Rachman, S., & Wilson, G. T. (1980). *The effects of psychological therapy.* Oxford: Pergamon.

Ramsden, R., Friedman, B. G., & Williamson, D. (1983). Treatment of childhood headache reports with contingency management procedures. *Journal of Clinical Child Psychology, 12*, 202–206.

Randolph, E. T., Eth, S., Glynn, S., Paz, G. B., Leong, G. B., Shaner, A. L., Strachan, A., Van Vort, W., Escobar, J., & Liberman, R. P. (In press). Behavioral family management in schizophrenia: Outcome from a clinic-based intervention. *British Journal of Psychiatry.*

Rapoff, M. A., Lindsley, C. B., & Christophersen, E. R. (1984). Improving compliance with medical regimens: A case study with juvenile rheumatoid arthritis. *Archives of Physical Medicine and Rehabilitation, 65*, 267–269.

Rapport, M. D. (1987). Attention deficit disorder with hyperactivity. In M. Hersen & V. B. Van Hasselt (Eds.), *Behavior therapy with children and adolescents: A clinical approach.* New York: Wiley.

Rapport, M. D., Jones, J. T., DuPaul, G. J., Kelly, K. L., Gardner, M. J., Tucker, S. B., & Shea, M. S. (1987). Attention deficit disorder and methylphenidate: Group and single-subjective analyses of dose effects on attention in clinic and classroom settings. *Journal of Clinical Child Psychology, 16*, 329–338.

Rapport, M. D., Murphy, A., & Bailey, J. S. (1982). Ritalin versus response cost in the control of hyperactive children: A within-subject comparison. *Journal of Applied Behavior Analysis, 15*, 205–216.

Raskin, A., Schulterbrandt, J. G., Reatig, N., & McKeon, J. J. (1970). Differential response to chlorpromazine, imipramine, and placebo: A study of subgroups of hospitalized depressed patients. *Archives of General Psychiatry, 23*, 164–173.

Rathus, S. A. (1973). A 30-item schedule for assessing assertive behavior. *Behavior Therapy, 4*, 398–406.

Raush, H. L, Barry, W. A., Hertel, R. K., & Swain, M. A. (1974). *Communication, conflict, and marriage.* San Francisco: Jossey-Bass.

Raw, M., & Russell, M. A. H. (1980). Rapid-smoking, cue exposure and support in the modification of smoking. *Behavior Research and Therapy, 18*, 363–372.

Razran, G. (1961). The observable unconscious and the inferable conscious in current Soviet psychophysiology: Interoceptive conditioning, semantic conditioning, and the orienting reflex. *Psychological Review, 68*, 81–150.

Reed, E. W., & Reed, S. C. (1965). *Mental retardation: A family study.* Philadelphia: W. B. Saunders.

Rehm, L. P. (1977). A self-control model of depression. *Behavior Therapy, 8*, 787–804.

Rehm, L P. (1981). Assessment of depression. In M. Hersen & A. S. Bellack (Eds.), *Behavioral assessment: A practical handbook*, (2nd ed., pp. 246–295). New York: Pergamon.

Rehm, L P., Fuchs, C. Z., Roth, D. M., Kornblith, S. J., & Romano, J. M. (1979). A comparison of self-control and assertion skills treatments of depression. *Behavior Therapy, 10*, 429–442.

Rehm, L P., Kornblith, S. J., O'Hara, M. W., Lamparski, D. M., Romano, J. M., & Volkin, J. I. (1981). An evaluation of major components in a self-control therapy program for depression. *Behavior Modification, 5*, 459–489.

Rehm, L. P., & Marston, A. R. (1968). Reduction of social anxiety through modification of self-reinforcement: An instigation therapy technique. *Journal of Consulting and Clinical Psychology, 32*, 565–574.

Reid, D. K. (1988). *Teaching the learning disabled.* Boston: Allyn & Bacon.

Reid, J. B. (Ed.) (1978). *A social learning approach to family intervention: Observation in home settings* (Vol. 2). Eugene, OR: Castalia.

Reid, J. B., Baldwin, D. V., Patterson, G. R., & Dishion, T. J. (1988). Observations in the assessment of childhood disorders. In M. Rutter, A. H. Tuma, & I. S. Lann (Eds.), *Assessment and diagnosis in child psychopathology* (pp. 156–195). New York: Guilford.

Reid, J. B., Hinojosa-Rivera, G., & Lorber, R. A. (1980). *A social learning approach to the outpatient treatment of children who steal.* Unpublished manuscript, Oregon Social Learning Center, Eugene, OR.

Reiss, S., Peterson, R. A., Gursky, D. M., & McNally, R. J. (1986). Anxiety sensitivity, anxiety frequency, and the prediction of fearfulness. *Behaviour Research and Therapy, 24*, 1–8.

Renneberg, B. Goldstein, A. J., Phillips, D., & Chambless, D. L. (1990). Intensive behavioral group therapy of avoidant personality disorder. *Behavior Therapy, 21*, 363–377.

Repp, A. C. (1983). *Teaching the mentally retarded.* Englewood Cliffs, NJ: Prentice-Hall.

Repp, A. C., Barton, L. E.,& Brulle, A. R. (1981). Correspondence between effectiveness and staff use of instructions for severely retarded persons. *Applied Research in Mental Retardation, 2*, 237–245.

Reschley, D. J. (1982). Assessing mild mental retardation: The influence of adaptive behavior, sociocultural status, and prospects for nonbiased assessment. In R. R. Reynolds, & T. B. Gutkin (Eds.), *The handbook of school psychology.* New York: Wiley.

Resnick, P. A., Jordan, C. G., Girelli, S. A., Hutler, C. K., & Marhoefer-Dvork, S. (1988). A comparative outcome study of behavioral group therapy for sexual assault victims. *Behavior Therapy, 19*, 384–401.

Revenstorf, D., Vogel, B., Wegener, C., Hahlweg, K., & Schindler, L. (1980). Escalation phenomena in interaction sequences: An empirical comparison of distressed and nondistressed couples. *Behavior analysis and Modification, 2*, 97–116.

Reynolds, B. S., Newsom, C. D., & Lovaas, O. I. (1974). Auditory overselectivity in autistic children. *Journal of Abnormal Child Psychology, 2*, 253–263.

Reynolds, W. M., Anderson, G., & Bartell, N. (1985). Measuring depression in children: A multi-method assessment investigation. *Journal of Abnormal Child Psychology, 13*, 513–526.

Reynolds, W. M., & Coats, K. I. (1986). A comparison of cognitive-behavioral therapy and relaxation training for the treatment of depression in adolescents. *Journal of Consulting and Clinical Psychology, 54*, 653–660.

Richter, I. L., McGrath, P. J., Humphreys, P. J., Goodman, J. T., Firestone, P., & Keene, D. (1986). Cognitive and relaxation treatment of pediatric migraine. *Pain, 25*, 195–203.

Rickard, K. (1988). The occurrence of maladaptive health-related behaviors and teacher-rated conduct problems in children of chronic low back pain patients. *Journal of Behavioral Medicine, 11*, 107–116.

Ricks, D. M., & Wing, L. (1975). Language, communication, and the use of symbols in normal and autistic children. *Journal of Autism and Childhood Schizophrenia, 5*, 191–22.

Riley, A. J., & Riley, E. (1978). Controlled study to evaluate directed masturbation in management of primary orgasmic failure in women. *British Journal of Psychiatry, 133*, 404–409.

Riley, D. M., Sobell, L. C., Leo, G. I., Sobell, M. B., & Klajner, F. (1987). Behavioral treatment of alcohol problems: A review and comparison of behavioral and nonbehavioral studies. In W. M. Cox (Ed.), *Treatment and Prevention of alcohol problems: A resource manual* (pp. 73–115). New York: Academic Press.

Rimland, B. (1964). *Infantile autism.* New York: Appleton-Century-Crofts.

Rimland, B. (1978). Inside the mind of an autistic savant. *Psychology Today, 12*, 68–80.

Rincover, A. (1978). Variables affecting stimulus fading and discriminative responding in psychotic children. *Journal of Abnormal Psychology, 87*, 541–553.

Rincover, A., Cook, R., Peoples, A., & Packard, D. (1979). Sensory extinction and sensory reinforcement principles for programming multiple adaptive behavior change. *Journal of Applied Behavior Analysis, 12*, 221–233.

Rincover, A., & Koegel, R. L. (1975). Setting generality and stimulus control in autistic children. *Journal of Applied Behavior Analysis, 8*, 235–246.

Rincover, A., & Koegel, R. L. (1977). Classroom treatment of autistic children: II. Individualized instruction in a group. *Journal of Abnormal Child Psychology, 5*, 113–126.

Risley, T. R., & Cuvo, A. (1980). Training mentally retarded adults to make emergency telephone calls. *Behavior Modification, 4*, 513–526.

Risley, T. R., & Wolf, M. (1967). Establishing functional speech in echolalia children. *Behavior Research and Therapy, 5*, 73–88.

Ritter, D. R. (1989). Teachers' perceptions of problem behavior in general and special education. *Exceptional Children, 55*, 559–564.

Ritvo, E. R., & Freeman, B. J. (1978). National Society for Autistic Children definition of the syndrome of autism. *Journal of Autism and Childhood Schizophrenia, 8*, 162–167.

Roazen, P. (1976). *Freud and his followers.* New York: Knopf.

Roberts, M. C. (1986). *Pediatric psychology: Psychological interventions and strategies for pediatric problems.* New York: Pergamon.

Roberts, M. C., & Broadbent, M. H. (1989). Increasing preschoolers' use of car safety devices: An effective program for day care staff. *Children's Health Care, 18*, 157–162.

Roberts, M. C., & Layfield, D. A. (1987). Promoting child passenger safety: A comparison of two positive methods. *Journal of Pediatric Psychology, 12*, 257–271.

Roberts, M. C., Layfield, D. A., & Fanurik, D. (1988). Motivating children's use of care safety devices. In M. Wolraich & D. Routh (Eds.), *Advances in developmental and behavioral pediatrics* (pp. 492–504). Greenwich, CT: JAI Press.

Roberts, M. C., Quevillon, R. P., & Wright, L. (1979). Pediatric psychology: A developmental report and survey of the literature. *Child and Youth Services, 2*, 1–9.

Roberts, M. C., & Turner, D. S. (1986). Rewarding parents for their children's use of safety seats. *Journal of Pediatric Psychology, 11*, 25–36.

Roberts, W. A., & Mazmanian, D. S. (1988). Concept learning at different levels of abstraction by pigeons, monkeys, and people. *Journal of Experimental Psychology: Animal Behavior Processes, 14*, 247–260.

Robins, E., & Guze, S. B. (1972). Classification of affective disorders: The primary-secondary, the endogenous-reactive, and the neurotic-psychotic concepts. In T. A. Williams, M. M. Katz, & J. A. Shield (Eds.), *Recent advances in the psychobiology of the depressive illness.* Washington, DC: U.S. Government Printing Office.

Robins, L. N. (1966). *Deviant children grown up.* Baltimore: Williams & Wilkins.

Robinson, E. A., Eyberg, S. M., & Ross, A. W. (1980). The standardization of an inventory of child conduct problem behaviors. *Journal of Clinical Child Psychology, 9*, 22–28.

Robinson, N. M., & Janos, P. M. (1987). The contribution of intelligence tests to the understanding of special children. In J. D. Day & J. G. Borkowski (Eds.), *Intelligence and exceptionality: New directions for theory, assessment, and instructional processes* (pp. 21–56). Norwood, NJ: Ablex.

Robinson, N., & Robinson, H. (1976). *The mentally retarded child: A psychological approach.* New York: McGraw-Hill.

Robinson, P. J., & Kobayashi, K. (1991). Development and evaluation of a presurgical preparation program. *Journal of Pediatric Psychology, 16*, 193–212.

Rogers, C. R. (1959). A theory of therapy, personality, and interpersonal relationships, as developed in the client-centered framework. In S. Koch (Ed.), *Psychology: A study of a science* (Vol. 3). New York: McGraw-Hill.

Rogers, C. R., Gendlin, E. G., Kiesler, D. J., & Truax, C. B. (Eds.). (1967). *The therapeutic relationship and its impact: Study of psychotherapy with schizophrenics.* Madison: The University of Wisconsin Press.

Rogers-Warren, P., & Baer, D. M. (1976). Correspondence between saying and doing: Teaching children to share and praise. *Journal of Applied Behavior Analysis, 9*, 335–354.

Rohsenow, D. J. (1983). Drinking habits and expectancies about alcohol's effects for self versus others. *Journal of Consulting and Clinical Psychology, 51*, 752–756.

Rolider, A., & Van Houten, R. (1985). Movement suppression time-out for undesirable behavior in psychotic and severely developmentally delayed children. *Journal of Applied Behavior Analysis, 18*, 275–288.

Rose, T. L. (1988). Current disciplinary practices with handicapped students: Suspensions and expulsions. *Exceptional Children, 55*, 230–239.

Rosen, A. J., Sussman, S., Mueser, K. T., Lyons, J. S., & Davis, J. M. (1981). Behavioral assessment of psychiatric inpatients and normal controls across different environmental contexts. *Journal of Behavioral Assessment, 3*, 25–36.

Rosen, J. C., & Leitenberg, H. (1984). Exposure plus response prevention treatment of bulimia. In D. M. Garner & P. E. Garfinkel (Eds.), *Handbook of psychotherapy for anorexia nervosa and bulimia.* New York: Guilford.

Rosen, L. A., O'Leary, S. G., Joyce, S. A., Conway, G., & Pfiffner, L. J. (1984). The importance of prudent negative consequences for maintaining the appropriate behavior of hyperactive students. *Journal of Abnormal Child Psychology, 12*, 581–604.

Rosen, M., Clark, G. R., & Kivitz, M. S. (1976). *The history of mental retardation.* Baltimore: University Park Press.

Rosenthal, T. L., & Bandura, A. (1978). Psychological modeling: Theory and practice. In S. L. Garfield & A. E. Bergin (Eds.), *Handbook of psychotherapy and behavior change.* New York: Wiley.

Rosnow, R. L., & Rosenthal, R. (1989). Statistical procedures and the justification of knowledge in psychological science. *American Psychologist, 44,* 1276–1284.

Ross, D. M., & Ross, S. A. (1973). Cognitive training for the EMR child: Situational problem-solving and planning. *American Journal of Mental Deficiency, 78,* 20–26.

Ross, D. M., & Ross, S. A. (1978). Cognitive training for EMR children: Choosing the best alternative. *American Journal of Mental Deficiency, 82,* 598–601.

Ross, D. M., & Ross, S. A. (1982). *Hyperactivity: Current issues, research, and theory* (2nd ed.). New York: Wiley.

Ross, D. M., & Ross, S. A. (1988). *Childhood pain: Current issues, research, and management.* Baltimore, MD: Urban & Schwarzenberg.

Rossiter, E. M., Agras, W. S., Losch, M., & Telch, C. F. (1988). Changes in self-reported food intake in bulimics as a consequence of antidepressant treatment. *International Journal of Eating Disorders, 7,* 779–784.

Rossiter, E. M., & Wilson, G. T. (1985). Cognitive restructuring and response prevention in the treatment of bulimia nervosa. *Behavior Research and Therapy, 23,* 349–359.

Rosvold, H. E., Mirsky, A. F., Sarason, I., Bransome, E. D., & Beck, L. H. (1956). A continuous performance test of brain damage. *Journal of Consulting Psychology, 20,* 343–350.

Roth, D., Bielski, R., Jones, M., Parker, W., & Osborn, G. (1982). A comparison of self-control therapy and combined self-control therapy and antidepressant medication in the treatment of depression. *Behavior Therapy, 13,* 133–144.

Rothbaum, B. O., & Foa, E. B. (1992). Cognitive-behavioral treatment of posttraumatic stress disorder. In P. A. Saigh (Ed.), *Posttraumatic Stress Disorder: A behavioral approach to assessment and treatment.* New York: Pergamon.

Rotholz, D. A., & Luce, S. C. (1983). Alternative reinforcement strategies for the reduction of self-stimulatory behavior in autistic youth. *Education and Treatment of Children, 6,* 363–377.

Routh, D. K. (1988). Introduction. In D. K. Routh (Ed.), *Handbook of pediatric psychology* (pp. 1–5). New York: Guilford.

Roy, A. (1986). Suicide in schizophrenia. In A. Roy (Ed.), *Suicide* (pp. 97–112). Baltimore: Williams & Wilkins.

Roy, A., Schreiber, J., Mazonson, A., & Picker, D. (1986). Suicidal behavior in chronic schizophrenia patients: A follow-up study. *Canadian Journal of Psychiatry, 31,* 737–740.

Rubin, K. H., Bream, L. A & Rose-Krasnor, L. (1991). Social problem solving and aggression in childhood. In D. J. Pepler & K. H. Rubin (Eds.), *The development and treatment of childhood aggression* (pp. 219–248). Hillsdale, NJ: Laurence Erlbaum.

Rusch, F. R., Morgan, T. K., Martin, J. E., Riva, M., & Agran, M. (1985). Competitive employment: Teaching mentally retarded employees self-instructional strategies. *Applied Research in Mental Retardation, 6,* 389–407.

Rusch, F. R., Rose, T., & Greenwood, C. R. (1988). *Introduction to behavior analysis in special education.* Englewood Cliffs, NJ: Prentice-Hall.

Rusch, F. R., & Schultz, R. P. (1981). Vocational and social work behavior: An evaluative review. In J. L. Matson & J. R. McCartney (Eds.), *Behavior modification with the mentally retarded.* New York: Plenum.

Rush, A. J., Beck, A. T., Kovacs, M., & Hollon, S. D. (1977). Comparative efficacy of cognitive therapy in the treatment of depressed outpatients. *Cognitive Therapy and Research, 1,* 17–36.

Russell, G. F. M. (1979). Bulimia nervosa: An ominous variant of anorexia nervosa. *Psychological Medicine, 9,* 429–448.

Rutter, M. (1965). Speech disorders in a series of autistic children. In A. W. Franklin (Ed.), *Children with communication problems.* London: Pitman.

Rutter, M. (1968). Concepts of autism: A review of research. *Journal of Child Psychology and Psychiatry, 9,* 1–25.

Rutter, M. (1978). Diagnosis and definition of childhood autism. *Journal of Autism and Childhood Schizophrenia. 8,* 139–161.

Rutter, M. (1986). The developmental psychopathology of depression: Issues and perspectives. In M. Rutter, C. Izard, & P. Read (Eds.), *Depression in young people: Developmental and clinical perspectives.* New York: Guilford.

Rutter, M., & Giller, H. (1983). *Juvenile delinquency: Trends and perspectives.* New York: Penguin.

Rutter, M., Graham, P., Chadwick, O., & Yule, W. (1976). Adolescent turmoil: Fact or fiction? *Journal of Child Psychology and Psychiatry, 17,* 35–56.

Rutter, M., & Lockyer, L. (1967). A five to fifteen year follow-up study of infantile psychosis: I. Description of sample. *British Journal of Psychiatry, 113,* 1169–1182.

Rutter, M., Tizard, J., & Whitmore, K. (Eds.). (1970/1978). *Education, health and behaviour.* Huntington, NY: Krieger. (Original work published 1970. London: Longmans).

Ryan, N. D. (1990). Pharmacotherapy of adolescent major depression: Beyond TCAs. *Psychopharmacology Bulletin, 26,* 75–79.

Ryan, N. D., Puig-Antich, J., Ambrosini, P., Rabinovich, H., Robinson, D., Nelson, B., Iyengar, S., & Twomey, J. (1987). The clinical picture of major depression in children and adolescents. *Archives of General Psychiatry, 44,* 854–861.

Ryan, N. D., Puig-Antich, J., Cooper, T., Rabinovich, H., Ambrosini, P., Davies, M., King, J., Torres, D., & Fried, J. (1986). Imipramine in adolescent major depression: Plasma level and clinical response. *Acta Psychiatrica Scandinavica, 73,* 275–288.

Rybstein-Blinchick, E. (1979). Effects of different cognitive strategies in the chronic pain experience. *Journal of Behavioral Medicine, 2,* 93–102.

Safer, R., & Allen, D. (1976). *Hyperactive children.* Baltimore: University Park Press.

Sailor, W. (1991). Special education in the restructured school. *Remedial and Special Education, 12,* 8–22.

Sainato, D. M., Strain, P. S., & Lefebvre, D., & Rapp, N. (1990). Effects of self-evaluation on the independent work skills of preschool children with disabilities. *Exceptional Children, 56,* 540–549.

Sajwaj, T., Libet, J., & Agras, S. (1974). Lemon-juice therapy: The control of life-threatening rumination in a six-month old infant. *Journal of Applied Behavior Analysis, 7,* 557–563.

Salter, A. (1949). *Conditioned reflex therapy.* New York: Farrar, Straus.

Sanchez-Craig, M., Annis, H. M., Bornet, A. R., & MacDonald, K. R. (1984). Random assignment to abstinence and controlled drinking: Evaluation of a cognitive-behavioral program for problem drinkers. *Journal of Consulting and Clinical Psychology, 52,* 390–403.

Sanchez-Craig, M., & Wilkinson, D. A. (1989). Brief treatments for alcohol and drug problems: Practical and methodological issues. In T. Loberg, W. R. Miller, P. E. Nathan, & G. A. Marlatt (Eds.), *Addictive behaviors: Prevention and early intervention.* Amsterdam: Swets and Zeitlinger.

Sanchez-Craig, M., & Wilkinson, D. A. (1987). Treating problem drinkers who are not severely dependent on alcohol. In M. Sobell & L. Sobell (Eds.), *Drugs and society,* (pp. 39–67). New York: Haworth Press.

Sanders, N. R., Rebgetz, M., Morrison, M., Bor, W., Gordon, A., Dadds, M., & Sheppero, R. (1989). Cognitive-behavioral treatment of recurrent nonspecific abdominal pain in children: An analysis of generalization maintenance, and side effects. *Journal of Consulting and Clinical Psychology, 57,* 294–300.

Sanders, S. H. (1983). Automated versus self-monitoring of "up-time" in chronic low back pain patients: A comparative study. *Pain, 15,* 399–406.

Sarrell, L. J., & Sarrell, P. (1979). *Sexual unfolding.* Boston: Little, Brown.

Satterfield, J. H., Hoppe, C. M., & Schell, A. M. (1982). A prospective study of delinquency in 110 adolescent boys with Attention Deficit Disorder and 88 normal adolescent boys. *American Journal of Psychiatry, 139,* 795–798.

Satterfield, J. H., Satterfield, B. T., & Schell, A. M. (1987). Therapeutic interventions to prevent delinquency in hyperactive boys. *Journal of the American Academy of Child and Adolescent Psychiatry, 26,* 56–64.

Scalfani, A., & Springer, D. (1976). Dietary obesity in adult rats: Similarities to hypothalamic and human obesity syndromes. *Physiology and Behavior, 17,* 461–471.

Scarborough, E., & Furomoto, L. (1987). *Untold lives: The first generation of American women psychologists.* New York: Columbia University Press.

Schaap, C. (1984). A comparison of the interaction of distressed and nondistressed married couples in a laboratory situation: Literature survey, methodological issues, and an empirical investigation. In K. Hahlweg & N. S. Jacobson (Eds.), *Marital interaction: Analysis and modification.* New York: Guilford.

Schachter, S., & Singer, J. E. (1962). Cognitive, social, and physiological determinants of emotional state. *Psychological Review, 69,* 379–399.

Schaughency, E. A., Hurley, L. K., Yano, K. E., Seeley, J., & Talarico, B. (1989, August). *Psychometric properties of the SESBI with clinic-referred children.* Paper presented at the meeting of the American Psychological Association, New Orleans.

Schepis, M. M., Reid, D. H., Fitzgerald, J. R., Faw, G. D., Van den Pol, R. A., & Welty, P. A. (1982). An incidental teaching program for increasing manual signing by autistic and profoundly retarded youth. *Journal of Applied Behavior Analysis, 15,* 363–379.

Schiavi, R., & Fisher, S. (1982). Measurement of nocturnal erections. In J. Bancroft (Ed.), *Diseases of sex and sexuality: Clinics in endocrinology and metabolism, 11*(3), 769–784.

Schilling, R. E., & McAlister, A. L. (1990). Preventing drug use in adolescents through media interventions. *Journal of Consulting and Clinical Psychology, 58,* 416–424.

Schinke, S. P., & Gilchrist, L. D. (1985). Preventing substance hypothetical constructs and intervening variables. *Psychological Review, 55,* 95–107.

Schleien, S. J., Weyman, P., & Kiernan, J. (1981). Teaching leisure skills to severely handicapped adults: An age-appropriate dart game. *Journal of Applied Behavior Analysis, 14,* 513–519.

Schnelle, J. F., Traughber, B., Sowell, V. A., Newman, D. R., Petrilli, C. O., & Ory, M. (1989). Prompted voiding treatment of urinary incontinence in nursing home staff. *Journal of the American Geriatric Society, 37,* 1051–1057.

Schooler, N. R., Hogarty, G., & Weissman, M. (1978). Social Adjustment Scale II (SAS-II). In W. A. Hargreaves, C. C. Atkisson, & J. E. Sorenson (Eds.), *Resource materials for community mental health program evaluations.* Rockville, MD: Department of Health, Education, and Welfare.

Schooler, C., & Spohn, H. E. (1982). Social dysfunction and treatment failure in schizophrenia. *Schizophrenia Bulletin, 8*, 85–98.

Schopler, E., & Reichler, R. J. (1971). Developmental therapy by parents with their own autistic child. In M. Rutter (Ed.), *Infantile autism: Concepts, characteristics, and treatment* (pp. 206–277). London: Churchill-Livingstone.

Schover, L. R., Friedman, J., Weiler, S., Heiman, J. R., & LoPiccolo, J. (1982). A multi-axial diagnostic system for sexual dysfunctions: An alternative to DSM-III. *Archives of General Psychiatry, 39*, 614–619.

Schover, L. R., & LoPiccolo, J. (1982). Treatment effectiveness for dysfunctions of sexual desire. *Journal of Sex and Marital Therapy, 8*, 179–197.

Schreibman, L. (1975). Effects of within-stimulus and extra-stimulus prompting on discrimination learning in autistic children. *Journal of Applied Behavior Analysis, 8*, 91–112.

Schreibman, L. (1988a). *Autism.* Newbury Park, CA: Sage Publications.

Schreibman, L. (1988b). Parenting training as a means of facilitating generalization in autistic children. In R. H. Horner, G. Dunlap, and R. L. Koegel (Eds.), *Generalization and maintenance: Lifestyle changes in applied settings* (pp. 21–40). New York: Paul H. Brookes.

Schreibman, L. (1990). Autism: Issues in the generalization of treatment effects. In G. Mayfield & T. H. Ollendick (Eds.), *Postgraduate advances in autism disorder.* Berryville, VA: Forum Medicum.

Schreibman, L., & Britten, K. R. (1984). Training parents as therapists for autistic children: Rationale, techniques, and results. In W. P. Christian, G. T. Hanna, & T. J. Glahn (Eds.), *Programming effective human services* (pp. 295–314). New York: Plenum.

Schreibman, L., & Carr, E. G. (1978). Elimination of echolalic responding to questions through the training of a generalized verbal response. *Journal of Applied Behavior Analysis, 11*, 453–463.

Schreibman, L., & Charlop, M. H. (1987). Autism. In V. B. Van Hasself & M. Hersen (Eds.), *Psychological evaluation of the developmentally and physically disabled* (pp. 155–177). New York: Plenum.

Schreibman, L., & Charlop, M. H. (1989). Infantile autism. In T. H. Ollendick & M. Hersen (Eds.), *Handbook of child psychopathology* (2nd Ed.). New York: Plenum.

Schreibman, L., Charlop, M. H., & Koegel, R. L. (1982). Teaching austic children to use extra stimulus prompts. *Journal of Experimental Child Psychology, 33*, 475–491.

Schreibman, L., Charlop, M. H., & Tryon, A. S. (1981, August). *The acquisition and generalization of appropriate spontaneous speech in autistic children.* Paper presented at the an-

nual convention of the American Psychological Association, Los Angeles.

Schreibman, L., & Koegel, R. L. (1981). A guideline for planning behavior modification programs for autistic children. In S. M. Turner, K. S. Calhoun, & H. E. Adams (Eds), *Handbook of clinical behavior therapy.* New York: Wiley.

Schreibman, L., & Koegel, R. L. (1982). Multiple cue responding in autistic children. In J. Steffen & P. Karoly (Eds.), *Advances in child behavior analysis and therapy: Autism and severe psychopathology* (Vol. II, pp. 81–99). Lexington, MA: Heath.

Schreibman, L., Koegel, R. L., & Craig, M. S. (1977). Reducing stimulus overselectivity in autistic children. *Journal of Abnormal Child Psychology, 5*, 425–436.

Schreibman, L., Kohlenberg, B., & Britten, K. R. (1986). Differential responding to content and intonation components of a complex auditory stimulus by autistic children. *Analysis and Intervention in Developmental Disabilities, 6*, 109–125.

Schrenk-Notzing, A. von. (1956). *The use of hypnosis in psychopathea sexualis, with special reference to contrary sexual interest.* New York: Julian. (First published in 1895.)

Schroeder, H. E., & Black, M. J. (1985). Unassertiveness. In M. Hersen & A. S. Bellack (Eds.), *Handbook of clinical behavior therapy with adults,* (pp. 509–530). New York: Plenum.

Schroeder, S. R., Gualtieri, C. T., & Van Bourgondien, M. E. (1986). Autism. In M. Hersen (Ed.), *Pharmacological and behavioral treatment: An integrative approach* (pp. 89–107). New York: Wiley.

Schroeder, S. R., Oldenquist, A., & Rojahn, J. (1990). A conceptual framework for judging the humaness and effectiveness of behavioral treatment. In A. C. Repp & N. N. Singh (Eds.), *Perspectives on the use of nonaversive and aversive interventions for persons with developmental disabilities* (pp. 103–118). Sycamore, Illinois: Sycamore.

Schull, W., & Sprenkle, T. (1980). Retarded ejaculation. *Journal of Sex and Marital Therapy, 6*, 234–246.

Schulz, S. C., & Pato, C. N. (Eds.). (1989). Advances in the genetics of schizophrenia. *Schizophrenia Bulletin, 15*, 361–464.

Schumaker, J. B., Hovell, M. F., & Sherman, J. A (1977). An analysis of daily report cards and parent-managed privileges in the improvement of adolescents' classroom performance. *Journal of Applied Behavior Analysis, 10*, 449–464.

Schwartz, G. E., & Weiss, S. M. (1978). What is behavioral medicine? *Psychosomatic Medicine, 36*, 377–381.

Schwartz, I. S., & Baer, D. M. (1991). Social validity assessments: Is current practice state-of-the art? *Journal of Applied Behavior Analysis, 24*, 189–204.

Schwartz, R. M., & Gottman, J. (1976). Toward a task analysis of assertive behavior. *Journal of Consulting and Clinical Psychology, 44*, 910–920.

Scogin, F., Jamison, C., & Gochneaur, K. (1989). Cognitive and behavioral bibliotherapy for mildly and moderately depressed older adults. *Journal of Consulting and Clinical Psychology, 57*, 403–407.

Scogin, F., Jamison, C., & Davis, N. (1990). A two year follow-up of the effects of bibliotherapy for depressed older adults. *Journal of Consulting and clinical Psychology, 58*, 665–667.

Sechrest, L. (1963). Incremental validity: A recommendation. *Education and Psychological Measurement, 23*, 153–158.

Selzer, M. L. (1971). The Michigan Alcoholism Screening Test: The quest for a new diagnostic instrument. *American Journal of Psychiatry, 127*, 1653–1658.

Semans, J. H. (1956). Premature ejaculation: A new approach. *Southern Medical Journal, 49*, 353–357.

Serber, M. (1974). Videotape feedback in the treatment of couples with sexual dysfunction. *Archives of Sexual Behavior, 3*, 377–380.

Sergis-Deavenport, E., & Varni, J. W. (1982). Behavioral techniques in teaching hemophilia factor replacement procedures to families. *Pediatric Nursing, 8*, 416–419.

Sergis-Deavenport, E., & Varni, J. W. (1983). Behavioral assessment and management of adherence to factor replacement therapy in hemophilia. *Journal of Pediatric Psychology, 8*, 367–377.

Shaffer, D. (1974). Suicide in childhood and early adolescence. *Journal of Child Psychology and Psychiatry, 15*, 275–291.

Shafii, M., Steltz-Lenarsky, J., Derrick, A. M., Beckner, C., & Whittinghill, J. R. (1988). Comorbidity of mental disorders in the post-mortem diagnosis of completed suicide in children and adolescents. *Journal of Affective Disorders, 15*, 227–233.

Shafto, F., & Sulzbacher, S. (1977). Comparing treatment tactics with a hyperactive preschool child: Stimulant mediation and programmed teacher intervention. *Journal of Applied Behavior Analysis, 10*, 13–20.

Shapiro, E. S. (1981). Self-control procedures with mentally retarded students. In M. Hersen, R. M. Eisler, & P. M. Miller (Eds.), *Progress in behavior modification* (Vol. 12, pp. 265–297). New York: Academic Press.

Shapiro, E. S. (1986). Behavior modification: Self-control and cognitive procedures. In R. P. Barrett (Ed.), *Severe behavior disorders in the mentally retarded* (pp. 61–97). New York: Plenum.

Shapiro, E. S. & Barrett, R. P. (1983). Behavioral assessment of mentally retarded. In J. L. Matson, & F. An-

drasik (Eds.), *Treatment issues and innovations in mental retardation*. New York: Plenum.

Shapiro, E. S., & Klein, R. D. (1980). Self-management of classroom behavior with retarded/disturbed children. *Behavior Modification, 4*, 83–97.

Shapiro, E. S., & Lentz, F. (1985). Assessing academic behavior: A behavioral approach. *School Psychology Review, 14*, 325–338.

Shapiro, E. S., McGonigle, J. J., & Ollendick, T. H. (1980). An analysis of self-assessment and self-reinforcement in a self-managed token economy with mentally retarded children. *Applied Research in Mental Retardation, 1*, 227–240.

Sharfstein, S. S. (1984). Sociopolitical issues affecting patients with chronic schizophrenia. In A. S. Bellack (Ed.), *Schizophrenia: Treatment, management and rehabilitation*. Orlando, FL: Grune & Stratton.

Shaw, B. F. (1977). Comparison of cognitive therapy and behavior therapy in the treatment of depression. *Journal of Consulting and Clinical Psychology, 45*, 543–551.

Sheehan, D. V. (1982). Panic attacks and phobias. *New England Journal of Medicine, 307*, 156–158.

Shiffman, S. (1982). Relapse following smoking cessation: A situational analysis. *Journal of Consulting and Clinical Psychology, 50*, 71–86.

Shiffman, S. (1984). Coping with temptations to smoke. *Journal of Consulting and Clinical Psychology, 52*, 261–267.

Shiffman, S. (1989). Conceptual issues in the study of relapse. In M. Gossop (Ed.), *Relapse and addictive behavior* (pp. 149–179). London: Tavistock/Routledge.

Shirk, S. R. (Ed.). (1988). *Cognitive development and child psychotherapy*. New York: Plenum.

Shure, M. B., & Spivack, G. (1978). *Problem-solving techniques in child-rearing*. San Francisco: Jossey-Bass.

Siegel, S. (1983). Classical conditioning, drug tolerance, and drug abuse with children and adolescents. *Journal of Consulting and Clinical Psychology, 53*, 596–602.

Simeon, J. G., Dinicola, V. F., Ferguson, H. B., & Copping, W. (1990). Adolescent depression: A placebo-controlled fluoxetine treatment study and follow-up. *Progress in Neuro-Psychopharmacology and Biological Psychiatry, 14*, 791–795.

Simon, N. (1976). Echolalic speech in childhood autism. In S. Chess & A. Thomas (Eds.), *Annual progress in child psychiatry and child development*. New York: Brunner/Mazel.

Simons, A. D., Murphy, G. E., Levine, J. L, & Wetzel, R. D. (1986). Cognitive therapy and pharmacotherapy for depression: Sustained improvement over one year. *Archives of General Psychiatry, 43*, 43–48.

Singh, N. N., & Winton, A. S. W. (1984). Behavioral

monitoring of pharmacological interventions for self-injury. *Applied Research in Mental Retardation, 5,* 161–170.

Sjoberg, L., & Person, L. (1979). A study of attempts by obese patients to regulate eating. *Addictive Behaviors, 4,* 349–359.

Skinner, B. F. (1953). *Science and human behavior.* New York: Free Press.

Skinner, B. F. (1971). *Beyond freedom and dignity.* New York: Knopf.

Skinner, B. F. (1974). *About behaviorism* New York: Vintage Books.

Skinner, B. F. (1984). The shame of American education. *American Psychologist, 39,* 947–954.

Skinner, B. F. (1987). What happened to psychology as the science of behavior? *American Psychologist, 42,* 780–786.

Skipper, J. K., & Leonard, R. C. (1968). Children, stress, and hospitalization: A field experiment. *Journal of Health and Social Behavior, 9,* 275–287.

Slade, P. D. (1972). The effects of systematic disensitization on auditory hallucinations. *Behaviour Research and Therapy, 10,* 85–91.

Slavin, R. E. (1986). The Napa evaluation of Madeline Hunter's ITIP: Lessons learned. *Elementary School Journal, 87,* 165–171.

Slavin, R. E., & Madden, N. A. (1987). *Effective classroom programs for students at risk* (Report No. 19). Baltimore, MD: Center for Research on Elementary and Middle Schools, Johns Hopkins University.

Slavin, R. E., Madden, N. A., & Leavey, M. (1984). Effects of team assisted individualization on the mathematics achievement of academically handicapped and nonhandicapped students. *Journal of Educational Psychology, 76,* 813–819.

Smith, D. J., Young, R., West, R. P., Morgan, D. P., & Rhode, G. (1988). Reducing the disruptive behavior of junior high school students: A classroom self-management procedure. *Behavior Disorders, 13,* 231–239.

Smith, K. E., Ackerson, J. D., & Blotcky, A. D. (1989). Reducing distress during invasive medical procedures: Relating behavioral interventions to preferred coping style in pediatric cancer patients. *Journal of Pediatric Psychology, 14,* 405–419.

Smith, M., & Meyers, A. (1979). Telephone skills training for retarded adults: Group and individual demonstrations with and without verbal instruction. *American Journal of Mental Deficiency, 83,* 581–587.

Smith, M. C., & Thelan, M. H. (1984). Development and validation of a test for bulimia. *Journal of Consulting and Clinical Psychology, 52,* 863–872.

Smith, R. C., & Lincoln, C. A. (1988). *America's shame,*

America's hope, twelve million youth at risk. Chapel Hill, NC: MDC.

Smith, R. E., & Smoll, F. L. (1991). Behavioral research and intervention in youth sports. *Behavior Therapy.*

Smith, R. E., Smoll, F. L., & Ptacek, J. T. (1990). Conjunctive moderator variables in vulnerability and resiliency research: Life stress, social support and coping skills, and adolescent sport injuries. *Journal of Personality and Social Psychology, 58,* 360–370.

Smith, R. W., Follock, M. J., & Ahern, D. K. (1986). Cognitive distortion and disability in chronic low back pain. *Cognitive Therapy and Research, 10,* 201–210.

Smyer, M. A., Zarit, S. H., & Qualls, S. H. (1990). Psychological intervention with the aging individual. In J. Birren & K. W. Schaie (Eds.), *Handbook of the Psychology of Aging* (3rd ed., pp. 375–403). New York: Academic Press.

Snell, M. E., & Smith, D. D. (1978). Intervention strategies. In M. E. Snell (Ed.), *Systematic instruction of the moderately and severely handicapped.* Columbus, OH: Charles E. Merrill.

Snow, J. S., Mercatoris, M., Beal, P., & Weber, . (1982). Development of standards of performance by mentally retarded children. *American Journal of Mental Deficiency, 81,* 338–379.

Sobell, M. B., Maisto, S. A., Sobell, L. C., Cooper, A. M., Cooper, T. C., & Sanders, B. (1980). Developing a protocol for evaluating alcohol treatment effectiveness. In L. C. Sobell, M. B. Sobell, & E. Ward (Eds.), *Evaluating alcohol and drug abuse treatment effectiveness: Recent advances,* (pp. 125–150). New York: Pergamon.

Sobell, L. C., & Sobell, M. B. (1982). Alcoholism treatment outcome methodology. In National Institute on Alcohol Abuse and Alcoholism Alcohol and Health Monograph No. 3. *Prevention, intervention and treatment: Concerns and models,* (pp. 293–321). Washington, D.C.: National Institute on Alcohol Abuse and Alcoholism.

Sobsey, D., & Ludlow, B. (1984). Guidelines for setting instructional criteria. *Education and Treatment of Children, 7,* 157–165.

Solnick, J. V., Rincover, A., & Peterson, C. R. (1977). Some determinants of the reinforcing and punishing effects of time-out. *Journal of Applied Behavior Analysis, 10,* 415–424.

Solomon, R. L., (1977). An opponent-process theory of acquired motivation: The affective dynamics of addiction. In J. E. Maser & M. E. P. Seligman (Eds.) *Psychopathology: Experimental models.* San Francisco: W. H. Freeman.

Soni, S. S., Morten, G. W., Pitner, S. E., Owens, D. A., & Powazek, M. (1975). Effects of central nervous systems irradiation on neuropsychological functioning of children with acute lymphocytic leukemia. *New England Journal of Medicine, 293,* 113–118.

Spanier, G. B. (1976). Measuring dyadic adjustment: New scales for assessing the quality of marriage and similar dyads. *Journal of Marriage and the Family, 38,* 15–28.

Sparrow, S., Balla, D. A., & Cicchetti, D. V. (1984). *Vineland Adaptive Behavior Scales.* Circle Pines, MN: American Guidance Service.

Spaulding, W. D. (1992). Design prerequisites for research on cognitive therapy for schizophrenia. *Schizophrenia Bulletin, 18,* 39–42.

Spiegel, C. N., & Lindaman, F. C. (1977). Children can't fly: A program to prevent childhood morbidity and mortality from window falls. *American Journal of Public Health, 67,* 1143–1147.

Spitz, H. H. (1973). Consolidating facts into the schematized learning and memory system of educable retardates. In N. R. Ellis (Ed.), *International review of research in mental retardation* (Vol 6, pp. 149–168). New York: Academic Press.

Spitz, H. H., & Winters, E. A. (1977). Tic tac toe performance as a function of maturational level of retarded adolescents and nonretarded children. *Intelligence, 1,* 108–117.

Spitz, R. (1946). Anaclitic depression. *Psychoanalytic Study of the Child, 2,* 313–342.

Spitzer, R. L., Endicott, J., & Robins, E. (1978). *Research diagnostic criteria for a selected group of functional disorders (3rd Ed.).* Biometrics Research Department, New York State Psychiatric Institute.

Spitzer, R. L., Forman, J. B., & Nee, J. (1979). DSM-III field trials: I. Initial interrater diagnostic reliability. *American Journal of Psychiatry, 136,* 815–817.

Spitzer, R. L., Sheeny, M., & Endicott, J. (1977). DSM-III: Guiding principles. In V. M. Rakoff, H. C. Stancer, & H. B. Kedward (Eds.), *Psychiatric diagnosis.* New York: Brunner/Mazel.

Spitzer, R. L, & Williams, J. B. W. (1985). *Structural Clinical Interview for DSM-III-R Personality Disorders (SCID-II, 7/1/85 Revision).* New York: Biometrics Research Department, New York State Psychiatric Institute.

Spivack, G., Platt, J. J., & Shure, M. B. (1976). *The problem-solving approach to adjustment.* San Francisco, CA: Jossey-Bass.

Spivack, G., & Shure, M. G. (1974). *Social adjustment in young children.* San Francisco: Jossey-Bass.

Spivack, G., & Shure, M. B. (1982). The cognition of social adjustment: Interpersonal cognitive problem solving thinking. In B. B. Lahey & A. E. Kazdin (Eds.), *Advances in clinical child psychology* (Vol. 5, pp. 323–372). New York: Plenum.

Sprenkle, D. (1975). A behavioral assessment of creativity, support, and power in clinic and non-clinic married

couples. Dissertation Abstracts International, Vol. 36 (6-A), 4066.

Spring, B. J., & Ravdin, L. (1992). cognitive remediation in schizophrenia: Should we attempt it? *Schizophrenia Bulletin, 18,* 15–20.

Stabler, B., Fernald, G. W., Johnson, M. R., Johnson, M. P., & Ryan, J. J. (1981). Facilitating positive prosocial adaptation in children with cystic fibrosis by increasing family communication and problem solving skills (Research Report). Chapel Hill, NC: University of North Carolina Cystic Fibrosis Foundation. (ERIC Document Reproduction Service No. ED 207 708.)

Stahmer, A. C., & Schreibman, L. (1992). Teaching children with autism appropriate play in unsupervised environments using a self-management treatment package. *Journal of Applied Behavior Analysis, 25,* 447–459.

Stalonas, P. M., Johnson, W. G., & Christ, M. (1978). Behavior modification for obesity: The evaluation of exercise, contingency management, and program adherence. *Journal of Consulting and Clinical Psychology, 46,* 463–469.

Stallings, J. A., & Krasavage, E. M. (1986). Program implementation and student achievement in a four-year Madeline Hunter Follow-through project. *Elementary School Journal, 87,* 118–138.

Stallings, J. A., & Stipek, D. (1986). Research on early childhood and elementary school teaching programs. In M. C. Wittrock (Ed.), *Handbook of research on teaching* (3rd Ed., pp. 727–753). New York: MacMillan.

Stamm, J. W. (1980). Cause of oral diseases and general approaches to their prevention. *Family and Community Health, 3,* 13–21.

Standoger, K. (1989). Structured interviews and the diagnosis of personality disorders. *Canadian Journal of Psychiatry, 34,* 906–912.

Starfield, B. (1977). Health needs of children. In *Children's medical care needs and treatments. Report of the Harvard Health Project* (Vol. 2, pp. 23–40). Cambridge, MA Ballinger.

Stark, K. D., & Brookman, C. S. (in press). Childhood depression: Theory and family-school intervention. In M. J. Fine & C. Carlson (Eds.), *Handbook of family-school intervention: A systems perspective.* New York: Grun & Stratton.

Stark, K. D., Reynolds, W. M., & Kaslow, N. J. (1987). A comparison of the relative efficacy of self-control therapy and a behavioral problem-solving therapy for depression in children. *Journal of Abnormal Child Psychology, 15,* 91–113.

Stark, K. D., Rouse, L. W., & Livingston, R. (in press). Treatment of depression during childhood and adolescence: Cognitive-behavioral procedures for the individual and the family. In P. C. Kendall (Ed.), *Child and adolescent therapy: Cognitive-behavioral procedures.*

Stark, L. J., Bowen, A. M., Tyc, V. L., Evans, S., & Passero, M. A. (1990). A behavioral approach to increasing calorie consumption in children with cystic fibrosis. *Journal of Pediatric Psychology, 15*, 309–326.

Stark, L. J., Collins, F. L., Osnes, P. G., & Stokes, T. F. (1986). Using reinforcement and cueing to increase healthy snack food choices in preschoolers. *Journal of Applied Behavior Analysis, 19*, 367–379.

Steffen, J. J., & Redden, J. (1977). Assessment of social competence in an evaluation-interaction analogue. *Human Communication Research, 4*, 30–37.

Stern, R. S., & Marks, I. (1973). Brief and prolonged flooding: A comparison of agoraphobic patients. *Archives of General Psychiatry, 28*, 270–276.

Sternbach, R., & Tursky, B. (1965). Ethic differences among housewives in psychophysical and skin potential responses to electric shock. *Psychophysiology, 1*, 241–246.

Still, G. F. (1902). Some abnormal psychical conditions in children. *Lancet, 1*, 1008–1012, 1077–1082, 1163–1168.

Stitzer, M. L., Bigelow, G. E., & McCaul, M. E. (1985). Behavior therapy in drug abuse treatment: Review and Evaluation. *National Institute of Drug Abuse Research Monograph, 58*, 31–50.

Stokes, T. F., & Baer, D. M. (1977). An implicit technology of generalization. *Journal of Applied Behavior Analysis, 10*, 349–368.

Stoneman, Z., & Brody, G. H. (1992, August). *Observational research on retarded children, their parents, and their siblings.* Paper presented at the National Institute of Child Development Lake Wilderness Conference, University of Washington, Seattle, WA.

Strain, P. (1975). Increasing social play of severely retarded preschoolers through sociodramatic activities. *Mental Retardation, 13*, 7–9.

Strain, P. S., McConnell, S. R., Carta, J. J., Fowler, S. A., Neisworth, J. T., & Wolery, M. (1992). Behaviorism in early intervention. *Topics in Early Childhood Special Education, 12*, 121–141.

Strain, P. S., Young, C. C., & Horowitz, J. (1981). Generalized behavior change during oppositional child training: An examination of child and family demographic variables. *Behavior Modification, 5*, 15–26.

Strauss, J. S., & Carpenter, W. T. (1977). Prediction of outcome in schizophrenia. *Archives of General Psychiatry, 34*, 159–163.

Strauss, J. S., & Carpenter, W. T. (1981). *Schizophrenia.* New York: Plenum.

Strauss, M. (1979). Measuring intrafamily conflict and violence: The conflict tactics scale. *Journal of Marriage and the Family, 41*, 54–88.

Stravynski, A., Grey, S., & Elie, R. (1987). Outline of the therapeutic process in social skills training with sociably dysfunctional patients. *Journal of Consulting and Clinical Psychology, 55*, 224–228.

Straw, M. K., Straw, R. B., Mahoney, M. J., Robergs, T., Mahoney, B. K., Craighead, L. W., & Stunkard, A. J. (1984). The Master Questionnaire: Preliminary reports of an obesity assessment device. *Addictive Behavior, 9*, 1–10.

Stremal, K. (1972). Language training: A program for retarded children. *Mental Retardation, 10*, 47–49.

Striefel, S., Wetherby, B., & Karlan, G. R. (1976). Establishing generalized verb-noun instruction following skills in retarded children. *Journal of Experimental Child Psychology, 22*, 247–260.

Strober, M. G., & Carlson, G. (1982). Bipolar illness in adolescents with major depression. *Archives of General Psychiatry, 39*, 549–555.

Strober, M., Freeman, R., & Rigali, J. (1990). The pharmacotherapy of depressive illness in adolescence: I. An open label trial of imipramine. *Psychopharmacology Bulletin, 26*, 80–84.

Strober, M. G., Green, J., & Carlson, G. (1981). Phenomenology and subtypes of major depressive disorders in adolescents. *Journal of Affective Disorders, 3*, 277–290.

Stuart, R. B. (1970). *Trick or treatment: How and when psychotherapy fails.* Champaign, IL: Research Press.

Stunkard, A. J., & Merrick, S. (1985). The three factor eating questionnaire to measure dietary restraint, disinhibition, and hunger. *Journal of Psychosomatic Research, 29*, 71–83.

Sturge, C. (1982). Reading retardation and antisocial behavior. *Journal of Child Psychology and Psychiatry, 23*, 21–31.

Sugai, G., & Colvin, G. (1989). Leveled behavior management systems: Development and operation. *Direct Instruction News, 8*, 17–19.

Suinn, R. (1983). *The seven steps to peak performance: Manual for mental training for athletes.* Fort Collins, CO: Colorado State University.

Sullivan, H. S. (1927). The onset of schizophrenia. *American Journal of Psychiatry, 7*, 105–134.

Sulzer-Azaroff, B., & Mayer, G. R. (1986). *Achieving educational excellence using behavioral strategies.* New York: Holt, Rinehart, & Winston.

Sumner, J. H., Mueser, S. T., Hsu, L., & Morales, R. G. (1974). Overcorrection treatment for radical reduction of aggressive-disruptive behavior in institutionalized mental patients. *Psychological Reports, 35*, 655–662.

Susser, E., Struening, E. L., & Conover, S. (1989). Psychiatric problems in homeless men. *Archives of General Psychiatry, 46*, 845–850.

Surwit, R. S., & Feinglos, M. N. (1983). The effects of relaxation on glucose tolerance levels in non-insulin-dependent diabetes. *Diabetes Care, 6,* 176–179.

Susen, G. S. (1978). Conditioned relaxation in a case of ulcerative colitis. *Journal of Behavior Therapy and Experimental Psychiatry, 9,* 283.

Swan, G. E., & McDonald, M. L. (1978). Behavior therapy in practice: A national survey of behavior therapists. *Behavior Therapy, 9,* 799–807.

Szasz, T. (1960). The myth of mental illness. *American Psychologist, 15,* 113–118.

Szykula, S. A., & Fleischman, M. J. (1985). Reducing out-of-home placement of abused children: Two controlled studies. *Child Abuse and Neglect, 9,* 277–284.

Tan, S. Y. (1982). Cognitive and cognitive-behavioral methods for pain control: A selective review. *Pain, 12,* 201–228.

Tanagho., T., Lue, F., & McClure, R. (Eds.) (1988). *Contemporary management of impotence and infertility.* Baltimore: Williams & Wilkins,

Tarnowski, K. J., King, D. R., Green, K., & Ginn-Pease, M. E. (1991). Congenital gastrointestinal anomalies: Psychosocial functioning of children with imperferete anus, gastroschisis, and omphalocele. *Journal of Consulting and Clinical Psychology, 59,* 587–590.

Tarrier, N., Barrowclough, C., Vaughn, C., Bamrah, J. S., Porceddu, R., Watts, S., & Freeman, H. (1989). Community management of schizophrenia: Two-year follow-up of a behavioral intervention with families. *British Journal of Psychiatry, 154,* 625–628.

Tarrier, N., Sharpe, L., Beckett, R., Harwood, S., Baker, A., & Yusopoff, L. (1993). A trial of two cognitive behavioural methods of treating drug resistant residual psychotic symptoms in schizophrenic patients: II. Treatment-specific changes in coping and problem solving skills. *Social Psychiatry & Psychiatric Epidemiology, 28,* 5–10.

Tate, B. G., & Baroff, G. S. (1966). Aversive control of self-injriouis behavior in a psychotic boy. *Behavior Research and Therapy, 4,* 281–287,

Taylor, F. G., & Marshall, W. L (1977). Experimental analysis of a cognitive-behavioral therapy for depression. *Cognitive Therapy and Research, 1,* 59–72.

Teri, L., & Gallagher, D. (1991). Cognitive-behavioral interventions for treatment of depression in Alzheimer's patients. *The Gerontologist, 31,* 413–416.

Teri, L, & Lewinsohn, P. M. (1985). Individual and group treatment of unipolar depression: Comparison of treatment outcome and identification of predictors of successful outcome. *Behavior Therapy, 17,* 215–228.

Teri, L., & Logsdan, R. (1990). Assessment and management of behavioral disturbances in Alzheimer's Disease. *Comprehensive Therapy, 16,* 36–42.

Terman, L. M., & Merrill, M. A. (1973). *The Stanford-Binet intelligence scale* (3rd ed.). Boston: Houghton Mifflin.

Test, M. A. (1984). Community support programs. In A. S. Bellack (Ed.), *Schizophrenia: Treatment, management, and rehabilitation* (pp. 347–374). Orlando, FL: Grune & Stratton.

Thomas, D. R., Becker, W. C., & Armstrong, M. (1968). Production and elimination of disruptive classroom behavior by systematically varying teacher's behavior. *Journal of Applied Behavior Analysis, 1,* 35–45.

Thompson, L. W., Gallagher, D. & Czirr, R. (1989). Personality disorder and outcome in the treatment of late-life depression. *Journal of Geriatric Psychiatry, 21,* 133–146.

Thorley, G. (1984). Review of follow-up and follow-back studies of childhood hyperactivity. *Psychological Bulletin, 96,* 116–132.

Tighe, R. J., & Groeneweg, G. (1985). A comparison of input and output alternatives with a computer-assisted basic concept program. In J. M. Berg (Ed.), *Science and service in mental retardation* (pp. 232–239).

Tisher, M., & Lang, M. (1983). The Children's Depression Scale: Review and further developments. In D. Cantwell & G. Carlson (Eds.), *Affective disorders in childhood and adolescence.* Jamaica, NY: Spectrum.

Tolman, R. M. (1987). *The development and validation of a scale of nonphysical abuse.* Paper presented at the Third National Family Violence Research Conference, University of New Hampshire, Durham, NH.

Touchette, P. E, MacDonald, R. F., & Langer, S. N. (1985). A scatter plot for identifying stimulus control of problem behavior. *Journal of Applied Behavior Analysis, 18,* 243–251.

Tremblay, R. E., LeBlanc, M., & Schwartzman, A. (1988). The predictive power of first-grade peer and teacher ratings of behavior: Sex differences in antisocial behavior and personality of adolescents. *Journal of Abnormal Child Psychology, 16,* 571–583.

Trower, P., Yardley, K., Bryant, B. M., & Shaw, P. (1978). The treatment of social failure: A comparison of anxiety-reduction and skills-acquisition procedures on two social problems. *Behavior Modification, 2,* 41–60.

Tu, J., & Tothstein, A. L. (1979). Improvement of jogging performance through application of personality specific motivational techniques. *Research Quarterly, 50,* 97–103.

Tuckman, B. W., & Hinkle, J. S. (1986). An experimental study of the physical and psychological effects of aerobic exercise on children. *Health Psychology, 5,* 197–207.

Tuma, A. H., & Maser, J. D. (1985). *Anxiety and the anxiety disorders*. Hillsdale, NJ: Laurence Erlbaum.

Tuma, J. M. (1975). Pediatric psychology? . . . Do you mean clinical child psychology? *Journal of Clinical Child Psychology, 4*, 9–12.

Tuma, J. M. (1982). *Handbook for the practice of pediatric psychology*. New York: Wiley.

Turk, D. C., & Flor, H. (1984). Etiological theories and treatments for chronic back pain: II. Psychological factors. *Pain, 19*, 209–233.

Turk, D. C., Meichenbaum, D. H., & Genest, M. (1983). *Pain and behavioral medicine: A cognitive-behavioral perspective*. New York: Guilford.

Turner, J. A. & Clancey, S. (1988). Chronic low back pain: Relationship to pain and disability. *Pain, 12*, 23–46.

Turner, R. M. (1989). Case study evaluations of a biocognitive-behavioral approach for the treatment of borderline personality disorder. *Behavior Therapy, 20*, 477–489.

Turner, S. M., Hersen, M., & Bellack, A. S. (1977). Effects of social disruption, stimulus interference, and aversive conditioning on auditory hallucinations. *Behavior Modification, 1*, 249–258.

Turnure, J., & Zigler E. (1964). Outer directedness in the problem-solving of normal and retarded children. *Journal of Abnormal and Social Psychology, 69*, 427–436.

Twentyman, C. T., & Zimering, R. T. (1979). Behavioral training of social skills: A critical review. In M. Hersen, R. M. Eisler, & P. M. Miller (Eds.), *Progress in behavior modification*, (Vol. 7). New York: Academic Press.

Ullmann, L. P., & Krasner, L. (1975). *A psychological approach to abnormal behavior* (2nd ed.). Englewood Cliffs, NJ: Prentice-Hall.

Urban, B. J. (1982). Therapeutic aspects in chronic pain: Modulation of nociception, alleviation of suffering and behavior analysis. *Behavior Therapy, 13*, 430–437.

Urey, J. R., Laughlin, C., & Kelly, J. A. (1979). Teaching heterosocial conversational skills to male psychiatric inpatients. *Journal of Behavior Therapy and Experimental Psychiatry, 10*, 323–328.

U.S. Congress, Office of Technology Assessment (1991). *Adolescent health*. (OTA-H-468). Washington, DC: U.S. Government Printing Office.

U.S. Department of Labor (1988, July). *Building a quality workforce*. Washington, DC: Office of Public Affairs.

U.S. Surgeon General (1988). *Health consequences of smoking*, (DHHS Publication # CDC 88–8406). Rockville, MD: U.S. Department of Health and Human Services.

Varni, J. W. (1981a). Behavioral medicine in hemophilia arthritic pain management: Two case studies. *Archives of Physical Medicine and Rehabilitation, 62*, 183–187.

Varni, J. W. (1981b). Self-regulation techniequest in the management of chronic arthritic pain in hemophilia. *Behavior Therapy, 12*, 185–194.

Varni, J. W. (1983). *Clinical behavioral pediatrics: An interdisciplinary biobehavioral approach*. New York: Pergamon.

Varni, J. W., Bessman, C. A., Russo, D. C., & Cataldo, M. F. (1980). Behavioral management of chronic pain in children: Case study. *Archives of Physical Medicine and Rehabilitation, 61*, 375–379.

Van den Hout, M. A., van der Molen, G. M., Griez, E., Lousberg, H., & Nansen, A. (1987). Reduction of carbon dioxide-induced anxiety after repeated carbon dioxide exposure. *American Journal of Psychiatry, 144*, 788–791.

Van Houten, R., & Doleys, D. M. (1983). Are social reprimands effective? In S. Axelrod & J. Apsche (Eds.), *The effects of punishment on human behavior* (pp. 45–70). New York: Academic Press.

Van Putten, T. & May, P. R. A. (1978). Akinetic depression in schizophrenia. *Archives of General Psychiatry, 35*, 1101–1107.

Van Wagenen, R. K., Meyerson, L., Kerr, N. J., & Mahoney, K. (1969). Field trials of a new procedure for toilet training. *Journal of Experimental Child Psychiatry, 8*, 147–159.

Van Wagenen, R. K., & Murdock, E. E. (1966). A transistorized signal-package for toilet-training of infants. *Journal of Experimental Child Psychiatry, 3*, 312–314.

VanderPlate, C., & Aral, S. (1987). Psychosocial aspects of genital herpes virus infections. *Health Psychology, 6*, 57–72.

Vaughn, C., & Leff, J. (1976). The measurement of expressed emotion in the families of psychiatric patients. *British Journal of social and Clinical Psychology, 15*, 157–165.

Vermilyea, J. A., Boice, R., & Barlow, D. H. (1984). Rachman and Hodgson (1974). A decade later: How do desynchronous response systems relate to the treatment of agoraphobia? *Behaviour Research and Therapy, 22*, 615–621.

Vieyra, M. A. B., Hoag, N. L., & Masek, B. J. (1991). Migraine in childhood: Developmental aspects of biobehavioral treatment. In J. P. Bush, & S. W. Harkin (Eds.), *Children in pain: Clinical and research issues from a developmental perspective* (pp. 373–396). New York: Springer Verlag.

Vincent, J. P., Weiss, R. L., & Birchler, G. R. (1975). A behavioral analysis of problem-solving in distressed and nondistressed married and stranger dyads. *Behavior Therapy, 6*, 475–487.

Voeltz, L. M., & Evans, I. M. (1982). The assessment of behavioral interrelationships in child behavior therapy. *Behavior Assessment, 4*, 131–165.

Von Korff, M., Dworkin, S. G., LeResche, L., & Kruger, A. (1988). An epidemiological comparison of pain complaints. *Pain, 32*, 173–184.

Vuchinich, R. E., Tucker, J. A., & Harllee, L. M. (1988). Behavioral assessment. In D. Donovan & G. A. Marlatt (Eds.), *Assessment of addictive behaviors* (pp. 51–83). New York: Guilford.

Vyse, S. A., & Rapport, M. D. (1989). The effects of methylphenidate on learning in children with ADDH: The stimulus equivalence paradigm. *Journal of Consulting and Clinical Psychology, 57,* 425–435.

Wacker, D. P., & Berg, W. K. (1983). Effects of picture prompts and the acquisition of complex vocational tasks by mentally retarded adolescents. *Journal of Applied Behavior Analysis, 16,* 417–433.

Wacker, D. P., & Berg, W. K. (1984). Training adolescents with severe handicaps to set up job tasks independently using picture prompts. *Analysis and Intervention Developmental Disabilities, 4,* 353–365.

Wadden, T. A., & Stunkard, A. J. (1986). Controlled trial of very low calorie diet, behavior therapy, and their combination in the treatment of obesity. *Journal of Consulting and Clinical Psychology, 4,* 482–488.

Wadden, T. A., Stunkard, A. J., & Liebschutz, J. (1989). Three year follow-up of the treatment of obesity by very low calorie diet, behavior therapy and their combination. *Journal of Consulting and Clinical Psychology, 56,* 925–928.

Wadsworth, M. (1979). *Roots of delinquency: Infancy, adolescence, and crime.* New York: Barnes & Noble.

Wahler, R. G. (1975). Some structural aspects of deviant child behavior. *Journal of Applied Behavior Analysis, 8,* 27–42.

Wahler, R. G. (1980). The insular mother: Her problems in parent-child treatment. *Journal of Applied Behavior Analysis, 13,* 207–219.

Wahler, R. G., & Dumas, J. (1986). Maintenance factors in coercive mother-child interactions: The compliance and predictability hypothesis. *Journal of Applied Behavior Analysis, 19,* 13–22.

Wahler, R. G., & Dumas, J. (1987). Stimulus class determinants of mother-child coercive interchanges in multidistressed families: Assessment and intervention. In J. D. Burchard & S. N. Bruchard (Eds.), *Prevention of delinquent behavior* (pp. 190–219). Newbury Park, CA: Sage.

Wahler, R. G., & Foxx, J. J. (1980a, October). *Response structure in deviant child-parent relationships: Implications for family therapy.* Paper presented to the Nebraska Symposium on Motivation, University of Nebraska, Lincoln.

Wahler, R. G., & Foxx, J. J. (1980b). Solitary toy play and time out: A family treatment package for children with aggressive and oppositional behavior. *Journal of Applied Behavior Analysis, 13,* 23–29.

Wahler, R. G. & Foxx, J. J. (1981). Setting events in applied behavior analysis: Toward a conceptual and methodological expansion. *Journal of Applied Behavior Analysis, 14,* 327–338.

Wahler, R. G., & Graves, M. G. (1983). Setting events in social networks: Ally or enemy in child behavior therapy? *Behavior Therapy, 14,* 19–36.

Wahler, R. G., House, A. E., & Stambaugh, E. E. (1976). *Ecological assessment of child problem behavior: A clinical package for home, school, and institutional settings.* New York: Pergamon.

Walco, G. A., & Varni, J. W. (1991). Chronic and recurrent pain: Hemophilia, juvenile rheumatoid arthritis, and sickle cell disease. In J. P. Bush & S. W. Harkins (Eds.), *Children in pain: Clinical and research issues from a developmental perspective* (pp. 297–336). New York: Springer Verlag.

Walker, C. E. (1979). Behavioral interventions in a pediatric setting. In J. R. MacNamara (Ed.), *Behavioral approaches in medicine: Application and analysis* (pp. 227–266). New York: Plenum.

Walker, H. M. (1983). Applications of response cost in school settings: Outcomes, issues, and recommendations. *Exceptional Education Quarterly, 3,* 47–55.

Walker, H. M. & Buckley, N. K. (1968). The use of positive reinforcement in conditioning attending behavior. *Journal of Applied Behavior Analysis, 1,* 245–250.

Walker, H. M., Hops, H., & Greenwood, C. R. (1981). RECESS: Research and development of a behavior management package for remediating social aggression in the school setting. In P. S. Strain (Ed.), *The utilization of classroom peers as behavior change agents* (pp. 261–303). New York: Plenum.

Walker, H. M., Mattson, R. H., & Buckley, N. K. (1971). The functional analysis of behavior with an experimental class setting. In W. C. Becker (Ed.), *An empirical basis for change education* (pp. 236–263). Chicago: Science Research Associates.

Wallace, C. J., Boone, S. E., Donahoe, C. P., & Foy, D. W. (1985). The chronically mentally disabled: Independent living skills training. In D. H. Barlow (Ed.), *Clinical handbook of psychological: A step-by-step treatment manual.* New York: Guilford.

Wallace, C. J., Liberman, R. P., MacKain, S. J., Blackwell, G., & Eckman, T. A. (1992). Effectiveness and replicability of modules for teaching social and instrumental skills to the severely mentally ill. *American Journal of Psychiatry, 149,* 654–658.

Wallace, C. J., Nelson, C. J., Liberman, R. P., Aitchison, R. A., Lukoff, D., Elder, J. P., & Ferris, C. (1980). A review and critique of social skills training with schizophrenic patients. *Schizophrenia Bulletin, 6,* 42–63.

Walter, H. I., & Gilmore, S. K. (1973). Placebo versus social learning effects in parent training procedures de-

454   **REFERENCES**

signed to alter the behaviors of aggressive boys. *Behavior Therapy, 4,* 361–377.

Walters, H. J., Hofman, A., Connelly, P. A., Barrett, L. T., & Kost, K. J. (1985). Preliminary prevention of chronic disease in childhood: Changes in risk factors after one year of intervention. *American Journal of Epidemiology, 122,* 772–781.

Walton, W. E. (1982). An evaluation of the Poison Prevention Packaging Act. *Pediatrics, 69,* 3673–370.

Wasserman, E. A., Kiedinger, R. E., & Bhatt, R. S. (1988). Conceptual behavior in pigeons: Categories, subcategories, and pseudocategories. *Journal of Experimental Psychology: Animal Behavior Processes, 14,* 235–246.

Watson, D., & Friend, R. (1969). Measurement of social-evaluative anxiety. *Journal of Consulting and Clinical Psychology, 33,* 448–457.

Watson, J. B. (1913). Psychology as the behaviorist views it. *Psychological Review, 20,* 158–177.

Watson, J. B. (1924). *Behaviorism.* Chicago: University of Chicago Press.

Watson, J. B., & Rayner, R. (1920). Conditioned emotional reactions. *Journal of Experimental Psychology, 3,* 1–20.

Watson, J. P., Mullett, G. E., & Pillay, H. (1973). The effects of prolonged exposure to phobic situations upon agoraphobic patients treated in groups. *Behaviour Research and Therapy, 11,* 531–545.

Webster-Stratton, C. (1985). Randomized trial of two parent-training programs for families with conduct-disordered children. *Journal of Consulting and Clinical Psychology, 52,* 666–678.

Webster-Stratton, C., Kolpacoff, M., & Hollinsworth, T. (1988). Self-administered videotape therapy for families with conduct problem children: Comparison with two cost-effective treatments and a control group. *Journal of Consulting and Clinical Psychology, 57,* 558–566.

Wechsler, D. (1967). *Manual for the Wechsler preschool and primary scale of intelligence.* New York: Psychological Corporation.

Wechsler, D. (1974). *The Wechsler intelligence scale for children—revised.* New York: Psychological Corporation.

Wegener, C., Revenstorf, D., Hahlweg, K., & Schlindler, L. (1979). Empirical analysis of communication in distressed and nondistressed couples. *Behavior analysis and Modification, 3,* 178–188.

Wehman, P., & Marchant, J. A. (1978). Improving free play skills of severely retarded children. *The American Journal of Occupational Therapy, 32,* 100–104.

Weinberg, W. A., Rutman, J., Sullivan, L., Penick, E. C., & Dietz, S. G. (1973). Depression in children referred to an educational diagnostic center. *Journal of Pediatrics, 83,* 1065–1072.

Weinberger, D. R., Wagner, R. L., & Wyatt, R. J. (1983). Neuropathological studies of schizophrenia: A selective review. *Schizophrenia Bulletin, 9,* 193–212.

Weinstein, D. J. (1976). Imagery and relaxation with a burn patient. *Behavior Research and Therapy, 14,* 481.

Weisberg, P. (1989). Direct instruction in preschool. *Education and Treatment of Children, 11,* 349–363.

Weiss, G., & Hechtman, L. (1986). *Hyperactive children grown up.* New York: Guilford.

Weiss, G., Hechtman, L., Milroy, T., & Perlman, T. (1985). Psychiatric status of hyperactives as adults: A controlled perspective 15-year follow-up of 63 hyperactive children. *Journal of the American Academy of Child Psychiatry, 24,* 211–220.

Weiss, G., Hechtman, L, & Perlman, T. (1978). Hyperactives as young adults: School, employer, and self-rating scales obtained during ten-year follow-up evaluation. *American Journal of Orthopsychiatry, 48,* 438–445.

Weiss, G., Hechtman, L., Perlman, T., Hopkins, J., & Wener, A. (1979). Hyperactives as young adults: A controlled prospective ten-year follow-up of 75 children. *Archives of General Psychiatry, 36,* 675–681.

Weiss, J. M. (1972). Psychological factors in stress and disease. *Scientific American, 226,* 104–113.

Weiss, R. L., Hops, H., & Patterson, G. R. (1973). A framework for conceptualizing marital conflict, technology for altering it, some data for evaluating it. In L. A. Hamerlynck, L. C. Handy, & E. J. Mash (Eds.), *Behavior change: Methdology, concepts and practice.* Champaign, IL: Research Press.

Weissman, M. M. (1979). The psychological treatments of depression: Research evidence for the efficacy of psychotherapy alone, in comparison and in combination with pharmacotherapy. *Archive of General Psychiatry, 36,* 1261–1269.

Weissman, M. M., & Klerman, G. (1977). Sex differences and the epidemiology of depression. *Archives of General Psychiatry, 34,* 98–111.

Weissman, M. M., Leckman, J. F., Merikangas, K. R., Gammon, G. D., & Prusoff, B. A. (1984). Depression and anxiety disorders in parents and children, Results from the Yale family study. *Archives of General Psychiatry, 41,* 845–852.

Wells, K. C. (1984). Review of a social learning approach, Vol. 3: Coercive family process. *Behavior Therapy, 15,* 121–127.

Wells, K. C., & Egan, J. (1988). Social learning and systems family therapy for childhood oppositional disorder: Comparative treatment outcome. *Comprehensive Psychiatry, 29,* 138–146.

Wells, K. C. & Forehand, R. (1981). Childhood behavior

problems in the home. In S. M. Turner, K. S. Calhoun, & H. E. Adams (Eds.), *Handbook of clinical behaviour therapy.* New York: Wiley.

Wells, K. C., & Forehand, R. (1985). Conduct and oppositional disorders. In P. H. Bornstein & A. E. Kazdin, Eds.), *Handbook of clinical behavior therapy with children.* Homewood, IL: Dorsey.

Wells, K. C., Forehand, R., & Griest, D. L. (1980). Generality of treatment effects from treated to untreated behaviors resulting from a parent training program. *Journal of Clinical Child Psychology, 9,* 217–219.

Wells, K. C., Griest, D. C., & Forehand, R. (1980). The use of a self control package to enhance temporal generality of a parent training program. *Behaviour Research and Therapy, 18,* 347–353.

Wells, K. B., Stewart, A., Hays, R. D., Bumam, A., Rogers, W., Daniels, M., Berry, S., Greenfield, S., & Ware, J. (1989). The functioning and well-being of depressed patients: Results from medical outcomes study. *Journal of the American Medical Association, 262,* 914–919.

Welner, Z., Reich, W., Herjanic, B., Jung, K. G., & Amado, H. (1987). Reliability, validity, and parent-child agreement studies of the Diagnostic Interview for Children and Adolescents (DICA). *Journal of the American Academy of Child and Adolescent Psychiatry, 26,* 649–653.

Wender, P. H. (1971). *Minimal brain dysfunction in children.* New York: Wiley.

Wender, P. H. (1987). *The hyperactive child, adolescent, and adult.* New York: Oxford.

Wender, P. H. Reimherr, F. W., & Wood, D. R. (1981). Attention deficit disorder ('Minimal brain dysfunction') in adults. *Archives of General Psychiatry, 38,* 449–456.

Werner, J. S., Minkin, N., Minkin, B. L., Fixsen, D. L., Phillips, E. L., & Wolf, M. M. (1975). "Intervention package": An analysis to prepare juvenile delinquents for encounters with police officers. *Criminal Justice and Behavior, 2,* 55–83.

Werry, J. (1968). Developmental hyperactivity. *Pediatric Clinics of North American, 19,* 9–16.

Werry, J., & Conners, C. K. (1979). Pharmacotherapy. In H. Quay & J. Werry (Eds.), *Psychopathological disorders of childhood* (2nd ed.). New York: Wiley.

Werry, J. S., & Sprague, R. L. (1970). Hyperactivity. In C. G. Costello (Ed.), *Symptoms of psychopathology* (pp. 397–417). New York: Wiley.

West, D. J. (1982). *Delinquency: Its roots, careers, and prospects.* Cambridge, MA: Harvard.

West, D. J. & Farrington, D. P. (1973. *Who becomes delinquent?* London: Heinemann.

West, R. P., & Young, K. R. (1990). Special issue: Precision teaching. *Teaching Exceptional Children, 22,* 4–75.

Whalen, C. K., & Henker, B. (1986). Cognitive behavior therapy for hyperactive children: What do we know? *Journal of Children in Contemporary Society, 19,* 123–142.

Whelan, J. P., Mahoney, M. J., & Meyers, A. W. (1991). Performance enhancement in sport: A cognitive behavioral domain. *Behavior Therapy, 22,* 307–327.

Whelan, J. P., Meyers, A. W., & Berman, J. S. (1989). Cognitive-behavioral interventions for athletic performance enhancement. In M. Greenspan (Chair), *Sport psychology intervention research: Reviews and issues.* Symposium conducted at meeting of the American Psychological Association. New Orleans, LA.

Whisman, M. S. (1989). *The use of booster maintenance sessions in behavioral marital therapy.* Paper presented at the 23rd Convention of the Association for the Advancement of Behavior Therapy. Washington, DC.

Whisman, M. A., Jacobson, N. S., Fruzzetti, A. E., & Waltz, J. A. (1989). Methodological issues in marital therapy. *Advances in Behavior Therapy, 11,* 175–189.

Whitaker, A., Johnson, J., Shaffer, D., Rapoport, J. L., Kalikow, K., Walsh, T. B., Davies, M., Braiman, S., & Dolinsky, A. (1990). Uncommon troubles in young people: Prevalence estimates of selected psychiatric disorders in a nonreferred adolescent population. *Archives of General Psychiatry, 47,* 487–496.

White, G. D., Nielsen, G., & Johnson, S. M. (1972). Time-out duration and the suppression of deviant behavior in children. *Journal of Applied Behavior Analysis, 5,* 111–120.

White, H. R., & Labouvie, E. W. (1989). Towards the assessment of adolescent problem drinking. *Journal of Studies on Alcohol, 50,* 30–37.

White, M. A. (1975). Natural rates of teacher approval and disapproval in the classroom. *Journal of Applied Behavior Analysis, 8,* 367–372.

White, O. R., & Haring, N. G. (1976). *Exceptional teaching* (1st ed.). Columbus, OH: Charles E. Merrill.

Whitman, T. L. (1987). Self-instruction, individual differences, and mental retardation. *American Journal on Mental Retardation, 92,* 213–223.

Whitman, T. L. (1990). Self-regulation and mental retardation. *American Journal on Mental Retardation, 94,* 347–362.

Whitman, T. L., Burgio, L., & Johnston, M. B. (1984). Cognitive behavior therapy with the mentally retarded. In A. Meyers & E. Craighead (Eds.), *Cognitive behavior therapy with children* (pp. 193–227). New York: Plenum.

Whitman, T. L., Hantula, B., & Spence, B. (1990). Current issues in behavior modification with mentally retarded persons. In J. L. Matson (Ed.), *Handbook of behavior modification with the mentally retarded* (2nd ed., pp. 9–50). New York: Plenum.

Whitman, T. L., Scibak, J. W., Butler, K. M., Richter,

R., & Johnson, M. R. (1982). Improving classroom behavior in mentally retarded children through correspondence training. *Journal of Applied Behavior Analysis, 15*, 545–564.

Whitman, T. L., Schibak, J., & Reid, D. (1983). *Behavior modification with the mentally retarded; Treatment and research perspectives*. New York: Academic Press.

Whitman, T. L., Spence, B. H., & Maxwell, S. E. (1987). A comparison of external and self-instructional teaching formats with mentally retarded adults in a vocational training setting. *Research in Developmental Disabilities, 8*, 371–388.

Whitman, T. L., Zakaras, M., & Chardos, S. (1971). Effects of reinforcement and guidance procedures on instruction following behavior of severely retarded children. *Journal of Applied Behavior Analysis, 4*, 283–290.

Wickramasekera, I. E. (1988). *Clinical behavioral medicine: Some concepts and procedures*. New York: Plenum.

Wiens, A. N., & Menustik, C. E. (1983). Treatment outcome and patient characteristics in an aversion therapy program for alcoholism. *American Psychologist, 38*, 1089–1096.

Wiggins, J. S. (1973). *Personality and prediction: Principles of personality assessment*. Reading, MA: Addison-Wesley.

Williams, D. A., & Thorn, B. E. (1989). An empirical assessment of pain beliefs. *Pain, 36*, 351–358.

Williams, J. A., Koegel, R. L., & Egel, A. L. (1981). Response reinforcer relationships and improved learning in autistic children. *Journal of Applied Behavior Analysis, 14*, 53–60.

Williams, J. R., & Gold, M. (1972). From delinquent behavior to official delinquency. *Social problems, 20*, 209–229.

Willis, D. J., Elliott, C. H., & Jay, S. M. (1982). Psychological effects of physical illness and its concomitants. In J. Tuma (Ed.), *Handbook for the practice of pediatric psychology* (pp. 28–66). New York: Wiley.

Wilson, G. L. Borstein, P. H., & Wilson, L. J. (1988). Treatment of relationship dysfunction: An empirical evaluation of group and conjoint behavioral marital therapy. *Journal of Consulting and Clinical Psychology, 56*, 929–931.

Wilson, G. T. (1987). Cognitive-behavioral treatment of bulimia nervosa. *Annals of Behavioral Medicine, 9*, 12–17.

Wilson, G. T., Rossiter, E. M., Kleinfield, E. J., & Lindholm, L. (1986). Cognitive-behavioral treatment of bulimia nervosa: A controlled evaluation. *Behavior Research and Therapy, 24*, 277–288.

Wilson, H. (1980). Parental supervision: A neglected aspect of delinquency. *British Journal of Criminology, 20*, 203–235.

Wiltz, N. A., & Patterson, G. R. (1974). An evaluation of parent training procedures designed to alter inappropriate aggressive behavior of boys. *Behavior Therapy, 5*, 215–221.

Wing, J. K. (Ed.). (1966). *Early childhood autism: Clinical, educational, and social aspects*. Oxford: Pergamon.

Wing, J. K., Cooper, J. E., & Sartorius, N. (1974). *The measurement and classification of psychiatric symptoms*. New York: Cambridge University Press.

Wing, J. K., & Brown, G. W. (1970). *Institutionalization and schizophrenia*. London: Cambridge University Press.

Wing, L. (1976). Diagnosis, clinical description and prognosis. In L. Wing (Ed.), *Early childhood autism: Clinical, educational, and social aspects* (2nd ed.). Oxford: Pergamon.

Winokur, G. (1979). Unipolar depression: Is it divisible into autonomous subtypes? *Archives of General Psychiatry, 36*, 47–52.

Wirt, R. D., Lachar, D., Klinedinst, J. K., & Seat, P. D. (1977). *Multidimensional description of child personality: A manual for the Personality Inventory for Children*. Los Angeles: Western Psychological Services.

Wolery, M., Bailey, D. B., & Sugai, G. M. (1988). *Effective teaching: Principles and procedures of applied behavior analysis with exceptional students*. Boston, MA: Allyn & Bacon.

Wolf, M. M. (1978). Social validity: The case for subjective measurement or how applied behavior analysis is finding its heart. *Journal of Applied Behavior Analysis, 11*, 203–214.

Wolf, M. M., Braukmann, C. J., & Ramp, K. A. (1987). Serious delinquent behavior as part of a significantly handicapping condition: Cures and supportive environments. *Journal of Applied Behavior Analysis, 20*, 347–359.

Wolf, M. M., Phillips, E. L., Fixsen, D. L., Braukmann, C. J., Kirigin, K. A ., Willner, A. G., & Schumaker, J. B. (1976). Achievement Place: The teaching-family model. *Child Care Quarterly, 5*, 92–103.

Wolf, M. M., Risley, T., & Mees, H. (1964). Application of operant conditioning procedures to the behavior problems of an autistic child. *Behavior Research and Therapy, 1*, 305–312.

Wolfe, B. E., & Goldfried, M. R. (1988). Research on psychotherapy integration: Recommendations and conclusions from an NIMH workshop. *Journal of Consulting and Clinical Psychology, 56*, 448–451.

Wolfe, D. A., Edwards, B., Manion, I., & Koverola, C. (1988). Early intervention for parents at risk of child abuse and neglect: A preliminary investigation. *Journal of Consulting and Clinical Psychology, 56*, 40–47.

Wolfe, D. A., Sandler, J., & Kaufman, K. (1981). A competency based parent training program for abusive parents. *Journal of Consulting and Clinical Psychology, 49*, 633–640.

Wolfe, V. V., Finch, A. J., Saylor, C. F., Blount, R. L., Pallmeyer, T. P., & Carek, D. J. (1987). Negative affectivity in children: A multitrait-multimethod investigation. *Journal of Consulting and Clinical Psychology, 55*, 245–250.

Wolfer, J. A., & Visintainer, M. A. (1975). Pediatric surgery patients' and parents' stress responses and adjustment. *Nursing Research, 24*, 244–255.

Wolpe, J. (1958). *Psychotherapy by reciprocal inhibition*. Stanford, CA: Stanford University Press.

Wong, S. E., Terranova, M. D., Bowen, L., Zarete, T., Massel, H. R., & Liberman, R. P. (1987). Providing independent recreational activities to reduce stereotypic vocalizations in chronic schizophrenics. *Journal of Applied Behavior Analysis, 20,* 77–81.

Wood, D. L. (1986). Designing microcomputer programs for disabled students. *Computers in Education, 10,* 35–42.

Wood, D. R., Reimherr, F. W., Wender, P. H., & Johnson, G. E. (1976). Diagnosis and treatment of minimal brain dysfunction in adults. *Archives of General Psychiatry, 33,* 1453–1460.

Woodcock, R. W., & Johnson, M. B. (1978). *Woodcock-Johnson Psycho-Educational Battery*. Allen, TX: DLM Teaching Resources.

Wooley, S. C., Blackwell, B., & Winget, C. (1978). A learning theory model of chronic illness behavior: Theory, treatment, and research. *Psychosomatic Research, 40,* 379–401.

Wright, D. F., Brown, R. A., & Andrews, M. E. (1978). Remission of chronic ruminative vomiting through a reversal of social contingencies. *Behaviour Research and Therapy, 16,* pp. 134–136.

Wright, L. (1967). The pediatric psychologist: A role model. *American Psychologist, 22,* 223–225.

Wynne, L., & Singer, M. (1963). Thought disorder and family relations of schizophrenics; I. A research strategy. II. A classification of forms. *Archives of General Psychiatry, 9,* 191–206.

Yeaton, W. H., & Bailey, J. S. (1978). Teaching pedestrian safety skills to young children: An analysis and one year follow-up. *Journal of Applied Behavior Analysis, 11,* 315–329.

Yoder, D. E., & Miller, J. F. (1972). What we may know and what we can do: Input toward a system. In J. E. McClean, D. E. Yoder, & R. L. Schiefellbrisch (Eds.), *Language intervention with the retarded* (pp. 89–103). Baltimore: University Park Press.

Young, J. E, (1990). *Cognitive therapy for personality disorders: A schema-focused approach*. Sarasota, FL: Professional Resource Exchange.

Young, J., & Beck, A. T. (1981). *The development of the Cognitive Therapy Scale*. Unpublished manuscript, Center for Cognitive Therapy, Philadelphia.

Youngren, M. A., & Lewinsohn, P. M. (1980). The functional relation between depression and problematic interpersonal behavior. *Journal of Abnormal Psychology, 89,* 333–341.

Zabel, M. K. (1986). Timeout use with behaviorally disordered students. *Behavioral Disorders, 12,* 15–21.

Zarate, R., Craske, M. G., Rapee, R. M., & Barlow, D. H. (1988). *The effectiveness of interoceptive exposure in the treatment of simple phobia*. Paper presented at the 22nd Annual Meeting of the Association for the Advancement of Behavior Therapy, New York.

Zastowny, T. R., Kirschenbaum, D. S., & Meng, A. L. (1986). Coping skills training for children: Effects on distress before, during, and after hospitalization for surgery. *Health Psychology, 5,* 231–247.

Zeaman, D., & House, B. J. (1963). The role of attention in retardate discrimination learning. In N. R. Ellis (Ed.), *Handbook of mental deficiency* (pp. 159–223). New York: McGraw-Hill.

Zeaman, D., & House, B. J. (1979). A review of attention theory. In N. R. Ellis (Ed.), *Handbook of mental deficiency: Psychology theory and research*, (pp. 63–120). Hillsdale, NJ: Laurence Erlbaum.

Zegiob, L., Klukas, N., & Junginger, J. (1978). Reactivity of self-monitoring procedures with retarded adolescents. *American Journal of Mental Deficiency, 83,* 156–163.

Zeiss, A. M., Lewinsohn, P. M., & Munoz, R. F. (1979). Nonspecific improvement effects in depression using interpersonal skills training, pleasant activity schedules, or cognitive training. *Journal of Consulting and Clinical Psychology, 47,* 427–439.

Zeiss, A. M., Rosen, G. M., & Zeiss, R. A. (1977). Orgasm during intercourse: A treatment strategy for women. *Journal of Consulting and Clinical Psychology, 45,* 891–895.

Zeltzer, L., & LeBaron, S. (1982). Hypnosis and nonhypnotic techniques for reduction of pain and anxiety during painful procedures in children and adolescents with cancer. *Journal of Pediatrics, 101,* 1032–1035.

Zentall, S. S. (1989). Self-control training with hyperactive and impulsive children. In J. N. Hughes & R. J. Hall (Eds.), *Cognitive behavioral psychology in the schools: A comprehensive handbook*. New York: Guilford.

Zilbergeld, B., & Evans, M. (1980, August). The inadequacy of Masters and Johnson. *Psychology Today*, pp. 29–43.

Zigler, E. (1966). Research on personality structure in the retardate. In N. R. Ellis (Ed.), *International review of research in mental retardation* (Vol 1). New York: Academic Press.

Zigler, E. (1967). Familial mental retardation: A continuing dilemma. *Science, 155,* 292–298.

Zigler, E., & Balla, D. (1982) *Mental retardation: The developmental-difference controversy*. Hillsdale, NJ: Erlbaum.

Zigler, E., & Phillips, L. (1961). Social competence and outcome in psychiatric disorder. *Journal of Abnormal and Social Psychology, 63,* 264–271.

Zis, A. P., & Goodwin, F. K (1979). Major affective disorder as a recurrent illness: A critical review. *Archives of General Psychiatry, 36,* 835–839.

Zitrin, C. M., Klein, D. F., & Woerner, M. G. (1980).

Treatment of agoraphobia with group exposure in vivo and imipramine. *Archives of General Psychiatry, 37,* 63–72.

Zlutnick, S., Mayville, W. J., & Moffat, S. (1975). Modification of seizure disorders: The interruption of behavioral chains. *Journal of Applied Behavior Analysis, 8,* 1–12.

Zubin, J., & Spring, B. (1977). Vulnerability—a new view of schizophrenia. *Journal of Abnormal Psychology, 86,* 103–126.

Zuckerman, M., & Lubin, B. (1965). *Manual for the Multiple Affective Adjective Check List.* San Diego: Educational and Industrial Testing Service.

Zung, W. W. K (1965). A self-rating depression scale. *Archives of General Psychiatry, 12,* 63–70.

Zuriff, G. E. (1985). *Behaviorism: A conceptual reconstruction.* New York: Columbia University Press.

462

Parent management training, 251–266, 288–292
and autism, 356–357
child behavior management, 241–243
concepts, 252–254
Hanf-Forehand parent training program, 254–260
Oregon Social Learning Center programs, 260–264
Parent Symptom Questionnaire, 276
Parents and family:
ADHD, 241
conduct disorder, 270–271
of chronically ill children, 364–365
medical treatment skills, 362
Patient Rejection Scale, 110
Patterson, G., 251–252
Pavlov, I., 2, 29–30
Peabody Individual Achievement Test (PIAT), 316
Peabody Picture Vocabulary test, 339
Pediatric psychology applications, 359–375
chronic diseases, 360–368
health promotion, 371–374
stress reduction, 368–371
Peer evaluations, 131, 276–277
Peer Nomination of Aggression, 273
Peer tutoring systems, 230
Penile stimulation, 191
Personality development, psychoanalytic theories, 302–303
Personality Inventory for Children, 276
Peterson, L., 359–375
Physiological arousal, 41
Physiological assessment, 79–80
panic disorders, 84–85
sexual dysfunction, 188–189
Piers-Harris Self-Concept Scale, 308, 310
Placebo, 42, 98, 101
Positive and negative contingencies of reinforcement, 220–222
Positive reinforcement, 31–33
definition of, 31
and depressed client, 99–100
side effects, 221
and weight gain, 154
Post-traumatic stress disorder, 378–379
definition of, 73
Predelinquent behavior, treatment approaches, 262–264
Premarital Relationship Enhancement Program (PREP), 179–180
Premature ejaculation, 190–191
definition of, 185
Present State Examination, 91
Primary negative reinforcers, 34
Primary reinforcer, definition of, 32
Probability value, 62
Problem solving, 40–41
definition of, 40

parents of chronically ill children, 364–365
and schizophrenics, 119–120
stages, 40
Problem-solving skills training, 57–58, 59, 285–288
for couples, 174–175
Program for Academic Survival Skills (PASS), 223
Projective tests, 19–20
Prompts, 37–38
definition of, 37
removing, 37–38
as stimuli, 228–229
within-stimulus, 349–350
Pronominal reversal, definition of, 336
Prosocial functioning, 280–281
Psychoanalytic model (Freud), 4
Psychoanalytic theory, 17–18, 20, 22, 302–303
Psychological practice, systems of, 2–5
Psychology:
definitions of, 2
schools of thought, 2, 3
Psychopathological problems, 3
Psychophysiological assessment:
pain management, 200, 204–205
stress management, 209
Psychosexual development, stages of, 18
punishment, 31, 32, 34–35
by application, 35
autism, 342–344
and classroom behaviors, 224–227
contingencies, 282–283
definition of, 34, 99
and discipline, 216, 218
as operant conditioning, 219
by removal, 35
side effects, 35, 218
Quasi-medical models, 17–22
Questionnaires, 76–77
Randomized time samples, 49
Raskin Depression Scale (RDS), 91
Rathus Assertiveness Scale, 131, 134
Rational-Emotive Therapy, 184, 307
"Reader in the text" concept, 13
Reattribution, negative cognition, 43
Reciprocal determinism, 25
Recovery, definition of, 36
Reinforcement, 31–34
contingencies, 282–283
negative, 33–34
as operant conditioning, 219
positive, 31–33
schedules of, 222–223
Reinforcer effectiveness, 222, 351
Relapse:
in addicts, 164–165, 166
in behavioral couples therapy, 178–179
depression, 97–98
and schizophrenia, 111, 116–117
Relationship distress, 169–171

Relaxation training, 210–211, 309, 369
Replication, 69
Research Diagnostic Criteria (RDC), 107
Research design, 50–51
definition of, 51
Respondents, definition of, 30
Response co-variation, definition of, 298
Response cost, 226, 322
Response-contingent positive reinforcement, 99–100
Reversal design, 55–57
Reversal phase, definition of, 55
Revised Behavior Problem Checklist, 239, 257, 276
Rewards, 31–32, 60
Reynolds Adolescent Depression Scale (RADS), 308, 310
Ritualistic behavior and autism, 337
Rorschach (measurement test), 279
Rutgers Alcohol Problem Inventory (RAPI), 161
Sampling method of data collection, 49–50
Scale for the Assessment of Negative Symptoms (SANS), 109
Schedule for Affective Disorders and Schizophrenia (SADS), 91–92, 108
Schedules of instructional activities, 228
Schizophrenia, 105–122
assessment, 107–110
behavioral interventions, 113–121
definition of, 107
early treatment, 106–107
symptoms, 105–106
token economy, 106–107
treatment, 110–113
School Behavior Checklist, 276
School intervention, examples of, 229–233
Schreibman, L., 335–358
Scientific evaluation, principles of, 45
Scientific methodology, 4
Scientific psychology, 1–2
Secondary negative reinforcers, 34
Secondary reinforcer, 33
definition of, 32
Seizure activity, 367–368
Self-concept behavior, 19
Self-control:
definition of, 101
therapy and depression, 101–103
Self-efficacy, definition of, 42
Self-help groups, 148
Self-help skills and mentally retarded, 318–319
Self-injurious behavior, autism, 338
Self-instructional training, 307
with mentally retarded, 324–325
and pain management, 204
Self-management training, 325–326, 329–330, 357

Self-monitoring, 77–78, 79
  depressed client, 93–94
  and stress management, 209
Self-report, 22
  addicts, 160
  assessment and social inadequacy,
    131–132
  by couple, 171–172
  schizophrenia, 109
  sexual dysfunction, 188
  and stress management, 209–210
Self-Report Delinquency Scale, 272
Self-statements, 43, 127
Sensitivity to interpersonal problems,
  definition of, 285
Sensory responsiveness and autism,
  337
Sex history interview, 187–188
Sex therapy (see Sexual dysfunction)
Sexual Arousal Inventory, 188
Sexual aversion, 185
Sexual desire, 185, 186, 187, 189–190
Sexual dysfunction, 175, 183–196
  assessment of, 187–189
  classification of, 184–187
  definition of, 185
  treatment, 189–195
Sexual Interaction Inventory, 188
Shaping, 36–37, 223
  definition of, 37
Sherman, D. D., 359–375
Sherrington, C., 13
Single-case experimental designs,
    54–62, 154
  changing-criterion design, 60–62
  multiple-baseline designs, 57–60
  reversal or ABAB design, 55–57
  and visual inspection, 63–64
Single-case research design, 51
Situation-specific social effectiveness,
  124
Skinner, B. F., 2, 6–7, 106
Social Adjustment Scale-II (SAS), 109
Social Avoidance and Distress Scale
  (SADS), 131, 134
Social aggression in families, 253–254
Social inadequacy and social skill,
    123–140
  anxiety, 126–127
  assertiveness, 129, 132–133
  assessment, 130–132
  behavioral consistency and
    behaviorism, 138–139
  case study, 133–135
  dating, 127–129
  depression, 125–126
  treatment, 132–135, 136
Social interaction tasks, 130–131
Social learning theory, 307
Social Performance Survey Schedule,
  131

Social phobia, definition of, 73
Social Phobia and Anxiety Inventory,
  131
Social skill, definition of, 125, 137
Social skills training (SST), 116–118,
    127–129, 132, 283–285
  and ADHD, 248
  definition of, 114, 123–124, 127
  and schizophrenics, 107, 108,
    114–118
  evaluations, 116–118
  procedures, 15
Speech and language training, autism,
  345–348
Spontaneous language, autism,
  346–347
Sports psychology, 389–390
Stanford-Binet intelligence scale, 316,
  339
Statistical evaluation, 62–63
Statistical tests, 10
Stimulus control:
  definition of, 219
  manipulation, 344–345
  as operant conditioning, 219
Stimulus overselectivity, 348–349, 354
Stream of consciousness (James), 2
Street, L. L., 71–87
Stress:
  definitions of, 208
  management, 207–212
  and pain, 200
  and schizophrenia, 113–114
Stress-related disorders, 208–209
Structuralism, 2
Structured Clinical Interview for
  DSM-III (SCID), 92, 108, 115
Subjectivity in statistical evaluation,
  62–63
Substance abuse, 159, 373–374
Superego, definition of, 18
Sutter-Eyberg Student Behavior
  Inventory (SESBI), 273, 275
Symptom substitution, definition
  of, 20
Symptoms, interventions to alleviate,
  365–368
Syndromal depression, 302
System of Multicultural Pluralistic
  Assessment (SOMPA), 316
Task analysis 220, 318–319
Temporal data, definition of, 48
Terminal goal, 37
Terminal response, 37
Terry, B., 215–234
Thematic Apperception Test, 279
Therapist-client team, 45
Therapy techniques, addictive
    behaviors, 162–165
  aversion therapy, 162–164
  contingency management, 163

relapse prevention, 164–165
skills training, 163–164
Thorndike, E. L., 2, 12
Time Line Follow-Back interview
  (TLFB), 161
Time sampling, 49
Time-Sample Behavioral Checklist
  (TSBC), 108
Time-out, 226–227, 255, 321, 343–344
Token economy, 33, 106–107, 114,
  246–247, 326
Tolerance to drugs, 158–159
Trainable mentally retarded (TMR),
  314
Trait theories, 18–19
Treatment matching and addiction
  behaviors, 165–166
Tricyclic antidepressants, 103, 153,
  307
Unconditioned stimulus, 30
Unconscious processes, 13
Uncontrollability, 72
Unipolar affective disorders, 90
Vaginismus, 195
  definition of, 185
Venipunctures, behavioral coping
  strategies, 368–369
Verbal instruction with mentally
  retarded, 323–325
Verbal reprimands, 225–226
Vicarious learning, 38–39
Vineland Adaptive Behavior Scales
  (VABS), 316–317
Visual inspection, 63–64, 66
Visual instruction with mentally
  retarded, 328–329
Visuo-motor behavior rehearsal
  (VMBR), 389
Vulnerability of schizophrenics,
  112–113
Walker, D., 215–234
Waltz, J., 169–181
Watson, J., 2, 11
Wechsler (IQ test), 339
Weekly Record of Anxiety and
  Depression, 77, 79
Weight loss, 143, 145
Weight maintenance, 143–144
Wells, K. C., 251–266
Whitman, T. L., 313–333
Wide Range Achievement
  Test-Revised (WRAT-R), 316
Wilson, G. T., 5
Withholding reinforcer, 36
Woodcock-Johnson Psychoeducational
  Battery, 316
Wundt, W., 1–2
Yale Conference on Behavioral
  Medicine, 197
Zink, M., 359–375
Zung Self-Rated Depression
  Inventory, 91